STREET ATLAS
East Sussex
Brighton and Hove

First published in 1998 by

Philip's, a division of
Octopus Publishing Group Ltd
2-4 Heron Quays, London E14 4JP

Third colour edition 2004
First impression 2004

ISBN-10 0-540-08648-7 (hardback)
ISBN-13 978-0-540-08648-1 (hardback)
ISBN-10 0-540-08649-5 (spiral)
ISBN-13 978-0-540-08649-8 (spiral)

© Philip's 2004

oiS Ordnance Survey®

This product includes mapping data licensed
from Ordnance Survey® with the permission of
the Controller of Her Majesty's Stationery Office.
© Crown copyright 2004. All rights reserved.
Licence number 100011710.

Printed and bound in Italy by Rotolito

Contents

III **Key to map symbols**

IV **Key to map pages**

VI **Route planning**

VIII **Administrative and Postcode boundaries**

1 **Street maps** at 3½ inches to 1 mile

189 **Street maps of centres of Brighton and Lewes**
at 7 inches to 1 mile

191 **Index** of towns and villages

193 **Index** of streets, hospitals, industrial estates, railway
stations, schools, shopping centres, universities
and places of interest

Digital Data

The exceptionally high-quality mapping found in this atlas is available as digital data in TIFF
format, which is easily convertible to other bitmapped (raster) image formats.

The index is also available in digital form as a standard database table. It contains all the details
found in the printed index together with the National Grid reference for the map square in which
each entry is named.

For further information and to discuss your requirements, please contact Philip's on
020 7644 6932 or james.mann@philips-maps.co.uk

Symbol	Description
22a	**Motorway** with junction number
	Primary route – dual/single carriageway
	A road – dual/single carriageway
	B road – dual/single carriageway
	Minor road – dual/single carriageway
	Other minor road – dual/single carriageway
	Road under construction
	Tunnel, covered road
	Rural track, private road or narrow road in urban area
	Gate or obstruction to traffic (restrictions may not apply at all times or to all vehicles)
	Path, bridleway, byway open to all traffic, road used as a public path
	Pedestrianised area
DY7	**Postcode boundaries**
	County and unitary authority boundaries
	Railway, tunnel, railway under construction
	Tramway, tramway under construction
	Miniature railway
Walsall	**Railway station**
	Private railway station
South Shields	**Metro station**
	Tram stop, tram stop under construction
	Bus, coach station

Symbol	Description
	Ambulance station
	Coastguard station
	Fire station
	Police station
+	**Accident and Emergency entrance to hospital**
H	**Hospital**
+	**Place of worship**
i	**Information Centre** (open all year)
P P&R	**Parking, Park and Ride**
PO	**Post Office**
	Camping site, caravan site
	Golf course
	Picnic site
Prim Sch	**Important buildings, schools, colleges, universities and hospitals**
	Built up area
	Woods
River Medway	**Water name**
	River, weir, stream
	Canal, lock, tunnel
	Water
	Tidal water
Church	**Non-Roman antiquity**
ROMAN FORT	**Roman antiquity**
87	**Adjoining page indicators and overlap bands** The colour of the arrow and the band indicates the scale of the adjoining or overlapping page (see scales below)
228	

Symbol	Description
	Railway or bus station building
	Place of interest
	Parkland

Acad	**Academy**	Inst	**Institute**	Recn Gd	**Recreation Ground**
Allot Gdns	**Allotments**	Ct	**Law Court**		
Cemy	**Cemetery**	L Ctr	**Leisure Centre**	Resr	**Reservoir**
C Ctr	**Civic Centre**	LC	**Level Crossing**	Ret Pk	**Retail Park**
CH	**Club House**	Liby	**Library**	Sch	**School**
Coll	**College**	Mkt	**Market**	Sh Ctr	**Shopping Centre**
Crem	**Crematorium**	Meml	**Memorial**	TH	**Town Hall/House**
Ent	**Enterprise**	Mon	**Monument**	Trad Est	**Trading Estate**
Ex H	**Exhibition Hall**	Mus	**Museum**	Univ	**University**
Ind Est	**Industrial Estate**	Obsy	**Observatory**	W Twr	**Water Tower**
IRB Sta	**Inshore Rescue Boat Station**	Pal	**Royal Palace**	Wks	**Works**
		PH	**Public House**	YH	**Youth Hostel**

■ The small numbers around the edges of the maps identify the 1 kilometre National Grid lines
■ The dark grey border on the inside edge of some pages indicates that the mapping does not continue onto the adjacent page

The scale of the maps on the pages numbered in blue is 5.52 cm to 1 km • 3½ inches to 1 mile • 1: 18103

0	¼	½	¾	1 mile
0	250 m	500 m	750 m	1 kilometre

The scale of the maps on pages numbered in red is 11.04 cm to 1 km • 7 inches to 1 mile • 1: 9051

0	220 yards	440 yards	660 yards	½ mile
0	125 m	250 m	375 m	½ kilometre

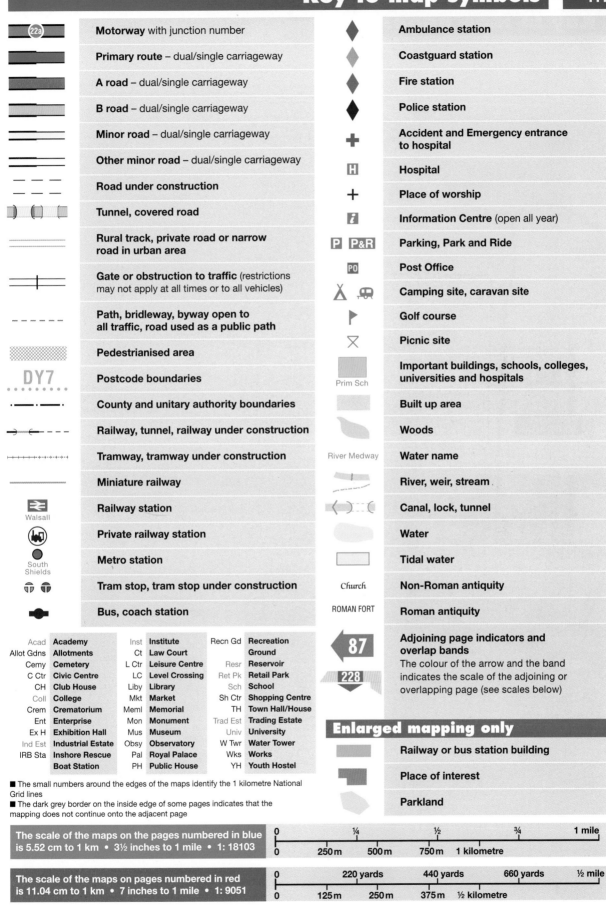

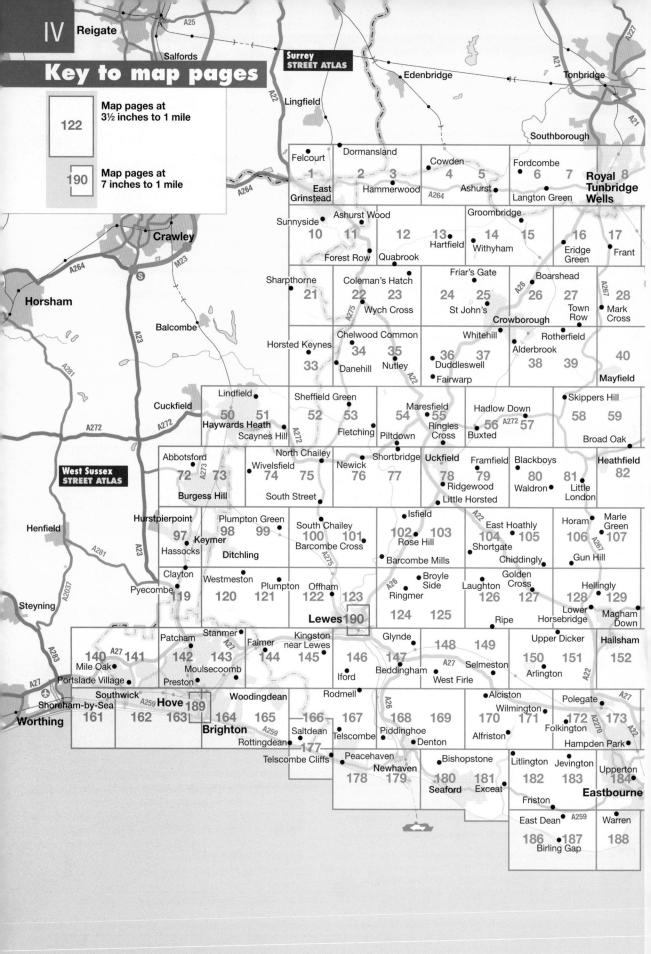

Salfords

Surrey STREET ATLAS

Edenbridge

Tonbridge

Key to map pages

Lingfield

Southborough

| 122 | Map pages at 3½ inches to 1 mile |
| 190 | Map pages at 7 inches to 1 mile |

Felcourt
Dormansland
Cowden
Fordcombe

1 East Grinstead
2
3
4
5 Ashurst
6
7
Royal Tunbridge Wells 8

Hammerwood
Langton Green

Sunnyside
Ashurst Wood
Groombridge

10
11 Forest Row
12
13 Hartfield
14 Withyham
15
16 Eridge Green
17 Frant

Quabrook

Sharpthorne
Coleman's Hatch
Friar's Gate
Boarshead

21
22
23
24
25 St John's
26
27 Town Row
28 Mark Cross

Wych Cross
Crowborough

Chelwood Common
Whitehill
Rotherfield

Horsted Keynes
Alderbrook

33
34
35
36
37
38
39
40 Mayfield

Danehill
Nutley
Duddleswell
Fairwarp

Lindfield
Sheffield Green
Maresfield
Hadlow Down
Skippers Hill

50
51 Haywards Heath
52
53
54
55 Ringles Cross
56
57
58
59

Scaynes Hill
Fletching
Piltdown
Buxted
Broad Oak

Cuckfield

Abbotsford
North Chailey
Shortbridge
Uckfield
Framfield
Blackboys
Heathfield

72
73
74 Wivelsfield
75
Newick
76
77
78
79
80
81
82

Burgess Hill
South Street
Ridgewood
Waldron
Little London

Little Horsted

Hurstpierpoint
Plumpton Green
Isfield
Horam
Marle Green

97
98
99
South Chailey
100
101 Barcombe Cross
102
103 Rose Hill
East Hoathly
104
105
106
107

Keymer
Hassocks
Ditchling
Barcombe Mills
Shortgate
Chiddingly
Gun Hill

Clayton
Westmeston
Plumpton
Offham
Broyle Side
Golden Cross
Hellingly

119
120
121
122
123
Ringmer
Laughton
126
127
128
129

Pyecombe
124
125
Ripe
Lower Horsebridge
Magham Down

Lewes **190**

Patcham
Stanmer
Falmer
Kingston near Lewes
Glynde
Upper Dicker
Hailsham

140
141
142
143
144
145
146
147
148
149
150
151
152

Mile Oak
Moulsecoomb
Beddingham
Selmeston
Arlington

Portslade Village
Preston
Iford
West Firle

Southwick
Woodingdean
Rodmell
Alciston
Polegate

Hove
Wilmington

Shoreham-by-Sea
161
162
163
189
164
165
166
167
168
169
170
171
172
173

Worthing
Brighton
Saltdean
Piddinghoe
Folkington

Rottingdean
Telscombe
Denton
Alfriston
Hampden Park

177

Telscombe Cliffs
Peacehaven
Bishopstone
Litlington
Jevington
Upperton

Newhaven
182
183
184

178
179
180
181
Exceat
Eastbourne

Seaford
Friston

East Dean
Warren

186
187
188

Birling Gap

Reigate

Crawley

Horsham

Balcombe

West Sussex STREET ATLAS

Henfield

Steyning

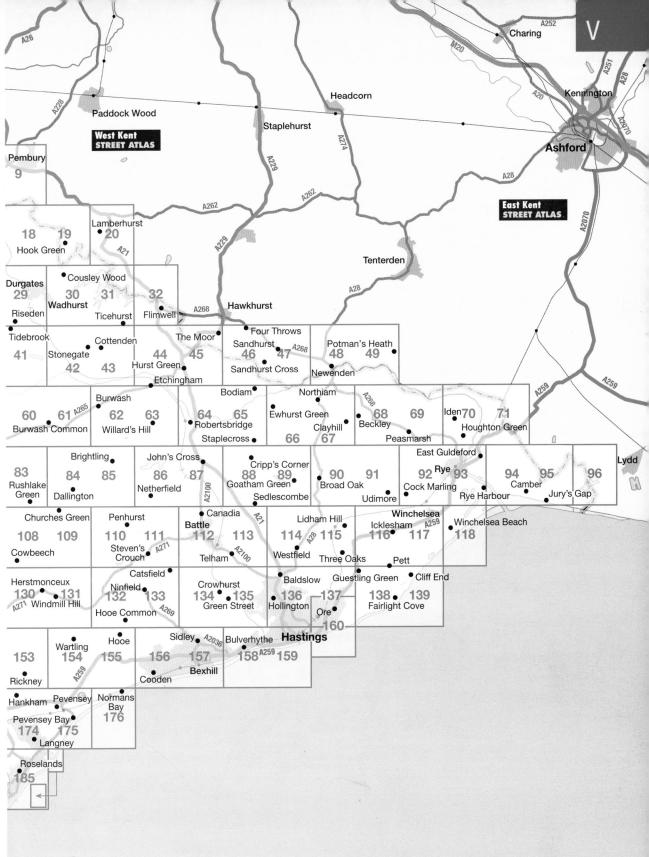

Charing

M20

Kennington

Headcorn

Staplehurst

A274

Ashford

A28

Paddock Wood

West Kent
STREET ATLAS

A228

A26

Pembury
9

A262

A262

A229

East Kent
STREET ATLAS

A2070

Lamberhurst
18 **19** **20**
Hook Green

A21

Tenterden

A28

A259

A259

Durgates
29 **30** **31** **32**
Riseden **Wadhurst**
Cousley Wood

Ticehurst Flimwell

A268 Hawkhurst

A259

Tidebrook
41 Stonegate Cottenden
42 **43** The Moor **45** **46** **47** **48** **49**
Hurst Green **44** Four Throws Potman's Heath
Sandhurst
Etchingham Sandhurst Cross A268
Newenden

A28

Lydd

Burwash
60 **61** A265 **62** **63** **64** **65** Northiam **68** **69** Iden **70** **71**
Burwash Common Willard's Hill Bodiam Ewhurst Green Beckley Houghton Green
Robertsbridge Clayhill Peasmarsh
Staplecross **66** **67**
A268

Brightling John's Cross Cripp's Corner East Guldeford
83 **84** **85** **86** **87** **88** **89** **90** **91** **92** Rye **93** **94** **95** **96**
Rushlake Netherfield Goatham Green Broad Oak Cock Marling Camber
Green Dallington Sedlescombe Udimore Rye Harbour Jury's Gap
A2100 A259

Churches Green Canadia **Winchelsea**
108 **109** Penhurst **110** **111** Battle **112** **113** **114** **115** Icklesham **116** **117** **118**
Cowbeech Steven's Lidham Hill Winchelsea Beach
Crouch A271 Telham Westfield A28 A259
A2100 Three Oaks Pett

Catsfield Baldslow Guestling Green Cliff End
Herstmonceux Ninfield Crowhurst **136** **137** **138** **139**
130 **131** **132** **133** **134** **135** Hollington Fairlight Cove
A271 Windmill Hill Green Street Ore
Hooe Common A269 **160**

Sidley Bulverhythe **Hastings**
153 Wartling Hooe **156** **157** A2036 **158** A259 **159**
154 **155** Bexhill
Rickney A259 Cooden
Hankham Pevensey Normans
Bay
Pevensey Bay **175** **176**
174 Langney

Roselands
185

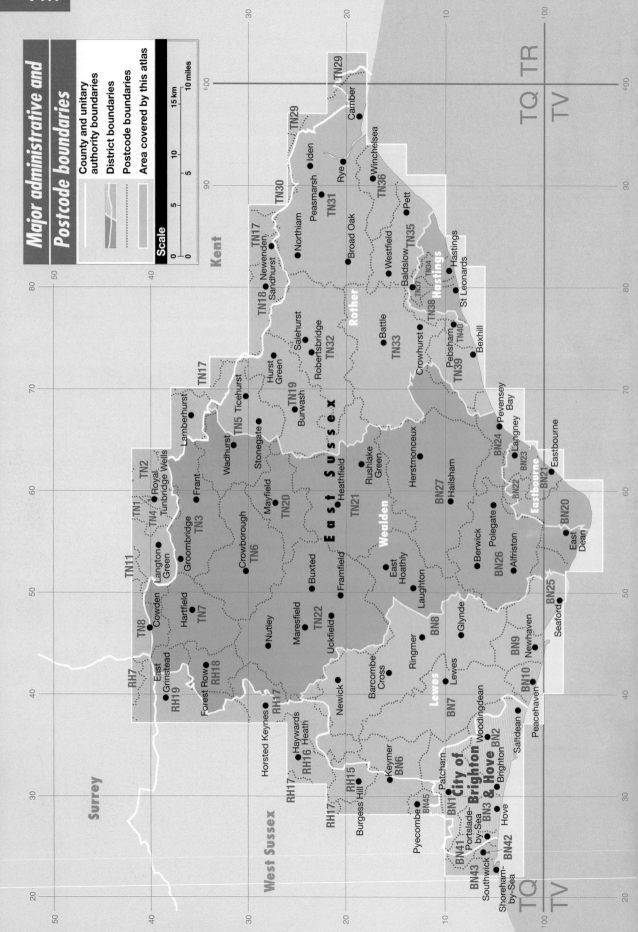

Surrey STREET ATLAS

C1
1 THE BROWNINGS
2 BYRON GR
3 CHAUCER AVE
4 TENNYSON RISE
5 THE SAYERS
6 WORDSWORTH RISE

D2
1 YEW CT
2 BIRCH HO
3 BEECH CL
4 ELM CT
5 FERNSIDE
6 SOUTHWICK HO

7 BEECH CT
8 ST CATHERINE'S CT

E1
1 GLENSIDE
2 GREGORY CT
3 WHITEHALL PAR
4 INSTITUTE WLK
5 CANTELUPE MEWS
6 NORMANS GDNS

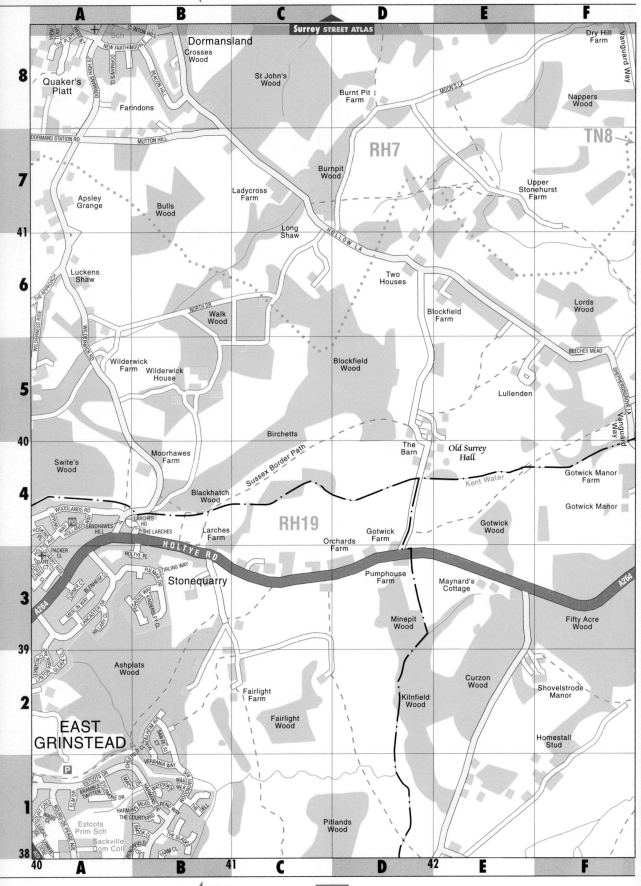

A B C D E F

8

7

41

6

5

40

4

3

39

2

1

38

Quaker's Platt

Dormansland

Crosses Wood

St John's Wood

Burnt Pit Farm

MOON'S LA

Dry Hill Farm

Vanguard Way

Farindons

DORMANS STATION RD

MUTTON HILL

RH7

Nappers Wood

TN8

Apsley Grange

Bulls Wood

Ladycross Farm

Burnpit Wood

Upper Stonehurst Farm

Luckens Shaw

Long Shaw

HOLLOW LA

Two Houses

Lords Wood

THE APPROACH

WILDERNESS RISE

WILDERWICK RD

NORTH DR

Walk Wood

Blockfield Farm

BEECHES MEAD

Wilderwick Farm

Wilderwick House

Blockfield Wood

Lullenden

SHEPHERDSGROVE LA

Vanguard Way

Swite's Wood

Moorhawes Farm

Birchetts

Sussex Border Path

The Barn

Old Surrey Hall

Kent Water

Gotwick Manor Farm

Gotwick Manor

WOODLANDS RD

Blackhatch Wood

RH19

Orchards Farm

Gotwick Farm

Gotwick Wood

SANDHAWES HILL

HOLLANDS WAY

THE LARCHES

LARCHES HO

Larches Farm

HOLTYE RD

Pumphouse Farm

Maynard's Cottage

A264

PACKER CL

HOLTYE PL

STIRLING WAY

Stonequarry

Minepit Wood

Fifty Acre Wood

MERLIN WAY

LANCASTER DR

HILARY CT

A264

Ashplats Wood

Curzon Wood

Shovelstrode Manor

Fairlight Farm

Kilnfield Wood

EAST GRINSTEAD

Fairlight Wood

Homestall Stud

CHESTNUT AVE

VERBANIA WAY

Estcots Prim Sch

Sackville Com Coll

Pitlands Wood

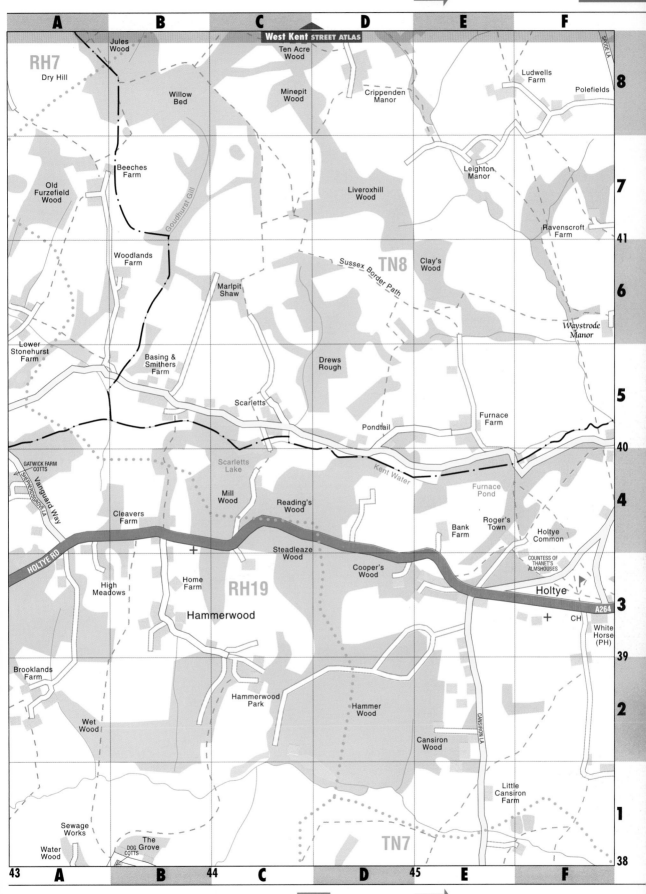

West Kent STREET ATLAS

RH7
Dry Hill
Jules Wood
Willow Bed
Beeches Farm
Old Furzefield Wood
Woodlands Farm
Goudhurst Gill
Lower Stonehurst Farm
Basing & Smithers Farm
Marlpit Shaw
Scarletts
Ten Acre Wood
Minepit Wood
Crippenden Manor
Liveroxhill Wood
Sussex Border Path
TN8
Clay's Wood
Drews Rough
Pondtail
Ludwells Farm
Polefields
SPODE LA
Leighton Manor
Ravenscroft Farm
Waystrode Manor
Furnace Farm
GATWICK FARM COTTS
SHEPHERDSGROVE LA
Vanguard Way
Cleavers Farm
Scarletts Lake
Mill Wood
Reading's Wood
Steadleaze Wood
Kent Water
Furnace Pond
Bank Farm
Roger's Town
Holtye Common
COUNTESS OF THANET'S ALMSHOUSES
HOLTYE RD
High Meadows
Home Farm
RH19
Hammerwood
Cooper's Wood
Holtye
A264
CH
White Horse (PH)
Brooklands Farm
Wet Wood
Hammerwood Park
Hammer Wood
Cansiron Wood
CANSIRON LA
Sewage Works
Water Wood
The Grove
DOG COTTS
TN7
Little Cansiron Farm

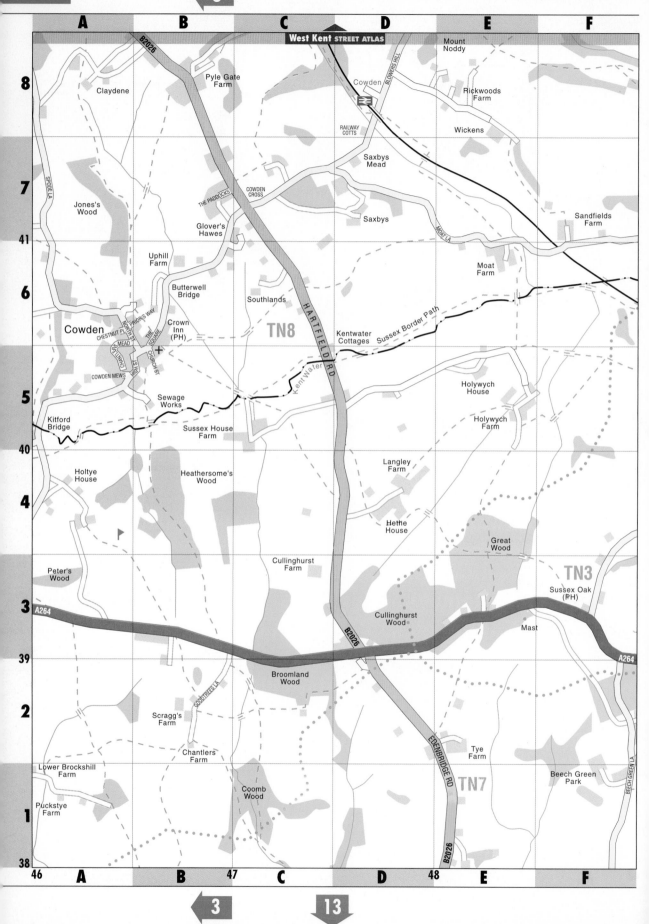

West Kent STREET ATLAS

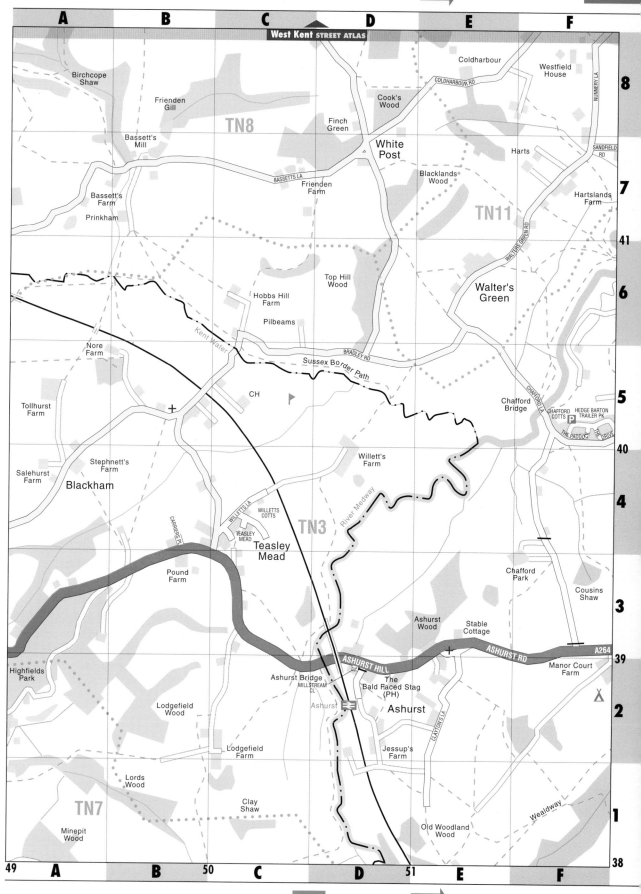

West Kent STREET ATLAS

A   B   C   D   E   F

8

Birchcope Shaw

Frienden Gill

TN8

Bassett's Mill

Bassett's Farm

Prinkham

Coldharbour

COLDHARBOUR RD

Westfield House

NUNNERY LA

Cook's Wood

Finch Green

White Post

Harts

SANDFIELD RD

7

BASSETTS LA

Frienden Farm

Blacklands Wood

TN11

Hartslands Farm

WALTER'S GREEN RD

41

Nore Farm

Hobbs Hill Farm

Pilbeams

Kent Water

Top Hill Wood

Walter's Green

6

BRADLEY RD

Sussex Border Path

CHAFFORD LA

Chafford Bridge

5

Tollhurst Farm

CH

Chafford Cotts

HEDGE BARTON TRAILER PK

THE PADDO'S

THE DRIVE

40

Salehurst Farm

Stephnett's Farm

Blackham

Willett's Farm

River Medway

4

CARRIERS PL

WILLETTS LA

WILLETTS COTTS

TEASLEY MEAD

Teasley Mead

TN3

Chafford Park

Cousins Shaw

3

Pound Farm

Ashurst Wood

Stable Cottage

ASHURST RD

A264

39

Highfields Park

Lodgefield Wood

Ashurst Bridge

MILLSTREAM CL

ASHURST HILL

Ashurst

The Bald Faced Stag (PH)

Ashurst

Manor Court Farm

CLAYTON'S LA

2

Lodgefield Farm

Jessup's Farm

Lords Wood

TN7

Clay Shaw

Old Woodland Wood

Wealdway

1

Minepit Wood

49   A   B   50   C   D   51   E   F   38

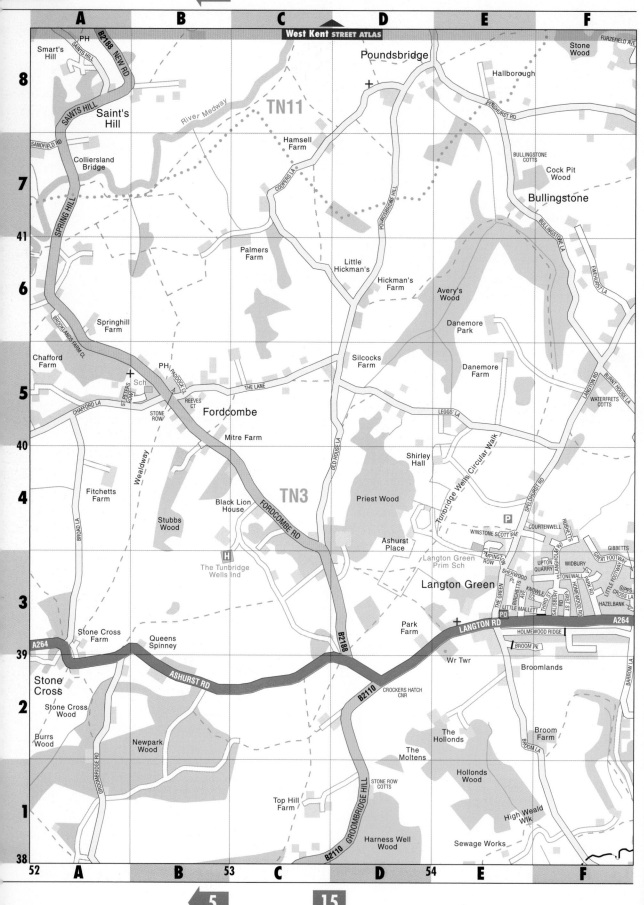

A B C D E F

8

7

41

6

5

40

4

3

39

2

1

38

52 A B 53 C D 54 E F

Smart's Hill
PH
B2188 NEW RD
SAINTS HILL
Saint's Hill
SAINTS HILL
River Medway
Poundsbridge
Hallborough
Stone Wood
FURZEFIELD AVE
TN11
SANDFIELD RD
Colliersland Bridge
SPRING HILL
Hamsell Farm
PENSHURST RD
BULLINGSTONE COTTS
Cock Pit Wood
Bullingstone
BULLINGSTONE LA
COOPERS LA
Palmers Farm
Little Hickman's
POUNDSBRIDGE HILL
Hickman's Farm
Avery's Wood
EWEHURST LA
BROOKLANDS FARM CL
Springhill Farm
Danemore Park
LANGTON RD
BURNT HOUSE LA
Chafford Farm
PH
Silcocks Farm
Danemore Farm
WATERFRETS COTTS
St PETERS ROW
Sch
PADDOCK PL
THE LANE
LEGGS' LA
CHAFFORD LA
REEVES CT
STONE ROW
Fordcombe
Tunbridge Wells Circular Walk
Mitre Farm
Shirley Hall
Wealdway
OLD HOUSE LA
TN3
SPELDHURST RD
Fitchetts Farm
BROAD LA
Black Lion House
FORDCOMBE RD
Priest Wood
COURTENWELL
RUSSETTS
P
GIBBETTS
Stubbs Wood
Ashurst Place
WINSTONE SCOTT AVE
Langton Green Prim Sch
UPTON
WIDBURY
GREAT FOOTWAY
H
The Tunbridge Wells Ind
MPING CT
SHERWOOD
LITTLE MALLETT
KNOWLE
THE GREEN
BIRCHETTS AVE
PL
THIRD ST
STONEWALL PARK RD
FIRST ST
HOMEWOOD RD
LITTLE FOOTWAY
HAZELBANK
Langton Green
Stone Cross Farm
Queens Spinney
B2188
Park Farm
LANGTON RD
SALISBURY RD
GIPPS CROSS LA
A264
A264
ASHURST RD
PO
Wr Twr
HOLMEWOOD RIDGE
BROOM PK
Broomlands
BARROW LA
Stone Cross
Stone Cross Wood
B2110
CROCKERS HATCH CNR
The Hollonds
BROOM LA
Broom Farm
Burrs Wood
Newpark Wood
The Moltens
Hollonds Wood
GROOMBRIDGE RD
GROOMBRIDGE HILL
Top Hill Farm
STONE ROW COTTS
High Weald Wlk
B2110
Harness Well Wood
Sewage Works

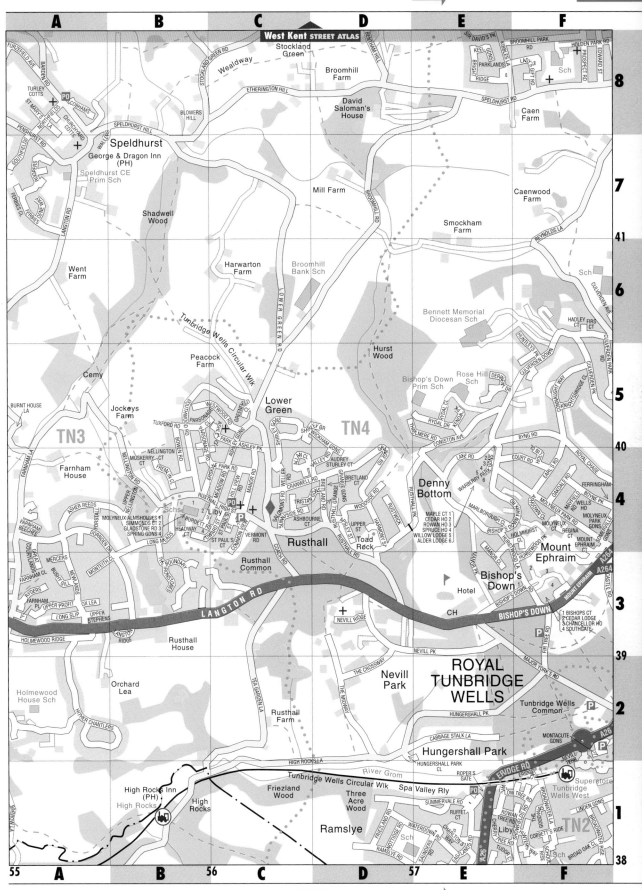

West Kent STREET ATLAS

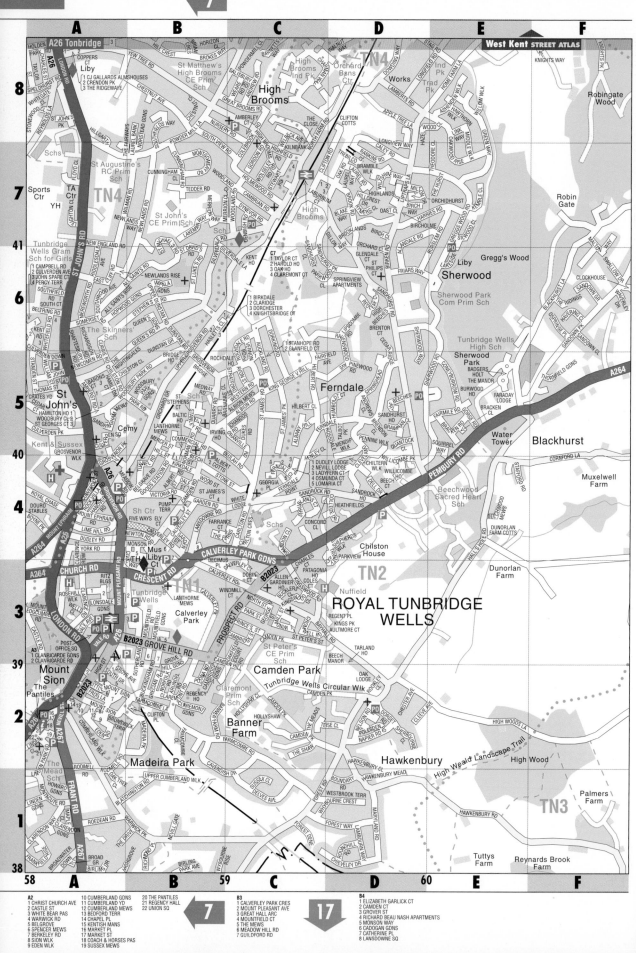

TN11

Sandhill Farm

Newbars Wood

Pembury Sch

Lower Green

Marshleyharbour Wood

Forest Wood

Snipe Wood

Pembury

Liby

Romford

Priory Farm

Henwood Green

Pembury Grange

Superstore

Woodhill Pk

Greenleas

The Paddock

Pembury

The Coach House

Oakley Sch

HASTINGS RD

A21 Hastings

West Kent STREET ATLAS

Larkfield Hall

Chalket Farm

TN2

High Weald Landscape Trail
Tunbridge Wells Circular Walk

Pastheap Farm

Fletchers

Fletchers Farm

Mouseden

Little Bayhall Farm

Great Bayhall

Brickhurst Wood

TN12

Great Bayhall Farm

Gull Rough Wood

Little Bayhall

TN3

Old Dundle

Dodhurst

River Teise

Dundale Farm

Dundale Wood

Brown's Lodge

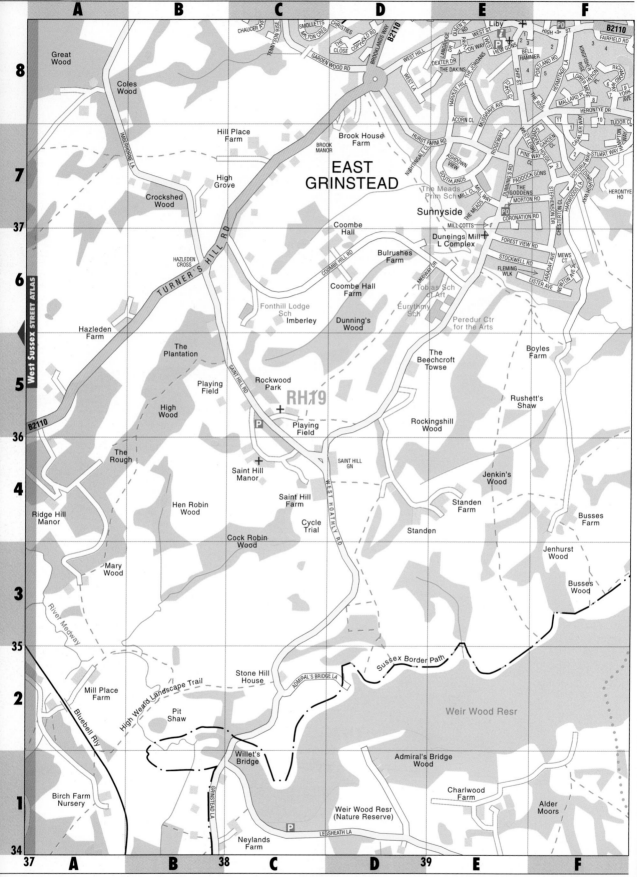

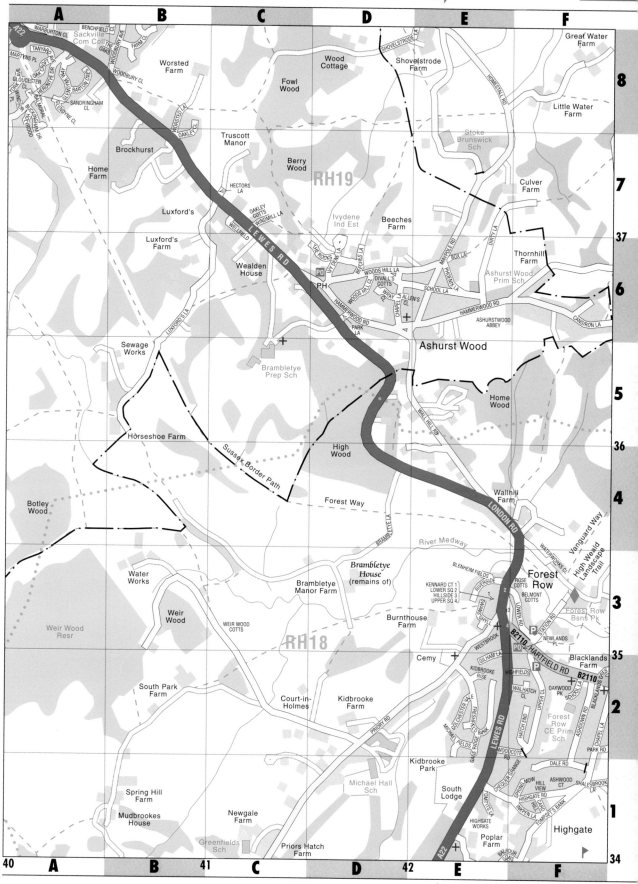

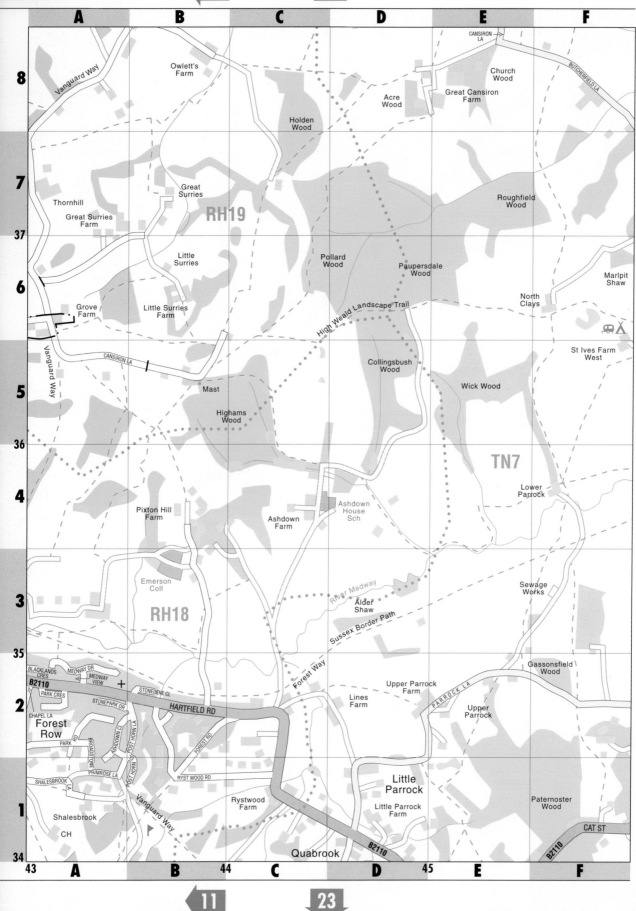
A   B   C   D   E   F

8

Vanguard Way

Owlett's Farm

CANSIRON LA

Church Wood

Acre Wood

Great Cansiron Farm

BUTCHERFIELD LA

Holden Wood

7

Thornhill

Great Surries

Roughfield Wood

RH19

37

Great Surries Farm

Little Surries

Pollard Wood

Paupersdale Wood

Marlpit Shaw

6

Grove Farm

Little Surries Farm

North Clays

High Weald Landscape Trail

Vanguard Way

CANSIRON LA

St Ives Farm West

Collingsbush Wood

Mast

Wick Wood

5

Highams Wood

36

TN7

Pixton Hill Farm

4

Ashdown Farm

Ashdown House Sch

Lower Parrock

Sewage Works

Emerson Coll

River Medway

3

RH18

Alder Shaw

Sussex Border Path

35

BLACKLANDS CRES

MEDWAY DR

MEDWAY VIEW

STONEDENE CL

Forest Way

Gassonsfield Wood

B2110

PARK CRES

STONEPARK DR

HARTFIELD RD

Upper Parrock Farm

PARROCK LA

2

CHAPEL LA

Forest Row

PARK

BROADSTONE

FOREST RD

POST HORN LA

Lines Farm

Upper Parrock

PRIMROSE LA

RYST WOOD RD

SHALESBROOK LA

Vanguard Way

Rystwood Farm

Little Parrock

Paternoster Wood

1

Shalesbrook

CH

Little Parrock Farm

CAT ST

B2110

B2110

Quabrook

34

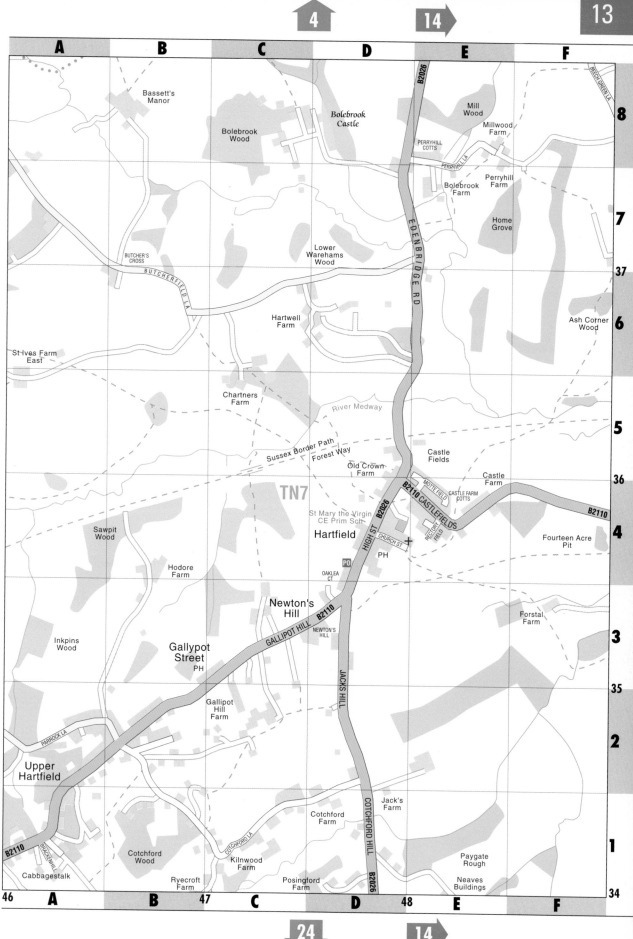

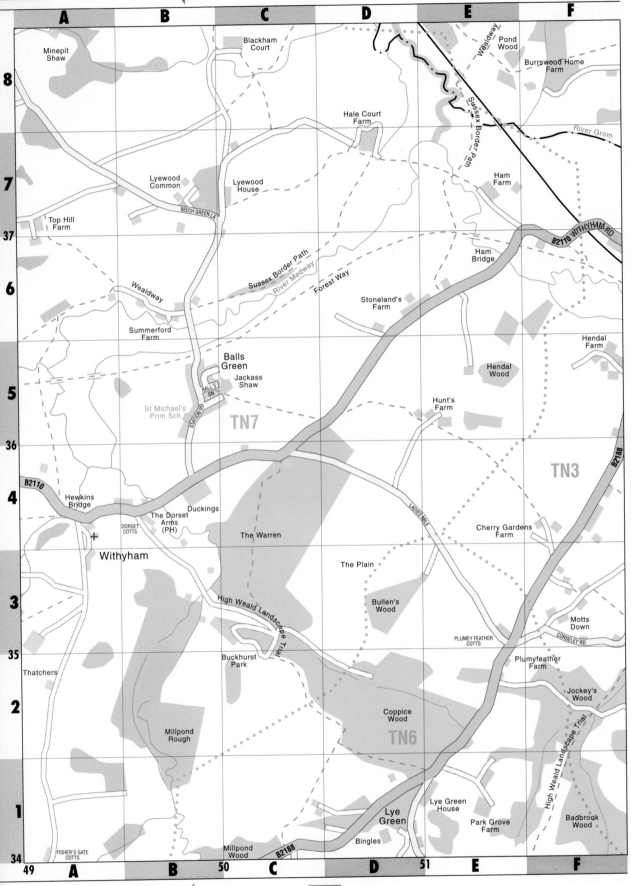

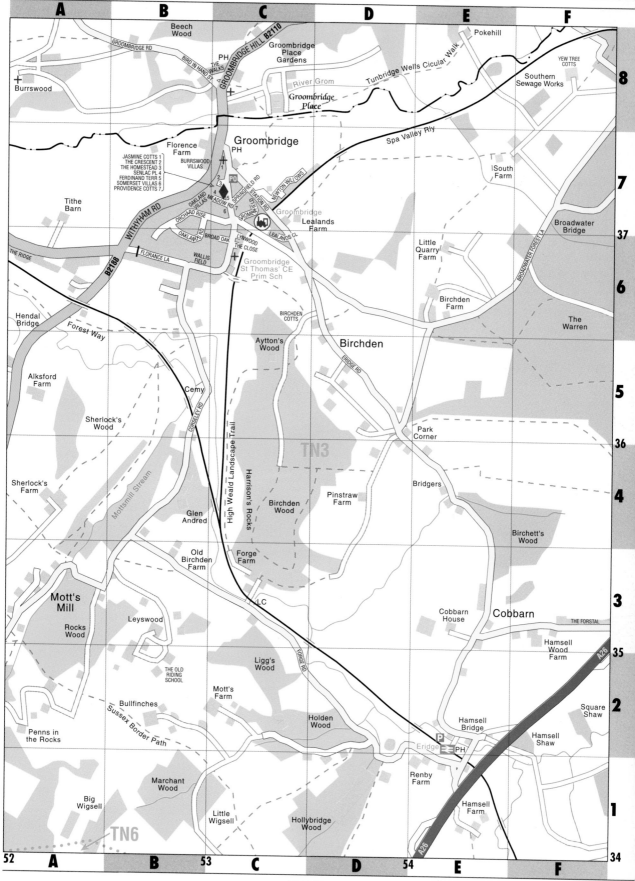

A B C D E F

8
7
37
6
5
36
4
3
35
2
1
34

Spa Valley Rly

LODGE LA

Broadwater
Forest

BROADWATER FOREST LA

The Firs

The Warren

Eridge
Rocks

Warren
Farm

The Nevill
Crest & Gun
(PH)

WARREN FARM LA

Eridge
Green

Crown House

A26

Steel
Bridge

Steel Bridge
Farm

Bushy
Wood

Great Robbins
Shaw

Ramslye
Wood

TN4

Ramslye
Farm

Strawberry
Hill

Ruffet
Wood

Spratsbrook
Farm

Broadwater
Lodge

Firtree
Plantation

The
Roundabouts

Eridge
Park

Eridge
Park

Mill
Wood

High Weald Landscape Trail

Forge
Wood

Bushy
Shaw

RAMSLYE RD

EASTLANDS
CL

ERIDGE RD

A26

SCOTTS
WAY

STUART CL

SIDNEY CL

LENDA DR

SCHFIELDS RD

ESSEX CL

FURNIVAL
CT

BROADWATER
LA

BROADCROFT

Sch

Court
Royal

BROADWATER
CT

KENTISH GDNS

BROADMEAD

SURREY CL

GLENMORE PK

ST GEORGE'S

BROADWATER DOWN

HARGATE CL

STRAWBERRY CL

Broadwater
Down

TN2

1 LEICESTER DR
2 DEVONSHIRE CL
3 BROADMEAD AVE

BARNFIELD

ST MARK'S RD

HARESCROFT

Strawberry Hill
Farm

Sprat's Brook

Hargate
Forest

BUNNY LA

Bohemia

Whitehill
Wood

TN3

Keepers
Cottages

Eridge
Old Park

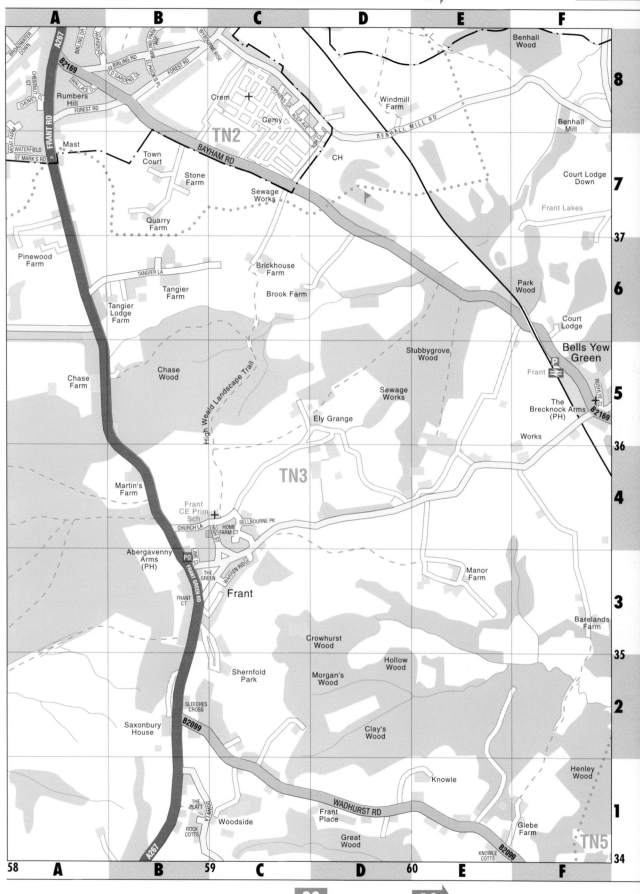

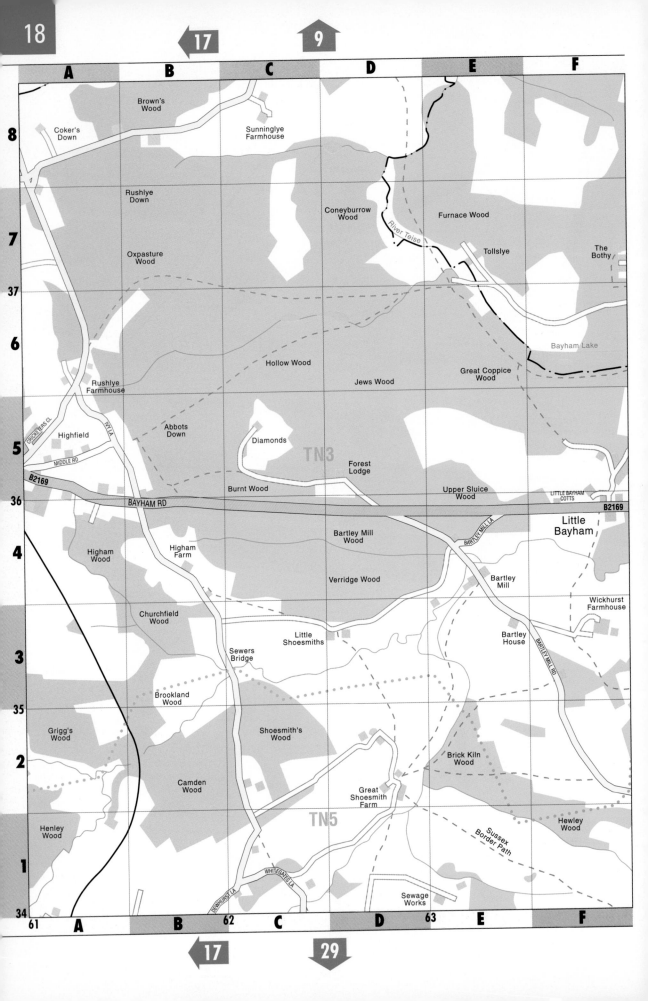

A B C D E F

8

Coker's Down

Brown's Wood

Sunninglye Farmhouse

Rushlye Down

Coneyburrow Wood

Furnace Wood

River Teise

7

Oxpasture Wood

Tollslye

The Bothy

37

6

Bayham Lake

Rushlye Farmhouse

Hollow Wood

Jews Wood

Great Coppice Wood

CROCKERS CL.

Highfield

IVY LA.

Abbots Down

Diamonds

TN3

5

MIDDLE RD

Forest Lodge

B2169

Burnt Wood

Upper Sluice Wood

LITTLE BAYHAM COTTS

36

BAYHAM RD

B2169

Little Bayham

BARTLEY MILL LA.

4

Higham Wood

Higham Farm

Bartley Mill Wood

Bartley Mill

Verridge Wood

Wickhurst Farmhouse

Churchfield Wood

Little Shoesmiths

BARTLEY MILL RD

Bartley House

Sewers Bridge

3

35

Brookland Wood

Grigg's Wood

Shoesmith's Wood

Brick Kiln Wood

2

Camden Wood

Great Shoesmith Farm

TN5

Henley Wood

Sussex Border Path

Hewley Wood

1

WHITEGATES LA.

DEWHURST LA.

Sewage Works

34

61 A B 62 C D 63 E F

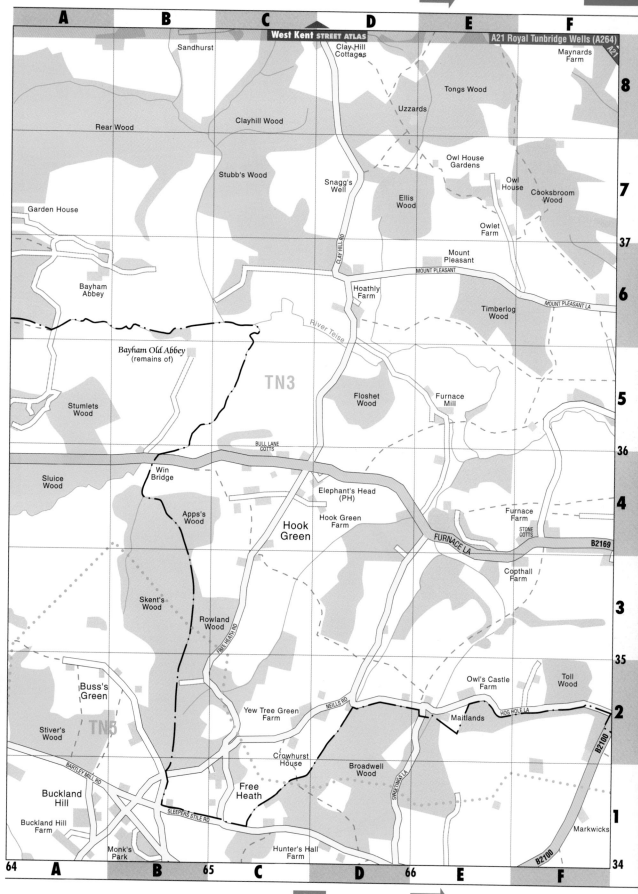

West Kent STREET ATLAS

A21 Royal Tunbridge Wells (A264)

Sandhurst

Clay Hill Cottages

Maynards Farm

Tongs Wood

Uzzards

Clayhill Wood

Rear Wood

Owl House Gardens

Stubb's Wood

Owl House

Cooksbroom Wood

Snagg's Well

Ellis Wood

Garden House

Owlet Farm

Mount Pleasant

MOUNT PLEASANT

Hoathly Farm

MOUNT PLEASANT LA

Bayham Abbey

Timberlog Wood

River Teise

Bayham Old Abbey (remains of)

TN3

Floshet Wood

Furnace Mill

Stumlets Wood

BULL LANE COTTS

Win Bridge

Sluice Wood

Elephant's Head (PH)

Apps's Wood

Hook Green Farm

Furnace Farm

Hook Green

STONE COTTS

FURNACE LA

B2169

Copthall Farm

Skent's Wood

Rowland Wood

Owl's Castle Farm

Toll Wood

Buss's Green

Yew Tree Green Farm

NEILLS RD

HOG HOLE LA

Maitlands

TN5

Stiver's Wood

B2100

BARTLEY MILL RD

Crowhurst House

Broadwell Wood

SWEETINGS LA

Buckland Hill

Free Heath

SLEEPERS STILE RD

Buckland Hill Farm

Markwicks

Monk's Park

Hunter's Hall Farm

B2100

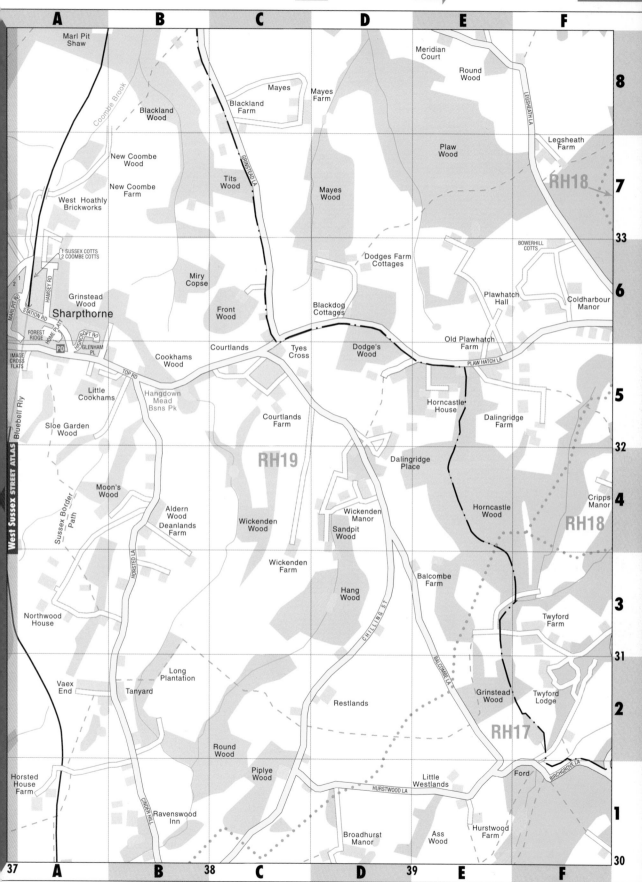

Marl Pit Shaw

Coombe Brook

Blackland Wood

New Coombe Wood

New Coombe Farm

West Hoathly Brickworks

1 SUSSEX COTTS
2 COOMBE COTTS

Grinstead Wood

Sharpthorne

FOREST RIDGE

HOME PLATT

STATION RD

HAMSEY RD

MARL PIT RD

ASHCROFT RD

GLENHAM PL

PO

IMAGE CROSS FLATS

Bluebell Rly

West Sussex STREET ATLAS

Little Cookhams

Cookhams Wood

TOP RD

Hangdown Mead Bsns Pk

Sloe Garden Wood

Moon's Wood

Sussex Border Path

HORSTED LA

Aldern Wood

Deanlands Farm

Northwood House

Vaex End

Tanyard

Long Plantation

CINDER HILL

Horsted House Farm

Ravenswood Inn

Mayes

Blackland Farm

Tits Wood

GRINSTEAD LA

Miry Copse

Front Wood

Courtlands

Courtlands Farm

RH19

Wickenden Wood

Wickenden Farm

Round Wood

Piplye Wood

Mayes Farm

Mayes Wood

Dodges Farm Cottages

Blackdog Cottages

Tyes Cross

Dodge's Wood

Dalingridge Place

CHILLING ST

Wickenden Manor

Sandpit Wood

Hang Wood

Restlands

BALCOMBE LA

Broadhurst Manor

HURSTWOOD LA

Meridian Court

Round Wood

Plaw Wood

LEGSHEATH LA

Legsheath Farm

RH18

BOWERHILL COTTS

Plawhatch Hall

Coldharbour Manor

Old Plawhatch Farm

PLAW HATCH LA

Horncastle House

Dalingridge Farm

Horncastle Wood

Cripps Manor

RH18

Balcombe Farm

Twyford Farm

Grinstead Wood

Twyford Lodge

RH17

Little Westlands

Ford

BIRCHGROVE LA

Ass Wood

Hurstwood Farm

8

7

33

6

5

32

4

3

31

2

1

30

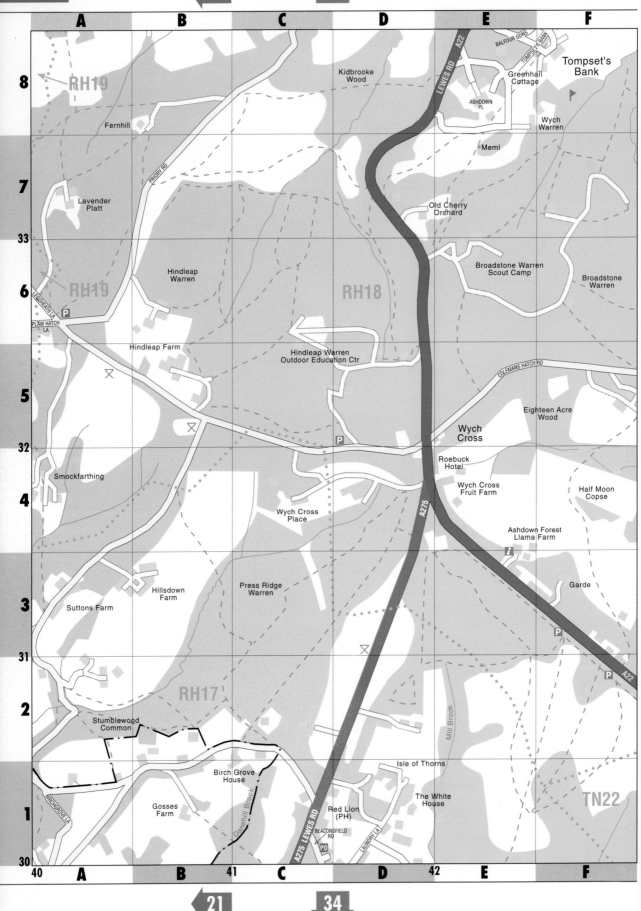

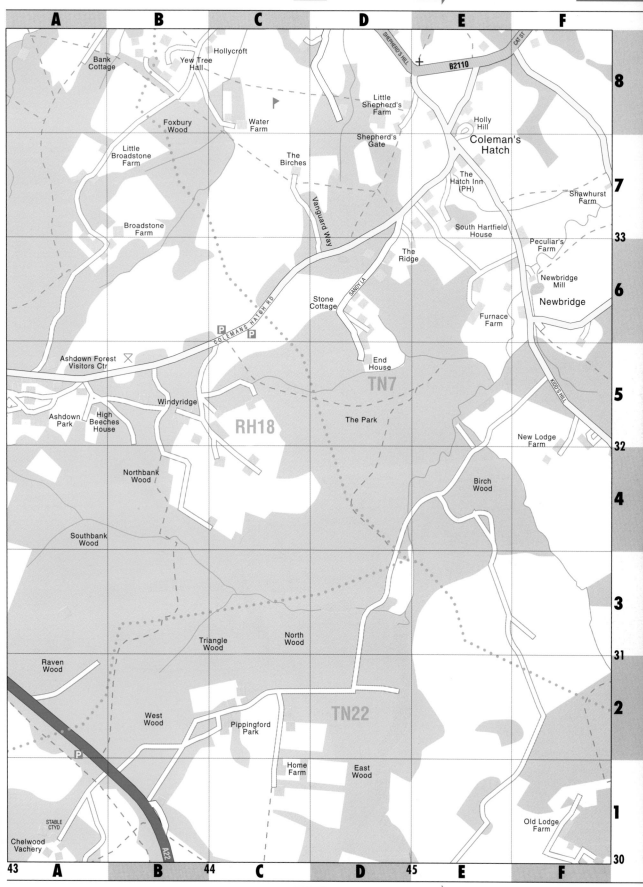

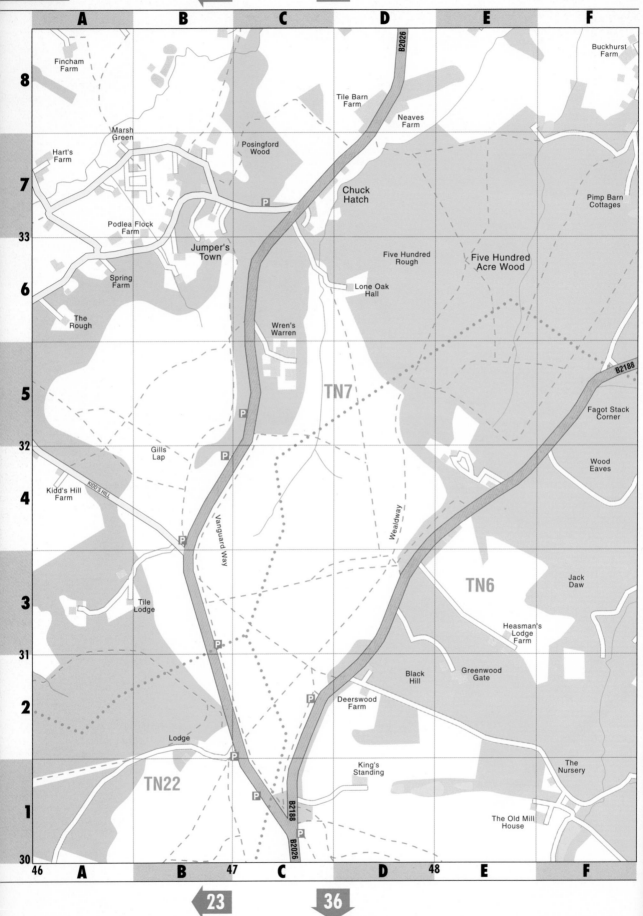

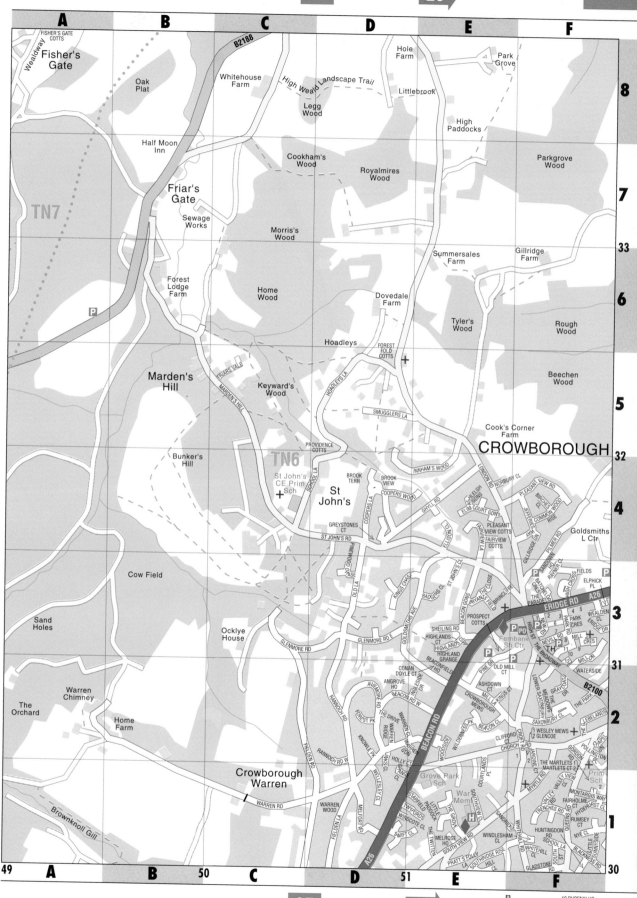

Fisher's Gate Cotts
Wealdway
Fisher's Gate
Oak Plat
Whitehouse Farm
B2188
High Weald Landscape Trail
Hole Farm
Park Grove
Littlebrook
Legg Wood
High Paddocks
Half Moon Inn
Cookham's Wood
Royalmires Wood
Parkgrove Wood
Friar's Gate
Sewage Works
Morris's Wood
Summersales Farm
Gillridge Farm
TN7
Forest Lodge Farm
Home Wood
Dovedale Farm
Tyler's Wood
Rough Wood
Hoadleys
Forest Fold Cotts
Marden's Hill
Friars Vale
Keyward's Wood
Beechen Wood
MARDEN'S HILL
SMUGGLERS LA
Cook's Corner Farm
Bunker's Hill
Providence Cotts
Innham's Wood
CROWBOROUGH
TN6
St John's CE Prim Sch
Brook Terr
Brook View
London Rd
Norbury Cl
St John's
Coopers Wood
Pleasant View Rd
Greystones Ct
Gryll Rd
Elim Court Gdns
Birches Cl
Common Wood Rise
St John's Rd
Coopers La
Pleasant View Cotts
Fairview Cotts
Goldsmiths L Ctr
Pinewood Chase
Cow Field
Kings Chase
Badgers Cl
St John's Cl
Beacon Edns
Bryants Fld
The Close
Bringliffe
Prospect Cotts
The Parade
Fields
Elphick Pl
Old La
Sand Holes
Ocklye House
Glenmore Rd
Glenmore Rd E
Goldsmiths Ave
Sheiling Rd
Highlands Ct
Highlands Grange
Highland Grange
Beaconfield
ERIDGE RD
A26
Park Cres
Wealden Cl
Eridge Dr
Pine Dr
Old Mill Ct
Waterside
B2100
Warren Chimney
The Orchard
Conan Doyle Ct
Angrove Ho
Aviemore Rd
The Drive
Warren Ridge
Warren Rd W
Beacon Rd W
Ashdown Ho
Mill La
Kings Gen
Crowborough Mews
Saxonbury Cl
Home Farm
Forest Pk
Rannoch Rd
Knowle Pk
Holly Cl
Wilderness Pk
Beacon Rd
Beacon Cl
Clifford Cl
Croft Rd
Church Rd
Wesley Mews
Glencoe
The Glebelands
Pollington
Crowborough Warren
WARREN RD
Warren Wood
Felden La
Wellesley Ct
Melfort Rd
Courtlands
Grove Park Sch
War Mem
Myrtle Rd
The Martlets
Martlets Ct
Prim Sch
Brownknoll Gill
Warren Rd
Stanford
Twyfords
Winscote Cl
The Twitten
Swift Cl
Melrose Ho
Pratt's Folly La
South View Rd
Windlesham Cl
Southridge Rise
Whitehill Rd
Gladstone Cl
Valley View
Trenches Rd
Fairholme Ct
Rumsey Ct
Huntingdon Rd
School La
Nye Cl
Montargis Way
Wydehurst Ct
Blackness Rd
Dunnside
A26

F3
1 THE LAURELS
2 LINK HO
3 MYRTLE COTTS
4 CROWBOROUGH CT
5 MAYVERN CT
6 PARK LA
7 NEVILL TERR
8 CROYDON COTTS
9 WARREN CT
10 PHOENIX HO
11 CROHAM RD
12 BARCOMBE PL

8
7
33
6
5
32
4
3
31
2
1

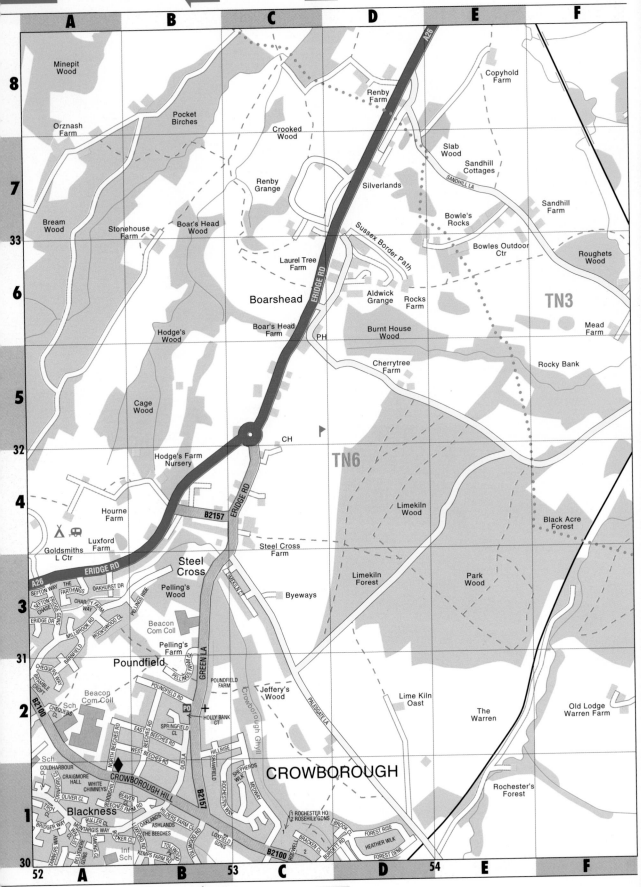

A B C D E F

Hamsell Manor

Rowland Wood

Stonewall Ghyll

Stitches Farm

Sham Farm

Danegate

Long Wood

Rocks Wood

Stonewall

Sussex Border Path

Spring Wood

Saxonbury Wood

TN3

Whitehouse Farm

Great Danegate

Saxonbury Hill

Marchant's Wood

Hoth Farm

Ashets

Blackdon Hill

Redgate Mill Farm

Lords Wood

Green Hedges Farm

Blackdon Hill Farm

Newhouse Farm

Card's Wood

Entryhill Wood

Towers Lodge Farm

Sewage Works

BRICKYARD LA

The Cants

Hoth Wood

Entry Hill

Forest Farm

Stone House Farm

Hornshurst Wood

The Gill

Lodge Farm

Little Millhole Wood

Big Millhole Wood

TN6

Markhouse Farm

B2100

FRIDGE LA

Greenhouse Farm

Town Row Green Farm

Orphanage Wood

Cemy

Heathfield Hall

Town Row

Chant Lane Farm

DOUGLAS RD

STATION CL

ASHLEY RD

Ashley Farm

Medway Farm

CATT'S HILL

Bletchingley Wood

Highgate Farm

CHANT LA

St Deny's Lodge

Biddenden Farm

STATION RD

NEW RD

PO

PH

BANDEN CL

YEWTREE LA

HOSMERS FIELD LA

Catt's Corner Cotts

SEYMOUR COTTS

Bletchingley Farm

Bletchinglye LA

HIGHGATE FLATS

B2100

8
7
33
6
5
32
4
31
2
1
30

55 A B 56 C D 57 E F

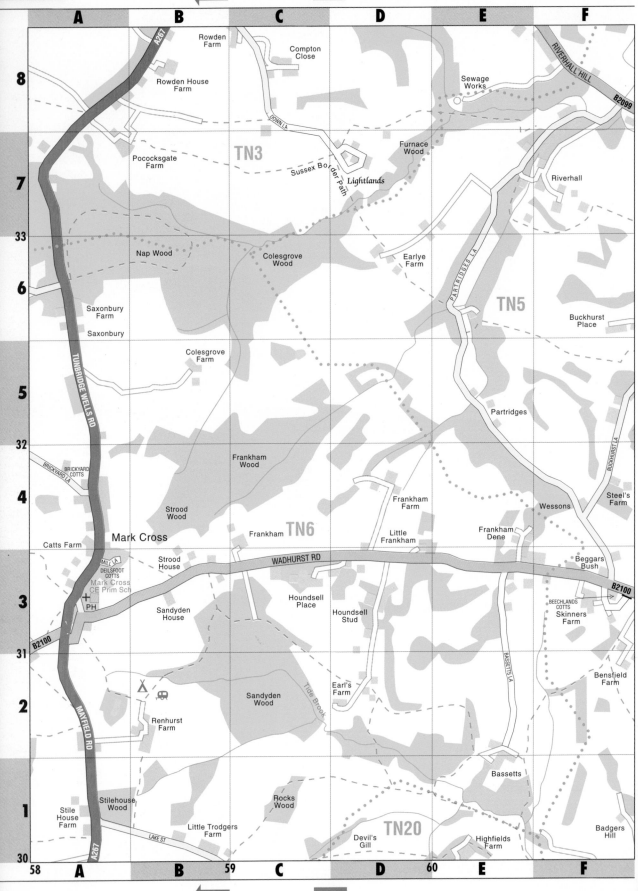

A **B** **C** **D** **E** **F**

8

Rowden
Farm

Compton
Close

Sewage
Works

RIVERHALL HILL

B2099

Rowden House
Farm

DOWN LA

TN3

Furnace
Wood

7

Pococksgate
Farm

Sussex Border Path

Lightlands

Riverhall

33

Nap Wood

Colesgrove
Wood

Earlye
Farm

PARTRIDGES LA

6

Saxonbury
Farm

TN5

Buckhurst
Place

Saxonbury

Colesgrove
Farm

BUCKHURST LA

5

Partridges

32

Frankham
Wood

BRICKYARD LA

BRICKYARD
COTTS

4

Strood
Wood

Frankham
Farm

Wessons

Steel's
Farm

Catts Farm

Mark Cross

Frankham

TN6

Little
Frankham

Frankham
Dene

TUNBRIDGE WELLS RD

MILL LA

DEILSFOOT
COTTS

Strood
House

WADHURST RD

Beggars
Bush

B2100

3

Mark Cross
CE Prim Sch

PH

Sandyden
House

Houndsell
Place

Houndsell
Stud

BEECHLANDS
COTTS

Skinners
Farm

B2100

31

BASSETTS LA

Bensfield
Farm

2

Renhurst
Farm

Sandyden
Wood

Tide Brook

Earl's
Farm

MAYFIELD RD

Bassetts

1

Stile
House
Farm

Stilehouse
Wood

Little Trodgers
Farm

Rocks
Wood

TN20

Devil's
Gill

Highfields
Farm

Badgers
Hill

LAKE ST

A267

30

58 **A** **B** 59 **C** **D** 60 **E** **F**

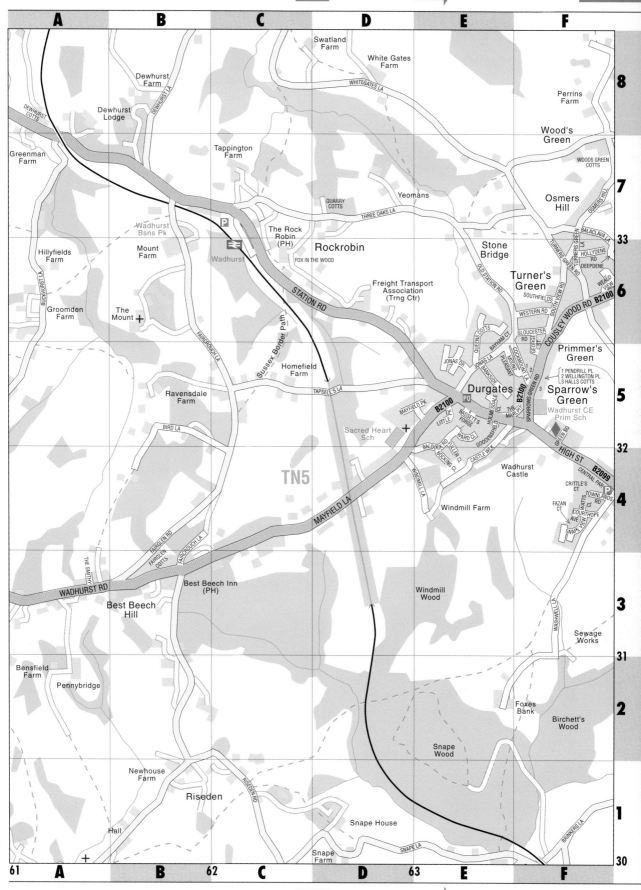

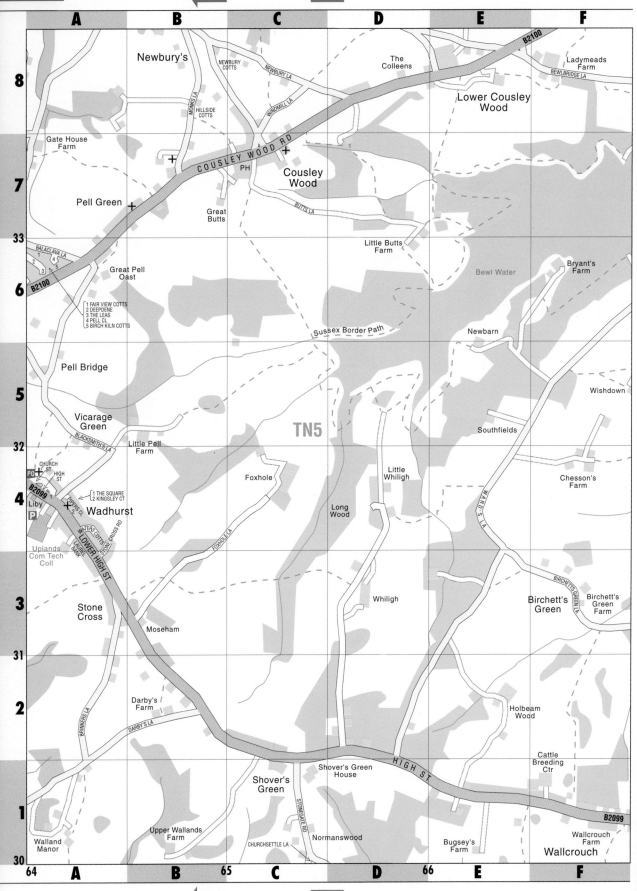

29

19

A B C D E F

8

Newbury's

Newbury Cotts

Newbury La

The Colleens

Ladymeads Farm

B2100

Bewlbridge La

Lower Cousley Wood

Monks La

Hillside Cotts

Windmill La

7

Gate House Farm

Cousley Wood Rd

PH

Cousley Wood

Pell Green

Great Butts

Butts La

Little Butts Farm

Bryant's Farm

33

Balaclava La

1
4
2
3 5

Great Pell Oast

Bewl Water

6

B2100

1 FAIR VIEW COTTS
2 DEEPDENE
3 THE LEAS
4 PELL CL
5 BIRCH KILN COTTS

Sussex Border Path

Newbarn

Pell Bridge

Wishdown

5

Vicarage Green

Blacksmith's La

Little Pell Farm

TN5

Foxhole

Little Whilligh

Southfields

Chesson's Farm

32

Church St

High St

PO

B2099

1 THE SQUARE
2 KINGSLEY CT

Cupers Cl

Liby

4

P

Wadhurst

Foxhole La

Long Wood

Ward's La

Uplands Com Tech Coll

Waters Cotts

Stone Cross Rd

Lower High St

Laurel Bank

Whilligh

Birchett's Green La

Birchett's Green

Birchett's Green Farm

3

Stone Cross

Moseham

Whilligh

31

Brinkers La

Darby's Farm

Holbeam Wood

2

Darby's La

Cattle Breeding Ctr

High St

1

Shover's Green

Stonegate Rd

Shover's Green House

Upper Wallands Farm

Normanswood

Bugsey's Farm

B2099

Wallcrouch Farm

Walland Manor

Churchsettle La

Wallcrouch

30

64 A B 65 C D 66 E F

29

42

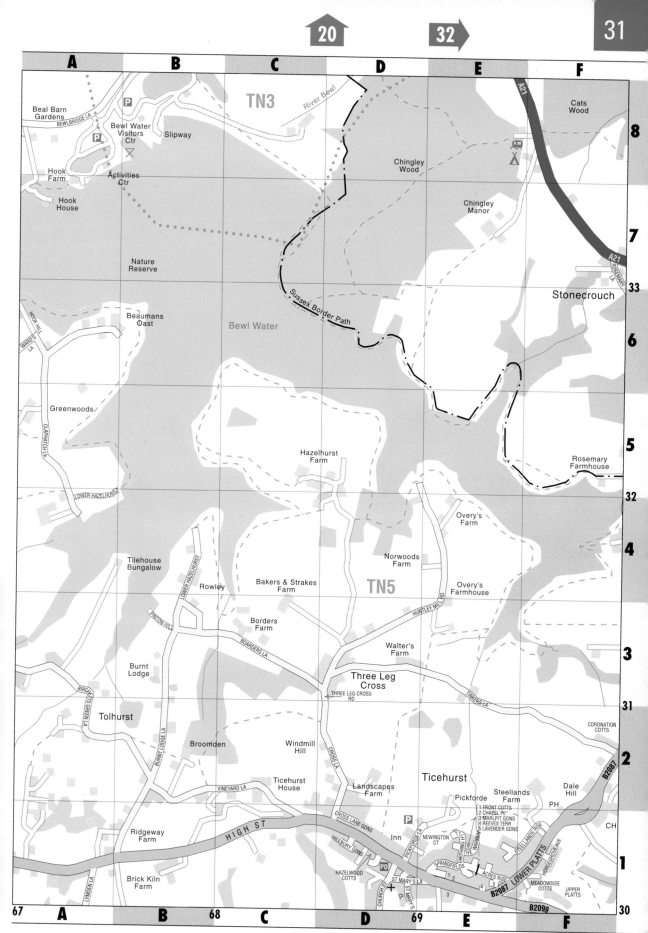

B2079

Combwell
Wood

P

Springwood
Lodge

Bedgebury
National Pinetum

Park
House

Bedgebury Park
Woods

TN17

Combwell Priory
Farm

LADY OAK LA

Stonecrouch
Farm House

A21

33

Starvegoose
Bank

Windmill Down

Flimwell
Grange

B2079

Windy
Ridge

Mast

Radio
Station

ROSEMARY LA

32

TN5

TN18

Ketley
Farm

Sussex Border Path

FLIMWELL
CL

Downash HO 1
Downash CT 2

1   2

BEWL BRIDGE CL

OLD WARDS DOWN

NURSERY CL

FRUITFIELDS

RED OAST
COTTS

BLENHEIM
WAY

PO

HIGH ST

LONDON RD

PH

PH

SUNNYBANK

Mount Pleasant
Farm

GINGERBREAD LA

A268 Hawkhurst

Flimwell

B2087

A268

HAWKHURST RD

A268

Union
Street

BROOM HILL
COTTS

UNION
ST

MEADOW VIEW

CLARK'S YD

31

B2087

Berner's
Hill

Quedley

West
Lodge

Seacox
Heath

Ringden
Wood

Keeper's
Cottage

Saw Mill

Sewage Works

TN19

Ringden
Farm

A21

30

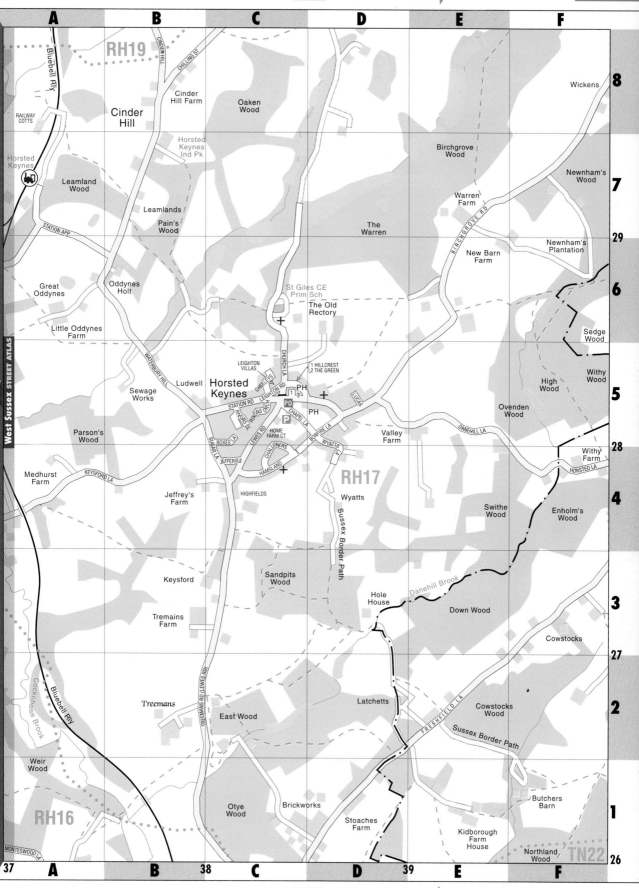

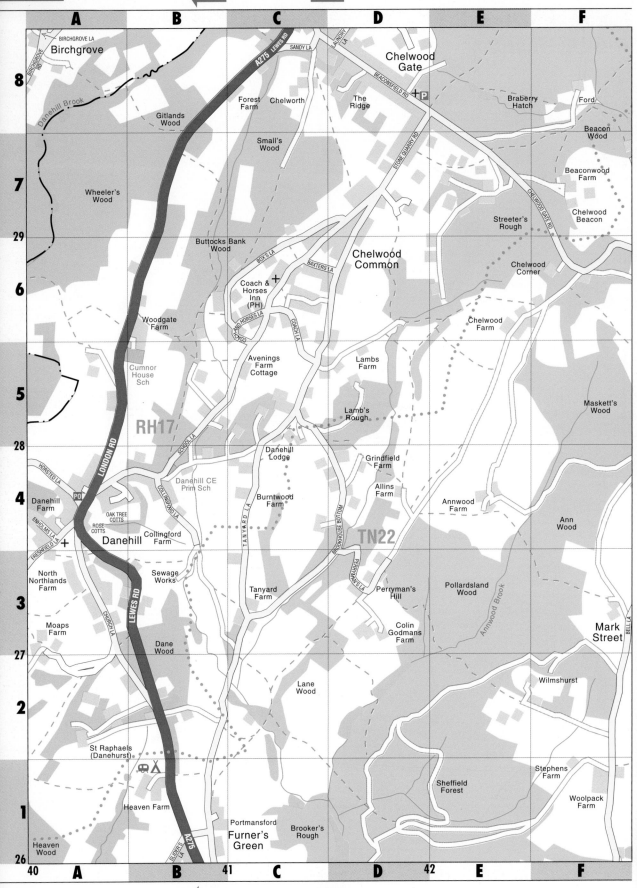

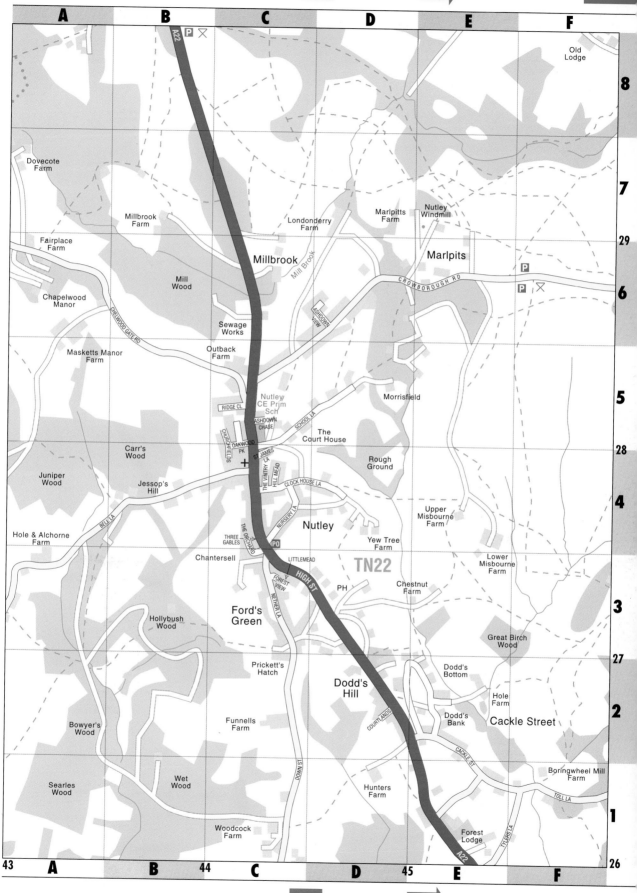

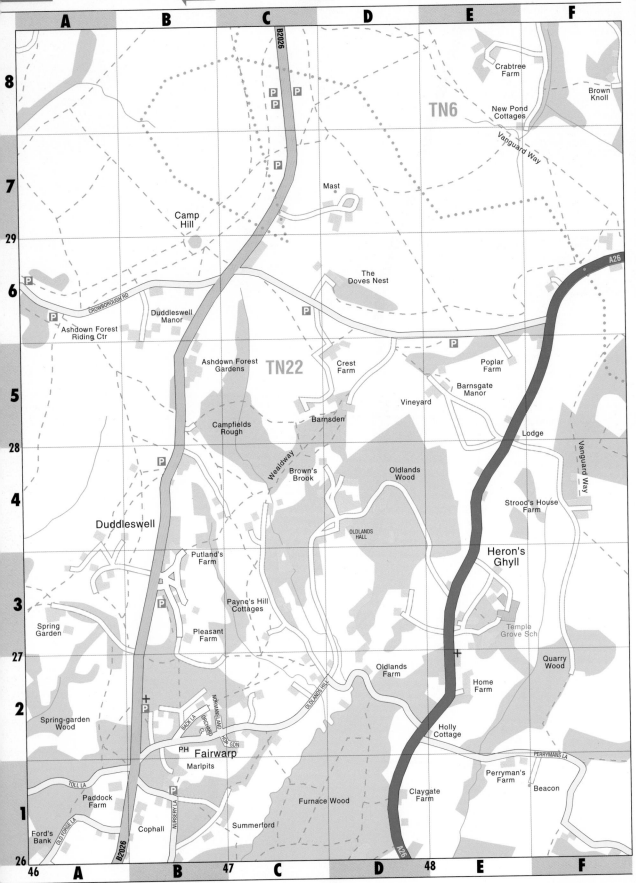

A B C D E F

8
7
29
6
5
28
4
3
27
2
1
26

TN6

TN22

A26

B2026

Crabtree Farm
Brown Knoll
New Pond Cottages
Vanguard Way

Camp Hill
Mast
The Doves Nest

CROWBOROUGH RD
Duddleswell Manor
Ashdown Forest Riding Ctr
Ashdown Forest Gardens
Crest Farm
Poplar Farm
Barnsgate Manor
Vineyard
Lodge
Vanguard Way

Campfields Rough
Barnsden
Oldlands Wood
Strood's House Farm

Wealdway
Brown's Brook
Oldlands Hall
Heron's Ghyll

Duddleswell
Putland's Farm
Temple Grove Sch
Quarry Wood

Spring Garden
Payne's Hill Cottages
Oldlands Farm
Home Farm

Pleasant Farm
Holly Cottage

Spring-garden Wood
BACK LA
NORMANSLAND
ORCHARD CT
HA
GDN
Fairwarp
Marlpits
Oldlands Hill
Perryman's Farm
Beacon
PERRYMANS LA

PH
Paddock Farm
NURSERY LA
Furnace Wood
Claygate Farm

Ford's Bank
TOLL LA
OLD FORGE LA
Cophall
Summerford
B2026
A26

46 A 47 B C 47 D 48 E F

F8
1 QUARRY VIEW
2 FERMOR ROW
3 CARLTON TERR
4 JUBILEE COTTS
5 MARLOW CT
6 HILLSIDE

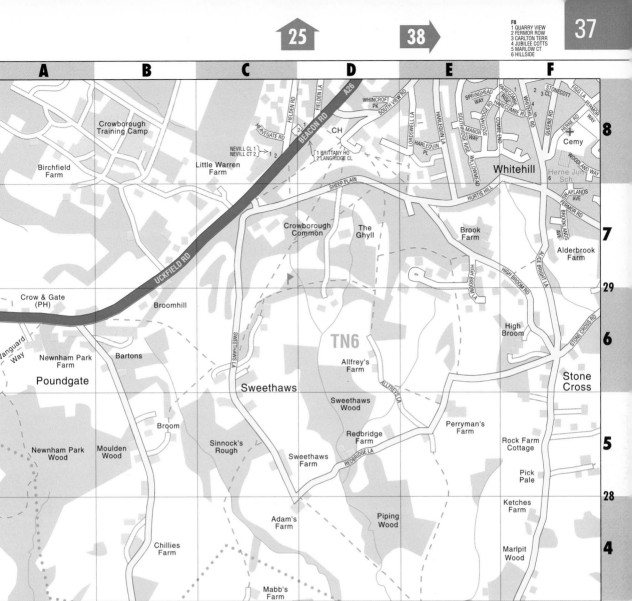

A · B · C · D · E · F

8
Crowborough Training Camp
Birchfield Farm
Little Warren Farm
NEVILL CL 1
NEVILL CT 2
HEVEGATE RD
FELDEN RD
FELDEN LA
BEACON RD
A26
WHINCROFT PK
SOUTH NEW RD
CH
1 BRITTANY HO
2 LANGRIDGE CL
LORDSWELL LA
HARLEQUIN LA
HARLEQUIN PL
SPRINGHEAD WAY
HARECOMBE RISE
PAREGREAVE RISE
SOUTHRIDGE RISE
MANOR WAY
COMBE END
WILLOWMEAD
WHITEHILL RD
QUEENS RD
STONECOTT
3 CL
FIGGS LA
FERMOR WAY
HERNE RD
WOODLAND WAY
Cemy
Herne Jun Sch
6
Whitehill

7
SHEEP PLAIN
Crowborough Common
The Ghyll
HURTIS HILL
Brook Farm
BROOKLANDS AVE
AYLANDS AVE
FERMOR RD
Alderbrook Farm

29
HIGH BROOM LA
HIGH BROOM RD
ALCE BRIGHT LA

6
Crow & Gate (PH)
Broomhill
TN6
High Broom
STONE CROSS RD
Stone Cross

Vanguard Way
Newnham Park Farm
Bartons
SWEETHAWS LA
Allfrey's Farm
Poundgate
Sweethaws

5
Broom
Sweethaws Wood
Perryman's Farm
Rock Farm Cottage
Newnham Park Wood
Moulden Wood
Sinnock's Rough
Redbridge Farm
ALLFREY'S LA
Pick Pale
Sweethaws Farm
REDBRIDGE LA

28
Ketches Farm

4
Adam's Farm
Piping Wood
Chillies Farm
Marlpit Wood

Broadfield Wood
Mabb's Farm
Grovehurst Farm
CHILLIES LA
Welchwood Farm

3
Vanguard Way
Greystones Farm
Oaky Wood
Oxley Wood
Brook House
Burnt Oak

27
Shadwell Farm
BURNT OAK RD
Burnt Oak Farm
FORDBROOK HILL

2
TN22
Holly Mount
Pickreed Wood
Grey Burchetts Wood
Wilding Wood
TIBBS MILL LA
Fordbrook Farm
MADLOW DOWN RD

Oldhall Farm
Lodge Wood
Pond Bay

1
High Hurstwood CE Prim Sch
High Hurstwood
Mount Pleasant Farm
Hurstwood Farm
The Rough
Kiln Farm
ROYAL OAK LA
FOWLY LA

26

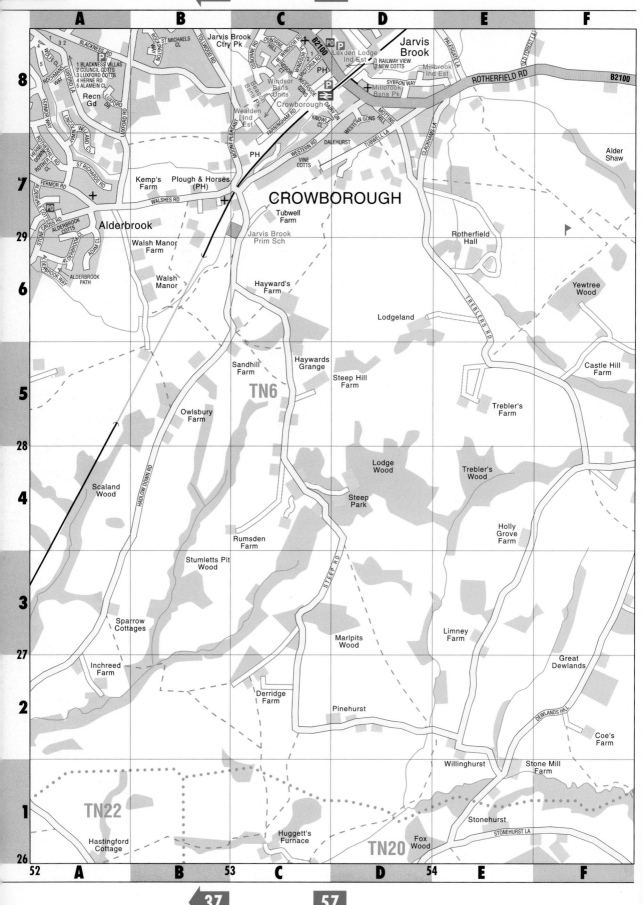

A B C D E F

8

7

29

6

5

28

4

3

27

2

1

26

52 A 53 B C 53 D 54 E F

CROWBOROUGH

Jarvis Brook

Alder Shaw

Rotherfield Hall

Yewtree Wood

Castle Hill Farm

Trebler's Farm

Lodgeland

Lodge Wood

Trebler's Wood

Holly Grove Farm

Steep Park

Limney Farm

Great Dewlands

Coe's Farm

Stone Mill Farm

Willinghurst

Stonehurst

Fox Wood

Marlpits Wood

Pinehurst

Derridge Farm

Huggett's Furnace

Hastingford Cottage

Inchreed Farm

Sparrow Cottages

Stumletts Pit Wood

Rumsden Farm

Scaland Wood

Owlsbury Farm

Sandhill Farm

Haywards Grange

Steep Hill Farm

Hayward's Farm

Walsh Manor

Walsh Manor Farm

Alderbrook

Kemp's Farm

Plough & Horses (PH)

Tubwell Farm

Jarvis Brook Prim Sch

WALSHES RD

TN6

TN22

TN20

Recn Gd

BLACKNESS RD

St Michaels Cl

Jarvis Brook Ctry Pk

TOLLWOOD RD

ROCKINGTON WAY

OSBORNE RD

WINDSOR RD

OSBORNE HILL

B2100

Lexden Lodge Ind Est

RAILWAY VIEW

NEW COTTS

Millbrook Ind Est

SYBRON WAY

Millbrook Bsns Pk

ROTHERFIELD RD

B2100

PALESGATE LA

OLD FOREST LA

CLACKHAMS LA

TREBLERS RD

STEEP RD

HADLOW DOWN RD

DEWLANDS HILL

STONEHURST LA

Windsor Bsns Units

Crowborough

Wealden Ind Est

FARNINGHAM RD

MOUNT PLEASANT

WESTERN RD

VINE COTTS

DALEHURST

WESTERN GDNS

TURWELL LA

MOTTING HILL

KNOWLE CL

RIVERSIDE GDNS

VICTORIA RD

PH

1 Blackness Villas
2 Council Cotts
3 Luxford Cotts
4 Herne Rd
5 Alamein Cl

LUXFORD LA
WOLFE CL
RICHMANS WAY
FERMOR WAY
LINCOLN WAY
WELAND CL
LUXFORD RD
ROTHERHILL DOWNS
HERNE RD
ROTHER CL
ST RICHARDS RD
FERMOR RD
ALDERVALE COTTS
STONE CROSS RD
ALDERBROOK CL
ADAM CL
ALDERBROOK COTTS
ALDERBROOK WAY
ALDERBROOK PATH

PO

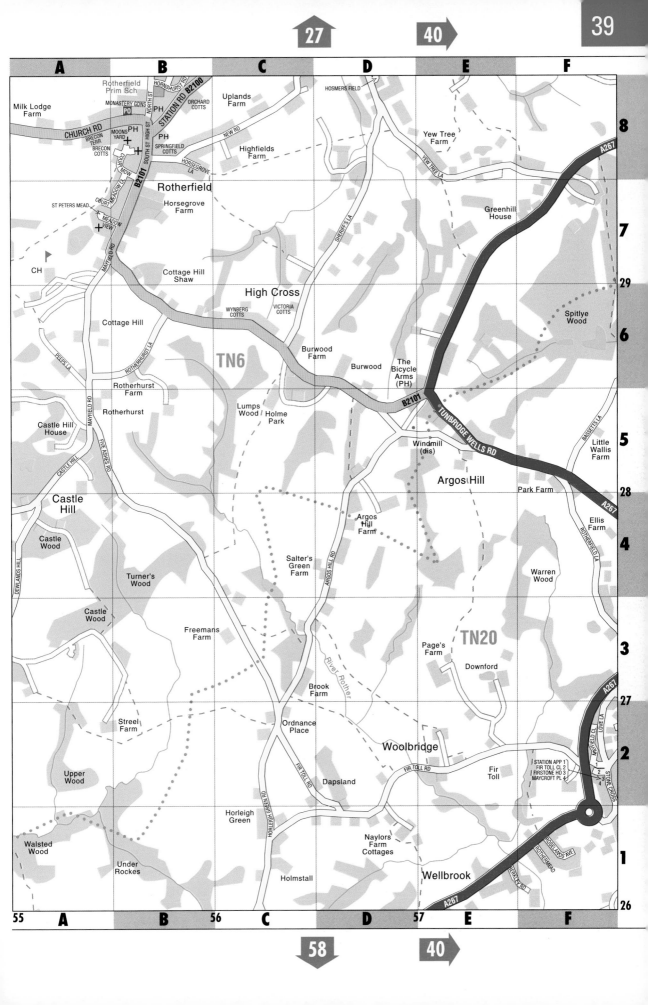

A B C D E F

Milk Lodge Farm

Rotherfield Prim Sch

MONASTERY GDNS
PO
CHURCH RD
BRECON TERR
BRECON COTTS
MOONS YARD
PH

STATION RD B2100
HORNSHURST RD
ORCHARD COTTS
NORTH ST
SOUTH ST HIGH ST
PH
PH
SPRINGFIELD COTTS
HORSEGROVE LA

Uplands Farm

NEW RD

Highfields Farm

HOSMERS FIELD

Yew Tree Farm

YEW TREE LA

A267

B2101

Rotherfield

St Peters Mead
MEADOW CL
COURT
MEADOW VIEW
MAYFIELD RD

Horsegrove Farm

SHERIFF'S LA

Greenhill House

CH

Cottage Hill Shaw

High Cross

WYNBERG COTTS
VICTORIA COTTS

Spitlye Wood

29

Cottage Hill

PEERS LA

ROTHERHURST LA

Burwood Farm

Burwood

The Bicycle Arms (PH)

6

TN6

Rotherhurst Farm

Rotherhurst

Lumps Wood

Holme Park

B2101

TUNBRIDGE WELLS RD

BASSETTS LA

Little Wallis Farm

5

Castle Hill House

Windmill (dis)

Argos Hill

Park Farm

A267

28

CASTLE HILL
FIVE ASHES RD
MAYFIELD RD

Castle Hill

Ellis Farm

ROTHERFIELD LA

Castle Wood

DEWLANDS HILL

Argos Hill Farm

Warren Wood

4

Turner's Wood

Salter's Green Farm

ARGOS HILL RD

TN20

Castle Wood

Freemans Farm

Page's Farm

Downford

A267

3

27

River Rother

Brook Farm

Ordnance Place

Woolbridge

STATION APP 1
FIR TOLL CL 2
FIRSTONE HO 3
MAYCROFT PL 4

MAYFIELD CL
LOVE LA
STONE CROSS

2

Streel Farm

FIR TOLL RD

Dapsland

Fir Toll

FIR TOLL RD

Upper Wood

HORLEIGH GREEN RD

Horleigh Green

Naylors Farm Cottages

ROSELANDS AVE

Walsted Wood

Under Rockes

Holmstall

Wellbrook

A267

ROTHERMEAD
PERACKS RD

26

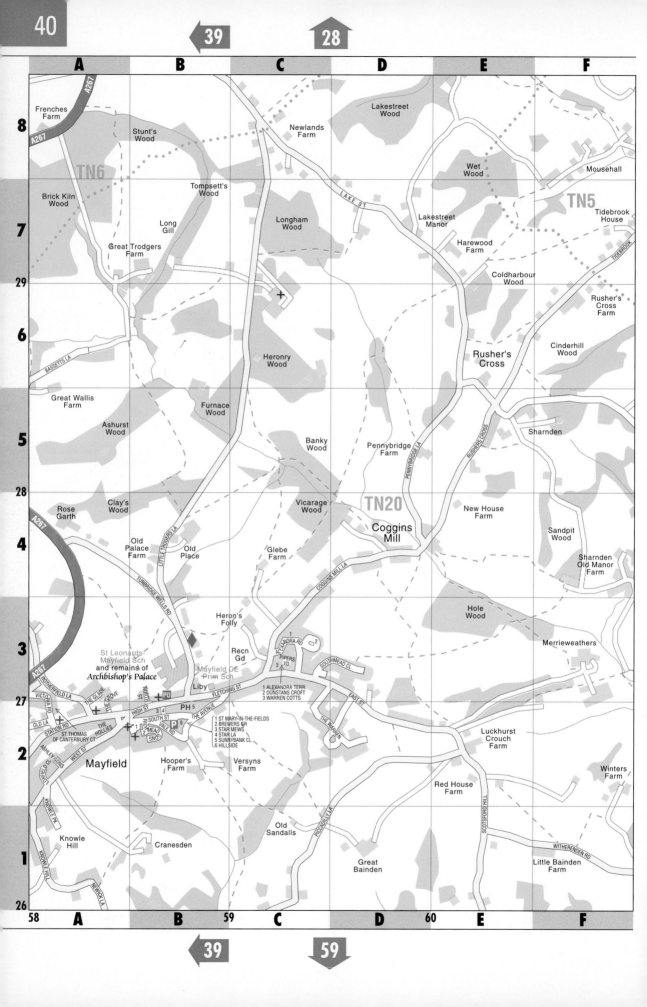

A B C D E F

8

Middle Wood

Slidingfield Wood

River Limden

The Olives

7

CHURCHSETTLE LA

Bricklehurst Manor

Bricklehurst Farm

BARDOWN RD

Bardown

Mabb's Hill Farm

MABB'S HILL

29

Churchsettle Farm

Longfield Shaw

Bardown Farm

Stonegate

LYMDEN LA

Peartree Wood

Maplesden Farm

Cooper's Farm

Cock Farm

THE ACORNS

LIMDEN CL

6

Maplesden

FORGE FIELD

COTTENDEN RD

Coalpit Wood

STONEGATE CT

OWLS GDNS

Stonegate CE Prim Sch

TN5

+

5

Dens Wood

Dens Farm

Hoadley Wood

STATION RD

28

4

Dens Bridge

Tide Brook

PEARTREE HILL

Marchant's Wood

Church Wood Shaws

3

Batt's Wood Cottages

Witherenden Farm

Stonegate

Hammerden

Newbridge Wood

27

Witherenden Mill

Cock's Wood

2

Bivelham Forge Farm

TN19

Witherenden Bridge

Alder Wood

Orchard Shaw

High Wood

Witherenden Hill

River Rother

Round Wood

1

Bines Farm

Bines Farm

Great Bines

Woodknowle Farm

Wreckery Bridge

26

64 A B 65 C D 66 E F

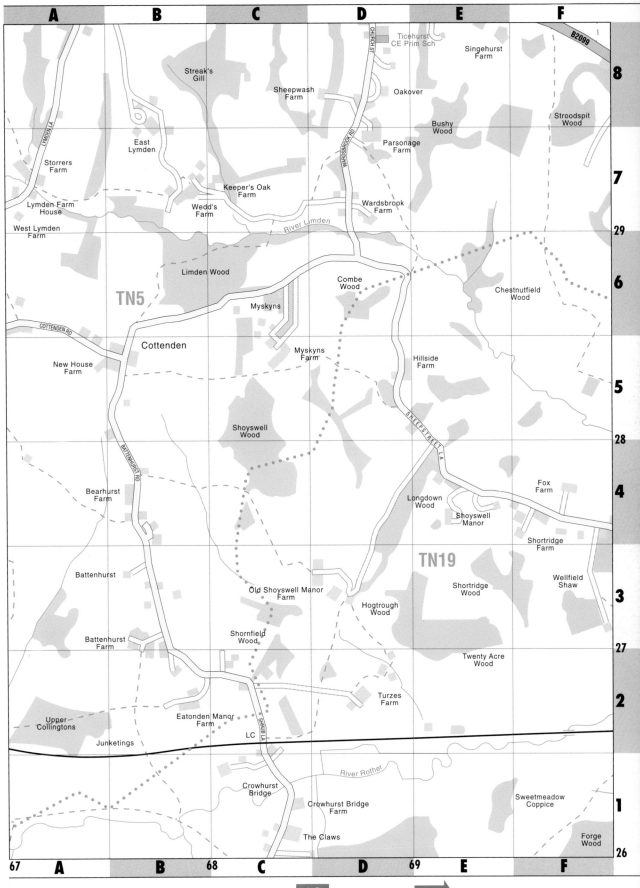

A B C D E F

8

Streak's Gill

Sheepwash Farm

CHURCH ST

Ticehurst CE Prim Sch

Singehurst Farm

Oakover

B2099

Stroodspit Wood

East Lymden

Storrers Farm

WARDSBROOK RD

Bushy Wood

Parsonage Farm

7

LYMDEN LA

Lymden Farm House

Keeper's Oak Farm

Wedd's Farm

Wardsbrook Farm

West Lymden Farm

River Limden

29

Limden Wood

Combe Wood

Chestnutfield Wood

6

TN5

Myskyns

COTTENDEN RD

Cottenden

Myskyns Farm

Hillside Farm

5

New House Farm

Shoyswell Wood

SHEEPSTREET LA

28

BATTENHURST RD

Longdown Wood

Shoyswell Manor

Fox Farm

4

Bearhurst Farm

Shortridge Farm

Battenhurst

TN19

Old Shoyswell Manor Farm

Hogtrough Wood

Shortridge Wood

Wellfield Shaw

3

Battenhurst Farm

Shornfield Wood

27

Twenty Acre Wood

2

Upper Collingtons

Eatonden Manor Farm

Turzes Farm

Junketings

LC

SHRUB LA

River Rother

Crowhurst Bridge

Sweetmeadow Coppice

1

Crowhurst Bridge Farm

The Claws

Forge Wood

26

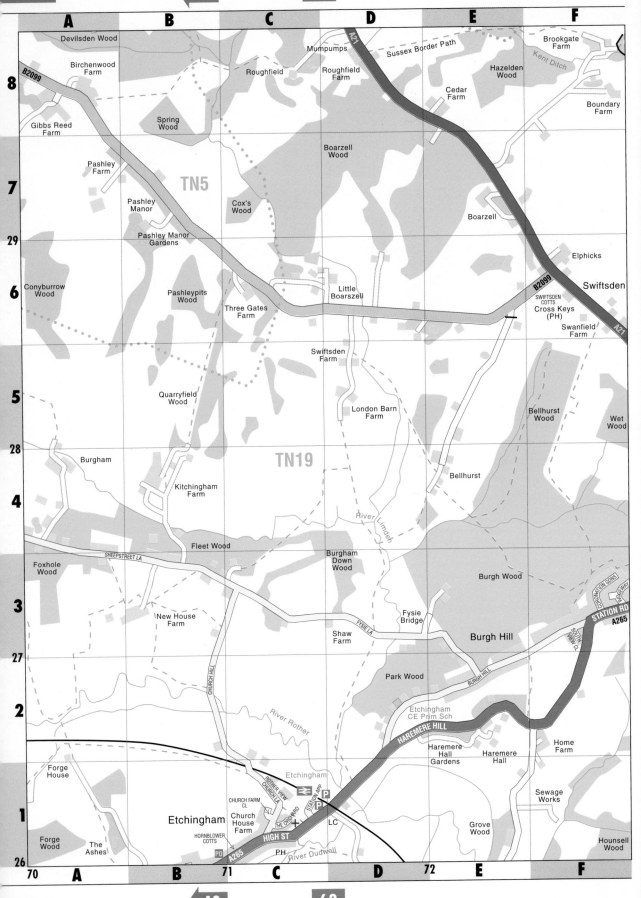

A B C D E F

8

B2099

Devilsden Wood

Birchenwood Farm

Gibbs Reed Farm

Mumpumps

A21

Sussex Border Path

Roughfield

Roughfield Farm

Cedar Farm

Hazelden Wood

Brookgate Farm

Kent Ditch

Boundary Farm

Spring Wood

Boarzell Wood

TN5

7

Pashley Farm

Pashley Manor

Cox's Wood

Boarzell

29

Pashley Manor Gardens

6

Conyburrow Wood

Pashleypits Wood

Three Gates Farm

Little Boarszell

B2099

Elphicks

Swiftsden

SWIFTSDEN COTTS

Cross Keys (PH)

Swanfield Farm

A21

Swiftsden Farm

5

Quarryfield Wood

London Barn Farm

Bellhurst Wood

Wet Wood

28

Burgham

Kitchingham Farm

TN19

Bellhurst

4

Foxhole Wood

SHEEPSTREET LA

Fleet Wood

River Limden

Burgham Down Wood

Burgh Wood

CORONATION GDNS

RISEWAY

3

New House Farm

CHURCH HILL

Shaw Farm

FYSIE LA

Fysie Bridge

Burgh Hill

STATION RD

A265

SOUTH VIEW CL

BURGH HILL

27

Park Wood

2

River Rother

Etchingham CE Prim Sch

HAREMERE HILL

Home Farm

Forge House

Etchingham

ROTHER VIEW

CHURCH LA

THE ORCHARD

STATION APP

P

P

Haremere Hall Gardens

Haremere Hall

Sewage Works

1

Etchingham

CHURCH FARM CL

Church House Farm

LC

Grove Wood

Hounsell Wood

Forge Wood

The Ashes

HORNBLOWER COTTS

PO

A265

HIGH ST

PH

River Dudwell

26

70 A B 71 C D 72 E F

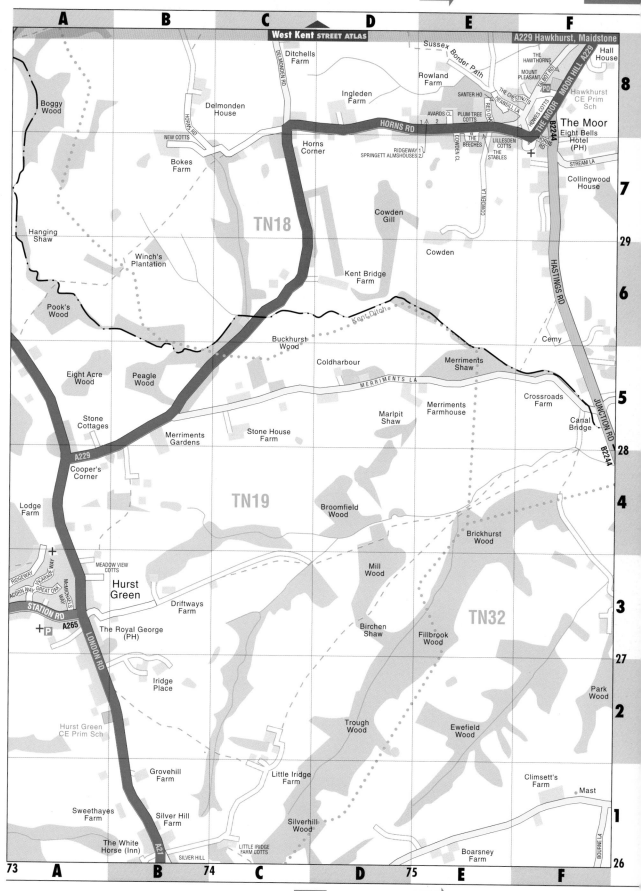

West Kent STREET ATLAS

A229 Hawkhurst, Maidstone

A B C D E F

8

7

29

6

5

28

4

3

27

2

1

26

Boggy Wood

Hanging Shaw

Pook's Wood

Delmonden House

New Cotts

Bokes Farm

Winch's Plantation

Eight Acre Wood

Peagle Wood

Stone Cottages

A229

Cooper's Corner

Lodge Farm

Ridgeway

Acorn Way

Scarf Way

Great Oak

McMichaels Way

MEADOW VIEW COTTS

Hurst Green

Station Rd

A265

London Rd

The Royal George (PH)

Iridge Place

Hurst Green CE Prim Sch

Grovehill Farm

Sweethayes Farm

Silver Hill Farm

The White Horse (Inn)

A21

SILVER HILL

TN18

TN19

Merriments Gardens

Driftways Farm

LITTLE IRIDGE FARM COTTS

Little Iridge Farm

Silverhill Wood

Delmonden Rd

Horns Rd

Ditchells Farm

Delmonden House

Horns Corner

SPRINGETT ALMSHOUSES

Buckhurst Wood

Coldharbour

Stone House Farm

Marlpit Shaw

MERRIMENTS LA

Broomfield Wood

Mill Wood

Birchen Shaw

Trough Wood

Silverhill Wood

Sussex Border Path

Ingleden Farm

Rowland Farm

Santer Ho

AVARDS CL

RIDGEWAY

HORNS RD

PLUM TREE COTTS

THE BEECHES

COWDEN CL

COWDEN LA

Cowden Gill

Cowden

Kent Bridge Farm

Kent Ditch

Merriments Shaw

Merriments Farmhouse

Brickhurst Wood

Fillbrook Wood

Ewefield Wood

Boarsney Farm

The Hawthorns

MOUNT PLEASANT

THE CHESTNUTS

HOWES COTTS

MOOR HILL A229

THE MOOR

HASTINGS RD

Hall House

Hawkhurst CE Prim Sch

The Moor

Eight Bells Hotel (PH)

Collingwood House

Cemy

Crossroads Farm

Canal Bridge

JUNCTION RD

B2244

TN32

Park Wood

Climsett's Farm

Mast

BOURNE LA

HEANSILL LA

RED OAK

LILLESDEN COTTS

THE STABLES

B2244

73 A B 74 C D 75 E F

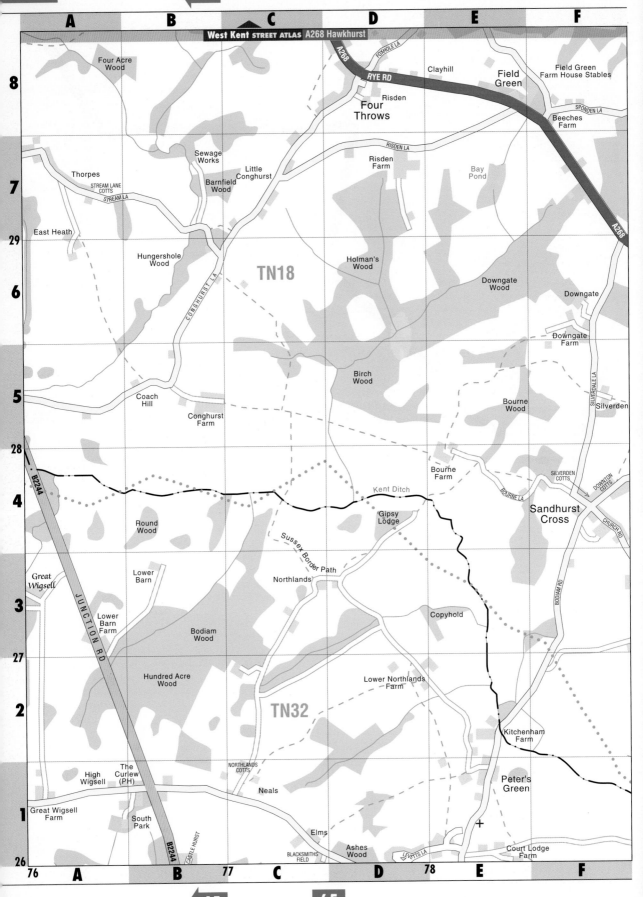

West Kent STREET ATLAS A268 Hawkhurst

A B C D E F

8

7

29

6

5

28

4

3

27

2

1

26

76 A B 77 C D 78 E F

Four Acre Wood

Thorpes

STREAM LANE COTTS

STREAM LA

East Heath

Hungershole Wood

Sewage Works

Barnfield Wood

Little Conghurst

TN18

Coach Hill

Conghurst Farm

CONGHURST LA

B2244

JUNCTION RD

B2244

CASTLE HURST

Great Wigsell

Lower Barn

Lower Barn Farm

Round Wood

Bodiam Wood

Hundred Acre Wood

TN32

Great Wigsell Farm

High Wigsell

The Curlew (PH)

South Park

Northlands

Sussex Border Path

Gipsy Lodge

Kent Ditch

NORTHLANDS COTTS

Neals

Elms

BLACKSMITHS FIELD

Ashes Wood

LEVETTS LA

Lower Northlands Farm

Copyhold

Peter's Green

Court Lodge Farm

Kitchenham Farm

RYE RD

FOXHOLE LA

A268

Four Throws

Risden

Clayhill

Field Green

Field Green Farm House Stables

SPONDEN LA

Beeches Farm

RISDEN LA

Risden Farm

Bay Pond

Holman's Wood

Downgate Wood

Downgate

A268

Birch Wood

Bourne Wood

Silverden

SILVERDALE LA

Bourne Farm

SILVERDEN COTTS

DOWNTON COTTS

Sandhurst Cross

BOURNE LA

CHURCH RD

BODIAM RD

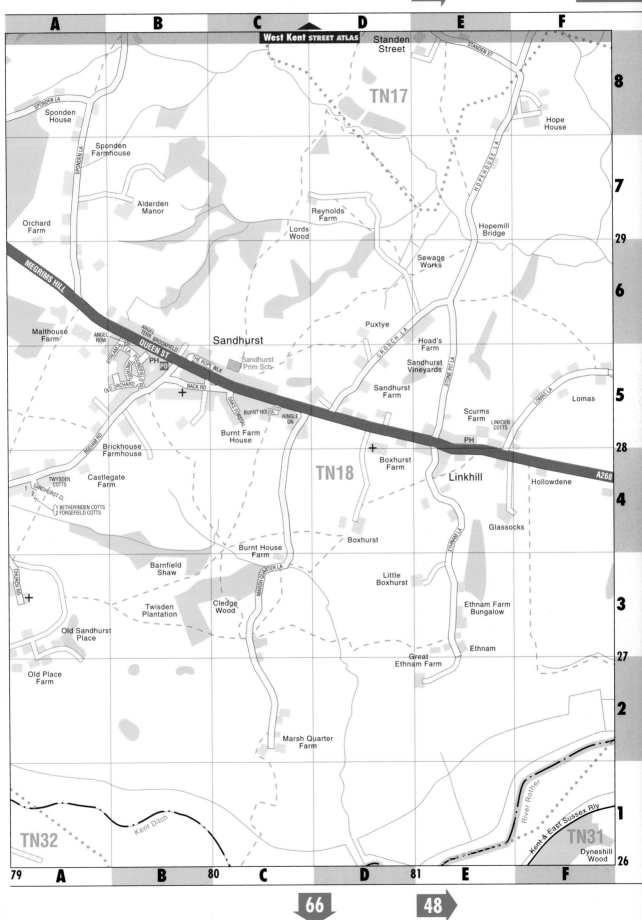

West Kent STREET ATLAS

Standen
Street

TN17

8

Hope
House

SPONDEN LA
Sponden
House

SPONDEN LA

HOPEHOUSE LA

7

Sponden
Farmhouse

Alderden
Manor

Reynolds
Farm

Lords
Wood

29

Orchard
Farm

Hopemill
Bridge

MEGRIMS HILL

Sewage
Works

6

Malthouse
Farm

ANGEL
ROW

ANGEL
TERR   BROOKFIELD

Sandhurst

Puxtye

CROUCH LA

Hoad's
Farm

QUEEN ST

STREAM PIT LA

POUNDFIELD RD

THE ROPE WLK

Sandhurst
Prim Sch

Sandhurst
Vineyards

STONE PIT LA

LOMAS LA

Lomas

5

PH
PO

Sandhurst
Farm

OLD ORCHARD

BACK RD

OAKS FENSTAL

BURNT HOUSE CT

Scurms
Farm

LINKDEN
COTTS

BODIAM RD

Brickhouse
Farmhouse

Burnt Farm
House

RINGLE
GN

PH

28

A268

TN18

Boxhurst
Farm

Linkhill

Hollowdene

4

TWYSDEN
COTTS

SANDHURST CL

Castlegate
Farm

Glassocks

1
2

1 BETHERINDEN COTTS
2 FORGEFIELD COTTS

Boxhurst

ETHNAM LA

Barnfield
Shaw

Burnt House
Farm

Little
Boxhurst

Ethnam Farm
Bungalow

3

CHURCH RD

MARSH QUARTER LA

Cledge
Wood

Twisden
Plantation

Ethnam

Old Sandhurst
Place

Great
Ethnam Farm

27

Old Place
Farm

2

Marsh Quarter
Farm

River Rother

Kent & East Sussex Rly

TN31

1

TN32

Kent Ditch

Dyneshill
Wood

26

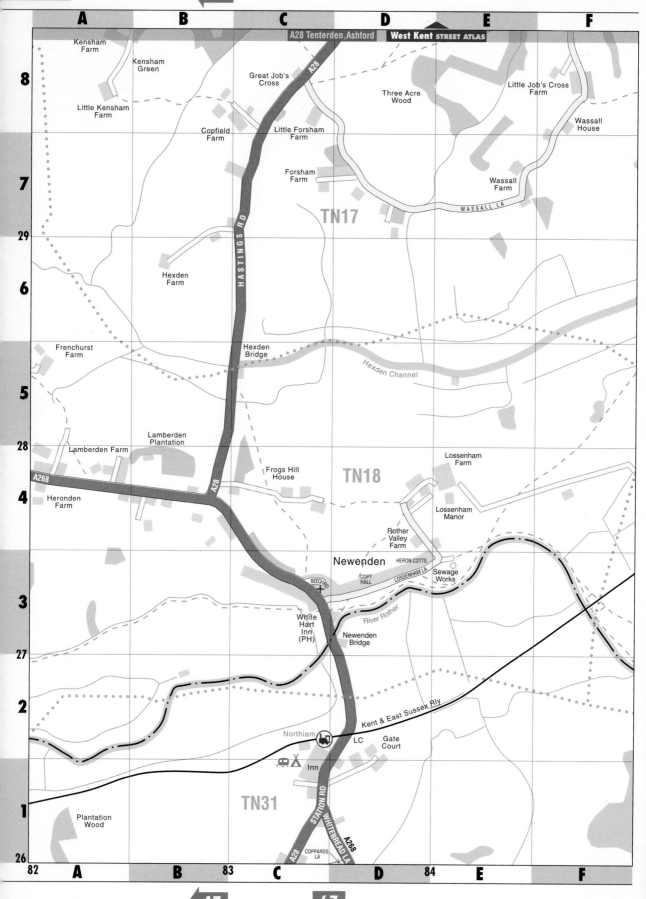

A28 Tenterden, Ashford

West Kent STREET ATLAS

Kensham Farm

Kensham Green

Little Kensham Farm

Great Job's Cross

Three Acre Wood

Little Job's Cross Farm

Wassall House

Copfield Farm

Little Forsham Farm

Forsham Farm

Wassall Farm

WASSALL LA

TN17

HASTINGS RD

A28

Hexden Farm

Frenchurst Farm

Hexden Bridge

Hexden Channel

Lamberden Plantation

Lamberden Farm

A268

Heronden Farm

TN18

Frogs Hill House

Lossenham Farm

Lossenham Manor

A28

Rother Valley Farm

Newenden

HERON COTTS

Sewage Works

BEECH RD

/COPT HALL

LOSSENHAM LA

White Hart Inn (PH)

Newenden Bridge

River Rother

Kent & East Sussex Rly

Northiam

LC

Gate Court

Inn

TN31

STATION RD

WHITEBREAD LA

A268

Plantation Wood

A28

COPPARDS LA

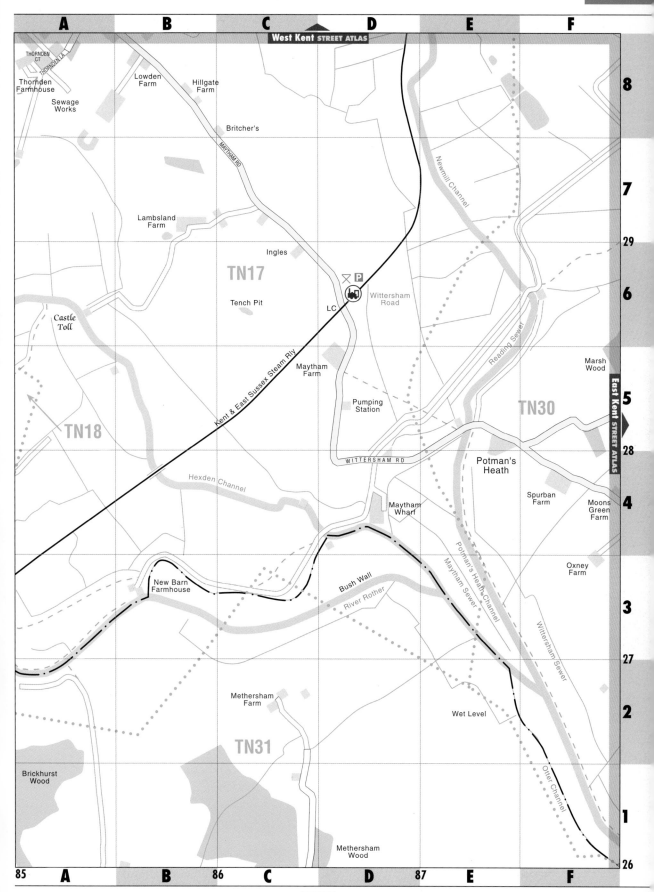

East Kent STREET ATLAS

THORNDEN
CT
Thornden
Farmhouse
Sewage
Works
THORNDEN LA

Lowden
Farm
Hillgate
Farm
Britcher's
MAYTHAM RD

Lambsland
Farm

Ingles

TN17

Tench Pit

Castle
Toll

Maytham
Farm

TN18

Kent & East Sussex Steam Rly

LC

Wittersham
Road

P

Pumping
Station

Newmill Channel

Reading Sewer

Marsh
Wood

TN30

5

28

Potman's
Heath

WITTERSHAM RD

Hexden Channel

Maytham
Wharf

Spurban
Farm

Moons
Green
Farm

New Barn
Farmhouse

Bush Wall

River Rother

Potman's Heath Channel

Maytham Sewer

Oxney
Farm

Wittersham Sewer

27

Methersham
Farm

TN31

Wet Level

Otter Channel

Brickhurst
Wood

Methersham
Wood

85   A   B   86   C   D   87   E   F

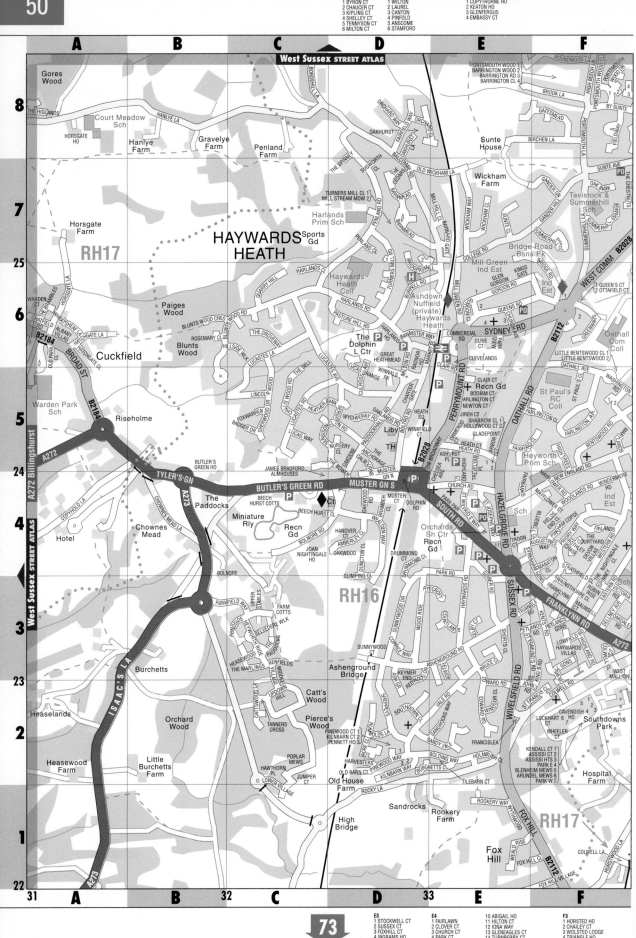

West Sussex STREET ATLAS

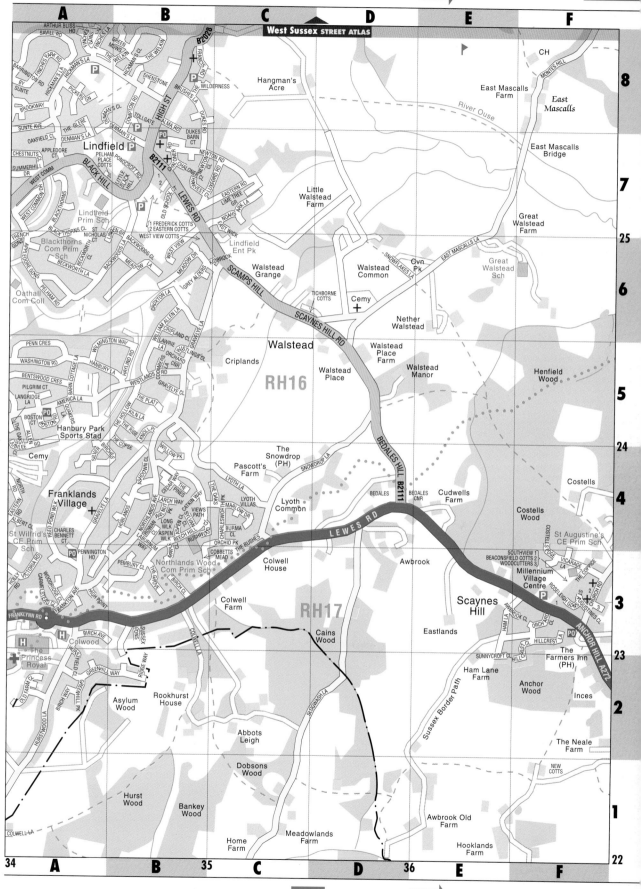

West Sussex STREET ATLAS

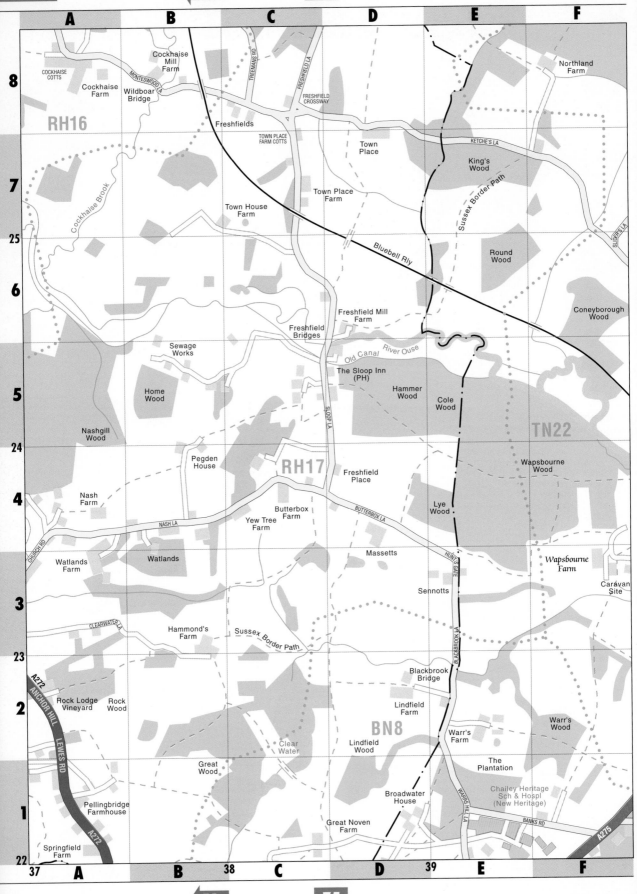

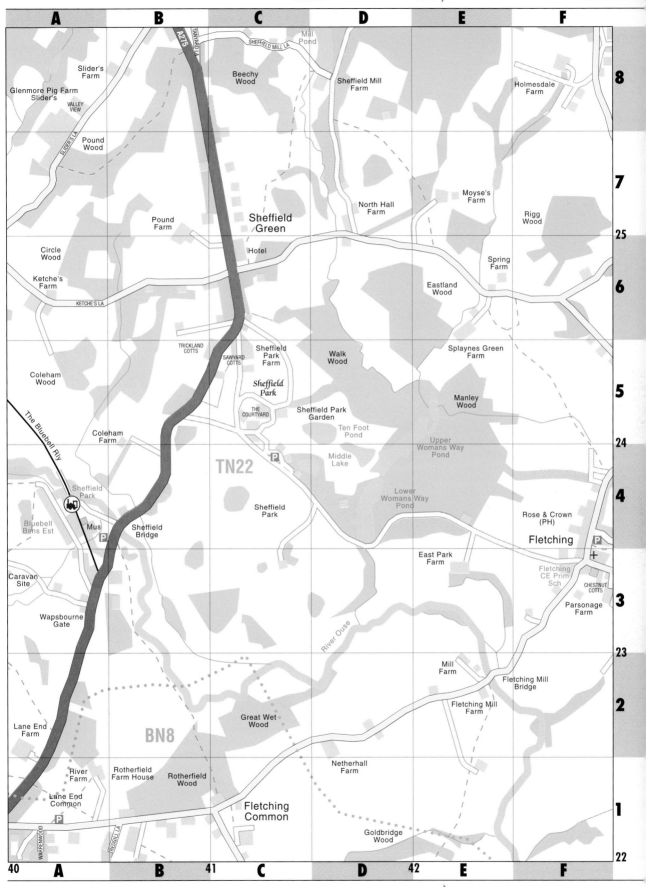

A   B   C   D   E   F

8

Slider's Farm

Glenmore Pig Farm
Slider's

VALLEY VIEW

Beechy Wood

Sheffield Mill Farm

Holmesdale Farm

A275

TANYARD LA

SHEFFIELD MILL LA

Mill Pond

SLIDER'S LA

Pound Wood

7

Pound Farm

Sheffield Green

North Hall Farm

Moyse's Farm

Rigg Wood

25

Hotel

Circle Wood

Ketche's Farm

KETCHE'S LA

Eastland Wood

Spring Farm

6

Coleham Wood

TRICKLAND COTTS

SAWYARD COTTS

Sheffield Park Farm

Walk Wood

Splaynes Green Farm

Sheffield Park

Manley Wood

5

THE COURTYARD

Sheffield Park Garden

Ten Foot Pond

Upper Womans Way Pond

24

TN22

P

Middle Lake

Coleham Farm

Bluebell Bsns Est

The Bluebell Rly

Sheffield Park

Mus

P

Sheffield Bridge

Sheffield Park

Lower Womans Way Pond

Rose & Crown (PH)

Fletching

P

4

Caravan Site

East Park Farm

Fletching CE Prim Sch

CHESTNUT COTTS

Wapsbourne Gate

Parsonage Farm

3

River Ouse

23

Mill Farm

Fletching Mill Bridge

2

Lane End Farm

BN8

Great Wet Wood

Fletching Mill Farm

River Farm

Rotherfield Farm House

Rotherfield Wood

Netherhall Farm

Lane End Common

P

Fletching Common

1

WARRENWOOD

REDGILL LA

Goldbridge Wood

22

40   A   B   41   C   D   42   E   F

53
35

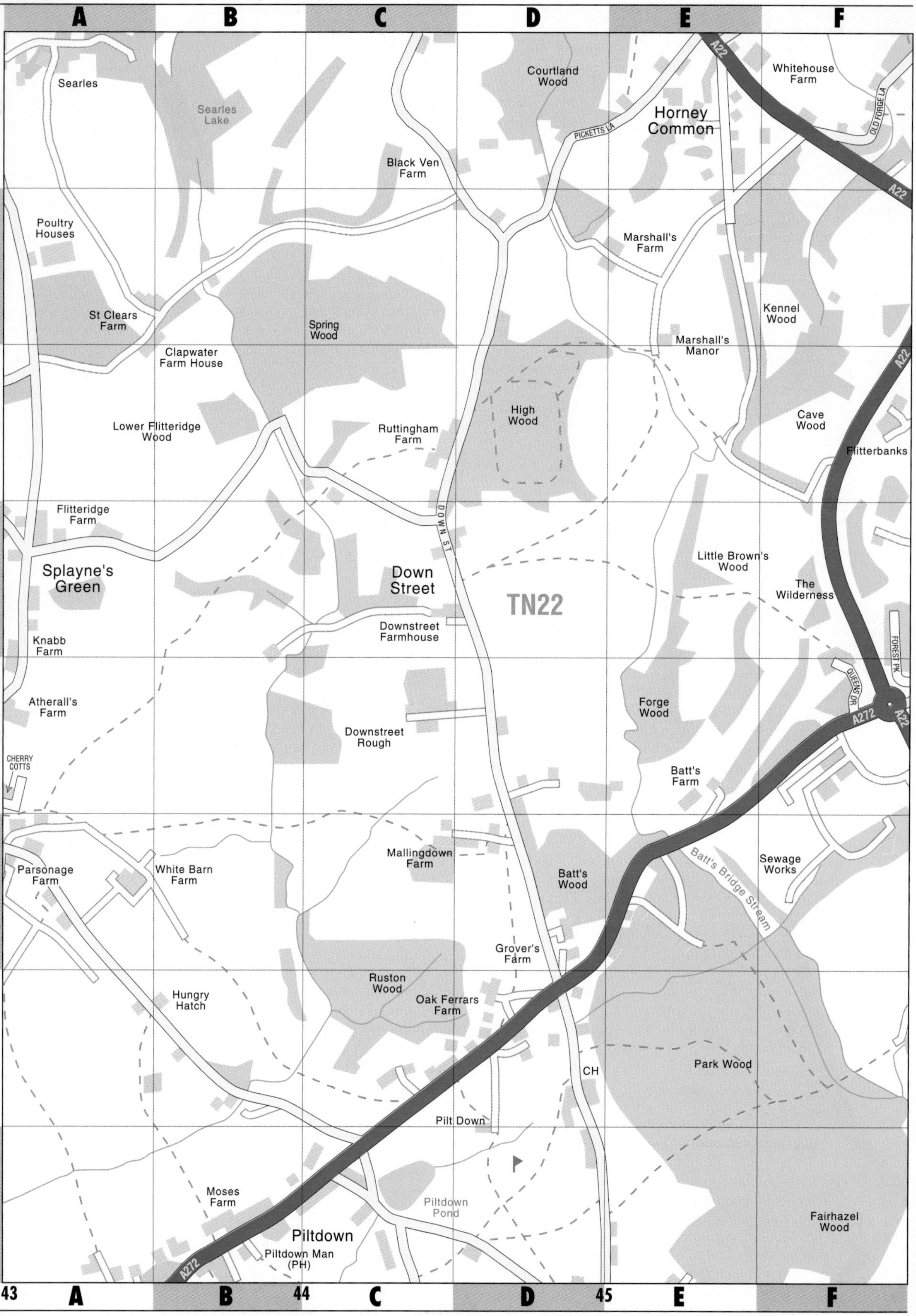

A B C D E F

8

Searles

Searles
Lake

Courtland
Wood

PICKETTS LA

Horney
Common

Whitehouse
Farm

OLD FORGE LA

A22

Black Ven
Farm

Poultry
Houses

7

Marshall's
Farm

Kennel
Wood

St Clears
Farm

25

Spring
Wood

Clapwater
Farm House

Marshall's
Manor

A22

6

Lower Flitteridge
Wood

Ruttingham
Farm

High
Wood

Cave
Wood

Flitterbanks

Flitteridge
Farm

DOWN ST

Little Brown's
Wood

The
Wilderness

Splayne's
Green

5

Down
Street

TN22

FOREST PK

Knabb
Farm

24

Downstreet
Farmhouse

QUEEN'S LA

Atherall's
Farm

4

Downstreet
Rough

Forge
Wood

A272

A22

CHERRY
COTTS

Batt's
Farm

Mallingdown
Farm

Batt's
Wood

Sewage
Works

Parsonage
Farm

3

White Barn
Farm

Batt's Bridge Stream

23

Hungry
Hatch

Ruston
Wood

Grover's
Farm

Oak Ferrars
Farm

Park Wood

2

CH

Pilt Down

Moses
Farm

1

Piltdown
Pond

Fairhazel
Wood

Piltdown

A272

Piltdown Man
(PH)

22

43 A B 44 C D 45 E F

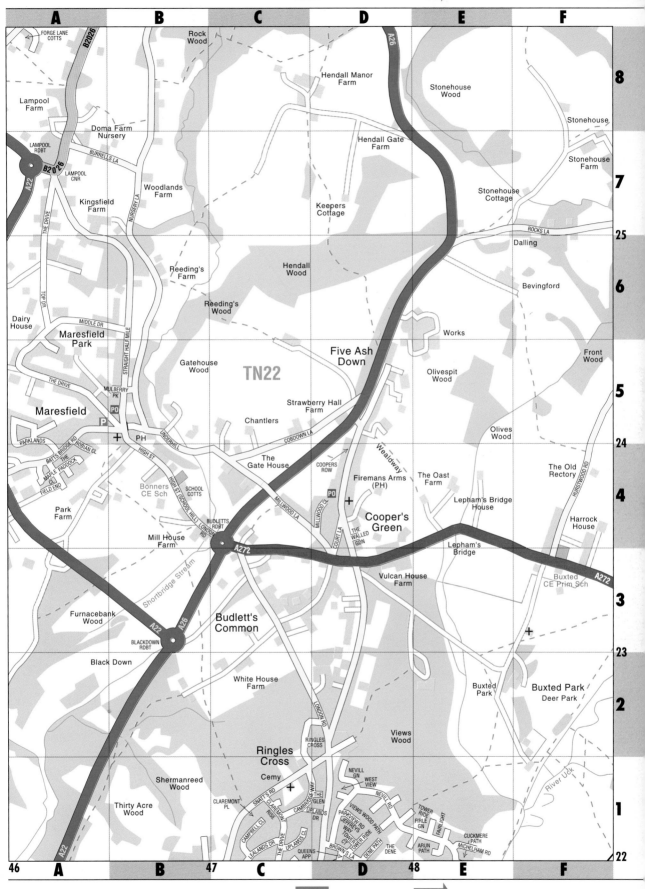

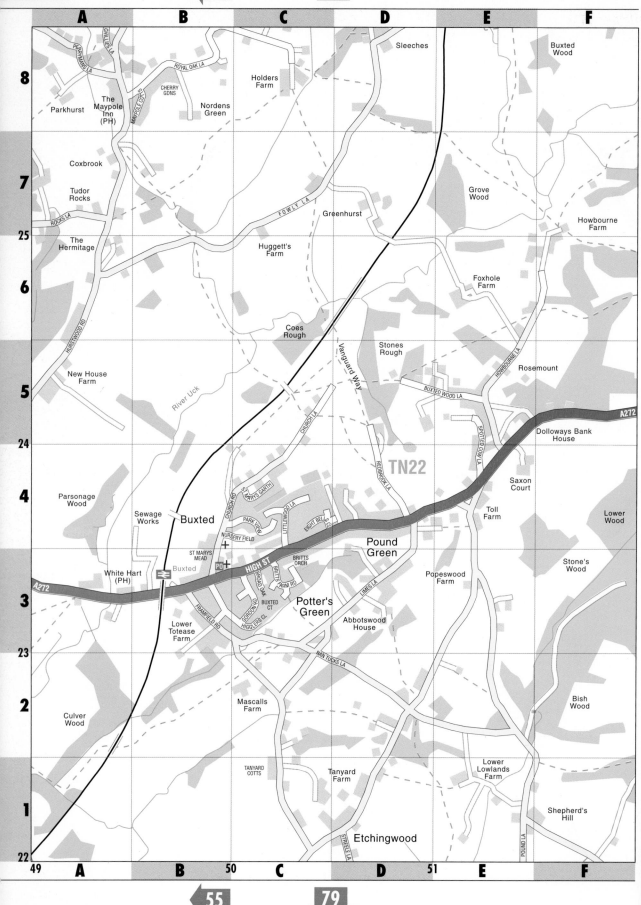

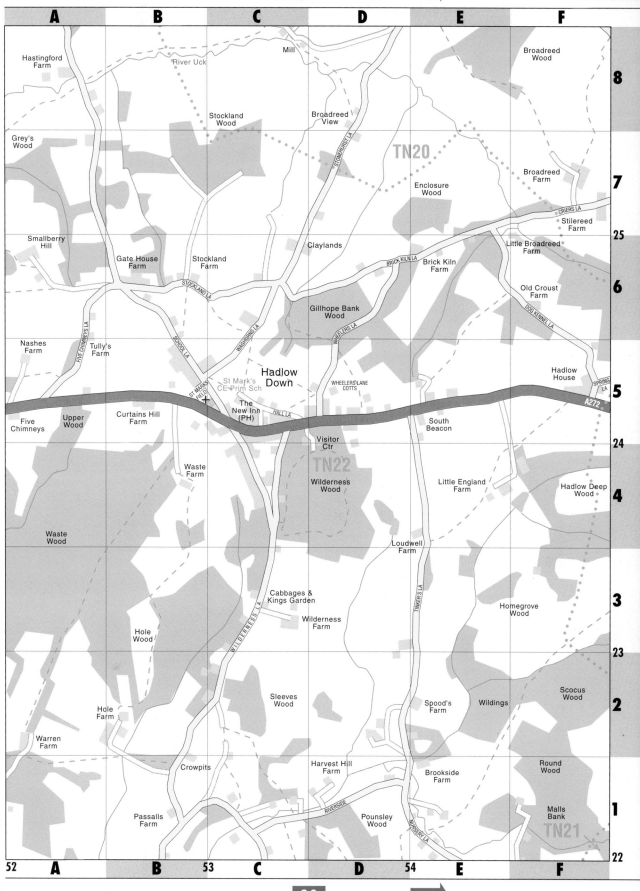

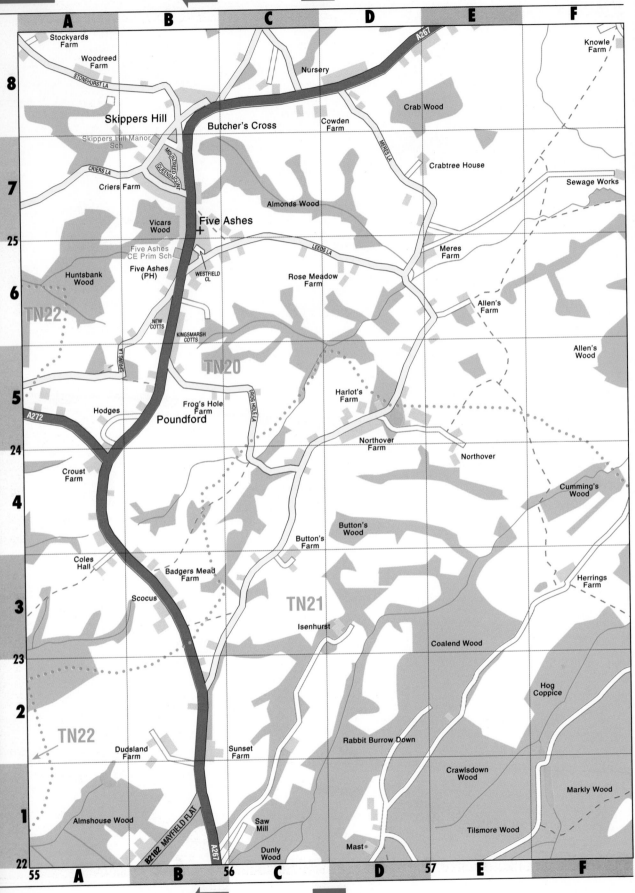

| | A | B | C | D | E | F |

8 Stockyards Farm
Woodreed Farm
STONEHURST LA
Nursery
A267
Crab Wood
Knowle Farm

Skippers Hill
Butcher's Cross
Cowden Farm
Crabtree House
MERES LA

Skippers Hill Manor Sch
MOUNTRED QUEENSMOON

7 CRIERS LA
Criers Farm
Almonds Wood
Meres Farm
Sewage Works

25 Vicars Wood
Five Ashes
LEEDS LA

Five Ashes CE Prim Sch
WESTFIELD CL
Rose Meadow Farm

6 Huntsbank Wood
Five Ashes (PH)
Allen's Farm

TN22
NEW COTTS
KINGSMARSH COTTS
TN20
Allen's Wood
SPRING LA

5 Hodges
Frog's Hole Farm
Poundford
FROG HOLE LA
Harlot's Farm

A272
24 Croust Farm
Northover Farm
Northover
Cumming's Wood

4 Button's Wood
Herrings Farm

Coles Hall
Badgers Mead Farm
Button's Farm

3 Scocus
TN21
Isenhurst
Coalend Wood

23 Hog Coppice

2 TN22
Dudsland Farm
Sunset Farm
Rabbit Burrow Down
Crawlsdown Wood
Markly Wood

1 Almshouse Wood
B2102 MAYFIELD FLAT
A267
Saw Mill
Mast
Tilsmore Wood

22 Dunly Wood

| 55 | A | B | 56 | C | D | 57 | E | F |

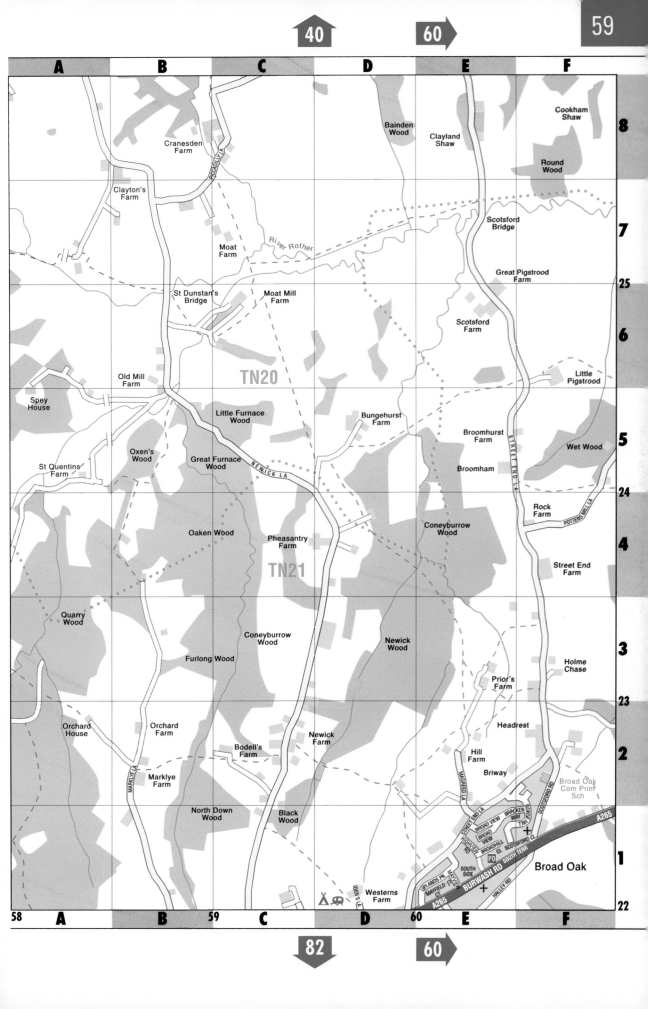

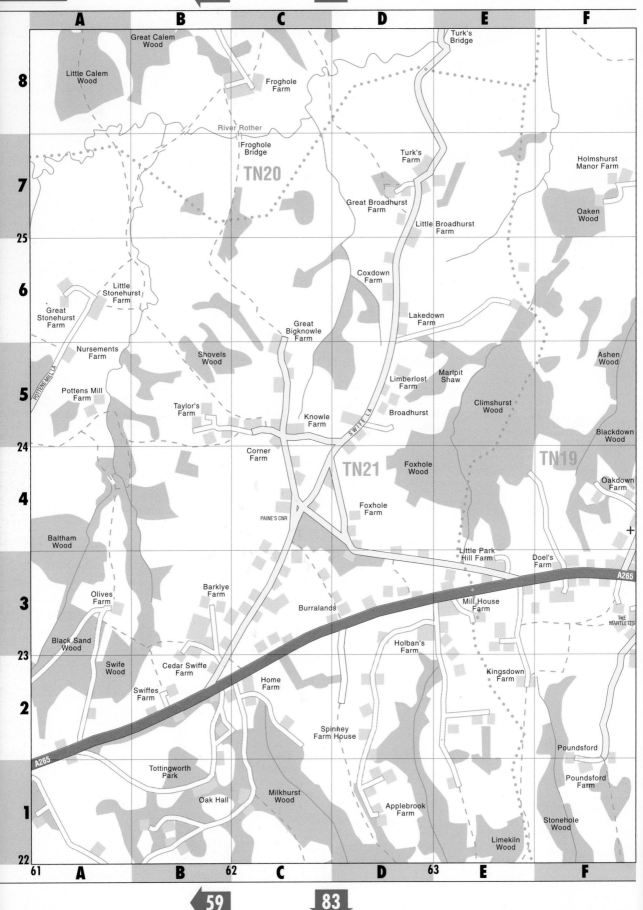

A | B | C | D | E | F

8

Little Calem Wood

Great Calem Wood

Froghole Farm

Turk's Bridge

River Rother

Froghole Bridge

7

TN20

Turk's Farm

Holmshurst Manor Farm

Great Broadhurst Farm

25

Little Broadhurst Farm

Oaken Wood

Little Stonehurst Farm

Coxdown Farm

6

Great Stonehurst Farm

Lakedown Farm

Great Bigknowle Farm

Nursements Farm

Shovels Wood

Limberlost Farm

Marlpit Shaw

Climshurst Wood

Ashen Wood

POTTENS MILL LA

5

Pottens Mill Farm

Taylor's Farm

Knowle Farm

Broadhurst

SWITE LA

Blackdown Wood

24

Corner Farm

TN21

Foxhole Wood

TN19

Oakdown Farm

4

Baltham Wood

PAINE'S CNR

Foxhole Farm

Little Park Hill Farm

Doel's Farm

3

Olives Farm

Barklye Farm

Burralands

Mill House Farm

A265

THE MARTLETTS

23

Black Sand Wood

Swife Wood

Cedar Swiffe Farm

Holban's Farm

Kingsdown Farm

2

Swiffes Farm

Home Farm

Poundsford

A265

Spinney Farm House

Poundsford Farm

Tottingworth Park

1

Oak Hall

Milkhurst Wood

Applebrook Farm

Stonehole Wood

Limekiln Wood

22

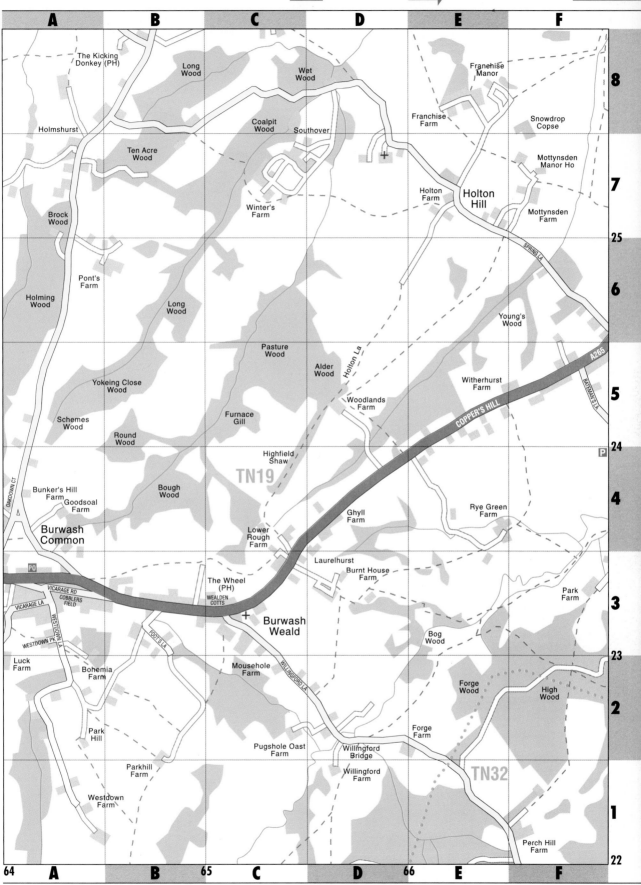

	A	B	C	D	E	F

8 The Kicking Donkey (PH), Long Wood, Wet Wood, Franchise Manor, Franchise Farm, Snowdrop Copse

7 Holmshurst, Ten Acre Wood, Coalpit Wood, Southover, Winter's Farm, Holton Farm, Holton Hill, Mottynsden Manor Ho, Mottynsden Farm

25

6 Brock Wood, Pont's Farm, Holming Wood, Long Wood, SPRING LA, Young's Wood, A265

5 Pasture Wood, Alder Wood, Holton La, Woodlands Farm, Witherhurst Farm, COPPER'S HILL, Yokeing Close Wood, BATEMAN'S LA

24 Schemes Wood, Round Wood, Furnace Gill, Highfield Shaw, P

4 TN19, Bunker's Hill Farm, Goodsoal Farm, Bough Wood, Ghyll Farm, Rye Green Farm

OAKDOWN CT, Burwash Common, Lower Rough Farm, Laurelhurst, Burnt House Farm, Park Farm

3 PO, VICARAGE RD, COBBLERS FIELD, VICARAGE LA, WESTDOWN PK, WESTDOWN LA, FOOT'S LA, The Wheel (PH), WEALDEN COTTS, Burwash Weald, Bog Wood

23 Luck Farm, Bohemia Farm, Mousehole Farm, WILLINGFORD LA, Forge Wood, High Wood

2 Park Hill, Pugshole Oast Farm, Willingford Bridge, Forge Farm, TN32

1 Parkhill Farm, Westdown Farm, Willingford Farm, Perch Hill Farm

22

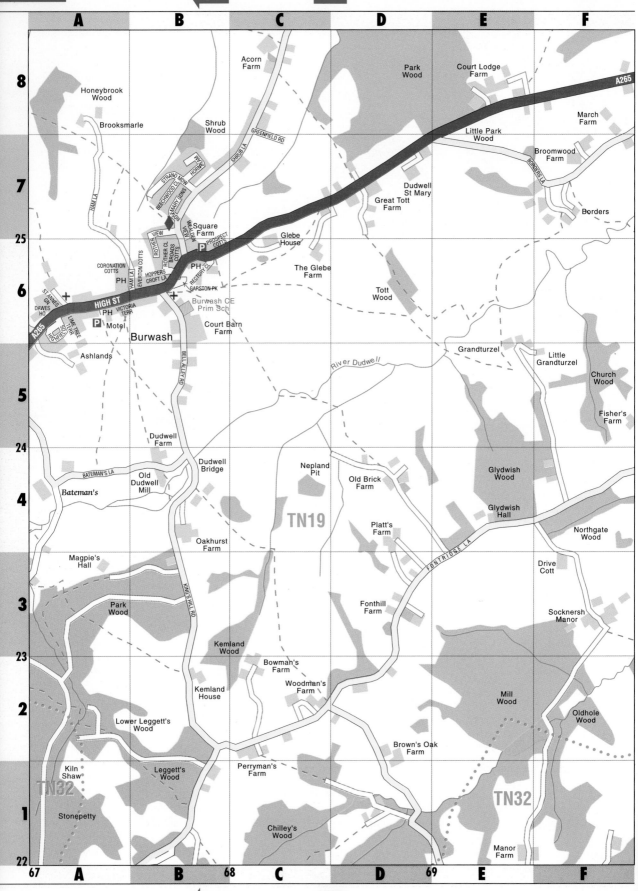

Honeybrook Wood

Brooksmarle

Shrub Wood

Acorn Farm

GREENFIELD RD

Park Wood

Court Lodge Farm

A265

March Farm

Little Park Wood

Broomwood Farm

BORDERS LA

Borders

SHRUB LA

HAM LA

STRAND MDW

BEECHWOOD CL

ST MARY GDNS

WEALDEN VIEW

ROTHER

VIEW

Square Farm

ROTHER CL

BROADS COTTS

PROSPECT COTTS

Dudwell St Mary

Great Tott Farm

Glebe House

CORONATION COTTS

PH

EVERTON COTTS

HOPPERS CROFT LA

PH

RECTORY CL

GARSTON PK

PH CL

The Glebe Farm

Tott Wood

Grandturzel

Little Grandturzel

Church Wood

ST IVES GDNS

DAWES HO

HIGH ST

PH

LIME TREE TERR

VICTORIA TERR

Burwash CE Prim Sch

A265

P

Motel

Burwash

Court Barn Farm

Fisher's Farm

Ashlands

BELL ALLEY RD

River Dudwell

Dudwell Farm

BATEMAN'S LA

Old Dudwell Mill

Dudwell Bridge

Nepland Pit

Old Brick Farm

Glydwish Wood

Glydwish Hall

Northgate Wood

Bateman's

Drive Cott

KING'S HILL RD

Oakhurst Farm

TN19

Platt's Farm

FONTRIDGE LA

Ssocknersh Manor

Magpie's Hall

Park Wood

Fonthill Farm

Kemland Wood

Bowman's Farm

Kemland House

Woodman's Farm

Mill Wood

Oldhole Wood

Lower Leggett's Wood

Kiln Shaw

TN32

Leggett's Wood

Perryman's Farm

Brown's Oak Farm

TN32

Stonepetty

Chilley's Wood

Manor Farm

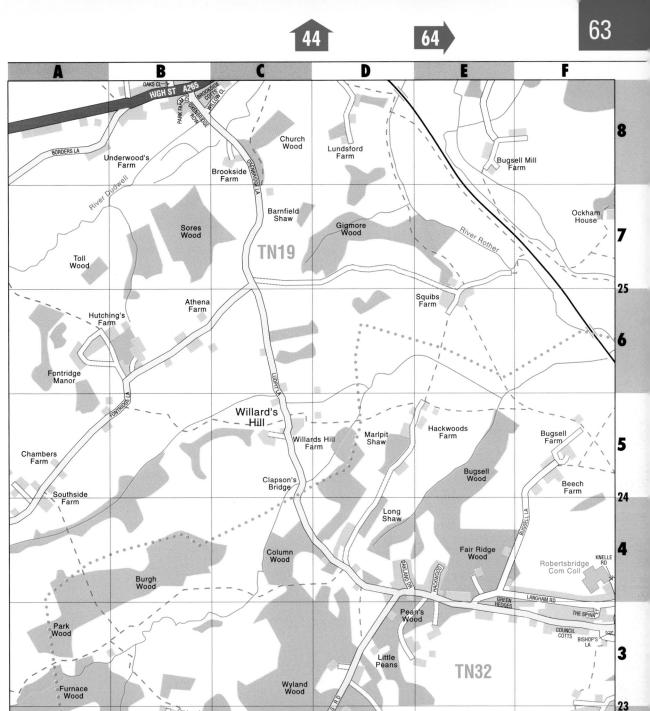

A B C D E F

8
7
25
6
5
24
4
3
23
2
1
22

TN19

TN32

OAKS CL.
HIGH ST A265
PARK FARM CL.
OXENBRIDGE ROW
BROOKSIDE COTTS
WILLOW CL.
BORDERS LA
Underwood's Farm
River Dudwell
Brookside Farm
Church Wood
Lundsford Farm
Bugsell Mill Farm
Ockham House
Sores Wood
Barnfield Shaw
Gigmore Wood
River Rother
Toll Wood
OXENBRIDGE LA
Athena Farm
Squibs Farm
Hutching's Farm
Fontridge Manor
LUDPIT LA
Willard's Hill
Willards Hill Farm
Marlpit Shaw
Hackwoods Farm
Bugsell Farm
Chambers Farm
FONTRIDGE LA
Clapson's Bridge
Bugsell Wood
Beech Farm
Southside Farm
Long Shaw
Column Wood
BUGSELL LA
Burgh Wood
Fair Ridge Wood
Robertsbridge Com Coll
KNELLE RD
OAKLAND DR
HACKWOOD
GREEN HEDGES
LANGHAM RD
THE SPINN
Park Wood
Pean's Wood
COUNCIL COTTS
BISHOP'S LA
Furnace Wood
Little Peans
Newhouse Farm
Wyland Wood
Darvell
Barnfield Wood
Middle Wood
BRIGHTLING RD
Scalands Farm
Brightling Hall
Scalands Wood
Bowden Wood
Sizzes Wood
Glottenham Stream
GLOTTENHAM FARM COTTS
Perryfield Wood
Ladds Wood
Glottenham Farm

70 A B 71 C D 72 E F

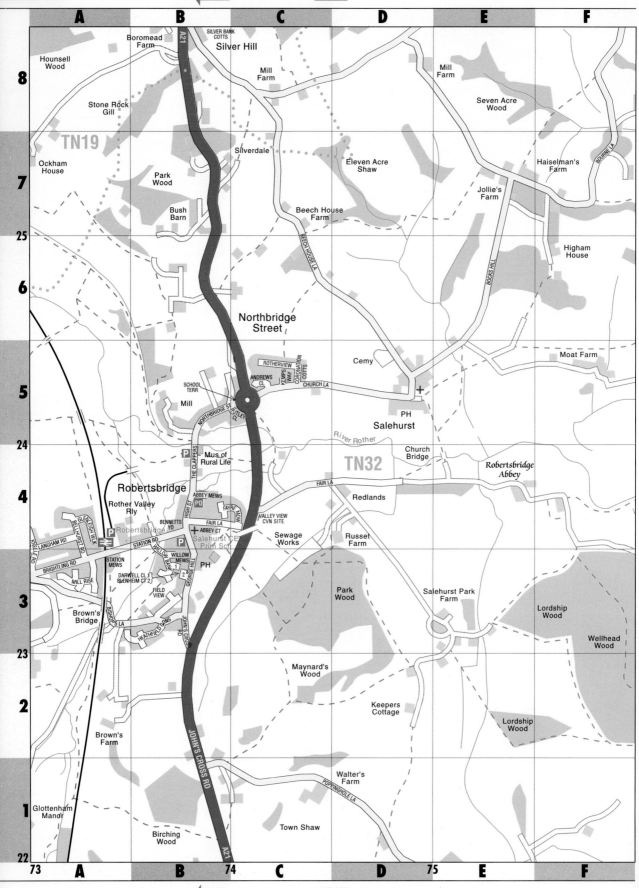

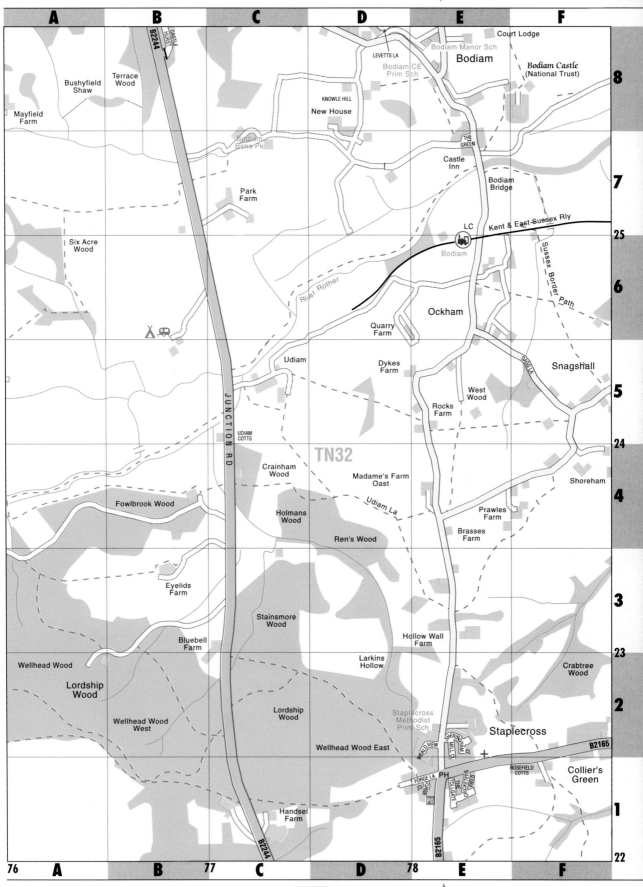

A | B | C | D | E | F

8 Bodiam

Court Lodge
Bodiam Manor Sch
Bodiam Castle
(National Trust)

Mayfield Farm
Bushyfield Shaw
Terrace Wood
LEVETTS LA
Bodiam CE Prim Sch
KNOWLE HILL
New House
B2244
CASTLE HURST

7 Six Acre Wood
Bodiam Bsns Pk
Park Farm
THE GREEN
Castle Inn
Bodiam Bridge

25 LC
Kent & East Sussex Rly
Bodiam

6 River Rother
Ockham
Sussex Border Path

5 Udiam
Quarry Farm
Dykes Farm
West Wood
Rocks Farm
Snagshall
B2165 LA

24 UDIAM COTTS
TN32

4 JUNCTION RD
Crainham Wood
Madame's Farm Oast
Udiam La
Prawles Farm
Shoreham
Fowlbrook Wood
Holmans Wood
Ren's Wood
Brasses Farm

3 Eyelids Farm
Stainsmore Wood
Hollow Wall Farm

23 Bluebell Farm
Wellhead Wood
Larkins Hollow
Crabtree Wood

2 Lordship Wood
Wellhead Wood West
Lordship Wood
Staplecross Methodist Prim Sch
Staplecross
B2165
Collier's Green

1 Wellhead Wood East
WEALD VIEW
SHERINGHAM
MILL CL
PH
FORGE LA
THE TOLLGATE
THE CRICKETERS FIELD
ROSEFIELD COTTS
PO
Handsel Farm
B2244
B2165

22

76 A | B 77 | C | D 78 | E | F

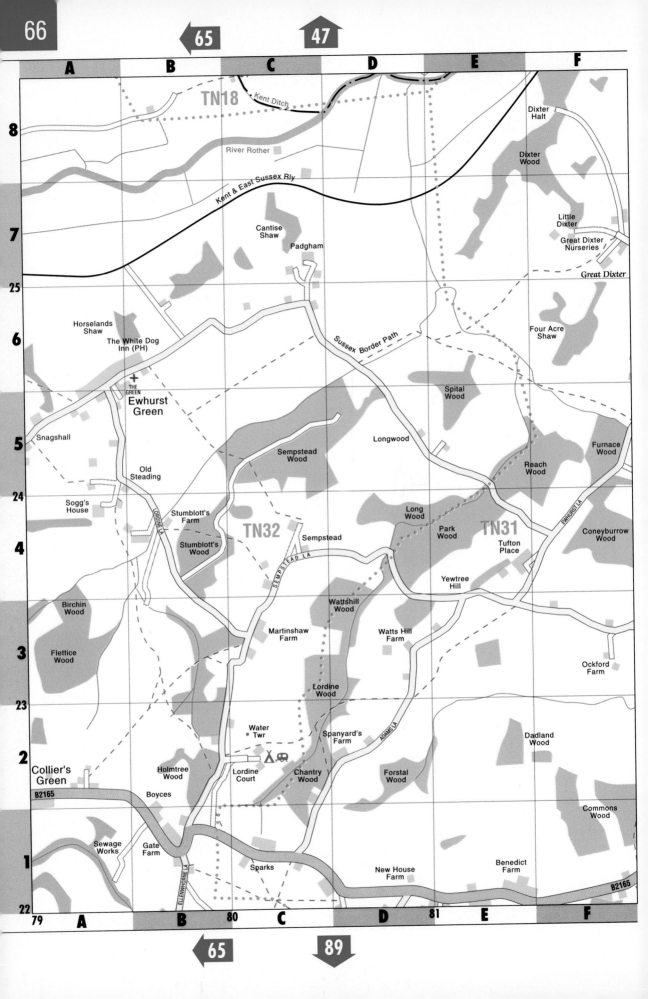

65
47

A   B   C   D   E   F

TN18

Kent Ditch

8

River Rother

Kent & East Sussex Rly

Dixter Halt

Dixter Wood

Cantise Shaw

Padgham

7

Little Dixter

Great Dixter Nurseries

Great Dixter

25

Horselands Shaw

Sussex Border Path

Four Acre Shaw

6

The White Dog Inn (PH)

THE GREEN

Ewhurst Green

Spital Wood

Snagshall

Longwood

Furnace Wood

5

Sempstead Wood

Reach Wood

Old Steading

24

Sogg's House

Stumblott's Farm

Long Wood

Coneyburrow Wood

LORDINE LA

TN32

Sempstead

Park Wood

TN31

Tufton Place

EWHURST LA

4

Stumblott's Wood

Birchin Wood

Yewtree Hill

SEMPSTEAD LA

Wattshill Wood

Watts Hill Farm

3

Flettice Wood

Martinshaw Farm

Ockford Farm

Lordine Wood

23

Water Twr

Spanyard's Farm

Dadland Wood

ADAMS LA

2

Collier's Green

Holmtree Wood

Lordine Court

Chantry Wood

Forstal Wood

B2165

Boyces

Commons Wood

Sewage Works

Gate Farm

1

Sparks

New House Farm

Benedict Farm

B2165

ELLENWHORNE LA

22

79   A   B   80   C   D   81   E   F

65
89

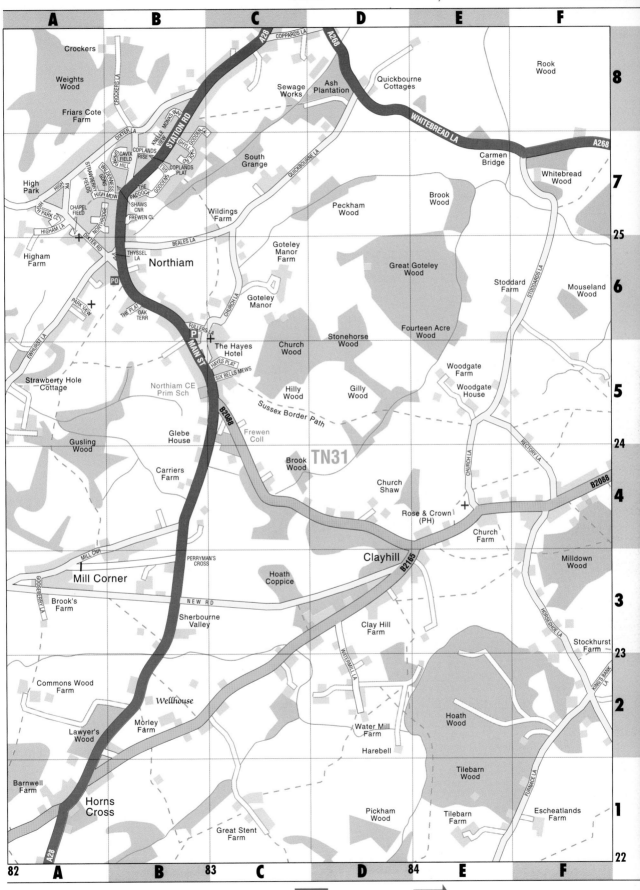

A B C D E F

8

Crockers

Weights Wood

Friars Cote Farm

CROCKERS LA

DIXTER LA

KNELLE MONKS WAY

STATION RD

COPPARDS LA

A28

A268

Sewage Works

Ash Plantation

Quickbourne Cottages

WHITEBREAD LA

Rook Wood

A268

7

High Park

HIGH PK

HIGH

HIGHAM LA

HIGH PARK CL

STRAWBERRY FIELDS

WILDERNESS

GDNS

HIGH MDW

HIGH HORSE RIDGE

CAVIX FIELD

COPSE HILL

CHAPEL FIELD

SPRING

DIXTER RD

THE PADDOCK

SHAWS CNR

FREWEN CL

KNELLE

COPLANDS RISE

GODDENS

GHYLL ST

GODDENS

COPLANDS PLAT

South Grange

QUICKBOURNE LA

Peckham Wood

Brook Wood

Carmen Bridge

Whitebread Wood

Higham Farm

THYSSEL LA

Northiam

BEALES LA

Wildings Farm

Goteley Manor Farm

CHURCH LA

Great Goteley Wood

Stoddard Farm

STODDARDS LA

Mouseland Wood

25

6

PARK VIEW

EWHURST LA

PO

THE PLAT

OAK TERR

FULLERS LA

P

MAIN ST

Goteley Manor

Church Wood

Stonehorse Wood

Fourteen Acre Wood

RECTORY LA

5

Strawberry Hole Cottage

The Hayes Hotel

HAYES PLAT

SIX BELLS MEWS

Northiam CE Prim Sch

Sussex Border Path

Hilly Wood

Gilly Wood

Woodgate Farm

Woodgate House

Gusling Wood

Glebe House

B2088

Frewen Coll

TN31

Brook Wood

Church Shaw

CHURCH LA

24

4

Carriers Farm

Church Farm

Rose & Crown (PH)

B2088

Milldown Wood

Mill Corner

MILL CNR

PERRYMAN'S CROSS

NEW RD

Clayhill

B2165

HORSSHOE LA

Stockhurst Farm

3

GOOSEBERRY LA

Brook's Farm

Sherbourne Valley

Hoath Coppice

Clay Hill Farm

WATERMILL LA

KING'S BANK LA

23

Commons Wood Farm

Wellhouse

Water Mill Farm

Harebell

Hoath Wood

2

Lawyer's Wood

Morley Farm

Pickham Wood

Tilebarn Wood

Tilebarn Farm

FURNACE LA

Escheatlands Farm

1

Barnwell Farm

Horns Cross

A28

Great Stent Farm

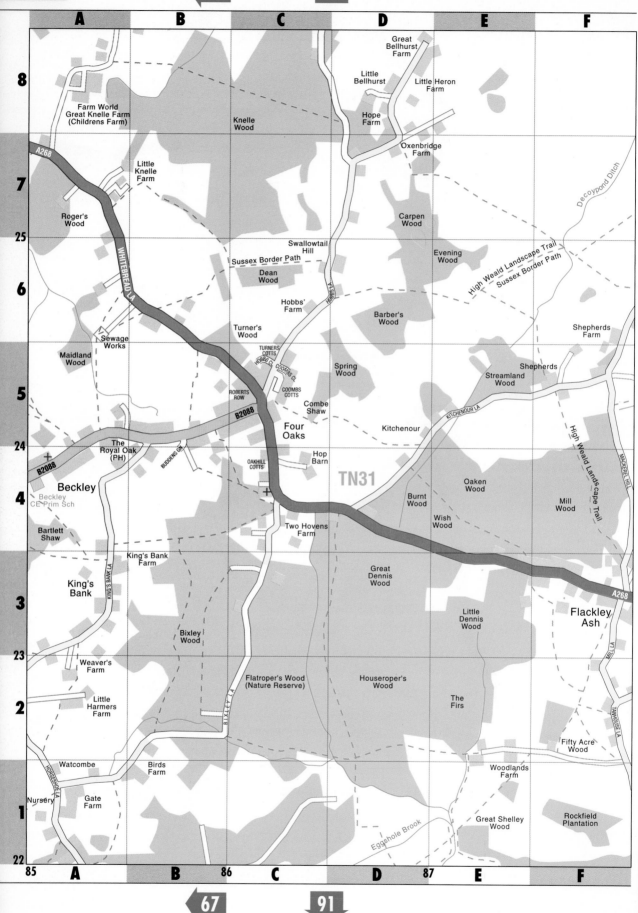

A B C D E F

8

Great Bellhurst Farm

Farm World Great Knelle Farm (Childrens Farm)

Little Bellhurst

Little Heron Farm

Knelle Wood

Hope Farm

Oxenbridge Farm

A268

7

Little Knelle Farm

Carpen Wood

Decoypond Ditch

Roger's Wood

25

Swallowtail Hill

Evening Wood

High Weald Landscape Trail

Sussex Border Path

Sussex Border Path

Dean Wood

WHITEBREAD LA

6

Hobbs' Farm

Barber's Wood

Shepherds Farm

Turner's Wood

Maidland Wood

Sewage Works

TURNERS COTTS

HOBBS CL

COOMBS CL

Spring Wood

Streamland Wood

Shepherds

High Weald Landscape Trail

5

ROBERTS ROW

COOMBS COTTS

Combe Shaw

Kitchenour

KITCHENOUR LA

B2088

24

The Royal Oak (PH)

BUDDENS GR

B2088

Four Oaks

Hop Barn

TN31

Oaken Wood

Mill Wood

MACKEREL HILL

Beckley

OAKHILL COTTS

Burnt Wood

4

Beckley CE Prim Sch

Two Hovens Farm

Wish Wood

Bartlett Shaw

King's Bank Farm

King's Bank

KING'S BANK LA

Great Dennis Wood

Little Dennis Wood

Flackley Ash

3

Bixley Wood

23

Weaver's Farm

BIXLEY LA

Flatroper's Wood (Nature Reserve)

Houseroper's Wood

MILL LA

Little Harmers Farm

The Firs

2

Fifty Acre Wood

TANHOUSE LA

Watcombe

Birds Farm

HORSESHOE LA

Woodlands Farm

Nursery

Gate Farm

Great Shelley Wood

Rockfield Plantation

1

Eggshole Brook

22

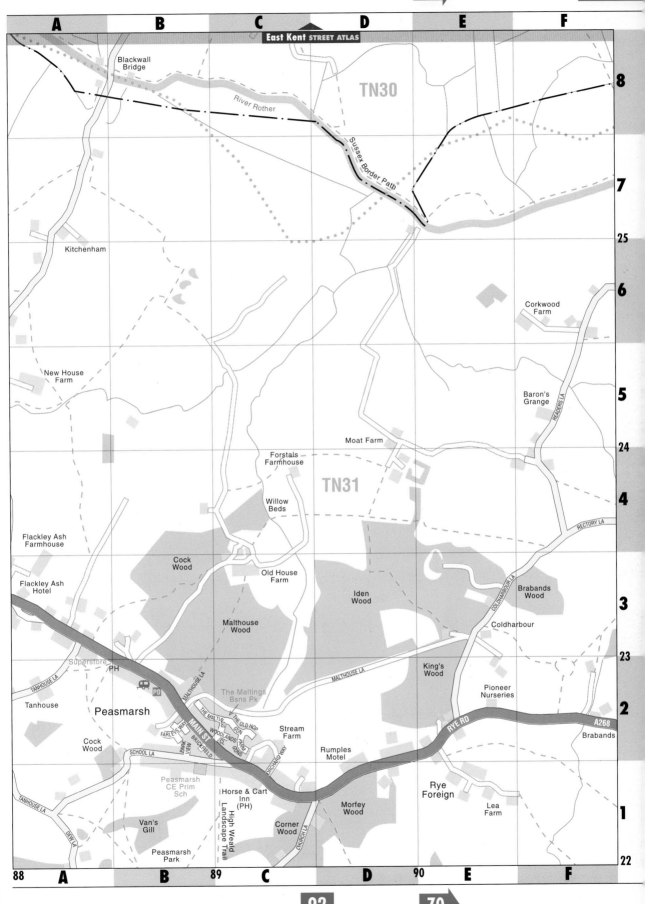

East Kent STREET ATLAS

A B C D E F

TN30

8

Blackwall
Bridge

River Rother

Sussex Border Path

7

25

Kitchenham

6

Corkwood
Farm

New House
Farm

Baron's
Grange

5

READERS LA

24

Moat Farm

Forstals
Farmhouse

TN31

RECTORY LA

Flackley Ash
Farmhouse

Willow
Beds

4

Cock
Wood

Old House
Farm

Flackley Ash
Hotel

Iden
Wood

Brabands
Wood

Coldharbour

3

COLDHARBOUR LA

Malthouse
Wood

23

Superstore

PH

King's
Wood

MALTHOUSE LA

Tanhouse

Peasmarsh

The Maltings
Bsns Pk

Pioneer
Nurseries

2

TANHOUSE LA

PO

MALTHOUSE LA

THE MALTINGS

THE OLD HOP

RYE RD

A268

Brabands

Cock
Wood

FARLEYS WAY

LBARK VIEW

WOODLANDS CL

GDNS

Stream
Farm

Rumples
Motel

Rye
Foreign

BRICKFIELD

Lea
Farm

SCHOOL LA

ORCHARD WAY

1

Peasmarsh
CE Prim
Sch

Horse & Cart
Inn
(PH)

Morfey
Wood

Van's
Gill

Corner
Wood

CHURCH LA

High Weald Landscape Trail

TANHOUSE LA

BENN LA

Peasmarsh
Park

22

88 A B 89 C D 90 E F

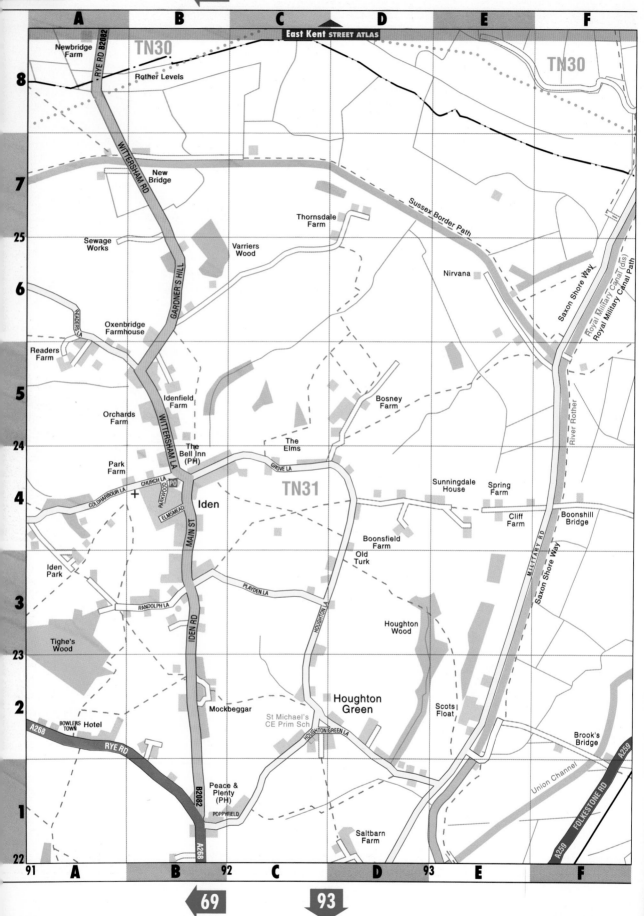

East Kent STREET ATLAS

TN30

TN30

Newbridge Farm

RYE RD B2082

Rother Levels

WITTERSHAM RD

New Bridge

GARDNER'S HILL

Sewage Works

Varriers Wood

Thornsdale Farm

Sussex Border Path

Nirvana

Saxon Shore Way

Royal Military Canal (dis)
Royal Military Canal Path

Oxenbridge Farmhouse

READERS LA

Readers Farm

Idenfield Farm

Bosney Farm

River Rother

Orchards Farm

WITTERSHAM LA

The Elms

Sunningdale House

Spring Farm

TN31

Park Farm

COLHARBOUR LA

CHURCH LA

PARK RD

PO

The Bell Inn (PH)

GROVE LA

ELMSMEAD

Iden

Boonsfield Farm

Old Turk

Cliff Farm

Boonshill Bridge

MILITARY RD

Saxon Shore Way

Iden Park

RANDOLPH LA

IDEN RD

PLAYDEN LA

HOUGHTON LA

Houghton Wood

Tighe's Wood

A268

BOWLERS TOWN

Hotel

RYE RD

Mockbeggar

Houghton Green

St Michael's CE Prim Sch

HOUGHTON GREEN LA

Scots Float

Brook's Bridge

A259

Union Channel

FOLKESTONE RD

B2082

Peace & Plenty (PH)

POPPYFIELD

Saltbarn Farm

A268

A259

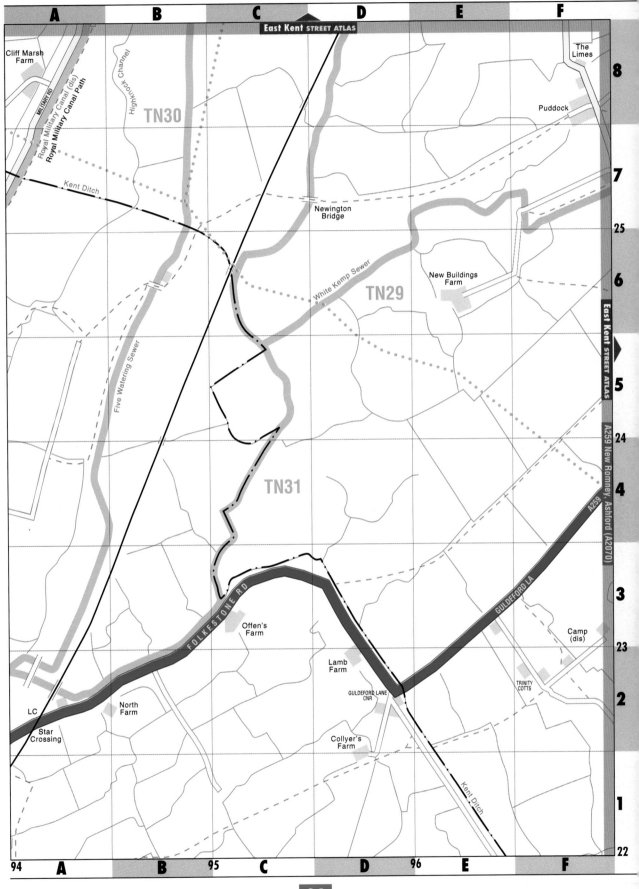

Cliff Marsh Farm

The Limes

Royal Military Canal (dis)
Royal Military Canal Path

MILITARY RD

Highknock Channel

TN30

Puddock

Kent Ditch

8

Newington Bridge

7

25

White Kemp Sewer

New Buildings Farm

TN29

6

East Kent STREET ATLAS

A259 New Romney, Ashford (A2070)

A259

5

Five Watering Sewer

24

TN31

4

23

FOLKESTONE RD

GULDEFORD LA

Offen's Farm

Camp (dis)

3

Lamb Farm

TRINITY COTTS

LC

North Farm

GULDEFORD LANE CNR

2

Star Crossing

Collyer's Farm

Kent Ditch

1

22

94   A   B   95   C   D   96   E   F

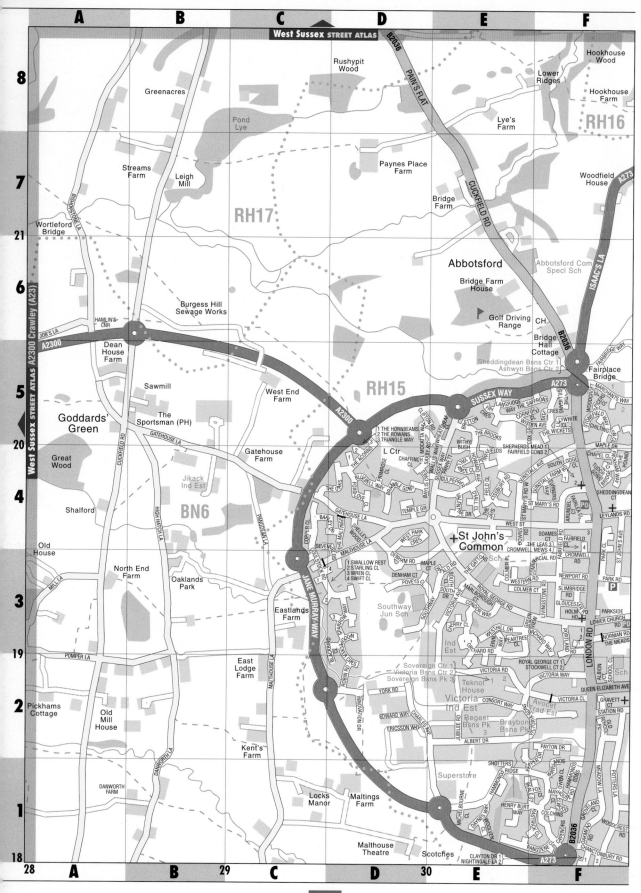

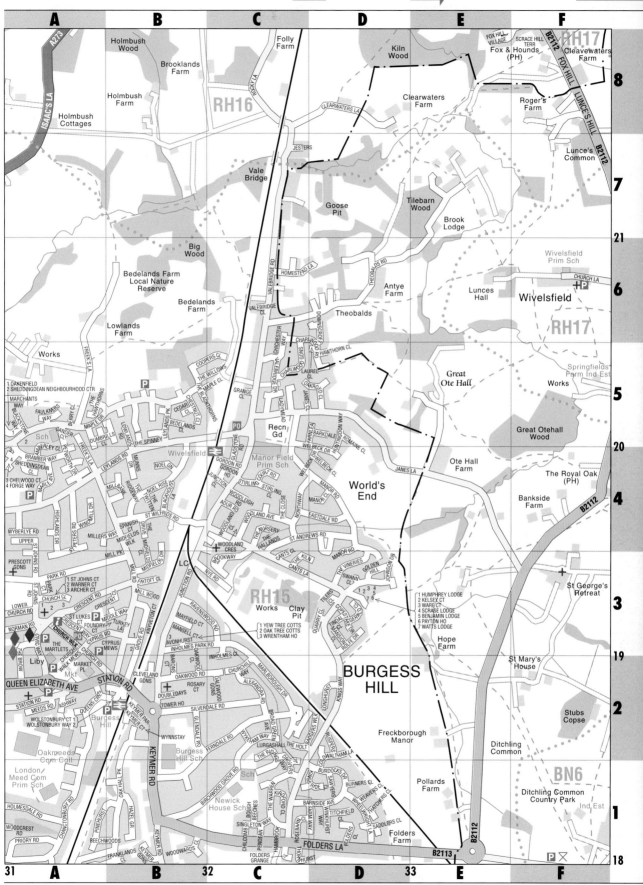

73 51

A | B | C | D | E | F

8

RH16

Ham Bridge

Ham Wood

Sussex Border Path

Ham La

Tylevel Wood

7

Fatting Hovel

B2112 LUNCE'S HILL

Wilderness Wood

Strood Wood

Holford Manor

21

CHURCH LA

Morehouse Farm Bsns Ctr
More House

Townings Place

Hole Farm

Wivelsfield Hall

Wivelsden Farm

Newhouse Wood

6

RH17

Roseland Wood

Strood Farm

Mann's Farm

Roselands

Longridge

Newhouse Farm

BLACKMORES

DIAMOND COTTS

TANNERS FIELD

PEPPER HALL COTTS

BALDINGS COTTS

GREEN RD

Wivelsfield

Fanners

Cock Inn (PH)

STROOD GATE

NORTH COMMON RD

Sedgebrook Wood

BN8

5

B2112

BALDINGS COTTS

Recn Gd

GREEN LA

PO

COPPARDS CL

FAIRPLACE

ALLWOOD CRES

FARNCOMBE CL

DOWNSVIEW RD

20

Lockstrood Farm

GREEN PARK CNR

EASTERN RD

WOODS GROUND

Coldharbour Farm

SOUTH RD

Grassy Wood

Longridge Wood

4

Wivelsfield Green

Purchase Wood

Woodlands Farm

3

Cemy

RH15

Sussex Border Path

West Wood

HUNDRED ACRE LA

Lashmar Wood

Melbourne Farm

Heath Farm

19

2

Park Farm

Park Farm Bsns Pk

Cottage Wood

Plumpton Wood

Beresford Manor

Ind Est

North America Farm

St Helena Farm

BN7

PLUMPTON CROSSWAYS

1

BN6

Hunt's Wood

ST HELENA LA

The Plough Inn (PH)

Shaw Farm

POTTERY COTTS

18

73 99

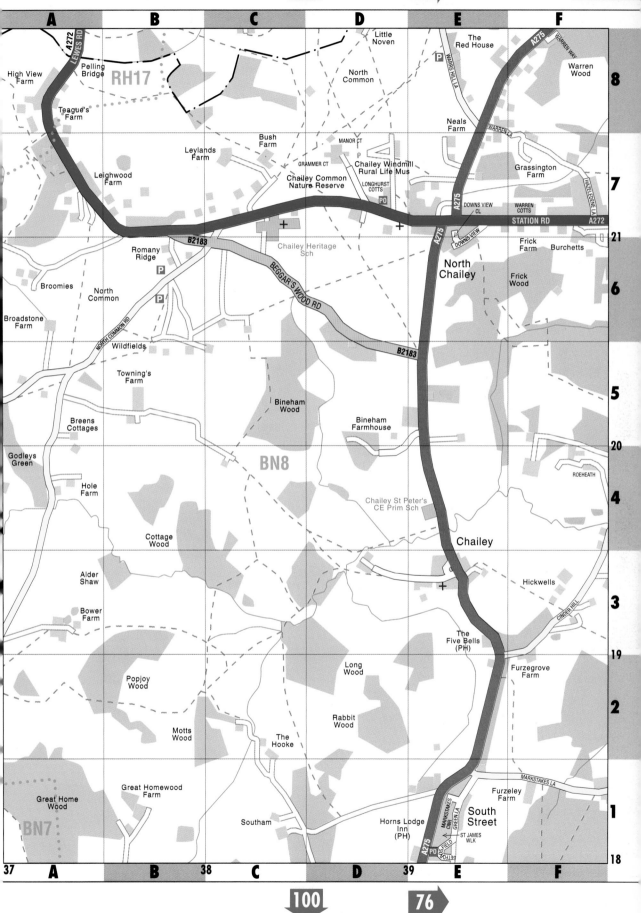

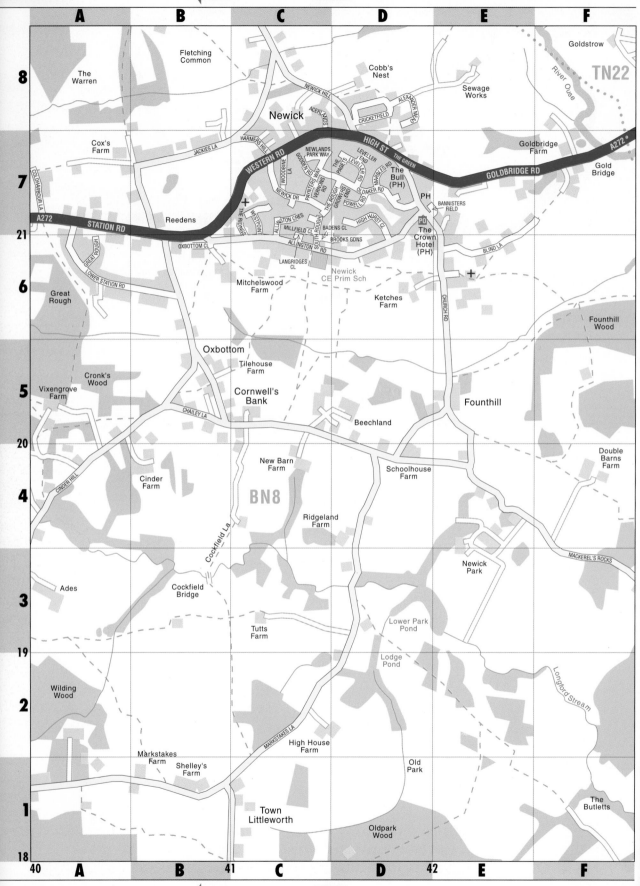

A B C D E F

8 The Warren
Fletching Common
Cobb's Nest
Goldstrow
River Ouse
TN22

Newick
Sewage Works

Cox's Farm
HARMERS HILL
NEWICK HILL
ACERLANDS
ALEXANDER RD
CRICKETFIELD
HIGH ST
THE GREEN
Goldbridge Farm
Gold Bridge

7 JACKIES LA
WESTERN RD
NEWLANDS PARK WAY
WOODBINE LA
GODWIN RD
PAYNTERS WAY
VERNONS
LEVELLER END
THE PAGETS
LEVELLS RD
MARBLES RD
OLDAKER RD
The Bull (PH)
GOLDBRIDGE RD
A272

A272
STATION RD
Reedens
NEWICK DR
THE RIDINGS
WESTPOINT
THE ROUGH
GROWERS END
POWELL
HIGH HURST CL
PH
BANNISTERS FIELD
BLIND LA

21 GREAT ROUGH
LOWER STATION RD
OXBOTTOM CL
ALLINGTON CRES
MILLFIELD CL
SOUTH ROUGH
ALLINGTON RD
BADENS CL
BROOKS GDNS
PO
The Crown Hotel (PH)

6 Great Rough
Mitchelswood Farm
LANGRIDGES CL
Newick CE Prim Sch
Ketches Farm
CHURCH RD
Founthill Wood

5 Vixengrove Farm
Cronk's Wood
Oxbottom
Tilehouse Farm
Cornwell's Bank
Beechland
Founthill

20 CHAILEY LA
New Barn Farm
Schoolhouse Farm
Double Barns Farm

4 CINDER HILL
Cinder Farm
BN8
Ridgeland Farm
MACKEREL'S ROCKS
Newick Park

COCKFIELD LA
Lower Park Pond
Longford Stream

3 Ades
Cockfield Bridge
Tutts Farm
Lodge Pond

19 Wilding Wood

2 Markstakes Farm
MARKSTAKES LA
High House Farm
Old Park

Shelley's Farm
Oldpark Wood
The Butletts

1 Town Littleworth

18
40 A B 41 C D 42 E F

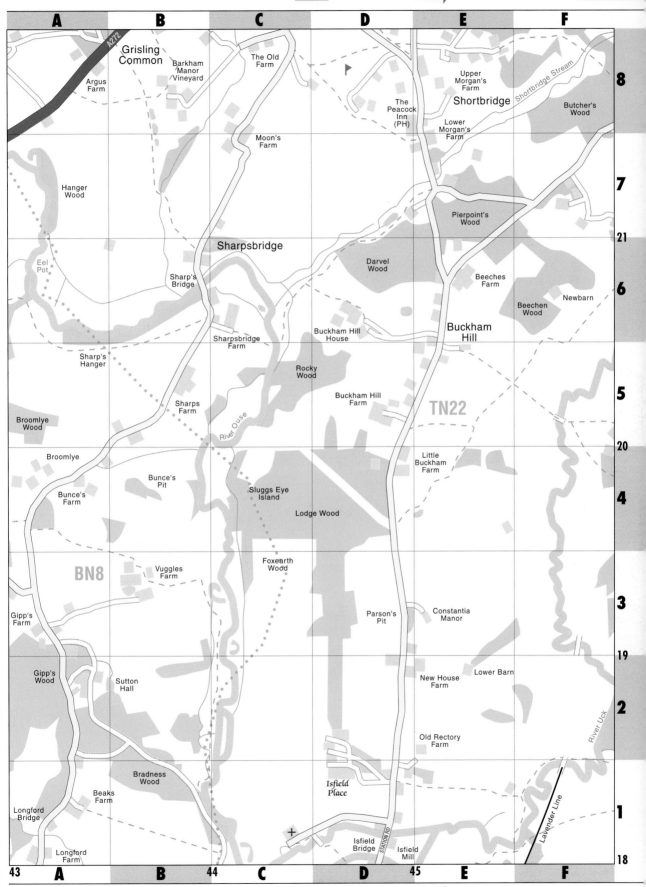

A272

Grisling
Common

Barkham
Manor
Vineyard

The Old
Farm

Argus
Farm

8

Upper
Morgan's
Farm

Shortbridge

Shortbridge Stream

Butcher's
Wood

Moon's
Farm

The Peacock
Inn
(PH)

Lower
Morgan's
Farm

Hanger
Wood

7

Pierpoint's
Wood

21

Sharpsbridge

Darvel
Wood

Eel
Pot

Sharp's
Bridge

Beeches
Farm

6

Beechen
Wood

Newbarn

Buckham
Hill

Sharpsbridge
Farm

Buckham Hill
House

Sharp's
Hanger

Rocky
Wood

Buckham Hill
Farm

TN22

5

Sharps
Farm

River Ouse

20

Broomlye
Wood

Little
Buckham
Farm

Broomlye

Bunce's
Pit

Sluggs Eye
Island

4

Bunce's
Farm

Lodge Wood

BN8

Vuggles
Farm

Foxearth
Wood

Parson's
Pit

Constantia
Manor

3

Gipp's
Farm

19

Gipp's
Wood

Sutton
Hall

New House
Farm

Lower Barn

2

Old Rectory
Farm

River Uck

Bradness
Wood

Isfield
Place

Beaks
Farm

Lavender Line

1

Longford
Bridge

STATION RD

Isfield
Bridge

Isfield
Mill

Longford
Farm

18

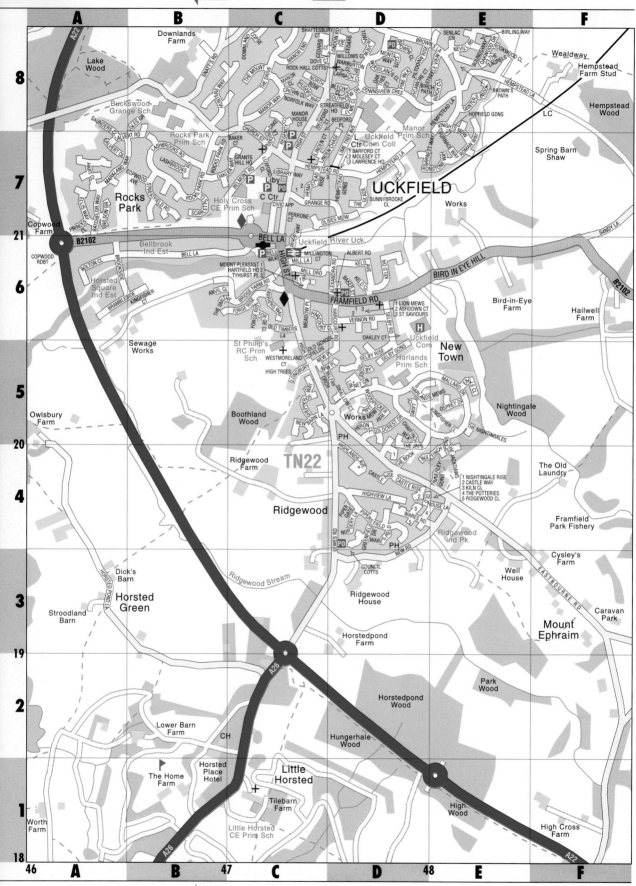

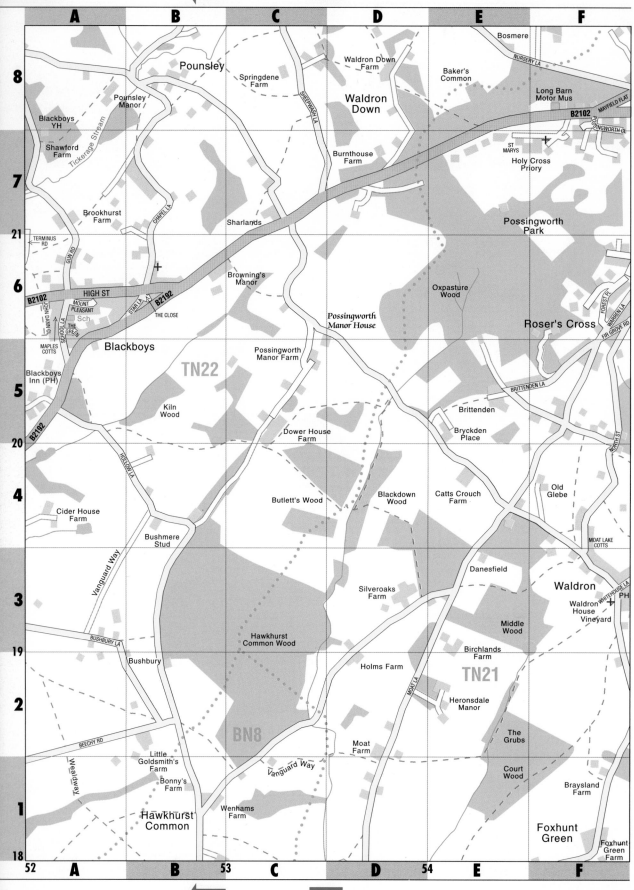

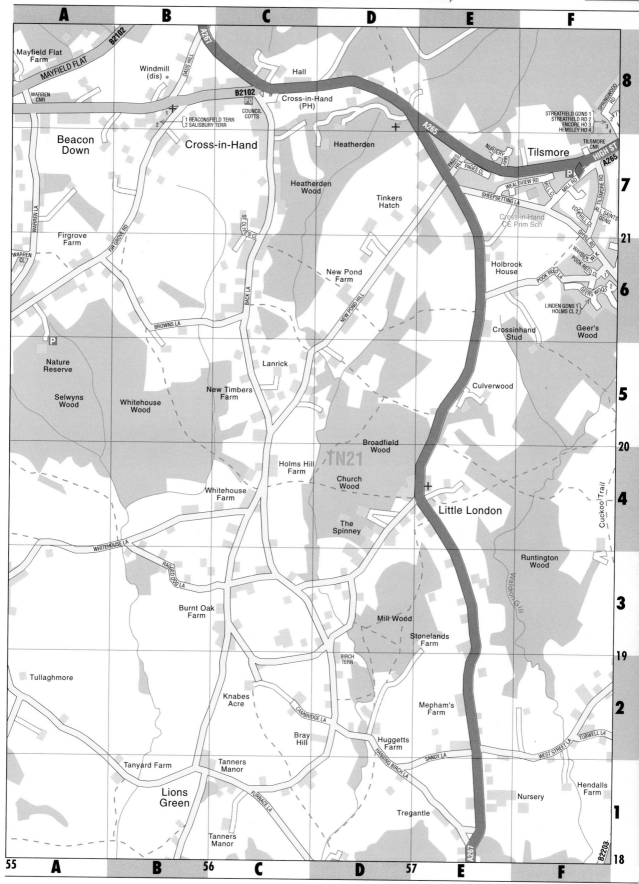

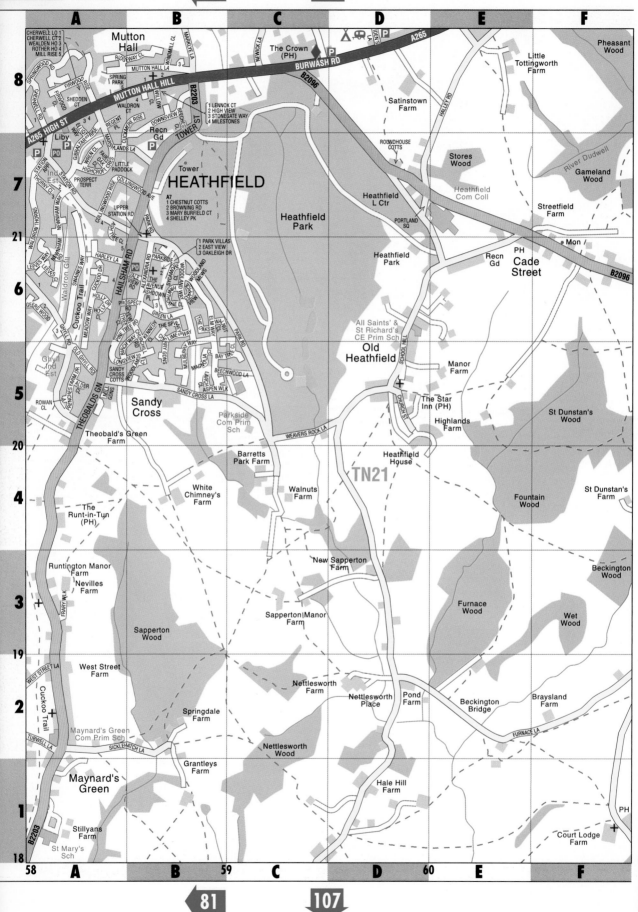

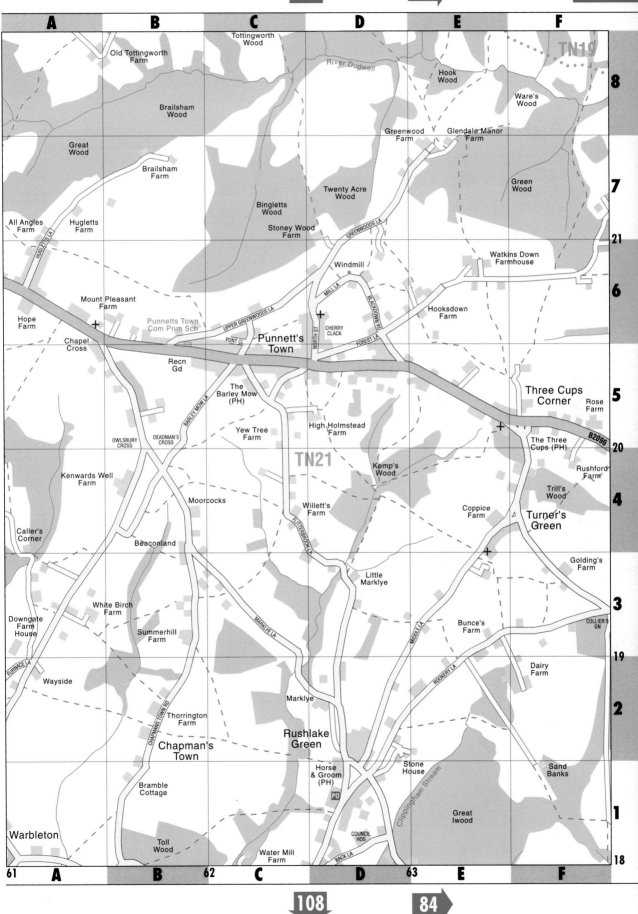

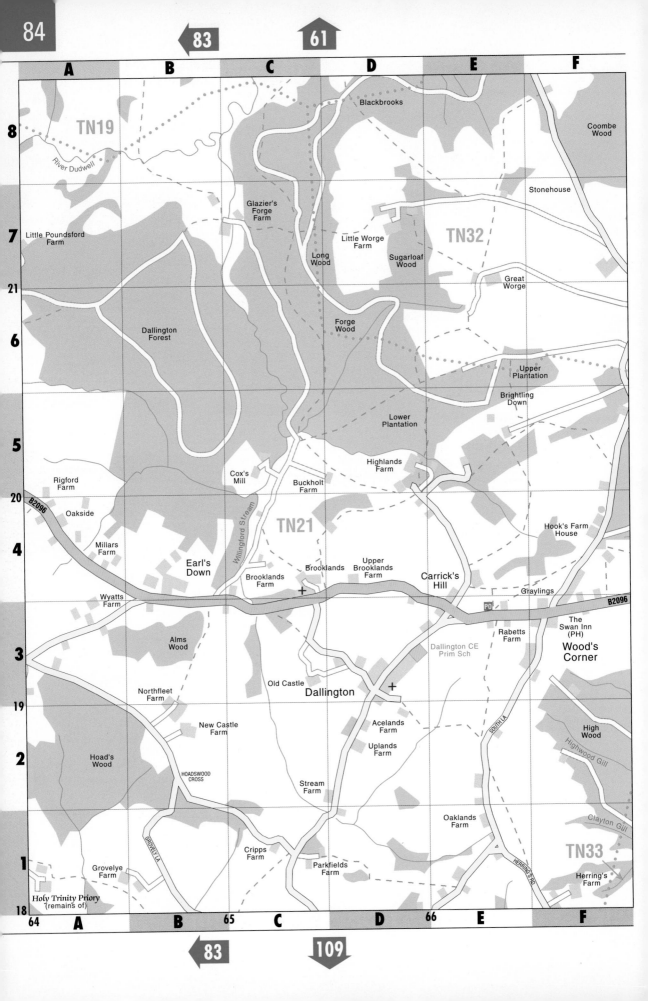

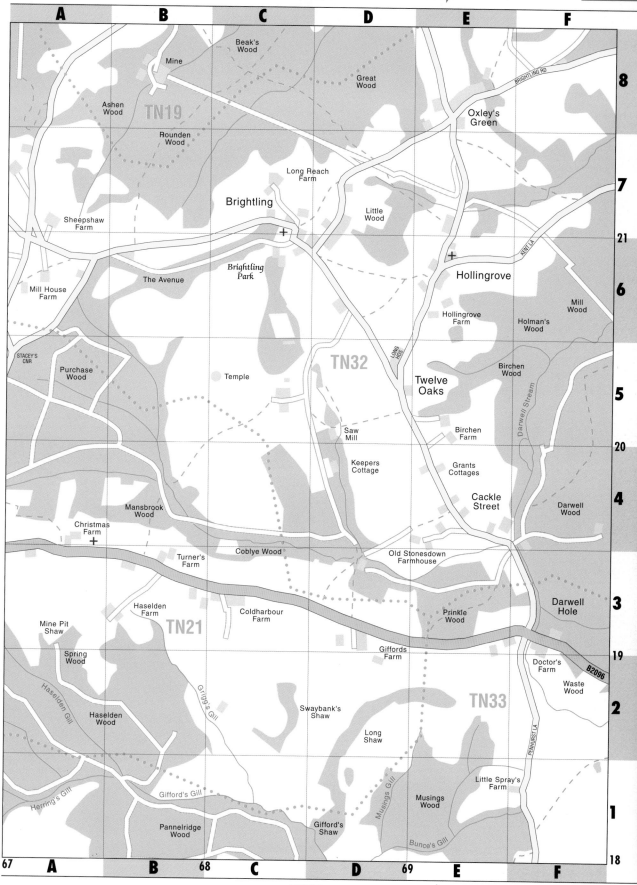

Beak's Wood
Mine
Great Wood
BRIGHTLING RD
8
Ashen Wood
TN19
Oxley's Green
Rounden Wood
Long Reach Farm
7
Brightling
Little Wood
21
Sheepshaw Farm
+
+
Hollingrove
6
Brightling Park
The Avenue
Hollingrove Farm
Mill Wood
Mill House Farm
Holman's Wood
STACEY'S CNR
Birchen Wood
Purchase Wood
TN32
Twelve Oaks
LONG HOS
Darwell Stream
5
Temple
Birchen Farm
20
Saw Mill
Keepers Cottage
Grants Cottages
Cackle Street
Darwell Wood
4
Mansbrook Wood
Coblye Wood
Old Stonesdown Farmhouse
Darwell Hole
3
Christmas Farm
+
Turner's Farm
Prinkle Wood
Haselden Farm
TN21
Coldharbour Farm
Mine Pit Shaw
Giffords Farm
Doctor's Farm
B2096
19
Spring Wood
Waste Wood
Haselden Gill
Griggs Gill
Swaybank's Shaw
TN33
2
Haselden Wood
Long Shaw
PENHURST LA
Little Spray's Farm
Herring's Gill
Gifford's Gill
Musings Gill
Musings Wood
1
Pannelridge Wood
Gifford's Shaw
Bunce's Gill
18

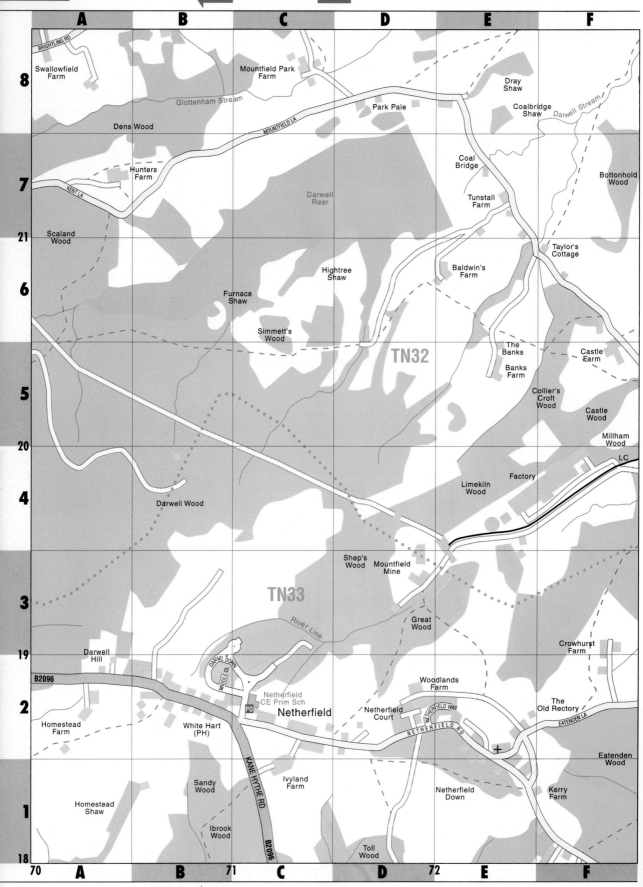

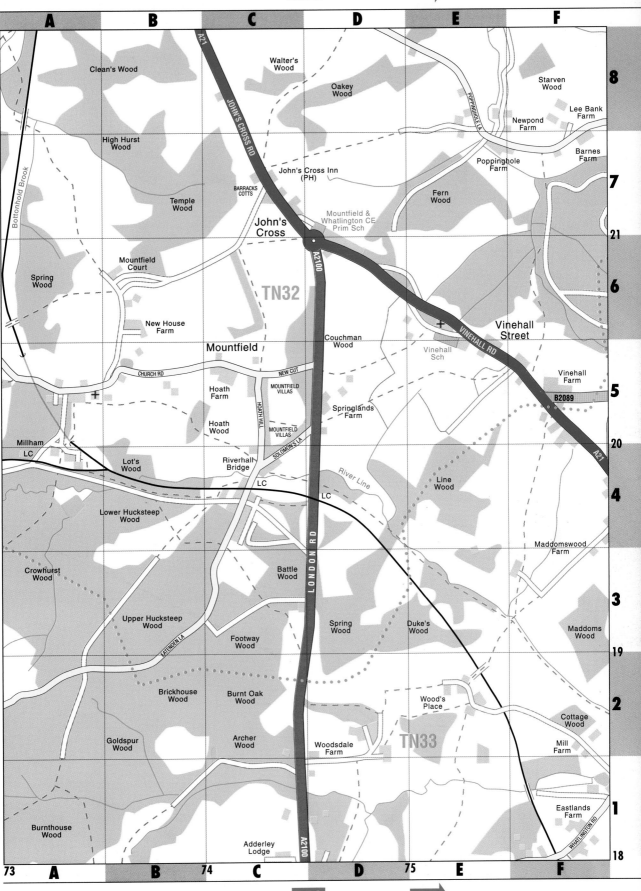

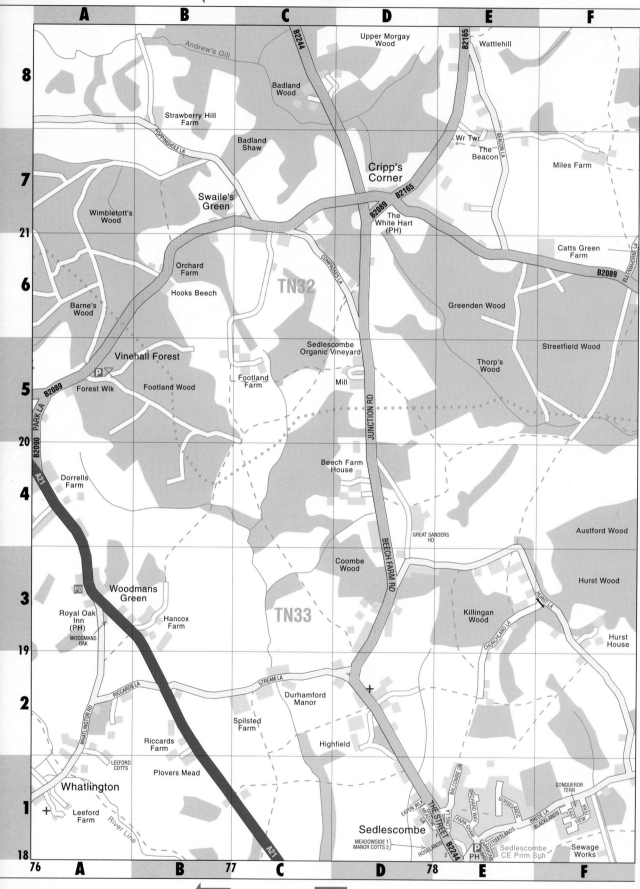

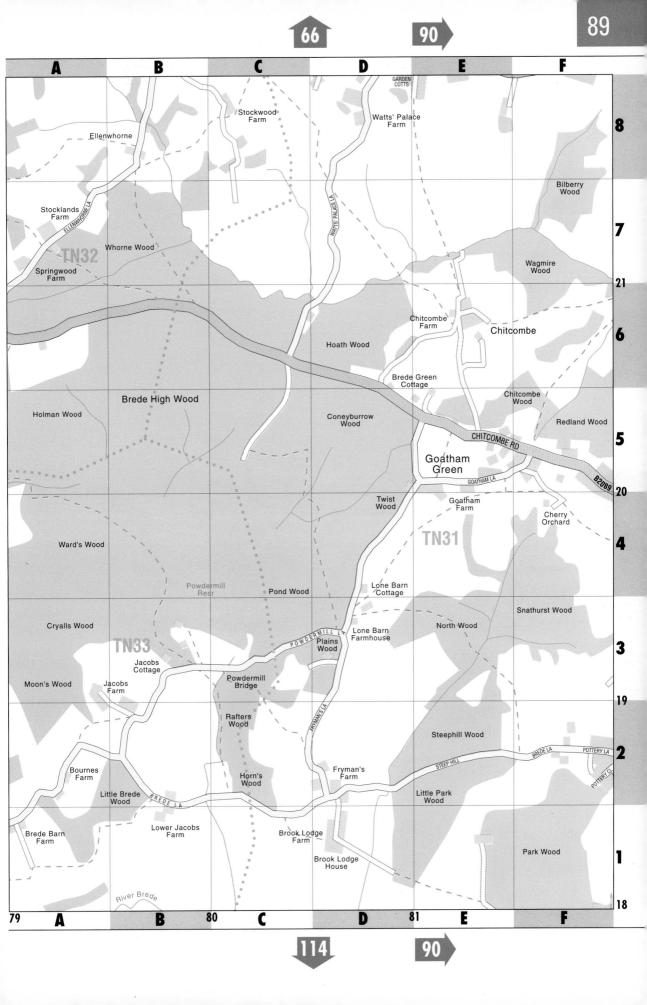

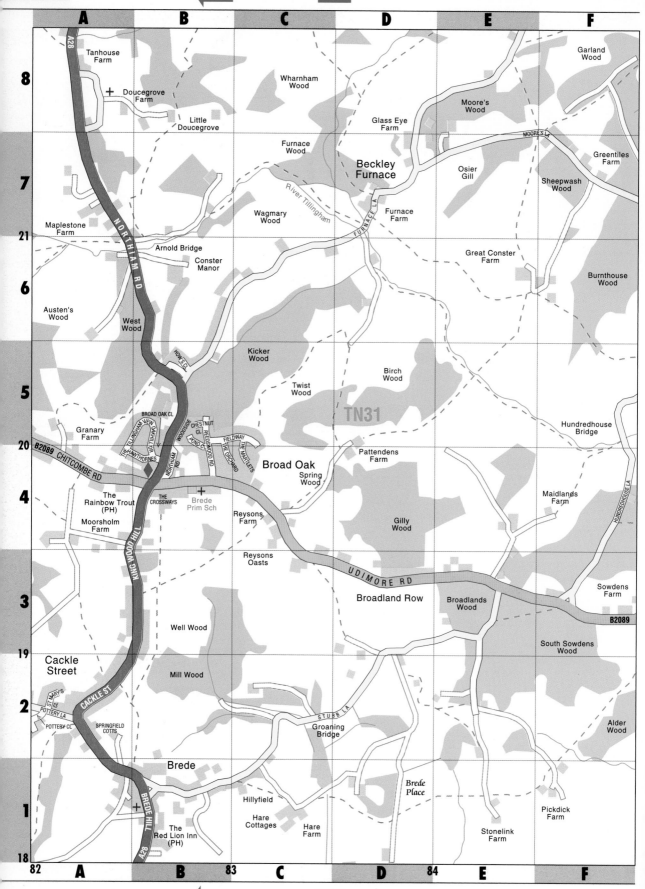

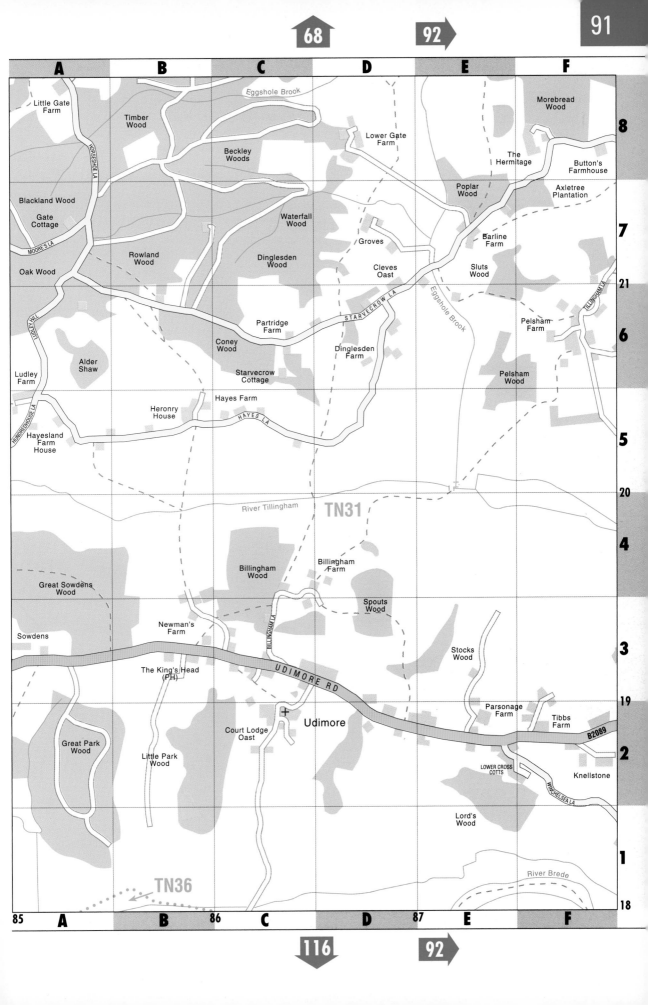

A B C D E F

8 7 21 6 5 20 4 3 19 2 1 18

Little Gate Farm

Timber Wood

Beckley Woods

Eggshole Brook

Lower Gate Farm

Morebread Wood

The Hermitage

Button's Farmhouse

Blackland Wood

Gate Cottage

HORSESHOE LA

MOORE'S LA

Poplar Wood

Axletree Plantation

Waterfall Wood

Rowland Wood

Groves

Barline Farm

Dinglesden Wood

Cleves Oast

Sluts Wood

Oak Wood

LUDLEY W.LL

STARVECROW LA

Eggshole Brook

TILLINGHAM LA

Partridge Farm

Pelsham Farm

Coney Wood

Dinglesden Farm

Ludley Farm

Alder Shaw

Starvecrow Cottage

Pelsham Wood

HUNDREDHOUSE LA

Heronry House

Hayes Farm

HAYES LA

Hayesland Farm House

River Tillingham

TN31

Great Sowdens Wood

Billingham Wood

Billingham Farm

Spouts Wood

Newman's Farm

Stocks Wood

Sowdens

BILLINGHAM LA

The King's Head (PH)

UDIMORE RD

Parsonage Farm

Tibbs Farm

Great Park Wood

Court Lodge Oast

Udimore

B2089

Little Park Wood

LOWER CROSS COTTS

Knellstone

WINCHELSEA LA

Lord's Wood

TN36

River Brede

85 A B 86 C D 87 E F

A **B** **C** **D** **E** **F**

Morebread Farm

Peasmarsh Place

CHURCH LA

Norland Wood

8

STARVECROW LA

DEW LA

Clayton Farm

Leasam Wood

Wr Twr

Cockney Hill Wood

Leasam House

Secret Wood

7

TILLINGHAM LA

21

Dew Farm

High Weald Landscape Trail

6

Ennets Wood

Tillingham Wood

River Tillingham

TILLINGHAM LA

Cottage Shaw

Tillingham Farm

5

Hooker's Wood

Calves Field Wood

20

Tillingham Bridge

Gillshaw Farm

B2089

CADBOROUGH CLIFF

OAST HOUSE DR

4

TN31

Wick Farm

Oaklands

Cadborough Farm

Turnpike Wood

Hotel

Wick Wood

Watlands

Cadborough Cliff

3

Knellstone Wood

UDIMORE RD

19

Farthing Wood

DUMB WOMAN'S LA

Cock Marling

2

B2089

1066 Country Wlk

The Plough (PH)

Nicholls Cottages

Padiam Sewer

Roadend Farm

WINCHELSEA LA

Newhouse Sewer

Winchelsea

LC

TN36

1

STATION RD

Float Farm

STATION COTTS

18

88 **A** **B** 89 **C** **D** 90 **E** **F**

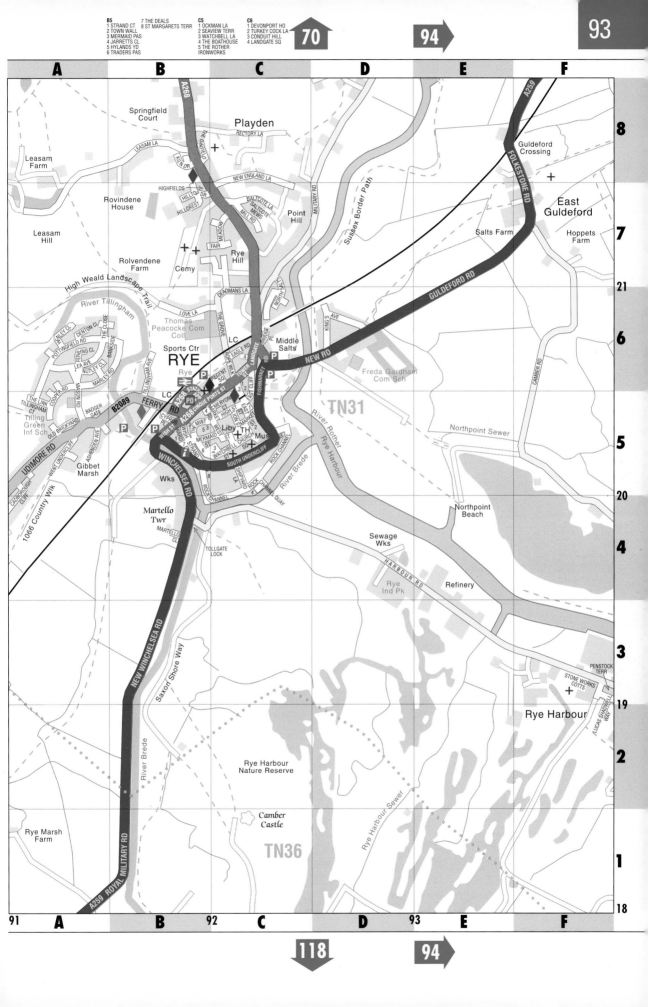

B5
1 STRAND CT
2 TOWN WALL
3 MERMAID PAS
4 JARRETTS CL
5 HYLANDS YD
6 TRADERS PAS

7 THE DEALS
8 ST MARGARETS TERR

C5
1 OCKMAN LA
2 SEAVIEW TERR
3 WATCHBELL LA
4 THE BOATHOUSE
5 THE ROTHER
   IRONWORKS

C6
1 DEVONPORT HO
2 TURKEY COCK LA
3 CONDUIT HILL
4 LANDGATE SQ

70 94

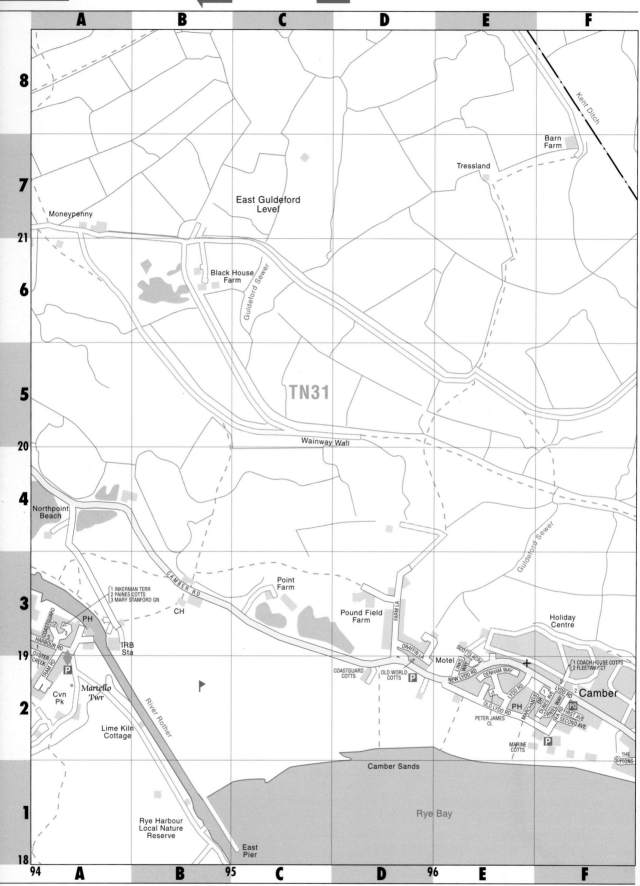

Moneypenny

East Guldeford
Level

Tressland

Barn
Farm

Kent Ditch

Black House
Farm

Guldeford Sewer

TN31

Wainway Wall

Guldeford Sewer

Northpoint
Beach

CAMBER RD

Point
Farm

Pound Field
Farm

FARM LA

Holiday
Centre

1 INKERMAN TERR
2 PAINES COTTS
3 MARY STANFORD GN

CH

DRAFFIN LA

Motel

SCOTTS ACRE

LINKS WAY

1 COACH HOUSE COTTS
2 FLEETWAY CT

COASTGUARD

PH

HARBOUR RD

OYSTER
CREEK

TRAM RD

P

Cvn
Pk

Martello
Twr

IRB
Sta

COASTGUARD
COTTS

OLD WORLD
COTTS

P

NEW LYDD RD

DENHAM WAY

LYDD RD

MARCHANTS

OLD LYDD RD

PH

DUNES AVE

DANIEL WAY

SEA RD

LYDD RD

FIRST AVE

SECOND AVE

Camber

PO

Lime Kiln
Cottage

River Rother

PETER JAMES
CL

MARINE
COTTS

P

THE
SUTTONS

Camber Sands

Rye Harbour
Local Nature
Reserve

Rye Bay

East
Pier

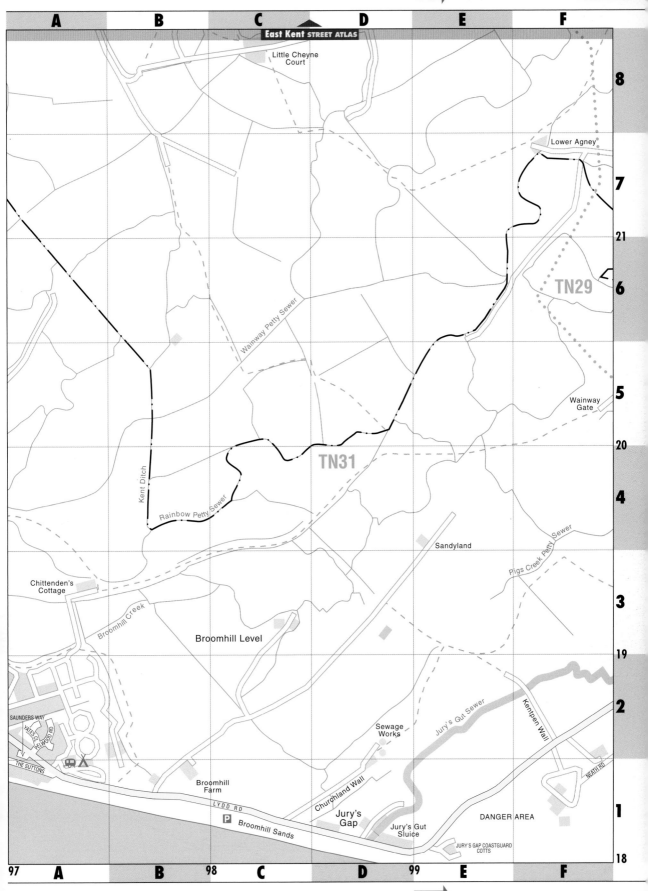

Little Cheyne
Court

Lower Agney

TN29

Wainway
Gate

TN31

Wainway Petty Sewer

Kent Ditch

Rainbow Petty Sewer

Sandyland

Pigs Creek Petty Sewer

Chittenden's
Cottage

Broomhill Creek

Broomhill Level

Jury's Gut Sewer

Kenpen Wall

SAUNDERS WAY

YATES CL

RELWOOD RD

THE SUTTONS

Sewage
Works

Churchland Wall

NEATH RD

DANGER AREA

Broomhill Farm

LYDD RD

P Broomhill Sands

Jury's
Gap

Jury's Gut
Sluice

JURY'S GAP COASTGUARD
COTTS

95

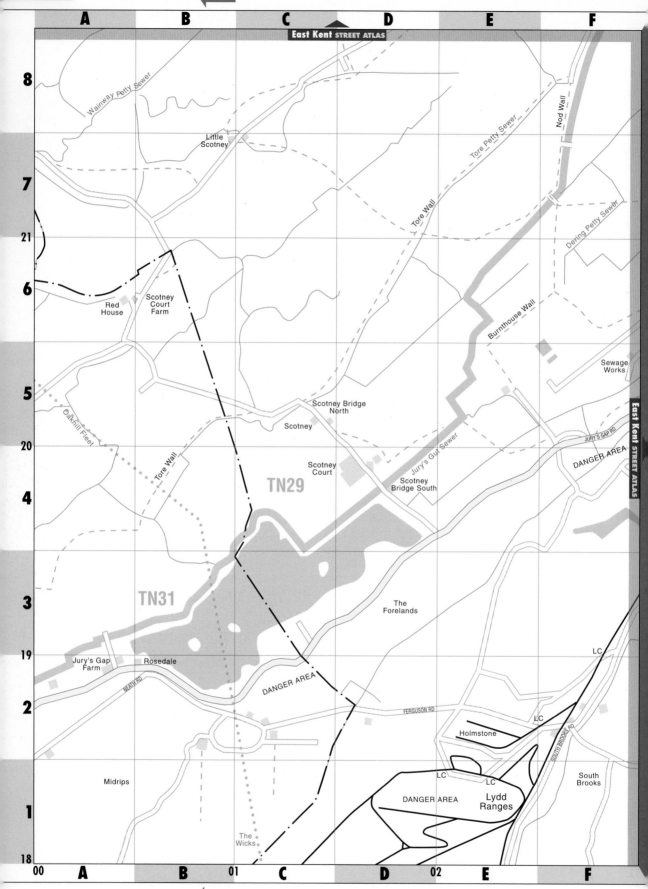

East Kent STREET ATLAS

East Kent STREET ATLAS

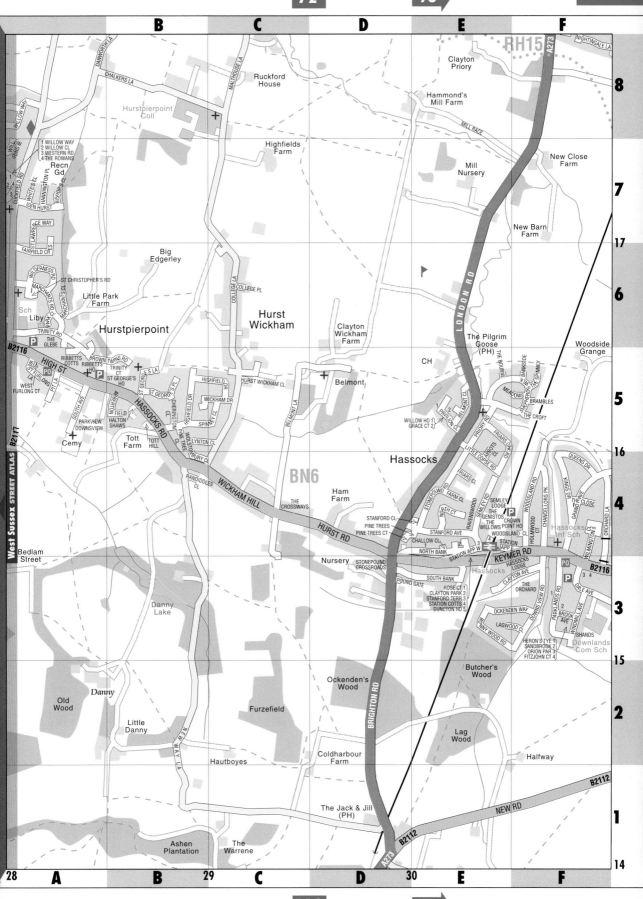

8

7

17

6

5

16

4

3

15

2

1

14

NIGHTINGALE LA
WINGATE TYE RD
GREENLANDS CL
GREENLANDS DR
High Chimneys
1 FRANKLANDS WAY
2 FRANKLANDS GDNS
KEYMER RD
BROADLANDS
Water Twr
The Blenheims
WELLHOUSE LA
Wellhouse Farm
Upper Furzefield
Hopkin's Crank
Fragbarrow Farm
Clearview Farm
B2112

RH15

OCKLEY LA
Ockley Wood
The Oaks Poultry Farm

OCKLEY HILL
The Tole
Broadhill Farm
Townmead
Swansyard Farm

COMMON LA
COTTAGE HOMES

Ockley Manor Farm
Court Gardens Farm
SOUTH VIEW
Oaktree Farm

Ockley Manor
Windmill
BN6
Stocks Farm

MACKIE AVE
FARNHAM AVE
SWEETLANDS
ANN CL
MANOR AVE
PH
Oldland
ORCHARD LA
Sussex Border Path

BROMLEY CL
GRAND AVE
OCKLEY LA
Newtons Farm

ADASTRA AVE
OLDLANDS AVE
Keymer
NORTH END
DUMBRELLS COURT RD
DUMBRELLS CT

PARKSIDE
FIR TREE WAY
QUADRANT
DAME N WAY
Lodge Hill
North End Farm
Stoneywish Nature Reserve
Sewage Farm
Spatham Gardens Nursery

KYNER SDALE
NEWLANDS CL
CHURCH MEAD
COOCH HILL LA
EAST GDNS
Ditchling
B2116
Stafford House
Liby
BODDINGTONS LA
THE TWITTEN
THE MILBERRY LA
SPATHAM LA

1 THE MINNELS
2 WILLOWBROOK WAY
3 THE POPLARS
4 ST ANNE'S GDNS
THE CRESCENT
SILVERDALE
Ditchling Mus
CHURCH LA
WEST ST
HIGH ST
PH
PO
EAST END LA
East End
Cemy

HIGHLANDS CL
DALE AVE
STAFFORD WAY
PH
KEYMER RD
BEACON HS
SOUTH ST
PH
CHARLTON GDNS
FIELDWAY
Prim Sch
FARM LA
BARNFIELD GDNS

TheWindmills Jun Sch
PARK AVE
CLAYTON RD
BEACON RD
NYE LA
SHIRLEYS
LEWES RD

LODGE LA
NEW RD
NEVILL COTTS
PARK LA
Molehilly Shaw
Jointer Copse
The Nye
Blackdog Hill

Lodge Farm
Bungalow Farm
NR COT
Ditchling Nurseries
Wellcroft Shaw

Millbrook Shaw
Park Barn Farm
NYE LA
B2116

B2112

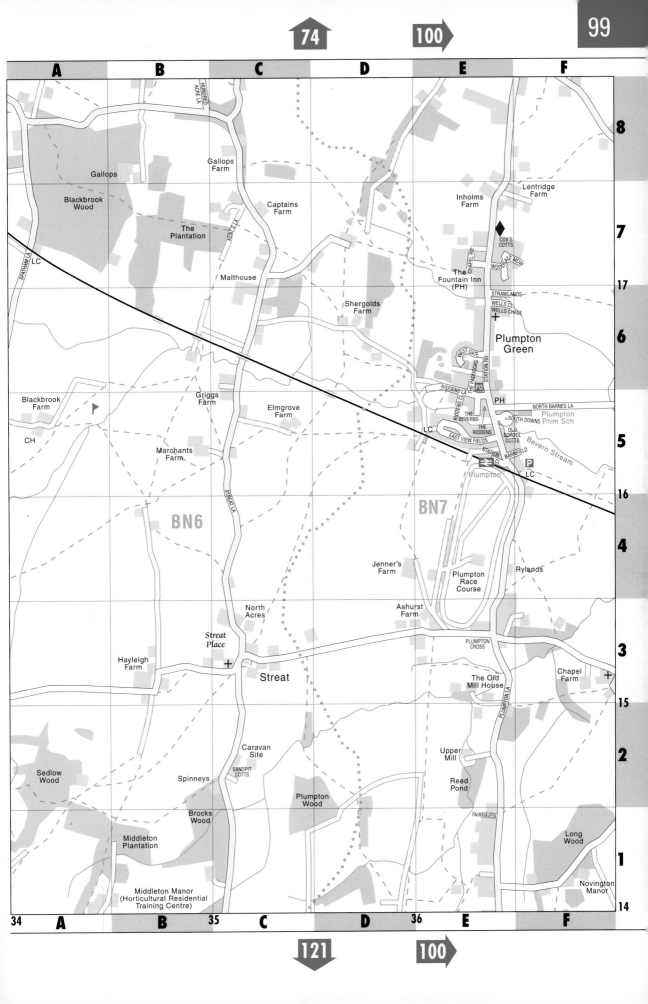

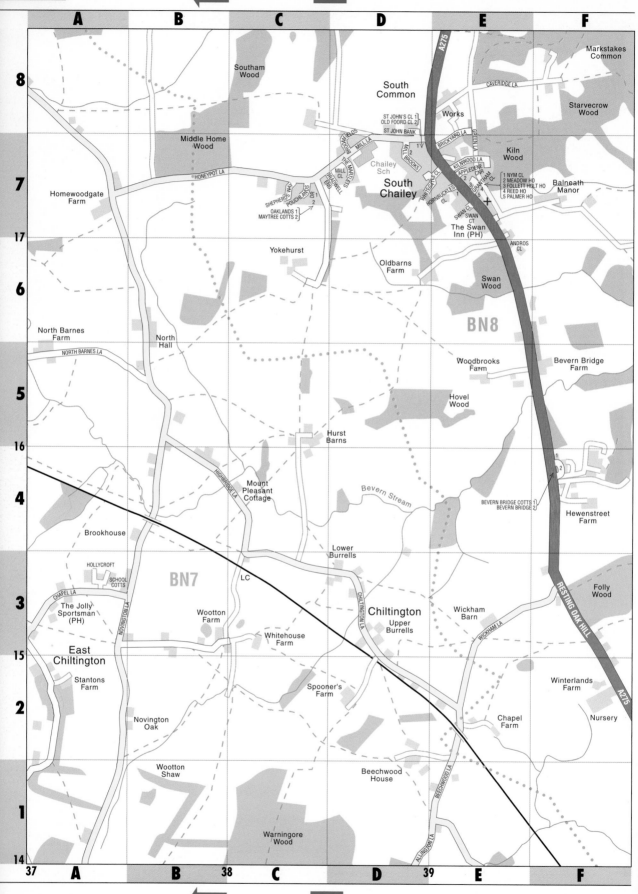

A B C D E F

8

St John's Cl 1
Old Foord Cl 2

St John Bank

South
Common

Works

Markstakes
Common

CAVERIDGE LA

Starvecrow
Wood

Kiln
Wood

Balneath
Manor

1 NYM CL
2 MEADOW HO
3 FOLLETT HOLT HO
4 REED HO
5 PALMER HO

Southam
Wood

Middle Home
Wood

HONEYPOT LA

Homewoodgate
Farm

17

Chailey
Sch

South
Chailey

The Swan
Inn (PH)

ANDROS
CL

Yokehurst

Oldbarns
Farm

Swan
Wood

BN8

6

North Barnes
Farm

NORTH BARNES LA

North
Hall

Woodbrooks
Farm

Bevern Bridge
Farm

5

Hovel
Wood

16

Hurst
Barns

Bevern Stream

4

HIGHBRIDGE LA

Mount
Pleasant
Cottage

BEVERN BRIDGE COTTS 1
BEVERN BRIDGE 2

Hewenstreet
Farm

Brookhouse

Lower
Burrells

Folly
Wood

RESTING OAK HILL

3

HOLLYCROFT

SCHOOL
COTTS

CHAPEL LA

The Jolly
Sportsman
(PH)

BN7

LC

Wootton
Farm

CHILTINGTON LA

Chiltington

Upper
Burrells

Wickham
Barn

WICKHAM LA

15

East
Chiltington

Whitehouse
Farm

Winterlands
Farm

2

Stantons
Farm

Novington
Oak

Spooner's
Farm

Chapel
Farm

Nursery

A275

1

Wootton
Shaw

Beechwood
House

ALLINGTON LA

BEECHWOOD LA

Warningore
Wood

14

37 A B 38 C D 39 E F

101
77

A **B** **C** **D** **E** **F**

8

River Uck

Longford Stream

Elms Farm

Tile Barn Farm

Lavender Line

Down Coppice

Dallas La

Agmond's Wood

White Bridge

Northfield Cotts

Tile Barn Cl

Station Rd

PO

Isfield

Oaks Farm

7

Burtenshaw's Wood

PH

Isfield

Horsted La

17

Birches Farm

6

Gallops Farm

Blunt's La

Iron River

Boathouse Farm

TN22

Lewes Rd

Brook Lodge Farm

Rose Hill

Scufflings

Delves Farm

Anchor La

The Halfway House (PH)

Kiln La

Plashett Park Gates

5

Banks Farm

Anchor Inn

Batchelor's Hall

Isfield Rd

A26

16

Lower Barn Cottage

River Ouse

BN8

Clay Hill Wood

Oaklands Park

4

Bevern Stream

Iron River

Stewards Enquiry (PH)

Beam Bridge (FB)

3

Barcombe Mills

Mill Farm

Barcombe Resr

Upper Clay Hill Farm

15

Barcombe House

Barcombe Mills Rd

2

Pikes Bridge

Ppg Sta

P

Plashett Park Farm

Works

Bridge Farm

Lower Clayhill

Clayhill House

Little Norlington

Norlington La

1

River Ouse

A26

Wellingham La

Swingate

Broyle La

14

43 **A** **B** **44** **C** **D** **45** **E** **F**

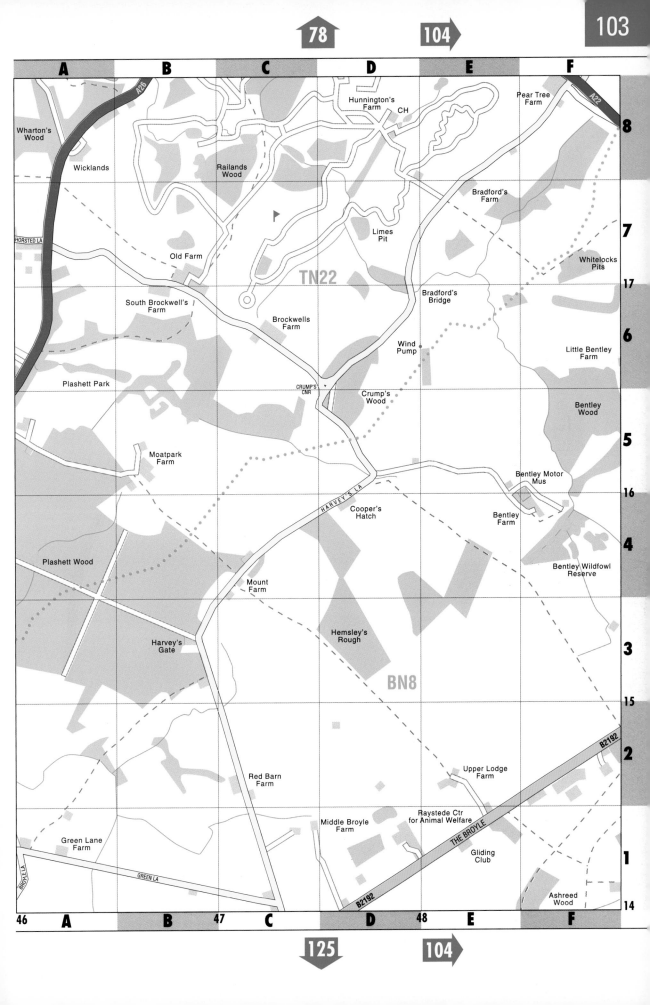

103
79

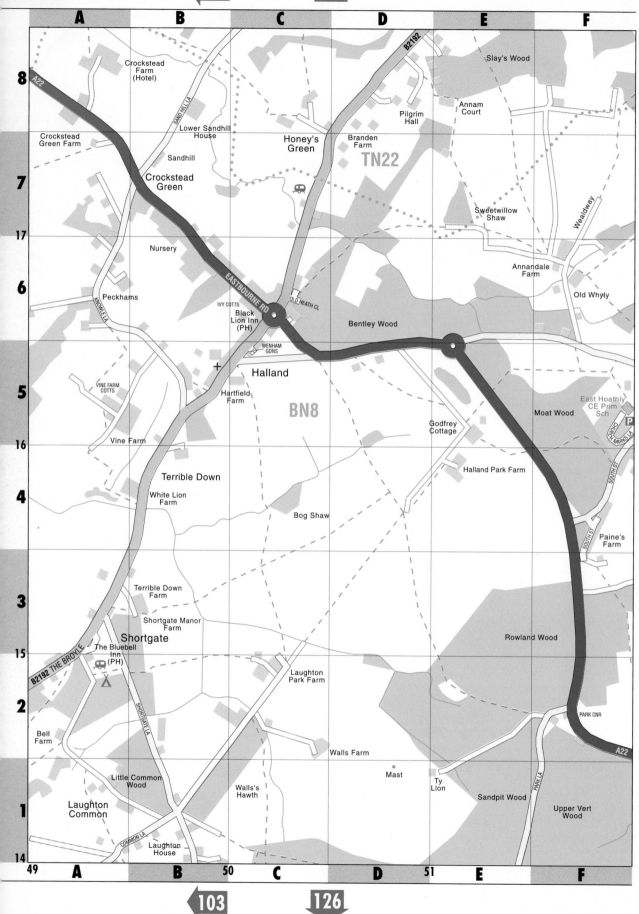

103
126

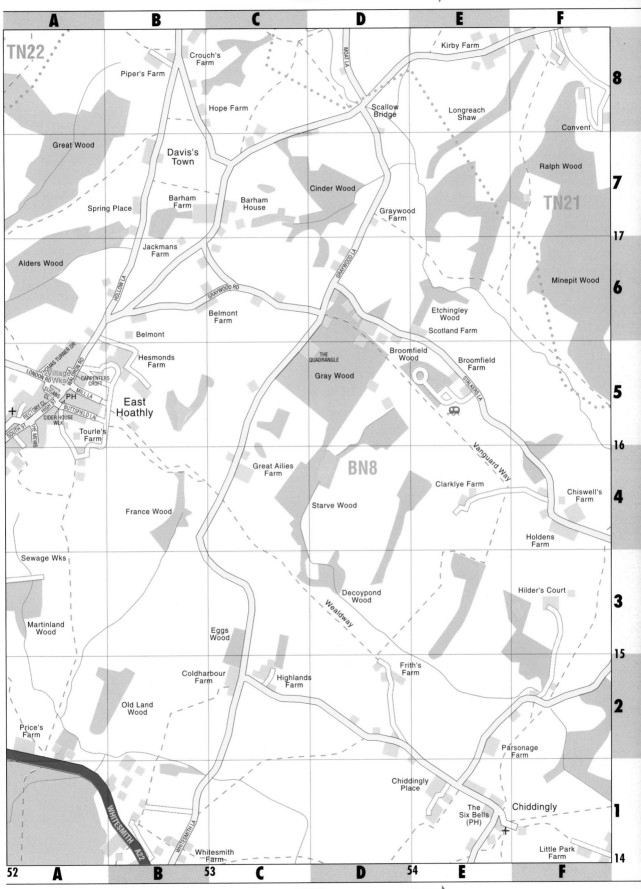

TN22

Crouch's Farm
Piper's Farm
Hope Farm
Scallow Bridge
Kirby Farm
Longreach Shaw
Convent

Great Wood
Davis's Town
Cinder Wood
Ralph Wood
TN21

Spring Place
Barham Farm
Barham House
Graywood Farm

Alders Wood
Jackmans Farm
Graywood Rd
Minepit Wood

HOLLOW LA
Belmont Farm
Etchingley Wood
Scotland Farm
GRAYWOOD LA

Belmont
THE QUADRANGLE
Broomfield Wood
Broomfield Farm

Hesmonds Farm
Gray Wood
STALKERS LA

THOMAS TURNER DR
CARPENTERS CROFT
Villages Wks
WALTON RD
MILL LA
LONDON RD
SUSANS CL
PH
East Hoathly
RECTORY CL
HIGH ST
BUTTSFIELD LA
CIDER HOUSE WLK
Tourle's Farm

Vanguard Way

SOUTH ST
THE MEWS
Great Ailies Farm
BN8
Clarklye Farm
Chiswell's Farm

France Wood
Starve Wood
Holdens Farm

Sewage Wks
Decoypond Wood
Hilder's Court

Wealdway

Martinland Wood
Eggs Wood

Coldharbour Farm
Highlands Farm
Frith's Farm

Old Land Wood
Parsonage Farm

Price's Farm
Chiddingly Place
Chiddingly

WHITESMITH A22
WHITESMITH LA
Whitesmith Farm
The Six Bells (PH)
Little Park Farm

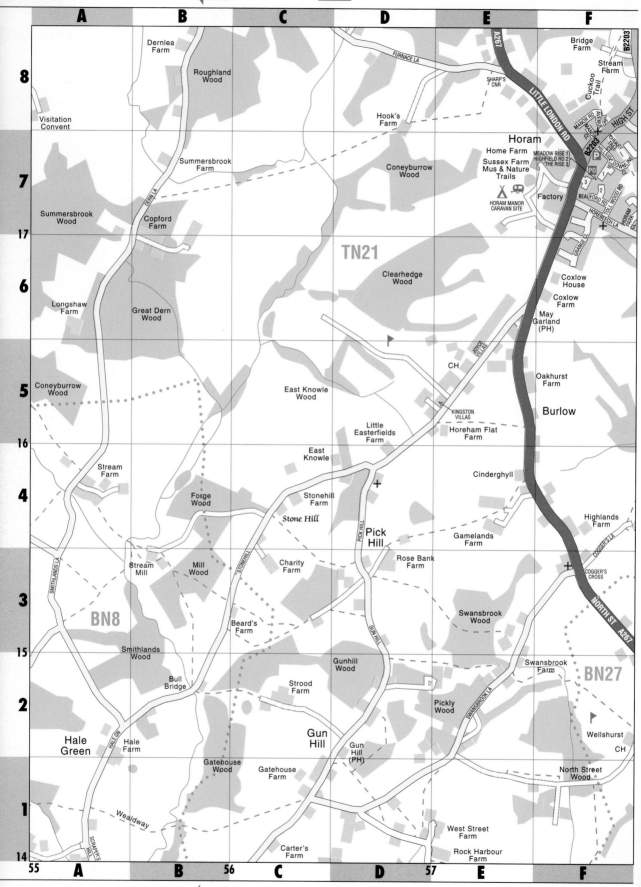

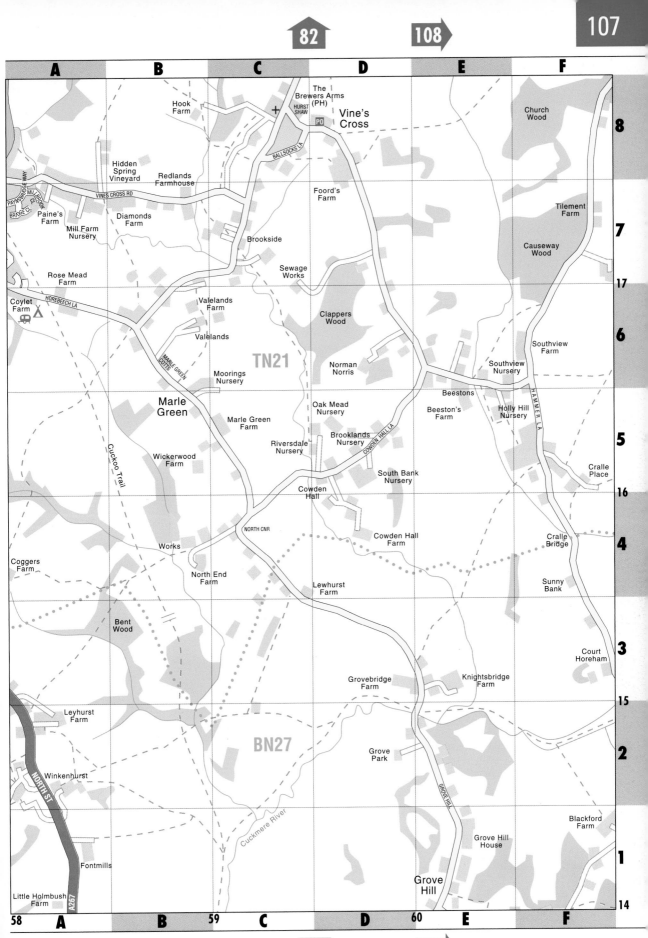

82
108

A **B** **C** **D** **E** **F**

8
7
17
6
5
16
4
3
15
2
1
14

Hook Farm

The Brewers Arms (PH)

HURST SHAW

PO

Vine's Cross

BALLSOCKS LA

Church Wood

Hidden Spring Vineyard

Redlands Farmhouse

VINES CROSS RD

Foord's Farm

Tilement Farm

PAYNSBRIDGE WAY

MILLBROOK CL

BRIDGE CL

Paine's Farm

Diamonds Farm

Brookside

Causeway Wood

Mill Farm Nursery

Sewage Works

Rose Mead Farm

HOREBEECH LA

Valelands Farm

Clappers Wood

Coylet Farm

Valelands

Southview Farm

MARLE GREEN COTTS

TN21

Norman Norris

Southview Nursery

Holly Hill Nursery

HAMMER LA

Moorings Nursery

Beestons

Marle Green

Marle Green Farm

Oak Mead Nursery

Beeston's Farm

Cuckoo Trail

Wickerwood Farm

Riversdale Nursery

Brooklands Nursery

COWDEN HALL LA

Cralle Place

Cowden Hall

South Bank Nursery

16

NORTH CNR

Cowden Hall Farm

Cralle Bridge

Works

North End Farm

Lewhurst Farm

Sunny Bank

Coggers Farm

Bent Wood

Court Horeham

Grovebridge Farm

Knightsbridge Farm

15

Leyhurst Farm

BN27

Grove Park

GROVE HILL

NORTH ST

Winkenhurst

Cuckmere River

Blackford Farm

Grove Hill House

Fontmills

A267

Grove Hill

Little Holmbush Farm

129
108

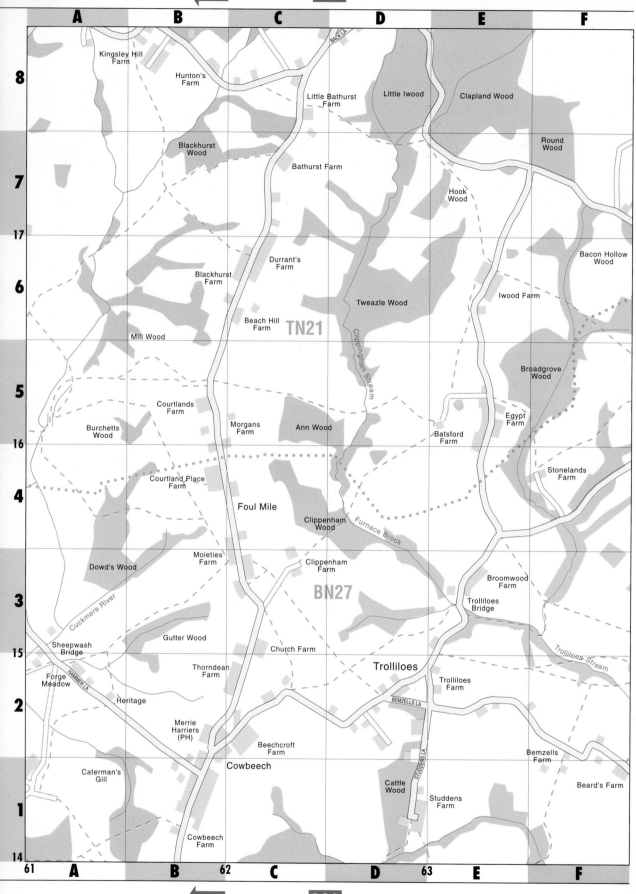

A B C D E F

8

Kingsley Hill
Farm

Hunton's
Farm

BACK LA

Little Bathurst
Farm

Little Iwood

Clapland Wood

Blackhurst
Wood

Round
Wood

7

Bathurst Farm

Hook
Wood

17

Durrant's
Farm

Bacon Hollow
Wood

6

Blackhurst
Farm

Tweazle Wood

Iwood Farm

Beach Hill
Farm

TN21

Clippingham Stream

Mill Wood

Broadgrove
Wood

5

Courtlands
Farm

Morgans
Farm

Ann Wood

Egypt
Farm

Burchetts
Wood

Batsford
Farm

16

Stonelands
Farm

4

Courtland Place
Farm

Foul Mile

Clippenham
Wood

Furnace Brook

Moieties
Farm

Clippenham
Farm

Dowd's Wood

Broomwood
Farm

3

BN27

Trolliloes
Bridge

Cuckmere River

Gutter Wood

Church Farm

Trolliloes Stream

15

Sheepwash
Bridge

Trolliloes

Forge
Meadow

HAMMER LA

Thorndean
Farm

Trolliloes
Farm

2

Heritage

BEMZELLS LA

Merrie
Harriers
(PH)

Beechcroft
Farm

STUDDENS LA

Bemzells
Farm

Cowbeech

Caterman's
Gill

Cattle
Wood

Beard's Farm

1

Studdens
Farm

Cowbeech
Farm

14

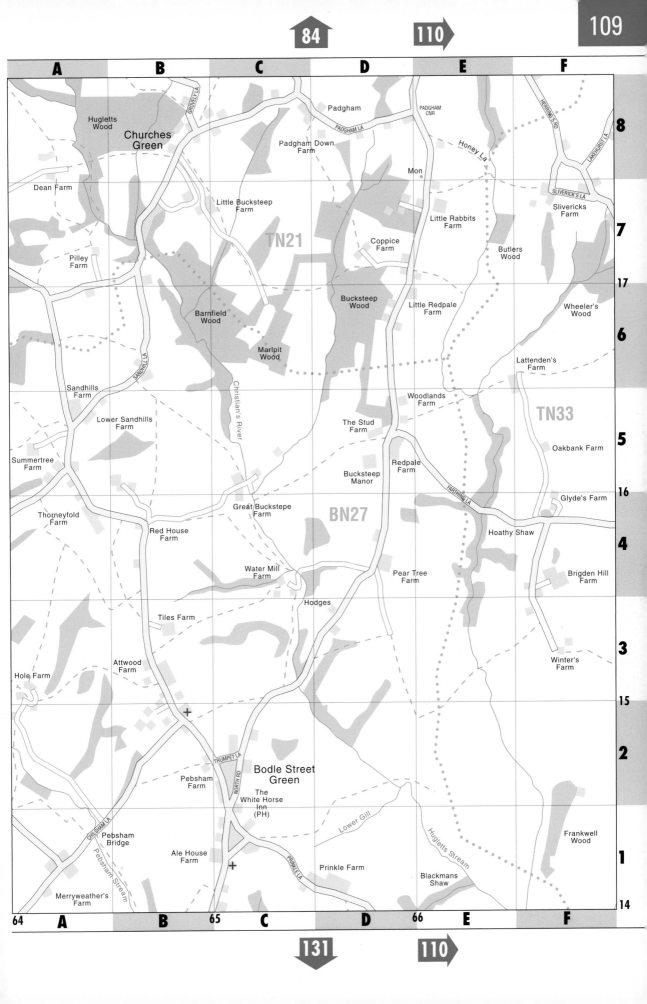

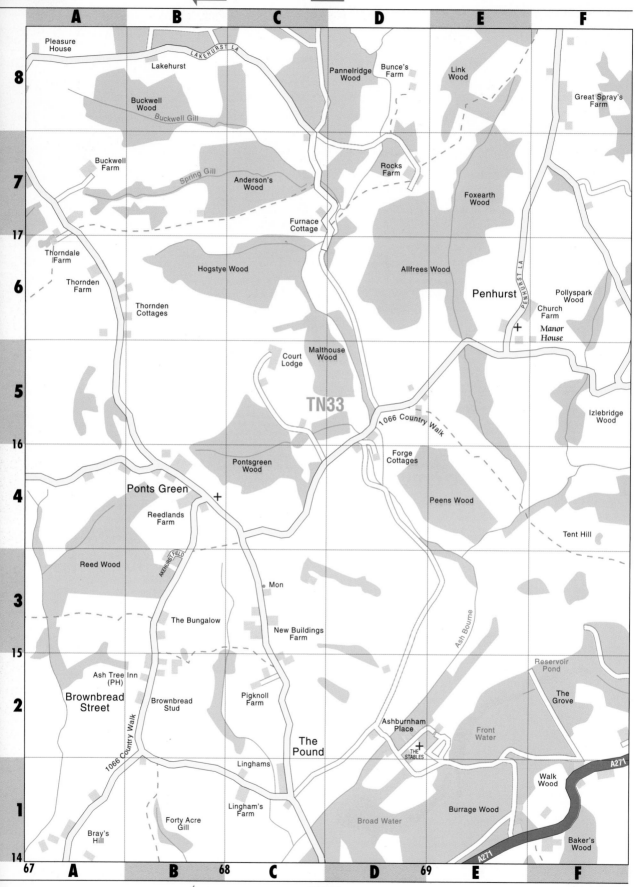

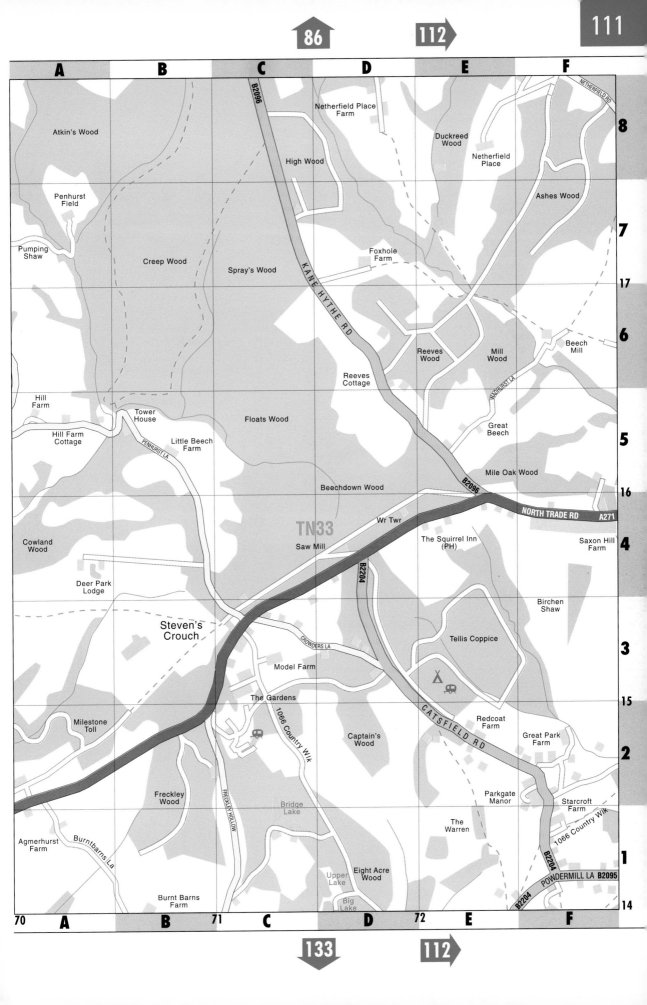

111 87

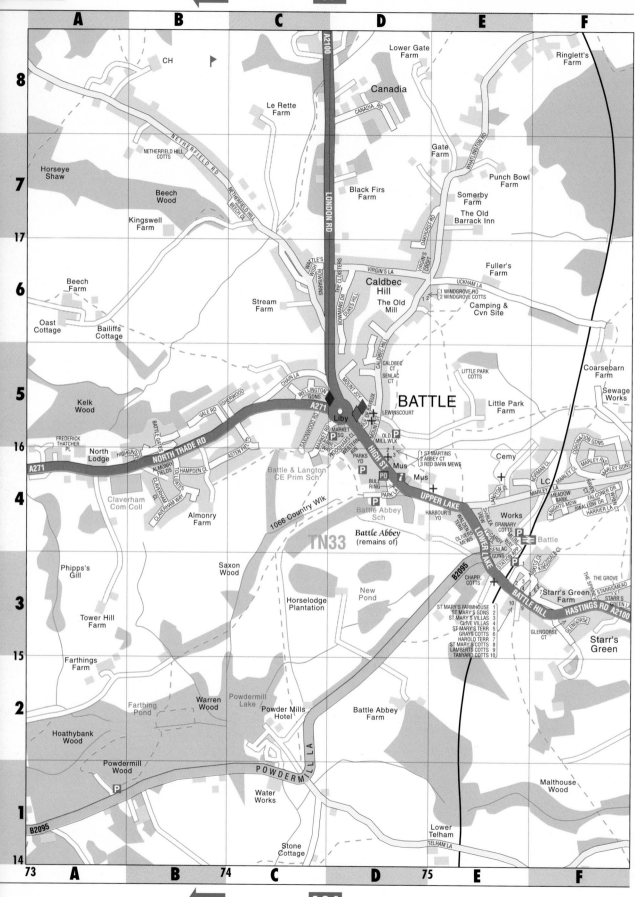

111 134

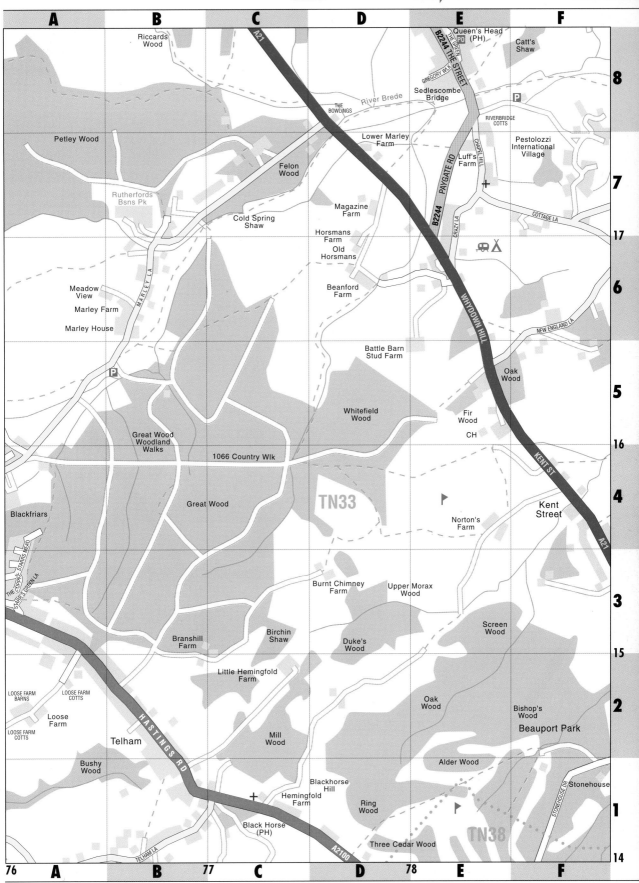

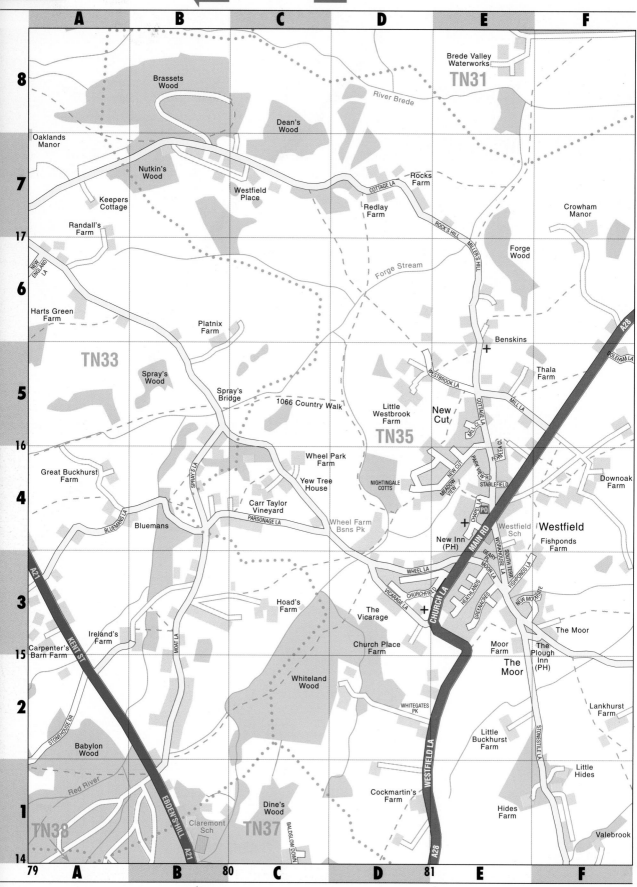

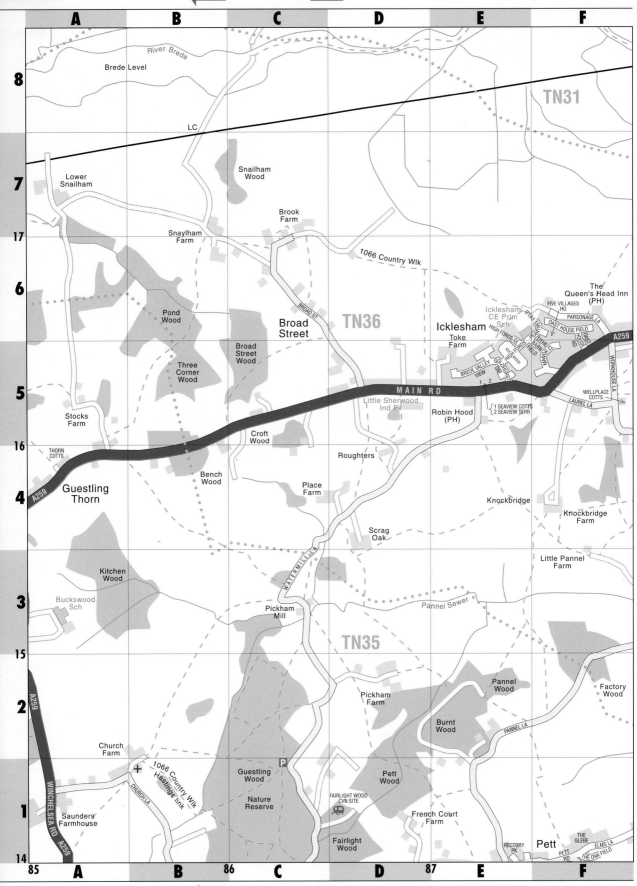

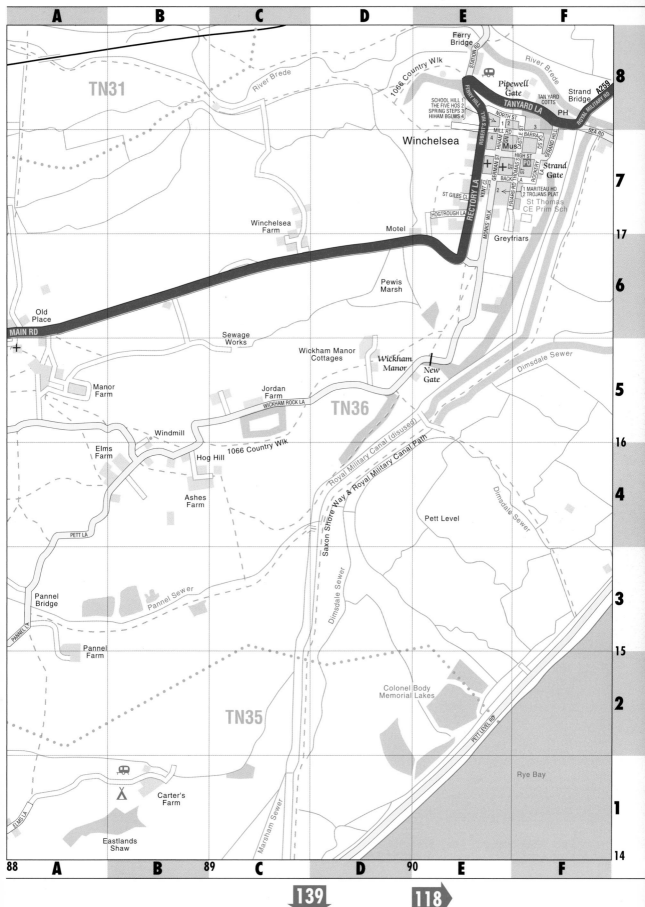

A **B** **C** **D** **E** **F**

8

TN31

River Brede

1066 Country Wlk

Ferry
Bridge

River Brede

Pipewell
Gate

Tan Yard
Cotts

Strand
Bridge

STATION RD

A259

ROYAL MILITARY RD

SCHOOL HILL 1
THE FIVE HOS 2
SPRING STEPS 3
HIHAM BGLWS 4

TANYARD LA

NORTH ST

1 2

3

MILL RD

FERRY HILL

ROBERTS HILL

PH

SEA RD

Winchelsea

HIHAM

4

BARRA
CASTLE ST

Mus

CS X

STRAND HILL

7

CHURCH

PO

High St

**Strand
Gate**

St Giles Cl

GERMAN ST

KENT CL

THOMAS S

BACK LA

ROOKERY LA

FRIARS RD

2

1 MARITEAU HO
2 TROJANS PLAT

HOGTROUGH LA

MONKS WLK

Greyfriars

St Thomas
CE Prim Sch

17

Winchelsea
Farm

Motel

RECTORY LA

6

Pewis
Marsh

Old
Place

MAIN RD

Sewage
Works

Wickham Manor
Cottages

Wickham
Manor

New
Gate

Dimsdale Sewer

5

Manor
Farm

Jordan
Farm

WICKHAM ROCK LA

TN36

16

Windmill

Elms
Farm

Hog Hill

1066 Country Wlk

Ashes
Farm

Saxon Shore Way & Royal Military Canal Path

Royal Military Canal (disused)

Pett Level

Dimsdale Sewer

4

PETT LA

Pannel
Bridge

Pannel Sewer

Dimsdale Sewer

3

PANNEL LA

Pannel
Farm

15

Colonel Body
Memorial Lakes

2

TN35

PETT LEVEL RD

ELMS LA

Carter's
Farm

Marsham Sewer

Rye Bay

1

Eastlands
Shaw

14

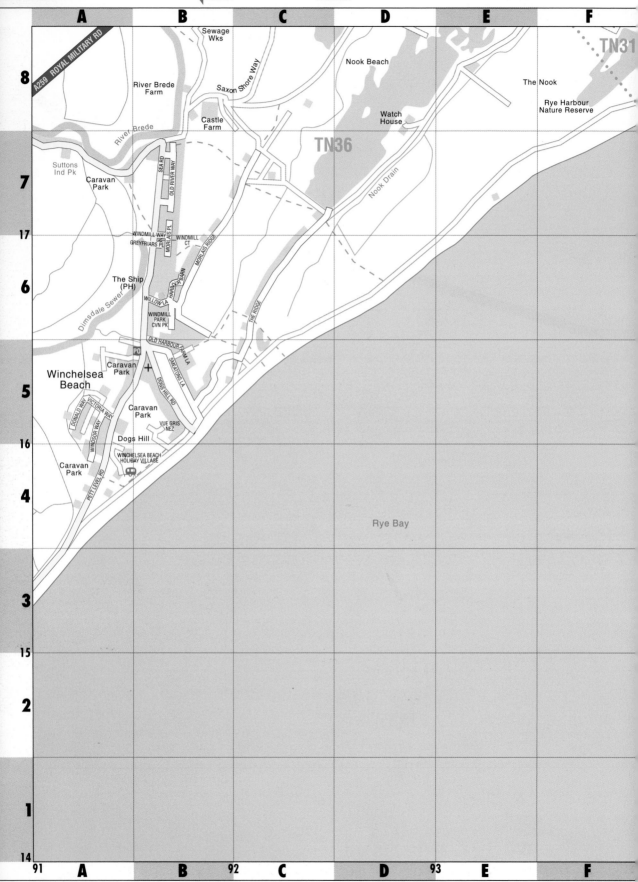

A B C D E F

TN31

ROYAL MILITARY RD

A259

8

Sewage
Wks

River Brede
Farm

River Brede

Saxon Shore Way

Nook Beach

The Nook

Castle
Farm

TN36

Watch
House

Rye Harbour
Nature Reserve

Suttons
Ind Pk

Caravan
Park

SEA RD

OLD RIVER WAY

7

Nook Drain

17

WINDMILL WAY
GREYFRIARS PL

MORLAIS PL

WINDMILL
CT

MORLAIS RIDGE

The Ship
(PH)

Dimsdale Sewer

HARBOUR BARN

WILLOW LA

6

WINDMILL
PARK
CVN PK

THE RIDGE

OLD HARBOUR FARM LA

PO

Caravan
Park

SMEATONS LA

DOGS HILL RD

Winchelsea
Beach

5

DONALD WAY

VICTORIA WAY

WINDSOR WAY

Caravan
Park

VUE GRIS
NEZ

Dogs Hill

16

WINCHELSEA BEACH
HOLIDAY VILLAGE

Caravan
Park

PETT LEVEL RD

4

Rye Bay

3

15

2

1

14

91 A B 92 C D 93 E F

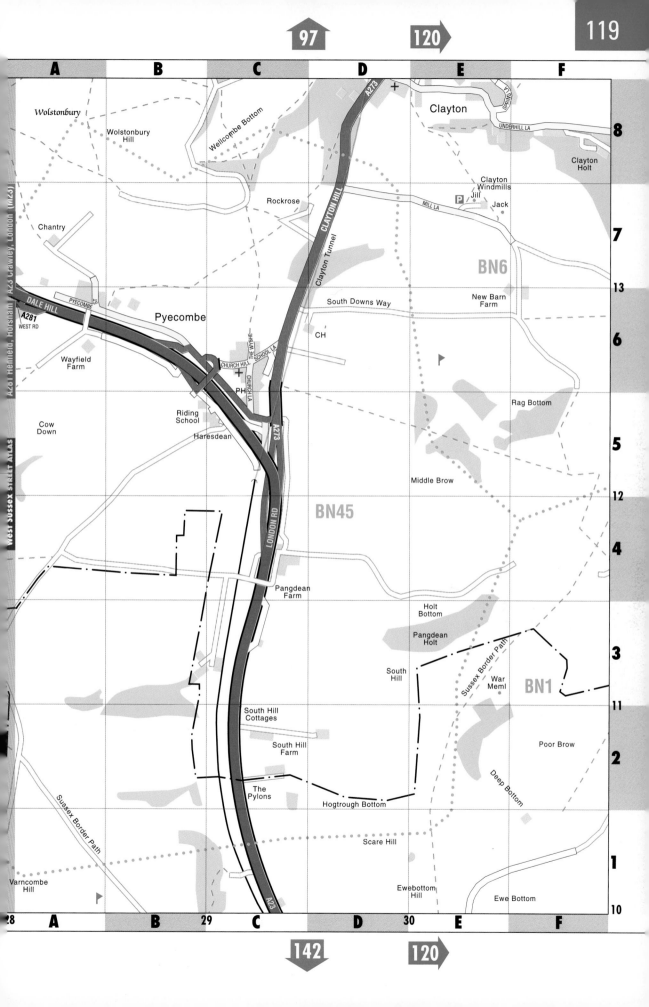

A B C D E F

8

Wolstonbury

Wolstonbury
Hill

Wellcombe Bottom

Clayton

UNDERHILL LA

Clayton
Holt

Rockrose

Clayton
Windmills

P

Jill

Jack

7

Chantry

Clayton Hill

Clayton Tunnel

MILL LA

BN6

New Barn
Farm

13

DALE HILL

PYECOMBE

A281
WEST RD

Pyecombe

South Downs Way

CH

6

Wayfield
Farm

CHURCH HILL

THE WYND

SCHOOL LA

PH

Rag Bottom

Cow
Down

Riding
School

Haresdean

A273

CHURCH LA

5

Middle Brow

12

BN45

LONDON RD

4

Pangdean
Farm

Holt
Bottom

Pangdean
Holt

Sussex Border Path

BN1

3

South
Hill

War
Meml

11

South Hill
Cottages

Poor Brow

2

South Hill
Farm

The
Pylons

Hogtrough Bottom

Deep Bottom

Sussex Border Path

Scare Hill

1

Varncombe
Hill

Ewebottom
Hill

Ewe Bottom

A23

10

A281 Henfield, Horsham, A23 Crawley, London (M23)

WEST SUSSEX STREET ATLAS

119
98

A B C D E F

8

Whitelands

LODGE LA

UNDERHILL LA

Coombe
Bottom

BURNTHOUSE BOSTALL

BEACON RD

NYE LA

Wick
Farm

DITCHLING BOSTALL

Saillards

Westmeston
Place

LEWES RD

B2116

B2116

Downview
Westmeston

THE STREET

Westmeston
Farm

7

Clayton
Holt

Burnthouse Bostall

South Downs Way

Ditchling Beacon
Nature Reserve

BN6

Ditchling
Beacon

P

Westmeston
Bostall

13

Sussex Border Path

Home Bottom

Middleton Bostall

Home Brow

6

Dencher
Bottom

Hogtrough
Bottom

Big Bottom

5

Heathy
Brow

12

North Bottom

4

Highpark
Corner

DITCHLING RD

High Park
Farm

White Thorn

Lower
Standean

Doddlis
Plantation

BN1

Highpark
Wood

3

Wonderhill
Plantation

New Barn

Green
Broom

Moon's
Bottom

11

Mid-down
House

Millbank
Wood

2

Piddingworth
Plantation

Granny's
Belt

Alpha Cottage

Beta
Cottage

Flint Heap

1

Tegdown
Hill

Upper Lodge
Wood

Limekiln
Wood

10

31   A   B   32   C   D   33   E   F

99
122

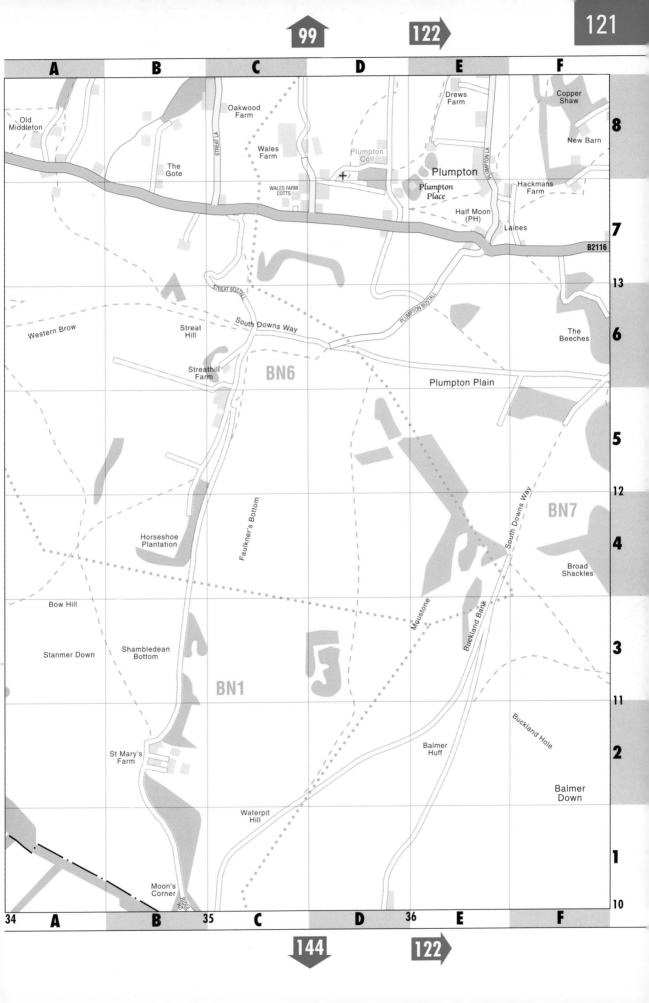

A **B** **C** **D** **E** **F**

Old Middleton

Oakwood Farm

STREAT LA

Wales Farm

The Gote

Plumpton Coll

Drews Farm

Copper Shaw

New Barn

8

Plumpton

PLUMPTON LA

WALES FARM COTTS

Plumpton Place

Hackmans Farm

Half Moon (PH)

Laines

7

B2116

13

STREAT BOSTALL

South Downs Way

Western Brow

Streat Hill

PLUMPTON BOSTALL

The Beeches

6

Streathill Farm

BN6

Plumpton Plain

5

Faulkner's Bottom

12

South Downs Way

BN7

Horseshoe Plantation

4

Broad Shackles

Bow Hill

Moustone

Buckland Bank

Buckland Hole

3

Stanmer Down

Shambledean Bottom

BN1

11

Balmer Huff

2

St Mary's Farm

Waterpit Hill

Balmer Down

1

Moon's Corner

HORSE RD

10

34 **A** **B** 35 **C** **D** 36 **E** **F**

121
100

A B C D E F

8

Warningore
House

Warningore
Farm

NOVINGTON LA

Allington
Farm

Russet
Shaw

ALLINGTON LA

Lower Tulleyswells
Farm

BEECHWOOD LA

Tulleyswells
Farm

BN8

7

Newstead
Farmhouse

Watershoot
Shaw

New
Barn

A275

B2116

13

Warningore Bostall

Courthouse
Farm

Mount Harry
House

B2116

6

Blackcap

Mount
Harry

Coombe
Place

Offham
Farm

Offham
House

5

Coombe
Plantation

PH

Offham

A275

12

Ashcombe
Bottom

BN7

Offham
Hill

4

Training Gallop

Landport
Bottom

HIGHDOWN RD

3

Cuckoo
Bottom

11

Training Gallop

FINLE CRES

2

South Downs Way

EAST
WAY

Balmer
Down

1

10

37 A B 38 C D 39 E F

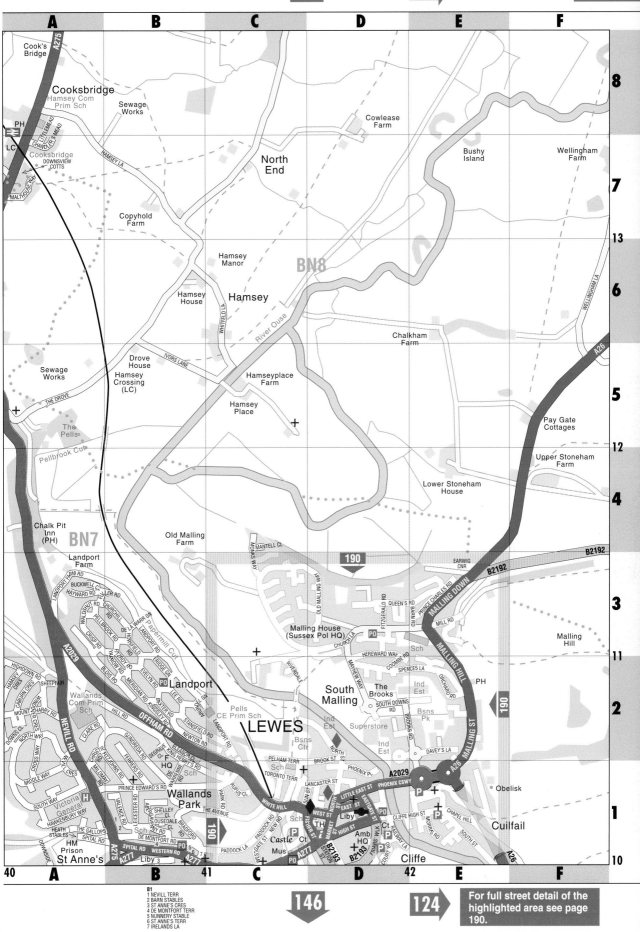

B1
1 NEVILL TERR
2 BARN STABLES
3 ST ANNE'S CRES
4 DE MONTFORT TERR
5 NUNNERY STABLE
6 ST ANNE'S TERR
7 IRELANDS LA

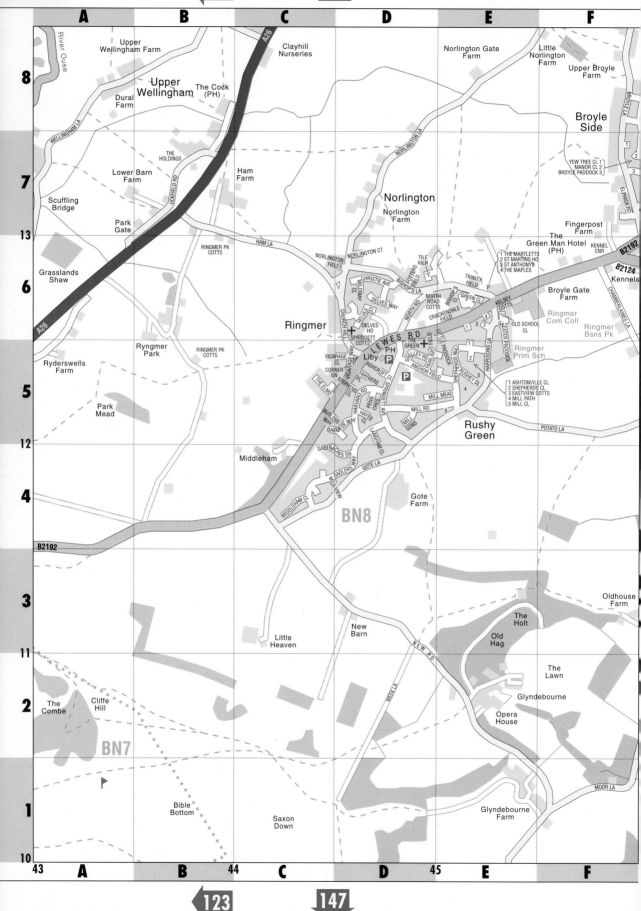

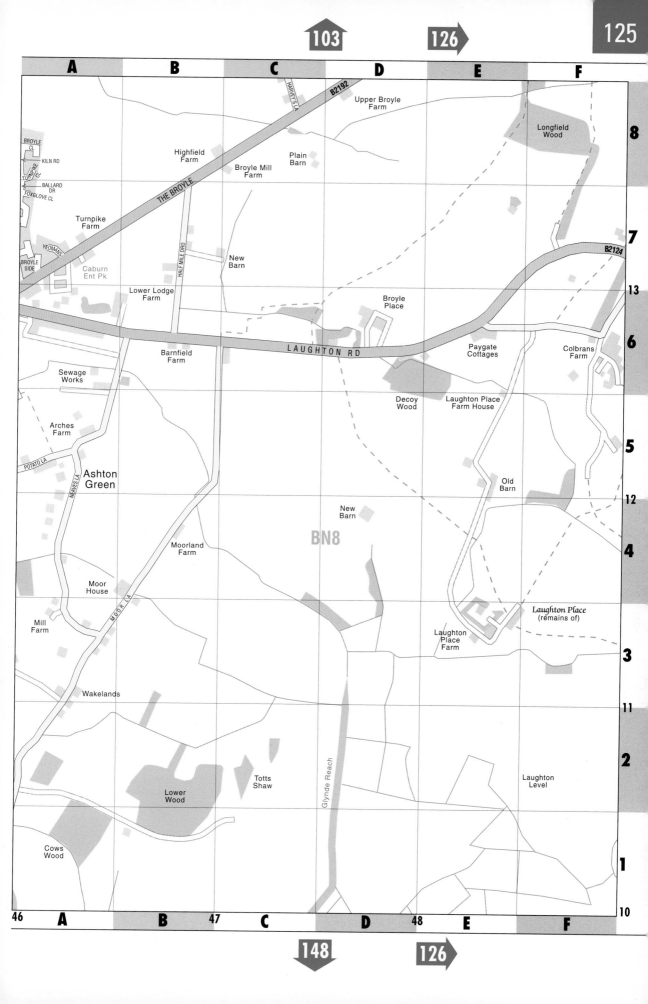

A   B   C   D   E   F

8

Brickhurst Wood

Laughton Common Wood

Lower Vert Wood

COMMON LA

LAUGHTON LODGE

BRICKHURST LA

SHORTGATE LA

Brickhurst Farm

Saw Mill

Averys Oak Farm

7

Laughton Manor

DUKE HO

ELM COTTS

ELM CL

The Roebuck (PH)

POUND LA

PARK LA

Helouan Farm

B2124 LAUGHTON RD

Home Farm

LEWES RD

Queeake

13

Laughton

Bowen Wood

6

Laughton Com Prim Sch

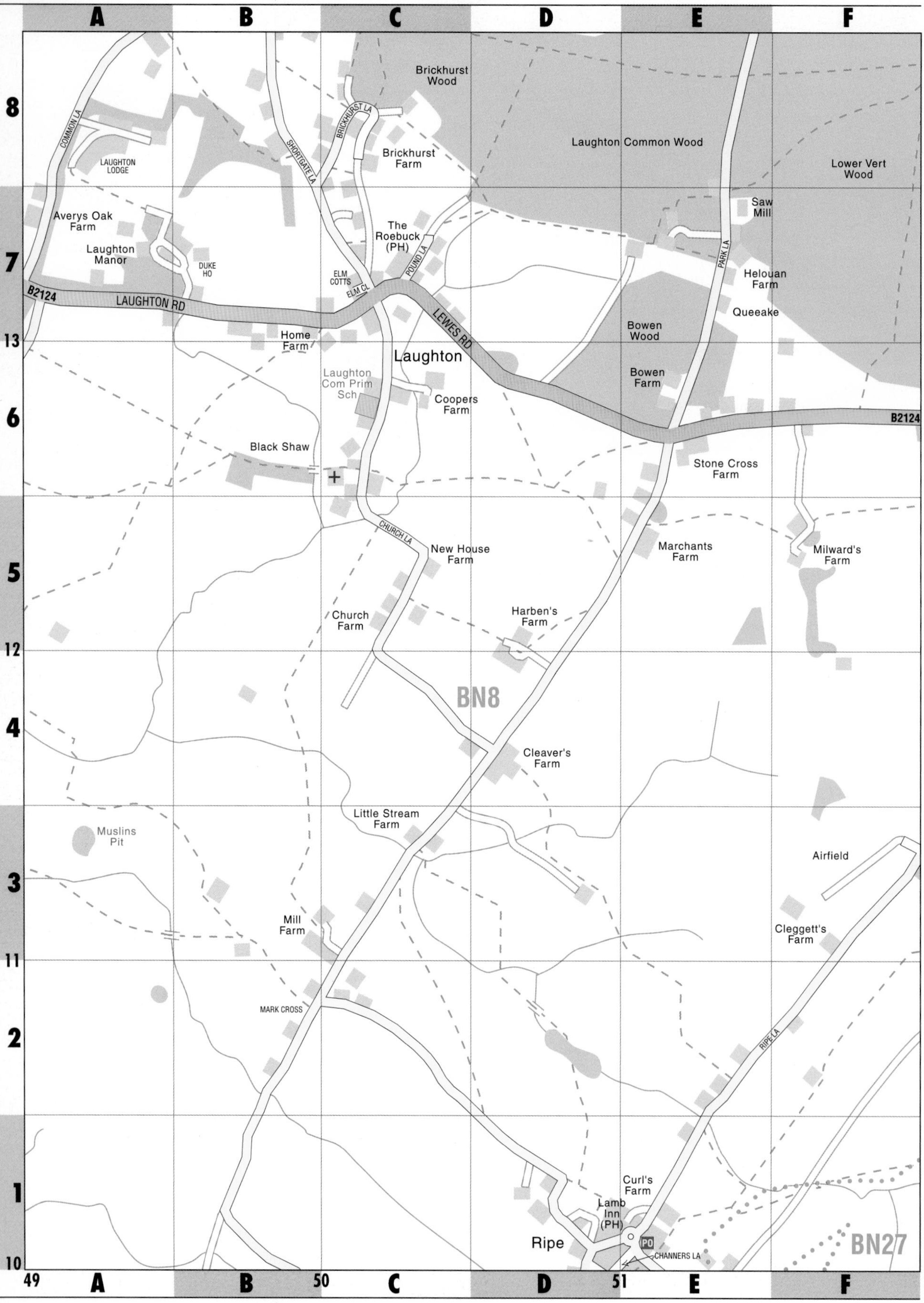

Coopers Farm

Bowen Farm

B2124

Black Shaw

Stone Cross Farm

CHURCH LA

New House Farm

Marchants Farm

Milward's Farm

5

Church Farm

Harben's Farm

12

BN8

4

Cleaver's Farm

Muslins Pit

Little Stream Farm

Airfield

3

Mill Farm

Cleggett's Farm

11

MARK CROSS

RIPE LA

2

Curl's Farm

1

Lamb Inn (PH)

Ripe

PO

CHANNERS LA

BN27

10

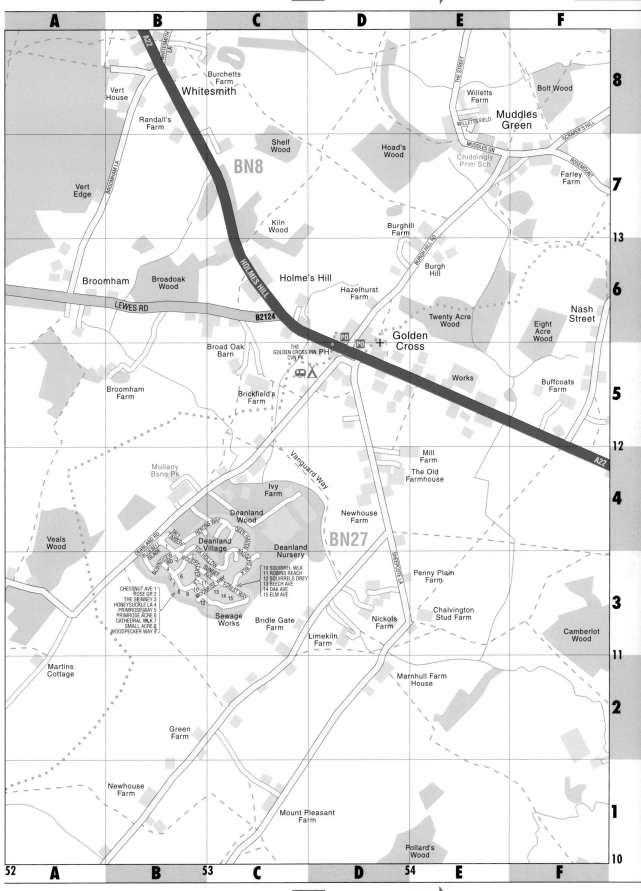

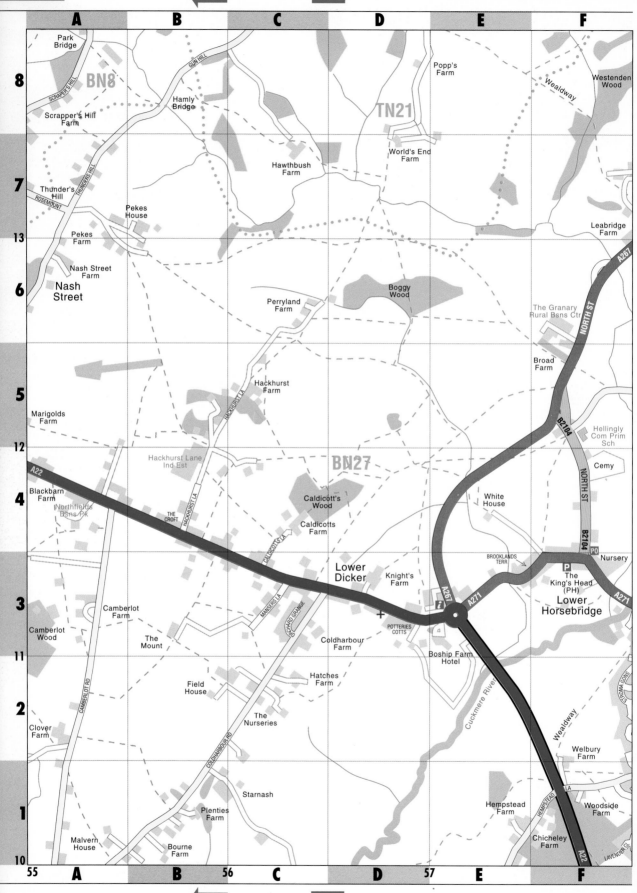

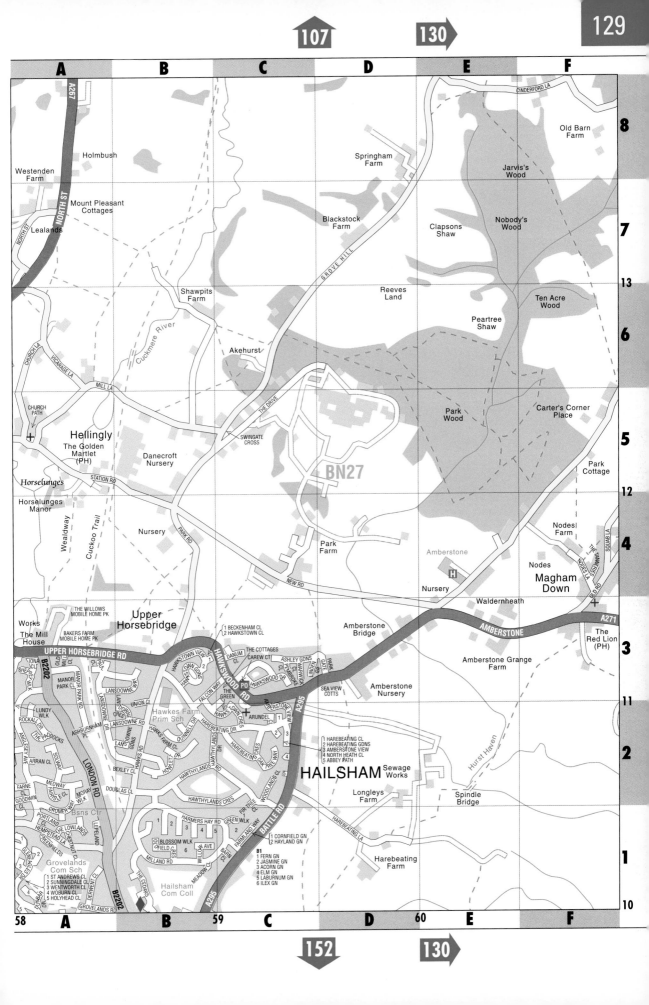

A B C D E F

8

7

13

6

5

12

4

11

2

1

10

Westenden Farm

North St

A267

Holmbush

Mount Pleasant Cottages

Lealands

North St

Church La

Vicarage La

Church Path

Hellingly

The Golden Martlet (PH)

Horselunges

Horselunges Manor

Wealdway

Cuckoo Trail

Mill La

Shawpits Farm

Cuckmere River

Akehurst

Danecroft Nursery

Station Rd

Nursery

Park Rd

Springham Farm

Blackstock Farm

Grove Hill

Reeves Land

Swingate Cross

The Drive

BN27

Park Farm

New Rd

Park Wood

Clapsons Shaw

Peartree Shaw

Nobody's Wood

Jarvis's Wood

Cinderford La

Old Barn Farm

Ten Acre Wood

Carter's Corner Place

Park Cottage

Nodes Farm

Amberstone

H

Nursery

Waldernheath

Amberstone

A271

Magham Down

Nodes

The Tannins

Nodes La

Squab La

The Red Lion (PH)

Works
The Mill House

Upper Horsebridge

The Willows Mobile Home Pk

Bakers Farm Mobile Home Pk

Upper Horsebridge Rd

B2202

Hawkstown View

Hawkswood Rd

Falcon Way

The Green

PO

Danum Cl

The Cottages

Carew Ct

Ashley Gdns

Warwick

Hawkswood Cl

1 BECKENHAM CL
2 HAWKSTOWN CL

Amberstone Bridge

Amberstone Nursery

Amberstone Grange Farm

Park Gate

Sea View Cotts

Amberstone View

A295

Hurst Haven

Manor Park Cl

Lundy Wlk

Rockal Dr

Anglesey Ave

Arran Cl

Solway

Old Mill Cl

Shearwalk

Iona Cl

Paul Cl

Manor Park Rd

Lansdowne Way

Ashburnham Pl

Lansdowne Cres

Union Cl

Lansdowne Dr

Lansdowne Gdns

Hawkes Farm Prim Sch

Hawks Farm Rd

Home Ct

Quinnell Dr

Harebeating Dr

Hawthylands Dr

Arundel

Hawks Town Cres

Harebeating Cres

Oak Tree Way

Woodlands Cl

Fir Tree Cl

Tye Way

1 HAREBEATING CL
2 HAREBEATING GDNS
3 AMBERSTONE VIEW
4 NORTH HEATH CL
5 ABBEY PATH

HAILSHAM

Longleys Farm

Sewage Works

Spindle Bridge

Farne Cl

Fairisle Cl

Goodwin Cl

Medway

Moray Wlk

Bexley Cl

Douglas Cl

Cromer Way

Portland Cl

The Lowlands

Hempstead La

The Chestnut Cl

Greenfields

Bsns Ctr

Hawthylands Cres

Harmers Hay Rd

Green Wlk

Blossom Wlk

Field Cres

Willow Ave

Barn Cl

Meadow Cl

Milland Rd

Farmland Way

Battle Rd

Harebeating La

1 CORNFIELD GN
2 HAYLAND GN

B1
1 FERN GN
2 JASMINE GN
3 ACORN GN
4 ELM GN
5 LABURNUM GN
6 ILEX GN

Harebeating Farm

Grovelands Com Sch

1 ST ANDREWS CL
2 SUNNINGDALE CL
3 WENTWORTH CL
4 WOBURN CL
5 HOLYHEAD CL

Derwent Cl

The Cedars

Hailsham Com Coll

Grovelands Rd

B2202

A295

Glynleigh Cl

London Rd

58 59 60

A B C D E F

129   108

	A	B	C	D	E	F

8

Cinderford La

Scrip Wood

Kiln Wood

Chilsham

Scripp Farm

Studdens La

Chilsham Farm

Greenway Fruit Farm

7

Cowbeech Hill Farm

Cowbeech Hill

Stunts Green

Old Court

13

Hollingwood

New Barn Farm

Nunningham Farm

Oaklands

Herstmonceux

COUNCIL HOS

6

West Terr

James Ave

Fairfield

Chestnut Cl

Monceux Rd

Bagham La

The Ridgeway

West End

Ginger's Green Farm

Ginger's Green

Starvecrow Wood

Fairlawns Dr

Fiennes Rd

Dacre Rd

PH

PH   PO

Twelveacres

P

Buckwell Rise

Queens Rd

Park View

GARDNER ST

Squirrel La

HAILSHAM RD

Herstmonceux CE Prim Sch

LIME CROSS

5

Buckwell Farm

Lime Park

The Welcome Stranger (PH)

Cooper's Croft

Deudney's Farm

12

Upper House Farm

Buckwell Place

Chapel Row

Old Rd

BN27

Lime End Farm

4

Magham Down Farm

Harkaway

CRICKETING LA

Butler's Farm

BUTLER LA

A271

Puckridge

UNDER RD

Flowers Green

3

Gilridge Lodge

Willow Farm

Chantler's Farm

Place Farm

11

Golden Cross

LOWER RD

Gildridge Farm

Sackville Farm

2

Puckridge Stream

Bowley Sewer

Ironcroft Cottage

Iron Stream

Cherry Croft Farm

Magham Sewer

1

Hurst Haven

Whelpley Level

Mill Stream

1066 Country Wlk

10

129   153

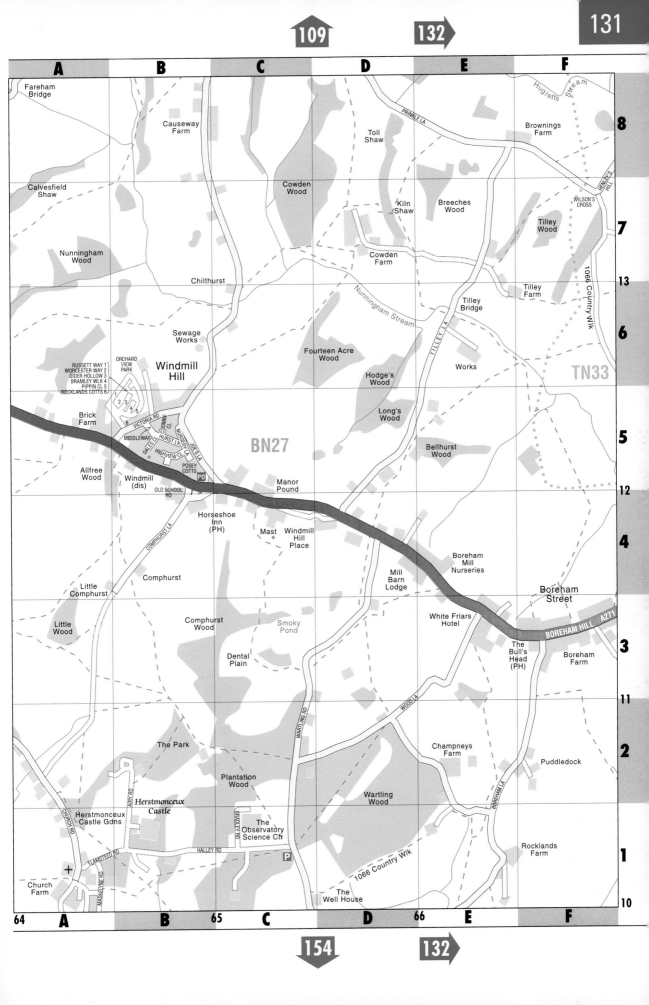

109
132

A B C D E F

8
7
13
6

TN33

5
12
4

11
2

1
10

64 A B 65 C D 66 E F

Fareham Bridge
Causeway Farm
Toll Shaw
PRINKLE LA
Brownings Farm
HENLEY'S HILL
Calvesfield Shaw
Cowden Wood
Kiln Shaw
Breeches Wood
WILSON'S CROSS
Tilley Wood
Nunningham Wood
Chilthurst
Cowden Farm
Nunningham Stream
Tilley Bridge
Tilley Farm
Tilley Wood
1066 Country Wlk
Sewage Works
Fourteen Acre Wood
TILLEY LA
Works
Windmill Hill
RUSSETT WAY 1
WORCESTER WAY 2
CIDER HOLLOW 3
BRAMLEY WLK 4
PIPPIN CL 5
ROCKLANDS COTTS 6
ORCHARD VIEW PARK
Hodge's Wood
Long's Wood
Bellhurst Wood
Brick Farm
1 2 3 4 5 6
VICTORIA RD
DALES CL
COOMBE CL
HURST LA
MIDDLEWAY
NURSERY LA
JOE'S LA
HIGHVIEW CL
PO
POSEY COTTS
BN27
Manor Pound
Allfree Wood
Windmill (dis)
OLD SCHOOL HO
Horseshoe Inn (PH)
Mast
Windmill Hill Place
Boreham Mill Nurseries
Boreham Street
COMPHURST LA
Comphurst
Little Comphurst
Comphurst Wood
Smoky Pond
Mill Barn Lodge
White Friars Hotel
BOREHAM HILL A271
Little Wood
Dental Plain
The Bull's Head (PH)
Boreham Farm
WARTLING RD
WOOD LA
The Park
Champneys Farm
Puddledock
Plantation Wood
AIRY RD
Herstmonceux Castle Gdns
Herstmonceux Castle
BRADLEY RD
The Observatory Science Ctr
Wartling Wood
BOREHAM LA
Rocklands Farm
CHURCH RD
FLAMSTEED RD
HALLEY RD
P
Church Farm
MASKELYNE RD
1066 Country Wlk
The Well House

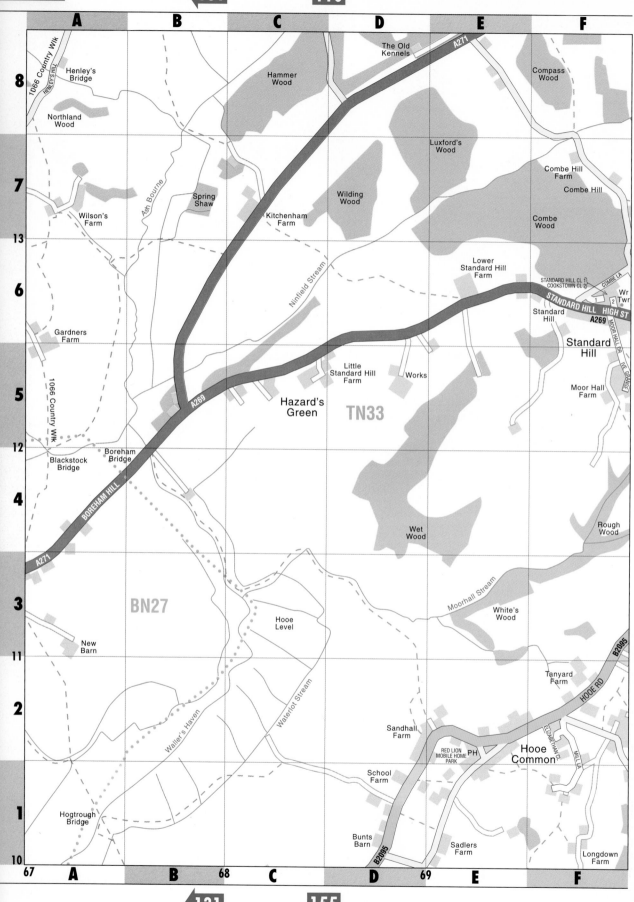

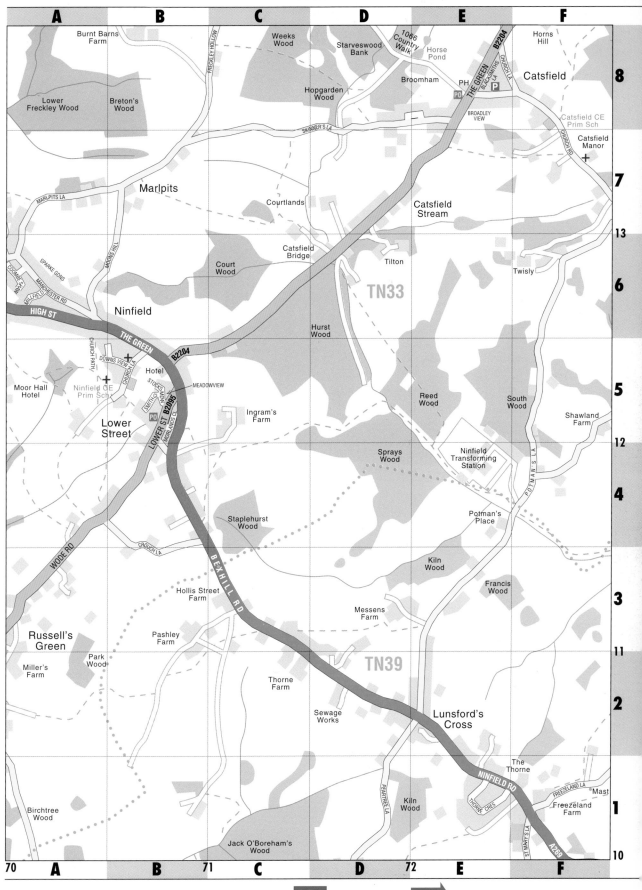

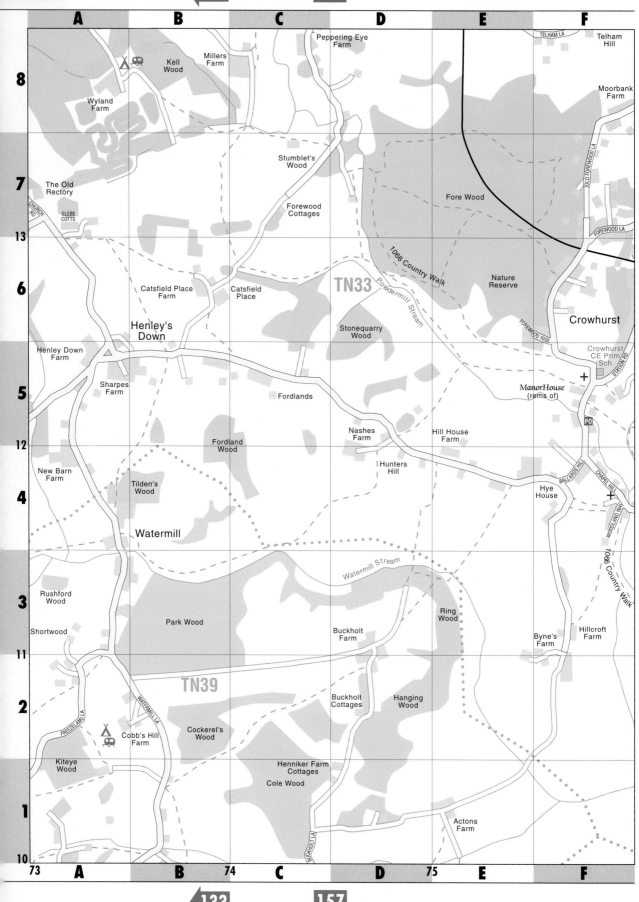

A B C D E F

8

Wyland Farm

Kell Wood

Millers Farm

Peppering Eye Farm

Moorbank Farm

Telham Hill

TELHAM LA

7

The Old Rectory

Stumblet's Wood

Forewood Cottages

Fore Wood

CHURCH RD

GLEBE COTTS

OLD FOREWOOD LA

FOREWOOD LA

13

6

Catsfield Place Farm

Catsfield Place

TN33

1066 Country Walk

Powdermill Stream

Nature Reserve

Crowhurst

FOREWOOD RISE

Henley's Down

Henley Down Farm

Stonequarry Wood

Crowhurst CE Prim Sch

STATION RD

5

Sharpes Farm

Fordlands

Hill House Farm

ManorHouse (rems of)

PO

12

New Barn Farm

Fordland Wood

Nashes Farm

Hunters Hill

Hye House

BALLARDS HILL

CHAPEL HILL

4

Tilden's Wood

WOODLAND WAY

1066 Country Walk

Watermill

Watermill Stream

3

Rushford Wood

Park Wood

Buckholt Farm

Ring Wood

Byne's Farm

Hillcroft Farm

Shortwood

11

TN39

WATERMILL LA

FREEZELAND LA

2

Cobb's Hill Farm

Cockerel's Wood

Buckholt Cottages

Hanging Wood

Kiteye Wood

Henniker Farm Cottages

Cole Wood

BUCKHOLT LA

1

Actons Farm

10

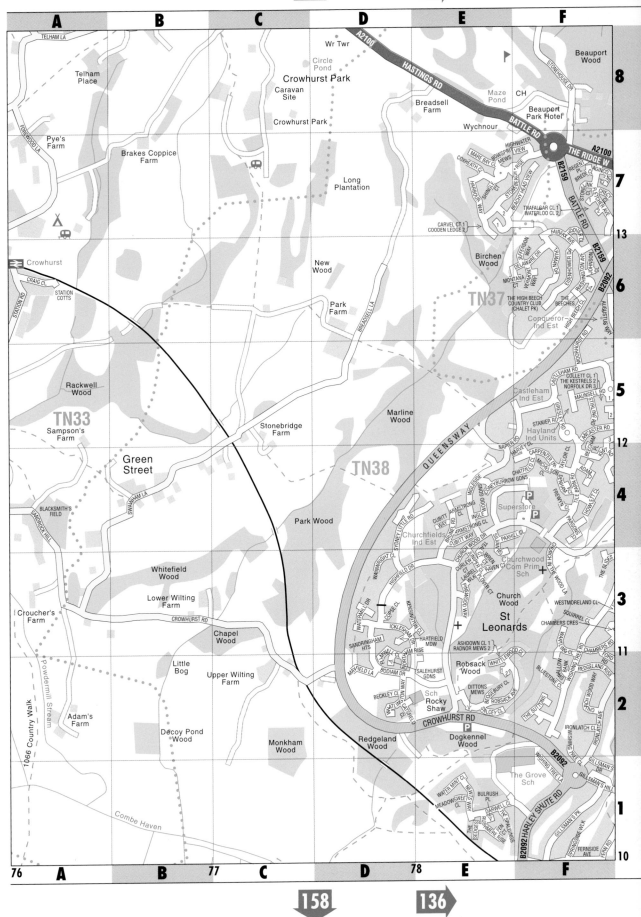

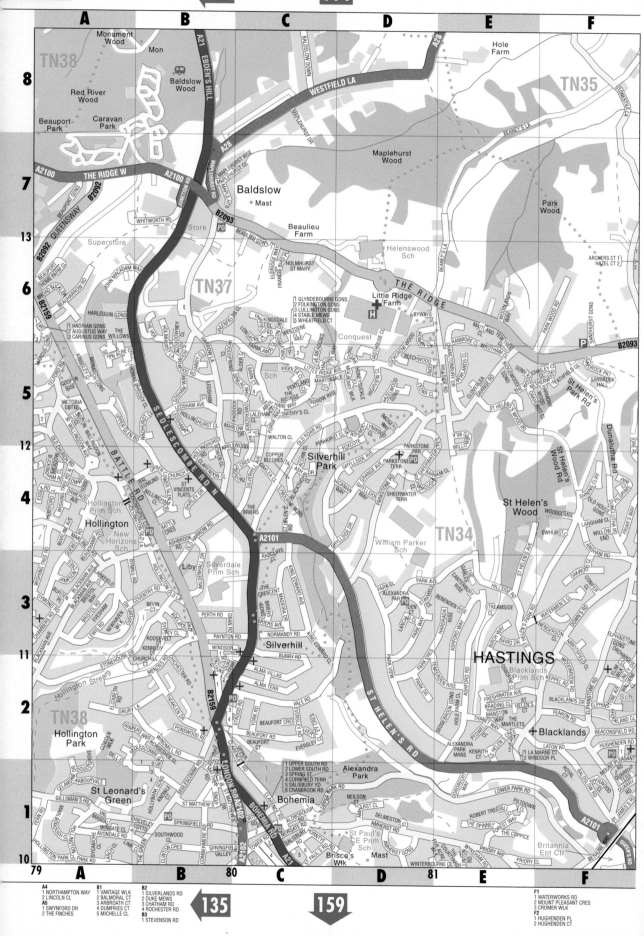

A4
1 NORTHAMPTON WAY
2 LINCOLN CL
A5
1 SWYNFORD DR
2 THE FINCHES

B1
1 VANTAGE WLK
2 BALMORAL CT
3 ARBROATH CT
4 DUMFRIES CT
5 MICHELLE CL

B2
1 SILVERLANDS RD
2 DUKE MEWS
3 CHATHAM RD
4 ROCHESTER RD
B3
1 STEVENSON RD

F1
1 WATERWORKS RD
2 MOUNT PLEASANT CRES
3 CROMER WLK
F2
1 HUGHENDEN PL
2 HUGHENDEN CT

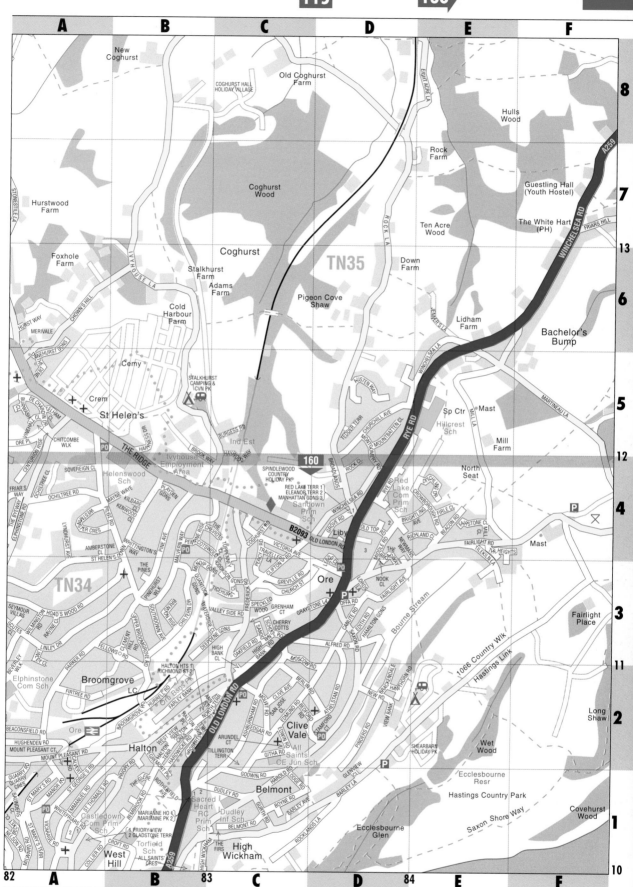

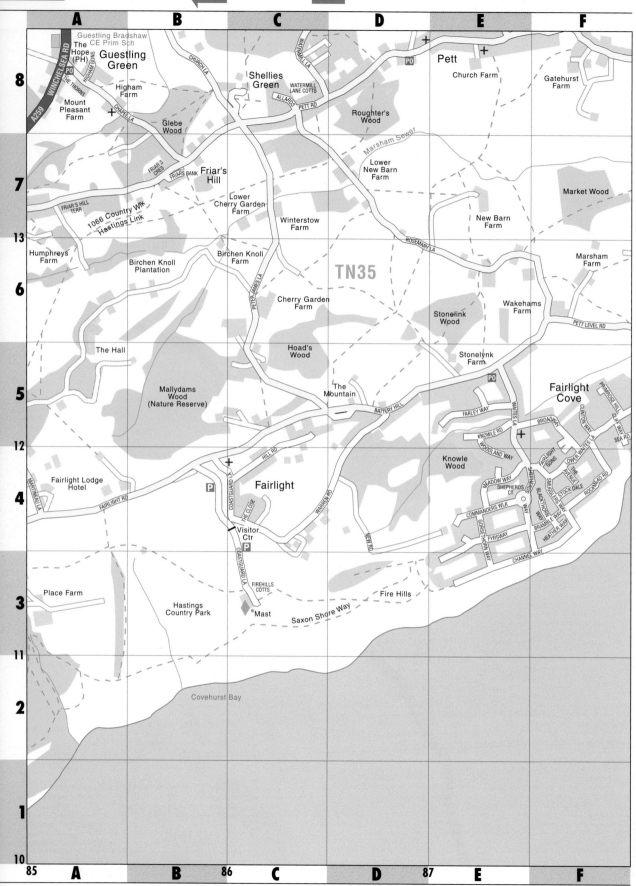

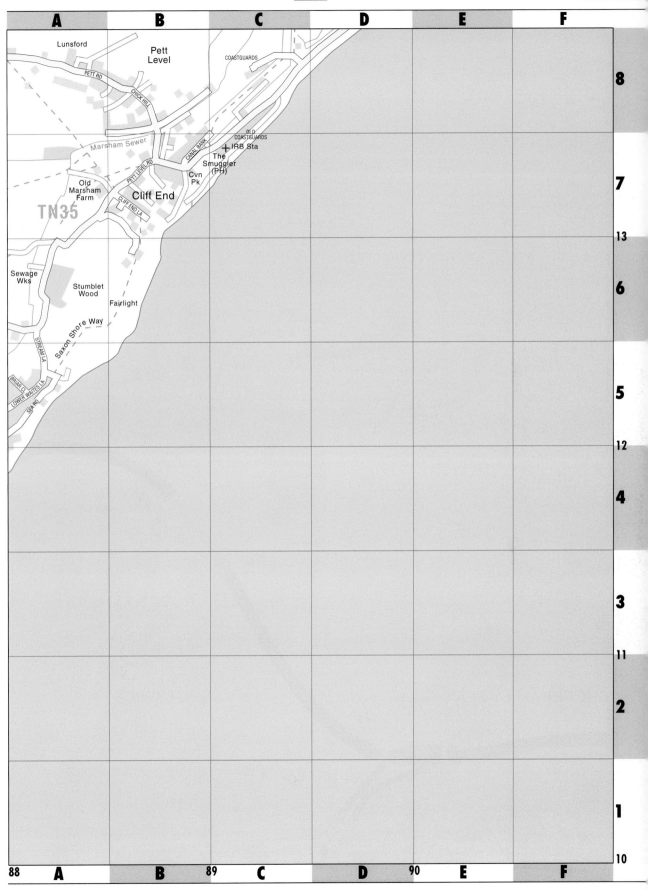

Lunsford

Pett Level

COASTGUARDS

PETT RD

CHICK HILL

OLD COASTGUARDS

Marsham Sewer

CANAL BANK

IRB Sta

The Smuggler (PH)

PETT LEVEL RD

Cvn Pk

Old Marsham Farm

Cliff End

TN35

CLIFF END LA

Sewage Wks

Stumblet Wood

Fairlight

Saxon Shore Way

STREAM LA

BRIAR CL

LOWER WAITES LA

SEA RD

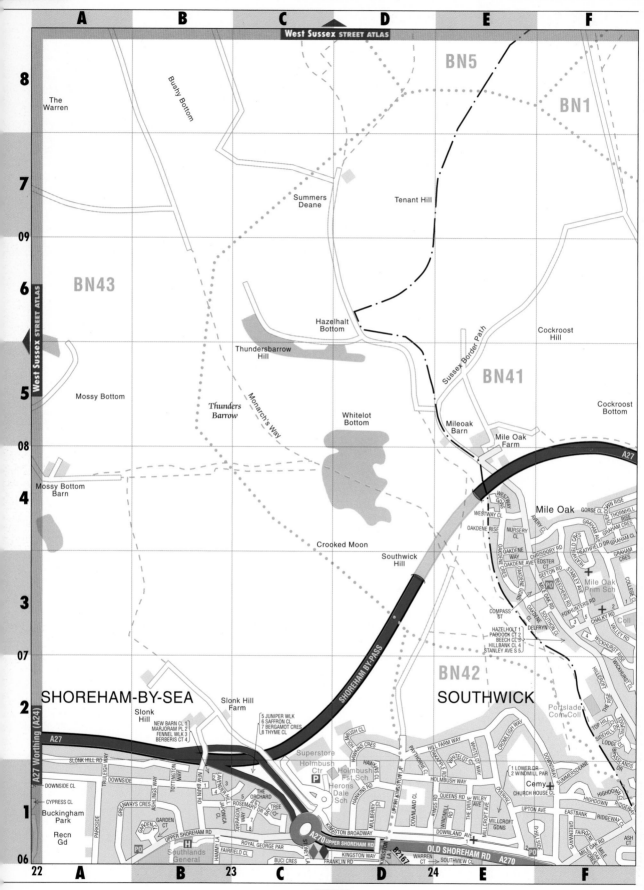

West Sussex STREET ATLAS

West Sussex STREET ATLAS

BN5

BN1

The Warren

Bushy Bottom

Summers Deane

Tenant Hill

BN43

Hazelhalt Bottom

Cockroost Hill

Thundersbarrow Hill

Sussex Border Path

BN41

Mossy Bottom

Thunders Barrow

Monarch's Way

Whitelot Bottom

Mileoak Barn

Mile Oak Farm

Cockroost Bottom

A27

Mossy Bottom Barn

Mile Oak

Crooked Moon

Southwick Hill

SHOREHAM-BY-BYPASS

Mile Oak Prim Sch

COMPASS PT

HAZELHOLT 1
PADDOCK CT 2
BEECH CL 3
HILLBANK CL 4
STANLEY AVE S 5

BN42

SHOREHAM-BY-SEA

Slonk Hill Farm

SOUTHWICK

Slonk Hill

NEW BARN CL 1
MARJORAM PL 2
FENNEL WLK 3
BERBERIS CT 4

5 JUNIPER WLK
6 SAFFRON CL
7 BERGAMOT CRES
8 THYME CL

Portslade Com Coll

A27 Worthing (A24)

A27

Superstore
Holmbush Ctr

Holmbush Fst Sch

1 LOWER DR
2 WINDMILL PAR

SLONK HILL RD WAY

DOWNSIDE CL
CYPRESS CL

DOWNSIDE

Herons Dale Sch

Cemy
CHURCH HOUSE CL

Buckingham Park Recn Gd

THE ORCHARD

Southlands General

A270 UPPER SHOREHAM RD

UPPER SHOREHAM RD

OLD SHOREHAM RD A270

B2161

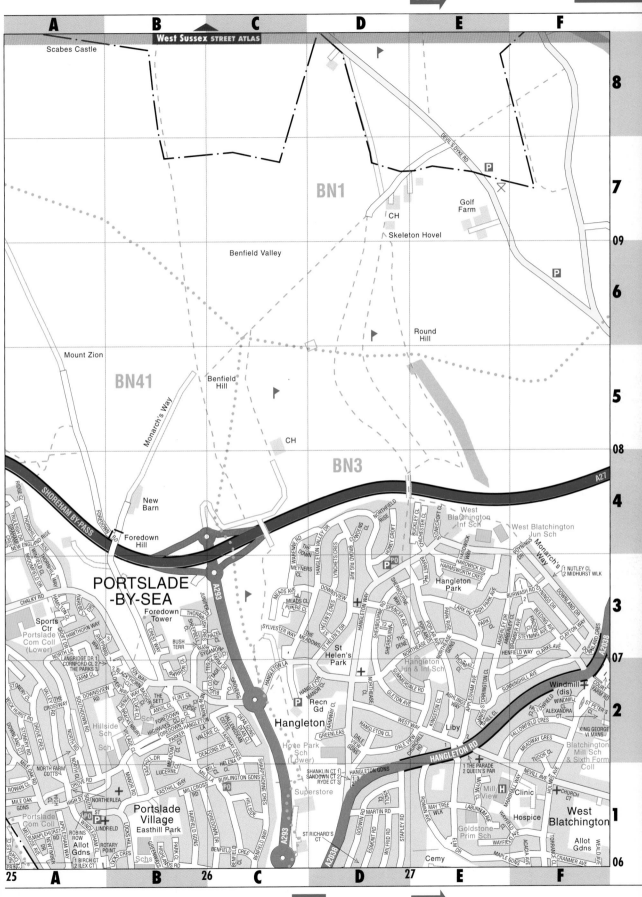

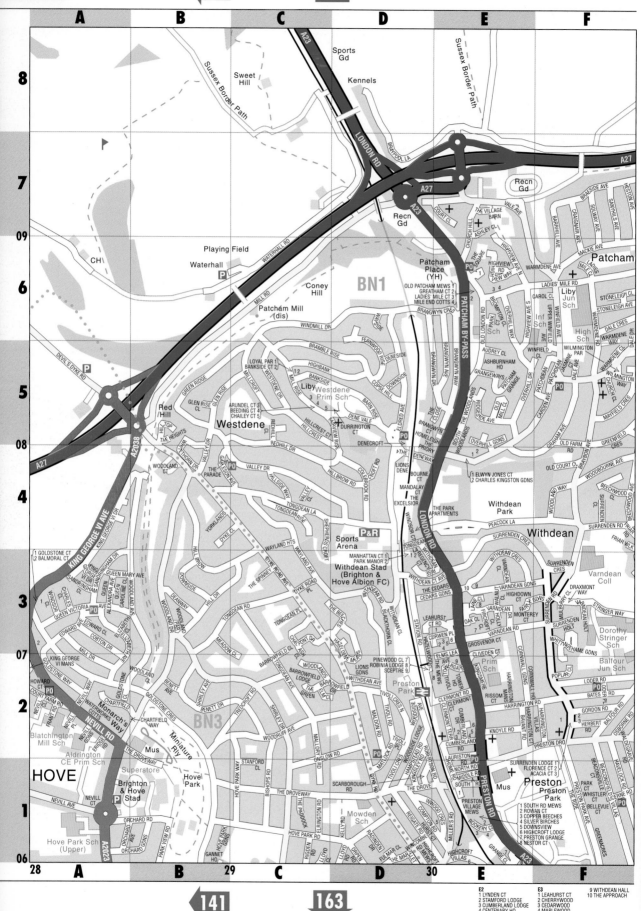

E2
1 LYNDEN CT
2 STAMFORD LODGE
3 CUMBERLAND LODGE
4 CENTENARY HO
5 SHAWCROSS HO
6 CARLTON HO

E3
1 LEAHURST CT
2 CHERRYWOOD
3 CEDARWOOD
4 MAPLEWOOD
5 PINEWOOD
6 BEECHWOOD
7 WITHDEAN CT
8 WELLINGTONIA CT

9 WITHDEAN HALL
10 THE APPROACH

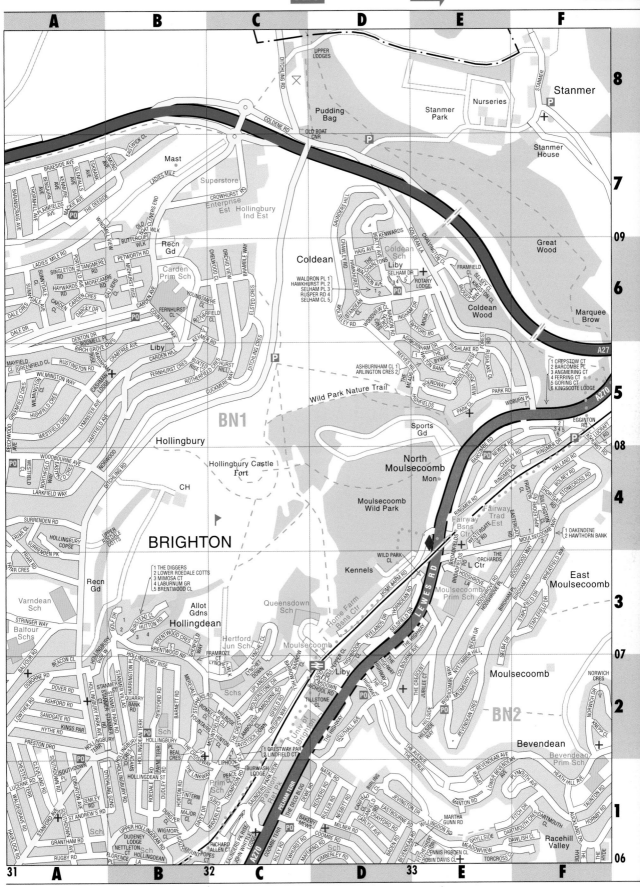

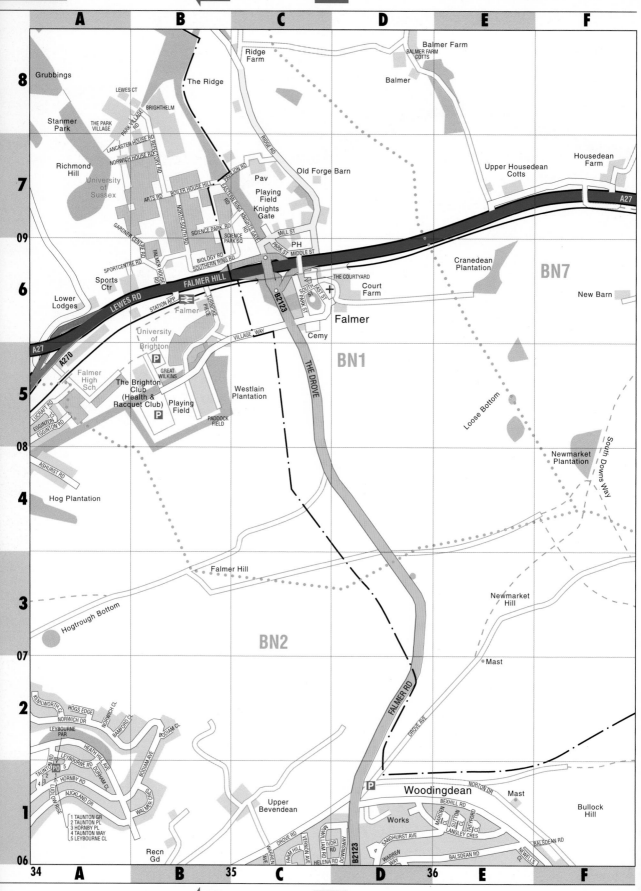

143
121

A B C D E F

8

Grubbings

Stanmer
Park

THE PARK
VILLAGE
Richmond
Hill

University
of Sussex

LEWES CT

PARK VILLAGE RD
BRIGHTHELM

The Ridge

Ridge
Farm

Balmer Farm
BALMER FARM
COTTS

Balmer

7

Lancaster HOUSE RD
NORWICH HOUSE RD
RECTORY RD

BOILER HOUSE HILL
ARTS RD
NORTH-SOUTH RD
PAVILION RD
EASTERN RING RD
KNIGHTS GATE RD

Pav

Playing
Field
Knights
Gate

Old Forge Barn

Upper Housedean
Cotts

Housedean
Farm

A27

09

GARDNER CENTRE RD
SCIENCE PARK RD
FALMER HOUSE RD
BIOLOGY RD
SOUTHERN RING RD
SPORTCENTRE RD

SCIENCE
PARK SQ

MILL ST

PARK ST
MIDDLE ST
PH

Cranedean
Plantation

BN7

6

Lower
Lodges

Sports
Ctr

LEWES RD
FALMER HILL
STATION APP
Falmer
TURNPIKE
PIECE

B2123

SOUTH ST
EAST ST

THE COURTYARD

Court
Farm

Falmer

New Barn

A27

A270

University
of
Brighton

P

GREAT
WILKINS

VILLAGE WAY

Cemy

THE DROVE

BN1

5

LUCRAFT RD
EGGINTON CL
EGGINTON RD

Falmer
High
Sch

The Brighton
Club
(Health &
Racquet Club)

P

Playing
Field

Westlain
Plantation

PADDOCK
FIELD

Loose Bottom

South Downs Way

08

ASHURST RD

Newmarket
Plantation

4

Hog Plantation

Falmer Hill

Newmarket
Hill

3

Hogtrough Bottom

BN2

Mast

07

2

KENILWORTH CL
HOGS EDGE
NORWICH DR
BAMFORD CL
BODIAM CL
HEATH HILL AVE
LEYBOURNE RD
DURHAM CL
BODIAM AVE

LEYBOURNE
PAR

PO

HORNBY RD
AUCKLAND DR
WALMER CRES

LUDLOW RISE

FALMER RD
DROVE AVE

NORTON DR

Mast

Woodingdean

P

BULLOCK
Hill

1

1 TAUNTON GR
2 TAUNTON PL
3 HORNBY PL
4 TAUNTON WAY
5 LEYBOURNE CL

Upper
Bevendean

Works

MARLER RD
BEXHILL RD
SUTTON CL
LANGLEY CRES
TREFFORD

Balsdean RD

06

Recn
Gd

DROVE RD
FARM HILL
VERNON AVE
WILLIAM RD
HELENA RD
B2123
SANDHURST AVE
DOWNSWAY
WARREN WAY
BALSDEAN RD
NEWELLS CL

34 A 35 B C 36 D E F

143
165

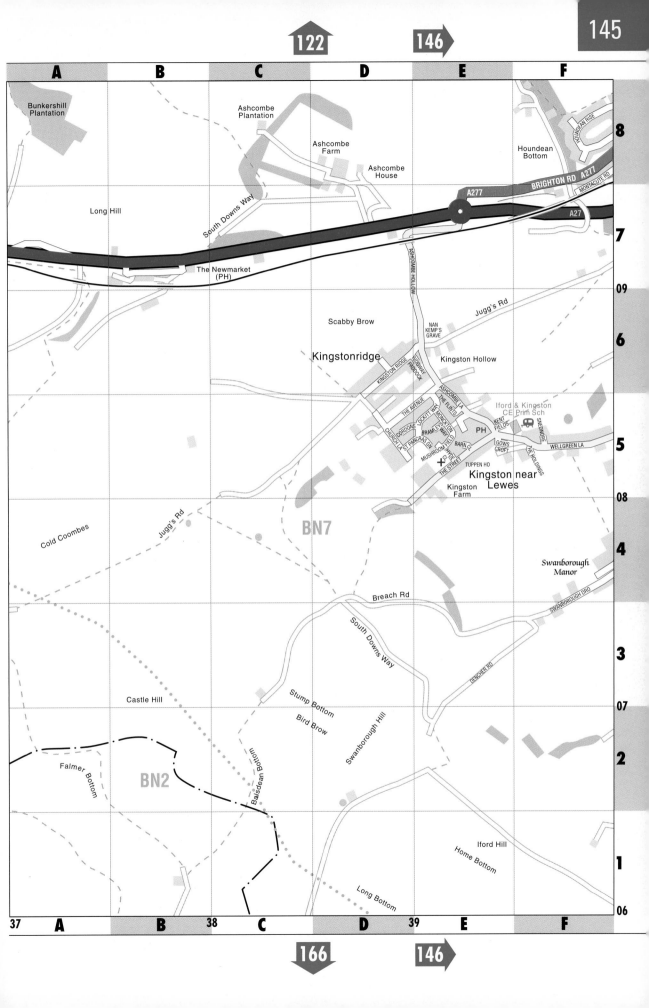

145 123

For full street detail of the highlighted area see page 190.

A B C D E F

8

DOWNSIDE
BRIGHTON RD A277
SOUTHDOWN AVE
HOUNDEAN RISE
HOUNDEAN CL
MONTACUTE RD
WARREN CL
LODGE LA
BISHOPS DR
WARREN CL
BARN HATCH CL
BARONS DOWN RD
BERKELEY ROW
DALE RD
DE LA WARE
CERNE CL
VALLEY RD
WINTERBOURNE LA
WINTERBOURNE CL
HILLYFIELD
BELL LA
JUGGS CL
1 CLEVEDOWN
2 BARONS WLK

Liby
St Anne's Sch
Cemy
City Hall
CHURCH LA
A277 HIGH ST
ROTTEN ROW
GRANGE RD
SOUTHOVER RD
EASTPORT LA
ST PANCRAS RD
POTTE'S LA
ST PANCRAS GDNS
CLEVE TERR
THE COURSE
BARBER CT
GREENE CT
DUMBRELL CT
MORLEY CL
B2193 SOUTHOVER HIGH ST
CLUNY ST
COCKSHUT RD
Schs
Mus
PRIORY ST
STATION RD
GARDEN ST
PINWELL RD
COURT RD
B2193
Sch
P
P
Lewes
P
PO
Sussex Downs Coll
MOUNTFIELD RD
Coll
Priory Sch
L Ctr
HAM LA
190
CH
A26
190
Cliffe Ind Est

Southover
The Cockshut
Southerham Farm

7

A27
JUGGS RD
CRANEDOWN
KINGSTON RD
LEWES
Sewage Works
River Ouse
A26
A27
BN8

09

Spring Barn Farm
Rise Farm
Upper Rise

6

WELLGREEN LA
Swanborough Fishing Lake
Celery Sewer
Rise Barn

5

THE DROVEWAY
Sewage Works
BN7
NORTON WALL
The Brooks
Lower Rise

08

4

SWANBOROUGH DRO
SWANBOROUGH COTTS
SWANBOROUGH HOLLOW
Swanborough Manor
Celery Sewer

Iford Farm
Iford
Iford Farm
SUTTON COTTS
SUTTON WALL

3

NORTHEASE WALL

07

2

WHITEWAYS COTTS
Northease Manor
BARLEY FIELD COTTS
Sewage Works

Northease Farm
Monk's House

1

WHITE WAY
Front Hill
Rodmell
Rodmell CE Prim Sch
South Farm
MARTENS FIELD

06

40 A B 41 C D 42 E F

145 167

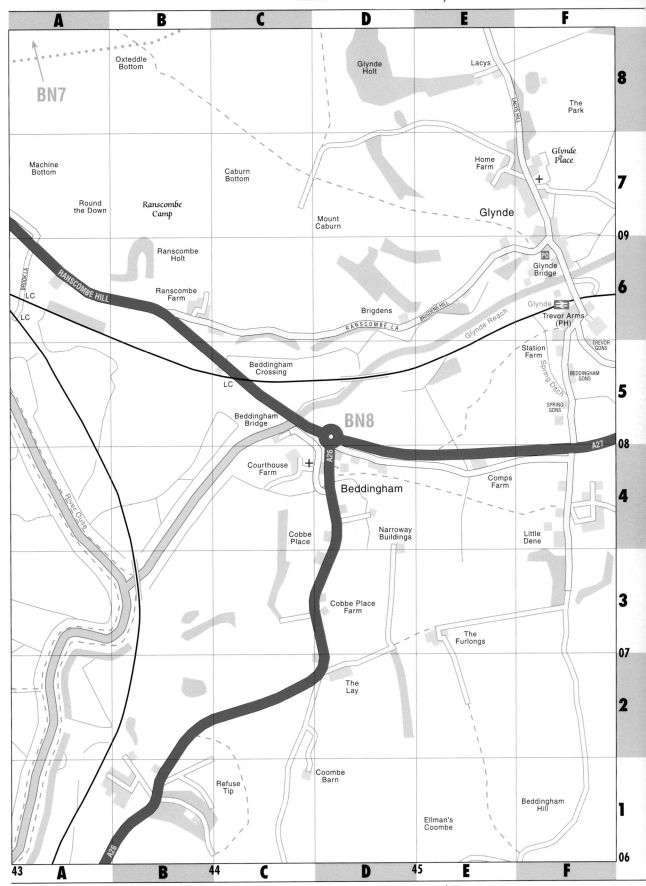

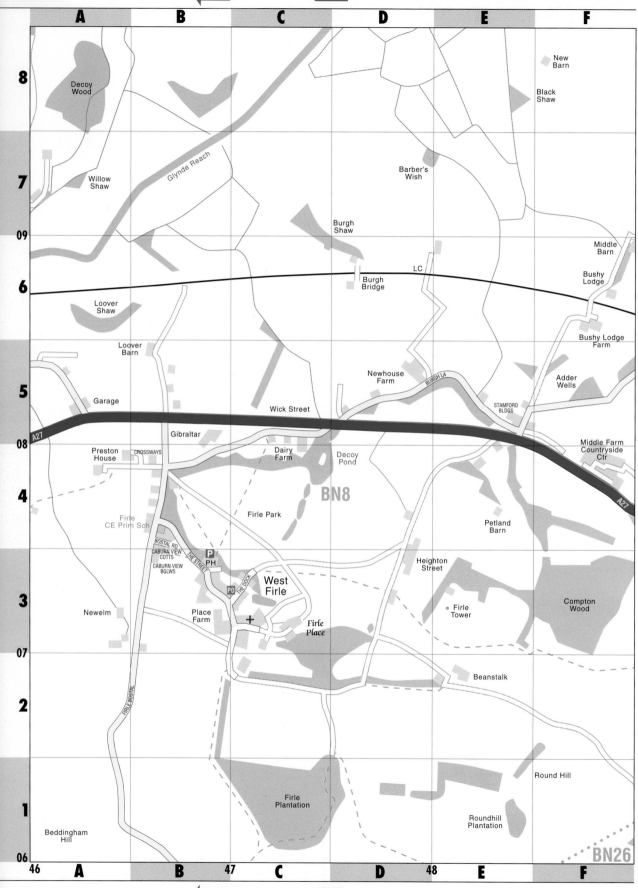

A B C D E F

8 Decoy Wood

New Barn

Black Shaw

7 Willow Shaw

Glynde Reach

Barber's Wish

09 Burgh Shaw

Middle Barn

6 LC

Burgh Bridge

Bushy Lodge

Loover Shaw

Bushy Lodge Farm

Loover Barn

Newhouse Farm

Adder Wells

5 Garage

Wick Street

BURGH LA

STAMFORD BLDGS

08 A27

Gibraltar

Middle Farm Countryside Ctr

Preston House

CROSSWAYS

Dairy Farm

Decoy Pond

A27

4 Firle CE Prim Sch

Firle Park

BN8

Petland Barn

BOSTAL RD

CABURN VIEW COTTS

P

PH

THE STREET

Heighton Street

CABURN VIEW BGLWS

3 Newelm

PO

THE DOCK

West Firle

Firle Tower

Compton Wood

Place Farm

+

Firle Place

07 FIRLE BOSTAL

Beanstalk

2 Round Hill

1 Firle Plantation

Roundhill Plantation

Beddingham Hill

BN26

06

46 A 47 B C 47 D 48 E F

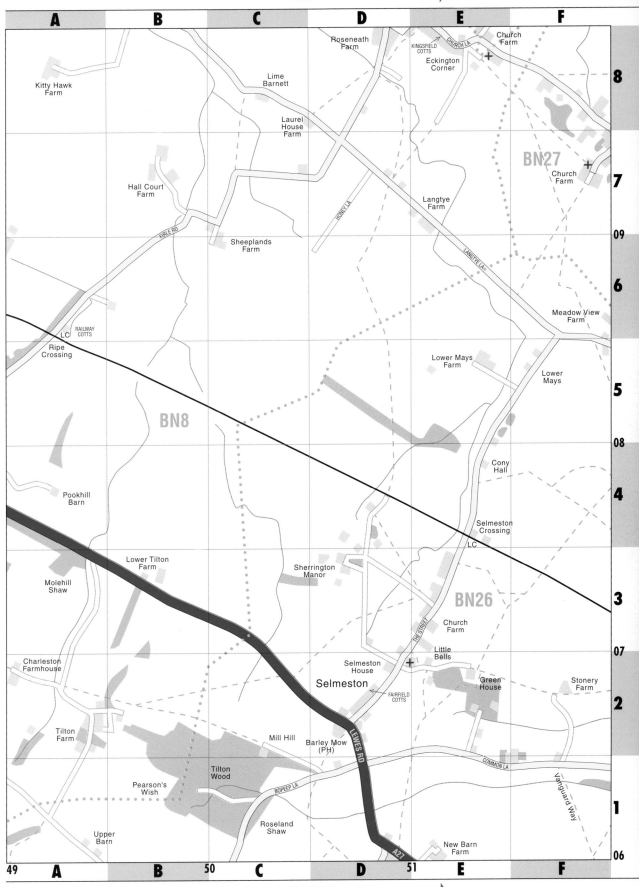

A   B   C   D   E   F

8

Yew Farm
Yew Tree (PH)
Diplocks Farm

BN27

SHEPCOTE LA
Selmeston Croft

Clifton Farm

The Plough (PH)

High Barn

Chalvington

7

Vanguard Way

Lower Claverham Farm

Park Wood

Claverham Manor

Wickstreet Farm

Parkwood Farm

09

Bungalow Farm

Wickstreet

6

Lower Claverham House

Batbrooks Farm House

Batbrook Cottages

Sessingham Farm

5

Cobb Court

Cuckmere River

BN26

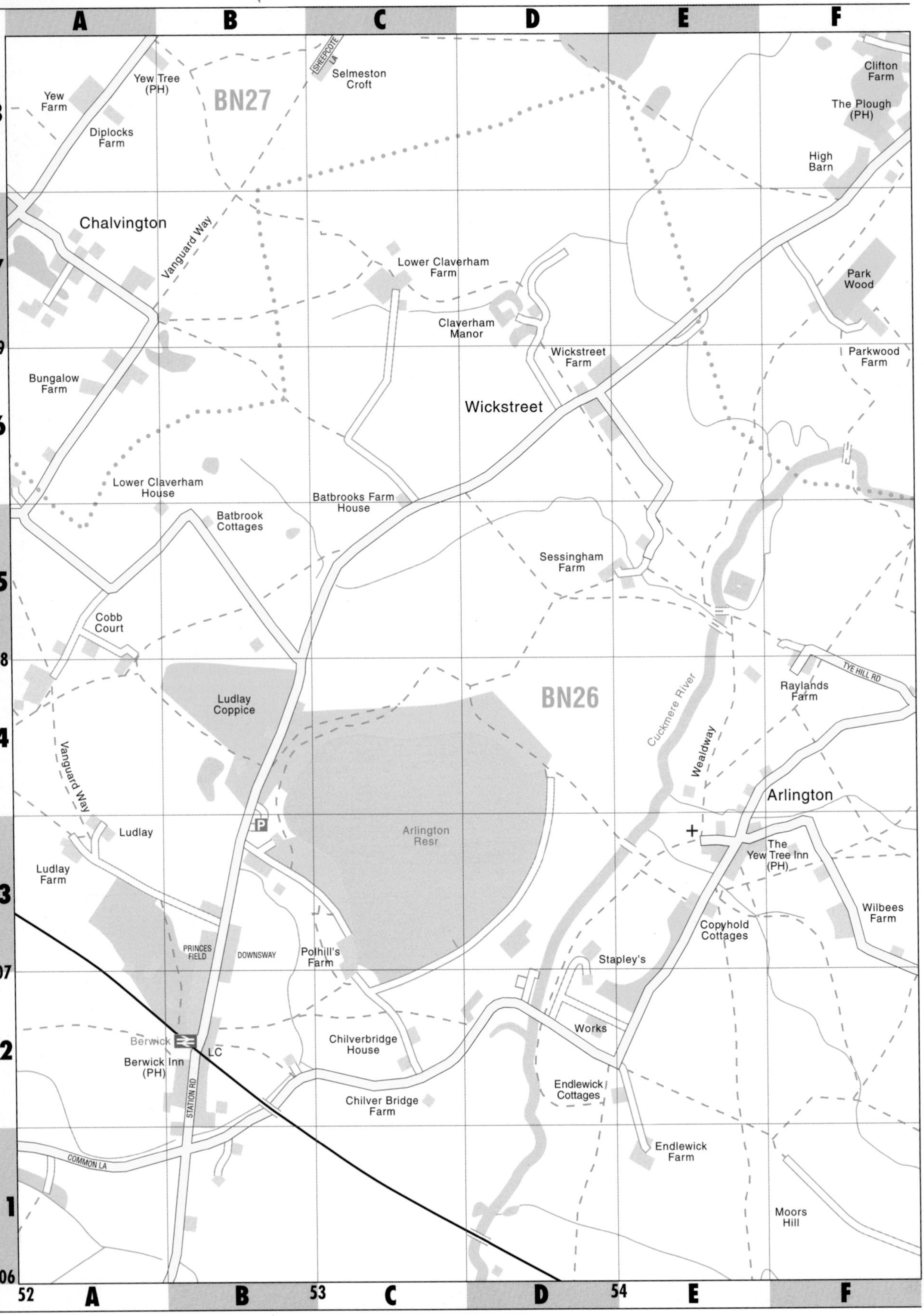

TYE HILL RD

08

Ludlay Coppice

Raylands Farm

4

Vanguard Way

Wealdway

Arlington

Ludlay

Arlington Resr

The Yew Tree Inn (PH)

Ludlay Farm

3

Wilbees Farm

PRINCES FIELD

DOWNSWAY

Polhill's Farm

Copyhold Cottages

07

Stapley's

Berwick
Berwick Inn (PH)

STATION RD

LC

Chilverbridge House

Works

2

Chilver Bridge Farm

Endlewick Cottages

COMMON LA

1

Endlewick Farm

Moors Hill

06

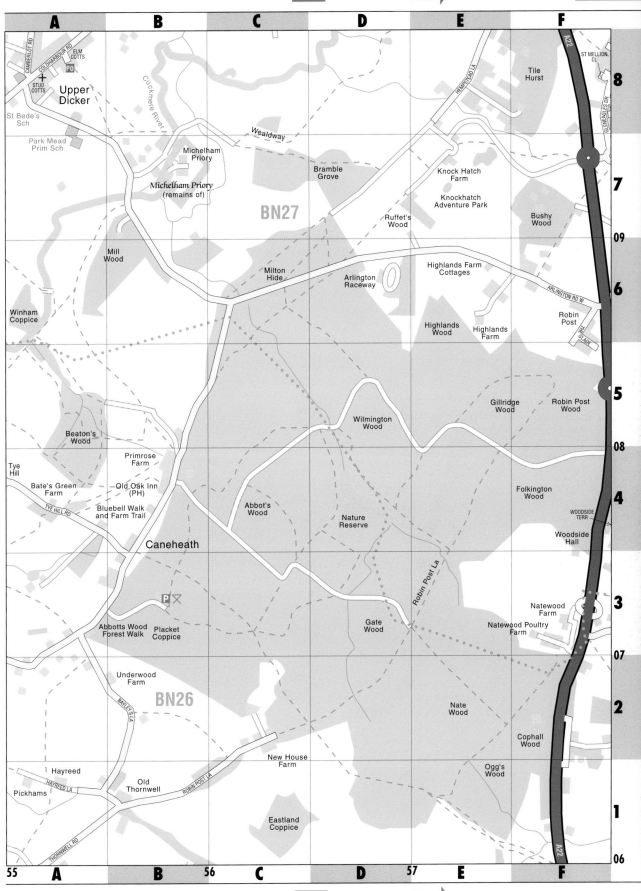

128
152

Tile Hurst

St Mellion CL

Upper Dicker

ELM COTTS

CAMBERLOT RD
COLDHARBOUR RD
PO
STUD COTTS

St Bede's Sch

Park Mead Prim Sch

Cuckmere River

Michelham Priory

Michelham Priory (remains of)

Wealdway

Bramble Grove

Knock Hatch Farm

Knockhatch Adventure Park

Bushy Wood

BN27

HEMPSTEAD LA

GLENEAGLES DR

A22

8

7

09

Mill Wood

Milton Hide

Arlington Raceway

Ruffet's Wood

Highlands Farm Cottages

ARLINGTON RD W

Highlands Wood

Highlands Farm

Robin Post

THE GLADE

6

Winham Coppice

Wilmington Wood

Gillridge Wood

Robin Post Wood

5

08

Beaton's Wood

Primrose Farm

Tye Hill

Bate's Green Farm

Old Oak Inn (PH)

Abbot's Wood

Nature Reserve

Folkington Wood

WOODSIDE TERR

Woodside Hall

4

TYE HILL RD

Bluebell Walk and Farm Trail

Caneheath

Robin Post La

Natewood Farm

Natewood Poultry Farm

3

07

P

Abbotts Wood Forest Walk

Placket Coppice

Gate Wood

Underwood Farm

BN26

BAYLEY'S LA

Nate Wood

Cophall Wood

2

Hayreed

HAYREED LA

Pickhams

Old Thornwell

ROBIN POST LA

New House Farm

Ogg's Wood

1

THORNWELL RD

Eastland Coppice

A22

06

← **151**

129

C7
1 MARKET SQ
2 ELIZABETH CT
3 SOUTHDOWN CT
4 ASHFORD CL
5 COBDEN PL
6 TERMINUS PL

C7
7 DEER PADDOCK LA

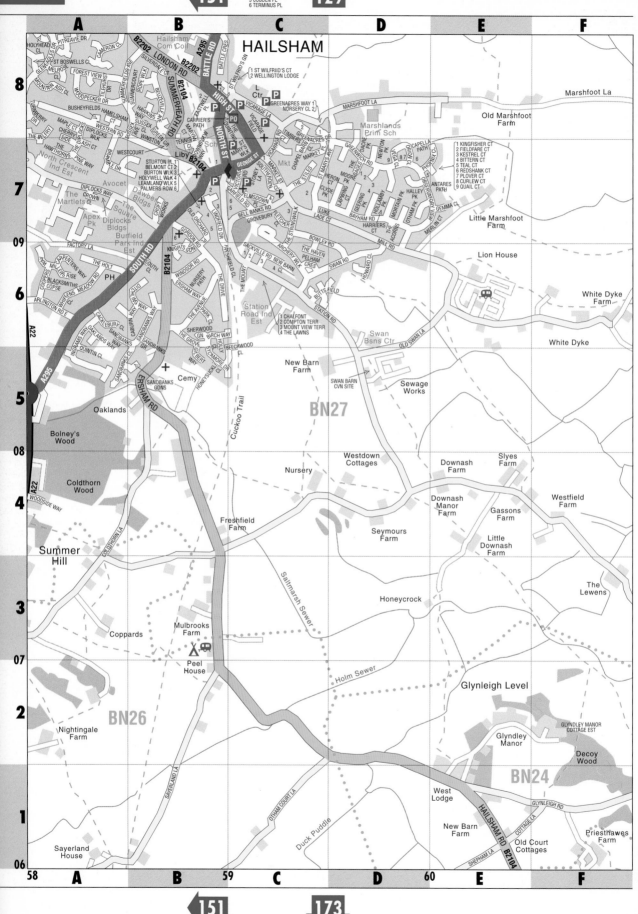

HAILSHAM

BN27

BN26

BN24

← **151**

173

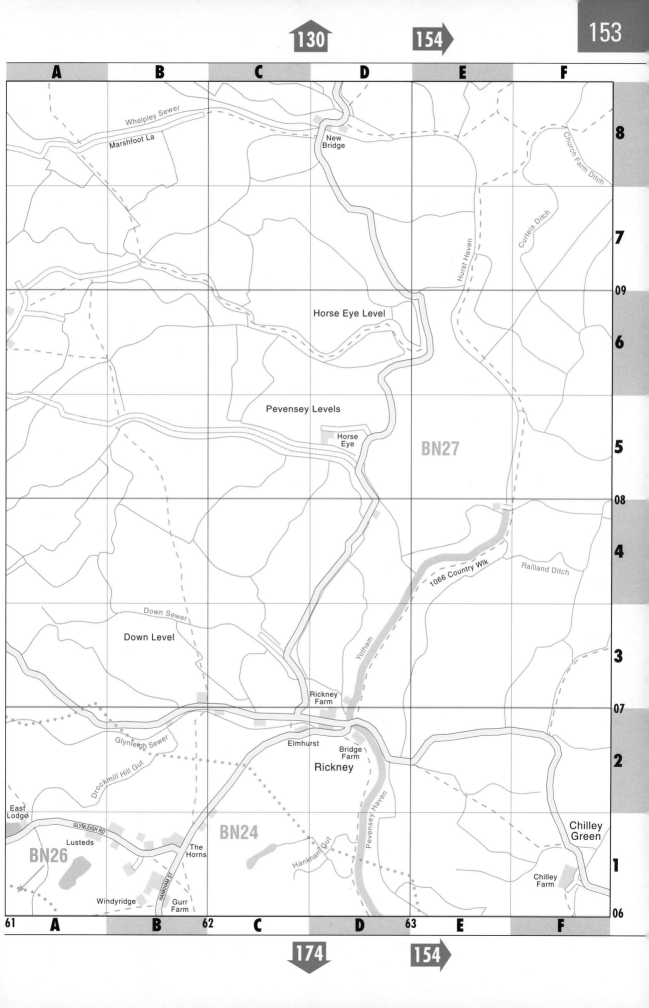

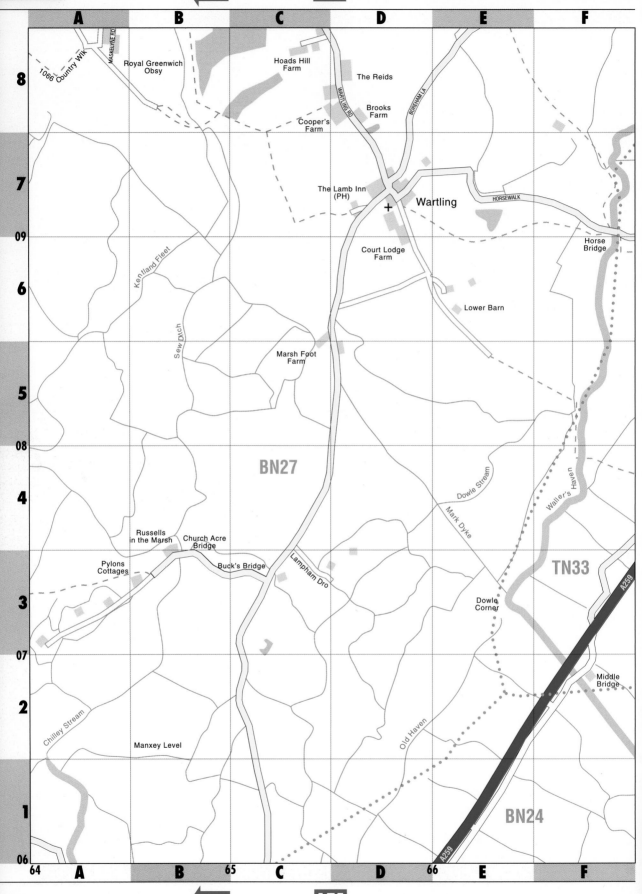

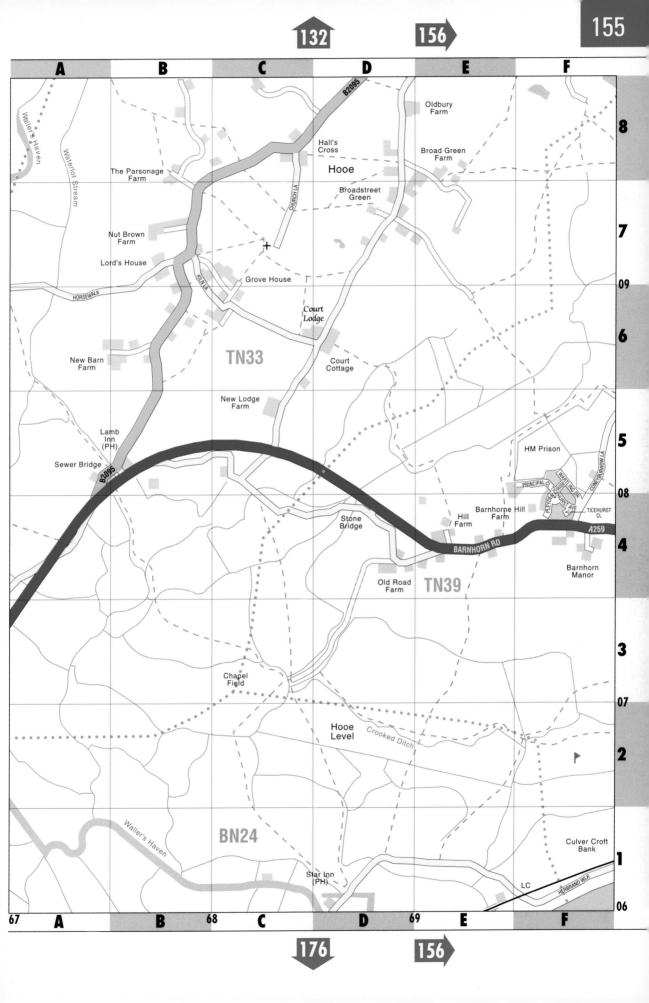

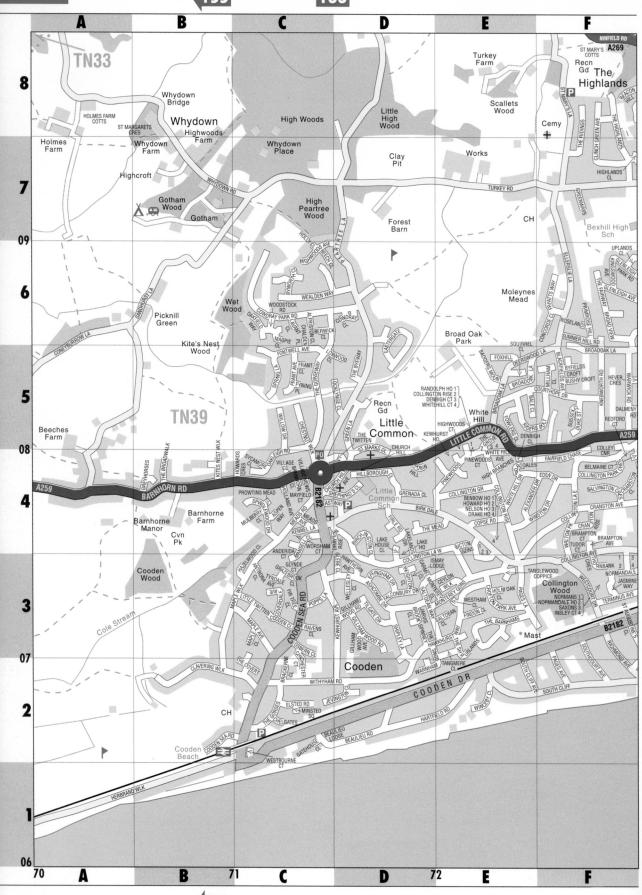

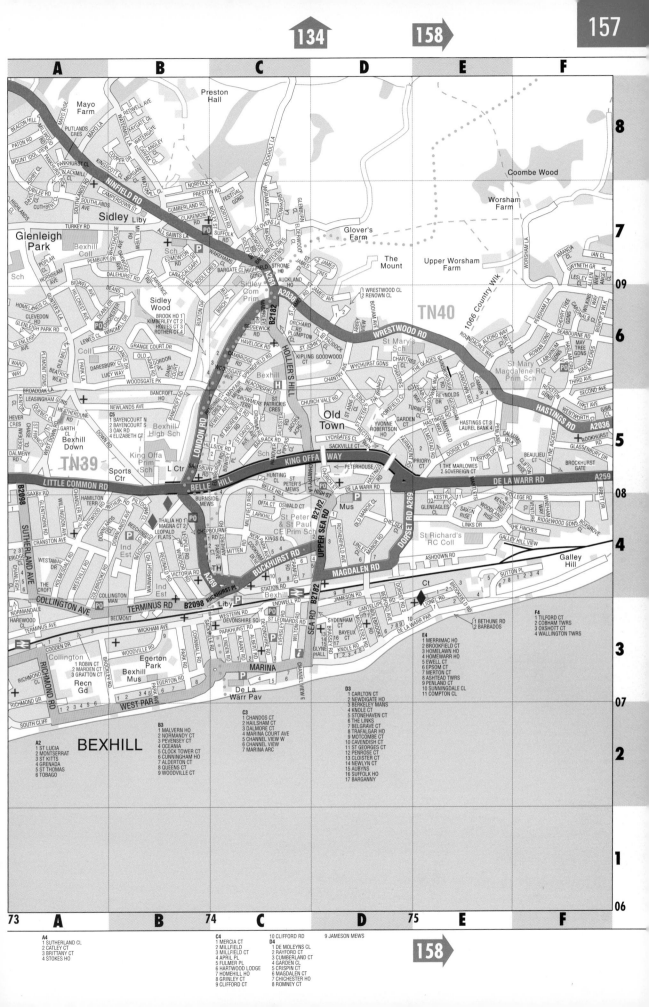

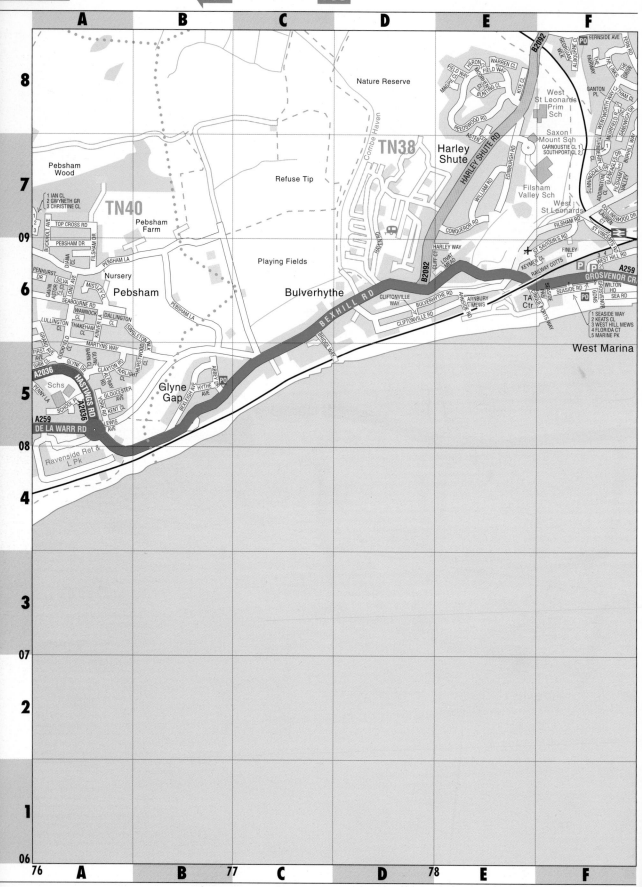

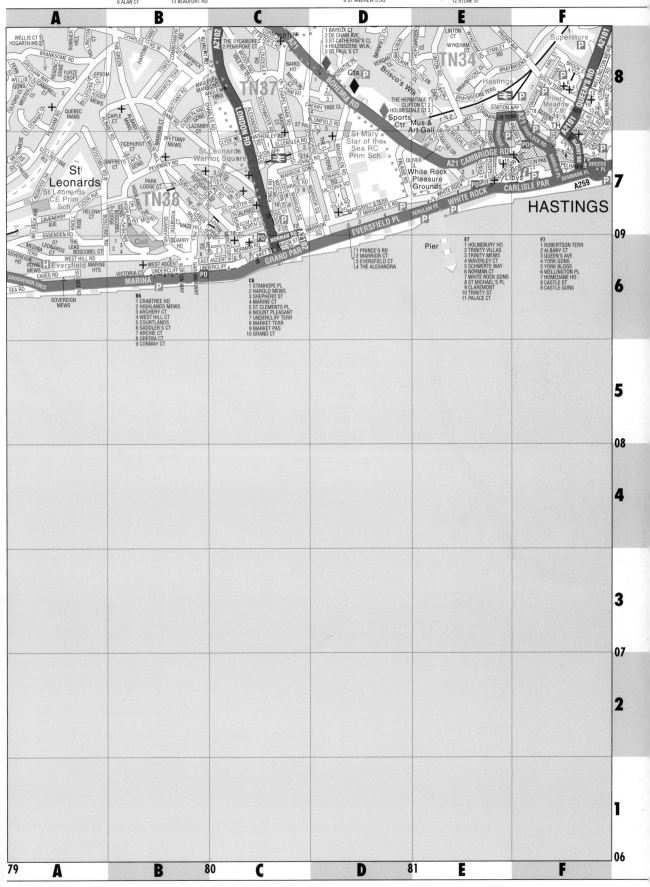

C7
1 STAINSBY ST
2 NORFOLK HO
3 ST RICHARDS HO
4 ROYAL TERR
5 EVERSFIELD MEWS N
6 ALAN CT

7 ASHLEY CT
8 ST MARY'S CT
9 CAVENDISH HO
10 DECIMUS BURTON WAY
11 UNION ST
12 MARLBOROUGH HO
13 BEAUFORT HO

14 ST GEORGES MOUNT
15 STOCKLEIGH CT
16 EVERSFIELD MEWS S
17 CHELSEA MEWS
18 ST MARYS COTTS

136

F8
1 WATERWORKS COTTS
2 STONEFIELD PL
3 ELFORD ST
4 WALDEGRAVE ST
5 CORNWALLIS ST
6 ST ANDREW'S SQ

160

F8
7 Robert Tressell Wkshps
8 QUEENS PAR
9 MIDDLE ST
10 KINGS WLK
11 PORTLAND COTTS
12 STONE ST

13 PORTLAND PL
14 WELLINGTON TERR
15 PORTLAND TERR
16 PORTLAND VILLAS
17 WELLINGTON HO
18 STATION RD

B6
1 CRABTREE HO
2 HIGHLANDS MEWS
3 ARCHERY CT
4 WEST HILL CT
5 COURTLANDS
6 SADDLER'S CT
7 ARCHIE CT
8 GREEBA CT
9 CONWAY CT

C6
1 STANHOPE PL
2 HAROLD MEWS
3 SHEPHERD ST
4 MARINE CT
5 ST CLEMENTS PL
6 MOUNT PLEASANT
7 UNDERCLIFF TERR
8 MARKET TERR
9 MARKET PAS
10 GRAND CT

D6
1 PRINCE'S RD
2 WARRIOR CT
3 EVERSFIELD CT
4 THE ALEXANDRA

E7
1 HOLMEBURY HO
2 TRINITY VILLAS
3 TRINITY MEWS
4 WAVERLEY CT
5 SCHWERTE WAY
6 NORMAN CT
7 WHITE ROCK GDNS
8 ST MICHAEL'S PL
9 CLAREMONT
10 TRINITY ST
11 PALACE CT

F7
1 ROBERTSON TERR
2 ALBANY CT
3 QUEEN'S AVE
4 YORK GDNS
5 YORK BLDGS
6 WELLINGTON PL
7 HOMEDANE HO
8 CASTLE ST
9 CASTLE GDNS

HASTINGS

← **136** ↑ **137** ↑ **138**

A B C D E F

HASTINGS

TN34 · TN35

Broomgrove · Halton · West Hill · Caves · Old Town · Belmont · High Wickham · Clive Vale · Ore · North Seat · Fairlight Place · Long Shaw · Covehurst Wood · Wet Wood · Hastings Country Park · Ecclesbourne Glen · Saxon Shore Way · 1066 Country Wlk · Hastings Link

Cliff Rly · Hastings Rly · Castle · Flamingo Family Fun Pk · Harbour · Heritage Ctr · Underwater World · LB Sta

A3
1 PELHAM ARC
2 BURDETT PL
3 WEST HILL ARC
4 ALBION LA
5 RUSSELL CT
6 MARKET PAS
7 CUTTER LA
8 SUN LA
9 SHELL LA

A4
1 UNICORN HO
2 CROFT TERR
3 GLOUCESTER COTTS
4 CAVENDISH PL
5 CHURCH PAS
6 COBOURG PL
7 CASTLEDOWN TERR
8 OAK PAS
9 SWAN AVE
10 POST OFFICE PAS

B4
1 OLD HUMPHREY AVE
2 HESTINGAS PLAT
3 HENRY TERR
4 WOOD'S PAS
5 STRONGS PAS
6 SWAINE'S PAS
7 EAST HILL PAS
8 TRAFALGAR COTTS

B4
9 OXFORD TERR
10 STARR'S COTTS
11 THE CREEK
12 BOURNE PAS
13 WATERLOO PL
14 GARDEN COTTS
15 WATERLOO PAS
16 PHILIP COLE CL
17 SINNOCK SQ
18 ROEBUCK ST
19 WELLESLEY CT
20 BOURNE CT
21 WINDING ST
22 EAST BOURNE ST
23 CROWN CT
24 TAMERISK STPS
25 PLEASANT ROW

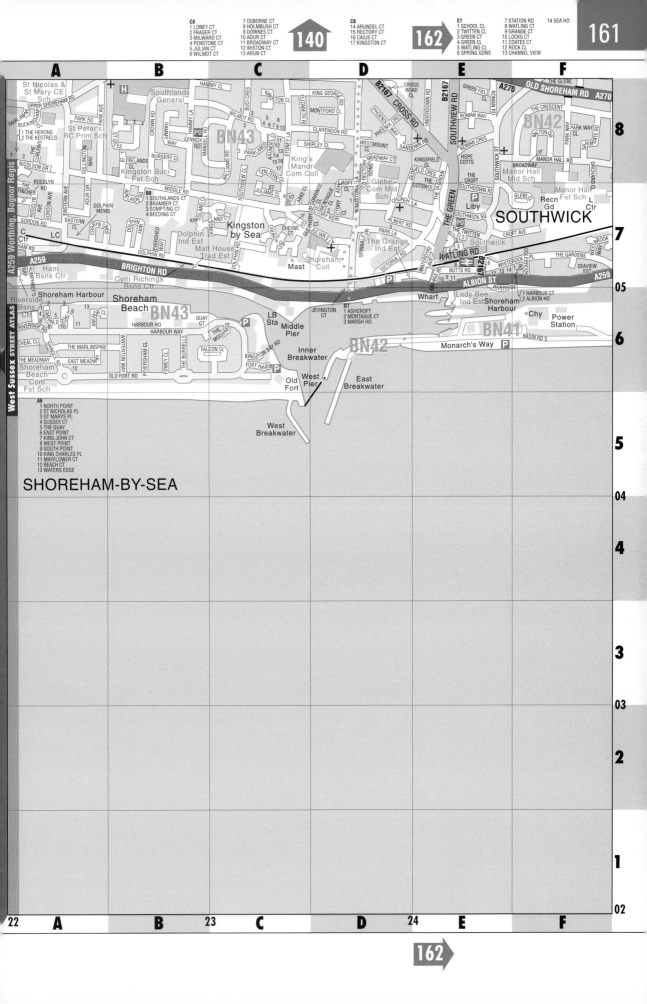

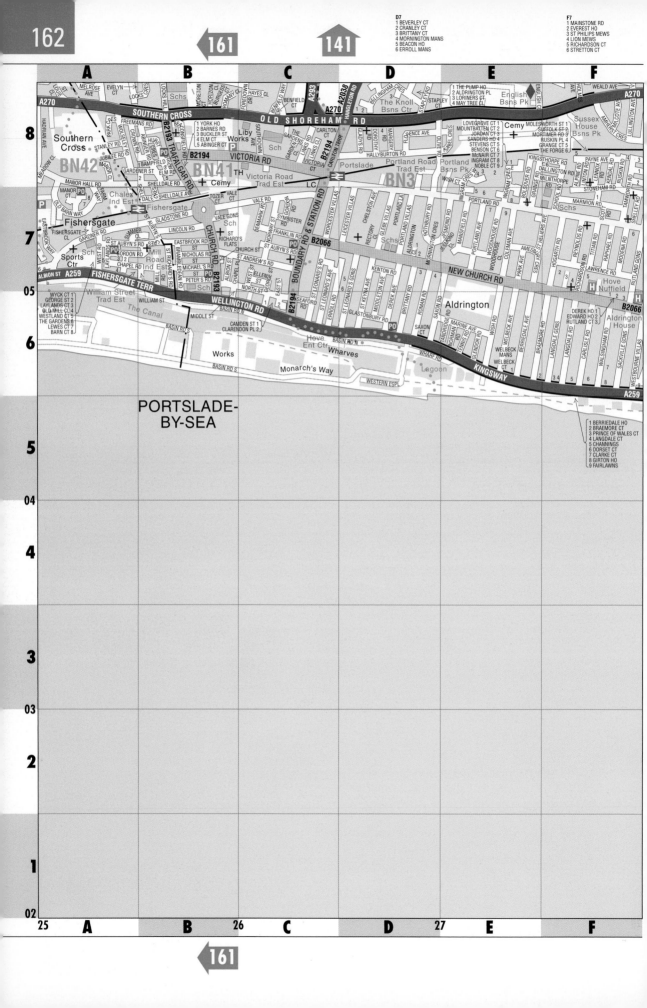

For full street detail of the highlighted area see page 189.

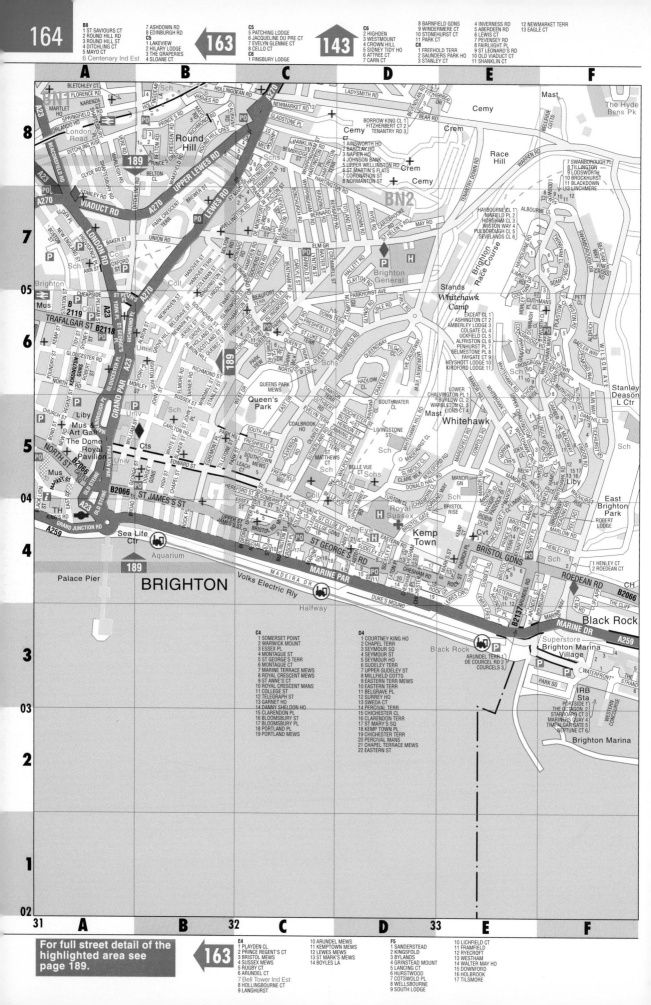

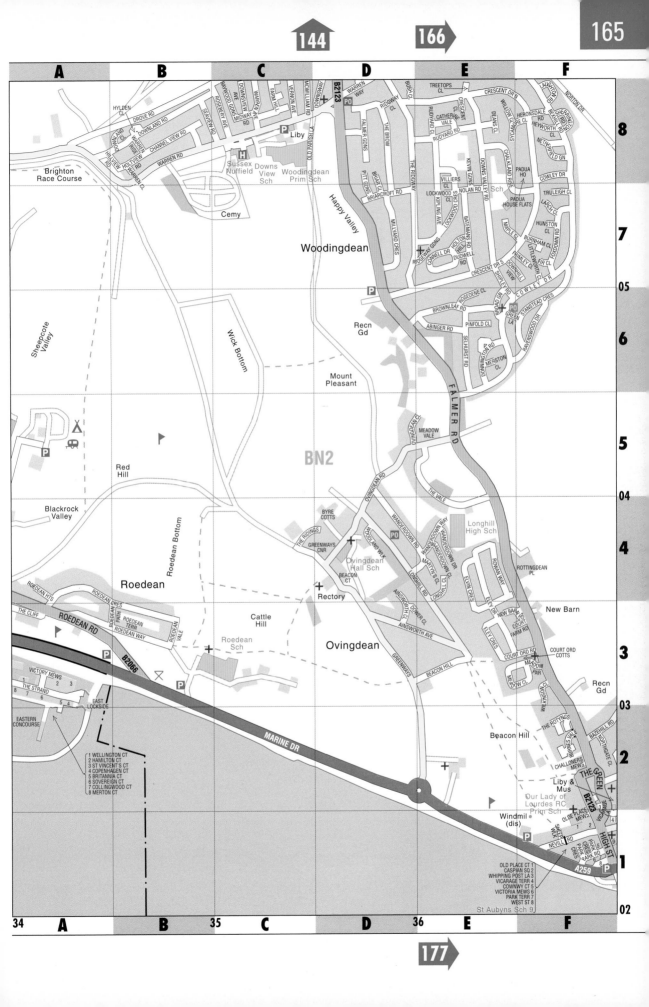

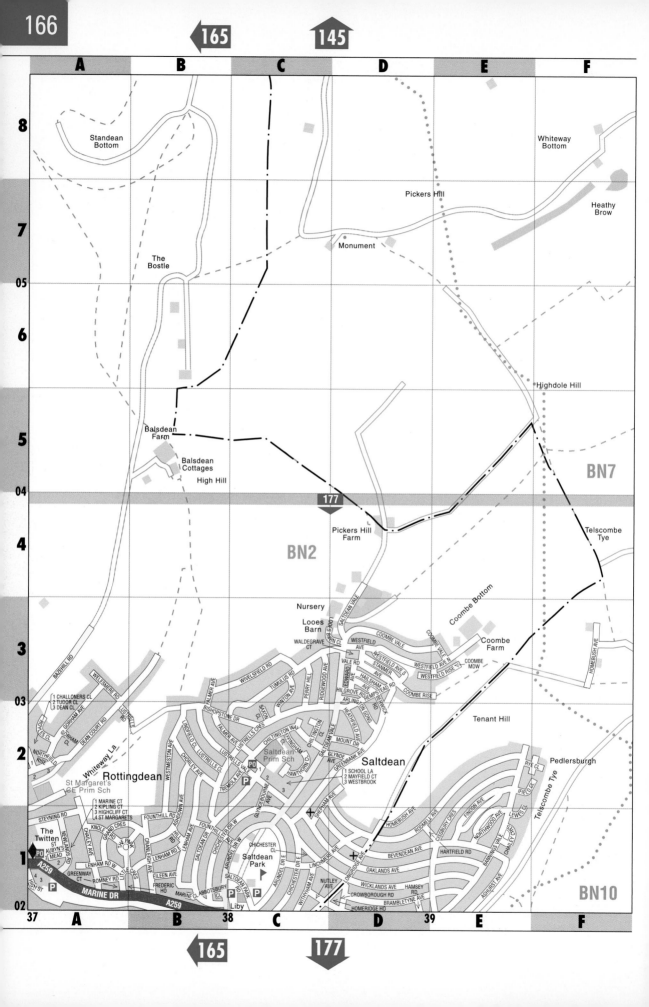

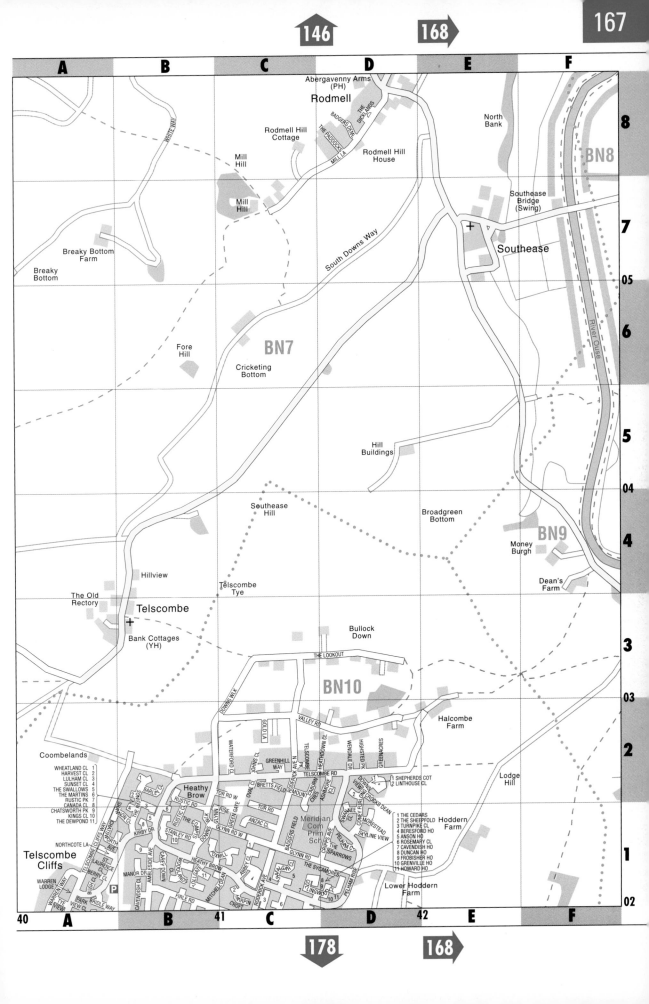

Rodmell
Abergavenny Arms (PH)
Rodmell Hill Cottage
Rodmell Hill House
Mill Hill
Mill Hill
THE PADDOCKS LA
THE DICK LANDS
BADGERS DEEN
MILL LA
North Bank
BN8
Southease Bridge (Swing)
Southease
South Downs Way
05
BN7
Fore Hill
Cricketing Bottom
River Ouse
6
Hill Buildings
5
Southease Hill
04
Broadgreen Bottom
BN9
4
Money Burgh
Dean's Farm
Hillview
Telscombe Tye
The Old Rectory
Telscombe
Bank Cottages (YH)
Bullock Down
THE LOOKOUT
BN10
Halcombe Farm
03
Coombelands
WHEATLAND CL 1
HARVEST CL 2
LULHAM CL 3
SUNSET CL 4
THE SWALLOWS 5
THE MARTINS 6
RUSTIC PK 7
CANADA CL 8
CHATSWORTH PK 9
KINGS CL 10
THE DEWPOND 11
Heathy Brow
Greenhill Way
BRETTS FIELD
VALLEY RD
TELSCOMBE RD
1 SHEPHERDS COT
2 LINTHOUSE CL
Lodge Hill
DOWNS VIEW
CROCKS DEAN
Meridian Com Prim Sch
MORESTEAD
SKYLINE VIEW
Hoddern Farm
1 THE CEDARS
2 THE SHEEPFOLD
3 TURNPIKE CL
4 BERESFORD HO
5 ANSON HO
6 ROSEMARY CL
7 CAVENDISH HO
8 DUNCAN HO
9 FROBISHER HO
10 GRENVILLE HO
11 HOWARD HO
Telscombe Cliffs
WARREN LODGE
NORTHCOTE LA
Lower Hoddern Farm
THE SYCAMORES
40 41 42 02

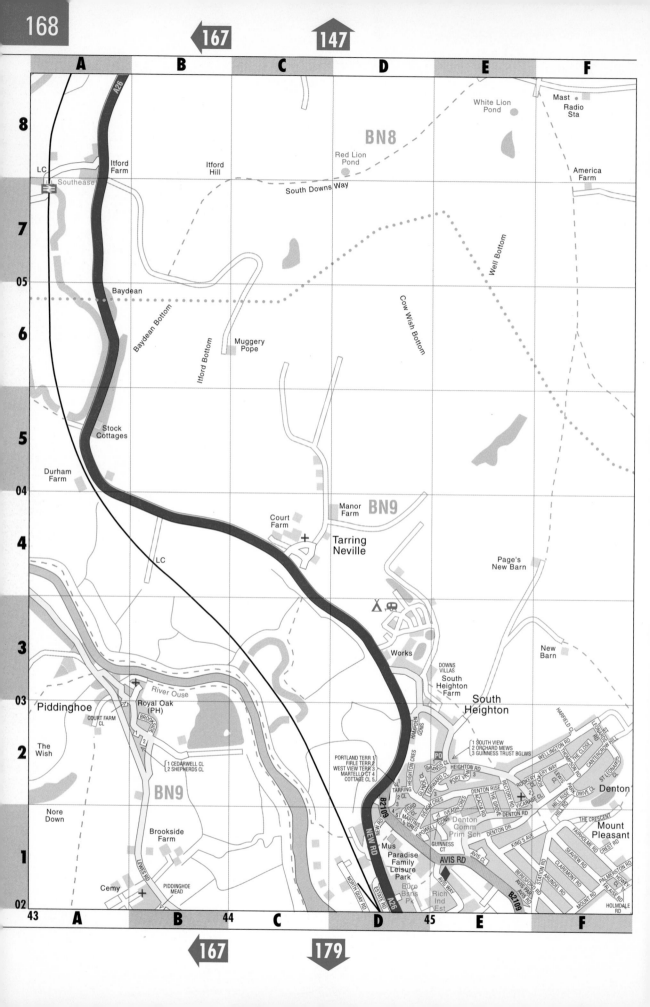

A B C D E F

8

BN8

White Lion Pond

Mast
Radio
Sta

LC
Southease
Itford
Farm

Itford
Hill

Red Lion
Pond

South Downs Way

America
Farm

7

Well Bottom

05

Baydean

Cow Wish Bottom

6

Baydean Bottom

Muggery
Pope

Itford Bottom

5

Stock
Cottages

Durham
Farm

04

Manor
Farm

BN9

Court
Farm

4

Tarring
Neville

Page's
New Barn

LC

3

Works

Downs
Villas
South
Heighton
Farm

New
Barn

03

Piddinghoe

River Ouse

Royal Oak
(PH)

South
Heighton

Denton

2

The Wish

COURT FARM
CL

1 CEDARWELL CL
2 SHEPHERDS CL

PORTLAND TERR 1
FIRLE TERR 2
WEST VIEW TERR 3
MARTELLO CT 4
COTTAGE CL 5

1 SOUTH VIEW
2 ORCHARD MEWS
3 GUINNESS TRUST BGLWS

PO

HEIGHTON RD

Mount
Pleasant

BN9

Nore
Down

Brookside
Farm

Denton
Comm
Prim Sch

1

Cemy

PIDDINGHOE
MEAD

Mus
Paradise
Family
Leisure
Park

Euro
Bsns
Pk

Rich
Ind
Est

AVIS RD

B2109

02

43

A

44

B

C

D

45

E

F

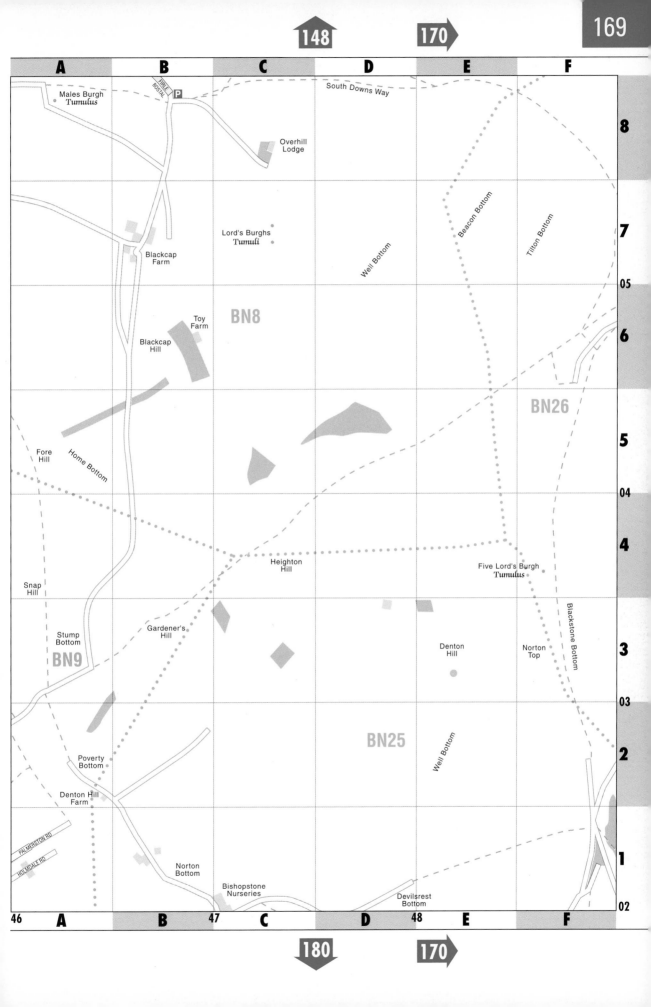

148
170

A B C D E F

8

Males Burgh
Tumulus

FIRE BOSTAL P

South Downs Way

Overhill
Lodge

7

Lord's Burghs
Tumuli

Blackcap
Farm

Well Bottom

Beacon Bottom

Tilton Bottom

05

BN8

Toy
Farm

6

Blackcap
Hill

BN26

Fore
Hill

Home Bottom

5

04

4

Heighton
Hill

Five Lord's Burgh
Tumulus

Snap
Hill

Stump
Bottom

Gardener's
Hill

Denton
Hill

Norton
Top

Blackstone Bottom

3

BN9

03

Poverty
Bottom

BN25

Well Bottom

2

Denton Hill
Farm

PALMERSTON RD

HOLMDALE RD

Norton
Bottom

Bishopstone
Nurseries

Devilsrest
Bottom

1

02

46 A B 47 C D 48 E F

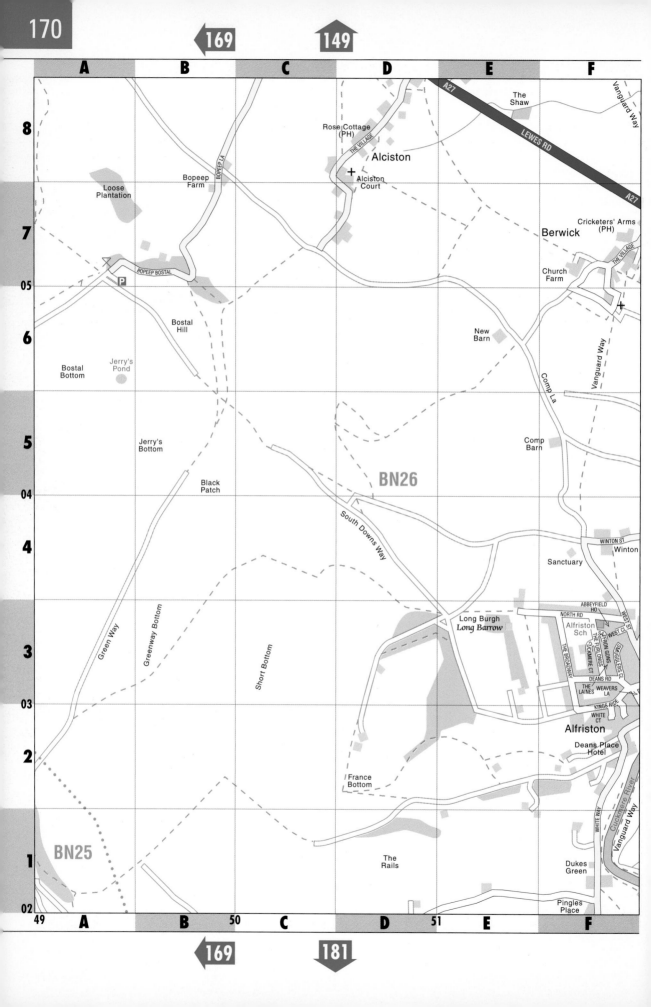

A B C D E F

8

The Shaw

A27

LEWES RD

Rose Cottage
(PH)

THE VILLAGE

Alciston

+
Alciston
Court

Bopeep
Farm

BOPEEP LA

7

Berwick

Cricketers' Arms
(PH)

THE VILLAGE

Loose
Plantation

Church
Farm

+

BOPEEP BOSTAL

P

05

Bostal
Hill

New
Barn

Vanguard Way

6

Bostal
Bottom

Jerry's
Pond

Comp La

Comp
Barn

5

Jerry's
Bottom

BN26

04

Black
Patch

South Downs Way

4

WINTON ST

Winton

Sanctuary

Green Way

Greenway Bottom

Short Bottom

3

Long Burgh
Long Barrow

ABBEYFIELD
HO

NORTH RD

Alfriston
Sch

WEST ST

THE FURLONGS

SAFFRON GDNS

OXENMERE CT

SMUGGLERS CL

THE BROADWAY

03

DEANS RD

THE
LAINES

WEAVERS
LA

KINGS RIDE

WHITE
CT

Alfriston

2

France
Bottom

Deans Place
Hotel

WHITE WAY

Cuckmere River

Vanguard Way

BN25

1

The
Rails

Dukes
Green

Pingles
Place

02

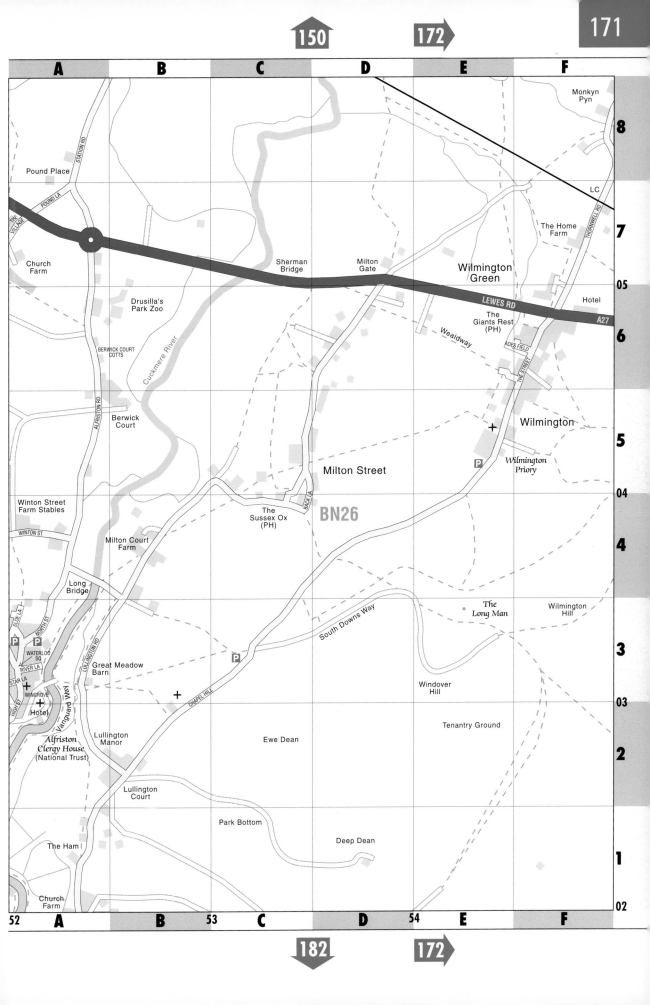

171
151

A B C D E F

8

7

05

6

5

04

4

3

03

2

1

02

171
183

55 A B 56 C D 57 E F

THORNWELL RD

Monkyn Pyn

Warren Farm

Hide Farm

Wootton Manor

A22

BAY TREE LA

Cophall Farm

A22

Cop Hall

A27

B2247

HAILSHAM RD

SILVERLAND RD

Newbarn Farm

POLEGATE BY-PASS

St LEONARDS TERR

BROOKSIDE AVE

GUARDIAN

VICTORIA CT

DIPLOCK RD

BROOK ST

GOSFORD WAY

A27

GRAND PAR 1

The BERNHARD BARON COTTAGE HOMES 2

A27

A2270

OLD DR

SOUTHDOWN CT

LEWES RD

The Flint House Farm

HYPERION AVE

SUNSTAR LA

CAINSBOROUGH LA

BAHRAM RD

GOLDEN MILLER LA

BROWN JACK AVE

GREYHOUNDSTOWN

The Stud Farm

SNO

BARONS WAY

BERNHARD

Recn Gd

WANNOCK RD

Puddingham Wood

Folkington Manor Farm

The Rough

HILARY CL

NORTHEND

Wannock Coppice

SOUTHFIELD

WANNOCK RD

GROSVENOR CL

The Links

Folkington Manor

FARMLANDS WAY

MAYFAIR CL

PADDOCK GDNS

LANCING WAY

MILL STREAM GDNS

The MILLCROFT

FARMLANDS AVE

PO

The Holt

FOLKINGTON RD

BN26

Wannock

MORTIMER GDNS

GLEN CL

MILL GDNS

Willingdon Com Sch

BROAD RD

Folkington

MILL LA

MILL CL

BROADWATER MEWS

HONEYWAN CL

MILL WAY

GOLDEN CL

MILL GDNS

FILCHING CL

WANNOCK AVE

WANNOCK LA

The PARAGON

THE GROVE

Folkington Bottom

Middle Brow

Cranedown Bottom

Crane Down

WAYFARING DOWN

Filching

JEVINGTON RD

Filching Manor Motor Mus

Hanging Hill

Willingdon Links

Folkington Hill

Ash Farm

Dean Wood

1066 COUNTRY WALK

BN20

Teddard's Bottom

Wealdway

Helling Down

The Combe

Hill Barn

South Downs Way

Hayward's Bottom

Jevington Holt

GREEN LA

Combe Hill

Wealdway

Holt Brow

Holt Bottom

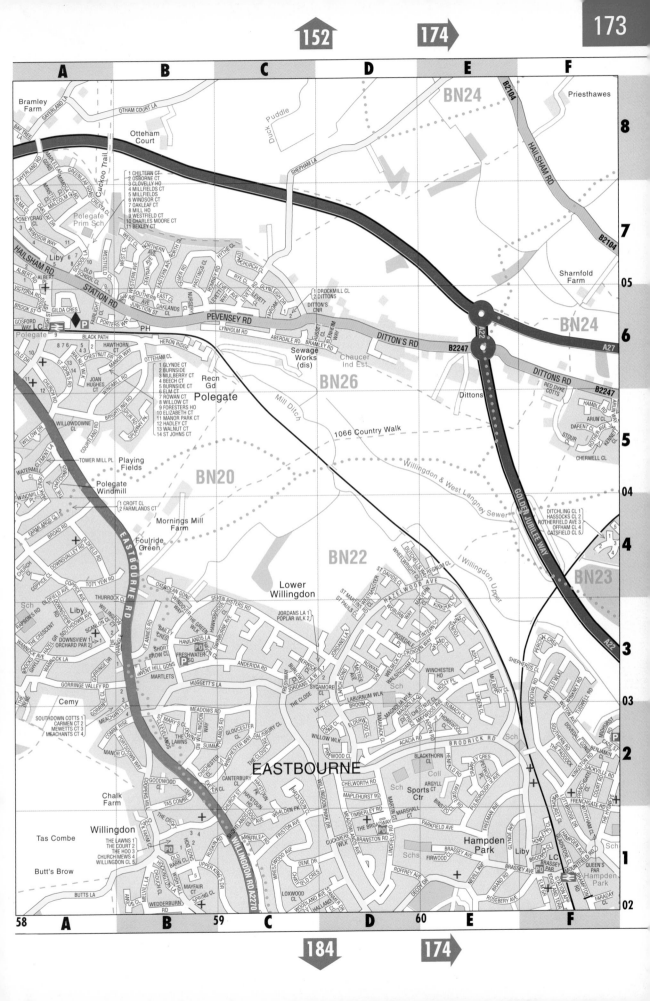

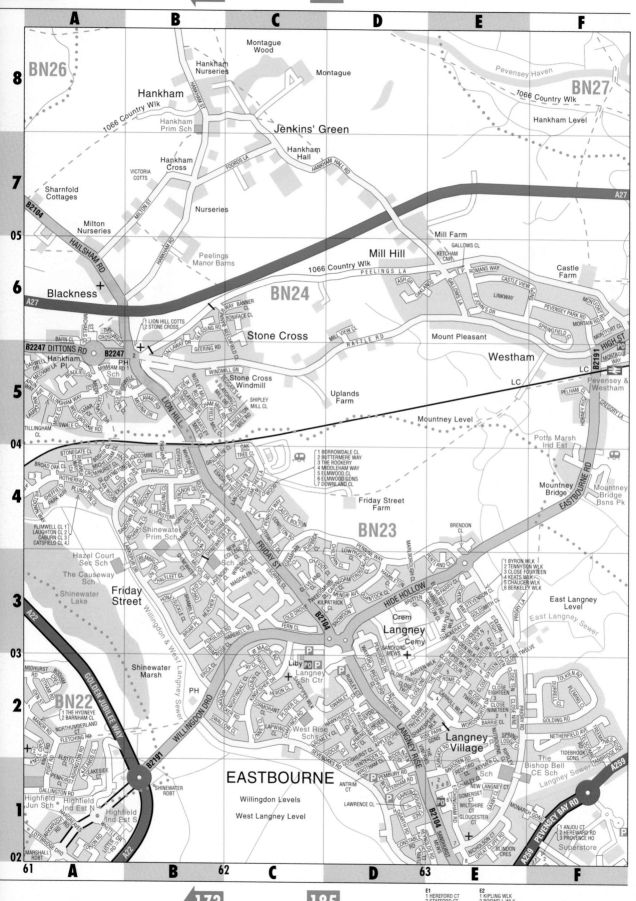

E1
1 HEREFORD CT
2 STAFFORD CT
3 RUTLAND CT
4 WARWICK CT
5 WORCESTER CT
6 HAMPSHIRE CT
7 WILLIAMS CT
8 PRIORY ORCH

E2
1 KIPLING WLK
2 BOSWELL WLK
3 SHELLEY WLK
4 CLOSE TWENTYFOUR
5 KEATS WLK
6 BROWNING WLK
7 COLERIDGE WLK

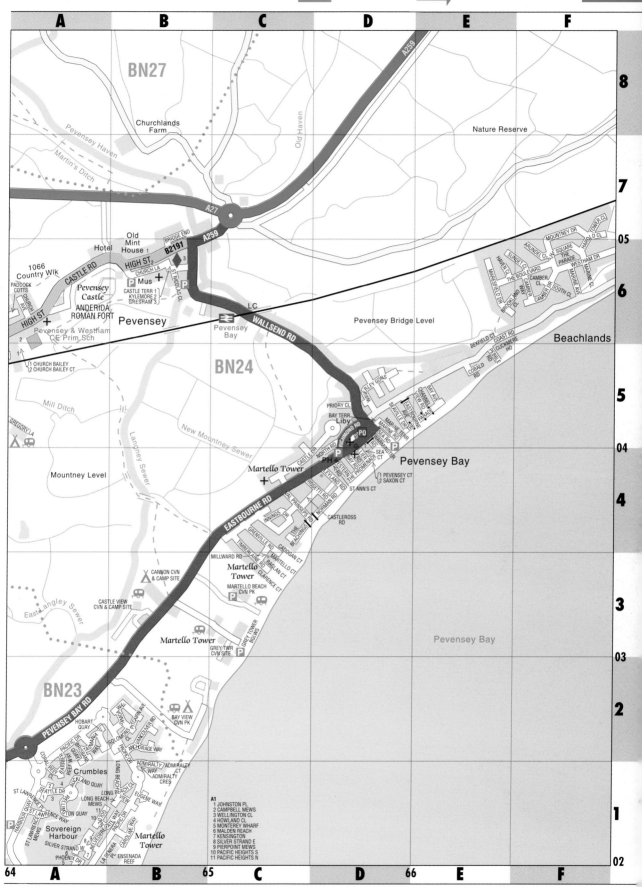

| A | B | C | D | E | F |

BN27

Churchlands Farm

Pevensey Haven

Martin's Ditch

A27

A259

Old Haven

A259

Nature Reserve

Old Mint House 1

Hotel

BRIDGE END

B2191

1066 Country Wlk

CASTLE RD

HIGH ST 2

CHURCH LA

ST NICOLAS CL

3

Mus

Pevensey Castle

ANDERIDA ROMAN FORT

PADDOCK COTTS

CHURCH AVE

HIGH ST

CASTLE TERR 1
KYLEMORE 2
GRESHAM 3

Pevensey

Pevensey & Westham CE Prim Sch

2

1

1 CHURCH BAILEY
2 CHURCH BAILEY CT

Pevensey Bay

WALLSEND RD

LC

05

Pevensey Bridge Level

Beachlands

MOUNTNEY DR

HAROLD CL

TOWER CL

ARUNDEL CL

THE SQUARE
THE PARADE

WESTHAM DR

HAVEN CL

SUNSET CL

THE BOULEVARD

CAMBER CL

MARINE AVE

MARESFIELD DR

BROOKLAND WAY

CAMBER DR

SOUTH CL

05

06

BEXFIELD CT

COAST RD

CUCKMERE HO

COBALD

PRIDE

COAST RD

BN24

Mill Ditch

New Mountney Sewer

Langley Sewer

GREGORY LA

Mountney Level

PRIORY CL

BAY TERR

Liby

WAVERLEY GDNS

CHANNEL VIEW RD
EASTERN RD

BAY AVE

MARINE TERR

SEAHILL DR
SEA RD
MARINE RD
NORMANS BAY

PO

CASTLE DR

NORTH RD

PH

P

RICHMOND RD

EASTERN RD

LELAND RD

THE PROMENADE

SEA CT

Pevensey Bay

Martello Tower

1 PEVENSEY CT
2 SAXON CT

ST ANN'S CT

EASTBOURNE RD

VAL PRINSEP RD

NORMAN RD

ROSETTI RD

INNINGS DR

THE BEACHINGS

CASTLEROSS RD

05

04

04

4

GRENVILLE RD

MARTELLO CT

CADOGAN CT

RABLAN CT

MILLWARD RD

TIMBER LAINE RD

CLARENCE CT

Martello Tower

CANNON CVN & CAMP SITE

CASTLE VIEW CVN & CAMP SITE

Martello Beach CVN PK

East Langley Sewer

GREY TOWER BGLWS

GREY TWR CVN SITE

Martello Tower

03

03

BN23

PEVENSEY BAY RD

HOBART QUAY

SOLOMONS CT

PITCAIRN AVE

VANCOUVER RD

ANCHORAGE WAY

BAY VIEW CVN PK

2

PACIFIC DR

BRISBANE AVE

PACIFIC DR

Crumbles

ADMIRALTY WAY

ADMIRALTY CT

ADMIRALTY CRES

CORAL REEF WAY

BARRIER REEF WAY

EASTERN QUAY

LONG BEACH

AUCKLAND QUAY

LONG BEACH MEWS

LONG BEACH VIEW

EUGENE WAY

St LAWRENCE

SEATTLE DR

ST LAWRENCE MEWS

ST LAWRENCE QUAY

WELLINGTON QUAY

SANDOS

PADDOCK

CAROLINE WAY

Sovereign Harbour

LA SENERA

BELVEDERE GATE

PHOENIX DR

SILVER STRAND W

ENSENADA REEF

Martello Tower

A1
1 JOHNSTON PL
2 CAMPBELL MEWS
3 WELLINGTON CL
4 HOWLAND CL
5 MONTEREY WHARF
6 MALDEN REACH
7 KENSINGTON
8 SILVER STRAND E
9 PIERPOINT MEWS
10 PACIFIC HEIGHTS S
11 PACIFIC HEIGHTS N

02

8

7

6

5

4

3

2

1

175
155

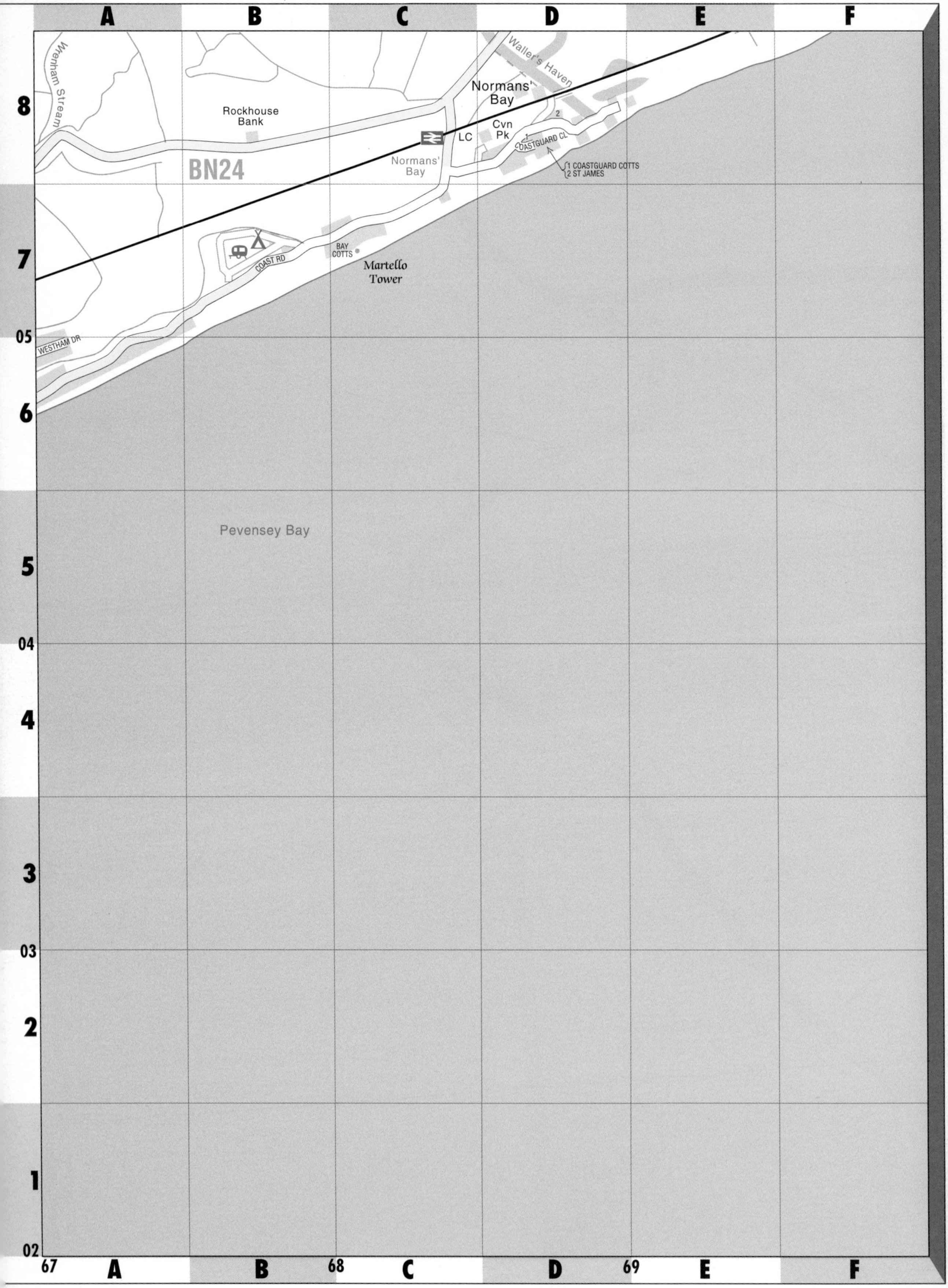

A B C D E F

Wrenham Stream

Rockhouse
Bank

Waller's Haven

Normans'
Bay

BN24

Normans'
Bay

LC

Cvn
Pk

COASTGUARD CL

2

1 COASTGUARD COTTS
2 ST JAMES

8

COAST RD

BAY
COTTS

Martello
Tower

7

WESTHAM DR

05

6

Pevensey Bay

5

04

4

3

03

2

02

1

67 A 68 B C 68 D 69 E F

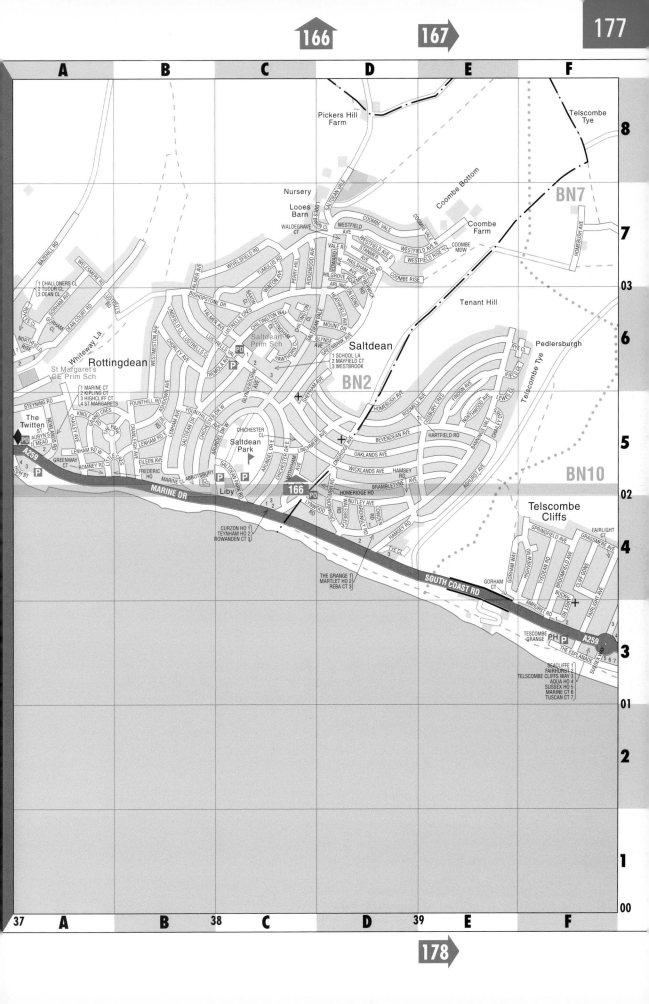

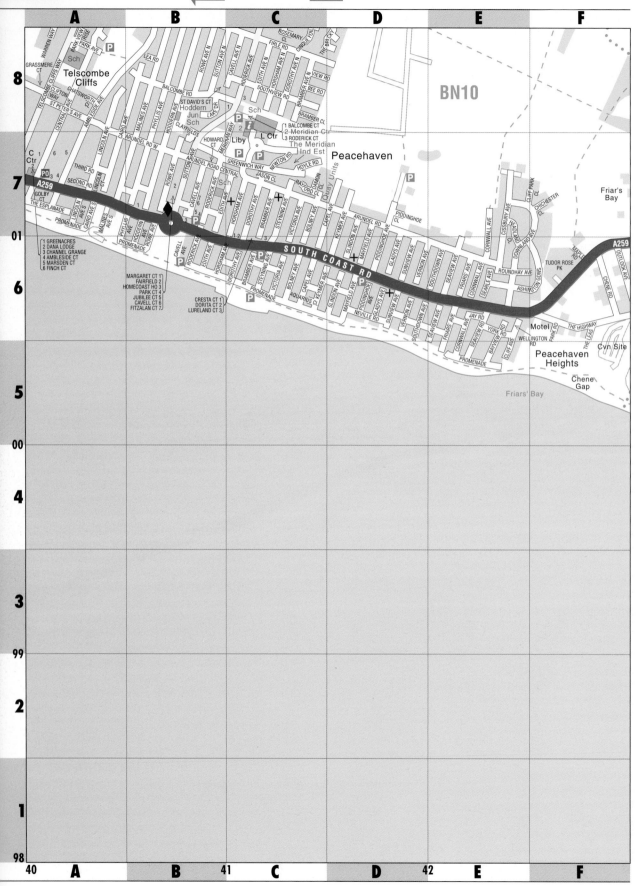

BN10

Telscombe
Cliffs

Peacehaven

1 Balcombe CT
2 Meridian Ctr
3 RODERICK CT
The Meridian
Ind Est

Friar's
Bay

SOUTH COAST RD

Peacehaven
Heights

Chene
Gap

Friars' Bay

C
Ctr

1 Greenacres
2 Dana Lodge
3 Channel Grange
4 Ambleside Ct
5 Marsden Ct
6 Finch Ct

Margaret Ct 1
Fairfield 2
Homecoast Ho 3
Park Ct 4
Jubilee Ct 5
Cavell Ct 6
Fitzalan Ct 7

Cresta Ct 1
Dorita Ct 2
Lureland Ct 3

Motel

Cvn Site

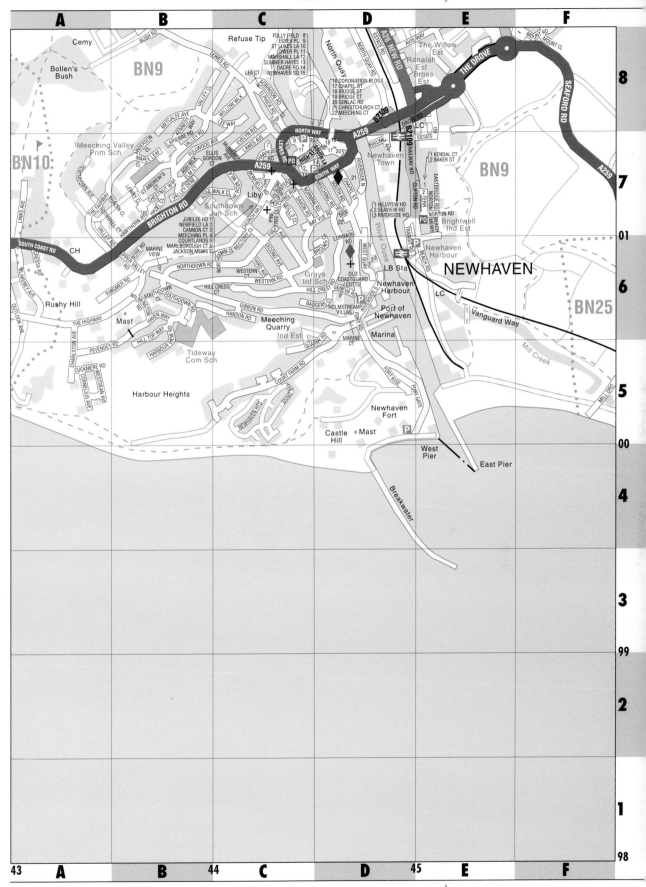

A B C D E F

8
7
01
6
5
00
4
3
99
2
1
98

46 47 48

Norton

Norton Farm

Beacon Hill

Blackstone Barn

Foxhole Farm

BN9

New Barn

Bullocks Barn

Stud Farm

Bishopstone Manor Farm

Bishopstone

Rookery Hill

CH

Crown Hill
The Lords
Duchess Dr

Whiteway Rd
Flint Cl

Bowden House Sch

CHALVINGTON CL

BN25

St John's Sch

East Blatchington

Tide Mills

LC

NEWHAVEN RD

Motel

BUCKLE BY-PASS

1 BLATCHINGTON HILL FLATS
2 PINE CT

Seaford Prim Sch

Buckle CVN Pk

Bishopstone

Sunnyside CVN Site

WEST BEACH CT

CLAREMONT RD

STATION APP

Liby

PO

Seaford

Recn Gd

Richmond Mews

SEAFORD

Seaford Bay

Chatham Pl

The Steyne

Seaford Head Com Coll

Seaford Mus of Local History

Groyne

Vanguard Way

Seaford Head Com Coll

C4
1 HAWTH VALLEY CT
2 SELMESTON CT
3 OFFHAM CT
4 LITLINGTON CT
5 RODMELL CT
6 NEW COASTGUARD COTTS

E2
1 SEAFORD CT
2 CHICHESTER CT
3 DANE HTS
4 PELHAM CT
5 TALLAND PAR
6 THE CROUCH
7 PELHAM YD
8 COURT LEET
9 FRENCH'S CT
10 CUNNINGHAM CT
11 GRANVILLE CT
12 MALLETT CL
13 THE CAUSEWAY
14 KINGS WELL CT
15 RAYFORD CT
16 STRATHNDEN CT
17 WEST VIEW CT
18 STEYNE CT
19 ESPLANADE MEWS
20 THE BOUNDARY
21 MARTELLO MEWS

E3
1 AVONDALE CT
2 RICHMOND TERR
3 OLD MARKET COTTS
4 CLINTON LA
5 CUCKMERE CT
6 SUTTON CROFT LA
7 CROFT CT
8 FITZGERALD HO
9 WELBECK CT

F2
1 KINGSFOLD CT
2 CROUCHFIELD CL
3 BRAMBER CL
4 STEYNE CL
5 SEA COTTS
6 CRICKETFIELD CT
7 WAVERLY CT

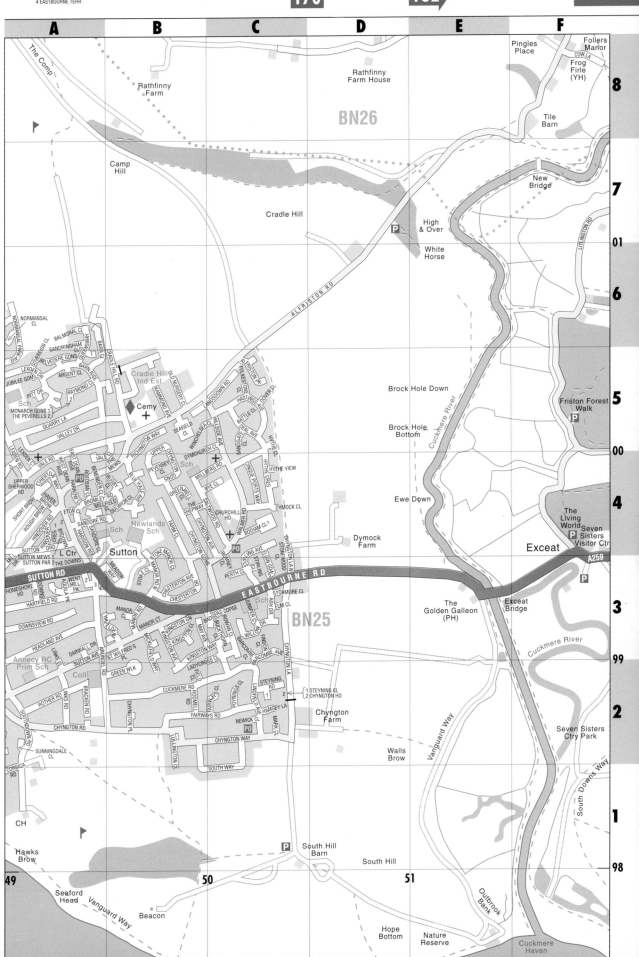

A3
1 WELLINGTON PK
2 BARN COTTS
3 SHEEP PEN LA
4 EASTBOURNE TERR

170

182

181

A   B   C   D   E   F

8
7
01
6
5
00
4
3
99
2
1
98

49   50   51

BN26

Pingles
Place

Follers
Manor

COW LA

Frog
Firle
(YH)

Rathfinny
Farm House

Tile
Barn

Rathfinny
Farm

Camp
Hill

New
Bridge

Cradle Hill

High
& Over

White
Horse

The Comp

ALFRISTON RD

Brock Hole Down

Brock Hole
Bottom

Cuckmere River

LITLINGTON RD

Friston Forest
Walk

NORMANSAL
CL

BALMORAL CL

SANDRINGHAM

BELVEDERE GDNS

ARGENT CL

BARN CL

CRADLE HILL RD

BARN RISE

OLD NURSERY CL

Cradle Hill
Ind Est

LANSDOWN RD

FOLKESTONE
CL

ALFRISTON RD

DOVER CL

Ewe Down

The
Living
World

Seven
Sisters
Visitor Ctr

Exceat

A259

LEXDEN DR

SOVEREIGN DR

JUBILEE GDNS

PITT DR

RAYMOND CL

Sch

MONARCH GDNS 1
THE PEVERELLS 2

QUARRY LA

VALLEY DR

KAMMOND AVE

Cemy

SEAFIELD
CL

RICHINGTON WAY

UPPER
CHYNGTON
GDNS

WINCHELSEA CL
HILLSIDE AVE

DYMCHURCH AVE

HASTINGS AVE

BATTLE CL

SANDGATE CL
DEAL AVE

HYTHE CL

HYTHE VIEW

HYTHE CRES

DYMOCK CL

Dymock
Farm

LEXDEN RD

VALE RD

UPPER
SHERWOOD
RD

SHORT BROW

ROUGH BROW

ETHER CT

VALE
WAY

BENFIELD CL

BROMLEY CL

MILL
RD

EATON CL

THE
MEWS

VALE
THE

BLUE HAZE AVE

PEVENSEY RD
SNOD

GREENWELL

THE
SHEPWAY

SHERWOOD RD

MILLBERG RD

RYE CL

CINQUE PORTS WAY

WALMER RD

Sch

CHURCHILL
HO

BODIAM CL

EAST DEAN RISE

WEST DEAN RISE

HARROW CL

HINDOVER RD

HINDOVER CRS

SANDORE RD

SANDORE CL

HARISON RD

DU WICH CL

FARM CL

CHYNGTON AVE

RIMNEY

STONEWOOD

CHYNGTON LA

Sch

Newlands
Sch

PO

Sutton

SUTTON MEWS

SUTTON PAR 2 THE DOWNS

SUTTON RD

WENT
HILL
PK

AQUILA PK

STONE CL

MANOR ROW

MEADON
WAY

ASTERTON AVE

CHESTERTON

LLNG AVE

ELGIN GDNS

PERTH CL

ELGIN
CL

SPRING
CL

EASTBOURNE RD

SYCAMORE CL

ELM CL

Sch

BN25

The
Golden Galleon
(PH)

Exceat
Bridge

HOMESHORE
HO

HARTFIELD RD

DOWNSVIEW RD

HEADLAND AVE

Annecy RC
Prim Sch

Coll

ROTHER RD

LINKS RD

CHYNGTON RD

MANOR
CL

MANOR CT

HAZEL DR

SUTTON AVE

ARUNDEL RD

DARWALL DR

St WILFRED'S
PL

GREEN WLK

BRACKEN RD

SUNNINGDALE
CL

CORSICA
RD

SOUTHDOWN RD

KINGSTON CN

KINGSTON CL

KINGSTON AVE

MICKLEFIELD WAY

LADYCROSS CL

CUCKMERE RD

RODMELL RD

FAIRWAYS RD

BADGERS COPSE

RIVIAN CL

BROOK LN

JUNIPER CL

MAX AVE

WILLON
DR

BARCOMBE CL

BUXTED CL

RINA'S CL

PEVINS CL

CHYNGTON PL

LINDFIELD AVE

NEWICK CL

CHYNGTON WAY

SOUTH WAY

HMSEY LA

MARK CL

STEYNING
RD

1 STEYNING CL
2 CHYNGTON HO

Chyngton
Farm

Walls
Brow

Vanguard Way

Cuckmere River

Seven Sisters
Cty Park

South Downs Way

CH

Hawks
Brow

Seaford
Head

Vanguard Way

Beacon

P

South Hill
Barn

South Hill

Hope
Bottom

Nature
Reserve

Outbrook
Bank

Cuckmere
Haven

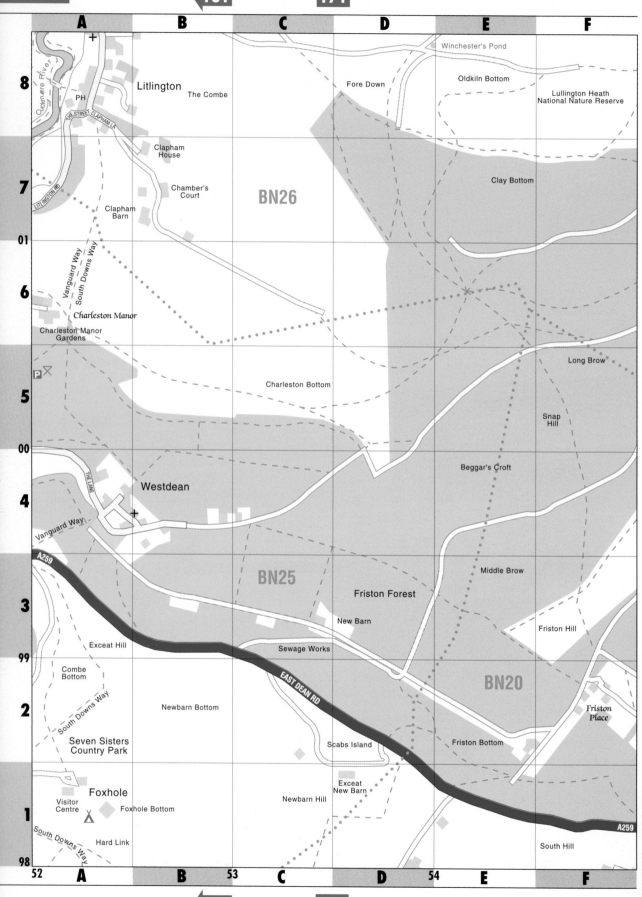

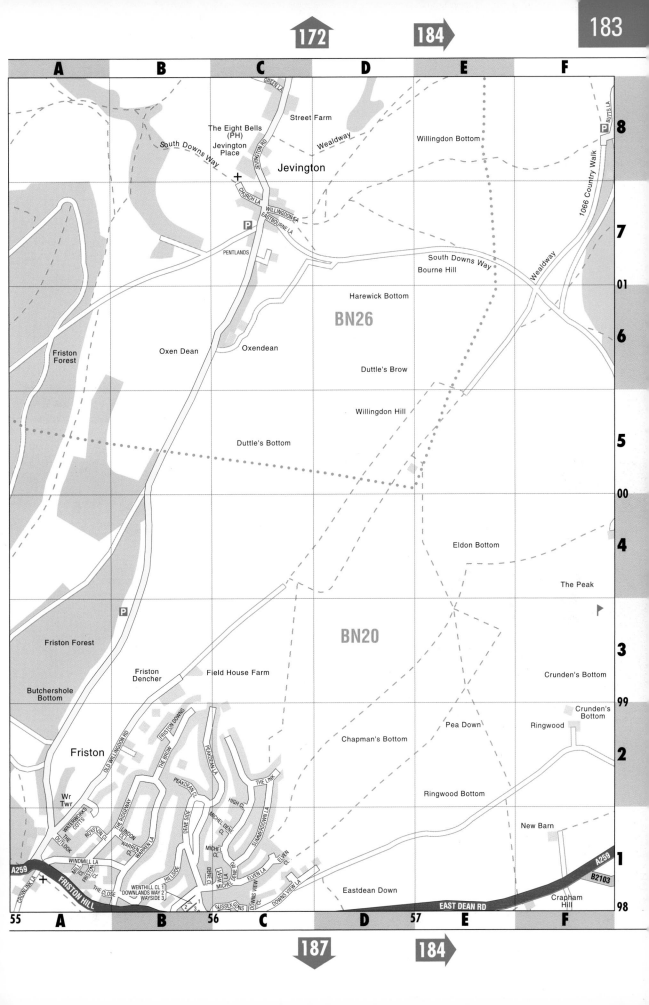

A   B   C   D   E   F

Map labels:

GREEN LA
Street Farm
The Eight Bells (PH)
Jevington Place
South Downs Way
Willingdon Bottom
BUTS LA
1066 Country Walk
Wealdway
Jevington
JEVINGTON RD
CHURCH LA
WILLINGDON EA
EASTBOURNE LA
South Downs Way
Bourne Hill
Wealdway
PENTLANDS
Harewick Bottom
BN26
Oxen Dean
Oxendean
Friston Forest
Duttle's Brow
Willingdon Hill
Duttle's Bottom
Eldon Bottom
The Peak
BN20
Friston Forest
Friston Dencher
Field House Farm
Crunden's Bottom
Butchershole Bottom
Crunden's Bottom
Pea Down
Ringwood
Chapman's Bottom
OLD WILLINGDON RD
FRISTON DOWNS
Friston
THE BROW
PEAKDEAN LA
Ringwood Bottom
PEAKDEAN CL
THE LINK
Wr Twr
WATERWORKS COTTS
ROYSTON CL
THE RIDGEWAY
THE LINDON CL
DENE SIDE
HIGH CL
MICHEL DENE CL
SUMMERDOWN LA
New Barn
THE OUTLOOK
WARREN CL
WARREN LA
HILLSIDE
MICHEL CL
ELVEN CL
WINDMILL LA
MILL CL
DENE CL
WEAL LA
MICHEL DENE RD
ELVEN LA
A259
B2103
THE CLOSE
WENTHILL CL 1
DOWNLANDS WAY 2
WAYSIDE 3
SUSSEX GDNS
DENE VIEW LA
DOWNS VIEW LA
Eastdean Down
EAST DEAN RD
Crapham Hill
CROSSLINK LA
FRISTON HILL
A259

01
6
5
00
4
3
99
2
1
98

8
7

55   56   57

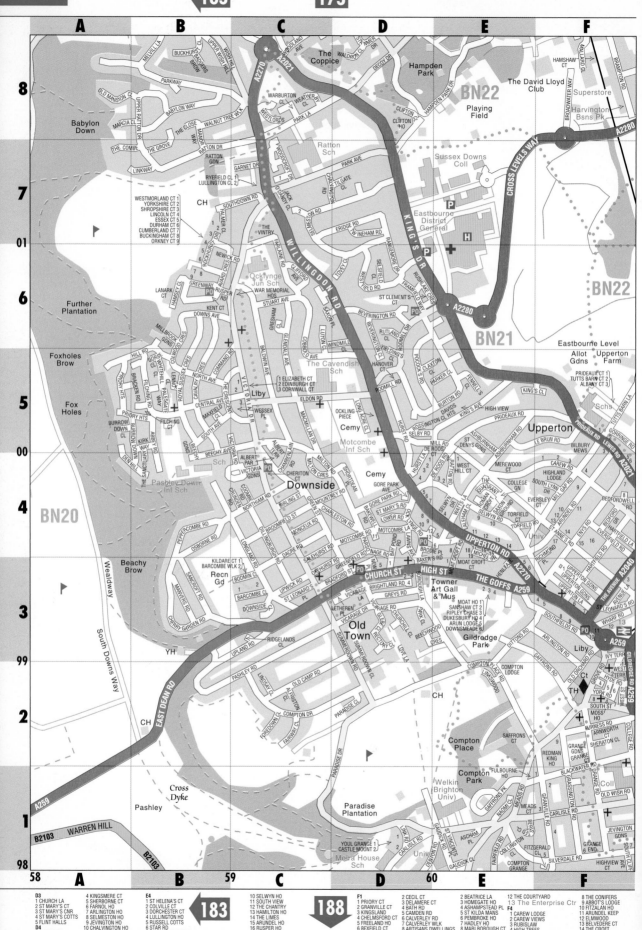

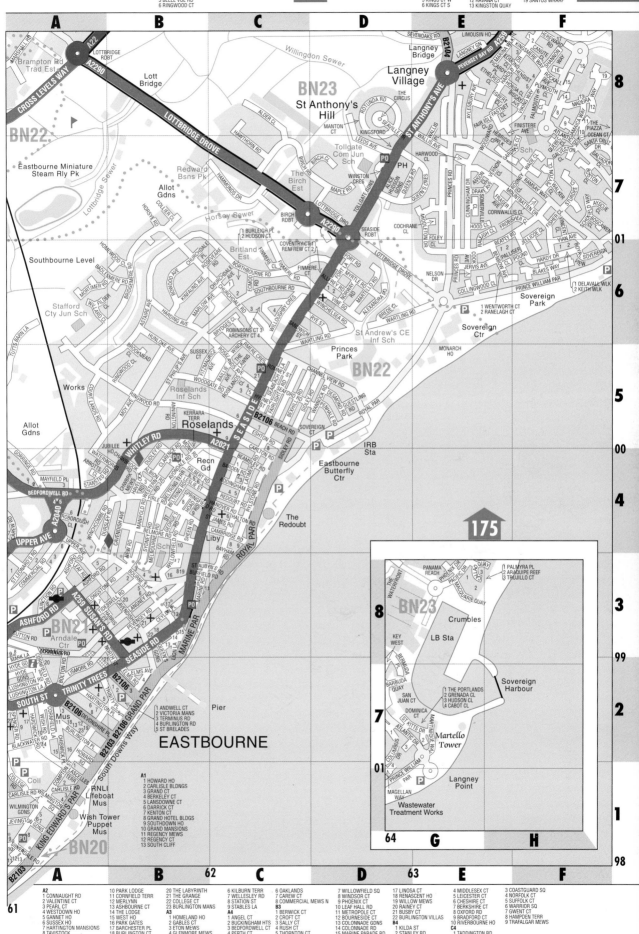

BN23
St Anthony's Hill
Langney Village
Langney Bridge

BN22

BN22
Princes Park

BN23
Roselands

EASTBOURNE

BN21
Arndale Ctr

BN20

175

BN23
Crumbles
LB Sta
Sovereign Harbour
Martello Tower
Langney Point
Wastewater Treatment Works
Panama Reach

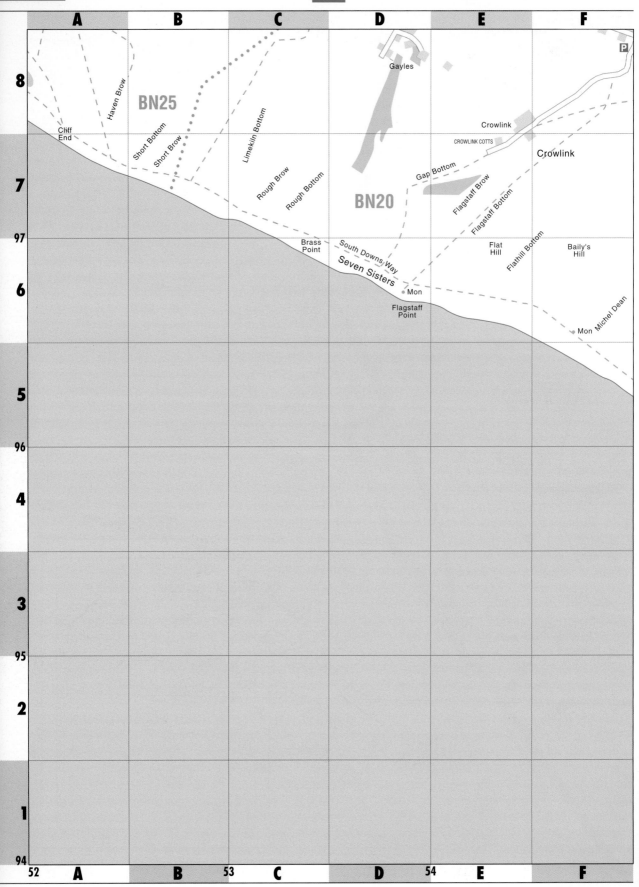

BN25

Haven Brow

Cliff
End

Short Bottom

Short Brow

Limekiln Bottom

Rough Brow

Rough Bottom

Brass
Point

South Downs Way

Seven Sisters

Gayles

Crowlink

CROWLINK COTTS

Crowlink

Gap Bottom

BN20

Flagstaff Brow

Flagstaff Bottom

Flat
Hill

Flathill Bottom

Baily's
Hill

Mon

Flagstaff
Point

Mon Michel Dean

Mon

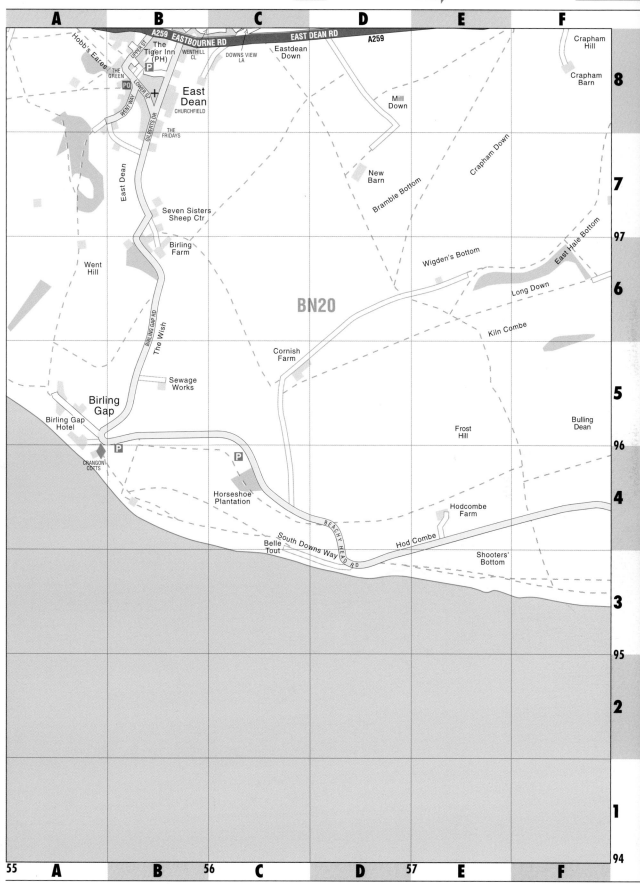

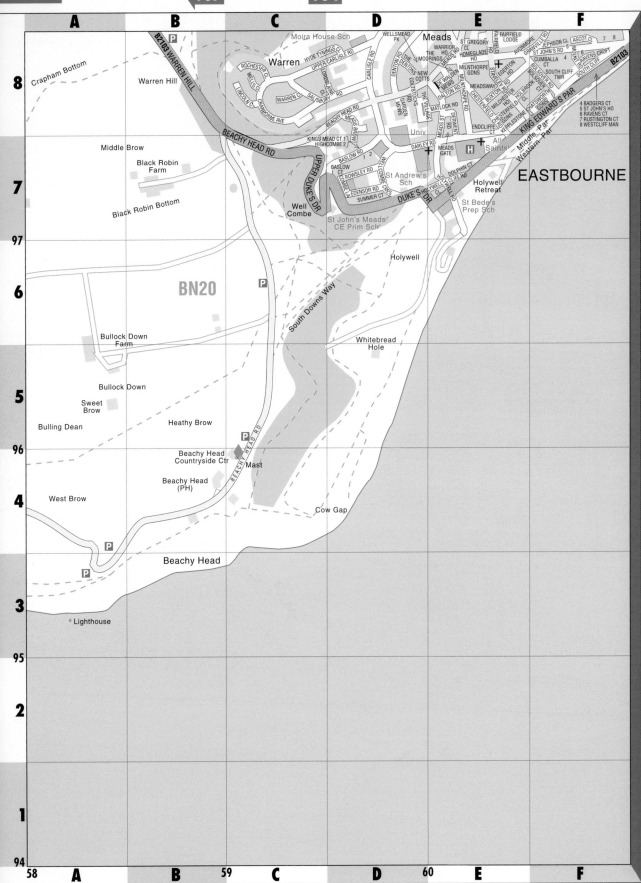

A B C D E F

8

Crapham Bottom

Warren Hill

Warren

Moira House Sch

Wellsmead Pk

Meads

St Gregory Cl

Fairfield Lodge

Ascot Cl 7 8

B2103

ROCHESTER CL

HYDE TYNINGS CL

WELLS CL

CRANBORNE AVE

WARREN CL

SALISBURY

LINCOLN CL

LORDSLAINE

UPPER CARLISLE RD

CARLISLE RD

DENTON RD

THE DENTONS

NEW COTTS

THE COLSTOCKS

WARRIOR THE HO MOORINGS

MEADS RD

HOMEGLADE HO

MILNTHORPE GDNS

GRANVILLE RD

JEPHSON CL

ST JOHN'S RD

AVONMORE

CUMBALLA CT

BUXTON

MILCHESTER HO

MEADSWAY

CHESTERFIELD GDNS

SOUTH CLIFF TWR

SOUTH CLIFF

KING EDWARD'S PAR

4 BADGERS CT
5 ST JOHN'S HO
6 RAVENS CT
7 RUSTINGTON CT
8 WESTCLIFF MAN

B2103 WARREN HILL

BEACHY HEAD RD

Middle Brow

Black Robin Farm

Black Robin Bottom

UPPER DUKE'S DR

Well Combe

BEACHY HEAD RD

KINGS MEAD CT 1
HIGHCOMBE 2

BASLOW RD

BASLOW CT

ROWSLEY RD

EDENSOR RD

SUMMER CT

St Andrew's Sch

DARLEY RD

MEADS GATE

All Saints

St John's Meads CE Prim Sch

DOLPHIN CT

HOLYWELL RD

CLIFF RD

Holywell Retreat

St Bede's Prep Sch

EASTBOURNE

Univ

MEADS ST

DUKE'S DR

Holywell

MIDDLE PAR

Western PAR

7

97

6

BN20

P

South Downs Way

Holywell

Bullock Down Farm

Whitebread Hole

Bullock Down

Sweet Brow

Bulling Dean

Heathy Brow

P

Beachy Head Countryside Ctr

Mast

Beachy Head (PH)

West Brow

Cow Gap

5

96

4

P

P

Beachy Head

3

Lighthouse

95

2

1

94

58 A B 59 C D 60 E F

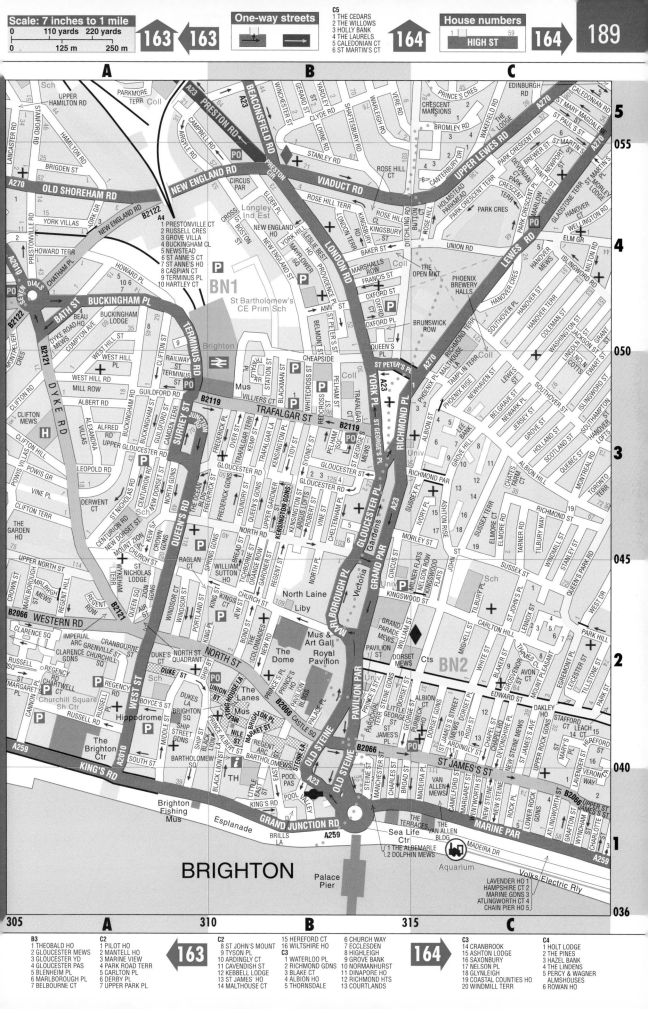

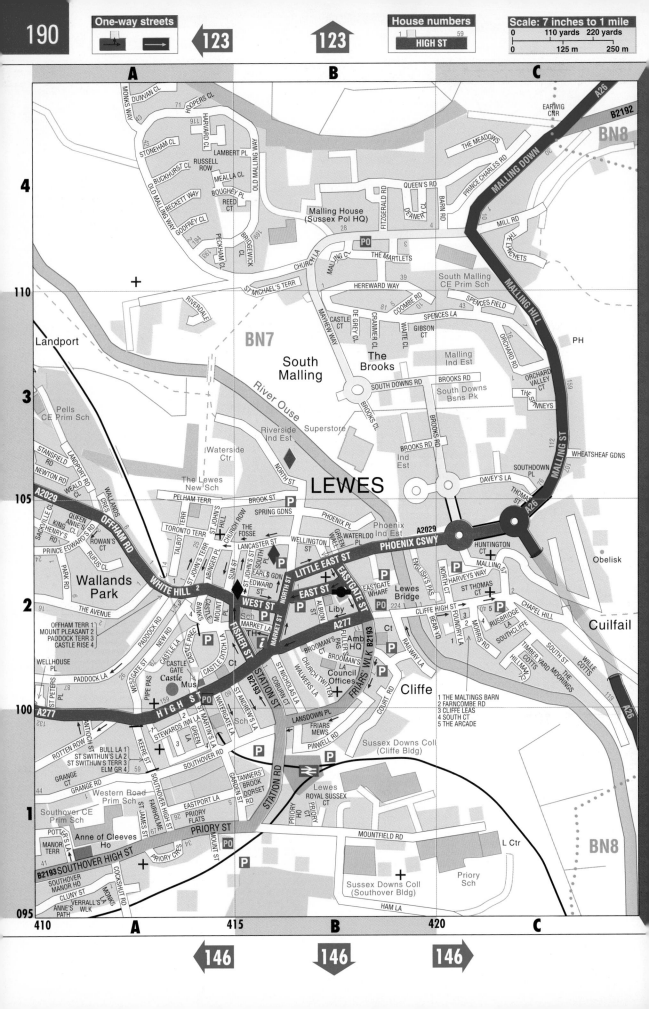

Index

Church Rd **6** Beckenham BR2..........**53** C6

Place name
May be abbreviated on the map

Location number
Present when a number indicates the place's position in a crowded area of mapping

Locality, town or village
Shown when more than one place has the same name

Postcode district
District for the indexed place

Page and grid square
Page number and grid reference for the standard mapping

Public and commercial buildings are highlighted in magenta **Places of interest** are highlighted in blue with a star ★

Abbreviations used in the index

Acad	Academy	Comm	Common	Gd	Ground	L	Leisure	Prom	Prom
App	Approach	Cott	Cottage	Gdn	Garden	La	Lane	Rd	Road
Arc	Arcade	Cres	Crescent	Gn	Green	Liby	Library	Recn	Recreation
Ave	Avenue	Cswy	Causeway	Gr	Grove	Mdw	Meadow	Ret	Retail
Bglw	Bungalow	Ct	Court	H	Hall	Meml	Memorial	Sh	Shopping
Bldg	Building	Ctr	Centre	Ho	House	Mkt	Market	Sq	Square
Bsns, Bus	Business	Ctry	Country	Hospl	Hospital	Mus	Museum	St	Street
Bvd	Boulevard	Cty	County	HQ	Headquarters	Orch	Orchard	Sta	Station
Cath	Cathedral	Dr	Drive	Hts	Heights	Pal	Palace	Terr	Terrace
Cir	Circus	Dro	Drove	Ind	Industrial	Par	Parade	TH	Town Hall
Cl	Close	Ed	Education	Inst	Institute	Pas	Passage	Univ	University
Cnr	Corner	Emb	Embankment	Int	International	Pk	Park	Wk, Wlk	Walk
Coll	College	Est	Estate	Intc	Interchange	Pl	Place	Wr	Water
Com	Community	Ex	Exhibition	Junc	Junction	Prec	Precinct	Yd	Yard

Index of localities, towns and villages

A

Abbotsford 72 E6
Alciston 170 D8
Alderbrook 38 A7
Aldrington 162 E6
Alfriston 170 F2
Argos Hill 39 E5
Arlington 150 F4
Ashurst 5 D2
Ashurst Wood 11 E5

B

Baldslow 136 C7
Baldwin's Hill 1 D4
Balls Green 14 C5
Banner Farm 8 C2
Barcombe 101 E2
Barcombe Cross 101 E4
Barcombe Mills 102 A3
Bardown 42 E7
Battle 112 D5
Beachlands 175 F6
Beacon Down 81 A7
Beckley 68 A4
Beckley Furnace 90 D7
Beddingham 147 D4
Bells Yew Green 17 F5
Belmont 137 C1
Berwick 170 F7
Best Beech Hill 29 B3
Bevendean 143 F7
Bexhill 157 A2
Birchden 15 D5
Birchett's Green 30 F3

Birchgrove 34 A8
Birling Gap 187 A5
Bishopstone 180 C6
Blackboys 80 A5
Blackham 5 A4
Blackhurst 8 F5
Blacklands 136 F2
Blackness Crowborough ..26 A1
Blackness Eastbourne ..174 A6
Black Rock 164 F3
Blackwell 1 E3
Boarshead 26 C6
Bodiam 65 E8
Bodle Street Green ..109 C2
Bohemia 136 C1
Boreham Street 131 F4
Brede 90 B1
Brightling 85 C7
Brighton 164 B4
Brighton 189 B1
Broadland Row 90 D3
Broad Oak Hastings ..90 C4
Broad Oak Heathfield .59 F1
Broad Street 116 C6
Broadwater Down 16 E7
Broomsgrove 137 A2
Brownbread Street ...110 A2
Broyle Side 124 F8
Buckham Hill 77 E6
Budlett's Common 55 C3
Bullingstone 6 E7
Bulverhythe 158 C6
Burgess Hill 73 D2
Burgh Hill 44 E3
Burlow 106 F5
Burnt Oak 37 F3
Burwash 62 B6
Burwash Common 61 A4
Burwash Weald 61 C3

Butcher's Cross 58 B8
Buxted 56 B4

C

Cackle Street Battle 85 E4
Cackle Street Hastings ..90 A2
Cackle Street Uckfield ..35 E2
Cade Street 82 E6
Caldbec Hill 112 D6
Camber 94 F2
Camden Park 8 C2
Canadia 112 D8
Caneheath 151 B4
Castle Hill 39 A4
Catsfield 133 F8
Catsfield Stream 133 E7
Chailey 75 E4
Chalvington 150 A7
Chapel Row 130 F5
Chapman's Town 83 B2
Chelwood Common 34 D6
Chelwood Gate 34 D8
Chiddingly 105 F1
Chiltington 100 D3
Chitcombe 89 E6
Chuck Hatch 24 D7
Churches Green 109 B8
Cinder Hill 33 B8
Clayhill 67 D3
Clayton 119 E8
Cliffe 190 B2
Cliff End 139 B7
Clive Vale 137 C2
Cobbarn 15 E3
Cock Marling 92 A2
Coggins Mill 40 D4

Coldean 143 D6
Coleman's Hatch 23 E7
Collier's Green 66 A2
Cooden 156 D2
Cooksbridge 123 A8
Cooper's Green 55 D4
Cornwell's Bank 76 C5
Cottenden 43 B5
Cousley Wood 30 C7
Cowbeech 108 C1
Cowbeech Hill 130 B7
Cowden 4 A6
Cripp's Corner 88 D7
Cross-in-Hand 81 B7
Crowborough 26 C1
Crowborough Warren ..25 C1
Crowhurst 134 F6
Crowlink 186 F7
Cuckfield 50 A6
Cuilfail 190 C2

D

Dallington 84 D3
Danehill 34 A4
Darwell Hole 85 F3
Deanland Village 127 B4
Denny Bottom 7 E4
Denton 168 F2
Ditchling 98 D3
Dodd's Hill 35 D2
Dormansland 2 B8
Dormans Park 1 E6
Downside 184 C4
Down Street 54 C5
Duddleswell 36 B4
Durgates 29 E5

E

Earl's Down 84 B4
East Blatchington ..180 E5
Eastbourne 185 B2
East Chiltington ...100 A3
East Dean 187 B8
East End 98 E3
East Grinstead 1 E2
East Guldeford 93 C7
East Hoathly 105 B5
East Moulsecoomb ..143 F3
Eridge Green 16 B3
Etchingham 44 B1
Etchingwood 56 D1
Ewhurst Green 66 B5
Exceat 181 F4

F

Fairlight 138 C4
Fairlight Cove 138 F5
Fairwarp 36 B2
Falmer 144 D6
Felbridge 1 A6
Felcourt 1 C8
Ferndale 8 C5
Filching 172 D3
Fishergate 162 A7
Five Ash Down 55 D5
Five Ashes 58 B7
Flackley Ash 68 F3
Fletching 53 F4
Fletching Common ...53 C1
Flimwell 32 C3
Flowers Green 130 F3

F (continued)

Folkington 172 B4
Fordcombe 6 B5
Ford's Green 35 C3
Forest Row 11 F3
Four Oaks 68 C5
Four Throws 46 D8
Foxhole 182 A1
Framfield 79 B6
Franklands Village 51 A4
Frant 17 C3
Friar's Gate 25 B7
Friar's Hill 138 B7
Friday Street 174 A3
Friston 183 A2
Furner's Green 34 C1

G

Gallypot Street 13 B3
Ginger's Green 130 C6
Glenleigh Park 157 A7
Glynde 147 E7
Glyne Gap 158 B5
Goatham Green 89 E5
Goddards' Green 72 A5
Golden Cross Hailsham . . 127 D6
Golden Cross
  Herstmonceux 130 E3
Green Street 135 B4
Grisling Common 77 B8
Groombridge 15 C7
Grove Hill 107 E1
Guestling Green 138 A8
Gun Hill 106 C2

H

Hadlow Down 57 C5
Hailsham 152 C8
Hale Green 106 A2
Halland 104 C5
Halton 137 B2
Hammerwood 3 B3
Hampden Park 173 E1
Hamsey 123 C6
Hangleton 141 C2
Hankham 174 B8
Harley Shute 158 E7
Hartfield 13 D4
Hassocks 97 E4
Hastings 159 F7
Hawkenbury 8 D2
Haywards Heath 50 C7
Hazard's Green 132 C5
Heathfield 82 B7
Hellingly 129 A5
Henley's Down 134 B6
Henwood Green 9 E6
Heron's Ghyll 36 E3
Herstmonceux 130 E6
High Brooms 8 C8
High Cross 39 C6
Highgate 11 F1
High Hurstwood 37 A1
High Wickham 137 C1
Holligdean 143 B3
Hollingbury 143 B5
Hollingrove 85 E6
Hollington 136 A4
Holton Hill 61 E7
Holtye 3 F3
Hooe 155 D8
Hooe Common 132 F2
Hook Green 19 C4
Horam 106 E7
Horney Common 54 E8
Horns Cross 67 A4
Horsted Green 78 A3
Horsted Keynes 33 C5
Houghton Green 70 D2
Hove 163 B5
Hungershall Park 7 E2
Hurst Green 45 B3
Hurstpierpoint 97 B6
Hurst Wickham 97 C6

I

Icklesham 116 E6
Iden 70 B4
Iford 146 B3
Isfield 102 E7

J

Jarvis Brook 38 D8
Jenkins' Green 174 C8
Jevington 183 C8
John's Cross 87 C7
Jury's Gap 95 D1

K

Kemp Town 164 D4
Keymer 98 B4
Kilndown 20 F3
Kings Bank 68 A3
Kingston by Sea 161 C7
Kingston near Lewes 145 E5
Kingstonridge 145 D6

L

Lamberhurst 20 B5
Landport 123 B2
Langney 174 D3
Langney Village 174 E2
Langton Green 6 E3
Laughton 126 C6
Lewes 123 C2
Lewes 190 B3
Lidham Hill 115 E6
Lindfield 51 A7
Linkhill 47 E4
Litlington 182 B8
Little Bayham 18 F4
Little Common 156 D5
Little Horsted 78 C1
Little London 81 E4
Little Norlington 102 F1
Little Parrock 12 D1
Lower Cousley Wood 30 E8
Lower Dicker 128 D3
Lower Green Pembury 9 D8
Lower Green
  Royal Tunbridge Wells 7 C5
Lower Horsebridge 128 F3
Lower Standean 120 A3
Lower Street 133 B5
Lower Willingdon 173 C4
Lunsford's Cross 133 E2
Lye Green 14 D1

M

Madeira Park 8 B2
Magham Down 129 F4
Marden's Hill 25 B5
Maresfield 55 A5
Maresfield Park 55 A6
Mark Cross 28 A4
Mark Street 34 F3
Marle Green 107 B5
Marlpits Bexhill 133 B7
Marlpits Crowborough . . . 35 E6
Mayfield 40 A2
Maynard's Green 82 A1
Meads 188 E8
Mile Oak 140 F4
Millbrook 35 C6
Mill Corner 67 A3
Mill Hill 174 D6
Milton Street 171 D5
Mott's Mill 15 A3
Moulsecoomb 143 E2
Mount Ephraim
  Royal Tunbridge Wells 7 F4
Mount Ephraim Uckfield . . 78 F3
Mountfield 87 C5
Mount Pleasant Lewes . . 101 F6
Mount Pleasant
  Newhaven 168 F1
Mount Sion 8 A2
Muddles Green 127 F8
Mutton Hall 82 A8

N

Nash Street 128 A6
Netherfield 86 C2
Nevill Park 7 D2
Newbridge 23 F6
Newbury's 30 B8
New Cut 114 E5
Newenden 48 D3
Newhaven 179 E6
Newick 76 C8
Newton's Hill 13 C3
New Town 78 E5
Ninfield 133 B6
Norlington 124 D7
Normans' Bay 176 D8
Northbridge Street 64 C6
North Chailey 75 E6
North End 1 B3
Northiam 67 B6
North Moulsecoomb 143 D4
Norton 180 C8
Nutley 35 C4

O

Offham 122 F5
Old Heathfield 82 D5
Old Town Bexhill 157 D5
Old Town Eastbourne . . . 184 D3
Old Town Hastings 160 B4
Ore 137 D3
Ovingdean 165 D3
Oxbottom 76 B5
Oxley's Green 85 E8

P

Patcham 142 F6
Peacehaven 178 D7
Peasmarsh 69 B2
Pebsham 158 A6
Pell Green 30 A7
Pembury 9 C6
Penhurst 110 E6
Pett 116 F1
Pett Level 139 B8
Pevensey 175 B6
Pevensey Bay 175 D4
Pick Hill 106 D4
Piddinghoe 168 A2
Piltdown 54 B1
Playden 93 C8
Plumpton 121 E8
Plumpton Green 99 E6
Polegate 173 B5
Ponts Green 110 B4
Portslade-by-Sea 162 B5
Portslade Village 141 B1
Potman's Heath 49 E4
Potter's Green 56 C3
Poundfield 26 A2
Poundford 58 B5
Poundgate 37 A6
Pound Green 56 D4
Poundsbridge 6 D8
Pounsley 80 B8
Preston 142 E1
Punnett's Town 83 C5
Pyecombe 119 B6

Q

Quabrook 12 C1

R

Ramslye 7 D1
Rickney 153 D2
Ridgewood 78 C4
Ringles Cross 55 C2
Ringmer 124 C6
Ripe 126 D1
Riseden 29 B1
Robertsbridge 64 B4
Rockrobin 29 D6
Rocks Park 78 A7
Rodmell 167 D8
Roedean 165 B4
Romford 9 F7
Rose Hill 102 F6
Roselands 185 B5
Roser's Cross 80 F6
Rotherfield 39 B7
Rottingdean 177 A6
Round Hill 164 B8
Royal Tunbridge Wells . . . 8 D3

S (top)

Rusher's Cross 40 E6
Rushlake Green 83 D2
Rushy Green 124 E5
Russell's Green 133 A3
Rusthall 7 C4
Rye 93 B6
Rye Foreign 69 E1
Rye Harbour 93 F2

S

St Annes 123 A1
St Anthony's Hill 185 C8
St Helen's 137 A5
St John's Crowborough . . 25 D4
St John's
  Royal Tunbridge Wells . . . 8 A5
St John's Common 72 E4
St Leonards 159 A7
St Leonard's Green 136 A1
Saint's Hill 6 A8
Salehurst 64 D5
Saltdean 177 D6
Sandhurst 47 C6
Sandhurst Cross 46 F4
Sandy Cross 82 B5
Scaynes Hill 51 E3
Seaford 180 D2
Sedlescombe 88 D1
Selmeston 149 D2
Sharpsbridge 77 C6
Sharpthorne 21 A6
Sheffield Green 53 C7
Shellies Green 138 C8
Sherwood 8 E6
Shoreham Beach 161 B6
Shoreham-by-Sea 161 A5
Shortbridge 77 E8
Shortgate 104 B3
Shover's Green 30 C1
Sidley 157 A7
Silver Hill 64 B8
Silverhill 136 C3
Silverhill Park 136 C4
Skippers Hill 58 B8
South Chailey 100 D7
Southease 167 E7
Southern Cross 162 A8
South Heighton 168 D2
South Malling 190 B3
Southover 146 B7
South Street 75 E1
Southwick 161 F7
Sparrow's Green 29 F5
Speldhurst 7 B7
Spithurst 101 F7
Splayne's Green 54 A5
Standard Hill 132 F6
Standen Street 47 D8
Stanmer 143 F8
Staplecross 65 E2
Starr's Green 112 F3
Steel Cross 26 B3
Steven's Crouch 111 B3
Stone Bridge 29 C5
Stone Cross Crowborough . 37 F6
Stone Cross Eastbourne . 174 C6
Stone Cross
  Royal Tunbridge Wells . . . 6 A2
Stonecrouch 31 F6
Stonegate 42 F6
Stonequarry 2 B3
Streat 99 C3
Stunts Green 130 F2
Summer Hill 152 A4
Sunnyside 10 D7
Sutton 181 B4
Sweethaws 37 C6
Swiftsden 44 F6

T

Tarring Neville 168 D4
Teasley Mead 5 C4
Telscombe 167 B3
Telscombe Cliffs 177 F4
The Brooks 190 B3
The Down 20 A3
The Highlands 156 F8
The Moor 45 F8
Three Cups Corner 83 F5
Three Leg Cross 31 D3
Three Oaks 115 E2
Ticehurst 31 E2

U

Tidebrook 41 A8
Tilsmore 81 F7
Tompset's Bank 22 F8
Town Littleworth 76 C1
Town Row 27 C2
Trolliloes 108 D2
Turner's Green 83 F4
Turner's Green 29 F6
Twelve Oaks 85 E5

U

Uckfield 78 D7
Udimore 91 D2
Union Street 32 B3
Upper Dicker 151 A8
Upper Hartfield 13 C4
Upper Horsebridge 129 B3
Upperton 184 F5
Upper Wellingham 124 B8

V

Vinehall Street 87 E6
Vine's Cross 107 D8

W

Wadhurst 30 A4
Waldron 80 F3
Waldron Down 80 D8
Wallands Park 123 B1
Walstead 51 C5
Walter's Green 5 E6
Wannock 172 E4
Warbleton 83 A1
Warren 188 C8
Wartling 154 D7
Wellbrook 39 E1
West Blatchington 141 F1
Westdean 182 B4
Westdene 142 B5
Westfield 114 F4
West Firle 148 C3
Westham 174 E5
West Hill 137 B1
West Marina 158 F5
Westmeston 120 F8
Whatlington 88 A1
Whitehawk 164 E5
Whitehill 37 F8
White Post 5 D7
Whitesmith 127 B8
Whydown 156 B8
Wickstreet 150 D6
Willard's Hill 63 C5
Willingdon 173 A1
Wilmington 171 F5
Wilmington Green 171 E7
Winchelsea 117 E7
Winchelsea Beach 118 A5
Windmill Hill 131 B6
Withdean 142 E4
Withyham 14 A3
Wivelsfield 74 B5
Wivelsfield Green 74 C4
Woodingdean 165 D7
Woodmans Green 88 A3
Wood's Corner 84 F3
Wood's Green 29 F8
Woolbridge 39 E2
World's End 73 D4
Wych Cross 22 C1

Abberton Field BN6 .....97 B5
Abbey Cl BN10 ....167 C1
Abbey Ct Battle TN33 ...112 D4
Robertsbridge TN32 .....64 B4
Abbey Dr TN38 ....158 B5
Abbey Mews TN32 ......64 B4
Abbey Path BN27 ......129 C2
Abbey Rd Brighton BN2 .164 D4
Eastbourne BN20 ....184 B5
Abbey View TN40 ......157 D6
Abbey Way TN33 ....112 D5
Abbeyfield Ho BN26 ....170 F3
Abbot's Lodge 9 BN21 .184 F4
Abbots Cl Battle TN33 ..112 D4
Hassocks BN6 ....97 A4
Abbotsbury Cl BN2 .....177 B5
Abbotsfield Cl TN34 ....136 F3
Abbotsford Com Specl Sch
RH15 ....72 E6
Abbotts 11 BN1 ....163 E5
Abbotts Cl BN22 ....185 A4
Abbotts Wood Forest Wlk*
BN26 ....151 B4
Aberdale Rd BN26 ......173 C6
Aberdeen Rd 5 BN2 ....164 C8
Abergavenny Rd BN7 ...123 B1
Abigail Ho 10 RH16 .....50 C4
Abinger Ct BN41 ....162 B8
Abinger Pl BN7 ....190 A2
Abinger Rd
Portslade-by-S BN41 ...162 B8
Woodingdean BN2 ......165 E6
Acacia Ave BN3 ....141 F1
Acacia Ct BN1 ....142 F2
Acacia Rd
Eastbourne BN22 ......173 D2
Newhaven BN9 ....168 E2
Acer Ave TN2 ....17 C8
Acerlands BN8 ....76 C8
Acorn Cl
East Grinstead RH19 ...10 E8
St Leonards TN37 ......136 C4
Acorn Gn 3 BN27 ......129 B1
Acorn Way TN19 ....45 A3
Acorns The
Burgess Hill RH15 ......72 D4
Hailsham BN27 ....152 D7
Stonegate TN5 ....42 F6
Acre Cl RH16 ....50 D2
Acres Rise TN5 ....31 E1
Adam Cl Crowborough TN6 38 A6
St Leonards TN38 ......135 F4
Adams Cl BN1 ....143 B2
Adams La TN31 ....66 D2
Adastra Ave BN4 ....98 A4
Addingham Rd BN22 ...185 C4
Addington Cl TN38 .....158 F7
Addison Rd BN3 ....163 E7
Adelaide Cl BN25 ......180 E5
Adelaide Cres BN3 .....163 C5
Adelaide Rd TN38 ......136 B3
Adelaide Sq BN43 ......161 B7
Ades Field BN26 ....171 F6
Admiral's Bridge La
RH19 ....10 C2
Admiralty Cres BN23 ..175 B1
Admiralty Ct BN23 .....175 B1
Admiralty Way BN23 ...175 B1
Adur Ct 10 BN43 ....161 C8
Adur Dr
Shoreham-by-S BN43 ...161 A4
Stone Cross BN24 ......174 A5
Adur Rd RH15 ....73 C4
Agincourt Cl TN37 .....135 F7
Agnes St BN2 ....164 C7
Ainsworth Ave BN2 ....165 D3
Ainsworth Cl BN2 .....165 D3
Ainsworth Ho 1 BN2 ..164 C7
Air St BN1 ....189 A2
Airlie Ho BN3 ....163 C6
Airy Rd BN27 ....131 B2
Akehurst Field TN33 ...110 B3
Alamein Cl TN6 ....38 A8
Alan Ct 6 TN37 ....159 C7
Alan Way BN2 ....164 F5
Albany Ct
Eastbourne BN21 ......184 F5
2 Hastings TN34 ......159 F7
Albany Hill TN2 ....8 C5
Albany Mans TN38 .....159 B8
Albany Mews BN3 .....163 B6
Albany Rd Bexhill TN40 .157 C3
Seaford BN25 ....180 C3
St Leonards TN38 .....159 B7
Albany Villas
Cuckfield RH17 ....50 A6
Hove BN3 ....163 B5
Albemarle Mans 9 BN3 163 B5
Albemarle The BN2 ....189 B1
Albert Cl RH16 ....51 A4
Albert Cotts TN1 ......8 B4
Albert Dr RH15 ....72 E2
Albert Mews BN3 ......163 C6
Albert Par BN21 ....184 C4
Albert Pl BN26 ....173 A7
Albert Rd Bexhill TN40 .157 C3
Brighton BN1 ....189 A3
Hastings TN34 ....159 F7
Polegate BN26 ....173 A2
Southwick BN42 ....161 C4
Uckfield TN22 ....78 D6
Albert St TN1 ....8 B4
Albert Terr BN21 ......184 C5
Albion Ct Brighton BN2 .189 C2
Burgess Hill RH15 ......72 F2

Albion Hill BN2 ....189 C3
Albion Ho
4 Brighton BN2 ....189 C3
Southwick BN42 ....161 F7
Albion La 4 TN34 .....160 A3
Albion Mews TN1 ......8 C5
Albion Rd
Eastbourne BN22 ......185 B4
Royal Tunbridge Wells TN1 ..8 C5
Albion St Brighton BN2 .189 C3
Lewes BN7 ....190 B2
Portslade-by-S BN41 ...162 B7
Southwick BN42 ....161 E7
Albourne Cl
Brighton BN2 ....164 F7
St Leonards TN38 ......158 F8
Alces Pl BN25 ....180 E5
Aldborough Rd TN37 ...136 C1
Aldenham Ct 1 BN21 ..184 F7
Alder Cl Eastbourne BN23 185 C8
Heathfield TN21 ....82 A5
St Leonards TN37 .....136 C5
Alder Lodge TN4 ......7 E4
Alderbrook Cl TN6 .....38 A6
Alderbrook Cotts TN6 ..38 A7
Alderbrook Path TN6 ...38 A6
Alderbrook Way TN6 ...38 A6
Alders Ave RH19 ......1 E3
Alders View Dr RH19 ...1 E3
Alderton Ct 7 TN39 ...157 B3
Aldervale Cotts TN6 ...38 A7
Aldrich Cl BN2 ....164 F6
Aldrington Ave BN3 ....163 A8
Aldrington CE Prim Sch
BN3 ....142 A2
Aldrington Cl BN3 .....162 F6
Aldrington House Hospl
BN3 ....162 F6
Aldrington Pl BN3 .....162 D8
Aldrington Sta BN3 ....163 A8
Alexander Dr TN39 ....156 E4
Alexander Mead BN8 ...76 D8
Alexandra Cl BN25 ....180 E5
Alexandra Ct BN3 .....141 F2
Alexandra Par TN34 ...136 C3
Alexandra Park Mans
TN34 ....136 E2
Alexandra Rd
Burgess Hill RH15 .....73 C2
Eastbourne BN22 ......185 D6
Heathfield TN21 ....82 B6
Mayfield TN20 ....40 C3
St Leonards TN37 .....159 C8
Uckfield TN22 ....78 D6
Alexandra Terr TN20 ...40 C3
Alexandra The TN37 ...159 D7
Alexandra Villas BN1 ..189 A3
Alford Way TN40 ......157 E6
Alfray Rd TN40 ....158 A4
Alfred Rd Brighton BN1 .189 A3
2 Eastbourne BN23 ...185 F8
Hastings TN35 ....160 D7
Alfred St TN38 ....159 C7
Alfriston Cl Bexhill TN39 156 C4
Brighton BN2 ....164 F6
Eastbourne BN20 ......184 C2
Alfriston Clergy Ho*
BN26 ....171 A4
Alfriston Pk BN25 .....181 C5
Alfriston Rd
Alfriston BN26 ....171 A5
Seaford BN25,BN26 ....181 D6
Alfriston St BN26 .....170 F3
Alice Bright La TN6 ....37 F7
Alice Cl 2 BN3 ....163 D5
Alice Hudson Gdns
BN23 ....185 D7
Alice St BN3 ....163 D5
All Saints CE Jun Sch
TN35 ....160 C6
All Saints CE Prim Sch
TN39 ....157 B7
All Saints Gdns TN21 ..81 F7
All Saints La TN39 .....157 B7
All Saints Rd TN4 .....8 B6
All Saints Rise TN4 ....8 B6
All Saints' & St Richard's CE
Prim Sch TN21 ....82 D6
All Saints' Cres TN35 ..160 B4
All Saints' Hospl BN20 .188 E7
All Saints' St TN34 ....160 B4
Allan Ct TN4 ....7 C4
Allandale Rd TN2 ......8 D7
Allards TN35 ....138 C8
Allegria Ct TN38 ......159 B7
Allen Gardiner Ho TN2 .8 C5
Allen Rd RH16 ....51 A4
Allen Way TN40 ....157 F7
Allen's Cl RH19 ....11 B1
Allfrey Rd BN22 ....185 D6
Allfreys La TN6 ....37 D6
Allington Cres BN8 ....76 C7
Allington La BN7 ......122 D7
Allington Rd BN8 ......76 C6
Allwood Cres RH17 ....74 C4
Alma Rd RH16 ....51 B8
Alma Terr TN37 ....136 C2
Alma Villas TN37 ......136 C2
Almonry Fields TN33 ..112 B4
Alpine Rd Hastings TN34 160 A4
Hove BN3 ....162 F8
Alverstone Rd BN23 ...174 D1
Amanda Cl TN40 ......157 D7
Ambassadors The 10
BN3 ....163 C6
Amber Ct 19 Hove BN3 .163 C6
8 Hove BN3 ....163 C6
Amberleaze Dr TN2 ...9 D6

Amberley Cl
Burgess Hill RH15 .....73 A4
Haywards Heath RH16 ..50 D4
Hove BN3 ....141 E3
Amberley Ct TN4 ......8 C8
Amberley Dr BN3 ......141 E3
Amberley Lodge
Brighton BN2 ....189 B4
Brighton,Whitehawk BN2 .164 F6
Amberley Rd BN22 ....173 C1
Amberstone BN27 .....129 E3
Amberstone Cl TN34 ..160 A8
Amberstone Hospl
BN27 ....129 E4
Amberstone View BN27 .129 C2
Ambleside Ave BN10 ..178 A8
Ambleside Cl BN10 ....178 A7
America La RH16 ......51 A5
Amesbury Cres BN3 ...162 F2
Amherst Cl TN34 ......136 D1
Amherst Cres BN3 .....162 F8
Amherst Gdns TN34 ...136 D1
Amherst Rd Bexhill TN40 157 C4
Hastings TN34 ....136 D1
Royal Tunbridge Wells TN4 ..8 A5
Amhurst Rd BN10 .....177 F3
Anchor Cl BN43 ....161 A6
Anchor Field BN8 .....124 D5
Anchor Hill RH17 ......52 A2
Anchor La BN8 ....102 B5
Anchorage The RH16 ..50 D5
Anchorage Way BN23 .175 B2
Anderida Ct TN39 .....156 C4
Anderida Rd BN22 ....173 C3
Anderson Cl TN39 .....179 B7
Andrew Rd TN4 ....8 C8
Andrews Cl
Northbridge Street TN32 ..64 C5
Royal Tunbridge Wells TN2 ..8 D5
Andros Cl BN8 ....100 E6
Andwell Ct BN21 ......185 B2
Angel Ct 1 BN21 .....185 A4
Angel Row BN18 ......47 B5
Angel Terr TN18 ......47 B6
Angela Ct TN40 ....157 F7
Anglesea Mans TN38 ..159 B8
Anglesea Terr TN37,
TN38 ....159 C8
Anglesey Ave BN27 ...129 A2
Angmering Ct BN1 ....143 F5
Angrove Ho TN6 ......25 D2
Angus Cl BN20 ....173 B1
Anjou Ct BN23 ....174 F1
Ann Cl BN6 ....98 A5
Ann St Brighton BN1 ..189 B4
Anne's Path BN7 ......190 A1
Annecy RC Prim Sch
BN25 ....181 A2
Annington Rd BN22 ...185 B5
Anscombe 5 RH16 ....50 D6
Anson Cl BN23 ....185 E4
Anson Ho BN10 ....167 C1
Ansty Cl BN2 ....164 E5
Antares Path BN27 ....152 E7
Antigua Cl 14 BN23 ...185 F8
Antioch St BN7 ....190 A1
Antony Cl BN25 ....180 B6
Antrim Ct BN23 ....174 D1
Antrona Ct TN39 ......156 C3
Anvil Cl
Portslade-by-S BN41 ...141 B2
Uckfield TN22 ....78 B6
Anvil Ct TN37 ....136 C5
Anzac Cl BN10 ....167 C1
Apex Pk BN27 ....152 A7
Apple Tree La TN2 ....8 D8
Appledene Cnr BN8 ...100 E7
Appledore Cl BN23 ...174 D2
Appledore Ct RH16 ...51 A7
Appledore Gdns RH16 .51 A6
Applesham Ave BN3 ..141 E4
Applesham Way BN41 .141 A1
Applewood Ct TN37 ..136 B5
Approach The
10 Brighton BN1 ......142 E3
Dormans Park RH19 ....1 F6
April Pl 4 TN40 ......157 C4
Apsley St TN4 ....7 D4
Aqua Ho BN1 ....177 F3
Aquarius Cl BN10 ....178 C6
Aquila Pk BN25 ....181 A3
Araquipe Reef BN23 ..185 G8
Arbor Ct TN4 ....8 B6
Arbourvale TN38 ......136 A1
Arbroath Ct 3 TN38 ..136 B1
Arcade The TN34 ......190 C2
Archer Ct RH15 ....73 A3
Archers TN35 ....136 F6
Archery Ct
Eastbourne BN22 .....185 C6
3 St Leonards TN38 ...159 B6
Archery Rd TN38 ......159 B7
Archery Wlk BN27 ....152 C6
Archie Ct 7 TN38 .....159 B6
Ardingly Ct 10 BN2 ...189 C2
Ardingly Rd BN2 ......177 D4
Ardingly St BN2 ......189 C2
Argent Cl BN25 ....181 A5
Argos Hill Rd TN20,TN6 ..39 D4
Argus Hill BN25 ....189 B3
Argus Lofts BN1 ......189 B3
Argyle Rd BN1 ....189 A4
Argyll Ct 3 Bexhill TN39 157 A4
Eastbourne BN22 .....173 E2

Arkendale RH19 ....1 A4
Arkwright Rd BN23 ....174 A1
Arlington Cres BN1 ...143 E5
Arlington Ct RH16 ....50 E5
Arlington Gdns BN2 ...177 D6
Arlington Ho 7 BN21 .184 D4
Arlington Rd BN21 ....184 F3
Arlington Rd E BN27 ..152 A6
Arlington Rd W BN27 .151 F6
Arlington Resr* BN26 .150 C3
Armstrong Cl TN38 ....135 E4
Arnbury Mews TN38 ..158 E6
Arnold St BN2 ....164 C7
Arnside Rd TN38 ......158 E6
Arnworth Ct BN21 ....184 F2
Arran Cl BN27 ....129 A2
Arthur Bliss Ho RH16 ..51 A8
Arthur Rd TN39 ....157 B4
Arthur St BN3 ....163 A8
Artisans Dwellings 8
BN21 ....184 F2
Arts Rd BN1 ....144 B7
Arun Cl BN24 ....173 D5
Arun Ct BN43 ....161 C8
Arun Lodge BN21 .....184 E3
Arun Path TN22 ......55 E1
Arun Way BN24 ....173 F5
Arundel Cl
Beachlands BN24 ......175 F6
Hailsham BN27 ....129 C2
Shoreham-by-S BN43 ..161 C8
Arundel Ct
6 Brighton BN2 ......164 E4
Brighton,Westdene BN1 ..142 C5
Burgess Hill RH15 ....72 F4
Hastings TN35 ....160 C6
Arundel Dr E BN2 .....177 C5
Arundel Dr W BN2 ....177 C5
Arundel Gn BN7 ......123 B2
Arundel Ho 15 BN21 ..184 E4
Arundel Keep 11 BN21 .184 F4
Arundel Mews
10 Brighton BN2 ......164 E4
Haywards Heath RH16 ..50 F2
Arundel Pl BN2 ....164 E3
Arundel Rd Brighton BN2 164 E4
Eastbourne BN21 .....184 F4
Newhaven BN9 ....168 F1
Peacehaven BN10 .....178 F8
Royal Tunbridge Wells TN1 ..8 C5
Seaford BN25 ....181 A3
Arundel Rd W BN10 ..178 B7
Arundel Road Central
BN10 ....178 B7
Arundel St BN2 ....164 E3
Arundel Terr BN2 .....164 E3
Ascham Pl BN20 ......184 E1
Ascot Cl BN20 ....188 F8
Ascot Mews TN38 ....159 A8
Ash Cl Eastbourne BN22 173 C3
Hove BN3 ....142 C3
Royal Tunbridge Wells TN2 ..17 D7
Ash Ct East Grinstead RH19 ..1 A7
Hailsham BN27 ....152 A7
Southwick BN42 ......140 F1
Ash Dr BN25 ....181 C3
Ash Gr
Haywards Heath RH16 ..50 D2
Westham BN24 ....174 D6
Ash Tree Cl TN21 .....82 A7
Ash Wlk BN9 ....179 B7
Ashampstead Pl 4
BN21 ....184 F3
Ashbourne Ct
13 Eastbourne BN21 ..185 A2
Rusthall TN4 ....7 D4
Ashbrook Rd TN38 ....136 B4
Ashburnham Cl BN1 ..143 E5
Ashburnham Dr BN1 ..143 E5
Ashburnham Gdns
BN21 ....184 E5
Ashburnham Ho BN1 ..142 E5
Ashburnham Pl BN27 .129 A2
Ashburnham Rd
Eastbourne BN21 .....184 D4
Hastings TN35 ....160 C6
Ashby Cl TN39 ....157 A8
Ashcombe Dr TN39 ...156 D3
Ashcombe Hollow BN7 .145 D2
Ashcombe La BN7 ....145 E5
Ashcroft 1 BN43 .....161 C8
Ashcroft Ringmer BN8 .124 D5
Shoreham-by-S BN43 ..161 D8
Ashdown 14 BN3 .....163 C6
Ashdown Ave BN2 ....177 D6
Ashdown Chase TN22 .35 C5
Ashdown Cl
Forest Row RH18 .....12 A2
Haywards Heath RH16 ..51 B4
Royal Tunbridge Wells TN4 ..7 F4
St Leonards TN38 .....135 E4
Ashdown Ct
Crowborough TN6 .....25 E2
Uckfield TN22 ....78 D6
Ashdown Forest Llama
Farm* RH18 ....22 E4
Ashdown Forest Riding Ctr
TN22 ....36 B6
Ashdown Forest Visitors
Ctr* RH18 ....23 A5
Ashdown Gate RH19 ..1 D2
Ashdown House Sch
RH18 ....12 C2
Ashdown Nuffield Hospl
RH16 ....50 D6

Ashdown Pl
Forest Row RH18 .....22 E8
Heathfield TN21 ....82 B6
Ashdown Rd
Bexhill TN40 ....157 E4
7 Brighton BN2 ......164 B8
Forest Row RH18 .....11 F2
Ashdown View
East Grinstead RH19 ..10 E7
Marlpits TN22 ....35 D6
Ashenden Ave TN31 ..93 A5
Ashenden Wlk TN2 ...8 E8
Ashengrove Cl 6 RH16 50 E3
Ashenground Rd RH16 .50 E3
Asher Reeds TN3 .....7 A4
Ashford Cl 4 BN27 ...152 C7
Ashford Rd Brighton BN1 143 A2
Eastbourne BN21 .....185 A3
Hastings TN34 ....136 E2
Ashford Sq BN21 .....185 A3
Ashford Way TN34 ....136 E2
Ashgate Rd BN25 .....174 E2
Ashington Ct BN2 .....164 F6
Ashington Gdns BN10 .178 F6
Ashington Rd BN22 ...174 A1
Ashlands TN6 ....26 B1
Ashleigh Gdns TN6 ...25 E4
Ashleigh Glegg Ho
BN25 ....180 C4
Ashley Cl BN1 ....142 E5
Ashley Ct Hove BN3 ..163 C5
7 St Leonards TN37 ..159 C7
Ashley Gdns
Hailsham BN27 ....129 C3
Mayfield TN20 ....40 A2
Rusthall TN4 ....7 C5
Ashley Park Cl TN4 ...7 C5
Ashley Pk TN4 ....7 C5
Ashley Rd TN6 ....27 C1
Ashlings Way Hove BN3 141 E2
Shoreham-by-S BN43 ..140 B1
Ashmore Cl BN10 .....167 C2
Ashtead Twrs 8 TN40 .157 E4
Ashton Lodge 15 BN2 .189 C3
Ashton Rise BN2 ......189 C3
Ashtonville Cl BN8 ....124 C5
Ashurst Ave BN2 .....177 C5
Ashurst Hill TN3 ......5 D2
Ashurst Pl RH16 ......50 E5
Ashurst Rd Brighton BN2 143 F5
Seaford BN25 ....180 C2
Stone Cross TN3 ......6 B2
Ashurst Sta TN3 ......5 D2
Ashurst Wood Prim Sch
RH19 ....11 E6
Ashurstwood Abbey
RH19 ....11 E6
Ashway RH15 ....73 B3
Ashwood Ct RH18 ....11 F1
Ashwyn Bsns Ctr RH15 .72 F5
Aspen Cl RH16 ....51 B4
Aspen Rd BN22 ....173 E2
Aspen Way TN39 .....156 C4
Aspen Wlk
Haywards Heath RH16 ..51 B4
Heathfield TN21 ....82 B5
Assissi Ct RH16 ......50 F2
Assissi Hts RH16 .....50 F2
Astaire Ave BN22 .....185 B6
Asten Cl TN38 ....158 E7
Asten Fields BN23 ....112 C4
Astra Ho 10 BN1 .....163 E5
Athelstan Cl 1 BN23 ..185 F8
Athelstan Rd TN35 ...160 D6
Athenaeum The 16 BN3 163 F7
Atlantic Dr BN23 ......185 F7
Atlingworth Ct BN2 ...189 C1
Atlingworth St BN2 ...189 C1
Attfield Wlk BN22 ....173 F3
Attree Ct 6 BN2 .....164 C6
Attree Dr BN2 ....164 C6
Aubyns 15 TN40 ......157 D3
Auckland Dr BN2 .....143 F1
Auckland Ho TN40 ...157 C7
Auckland Quay BN23 .175 A1
Auckland Rd TN1 .....8 C5
Audrey Cl Brighton BN1 142 E5
Seaford BN25 ....180 D5
Audrey Sturley Ct TN4 .7 D4
Augustines Way RH16 .50 F4
Augustus Way TN37 ..135 F6
Aultmore Ct TN2 .....8 D3
Austen Cl RH19 ......1 B1
Austen Way TN35 ....137 D5
Austen Wlk BN23 .....174 D2
Avard Cres BN20 .....184 B6
Avards Cl TN38 ....45 E8
Avenue Cl 20 BN3 ...163 C6
Avenue La BN21 ......184 F3
Avenue The
Brighton BN2 ....143 E1
Eastbourne BN21 .....184 F3
Fairlight Cove TN35 ...138 C4
Hailsham BN27 ....152 B6
Heathfield TN21 ....82 B6
Horam TN21 ....106 F8
Kingston near Lewes BN7 .145 D2
Lewes BN7 ....190 A2
Mayfield TN20 ....40 B2
Avery Cl BN41 ....140 F4
Aviemore Rd TN6 .....25 D2
Avis Cl BN9 ....168 E1
Avis Par BN9 ....168 E1
Avis Rd BN9 ....168 E1
Avis Way BN9 ....168 E1

Avocet BN27 . . . .**152** A7
Avocet Trad Est RH15 . . . . .**72** F2
Avon Ct BN2 . . . .**189** C2
Avon St TN1 . . . .**8** C5
Avondale Ct **1** BN25 . . .**180** E3
Avondale Rd
　Eastbourne BN22 . . . .**185** B4
　Hove BN3 . . . .**163** D7
　Seaford BN25 . . . .**180** F3
　St Leonards TN38 . . . . . .**136** A1
Avonhurst RH15 . . . .**73** B3
Avonmore BN20 . . . .**188** E8
Awbrook Cl RH17 . . . .**51** F3
Aylesbury BN3 . . . .**163** E6
Aylesbury Ave BN23 . . . . .**185** E8
Aymer Ho **4** BN3 . . . . . .**163** A6
Aymer Rd BN3 . . . .**163** A6
Aynsley Ct BN3 . . . .**163** C8
Ayscue Ct BN23 . . . .**185** F4

B

Babylon Way BN20 . . . . . .**184** B8
Back La Alfriston BN26 . . .**171** C4
　Cross-in-H TN21 . . . .**81** C6
　Fairwarp TN22 . . . .**36** B2
　Rushlake Green TN21 . . . . . .**83** D1
　Winchelsea TN36 . . . .**117** E7
Back Rd TN18 . . . .**47** B5
Backwoods Cl RH16 . . . . . .**51** B6
Backwoods La RH16 . . . . . .**51** B6
Baden Rd BN2 . . . .**143** C5
Badens Cl BN8 . . . .**76** C6
Badger Cl BN41 . . . .**141** B2
Badger Dr RH16 . . . .**50** C5
Badger Gate TN31 . . . .**93** A5
Badger Way BN1 . . . .**143** E6
Badgers Brow BN20 . . . . . .**184** B8
Badgers Cl
　Crowborough TN6 . . . .**25** C3
　Newhaven BN9 . . . .**179** D6
Badgers Copse BN25 . . . .**181** C3
Badgers Ct BN20 . . . .**188** F8
Badgers Dene BN7 . . . . . .**167** D8
Badgers Field BN10 . . . . .**167** C1
Badgers Holt TN2 . . . .**8** E5
Badgers Mount TN39 . . . .**156** E5
Badgers Way
　East Grinstead RH19 . . . .**1** F2
　Hastings TN34 . . . .**136** D5
Badgers Wlk
　Burgess Hill RH15 . . . .**73** D2
　Golden Cross BN27 . . . . . .**127** C3
Badlesmere Rd BN22 . . . .**185** B6
Bagham La BN27 . . . .**130** F6
Bahram Rd BN26 . . . .**172** F6
Bailey Cres BN22 . . . .**173** B3
Baillie Ave BN22 . . . .**185** C5
Bainbridge Cl BN25 . . . . .**180** F3
Bainden Cl TN6 . . . .**27** D1
Baird Dr BN3 . . . .**136** E3
Baird Ho TN37 . . . .**159** C8
Baker Ct TN22 . . . .**78** C7
Baker St Brighton BN1 . . .**189** B4
　Newhaven BN9 . . . .**179** E7
　Uckfield TN22 . . . .**78** D6
Baker's Rd BN21 . . . .**184** C3
Bakers Farm Mobile Home
　Pk BN27 . . . .**129** A3
Bakery Mews BN1 . . . . . .**143** C1
Bakewell Rd BN21 . . . . . .**184** D4
Bal Edmund TN37 . . . .**136** B4
Balaclava La TN5 . . . .**30** A6
Balcombe Ct BN10 . . . . . .**178** C8
Balcombe Gn TN33 . . . .**88** E1
Balcombe La RH17,RH19 . . .**21** E2
Balcombe Rd
　Haywards Heath RH16 . . . .**50** D7
　Peacehaven BN10 . . . . . .**178** B8
Baldings Cotts RH17 . . . . .**74** B5
Baldock Rd TN5 . . . .**29** E4
Baldslow Down TN37 . . . .**136** C8
Baldslow Rd TN34 . . . . . .**136** F1
Baldwin Ave BN21 . . . . . .**184** C5
Baldwins Field RH19 . . . .**1** C4
Baldwins Hill Prim Sch
　RH19 . . . .**1** D3
Bale Cl TN39 . . . .**156** C5
Balfour Gdns RH18 . . . .**11** E1
Balfour Inf Sch BN1 . . . . .**143** A3
Balfour Jun Sch BN1 . . . . .**143** A3
Balfour Rd BN1 . . . .**143** A2
Ball's Gn TN7 . . . .**14** B5
Ballard Dr BN8 . . . .**125** A7
Ballards Hill TN33 . . . .**134** F4
Ballsocks La TN21 . . . . . .**107** C8
Balmer Farm Cotts BN7 . .**144** D8
Balmoral RH19 . . . .**11** A8
Balmoral Ct BN25 . . . .**181** A6
Balmoral Ct Hove BN3 . . .**142** A3
　2 St Leonards TN38 . . .**136** B1
Balsdean Rd BN2 . . . .**144** F1
Baltic Ho TN1 . . . .**8** B5
Baltimore Ct **9** BN3 . . . .**163** C7
Bamford Cl BN2 . . . .**144** A2
Bampfield St BN41 . . . . . .**162** B8
Bancroft Ho TN39 . . . .**157** B5
Bancroft Rd TN39 . . . .**157** B5
Bank Rd TN39 . . . .**157** C7
Banks Rd BN8 . . . .**52** F1
Bankside Brighton BN1 . . .**142** C5
　Durgates TN5 . . . .**29** E5
　Hassocks BN6 . . . .**97** F5
　Rye TN31 . . . .**93** B6

Bankside Ct BN1 . . . .**142** C5
Banner Cl BN21 . . . .**184** D4
Banner Farm Rd TN2 . . . .**8** B2
Banner Way BN2 . . . .**174** C6
Bannings Vale BN2 . . . . . .**177** E5
Bannister Way BN16 . . . . . .**50** D6
Bannisters Field BN8 . . . . .**76** D7
Baranscraig Ave BN1 . . . .**143** A7
Barbados BN40 . . . .**157** E3
Barber Ct BN7 . . . .**146** B8
Barbican House Mus★
　BN7 . . . .**190** A2
Barbuda Quay BN23 . . . . .**185** G7
Barchester Pl **17** BN21 . .**185** A2
Barclay Ho **2** BN2 . . . . .**164** C7
Barcombe Ave BN25 . . . . .**181** C3
Barcombe CE Prim Sch
　BN8 . . . .**101** D5
Barcombe Cl
　Eastbourne BN20 . . . .**184** C3
　Seaford BN25 . . . .**181** C3
Barcombe Mills Rd BN8 101 E4
Barcombe Pl
　Brighton BN1 . . . .**143** F5
　12 Crowborough TN6 . . . . .**25** F3
Barcombe Rd BN1 . . . .**143** E4
Barcombe Wlk BN20 . . . . .**184** C3
Barden Rd
　Eastbourne BN22 . . . .**185** C4
　Speldhurst TN3 . . . .**7** A8
Bardown Rd TN5 . . . .**42** E7
Barford Ct TN22 . . . .**78** C7
Barganny **17** TN40 . . . . .**157** D3
Bargate Cl TN39 . . . .**157** C7
Barham Cl TN34 . . . .**136** D4
Barkdale RH15 . . . .**73** D5
Barley Ave TN35 . . . .**160** C5
Barley Cl BN10 . . . .**167** B2
Barley Dr RH15 . . . .**72** D4
Barley Field Cotts BN7 . . .**146** D1
Barley La TN35 . . . .**160** D5
Barley Mow La TN21 . . . . . .**83** B5
Barming Cl BN23 . . . .**174** C2
Barn Cl Hailsham BN27 . . .**129** C1
　Kingston near Lewes BN7 . . .**145** C3
　Seaford BN25 . . . .**181** A6
　Stone Cross BN24 . . . .**174** A6
Barn Cottage La RH16 . . . .**51** A5
Barn Cotts **2** BN25 . . . .**181** A3
Barn Ct Southwick BN42 . . .**162** A7
　St Leonards TN37 . . . .**136** C5
Barn Hatch Cl BN7 . . . . . .**146** A8
Barn Ho The BN25 . . . . . .**180** E5
Barn La TN22 . . . .**79** D8
Barn Rd BN7 . . . .**190** C4
Barn Rise Brighton BN1 . . .**142** D5
　Seaford BN25 . . . .**181** A5
Barn Stables **2** BN2 . . .**123** B1
Barnard Gate RH16 . . . . . .**50** E7
Barnes Rd BN41 . . . .**162** B8
Barnet Way BN1 . . . .**141** E3
Barnett Rd BN1 . . . .**143** B2
Barnett Way TN22 . . . .**78** D7
Barnetts Way TN4 . . . .**8** C8
Barnfield
　Crowborough TN6 . . . .**26** A3
　Plumpton Green BN7 . . . . . .**99** E5
　Royal Tunbridge Wells TN2 . .**16** F7
Barnfield Cl TN34 . . . .**159** D8
Barnfield Gdns
　8 Brighton BN2 . . . . . .**164** C6
　Ditchling BN6 . . . .**98** E3
Barnham Cl BN22 . . . .**174** A2
Barnhams The TN39 . . . . .**156** E3
Barnhorn Cl TN39 . . . .**156** C4
Barnhorn Rd TN39 . . . . . .**156** B4
Barnmead RH16 . . . .**50** E7
Barnsgate Manor Vineyard★
　TN22 . . . .**36** E5
Barnside Ave RH15 . . . . . .**73** D1
Barons Cl BN25 . . . .**180** C5
Barons Ct
　Burgess Hill RH15 . . . .**73** B2
　Royal Tunbridge Wells TN2 . . .**8** A5
Barons Down Rd BN7 . . . .**146** A8
Barons Way BN26 . . . .**172** F5
Barons Wlk BN7 . . . .**146** A8
Barrack Rd TN39 . . . .**157** C5
Barrack Sq TN36 . . . .**117** F7
Barracks Cotts TN32 . . . . .**87** C7
Barrhill Ave BN1 . . . .**142** F7
Barrie Rd BN23 . . . .**174** E2
Barrier Reef Way BN23 . . .**175** A1
Barrington Cl RH16 . . . . . .**50** F8
Barrington Rd RH16 . . . . . .**51** A8
Barrington Wood RH16 . . . .**50** F8
Barrow Cl BN1 . . . .**143** C2
Barrow Hill BN1 . . . .**143** C2
Barrow La TN3 . . . .**6** F2
Barrow Rise TN37 . . . .**136** C5
Barrowfield Cl BN3 . . . . . .**142** C3
Barrowfield Dr BN3 . . . . . .**142** D2
Barrowfield Lodge BN3 142 C2
Barry Wlk BN2 . . . .**164** C6
Bartholomew Sq BN1 . . . .**189** B2
Bartholomews BN1 . . . . . .**189** B2
Bartley Mill Rd BN24 . . . .**174** B5
Bartley Mill La TN3 . . . .**18** E4
Bartley Mill Rd TN3 . . . .**18** F3
Barton Cres RH19 . . . .**11** A8
Basin Rd N BN41 . . . .**162** B6
Basin Rd S BN3,BN41 . . . .**162** B6
Baslow Cl BN20 . . . .**188** D7
Baslow Rd BN20 . . . .**188** D7
Bassett's Forge TN5 . . . . . .**29** E5
Bassetts La
　Argos Hill TN20 . . . .**39** F5
　Mark Cross TN6 . . . .**28** E2

Bassetts La continued
　White Post TN8,TN11 . . . .**5** C7
Batchelor Cres TN6 . . . . . .**25** F3
Batchelor Way TN22 . . . . . .**78** A7
Batchelors TN2 . . . .**9** E8
Bates Rd BN1 . . . .**142** F2
Bath Cl BN3 . . . .**163** A5
Bath Rd **4** BN21 . . . . . .**184** F2
Bath St BN1 . . . .**189** A4
Bathford Cl BN23 . . . .**174** D2
Battenhurst Rd TN5 . . . .**43** B4
Battery Hill TN35 . . . .**138** D5
Battle & Langton CE Prim
　Sch TN33 . . . .**112** C4
Battle Abbey★ TN33 . . . .**112** D4
Battle Abbey Sch TN33 . . .**112** D4
Battle Cl BN25 . . . .**181** C5
Battle Cres
　Hailsham BN27 . . . .**152** B8
　St Leonards TN37 . . . .**136** B4
Battle Gates TN33 . . . .**112** B5
Battle Hill TN33 . . . .**112** E3
Battle Rd Hailsham BN27 .**129** C1
　St Leonards TN37 . . . .**136** A4
Battle Sta TN33 . . . .**112** C4
Batts Bridge Rd TN22 . . . . .**55** A4
Bavant Rd BN1 . . . .**142** E2
Baxter Rd BN7 . . . .**123** B2
Baxter St BN2 . . . .**164** C7
Baxters La RH17 . . . .**34** C6
Bay Ave BN24 . . . .**175** E5
Bay Cotts BN24 . . . .**176** C7
Bay Pond Rd BN21 . . . . . .**184** D4
Bay Rd BN24 . . . .**175** D4
Bay Terr BN24 . . . .**175** D5
Bay Tree Cl
　Heathfield TN21 . . . .**82** C5
　Shoreham-by-S BN43 . . . .**140** C1
Bay Tree La BN26 . . . .**172** F8
Bay View Cvn Pk BN24 . . .**175** B2
Bay Vue Rd BN9 . . . .**179** D7
Bayencourt N **1** TN40 . .**157** C5
Bayencourt S **2** TN40 . . .**157** C5
Bayeux Rd Bexhill TN40 . .**157** D3
　St Leonards TN37 . . . .**159** D8
Bayhall Rd TN2 . . . .**8** C3
Bayham Old Abbey★
　TN3 . . . .**19** B5
Bayham Rd
　Bells Yew Green TN3 . . . . . .**18** B4
　Eastbourne BN22 . . . .**185** B4
　Hailsham BN27 . . . .**152** D7
　Royal Tunbridge Wells TN2,
　TN3 . . . .**17** C7
Bayley's La BN26 . . . .**151** B2
Baylis Cres RH15 . . . .**72** D4
Bayview Rd BN10 . . . .**178** E5
Baywood Gdns BN2 . . . . .**165** C8
Bazehill Rd BN2 . . . .**165** F2
Beach Cl BN25 . . . .**180** D3
Beach Cotts BN25 . . . .**180** C4
Beach Ct **12** BN43 . . . . .**161** A6
Beach Mews
　7 Eastbourne BN22 . . . .**185** C5
　Newhaven BN9 . . . .**179** E7
Beach Rd
　Eastbourne BN22 . . . .**185** C5
　Newhaven BN9 . . . .**179** E6
Beachings The BN24 . . . . .**175** C4
Beachy Head Countryside
　Ctr★ **188** B4
Beachy Head Rd
　Eastbourne BN20 . . . .**188** C4
　Eastbourne BN20 . . . .**188** D8
Beachy Head View
　TN37 . . . .**135** F7
Beacon Bsns Pk TN6 . . . . .**38** C8
Beacon Cl Brighton BN1 . .**143** A2
　Crowborough TN6 . . . .**25** E2
　Seaford BN25 . . . .**180** D5
Beacon Com Coll
　Crowborough TN6 . . . .**26** A2
　Crowborough TN6 . . . .**26** B3
Beacon Ct BN2 . . . .**165** D4
Beacon Dr BN25 . . . .**180** E5
Beacon Gdns TN6 . . . .**25** E2
Beacon Hill Bexhill TN39 . .**157** A8
　Dormansland RH7 . . . .**2** B3
　Ovingdean BN2 . . . .**165** E3
Beacon Ho **5** BN3 . . . . .**162** D7
Beacon Hurst BN6 . . . .**98** B3
Beacon La TN32 . . . .**88** E7
Beacon Rd
　Crowborough TN6 . . . .**25** E2
　Ditchling BN6 . . . .**98** D2
　Hastings TN35 . . . .**160** E8
　Seaford BN25 . . . .**180** D4
Beacon Rd W TN6 . . . .**25** D2
Beaconfield Ho TN6 . . . . . .**25** E2
Beaconsfield Cotts RH17 .**51** F3
Beaconsfield Rd
　Bexhill TN40 . . . .**157** C6
　Brighton BN1 . . . .**164** A8
　Chelwood Gate RH17 . . . . . .**34** D8
　Hastings TN34 . . . .**136** F2
　Portslade-by-S BN41 . . . . .**162** B8
Beaconsfield Terr TN21 . . .**81** D4
Beaconsfield Villas BN1 142 F1
Beaconsville BN1 . . . .**142** F1
Beagles Wood Rd TN2 . . . . .**9** E7
Beal Cres BN1 . . . .**143** B2
Beale St RH15 . . . .**72** F1
Beales La TN31 . . . .**67** B6
Beame Ct BN25 . . . .**180** D3

Beamsley Rd BN22 . . . . . .**185** C4
Beaney's La TN34,TN35 . .**136** E6
Bear Rd BN2 . . . .**164** D8
Bear Yd BN7 . . . .**190** B2
Beatrice La **2** BN21 . . . .**184** F4
Beatrice Wlk TN39 . . . . . .**157** A6
Beatty Ave BN1 . . . .**143** D6
Beatty Rd BN23 . . . .**185** E7
Beau Ho BN1 . . . .**189** A4
Beauchamp Rd TN38 . . . .**136** A4
Beauford Rd TN21 . . . . . .**106** F7
Beaufort Cres TN37 . . . . .**136** C2
Beaufort Ct TN37 . . . .**136** C2
Beaufort Ho **18** TN37 . . .**159** C7
Beaufort Rd TN37 . . . .**136** C2
Beaufort Terr BN2 . . . .**164** C6
Beauharrow Rd TN37 . . . .**136** A6
Beaulieu Ct TN40 . . . .**157** C5
Beaulieu Dr BN24 . . . .**174** A5
Beaulieu Gdns TN37 . . . . .**136** C6
Beaulieu Lodge TN39 . . . .**156** C2
Beaulieu Rd TN39 . . . .**156** D2
Beauport Gdns TN37 . . . .**136** A7
Beauport Home Farm Cl
　TN37 . . . .**136** A6
Beaver Cl TN6 . . . .**26** A1
Beckenham Cl BN27 . . . . .**129** B3
Becket Cl TN34 . . . .**160** A5
Beckets Way TN22 . . . .**79** B5
Beckett Way
　11 East Grinstead RH19 . . .**10** C3
　Lewes BN7 . . . .**190** A4
Beckley CE Prim Sch
　TN31 . . . .**68** A4
Beckley Cl Brighton BN2 .**164** E5
　St Leonards TN38 . . . .**135** D2
Beckworth Cl RH16 . . . . . .**51** A6
Beckworth La RH16 . . . . . .**51** A6
Bedales RH17 . . . .**51** D4
Bedales Cnr RH17 . . . .**51** D5
Bedales Hill RH16,RH17 . . .**51** D4
Beddingham Gdns BN8 . . .**147** F5
Bedelands Cl RH15 . . . . . .**73** B5
Bedford Ave TN40 . . . .**157** D3
Bedford Ct TN22 . . . .**78** D8
Bedford Gr BN21 . . . .**184** F4
Bedford Pl Brighton BN1 . .**163** E5
　Uckfield TN22 . . . .**78** C8
Bedford Rd TN35 . . . .**160** C6
Bedford Sq BN1 . . . .**163** E5
Bedford St BN2 . . . .**164** C4
Bedford Terr **13** TN1 . . . . .**8** B4
Bedford Twrs **9** BN1 . . . .**163** E5
Bedfordwell Ct **3** BN22 .**185** A4
Bedfordwell Rd BN22 . . . .**185** A4
Bedgebury Ct TN38 . . . . . .**135** C2
Bedgebury National
　Pinetum★ TN17 . . . .**32** E8
Bee Rd BN10 . . . .**178** E8
Beech Ave BN23 . . . .**127** C3
Beech Cl Battle TN33 . . . .**112** C4
　Bexhill TN39 . . . .**156** C6
　3 East Grinstead RH19 . . . .**1** D2
　Portslade-by-S BN41 . . . . .**140** C4
Beech Ct
　7 East Grinstead RH19 . . . .**1** D1
　Polegate BN26 . . . .**173** A6
　Royal Tunbridge Wells TN2 . . .**8** D4
Beech Gr BN2 . . . .**143** E3
Beech Green La TN7 . . . . . .**14** B7
Beech Hill RH16 . . . .**51** B6
Beech House La TN19,
　TN32 . . . .**64** C6
Beech Hurst TN2 . . . .**9** D7
Beech Hurst Cl RH16 . . . . .**50** C4
Beech Hurst Cotts RH16 . .**50** C4
Beech Manor TN2 . . . .**8** D3
Beech Rd TN18 . . . .**48** C3
Beech St TN1 . . . .**8** B5
Beech Villas **1** TN21 . . . .**82** A6
Beecham Pl TN38 . . . .**135** F4
Beechers Rd BN41 . . . . . .**140** F3
Beeches Cl
　Heathfield TN21 . . . .**82** B5
　Uckfield TN22 . . . .**78** D8
Beeches Farm Rd TN6 . . . .**26** A1
Beeches La RH19 . . . .**11** D6
Beeches Mead RH19 . . . . . .**2** F5
Beeches Rd TN6 . . . .**26** B2
Beeches The
　Brighton BN1 . . . .**142** D3
　Crowborough TN6 . . . .**26** B1
　Royal Tunbridge Wells TN2 . . .**8** D5
　St Leonards TN37 . . . .**135** F6
　The Moor TN18 . . . .**45** E7
Beechfield Cl BN24 . . . . . .**174** B6
Beechfields RH19 . . . .**1** F4
Beeching Cl TN39 . . . .**157** B4
Beeching Park Ind Est
　TN39 . . . .**157** B4
Beeching Rd TN39 . . . . . .**157** B4
Beeching Way RH19 . . . . . .**1** F1
Beechlands Cotts TN5 . . . .**28** C3
Beechwood **6** BN1 . . . . .**142** E3
Beechwood Ave BN1 . . . . .**142** F4
Beechwood Cl
　Brighton BN1 . . . .**142** F4
　Burwash TN19 . . . .**62** B7
　Hailsham BN27 . . . .**152** C5
Beechwood Cres BN20 . . .**184** D3
Beechwood La
　Cooksbridge BN7,BN8 . . . .**122** F8
　Heathfield TN21 . . . .**82** B5
Beechwood Mews TN2 . . . .**8** E4
Beechwood Sacred Heart Sch
　TN2 . . . .**8** E4

Beechwoods RH15 . . . .**73** A1
Beechy Ave BN20 . . . .**184** B5
Beechy Gdns BN20 . . . . . .**184** B5
Beechy Rd TN22 . . . .**80** A2
Beeding Ave BN3 . . . .**141** F3
Beeding Ct Brighton BN1 142 C5
　4 Shoreham-by-S BN43 . .**161** B8
Beggar's La BN24 . . . .**174** B5
Beggar's Wood Rd BN8 . . .**75** C6
Belbourne St **7** BN1 . . . .**189** B3
Belfast St BN3 . . . .**163** B7
Belfield Rd TN2 . . . .**9** D6
Belfry Orch TN22 . . . .**78** D5
Belfry The BN27 . . . .**152** A8
Belgrave Cres BN25 . . . . .**180** F5
Belgrave Ct **7** TN40 . . . .**157** D3
Belgrave Pl **11** BN2 . . . .**164** D4
Belgrave Rd
　Royal Tunbridge Wells TN1 . . .**8** B4
　Seaford BN25 . . . .**180** E4
Belgrave St BN2 . . . .**189** C3
Belgrove **5** TN1 . . . .**8** A2
Bell Alley Rd TN19 . . . .**62** B5
Bell Banks Rd BN27 . . . . .**152** C7
Bell Hammer RH19 . . . .**10** E8
Bell La Lewes BN7 . . . . . .**146** B8
　Nutley TN22 . . . .**35** A4
　Uckfield TN22 . . . .**78** B6
　Uckfield TN22 . . . .**78** C6
Bell Tower Ind Est **7**
　. . . . .**164** E4
Bell Wlk TN22 . . . .**78** C6
Bellbrook Ind Est TN22 . . .**78** B6
Belle Hill Bexhill TN40 . . .**157** B5
　Bexhill TN40 . . . .**157** C5
Belle Vue Ct BN2 . . . .**164** D5
Belle Vue Gdns BN2 . . . . .**164** D4
Belle Vue Rd **5** BN22 . . .**185** C5
Bellevue Cotts BN2 . . . . . .**164** E5
Bellevue Ct Brighton BN1 142 F1
　3 Eastbourne BN22 . . . .**185** C5
Bellhurst Rd TN32 . . . .**64** A4
Bellingham Cl TN37 . . . . .**136** B4
Bellingham Cres BN3 . . . .**162** D8
Bellmead **7** BN3 . . . . . .**163** D7
Belmaine Ct TN39 . . . .**156** F4
Belmont Bexhill TN39 . . . .**157** B3
　Brighton BN1,BN3 . . . . . .**163** E7
Belmont Cotts BN18 . . . . . .**11** F3
Belmont Ct
　4 Brighton BN1 . . . . . .**163** E7
　Hailsham BN27 . . . .**152** B7
Belmont La BN6 . . . .**97** E5
Belmont Rd
　Hastings TN35 . . . .**160** C5
　Uckfield TN22 . . . .**78** C7
Belmont St BN1 . . . .**189** B3
Belmore Rd BN22 . . . .**185** B4
Belton Cl BN2 . . . .**164** B8
Belton Rd BN2 . . . .**164** B8
Beltring Rd
　Eastbourne BN22 . . . .**185** B4
　Royal Tunbridge Wells TN4 . . .**8** A6
Beltring Terr BN22 . . . . . .**185** B4
Belvedere Brighton BN1 . .**163** E8
　Brighton BN23 . . . .**175** A1
Belvedere Ct **13** BN21 . .**184** F4
Belvedere Gdns
　Crowborough TN6 . . . .**26** A1
　Seaford BN25 . . . .**181** A5
Belvedere Pk TN38 . . . . . .**159** A8
Belvedere Terr **5** BN1 . . .**163** E6
Belvedere Wlk RH16 . . . . .**50** C3
Bembridge Rd BN23 . . . . .**174** B3
Bembridge St BN2 . . . . . .**164** C8
Bembrook Rd TN34 . . . . . .**160** B5
Bemzells La BN27 . . . .**108** D2
Benbow Ave BN23 . . . . . .**185** E6
Benbow Ho TN39 . . . .**156** E4
Benchfield Cl RH19 . . . .**2** B1
Bending Cres TN40 . . . . . .**157** C5
Benenden Cl BN25 . . . . . .**181** A4
Benenden Rise TN34 . . . . .**136** E3
Benett Ave BN3 . . . .**142** B2
Benett Dr BN3 . . . .**142** B2
Benfield Cl BN41 . . . .**141** C1
Benfield Cres BN41 . . . . . .**141** C1
Benfield Cl BN41 . . . .**162** C8
Benfield Jun Sch BN41 . . .**162** C8
Benfield Way BN41 . . . . . .**141** C1
Bengairn Ave BN1 . . . .**143** A7
Benhall Mill Rd TN2,TN3 . .**17** D8
Benham Ct **3** BN3 . . . . .**163** B5
Benjamin Cl BN22 . . . . . .**173** F2
Benjamin Lodge RH15 . . . .**73** D3
Bennett Meml Diocesan Sch
　TN4 . . . .**7** E6
Bennett Rd BN2 . . . .**164** E4
Bennetts Yd TN32 . . . .**64** B4
Benson Ct BN3 . . . .**162** E7
Bentham Hill TN3 . . . .**7** D8
Bentham Rd BN2 . . . .**164** C7
Bentley Motor Mus★
　BN8 . . . .**103** F5
Bentley Wildfowl Reserve★
　BN8 . . . .**103** F4
Bentswood Cres RH16 . . . .**51** A5
Bentswood Rd RH16 . . . . .**50** F5
Berberis Ct BN43 . . . .**140** B1
Beresford Cl TN17 . . . .**20** F2
Beresford Ct **12** BN3 . . .**163** D7
Beresford Ho BN10 . . . . . .**167** C1
Beresford Rd
　Brighton BN2 . . . .**164** D5
　Newhaven BN9 . . . .**168** E1
Bergamot Cres BN43 . . . .**140** C1
Beristede Cl BN20 . . . .**184** E1

Berkeley Cl TN2 . . . . .9 E7
Berkeley Ct
 4 Eastbourne BN21 . . . . .185 A1
 6 Hove BN3 . . . . .163 E7
Berkeley Mans **3** TN40 .157 D3
Berkeley Rd **7** TN1 . . . . . . .8 A2
Berkeley Row BN7 . . . . .146 A8
Berkeley Wlk BN23 . . . . .174 E3
Berkley Rd TN20 . . . . .39 E1
Berkshire Ct **7** BN21 . . . .185 B4
Berlin Rd TN35 . . . . .160 C6
Bermuda Pl BN23 . . . . . .185 G8
Bernard La **1** BN21 . . . .184 F3
Bernard Pl BN2 . . . . .164 C7
Bernard Rd BN2 . . . . .164 C7
Bernhard Baron Cottage
 Homes The BN26 . . . . . .172 F6
Bernhard Gdns BN26 . . . .172 F5
Berriedale Ave BN3 . . . . .162 E6
Berriedale Ho BN3 . . . . . .162 E6
Berry Cl Burgess Hill RH15 73 A5
 Telscombe Cliffs BN10 . .167 A1
Berwick Cl Bexhill TN39 .156 C6
 Eastbourne BN22 . . . . . .173 C3
 Seaford BN25 . . . . .180 D4
Berwick Court Cotts
 BN26 . . . . .171 A6
Berwick Ct **1** BN21 . . . .185 B3
Berwick Rd BN26 . . . . . .177 D7
Berwick Sta TN39 . . . . . .150 B2
Betchley Cl RH19 . . . . .1 E3
Betherinden Cotts TN18 .47 A4
Bethune Rd TN40 . . . . . . .157 E3
Bethune Way TN34 . . . . .136 F1
Beulah Rd TN1 . . . . .8 C4
Beuzeville Ave BN27 . . . .152 B8
Bevendean Ave BN27 . . . .177 D5
Bevendean Cres BN2 . . . .143 E2
Bevendean Prim Sch
 BN2 . . . . .143 F1
Bevendean Rd BN2 . . . . .143 D1
Beverington Cl BN21 . . . .184 D6
Beverington Rd BN21 . . . .184 D6
Beverley Ct **1** BN2 . . . . .162 D7
Beverley Wlk TN34 . . . . .160 A6
Bevern Bridge BN8 . . . . .100 F4
Bevern Bridge Cotts
 BN8 . . . . .100 F4
Beverns The BN7 . . . . .99 E5
Bevin Ct TN38 . . . . .136 B3
Bewl Bridge Cl TN5 . . . . . .32 B3
Bewl Water★ TN5 . . . . . .31 C6
Bewl Water Visitors Ctr★
 TN3 . . . . .31 B8
Bewlbridge La
 Lamberhurst TN3,TN5 . . .20 B1
 Lower Cousley Wood TN5 .30 F8
Bexfield Ct
 Beachlands BN24 . . . . . .175 E6
 6 Eastbourne BN24 . . . .184 F1
Bexhill Coll TN39 . . . . . . .157 A6
Bexhill High Sch TN39 . . .157 B5
Bexhill High Sch (Lower)
 TN39 . . . . .157 A7
Bexhill Hospl TN40 . . . . . .157 C5
Bexhill Mus★ TN39 . . . . .157 B3
Bexhill Rd
 Eastbourne BN22 . . . . . .185 C5
 Lower Street TN33,TN39 .133 C3
 St Leonards TN38,TN40 . .158 D6
 Woodingdean BN2 . . . . .144 E1
Bexhill Sta TN40 . . . . . . .157 C4
Bexleigh Ave TN38 . . . . .158 B3
Bexley Cl BN27 . . . . .129 B2
Bexley Ct BN26 . . . . .173 C4
Bicton Gdns TN39 . . . . . .156 E4
Biddenden Cl BN23 . . . . .174 D2
Bidwell Ave TN39 . . . . . .157 A7
Bigwood Ave BN3 . . . . . .163 D8
Bilbury Mews BN21 . . . . .184 F5
Billingham La TN31 . . . . . .91 C3
Binsted Cl BN22 . . . . .173 E1
Biology Rd BN1 . . . . .144 B6
Birch Ave RH17 . . . . .51 A3
Birch Cl Eastbourne BN23 185 D7
 Haywards Heath RH17 . . .51 B3
 Royal Tunbridge Wells TN2 . .8 D7
 Uckfield TN22 . . . . .78 E8
Birch Ct BN42 . . . . .141 A4
Birch Est The BN23 . . . . .185 C7
Birch Grove Cres BN1 . . .143 A5
Birch Ho **2** RH19 . . . . .1 D2
Birch Kiln Cotts TN5 . . . . . .30 A6
Birch Path TN22 . . . . .78 D8
Birch Rd BN23 . . . . .185 C7
Birch Rdbt BN23 . . . . . . .185 C7
Birch Terr TN21 . . . . .81 D2
Birch View TN39 . . . . .157 C6
Birch Way
 Hailsham BN27 . . . . .152 B6
 Hastings TN34 . . . . .136 E3
 Haywards Heath RH17 . . .51 A2
 Heathfield TN21 . . . . .82 A5
 Royal Tunbridge Wells TN2 . .8 D7
Birchden Cotts TN3 . . . . . .15 C6
Birchen La RH16 . . . . .50 F8
Birches Cl TN16 . . . . .25 F4
Birches Ind Est RH19 . . . . . .1 A3
Birchetts Ave TN3 . . . . . . .16 E3
Birchetts Green La TN5 . .31 C3
Birchgrove La RH17 . . . . . .22 A1
Birchgrove Rd RH17 . . . . . .33 E7
Birchington Cl TN39 . . . .156 D4
Bircholme TN2 . . . . .9 A2
Birchwood Grove Com Prim
 Sch RH15 . . . . .73 C1
Birchwood Grove Rd
 RH15 . . . . .73 C1

Bird In Eye Hill TN22 . . . .78 E6
Bird in Hand St TN3 . . . . .15 B8
Bird La TN1 . . . . .29 B5
Birdham Pl BN2 . . . . .143 E3
Birdham Rd BN2 . . . . . . .143 F3
Birk Dale TN39 . . . . .156 D4
Birkdale TN1 . . . . .8 B6
Birken Rd TN2 . . . . .8 D6
Birling Cl Brighton BN2 . .143 D1
 Seaford BN25 . . . . .180 D4
Birling Dr TN2 . . . . .8 A1
Birling Gap Rd BN20 . . . .187 B6
Birling Park Ave TN2 . . . . .17 B8
Birling Rd TN2 . . . . .17 B8
Birling St BN21 . . . . .184 C4
Birling Way TN22 . . . . .78 E8
Biscay Ave BN23 . . . . . . .185 F8
Bishop Bell CE Sch The
 BN23 . . . . .174 E1
Bishop's Cl
 Hurstpierpoint BN6 . . . . .97 A7
 Ringmer BN8 . . . . .124 A6
Bishop's Down TN4 . . . . . . .7 F3
Bishop's Down Park Rd
 TN4 . . . . .7 F4
Bishop's Down Prim Sch
 TN4 . . . . .7 E5
Bishop's Down Rd TN4 . . . .7 F5
Bishop's La Ringmer BN8 124 D6
 Robertsbridge TN32 . . . . .64 A3
Bishop's Wlk TN40 . . . . .157 F6
Bishops Cl BN25 . . . . . . .180 C4
Bishops Ct TN4 . . . . .7 F3
Bishops Dr BN7 . . . . .146 A8
Bishops Rd BN3 . . . . .142 C1
Bishopstone Dr BN2 . . . .177 B6
Bishopstone La BN6,RH17 72 A7
Bishopstone Rd BN25 . . .180 C6
Bishopstone Sta BN25 . . .180 B4
Bittern Ct BN27 . . . . .152 D7
Bixley La TN31 . . . . .68 B2
Black Hill RH16 . . . . .51 A7
Black Lion La BN1 . . . . . .189 A2
Black Lion St BN1 . . . . . .189 B1
Black Path BN26 . . . . . . .173 A6
Black Rock (for Marina)
 Sta★ 164 E3
Blackberry La RH19,RH7 . . .1 D8
Blackberry Rd RH19,RH7 . . .1 D8
Blackbird Cl RH15 . . . . . . .72 D3
Blackboys CE Prim Sch
 TN22 . . . . .80 A6
Blackboys YH★ TN22 . . . .80 A8
Blackbrook La BN8,RH17 .52 E2
Blackdon Hill TN3 . . . . . . .27 B6
Blackdown BN2 . . . . .164 F7
Blackdown Rd TN21 . . . . .83 D6
Blackdown Rdbt TN22 . . . .55 B3
Blackfields Ave TN39 . . . .156 F5
Blackhorse Mews TN2 . . . . .9 C6
Blackhouse La RH15 . . . . .73 B4
Blackhurst La TN2 . . . . .8 F6
Blacklands TN33 . . . . .88 F1
Blacklands Cres RH18 . . . .11 F2
Blacklands Dr TN34 . . . . .136 F2
Blacklands Prim Sch
 TN34 . . . . .136 E2
Blackman Ave TN38 . . . . .136 A3
Blackman St BN1 . . . . . . .189 B3
Blackmill Cl TN39 . . . . . . .157 A8
Blackmores RH17 . . . . . . .74 A5
Blackness Rd TN6 . . . . . . .38 A8
Blackness Villas TN6 . . . . .38 A8
Blacksmith's Field TN33 135 A4
Blacksmith's La TN5 . . . . .30 A5
Blacksmiths Copse
 BN27 . . . . .152 A6
Blacksmiths Field TN32 .46 C1
Blacksmiths La TN33 . . . .133 E8
Blackstone Way RH15 . . .73 A5
Blackthorn Cl
 Brighton BN1 . . . . .142 D3
 Eastbourne BN22 . . . . . .173 E2
 Portslade-by-S BN41 . . . .141 B2
 St Leonards TN37 . . . . . .136 C4
Blackthorn Way TN35 . . .138 F4
Blackthorns RH16 . . . . . . .51 A4
Blackthorns Cl RH16 . . . . .51 A6
Blackthorns Com Prim Sch
 RH16 . . . . .51 A6
Blackthorns The RH15 . . .73 B5
Blackwater Rd BN20,
 BN21 . . . . .184 F1
Blackwell Farm Rd RH19 . .1 F1
Blackwell Hollow RH19 . . . .1 E2
Blackwell Prim Sch RH19 . .1 E2
Blackwell Rd RH19 . . . . . . .1 F2
Blake Ct **3** BN2 . . . . . . .189 C3
Blake Way TN2 . . . . .8 D7
Blakeney Ave BN10,BN9 .179 A6
Blaker St BN2 . . . . .189 C2
Blakes Way BN23 . . . . . . .185 F6
Blatchington Cl BN25 . . .180 E4
Blatchington Hill BN25 . .180 E4
Blatchington Hill Flats
 BN25 . . . . .180 F5
Blatchington Mill Dr
 BN24 . . . . .174 C5
Blatchington Mill Sch & Sixth
 Form Coll BN3 . . . . .141 F2
Blatchington Rd
 Hove BN3 . . . . .163 B3
 Royal Tunbridge Wells TN1 . .8 B1
 Seaford BN25 . . . . .180 E3
Blenheim Cl RH19 . . . . .2 A3
Blenheim Ct
 1 Hove BN3 . . . . .163 A6
 Robertsbridge TN32 . . . . .64 B3

Blenheim Fields RH18 . . . .11 E3
Blenheim Mews RH16 . . . .50 F2
Blenheim Pl **5** BN1 . . . .189 B3
Blenheim Way
 Flimwell TN5 . . . . .32 C3
 Polegate BN26 . . . . .173 D6
Bletchinglye La TN6 . . . . .27 E1
Bletchley Ct BN1 . . . . . . .164 A8
Blind La BN8 . . . . .76 E6
Blois Rd BN7 . . . . .123 B2
Blomfield Rd TN39 . . . . . .157 D8
Bloomsbury Pl **17** BN2 .164 C4
Bloomsbury St **16** BN2 .164 C4
Blossom Wlk BN27 . . . . .129 B1
Blount Ave RH19 . . . . .1 C1
Blowers Hill Cowden TN8 . .4 D8
 Speldhurst TN3 . . . . .7 B8
Blue Haze Ave BN5 . . . . .181 B4
Bluebell Bsns Est TN22 . .53 A4
Bluebell Cl
 East Grinstead RH19 . . . . .1 B1
 Haywards Heath RH16 . . .50 F4
Bluebell Glade BN27 . . . .127 B4
Bluebell Rly★ RH17,RH19,
 .21 A5
Bluebell Rly Mus★ TN22 .53 A4
Bluebell Rly The★ TN22 . .53 A4
Bluebell Walk & Farm Trail★
 BN26 . . . . .151 B4
Bluebell Way RH15 . . . . . .72 D4
Bluebird Cl **11** BN3 . . . .163 A6
Bluemans La TN33 . . . . . .114 A4
Bluestone Cl TN38 . . . . . .135 F2
Blunts Wood Cres RH16 . .50 B6
Blunts Wood Rd RH16 . . . .50 C6
Blytons The RH19 . . . . .1 B1
Boarders La TN5 . . . . .31 C3
Boast La BN8 . . . . .101 F5
Boathouse The **4** TN31 . .93 C5
Bocking TN5 . . . . .29 E4
Bocks Hill TN32 . . . . .64 E6
Boddingtons La BN6 . . . . .98 D3
Bodiam Ave Bexhill TN40 157 D6
Bodiam Bsns Pk TN32 . . .65 C7
Bodiam Castle (NT)★
 TN32 . . . . .65 F8
Bodiam CE Prim Sch
 TN32 . . . . .65 E6
Bodiam Cl Brighton BN2 . .144 B2
 Seaford BN25 . . . . .181 C4
Bodiam Cres BN22 . . . . . .174 A2
Bodiam Ct RH16 . . . . .50 E5
Bodiam Dr TN38 . . . . .135 D2
Bodiam Manor Sch TN32 65 E8
Bodiam Rd TN18,TN32 . . . .46 F3
Bodiam Sta★ TN32 . . . . . .65 E6
Bodiam Ho **15** BN3 . . . .163 D7
Bodle Cres BN39 . . . . . . .157 B7
Bodmin Cl BN20 . . . . .184 C3
Bohemia Rd TN34,TN37 .159 D8
Boiler House Hill BN1 . . .144 B7
Bolding Way RH16 . . . . . . .50 E2
Bolebrooke Rd TN40 . . . .157 D3
Bolney Ave BN10 . . . . . . .178 C6
Bolney Rd BN2 . . . . .143 F4
Bolnore Rd RH16 . . . . .50 B4
Bolnore Rd RH16 . . . . .50 C4
Bolsover Ct BN20 . . . . . . .188 F8
Bolsover Rd
 Eastbourne BN20 . . . . . .188 F8
 Hove BN3 . . . . .162 E8
Bolton Cl TN22 . . . . .78 A6
Bolton Rd BN21 . . . . .185 A2
Boltro Rd RH16 . . . . .50 D5
Bonchurch Rd BN2 . . . . .164 C7
Bond St BN1 . . . . .189 B2
Bonfire La RH17 . . . . .33 D5
Boniface Cl BN24 . . . . . . .174 C6
Bonners CE Sch TN22 . . . .55 B4
Bonny Wood Rd BN6 . . . . .97 E3
Booker Cl TN6 . . . . .26 A1
Booth Mus of Natural
 History★ BN1 . . . . .163 E8
Bopeep Bostal BN26 . . . .170 B7
Bopeep La BN26 . . . . . . .170 B8
Bordehill la RH16 . . . . .50 C8
Border Ct RH19 . . . . .1 F4
Borders La TN19 . . . . .62 F7
Boreham Hill BN27,TN33 132 A4
Boreham Ct BN21 . . . . . .131 E2
Borodales TN39 . . . . .156 E4
Borough La BN20 . . . . . . .184 D3
Borough St BN1 . . . . .163 E6
Borrow King Cl BN2 . . . . .164 D8
Borrowdale Cl BN23 . . . . .174 C4
Boscawen Cl BN23 . . . . . .185 F7
Boscobel Ct TN38 . . . . . .159 A6
Boscobel Lodge TN38 . . .159 B7
Boscobel Rd TN38 . . . . . .159 A7
Boscobel Rd N TN38 . . . .159 A7
Boship Cl BN23 . . . . .174 A4
Bostal La BN8 . . . . .148 B4
Boston Cl BN23 . . . . .185 F7
Boston Rd RH16 . . . . .51 A5
Boston Rd RH16 . . . . .51 A5
Boston St BN1 . . . . .189 B4
Boswell Wlk **2** BN23 . . .174 E2
Bough Beeches RH15 . . . .73 C1
Boughey Pl TN7 . . . . .190 A4
Boulevard The BN24 . . . .175 F6
Boundary Pas **10** BN3 .163 E6
Boundary Rd
 Brighton BN2 . . . . .164 F4
 Portslade-by-S BN3,BN41 .162 C7
 Royal Tunbridge Wells TN2 . .8 D1
Boundary The
 Langton Green TN3 . . . . . .7 B3

Boundary The continued
 20 Seaford BN25 . . . . . .180 E2
Boundsway TN22 . . . . .78 E8
Bourg-de-Peage Ave
 RH19 . . . . .2 A1
Bourne Ct Brighton BN1 .142 D4
 20 Hastings TN35 . . . . .180 B4
Bourne La
 Northbridge Street TN32 . .64 F7
 Sandhurst Cross TN18 . . .46 E4
Bourne Pas **12** TN34 . . .160 B4
Bourne Prim Sch BN22 . .185 B3
Bourne St BN21 . . . . .185 B3
Bourne The Hassocks BN6 .97 E5
 Hastings TN34 . . . . .160 B4
Bourneside Ct **12** BN22 .185 B3
Bowden House Sch
 BN25 . . . . .180 F6
Bowden Rise BN25 . . . . . .180 E6
Bowen Ct **11** BN3 . . . . .163 C6
Bowen Rd TN4 . . . . .7 B4
Bower Cl TN37 . . . . .136 B4
Bower The RH16 . . . . .50 D5
Bowerhill Cotts RH19 . . . .21 E7
Bowlers Town TN31 . . . . . .70 A2
Bowles Outdoor Ctr TN6 .26 C6
Bowley Rd BN27 . . . . .152 C7
Bowlings The TN33 . . . . . .113 D8
Bowmans Dr TN33 . . . . . .112 D6
Bowood Ave BN22 . . . . . .185 B6
Bowrey Pl TN40 . . . . .157 C5
Bowring Way BN2 . . . . . .164 D4
Bowsprit Mews TN38 . . . .135 E7
Box Rd RH19 . . . . .11 E6
Box's La RH17 . . . . .34 C6
Boxes La RH17 . . . . .33 C5
Boxgrove Cl TN40 . . . . . .157 F4
Boyce's St BN1 . . . . .189 A2
Boyles La **14** BN2 . . . . .164 E4
Boyne Pk TN4 . . . . .7 F4
Boyne Rd TN35 . . . . .160 C5
Bracken Cl
 Crowborough TN6 . . . . . .26 C1
 Royal Tunbridge Wells TN2 . .8 E5
Bracken Rd
 Eastbourne BN20 . . . . . .184 B5
 Royal Tunbridge Wells TN2 . .8 E5
 Seaford BN25 . . . . .181 A2
Bracken Way TN21 . . . . . . .59 E1
Brackenbury Cl BN41 . . . .141 B2
Brackendale TN35 . . . . . .160 D6
Brackenhill TN7 . . . . .13 A1
Brackerne Cl TN39 . . . . . .156 C2
Bradford Ct **9** BN22 . . . .185 B4
Bradford Rd BN7 . . . . . . .123 B4
Bradford St BN21 . . . . . . .184 D3
Brading Cl
 Eastbourne BN23 . . . . . .174 B4
 Hastings TN34 . . . . .136 E2
Brading Rd BN2 . . . . .164 C7
Bradley Rd
 Wartling BN27 . . . . .131 C1
 White Post TN3 . . . . .5 D5
Braemar Ct **2** TN39 . . . .157 A4
Braemar Ho **11** BN3 . . . .163 E6
Braemore Cl BN3 . . . . . . .162 E6
Braemore Rd BN3 . . . . . .162 E6
Braeside Ave BN1 . . . . . .143 A7
Bramber Ave Hove BN3 . .141 F3
 Peacehaven BN10 . . . . . .178 C6
Bramber Ave N BN10 . . . .178 C8
Bramber Cl
 Haywards Heath RH16 . . .50 D4
 Peacehaven BN10 . . . . . .178 C8
 3 Seaford BN25 . . . . . .180 F2
Bramber Ct **8** Hove BN3 163 B7
 2 Shoreham-by-S BN43 .161 B8
Bramber Ho **17** BN21 . . .184 E4
Bramber La BN25 . . . . . . .180 F2
Bramber Rd BN25 . . . . . .180 F2
Bramber Way RH15 . . . . . .73 A4
Bramble Cl BN23 . . . . . . .174 B3
Bramble Croft TN6 . . . . . . .26 A2
Bramble Dr BN27 . . . . . . .152 A7
Bramble Gdns RH15 . . . . .72 D4
Bramble Rise BN2 . . . . . .142 C5
Bramble Twitten RH19 . . . . .2 A1
Bramble Way
 Brighton BN1 . . . . .143 C6
 Fairlight Cove TN35 . . . .138 F4
Bramble Wlk TN2 . . . . .8 D7
Brambledean Rd BN41 . . .162 B7
Brambles BN2 . . . . .97 F5
Brambles The RH17 . . . . . .50 A6
Brambleside TN22 . . . . . . .78 A6
Brambletye La RH18 . . . . .11 D3
Brambletye Prep Sch
 RH19 . . . . .11 C5
Brambletyne Ave BN2 . . .177 D5
Bramley Rd BN26 . . . . . . .173 D6
Bramley Wlk BN27 . . . . . .131 B5
Bramleys BN7 . . . . .145 E5
Brampton Ave TN39 . . . . .156 F4
Brampton Ct TN39 . . . . . .156 F4
Brampton Rd BN22 . . . . . .184 F8
Brampton Road Trad Est
 BN22 . . . . .185 A8
Brand Rd BN22 . . . . .173 E1
Brands Cl BN9 . . . . .168 E2
Brangwyn Ave BN1 . . . . . .142 F5
Brangwyn Cres BN1 . . . . .142 E6
Brangwyn Ct BN1 . . . . . . .142 E5
Brangwyn Dr BN1 . . . . . . .142 E5
Brangwyn Way BN1 . . . . .142 E5
Branksome Rd TN38 . . . . .159 A8
Branston Rd BN22 . . . . . .173 D1
Brassey Ave BN22 . . . . . .173 E1
Brassey Par BN22 . . . . . .173 E1

Brassey Rd TN40 . . . . . . .157 D3
Brasslands Dr BN41 . . . . .140 F1
Braybon Ave BN1 . . . . . . .142 F4
Braybon Bsns Pk RH15 . . .72 E2
Braybrooke Cl TN34 . . . . .159 E8
Braybrooke Rd TN34 . . . .159 F8
Braybrooke Terr TN34 . . .159 E8
Braypool La BN1 . . . . .142 D7
Brazen Cl BN9 . . . . .179 B7
Bread St BN1 . . . . .189 B3
Breadsell La TN38 . . . . . .135 D6
Brecon Cotts TN6 . . . . . . .39 A8
Brecon Ct **6** BN3 . . . . . .163 C7
Brecon Terr TN6 . . . . .39 A8
Brede Cl Brighton BN2 . . .164 F5
 Eastbourne BN22 . . . . . .185 D6
 St Leonards TN37 . . . . . .135 F4
Brede Hill TN31 . . . . .115 B8
Brede La Brede TN31 . . . . .89 C3
 Sedlescombe TN31,TN33 . .89 B2
Brede Prim Sch TN31 . . . .90 B4
Brede Valley View TN36 . .116 E5
Breeds Pl TN34 . . . . .159 F7
Brendon Cl
 Eastbourne BN23 . . . . . .174 E4
 Royal Tunbridge Wells TN2 . .8 D5
Brendon Rise TN34 . . . . . .160 B7
Brentor Ct TN2 . . . . .8 D6
Brentwood Cl BN1 . . . . . .143 B3
Brentwood Cres BN1 . . . .143 B3
Brentwood Rd BN1 . . . . . .143 B3
Bretland Ct TN1 . . . . .7 D4
Bretland Rd TN4 . . . . .7 D4
Brett Dr BN27 . . . . .157 F4
Bretton RH15 . . . . .72 E5
Bretts Cotts TN22 . . . . . . .79 B7
Bretts Field BN10 . . . . . .167 C6
Brewer St Brighton BN2 . .189 C4
 Lamberhurst TN3 . . . . . . .20 A5
Brewers Gr TN20 . . . . .40 B2
Brian Cres TN4 . . . . .8 B8
Briar Cl
 Fairlight Cove TN35 . . . .139 A5
 Woodingdean BN2 . . . . .165 D7
Briar Pl BN23 . . . . .174 B3
Briarcroft Rd BN2 . . . . . . .165 D7
Briary The TN40 . . . . .157 D5
Brick Kiln La TN20,TN22 . .57 E6
Brickfield TN31 . . . . .69 B2
Brickfields TN2 . . . . .9 E8
Brickhurst La BN8 . . . . . .126 C8
Bricky The BN10 . . . . .178 D8
Brickyard Cotts TN6 . . . . . .28 A4
Brickyard La
 Mark Cross TN6 . . . . .27 E5
 South Chailey BN8 . . . . . .100 A3
Bridge Cl
 Burgess Hill RH15 . . . . . . .72 E4
 Horam TN21 . . . . .107 A7
Bridge Ct BN9 . . . . .179 D7
Bridge End BN24 . . . . . . .175 E4
Bridge Farm Rd TN22 . . . .78 C6
Bridge Ho TN4 . . . . .8 B1
Bridge Pl TN31 . . . . .93 C6
Bridge Rd RH16 . . . . .50 F7
Bridge Road Bsns Pk
 RH16 . . . . .50 F7
Bridge St BN9 . . . . .179 D7
Bridge Way TN38 . . . . . . .158 C6
Bridgelands BN8 . . . . . . .101 B4
Bridgemere Rd BN22 . . . .185 B6
Bridger Way TN6 . . . . .26 A1
Bridgersmill RH16 . . . . . . .50 D6
Bridgewick Cl BN7 . . . . . .190 B4
Bridle Way BN10 . . . . . . .167 A1
Briers Ave TN34 . . . . .136 C3
Briers Gdns TN34 . . . . . . .136 C4
Briers The TN37 . . . . .136 C4
Brigden St BN1 . . . . .189 A4
Brigdens Hill BN8 . . . . . . .147 E6
Bright Ridge TN4 . . . . .7 E8
Brighthelm BN1 . . . . .144 B8
Brightland Rd BN20 . . . . .184 D3
Brightling Ave TN35 . . . . .160 E8
Brightling Rd
 Polegate BN26 . . . . .173 B5
 Robertsbridge TN32 . . . . .63 D2
Brighton & Hove High Sch
 BN1 . . . . .163 E6
Brighton & Hove Stad
 BN3 . . . . .142 B1
Brighton Coll BN2 . . . . . .164 C5
Brighton College Pre-Prep
 Sch BN2 . . . . .164 C5
Brighton Fishing Mus★
 BN1 . . . . .189 A1
Brighton General Hospl
 BN2 . . . . .164 D7
Brighton Marina BN2 . . . .164 F2
Brighton Marina Village
 BN2 . . . . .164 F3
Brighton Mus & Art Gall★
 BN1 . . . . .189 B2
Brighton Mus of Childhood★
 BN1 . . . . .189 B2
Brighton Pl BN1 . . . . .189 B2
Brighton Race Course
 BN2 . . . . .165 A8
Brighton Rd
 Hassocks BN6 . . . . .97 D2
 Lewes BN7 . . . . .146 A8
 Newhaven BN9 . . . . .179 B7
 Shoreham-by-S BN43 . . .161 B7
Brighton Sea Life Ctr★
 BN1 . . . . .189 B1

Brighton Sq BN1 ....189 B2
Brighton Sta BN1 ......189 B3
Brighton Steiner Sch Ltd
(John Howard Ho)
BN2 ....164 F4
Brighton Toy & Model Mus
The★ BN1 ....189 B3
Brighton, Hove & Sussex
Sixth Form Coll BN3 ..163 E8
Brightwell Ind Est BN9 .179 E7
Brills La BN1 ....189 B1
Brincliffe TN6 ....25 E3
Brinkers La TN5 ....30 A2
Brisbane Quay BN23 ....175 A2
Bristol Gate BN2 ....164 D4
Bristol Gdns BN2 ....164 E4
Bristol Mews 3 BN2 ....164 E4
Bristol Pl BN2 ....164 E4
Bristol Rd Brighton BN2 .164 E4
  St Leonards TN38 .....136 A3
Bristol Rise BN2 ....164 D4
Bristol St BN2 ....164 E4
Bristol Way TN38 ......136 A3
Britannia Ct BN2 ......165 A3
Britannia Ent Ctr TN34 .138 F1
British Engineerium Mus★
BN3 ....142 B2
Britland Est BN22 .....185 C6
Brittany Ct
  5 Bexhill TN39 ......157 A4
  3 Hove BN3 ....162 D7
Brittany Ho TN6 ....37 D8
Brittany Mews TN38 ...159 B7
Brittany Rd Hove BN3 ..162 D6
  St Leonards TN37,TN38 .159 A8
Britten Cl BN23 ....174 D3
Brittenden La TN21 .....80 E5
Britts Orch TN22 ....56 C3
Broad Buckler TN37 ...136 A6
Broad Gn BN2 ....165 E6
Broad Gr TN2 ....8 A1
Broad Green Ave RH15 .73 C2
Broad La TN3 ....6 A4
Broad Oak Buxted TN22 .56 C3
  Groombridge TN3 .....15 C6
Broad Oak Cl
  Broad Oak TN31 ......90 B5
  Eastbourne BN23 .....174 A4
  Royal Tunbridge Wells TN2 .7 F1
Broad Oak Com Prim Sch
  TN21 ....59 F2
Broad Rd BN20 ....173 A4
Broad Rig Ave BN3 ....141 D3
Broad St Brighton BN2 .189 B1
  Cuckfield RH17 ....50 A4
  Icklesham TN36 .....116 C6
  Seaford BN25 ....180 E3
Broad View Bexhill TN39 156 F6
  Broad Oak TN31 ......59 E1
Broadcroft TN2 ....16 F8
Broadfields BN2 ....143 E3
Broadfields Rd BN2 ...143 E3
Broadhill Cl TN21 ......59 E1
Broadlands
  Burgess Hill RH15 ....98 B8
  Hastings TN35 ....160 D8
Broadley View TN33 ...133 E8
Broadmead TN2 ....16 F8
Broadmead Ave TN2 ...16 F8
Broadoak La
  Bexhill TN39 ....156 E5
  Bexhill TN39 ....156 F5
Broads Cotts TN19 .....62 B6
Broadstone RH18 ....12 A2
Broadview CI BN20 ....172 F4
Broadwalk The TN6 ...156 B4
Broadwater Ct TN2 ....16 E8
Broadwater Down TN2 .16 F8
Broadwater Down Prim Sch
  TN2 ....7 F1
Broadwater Forest La
  TN3 ....16 B7
Broadwater La
  Royal Tunbridge Wells TN2 .16 F8
  Royal Tunbridge Wells TN2,
  TN4 ....7 F1
Broadwater Mews TN26 172 E3
Broadwater Rise TN2 ....7 F1
Broadwater Way BN22 .184 F8
Broadway
  Fairlight Cove TN35 ..138 F5
  Southwick BN42 .....161 C8
Broadway Ct 11 BN43 .161 C8
Broadway The
  Alfriston BN26 ....170 F3
  Brighton BN2 ....164 F4
  Crowborough TN6 .....25 F3
  Eastbourne BN22 ....173 D1
  Hastings TN35 ....160 D8
  Haywards Heath RH16 ..50 E5
  Lamberhurst TN3 .....20 B5
Brockhurst BN2 ....164 F7
Brockhurst Gate TN40 .157 F5
Brockley Rd TN39 .....157 A3
Brocks Ghyll BN20 ....173 A3
Brodie Pl BN21 ....184 D4
Brodrick Cl BN22 .....173 F1
Brodrick Rd BN22 .....173 E2
Brokes Way TN4 ....8 B8
Bromley Cl
  Eastbourne BN23 ....174 C2
  Keymer BN6 ....98 A4
Bromley Rd
  Brighton BN2 ....189 C5

Bromley Rd *continued*
  Seaford BN25 ....181 A4
Brompton Cl BN1 .....142 E6
Brontes The RH19 ....1 D1
Brook Ave BN6 ....97 F3
Brook Cl Crowborough TN6 26 D1
  East Grinstead RH19 ....2 B1
Brook Ho TN39 ....157 C6
Brook La
  Beddingham BN8 .....147 A6
  Haywards Heath RH16 ..50 F8
Brook Manor RH19 .....10 C7
Brook Rd TN2 ....8 D7
Brook St Hastings TN34 159 F8
  Lewes BN7 ....190 B2
  Polegate BN26 ......172 F6
Brook Terr TN6 ....25 D4
Brook View TN6 ....25 D4
Brook Way TN35 ......160 B8
Brooker Pl BN3 ....163 A7
Brooker St BN3 ....163 A7
Brookfield TN18 ....47 B5
Brookfield Ct 2 TN40 .157 E4
Brookfield Rd TN40 ...157 E4
Brookhouse Bottom
  TN22 ....34 D4
Brookhouse La TN22 ...79 A5
Brookhouse Rd TN22 ...79 A4
Brookland Cl
  Beachlands BN24 ....175 E6
  Hastings TN34 ......136 F2
Brookland Ho RH19 ......1 E1
Brooklands TN2 ....8 D7
Brooklands Ave TN6 ....37 F7
Brooklands Farm Cl TN3 ..6 A6
Brooklands Way RH16 ..10 D8
Brooklyn Rd BN25 ....180 E3
Brookmead Cl BN2 ....185 B5
Brooks Cl Lewes BN7 ..190 B3
  Newhaven BN9 ......179 D6
Brooks Gdns BN8 ....76 D6
Brooks Rd BN7 ....190 B3
Brooks The RH15 ....72 E5
Brookside
  Piddinghoe BN9 .....168 B2
  Uckfield BN26 ....78 A6
Brookside Ave BN26 ..172 F7
Brookside Cotts TN19 ..63 B8
Brookway
  Burgess Hill RH15 ....73 C3
  Lindfield RH16 ....51 A8
Broom Cl BN22 ....173 D2
Broom Hill Cotts TN5 ..32 B3
Broom La TN3 ....6 E3
Broom Pk TN3 ....6 E3
Brooman's Ct BN7 ....190 B2
Broomans La BN7 .....190 B2
Broomfield Ave BN10 ..177 F4
Broomfield Dr BN41 ...141 A3
Broomfield St BN20,
  BN21 ....184 C4
Broomgrove Rd TN34 ..160 B6
Broomham La BN8 ....127 B7
Broomhill Bank Sch TN3 .7 C6
Broomhill Park Rd TN4 ...7 F8
Broomhill Rd TN3 ....7 D7
Bross Est BN9 ....179 D6
Brow The
  Burgess Hill RH15 ....73 A2
  Friston BN20 ....183 B2
  Woodingdean BN2 ...165 D8
Brown Jack Ave BN7 ..172 F6
Brown Twins Rd BN6 ...97 B5
Brown's La TN22 ....78 D8
Brown's Path TN22 ....78 E8
Browning Rd 2 TN21 ..82 A7
Browning Wlk 5 BN23 .174 E2
Brownings The 1 RH19 .1 C1
Brownleaf Rd BN2 ....165 E6
Browns Cl TN22 ....78 D8
Browns La TN21 ....81 B6
Browns Wood RH19 .....1 E4
Broyle Cl BN8 ....125 A8
Broyle La BN8 ....124 F8
Broyle Paddock BN8 ..124 F7
Broyle The BN8 ....125 B7
Broyleside BN8 ....125 A7
Bruce Cl RH16 ....50 E3
Brunel Rd TN38 ......135 E4
Brunswick Mews 3
  BN3 ....163 D5
Brunswick Pl BN3 ....163 D6
Brunswick Rd BN3 ....163 D6
Brunswick Row BN1 ...189 B4
Brunswick Sq BN3 ....163 D5
Brunswick St E BN3 ..163 D5
Brunswick St W BN3 ..163 D5
Brunswick Terr
  Hove BN1,BN3 ......163 D5
  Royal Tunbridge Wells TN1 ..8 A2
Brushes La RH16 ....51 B8
Bryants Field TN6 .....25 E3
Brydges Cl BN22 .....185 C6
Buci Cres BN43 ......140 C1
Buckholt Ave TN40 ...158 A4
Buckholt La TN39 ....157 C8
Buckhurst Cl
  East Grinstead RH19 ...1 C3
  Eastbourne BN20 ...184 B8
  Lewes BN7 ....190 A4
Buckhurst La TN5 ......29 A6
Buckhurst Mead TN5 ...29 A6
Buckhurst Pl TN39 ...157 C4
Buckhurst Rd
  Bexhill TN40 ....157 C4
  Telscombe Cliffs BN10 .177 F3

Buckhurst Way RH19 .....1 C3
Buckingham Cl
  4 Brighton BN1 .....189 A4
  Seaford BN25 ....180 E4
  Shoreham-by-S BN43 .161 A8
Buckingham Ct BN20 .184 B6
Buckingham Dr RH19 ..11 A8
Buckingham Hts 2
  BN22 ....185 A4
Buckingham Lodge
  BN1 ....189 A4
Buckingham Pl BN1 ...189 A4
Buckingham Rd
  Brighton BN1 ....189 A3
  Royal Tunbridge Wells TN1 ..8 B2
  St Leonards TN38 ...136 A4
Buckingham St BN1 ...189 A3
Buckland Rd BN25 ....180 F5
Buckle By-Pass BN25 .180 C4
Buckle Cl BN25 ....180 C4
Buckle Cvn Pk BN25 ..180 B4
Buckle Dr BN25 ......180 C4
Buckle Rise BN25 ....180 C4
Buckler BN41 ....162 B8
Bucklers Cl TN2 ....8 C3
Buckley Cl BN3 ......141 E4
Buckswood Grange Sch
  TN22 ....78 B8
Buckswood Sch TN35 .116 A3
Buckthorn Cl BN25 ...181 C3
Buckwell Ct BN7 .....123 A3
Buckwell Rise BN27 ..130 E5
Buddens Gn TN31 ......68 B5
Budletts Rdbt TN22 ....55 C4
Bugsell La TN32 ....63 F4
Bull La BN7 ....190 A1
Bull Lane Cotts TN3 ...19 C4
Bull Ring TN33 ....112 D4
Buller Cl TN6 ....26 A1
Buller Rd BN2 ....143 D1
Bullfinch Gdns TN22 ...78 E4
Bullingdon Cotts TN3 ...6 F7
Bullingstone La TN3 ....6 F7
Bulls Pl TN2 ....9 D6
Bulrush Pl TN38 .....135 E1
Bulverhythe Rd TN38 .158 D6
Bungalows The TN22 ..79 B5
Bunny La TN3 ....16 E5
Bunting Cl TN38 .....158 E8
Burchetts Cl RH16 ....50 E2
Burden Pl TN38 ......136 A3
Burdett Pl 2 TN34 ...160 A3
Burdett Rd
  Crowborough TN6 ....26 C1
  Rusthall TN4 ....7 A4
Burdocks Dr RH15 .....73 D1
Burfield Park Ind Est
  BN27 ....152 B6
Burfield Rd BN22 ....185 B3
Burgess Ct BN41 .....162 B8
Burgess Rd TN35 ....137 C5
Burgess Hill Sch RH15 .73 B2
Burgess Hill Sta RH15 .73 B2
Burgh Hill TN19 ....44 B7
Burgh Hill Rd BN8 ...127 E6
Burgh La BN8 ....148 E5
Burgundy Ho 3 BN23 .185 F8
Burhill Way TN38 ....158 F7
Burleigh Pl BN22 ....185 C6
Burlington Ct 18 BN21 185 A2
Burlington Gdns BN41 141 C1
Burlington Mans 23
  BN21 ....185 A2
Burlington Pl BN21 ..185 A2
Burlington Rd BN21 ..185 B2
Burlington St BN2 ...164 C4
Burlington Villas 22
  BN21 ....185 B3
Burlow Cl Brighton BN2 164 E5
  Eastbourne BN22 ...173 C3
Burma Cl RH16 ....51 C4
Burners Cl RH15 ....73 D1
Burnes Vale BN2 .....165 F2
Burnham Cl BN2 .....165 F7
Burns Way RH19 ....1 C1
Burnside BN26 ......173 A6
Burnside Ct BN26 ...173 A6
Burnside Mews TN39 .157 B4
Burnt House Cl TN18 ..47 C5
Burnt House La TN3 ....7 A5
Burnt Lodge La TN5 ...31 B2
Burnt Oak Rd TN22,TN6 .37 C2
Burnthouse Bostall
  BN6 ....120 C8
Burrell Rd RH16 ....50 D6
Burrells La TN22 ....55 A7
Burrells The BN43 ...161 B6
Burrow Down BN20 ..184 B5
Burrow Down Cl BN20 184 A5
Burrswood Villas TN3 ..15 B7
Burry Rd TN37 ......136 C3
Burslem Rd TN2 ....8 E7
Burstead Cl BN1 .....143 B3
Burston Gdns RH19 ....1 D4
Burton Rd BN21 .....184 E5
Burton Villas BN3 ...163 D8
Burton Way TN38 ....159 B6
Burton Wlk BN27 ....152 B7
Burwash CE Prim Sch
  TN19 ....62 B6
Burwash Cl
  Eastbourne BN23 ...174 B4
  Hastings TN34 ......137 A5
Burwash Lodge BN1 ..143 C1
Burwash Rd
  Broad Oak TN21 ......82 C8
  Hove BN3 ....141 F3
Burwood Ho TN2 ....8 E5

Busby Ct 21 BN21 ......185 B3
Bush Cottage Cl BN41 .141 C2
Bush Farm Dr BN41 ..141 C1
Bush Rd BN9 ....179 B8
Bush Terr BN41 ......141 B3
Bushbury La TN22 .....80 A3
Busheyfields BN27 ...152 A8
Bushy Croft TN39 ....156 F5
Bushy Gill TN3 ....7 A3
Butcher's Cross TN7 ...13 B7
Butcher's La TN35 ...115 E2
Butcherfield La TN7 ...13 B6
Bute St BN2 ....164 C4
Butler's Green Ho RH16 .50 B5
Butler's Green Rd RH16 .50 C4
Butler's La TN35 .....130 C3
Butlers Way BN8 .....124 C5
Butterbox La RH17 ....52 D4
Buttercup Wlk BN1 ..143 B7
Butterfield RH19 ....1 A2
Buttermere Way BN23 174 C4
Button Ct BN2 ....189 C4
Button St BN2 ....164 C4
Butts Cl Cousley Wood TN5 .30 C7
  Eastbourne BN20 ...173 A1
Butts Rd BN42 ....161 E7
Buttsfield La BN8 ....105 A5
Buxted CE Prim Sch
  TN22 ....55 F3
Buxted Ct TN22 ....56 C3
Buxted Rise BN1 .....143 B5
Buxted Sta TN22 ......56 B3
Buxted Wood La TN22 .56 E5
Buxton Dr TN39 .....156 D4
Buxton Rd Brighton BN1 163 E7
  Eastbourne BN20 ...188 E8
By Sunte RH16 ....50 F8
Bydown BN25 ....181 A4
Bye-Law Cotts BN8 ...101 E6
Byeway The Bexhill TN39 156 D5
  Hastings TN34 ......160 A8
Byeways The BN25 ...180 E4
Byfields Croft TN39 ..156 F5
Byland Cl BN2 ....173 E3
Bylands 3 BN2 ......164 F5
Byng Rd TN4 ....7 F5
Byre Cotts BN2 ......165 D4
Byron Cl 1 RH16 ......50 D5
Byron Gr 2 RH19 ......1 C1
Byron Rd BN3 ....163 A7
Byron Terr 1 BN3 ....163 A7
Byron Wlk BN23 .....174 E3
Byway The BN1 ......143 E5
Byways TN34 ....136 D6
Byworth Cl Bexhill TN39 156 C6
  Brighton BN2 ......164 C6

C

Cabbage Stalk La TN4 ...7 E2
Cabbages & Kings Gdn★
  TN22 ....57 C3
Cabot Cl BN23 ....185 G2
Caburn Cl BN23 .....174 A4
Caburn Cres BN7 ....123 A2
Caburn Ent Pk BN23 .125 A7
Caburn Rd BN3 ......163 E7
Caburn View Bglws
  BN8 ....148 B3
Caburn View Cotts BN8 148 B3
Caburn Way BN27 ...152 B6
Cackle St
  Cackle Street TN31 ...90 A2
  Dodd's Hill TN22 ......35 E2
Cacklebury Cl BN27 ..152 A6
Cadborough Cliff TN31 ..93 A4
Cade St TN21 ....173 F2
Cadogan Ct
  Pevensey Bay BN24 ..175 C4
  3 Brighton BN1 .....163 E7
Cadogan Gdns 6 TN1 ..8 B4
Cairngorm Cl BN23 ..174 D3
Cairo Ave BN10 .....178 A8
Cairo Ave S BN10 ...178 A7
Caister's Cl BN3 ....163 C8
Caius St 16 BN43 ...161 C8
Calbourne RH16 ....50 D5
Caldbec Ct TN33 ....112 C5
Caldbec Hill TN33 ...112 D5
Caldicotts La BN27 ..128 C2
Caledonian Cl 5 BN2 .189 C5
Caledonian Rd BN2 ..189 C5
Caley Rd TN2 ....8 D7
Calgary Rd TN39 ....157 B7
Callao Quay BN23 ...185 G8
Callums Wlk TN40 ...157 E5
Calverley Ct TN1 ......8 C3
Calverley Park Cres 1
  TN1 ....8 B3
Calverley Park Gdns TN1 .8 C4
Calverley Pk TN1 ......8 B3
Calverley Rd
  6 Eastbourne BN21 ..184 F2
  Royal Tunbridge Wells TN1 ..8 C4
  Royal Tunbridge Wells TN1 ..8 B4
Calverley St TN1 ......8 B4
Calverley Wlk 7 BN21 184 F2
Calvert Cl TN22 ....78 A7
Calvert Rd Hastings TN34 160 A6
  Uckfield TN22 ....78 A7
Camber Castle★ TN36 ..93 C1
Camber Cl
  Beachlands BN24 ...175 F6
  Bexhill TN40 ....157 E6

Camber Cl *continued*
  Brighton BN2 ....164 F5
Camber Dr BN24 .....175 F6
Camber Rd TN31 ......94 B3
Camber Way BN24 ...175 F6
Camberlot Rd BN27 ..128 A2
Cambrian Rd TN4 ......8 C7
Cambridge Gdns
  Hastings TN34 ......159 E7
  Royal Tunbridge Wells TN2 ..8 B2
Cambridge Gr BN3 ...163 C7
Cambridge La TN21 ...81 C2
Cambridge Mews BN3 163 C7
Cambridge Rd
  Bexhill TN40 ....157 C6
  Eastbourne BN22 ...185 C4
  Hastings TN34 .....159 F7
  Hove BN3 ....163 D6
Cambridge St TN2 .....8 C3
Cambridge Way TN22 ..55 C1
Camden Ave TN2 ....9 C6
Camden Ct Pembury TN2 ..9 D6
  2 Royal Tunbridge Wells
  TN1 ....8 B4
Camden Hill TN2 ....8 B3
Camden Pk TN2 ....8 C2
Camden Rd
  5 Eastbourne BN21 ..184 F2
  Royal Tunbridge Wells TN1 ..8 B4
Camden St BN41 .....162 C6
Camden Terr BN1 ....189 A3
Camelford St BN2 ....189 C1
Cameron Cl BN27 ....152 A8
Campbell Cl TN22 .....55 C1
Campbell Cres RH19 ...1 B1
Campbell Ct TN38 ...159 A8
Campbell Mews 2
  BN23 ....175 A1
Campbell Rd
  Brighton BN1 ....189 A5
  Royal Tunbridge Wells TN4 ..8 B4
Camperdown St TN39 157 B7
Canada Cl BN10 .....167 B1
Canada Way TN39 ...157 B7
Canadia Rd TN33 ....112 D8
Canal Bank TN35 ....139 B7
Canary Quay 15 BN23 185 F8
Canfield Cl BN2 .....143 D1
Canfield Rd BN2 ....143 D1
Canning St BN2 .....164 C4
Cannon Cvn & Camp Site
  BN24 ....175 B3
Cannon Pl BN1 ......189 A2
Cansiron La
  Ashurst Wood RH19 ..11 F6
  Holtye TN7,TN8 ....3 E2
Cantelupe Mews 5 RH19 .1 E1
Cantelupe Rd
  Bexhill TN40 ....157 D3
  East Grinstead RH19 ...1 F1
Canterbury Cl BN22 ..173 C2
Canterbury Dr 5 BN2 .164 C4
Canterbury Rd TN2 ....9 E6
Canterbury Rise TN34 136 E3
Cantercrow Hill BN9 .168 F2
Canton 3 RH16 ......50 D6
Cants Cl RH15 ....73 C3
Cants La RH15 ....73 C3
Canute Cl BN23 .....185 F8
Canute Rd TN35 .....160 D7
Capel Ave RH10 .....178 D7
Capella Path BN27 ..152 D7
Capenors RH15 ....72 F1
Caple Ct TN38 ......159 B8
Caple Gdns TN38 ...159 B7
Card Hill RH18 ....11 F1
Carden Ave BN1 ....143 B6
Carden Cl BN1 ......143 A6
Carden Cres BN1 ...143 A6
Carden Hill BN1 ....143 B5
Carden Prim Sch BN1 143 B6
Cardiff Rd TN38 ....159 C7
Cardinal Newman RC Sch
  BN3 ....163 D8
Cardinals Cl TN40 ...157 C6
Carew Ct
  7 Eastbourne BN21 .185 A4
  Hailsham BN27 .....129 C3
Carew Lodge 1 BN21 184 F4
Carew Rd BN21 .....184 F4
Carew Views 2 BN21 184 F4
Carey Down BN10 ...167 B1
Carfax TN39 ....157 B8
Carinus Gdns TN37 ..136 A6
Carisbrooke Cl BN23 174 B4
Carisbrooke Rd
  Brighton BN2 ......164 F7
  St Leonards TN38 ..159 C7
Carlisle Bldgs 2 BN21 185 A1
Carlisle Par TN34 ...159 F7
Carlisle Rd
  Eastbourne BN20,BN21 184 F1
  Hove BN3 ....162 F6
Carlton Cl BN25 ....180 E4
Carlton Cres TN1 ......8 C4
Carlton Ct
  1 Bexhill TN40 .....157 D3
  Portslade-by-S BN41 .162 C8
Carlton Hill BN2 ....189 C2
Carlton Hill Prim Sch
  BN2 ....189 C2
Carlton Ho 6 BN1 ...142 E2
Carlton Pl 5 BN2 ...189 C2
Carlton Rd
  Eastbourne BN22 ...185 C4
  Royal Tunbridge Wells TN1 ..8 B4
  Seaford BN25 ......180 D4

Carlton Terr
　🔳 Crowborough TN6 ......37 F8
　Portslade-by-S BN3,BN41 ..162 C8
Carlyle Ave BN2 ....143 D1
Carlyle St BN2 ....164 C7
Carmel Cl TN39 ....156 D3
Carmel Ho BN3 ....163 A7
Carmelstead Cl RH16 ....51 A3
Carmen Ct BN20 ....173 B3
Carn Ct 🔳 BN2 ....164 C6
Carnoustie Cl TN38 .....158 F4
Carnoustie Ct 🔳 RH16 ..50 E4
Carol Cl BN1 ....142 F6
Caroline Cl BN25 ....180 D5
Caroline Way BN23 .....175 B1
Carpenter Dr TN38 .....135 F4
Carpenters Croft BN8 ...105 A5
Carpenters Way BN27 ...152 A6
Carr Taylor Vineyard★
　TN35 ....114 C4
Carrier's Path BN27 .....152 B8
Carriers Pl TN3 ....5 B4
Carroll Wlk BN23 ....174 E2
Carvel Ct TN37 ....135 E7
Cashman Lodge BN1 ....143 A3
Caspian Ct 🔳 BN1 ......189 A4
Caspian Sq BN1 ....165 F1
Castle Banks BN7 ......190 A2
Castle Bolton BN23 .....174 C4
Castle Ct BN7 ....190 B3
Castle Ditch La BN7 ....190 A2
Castle Dr BN24 ....175 C4
Castle Farm Cotts TN7 ..13 C4
Castle Gate BN7 ....190 A2
Castle Gdns 🔳 TN34 ...159 F7
Castle Hill TN6 ....39 A5
Castle Hill Pas TN34 ...159 F8
Castle Hill Rd TN34 ....159 F7
Castle Hurst TN32 ....65 B8
Castle La BN7 ....190 A2
Castle Mount BN20 .....184 D1
Castle Prec BN7 ....190 A2
Castle Rd Pevensey BN24 175 A6
　Royal Tunbridge Wells TN4 ..8 A3
Castle Rise Lewes BN7 ..190 A2
　Uckfield TN22 ....78 D4
Castle Sq BN1 ....189 B2
Castle St Brighton BN1 ..163 E5
　🔳 Hastings TN34 ......159 F7
　🔳 Royal Tunbridge Wells
　TN1 ....8 A2
　Winchelsea TN36 ......117 F7
Castle Terr BN24 ....175 B6
Castle View Cvn & Camp Site
　BN24 ....175 B3
Castle View Gdns BN24 .174 E6
Castle Way TN22 ....78 D4
Castle Wlk TN5 ....29 E4
Castledean Sch BN1 ....143 C2
Castledown Ave TN34 ...160 A4
Castledown Com Prim Sch
　TN34 ....160 A5
Castledown Terr 🔳
　TN34 ....160 A4
Castlefields TN7 ....13 E4
Castleham Ind Est TN38 135 F5
Castleham Rd TN38 .....135 F5
Castleross Rd BN24 ....175 C4
Castleview Mews TN34 ..160 A4
Cat St TN7 ....12 F1
Cathedral Wlk BN27 ....127 B3
Catherine Pl 🔳 TN1 .....8 B4
Catherine Vale BN2 .....165 E8
Catkin Way RH16 ....51 B4
Catley Ct 🔳 TN39 ......157 A4
Catsfield CE Prim Sch
　TN33 ....133 F8
Catsfield Cl
　Eastbourne BN23 .....173 F4
　St Leonards TN38 .....135 D2
Catsfield Rd TN33 ......111 C2
Catt's Corner Cotts TN6 .27 D1
Catt's Hill TN6 ....27 E1
Cattswood La RH16 .....50 C2
Causeway Sch The
　BN23 ....174 A3
Causeway The
　Brighton BN2 ....164 D6
　🔳 Seaford BN25 ......180 E2
Cavalier Way RH19 .....10 F7
Cavalry Cres BN20 .....184 B5
Cavendish Mews 🔳
　BN1 ....163 D5
Cavell Ave BN10 ....178 B7
Cavell Ave N BN10 .....178 C8
Cavell Ct BN10 ....178 B7
Cavendish Ave
　Eastbourne BN22 .....185 B4
　St Leonards TN38 .....159 A7
Cavendish Cl BN10 .....167 B1
Cavendish Ct 🔳 TN40 ..157 D3
Cavendish Dr TN2 ....8 B1
Cavendish Ho
　🔳 Brighton BN1 ......163 E5
　Haywards Heath RH16 ..50 F2
　Peacehaven BN10 .....167 C1
　🔳 St Leonards TN37 ..159 C7
Cavendish Pl
　Brighton BN1 ....163 E5
　Eastbourne BN21 .....185 B3
　🔳 Hastings TN34 .....160 A4
Cavendish Sch The
　BN21 ....184 C5
Cavendish St 🔳 BN2 ...189 C5
Caveridge La BN8 ......100 E8
Caves Rd TN38 ....159 A6
Cavix Field TN31 ....67 B7
Caxton Way 🔳 RH16 ...50 E4

Cecil Ct 🔳 BN21 ....184 F2
Cedar Cl Burgess Hill RH15 73 B5
　Eastbourne BN22 .....173 D2
　St Leonards TN37 ....136 D5
Cedar Ct TN4 ....8 A5
Cedar Ho TN4 ....7 E4
Cedar Lodge TN4 ....7 F3
Cedar Ridge TN7 ......51 B4
Cedar Way RH16 ......51 B4
Cedars Cl TN22 ....78 C8
Cedars Gdns BN1 .....142 E3
Cedars The
　🔳 Brighton BN2 .....189 C5
　Brighton,Withdean BN1 142 E3
　Hailsham BN27 ....129 B1
　Haywards Heath RH16 ..50 D7
　Peacehaven BN10 ....167 C1
　Uckfield TN22 ....78 D8
Cedarwell Cl BN9 ......168 B2
Cedarwood 🔳 BN1 ....142 E3
Celandine Dr TN38 ....136 A1
Cello Ct 🔳 BN1 ....164 C5
Centenary Ho 🔳 BN1 ..142 E2
Centenary Ind Est 🔳
　BN2 ....164 B8
Central Ave
　Eastbourne BN20 ....184 B5
　Polegate BN26 ......173 B7
　Telscombe Cliffs BN10 .178 A8
Central Par TN5 ....29 F4
Centurion Rd BN1 .....189 A3
Centurion Rise TN34 ..160 A8
Ceylon Pl BN21,BN22 ..185 B3
Ceylon Wlk TN39 .....156 E3
Chadborn Cl BN2 .....164 D5
Chaffinch Cl RH15 .....72 D4
Chaffinch Rd BN23 ....174 C2
Chaffinch Wlk TN38 ....78 D5
Chafford Cotts TN3 .....5 F5
Chafford La TN3 ....5 F5
Chailey Ave BN2 ......177 A5
Chailey Cl
　Eastbourne BN23 ....174 E1
　Hastings TN34 ....136 F5
Chailey Common Nature
　Reserve★ BN8 ....75 D7
Chailey Cres BN2 .....177 A5
Chailey Ct Brighton BN1 50 F3
　🔳 Haywards Heath RH16 50 F3
Chailey Heritage Sch
　BN8 ....75 C7
Chailey Heritage Sch & Hospl
　(New Heritage) BN8 ..52 E1
Chailey La BN8 ....76 B5
Chailey Rd BN1 ....143 E4
Chailey Sch BN8 ......100 D7
Chailey St Peter's CE Prim
　Sch BN8 ....75 E4
Chailey Windmill Rural Life
　Mus★ BN8 ....75 D7
Chain La TN33 ....112 C5
Chain Pier Ho BN2 ....189 C1
Chalden Pl TN39 ......156 C6
Chalex Ind Est BN42 ..162 A7
Chalfont Cl BN27 .....152 C6
Chalfont Dr BN3 ......142 C3
Chalk Farm Cl BN20 ..173 B1
Chalkers La BN6 ......97 B8
Chalket La TN2 ....9 C5
Chalkland Rise BN2 ...165 E8
Chalky Rd BN41 ......141 A3
Challoners Cl BN2 .....165 F2
Challoners Cl RH17 ...33 C4
Challoners Mews BN2 ..165 F2
Challow Cl BN6 ....97 E4
Chaloner Cl RH16 .....51 B7
Chaloner Rd RH16 ....51 B7
Chalvington Cl
　Brighton BN1 ....143 E6
　Seaford BN25 ....180 F6
Chalvington Dr TN37 ..136 C6
Chalvington Ho 🔳
　BN21 ....184 D4
Chalvington Rd BN21 ..184 C7
Chamberlain Rd BN21 ..184 C4
Chamberlaines La BN8 124 F6
Chambers Cres TN38 ..135 F3
Chambers Rd TN38 ...135 F3
Champions Row BN3 ..163 C8
Chancellor Ho TN4 ...7 F3
Chancellors Pk BN6 ..97 E4
Chanctonbury Dr TN34 136 E5
Chanctonbury Rd
　Burgess Hill RH15 ....73 A1
　Hove BN3 ....163 F2
Chandler Rd TN39 ....157 A4
Chandler's Mead BN8 .123 A7
Chandos Ct 🔳 TN40 ..157 C3
Chandos Rd TN1 ......8 C5
Channel Grange BN10 178 A7
Channel View
　🔳 Bexhill TN40 .....157 C3
　🔳 Southwick BN42 ..161 E7
Channel View E TN40 ..157 C3
Channel View Rd
　Eastbourne BN22 ....185 D5
　Pevensey Bay BN24 ..175 C4
　Woodingdean BN2 ...165 B8
Channel View W 🔳
　TN40 ....157 C3
Channel Way TN35 ...138 E3
Channers La BN6 .....126 E1
Chant La TN6 ....25 F2
Chantlers Cl RH19 .....1 C2
Chantlers Mead TN8 ...4 A1
Chantry Ave TN40 ....157 D6
Chantry Com Prim Sch
　TN40 ....157 C5

Chantry La TN40 ......157 C5
Chantry The 🔳 BN21 ..184 E4
Chapel Barn Cl BN27 ..152 C7
Chapel Cl
　Burgess Hill RH15 ....72 F4
　Seaford BN25 ....180 E4
Chapel Cotts TN33 ....112 E3
Chapel Field TN31 .....67 A7
Chapel Gn TN6 ....25 F2
Chapel Hill
　Alfriston BN26 ......171 B3
　Crowhurst TN33 .....134 F4
　Lewes BN7 ....190 C2
　Sedlescombe TN33 ..113 E7
Chapel Ho BN2 ......189 C2
Chapel La
　Ashurst Wood RH19 ..11 D6
　Blackboys TN22 .....80 B7
　East Chiltington BN7 .100 A3
　Forest Row RH18 ...11 F2
　Guestling Green TN35 138 A8
　Horsted Keynes RH17 .33 C5
　Westfield TN35 .....114 C4
Chapel Mews 🔳 BN3 ..163 D5
Chapel Park Rd TN37 ..159 C8
Chapel Pl
　Portslade-by-S BN41 ..162 B7
　🔳 Royal Tunbridge Wells
　TN1 ....8 A2
　Ticehurst TN5 ....31 E1
Chapel Rd
　Plumpton Green BN7 ..99 E7
　Portslade-by-S BN41 ..162 A7
　Newhaven BN9 .....179 D7
Chapel Terr 🔳 BN2 ...164 D4
Chapel Terrace Mews 🔳
　BN2 ....164 D4
Chapman Way TN2 ....8 C8
Chapman's La
　East Grinstead RH19 ...1 B1
　East Grinstead RH19 ...1 D1
Chapman's Town Rd
　TN21 ....83 B2
Charis Ct 🔳 BN3 .....163 C7
Charity Farm Way TN6 ..26 A3
Charles Ave RH15 .....72 D2
Charles Bennett Ct RH16 51 A4
Charles Cl Hove BN3 ..142 A3
　Seaford BN25 ....180 D5
Charles Ct TN2 ....8 C3
Charles Kingston Gdns
　BN1 ....142 E4
Charles Moore Ct BN26 173 A7
Charles Rd TN38 .....159 C8
Charles Rd W TN38 ..159 B8
Charles St Brighton BN2 189 B1
　Royal Tunbridge Wells TN4 ..8 A8
Charleston Farmhouse★
　BN8 ....149 A2
Charleston Manor Gdns★
　BN25 ....182 A6
Charleston Rd BN21 ..184 D4
Charlesworth Pk RH16 ..51 C4
Charlotte St BN2 .....189 C1
Charlston Ave BN9 ...179 A5
Charlton Gdns BN6 ...98 D3
Charlton's Way TN4 ...7 E1
Charltons The BN1 ...143 D6
Charlwood Gdns RH15 .73 C5
Charlwood Rd RH15 ...73 D6
Charlwoods Bsns Ctr
　RH19 ....1 D2
Charlwoods Pl RH19 ...1 E3
Charlwoods Rd RH19 ...1 E3
Charter Gate RH16 ...50 D5
Charters Ancaster Coll
　TN40 ....157 A6
Charters Ancaster Sch
　TN40 ....157 F5
Chartfield BN3 ....142 A2
Chartfield Way BN3 ..142 B2
Chartres TN40 ....157 D6
Chartres Cl TN40 ....157 D6
Chartwell Cl BN25 ...180 E6
Chartwell Ct BN1 ....189 A4
Chates Farm Ct BN2 .189 C3
Chatfield Cres TN38 ..135 F4
Chatfield Cres BN22 ..173 C1
Chatfield Rd RH17 ....50 A4
Chatham Pl
　Brighton BN1 ....189 A4
　Seaford BN25 ......180 E2
Chatham Rd 🔳 TN37 .136 B2
Chatsworth Ave BN10 167 A1
Chatsworth Cl BN10 ..178 A8
Chatsworth Ct BN1 ..163 E8
Chatsworth Gdns BN20 188 F8
Chatsworth Pk BN10 ..167 B1
Chatsworth Rd BN1 ..163 E8
Chatsworth Sq BN3 ..163 D7
Chaucer Ave 🔳 RH19 ..1 C1
Chaucer Ct 🔳 RH16 ..50 F2
Chaucer Ind Est BN26 173 D6
Chaucer Wlk BN23 ...174 E3
Chawbrook Mews BN22 185 B4
Chawbrook Rd BN22 ..185 B4
Cheal Cl BN43 ....161 A6
Cheapside BN1 ......189 B3
Cheeleys RH17 ....33 C5
Chelgates TN6 ....25 F2
Chelmsford Ct 🔳 BN20 184 F1
Chelsea Arc RH16 ....50 F2
Chelsea Ct TN40 ....157 D4
Chelsea Mews 🔳 TN38 159 C7
Chelston Ave BN3 ....162 D2
Cheltenham Pl BN1 ..189 B3
Chelwood Cl BN1 ....143 C6

Chelwood Ct RH15 .....73 A4
Chelwood Gate Rd RH15,
　TN22 ....34 D7
Chelworth Rd BN22 ...173 D2
Chene Rd BN10 ....178 B5
Chenies TN2 ....17 A8
Chepbourne Rd TN40 .157 C4
Chepstow Ct BN1 ....143 F5
Chequer Grange RH18 .11 E1
Chequer Mead Arts Ctr
　RH19 ....1 F1
Chequer Rd RH19 .....1 F1
Chequers Cl TN6 .....26 A2
Chequers Way TN6 ...26 A2
Cherington Cl BN6 ...97 B5
Cherith Cotts 🔳 TN21 .82 A6
Cheriton TN20 ....184 C1
Cherry Cl RH15 ....72 E3
Cherry Clack TN21 ...83 C6
Cherry Cotts
　Fletching TN22 ......54 A4
　Hastings TN35 ......160 C7
Cherry Garden Rd BN20 184 B3
Cherry Gdns
　Heathfield TN21 .....82 B5
　High Hurstwood TN22 56 B8
Cherry Side BN27 ....152 A7
Cherry Tree Cl TN37 ..159 D8
Cherry Tree Ct TN21 ..106 F3
Cherry Tree Gdns TN40 157 F6
Cherry Tree Rd TN2 ...7 E1
Cherrywood 🔳 BN1 ..142 E3
Cherwell Cl BN24 ....173 F5
Cherwell Ct TN21 ....82 A8
Cherwell Lo BN2 ....82 A8
Cherwell Rd TN21 ...82 A8
Chesham Pl BN2 ....164 D4
Chesham Rd BN2 ....164 D4
Chesham St BN2 ....164 D4
Cheshire Ct 🔳 BN22 ..185 B4
Chester Ave TN2 ....8 D2
Chester Ct 🔳 BN3 ...163 E7
Chester Terr BN1 ....143 A1
Chesterfield Gdns BN20 188 E8
Chesterfield Rd BN20 ..188 E8
Chesterton Ave BN25 ..181 B3
Chesterton Cl RH19 ...10 F7
Chesterton Dr BN25 ..181 B3
Chestnut Ave
　Golden Cross BN27 ..127 B4
　Royal Tunbridge Wells TN4 ..8 B8
Chestnut Cl
　Broad Oak TN31 .....90 B5
　Burgess Hill RH15 ...73 B5
　East Grinstead RH19 ..2 A1
　Eastbourne BN22 ....173 E2
　Hailsham BN27 .....129 A1
　Herstmonceux BN27 .130 E6
　Royal Tunbridge Wells TN4 ..8 B8
Chestnut Cotts
　Fletching TN22 .....53 F3
　🔳 Heathfield TN21 ..82 A7
Chestnut Ct TN2 .....17 A8
Chestnut Dr BN26 ...173 A6
Chestnut Pl TN8 .....4 A6
Chestnut Way BN9 ..179 B7
Chestnut Wlk
　Bexhill TN39 ....156 C5
　Felcourt RH19 ....1 C8
Chestnuts Cl RH16 ...51 A7
Chestnuts The
　Haywards Heath RH16 50 F7
　The Moor TN18 .....45 F8
Chetnole RH19 ....1 D2
Cheviot Cl BN23 .....174 C3
Cheviots The TN34 ..160 C8
Cheyne Ct BN43 .....161 C7
Chichester Cl
　Bexhill TN39 ....157 B6
　Eastbourne BN22 ...173 B2
　Hove BN3 ....141 E4
　Peacehaven BN10 ..178 F7
　Saltdean BN2 ....177 C5
　Seaford BN25 ....180 E3
Chichester Ct
　Bexhill TN39 ....156 C3
　🔳 Seaford BN25 ....180 E2
Chichester Dr E BN2 ..177 C5
Chichester Dr W BN2 ..177 B5
Chichester Ho 🔳 TN40 157 C3
Chichester Lodge BN25 180 E3
Chichester Pl 🔳 BN2 ..164 D4
Chichester Rd
　Seaford BN25 ......180 E3
　St Leonards TN38 ...136 B3
Chichester Terr 🔳 BN2 164 D4
Chichester Way RH15 ..73 C5
Chick Hill TN35 ......139 B8
Chicks La TN7 ....20 F2
Chiddingly Cl BN2 ...164 F5
Chiddingly Ho 🔳 BN3 163 D7
Chiddingly Prim Sch
　BN8 ....127 C2
Chieveley Cotts TN38 136 B1
Chieveley Dr TN2 ....8 D1
Chilcomb RH15 ......73 C1
Chilham Cl BN23 ....174 D2
Chillies La TN22,TN6 ..37 B3
Chilling St RH19 ......21 D3
Chillis Wood Rd RH16 ..50 C5
Chilsham La BN27 ....130 E2
Chilston Ct TN4 .....8 A5
Chilston Rd TN4 ....8 A5
Chiltern Cl
　Eastbourne BN23 ...174 D3
　Shoreham-by-S BN43 161 C8
Chiltern Ct BN26 ....173 A7

Chiltern Dr TN34 .....160 B7
Chiltern Wlk TN2 ....8 D4
Chiltington Cl
　Burgess Hill RH15 ...72 F5
　Saltdean BN2 ....177 C6
Chiltington La TN7 ....100 D3
Chiltington Way BN2 ..177 C6
Chiswick Pl BN21 ....185 A2
Chitcombe Rd TN31 ..89 C5
Chitcombe Wlk TN34 ..137 A5
Chorley Ave BN2 ....177 B6
Chown's Hill TN35 ...137 A6
Chownes Mead La RH16 50 B4
Chrisdory Rd BN41 ...140 F3
Christ Church Ave 🔳 TN1 ..8 A2
Christ Church CE Prim Sch
　TN37 ....136 C1
Christchurch Ct TN9 ..179 D7
Christie Ave BN8 ....124 D6
Christie Rd BN7 .....123 A2
Christies RH19 ......10 D8
Christine Cl TN40 ....158 A7
Christopher Rd BN19 ..1 E1
Church App TN22 ....79 B5
Church Ave
　Haywards Heath RH16 50 E6
　Westham BN24 ......175 A6
Church Bailey BN24 ..175 A5
Church Bailey Ct BN24 175 A5
Church Cl Brighton BN1 142 F5
　Burgess Hill RH15 ...73 A3
　Eastbourne BN20 ...173 A4
Church Ct
　🔳 Haywards Heath RH16 50 E4
　Hove BN3 ....141 F1
Church Farm Cl TN19 ..44 C1
Church Gn BN43 .....161 C7
Church Hill Bexhill TN39 156 D4
　Brighton BN1 ....142 E7
　Etchingham TN19 ...44 B2
　Newhaven BN9 .....179 C7
　Pyecombe BN45 ...119 C6
　Ringmer BN8 ....124 D6
Church Hill Ave TN39 .156 D4
Church House Cl BN42 140 F4
Church La
　Burgess Hill RH17 ...73 F6
　Buxted TN22 ....56 C5
　Catsfield TN33 ......133 E8
　Clayhill TN31 ....67 E4
　Danehill RH17 ....34 A3
　Ditchling BN6 ....98 D3
　East Grinstead RH19 ..1 F1
　🔳 Eastbourne BN21 ..184 D3
　Etchingham TN19 ...44 C1
　Frant TN3 ....17 B4
　Guestling Green TN35 116 B1
　Hellingly BN27 ......129 A6
　Hooe TN33 ....155 C7
　Horsted Keynes RH17 .33 C5
　Iden TN31 ....70 D7
　Jevington BN26 .....183 C7
　Kingston near Lewes BN7 145 D5
　Laughton BN8 ......126 C5
　Lewes,South Malling BN7 190 B4
　Lewes,St Anne's BN7 146 B8
　Ninfield TN33 ....133 B5
　Northbridge Street TN32 .64 C5
　Northiam TN31 ......67 C6
　Pevensey BN24 .....175 B6
　Pyecombe BN45 ...119 C6
　Ripe BN27,TN8 .....149 E8
　Rye Foreign TN31 ...92 B8
　Seaford BN25 ....180 E2
　Southwick BN42 ....161 D7
　Westfield TN35 .....114 C4
Church Marks La BN8 ..104 F5
Church Mead BN6 ...98 B3
Church Mews BN26 ..173 B1
Church Pas 🔳 TN34 ..160 A4
Church Path
　Hellingly BN27 ......129 A5
　Ninfield TN33 ....133 A5
Church Pl BN2 ....164 E4
Church Rd
　Barcombe BN8 ......101 E2
　Burgess Hill RH15 ...73 A3
　Buxted TN22 ....56 B4
　Catsfield TN33 ......133 F7
　Crowborough TN6 ...25 F2
　Flowers Green BN27 .131 A1
　Haywards Heath RH16 50 E4
　Hove BN3 ....163 B6
　Kilndown TN17 ......20 F3
　Lamberhurst TN3 ...20 C6
　Mountfield TN32 ....87 B5
　Newick BN8 ....76 B6
　Pembury TN2 ....9 D8
　Polegate BN26 .....173 A6
　Portslade-by-S BN41 ..162 B7
　Rotherfield TN6 .....39 A8
　Royal Tunbridge Wells TN1 ..8 A3
　Sandhurst Cross TN18 ..46 F4
　Scaynes Hill RH17 ...51 F3
　St Leonards TN37 ...159 D7
Church Row BN7 .....190 A2
Church Sq TN35 .....93 C5
Church St Bexhill TN40 157 D5
　Brighton BN1 ....189 B2
　Cowden TN8 ....4 B5
　Eastbourne,Old Town
　BN20,BN21 ....184 D3

Church St continued
Hartfield TN7 . . . .**13** D4
Hastings TN35 . . . .**160** C7
Old Heathfield TN21 . . . . . .**82** D5
Portslade-by-S BN41 . . . . .**162** B7
Seaford BN25 . . . .**180** E2
Ticehurst TN5 . . . .**31** D1
Uckfield TN22 . . . .**78** C7
Wadhurst TN5 . . . .**30** A4
Church Twitten BN7 . . . . .**190** B2
Church Vale Rd TN40 . . . .**157** D5
Church Walk Mews RH15 73 A3
Church Way 6 BN2 . . . . .**189** C3
Church Wlk RH15 . . . .**73** A3
Church Wood Dr TN38 . .**135** E4
Church Wood Way
TN38 . . . .**135** F2
Churchdale Ave BN22 . . .**185** C6
Churchdale Pl BN22 . . . . .**185** B6
Churchdale Rd BN22 . . . .**185** C6
Churchfield
East Dean BN20 . . . .**187** B8
Westfield TN35 . . . .**114** D3
Churchfield Sq 16 BN21 .**184** F4
Churchfields TN22 . . . . . .**35** C4
Churchfields Ind Est
TN38 . . . .**135** E4
Churchill Ave TN35 . . . . .**137** D5
Churchill Cl BN20 . . . . . .**184** D3
Churchill Ct TN38 . . . . . .**136** B2
Churchill Ho Hove BN3 . .**141** E2
Seaford BN25 . . . .**181** C4
Churchill Rd
Heathfield TN21 . . . .**82** B6
Lewes BN7 . . . .**123** B3
Seaford BN25 . . . .**180** D5
Churchill Sq BN1 . . . . . .**189** A2
Churchill Square Sh Ctr
BN1 . . . .**189** A2
Churchill Way RH15 . . . . .**73** C2
Churchland La TN33 . . . . .**88** E3
Churchsettle La TN5 . . . . .**42** B7
Churchwood Com Prim Sch
TN38 . . . .**135** F2
Churchyard Cotts TN3 . . .**7** A8
Chyngton Ave BN25 . . . .**181** B4
Chyngton Cl BN23 . . . . . .**174** A4
Chyngton Gdns BN25 . . .**181** B4
Chyngton Ho BN25 . . . . .**181** C2
Chyngton La BN25 . . . . . .**181** C3
Chyngton La N BN25 . . . .**181** C3
Chyngton Pl BN25 . . . . . .**181** B2
Chyngton Rd BN25 . . . . . .**181** A2
Chyngton Sch BN25 . . . . .**181** B4
Chyngton Way BN25 . . . .**181** C2
Cider Hollow BN27 . . . . . .**131** B5
Cider House Wlk BN8 . . .**105** A5
Cinder Hill Chailey BN8 . .**75** F3
Cinder Hill RH16 . . . .**21** B1
Cinderford La TN22 . . . . .**129** F8
Cinque Ports St TN31 . . . .**93** B5
Cinque Ports Way
Seaford BN25 . . . .**181** C4
St Leonards TN38 . . . .**158** C4
Cinquefoil BN10 . . . .**178** C4
Circus Par BN1 . . . .**189** B4
Circus St BN2 . . . .**189** B2
Circus The BN23 . . . .**185** D8
Cissbury Ave BN10 . . . . .**178** E7
Cissbury Cres BN2 . . . . .**177** E5
Cissbury Rd
Burgess Hill RH15 . . . .**72** C4
Hove BN3 . . . .**163** E7
City Coll Brighton & Hove
Brighton BN1 . . . .**189** A5
Brighton BN1 . . . .**189** B3
Brighton BN2 . . . .**189** C4
Hove BN3 . . . .**163** A6
Civic App TN22 . . . .**78** C7
Civic Way
Burgess Hill RH15 . . . .**73** A4
Royal Tunbridge Wells TN1 . .**8** A3
CJ Gallards Almshouses
TN4 . . . .**8** A8
Clackhams La TN6 . . . . . .**38** D7
Clair Ct RH16 . . . .**50** E5
Clair Rd RH16 . . . .**50** E5
Clanricarde Gdns 1 TN1 .**8** A3
Clanricarde Rd 2 TN1 . . . .**8** A3
Clapham La BN26 . . . . . .**182** A8
Claphatch La TN5 . . . .**31** A5
Clappers The TN32 . . . . . .**64** B4
Clare Rd BN7 . . . .**123** A2
Clare Wlk BN2 . . . .**164** D5
Claremont 9 TN34 . . . . . .**159** E7
Claremont Ct
4 Royal Tunbridge Wells
TN2 . . . .**8** C7
Seaford BN25 . . . .**180** D3
Claremont Gdns TN2 . . . . .**8** A2
Claremont Pl TN22 . . . . . .**55** C1
Claremont Prim Sch TN2 . .**8** B2
Claremont Rd
Bexhill TN39 . . . .**157** B7
Newhaven BN9 . . . .**168** F1
Royal Tunbridge Wells TN1 . .**8** B2
Seaford BN25 . . . .**180** D3
Claremont Rise TN22 . . . .**55** C1
Claremont Sch TN37 . . . . .**114** B1
Clarence Ct BN24 . . . . . .**175** C3
Clarence Dr 2 RH19 . . . . .**10** F7
Clarence Gdns BN1 . . . . .**189** A2
Clarence Rd
Eastbourne BN22 . . . .**185** B4
Royal Tunbridge Wells TN1 . .**8** A3

Clarence Rd continued
St Leonards TN37 . . . .**136** C1
Clarence Row TN1 . . . .**8** A3
Clarence Sq BN1 . . . .**189** A2
Clarendon Cl TN37 . . . . . .**136** B4
Clarendon Gdns TN2 . . . . .**8** A1
Clarendon Ho 2 BN3 . . . .**163** B7
Clarendon Pl
15 Brighton BN2 . . . .**164** C4
Portslade-by-S BN41 . . . . .**162** C6
Clarendon Rd Hove BN3 . .**163** B7
Shoreham-by-S BN42,
BN43 . . . .**161** D8
Clarendon Terr 16 BN2 . . .**164** D4
Clarendon Villas BN3 . . . .**163** B7
Clarendon Way TN2 . . . . . .**8** A1
Claridge TN1 . . . .**8** B6
Clark's Yd TN5 . . . .**32** A3
Clarke Ave BN3 . . . .**141** F3
Clarke Ct BN3 . . . .**162** F6
Clarks Inn BN3 . . . .**163** B8
Claverham Cl TN33 . . . . . .**112** B4
Claverham Com Coll
TN33 . . . .**112** A4
Claverham Way TN33 . . . .**112** B4
Clavering Wlk TN39 . . . . .**156** B2
Claxton Cl BN21 . . . .**184** D5
Claxton Rd TN40 . . . .**158** A5
Clay Cnr BN8 . . . .**101** F6
Clay Hill Rd TN3 . . . .**19** D6
Clayfields BN10 . . . .**178** B7
Clays Cl RH19 . . . .**10** E8
Clayton Ave BN6 . . . .**97** F3
Clayton Dr BN25 . . . .**72** F1
Clayton Hill BN6,BN45 . . .**119** D7
Clayton Mill Rd BN24 . . . .**174** B5
Clayton Pk BN6 . . . .**97** E4
Clayton Rd Brighton BN2 .**164** D7
Ditchling BN6 . . . .**98** C3
Clayton Way BN3 . . . .**141** F3
Clayton Windmills★
BN6 . . . .**119** E7
Clayton's La TN3 . . . .**5** E2
Clearwater La RH17 . . . . . .**52** A3
Clearwaters La RH16 . . . . .**73** D8
Cleeve Ave TN2 . . . .**8** D2
Cleevelands BN22 . . . . . .**173** B4
Clement Hill Rd TN34 . . . .**160** B7
Clement La BN26 . . . .**173** A5
Clementine Ave BN25 . . . .**180** D5
Clerks Acre BN6 . . . .**98** A4
Clermont Ct BN1 . . . .**142** E2
Clermont Rd BN1 . . . .**142** E2
Clermont Terr BN1 . . . . . .**142** E2
Cleve TN22 . . . .**79** B5
Cleve Terr BN7 . . . .**146** B8
Clevedon Rd TN39 . . . . . .**157** A6
Clevedown BN7 . . . .**146** A8
Cleveland TN2 . . . .**8** D4
Cleveland Cl BN23 . . . . . .**174** C3
Cleveland Gdns RH15 . . . .**73** B2
Cleveland Rd BN1 . . . . . .**143** A1
Clevelands RH16 . . . .**50** E6
Cliff App BN2 . . . .**164** F4
Cliff Ave BN10 . . . .**178** E5
Cliff Cl BN25 . . . .**180** F1
Cliff Ct TN38 . . . .**158** D6
Cliff End La TN35 . . . .**139** B7
Cliff Gdns Seaford BN25 .**180** F1
Telscombe Cliffs BN10 . . . .**177** F4
Cliff Park Cl BN10 . . . . . .**178** F7
Cliff Rd Brighton BN2 . . . .**164** F4
Eastbourne BN20 . . . .**188** E7
Seaford BN25 . . . .**180** F1
Cliff The BN2 . . . .**164** F4
Cliff Way TN35 . . . .**138** F5
Cliffe Ave BN3 . . . .**141** F3
Cliffe High St BN7 . . . . . .**190** B2
Cliffe Ind Est BN8 . . . .**146** F8
Cliffe Leas BN7 . . . .**190** C2
Clifford Ave BN1 . . . .**184** C6
Clifford Ct
9 Bexhill TN40 . . . .**157** C4
Crowborough TN6 . . . .**25** F2
Clifford Rd 10 TN40 . . . . .**157** C4
Clifton Cl BN22 . . . .**184** D8
Clifton Cotts TN2 . . . .**8** D8
Clifton Ct TN34 . . . .**159** E8
Clifton Hill BN1 . . . .**189** A3
Clifton Ho BN21 . . . .**184** D8
Clifton Mews BN1 . . . .**189** A3
Clifton Pl Brighton BN1 . . .**163** E6
Royal Tunbridge Wells TN1 . .**8** B2
Clifton Rd Brighton BN1 . . .**189** A3
Burgess Hill RH15 . . . .**72** D5
Hastings TN35 . . . .**160** C7
Newhaven BN9 . . . .**179** D7
Royal Tunbridge Wells TN2 . .**8** C7
Clifton Rise TN40 . . . .**157** F5
Clifton St BN1 . . . .**189** A4
Clifton Terr BN1 . . . .**189** A3
Clifton Way BN10 . . . .**178** A3
Cliftonville Ct 6 BN3 . . . .**163** B7
Cliftonville Rd TN38 . . . . .**158** C4
Cliftonville Way TN38 . . . .**158** D6
Climping Cl RH16 . . . .**50** D5
Clinch Green Ave TN39 . .**156** F7
Clinton Cres TN38 . . . . . .**136** B1
Clinton Hill RH7 . . . .**2** A8
Clinton La 4 BN25 . . . . . .**180** E3
Clinton Pl BN25 . . . .**180** E3
Clinton Way TN35 . . . .**138** F5
Clive Ave TN35 . . . .**160** C6
Clive Ct RH16 . . . .**50** E6
Clive Villas BN1 . . . .**112** E3
Cliveden Ct BN1 . . . .**142** E3
Clock House La TN2 . . . . . .**8** B1
Clock Tower Ct 5 TN39 157 B3
Clockhouse TN2 . . . .**8** F6

Cloister Ct 13 TN40 . . . . .**157** D3
Cloisters BN9 . . . .**179** C7
Cloisters The
Battle TN33 . . . .**112** D6
Eastbourne BN22 . . . .**173** C2
St Leonards TN37 . . . .**159** D7
Close Eight BN23 . . . .**174** E3
Close Eighteen BN23 . . . .**174** E2
Close Eleven BN23 . . . . . .**174** E3
Close Fifteen 6 BN23 . . . .**174** E2
Close Five BN23 . . . .**174** E2
Close Four BN23 . . . .**174** E2
Close Fourteen BN23 . . . .**174** E2
Close Nine BN23 . . . .**174** E2
Close Nineteen BN23 . . . .**174** E2
Close One BN23 . . . .**174** E3
Close Seven BN23 . . . . . .**174** E3
Close Seventeen BN23 . . .**174** E2
Close Six BN23 . . . .**174** E3
Close Sixteen BN23 . . . . .**174** E2
Close Ten BN23 . . . .**174** E2
Close The Blackboys TN22 .**80** B6
Brighton BN1 . . . .**164** D4
Burgess Hill RH15 . . . .**73** C4
Crowborough BN6 . . . .**25** E3
East Grinstead RH19 . . . . .**10** D8
Eastbourne BN21 . . . .**184** B8
Eastbourne BN22 . . . .**173** C3
Fairlight TN35 . . . .**138** C4
Friston BN20 . . . .**183** A1
Groombridge TN3 . . . .**15** C6
Hassocks BN6 . . . .**97** F4
Newhaven BN9 . . . .**168** F2
Royal Tunbridge Wells TN2 . .**8** C8
Rye TN31 . . . .**93** A6
Seaford BN25 . . . .**180** F2
Close Three BN23 . . . .**174** E3
Close Twelve BN23 . . . . . .**174** E2
Close Twenty BN23 . . . . . .**174** E2
Close Twentyfive BN23 . . .**174** D2
Close Twentyfour 4
BN23 . . . .**174** E2
Close Two BN23 . . . .**174** D2
Cloudesley Rd TN37 . . . . .**159** C8
Clovelly Ho BN26 . . . .**173** A7
Clover Ct 2 RH16 . . . .**50** E4
Clover Way BN41 . . . .**141** F3
Cloverlea TN39 . . . .**136** E5
Clovers End BN1 . . . .**143** B7
Cluny St BN7 . . . .**190** A1
Clyde Pk BN27 . . . .**152** C7
Clyde Rd Brighton BN1 . . .**189** B5
St Leonards TN37,TN38 . .**159** C7
Coach & Horses La RH17 34 C6
Coach & Horses Pas 18
TN2 . . . .**8** A2
Coach House Cotts TN31 94 F2
Coach La RH17 . . . .**34** C6
Coach Rd TN4 . . . .**7** C3
Coalbrook Ho BN2 . . . . . .**164** C5
Coast Rd BN24 . . . .**176** B7
Coastal Counties Ho 19
BN2 . . . .**189** C3
Coastguard Cl BN24 . . . . .**176** D8
Coastguard Cotts
Camber TN31 . . . .**94** D2
Normans' Bay BN24 . . . . .**176** D8
Coastguard La TN35 . . . . .**138** C4
Coastguard Sq
3 Eastbourne BN22 . . . . .**185** C4
Rye Harbour TN31 . . . .**94** A3
Coastguards TN35 . . . . . .**139** C8
Coates Ct 11 BN42 . . . . . .**161** E7
Cobald Rd BN24 . . . .**175** C5
Cobbett's Ride TN2 . . . .**7** F1
Cobbetts Mead RH16 . . . . .**51** B3
Cobblers Field TN19 . . . . . .**61** A3
Cobbold Ave BN1 . . . .**184** C5
Cobden Pl 5 BN27 . . . . . .**152** C7
Cobden Rd BN2 . . . .**164** C7
Cobdown La TN22 . . . .**55** C5
Cobham Twrs 2 TN40 . . . .**157** F4
Cobhams TN3 . . . .**7** A8
Cobourg Pl 6 TN34 . . . . .**160** A4
Cobton Dr BN3 . . . .**142** A3
Coburn Ct BN7 . . . .**190** B2
Cochrane Cl BN23 . . . . . .**185** E7
Cockcrow Wood TN37 . . . .**136** D5
Cockhaise Cotts RH16 . . . .**52** M4
Cockmount La TN5 . . . .**29** F5
Cockshut Rd BN7 . . . .**190** A1
Cogger's Cross TN21 . . . .**106** F3
Cogger's La TN21 . . . .**106** F4
Coggins Mill La TN20 . . . . .**40** D4
Coghurst Hall Holiday Village
TN35 . . . .**137** C8
Coghurst Rd TN35 . . . . . .**160** C8
Colbourne Ave BN2 . . . . .**143** D2
Colbourne Rd BN3 . . . . . .**163** E7
Colchester Vale RH18 . . . .**11** E2
Colchins RH15 . . . .**72** F1
Coldean La BN1 . . . .**143** E6
Coldean Prim Sch BN1 . . .**143** D6
Coldene Rd BN1 . . . .**143** C8
Coldharbour Cl TN6 . . . . . .**26** A1
Coldharbour La
Iden TN31 . . . .**70** A4
Newick BN8 . . . .**76** A7
Peasmarsh TN31 . . . .**69** E3
Coldharbour Rd
Lower Dicker BN27 . . . . . .**128** B2
White Post TN8,TN11 . . . . .**5** E8
Coldthorn La BN26,BN27 152 A4
Coldwaltham La RH15 . . . .**73** D2
Colebrook Rd
Brighton BN1 . . . .**142** D4
Royal Tunbridge Wells TN4 . .**8** C8
Southwick BN42 . . . .**161** F7

Colebrooke Rd TN39 . . . .**157** A4
Coleman Ave BN3 . . . . . .**162** E7
Coleman St BN2 . . . .**189** C4
Colemans Hatch Rd
RH18,TN7 . . . .**23** C6
Coleridge St BN3 . . . .**163** A7
Coleridge Wlk 7 BN23 . . .**174** E2
Coles Ct TN2 . . . .**8** C3
Colgate Cl BN2 . . . .**164** F6
College Cl
East Grinstead RH19 . . . . . .**1** F1
Portslade-by-S BN41 . . . . .**140** F3
College Ct 22 BN21 . . . . .**185** A2
College Dr TN2 . . . .**8** D4
College Gdns BN2 . . . . . .**164** C4
College Gn BN21 . . . .**184** E4
College La
East Grinstead RH19 . . . . . .**1** F1
Hurst Wickham BN6 . . . . . .**97** C6
College Pl Brighton BN2 . .**164** C4
Hurst Wickham BN6 . . . . . .**97** C6
College Rd Bexhill TN40 . .**157** F5
Brighton BN2 . . . .**164** C4
Eastbourne BN21 . . . .**184** F2
Seaford BN25 . . . .**180** F2
College St 11 BN21 . . . . .**164** C4
College Terr BN2 . . . .**164** D5
Collett Ct TN38 . . . .**135** F5
Collier Cl BN22 . . . .**184** C2
Collier Rd Hastings TN34 .**160** A5
Pevensey Bay BN24 . . . . .**175** D4
Collier's Gn TN21 . . . .**83** F3
Collingford La RH17 . . . . .**34** B4
Collington Ave TN39 . . . .**156** F3
Collington Cl BN20 . . . . . .**184** E1
Collington Gr TN39 . . . . . .**156** E4
Collington La E TN39 . . . .**156** F4
Collington La W TN39 . . . .**156** D3
Collington Man TN39 . . . .**157** B3
Collington Park Cres
TN39 . . . .**156** F4
Collington Rise
Bexhill TN39 . . . .**156** E4
Bexhill TN39 . . . .**156** E5
Collington Sta TN39 . . . . .**157** A3
Collingwood Ave TN21 . . .**82** B7
Collingwood Cl
4 East Grinstead RH19 . . .**10** F7
Eastbourne BN23 . . . .**185** E6
Peacehaven BN10 . . . .**167** D1
Collingwood Ct BN2 . . . . .**165** A3
Collingwood Rise TN21 . . .**82** A7
Collinstone Rd TN38 . . . . .**159** A7
Collinswood Dr TN38 . . . .**159** A7
Colmer Ct RH15 . . . .**72** C3
Colmer Pl RH15 . . . .**72** C3
Colonnade Gdns 13
BN21 . . . .**185** B3
Colonnade Rd 14 BN21 . .**185** B3
Colonnades The BN1 . . . .**189** B2
Coltstocks Rd BN20 . . . . .**188** D8
Columbus Dr BN3 . . . . . .**185** G7
Colville Ct 2 BN21 . . . . . .**184** E4
Colwell Cl RH16 . . . .**50** F3
Colwell Gdns RH16 . . . . . .**50** F3
Colwell La
Haywards Heath RH17 . . . .**50** E1
Haywards Heath RH17 . . . .**51** B3
Colwell Rd RH16 . . . .**50** F2
Colwood Cres BN20 . . . . .**184** B6
Colwood Hospl RH17 . . . . .**51** A3
Combe End TN6 . . . .**37** E8
Combe La
Eastbourne BN20 . . . .**188** D7
Standard Hill TN33 . . . . . .**132** F6
Combe Rise BN20 . . . . . .**173** A2
Combe The BN20 . . . .**184** A4
Combermere Rd TN38 . . .**136** B1
Command Rd BN20 . . . . .**184** B5
Commanders Wlk TN35 138 E4
Commercial Mews N 8
BN21 . . . .**185** A4
Commercial Rd
Burgess Hill RH15 . . . .**72** C3
Eastbourne BN21 . . . .**185** A3
Royal Tunbridge Wells TN1 . .**8** B5
Commercial Sq RH16 . . . . .**50** E6
Common La Ditchling BN6 . .**98** D6
Laughton BN8 . . . .**126** A8
Selmeston BN26 . . . .**149** E1
Common View TN4 . . . .**7** C4
Common Wood Rise TN6 25 F4
Compass BN41 . . . .**140** E3
Compasses La TN32 . . . . . .**88** C6
Comphurst La BN27 . . . . .**131** B4
Compton Ave BN1 . . . . . .**189** A4
Compton Cl 11 TN40 . . . . .**157** E4
Compton Dr BN20 . . . . . .**184** C2
Compton Grange BN20 . .**184** E1
Compton Lodge BN21 . . .**184** E2
Compton Place Rd
BN20,BN21 . . . .**184** E2
Compton Rd
Brighton BN1 . . . .**142** D1
Lindfield RH16 . . . .**51** B8
Compton St BN21 . . . .**185** A1
Compton Terr BN27 . . . . .**152** C7
Compts The BN10 . . . .**167** B1
Conan Doyle Ct TN6 . . . . .**25** E2
Concord Cl TN2 . . . .**8** C4
Concorde Ct TN39 . . . . . .**156** F6
Condor Way RH15 . . . .**72** E3
Conduit Hill 3 TN31 . . . . . .**93** C6
Coney Furlong BN10 . . . . .**167** D4
Coneyburrow Gdns
TN38 . . . .**135** E4

Coneyburrow La TN39 . . .**155** F5
Coneyburrow Rd TN2 . . . . .**8** E5
Conghurst La TN18 . . . . . .**46** B6
Conifer Cl TN34 . . . .**136** F3
Conifers The 8 BN21 . . . .**184** F4
Coniston Ave TN4 . . . .**7** E5
Coniston Ct 9 BN3 . . . . . .**163** D7
Coniston Rd BN23 . . . . . .**174** C4
Connaught Rd
1 Eastbourne BN21 . . . . .**185** A2
Hove BN3 . . . .**163** A6
Seaford BN25 . . . .**180** C3
Connaught Terr BN3 . . . . .**163** B7
Connaught Way TN4 . . . . . .**7** F5
Connell Dr BN2 . . . .**165** F2
Conqueror Ind Est TN38 135 F6
Conqueror Rd TN38 . . . . .**158** E7
Conqueror Terr TN33 . . . . .**88** F1
Conquest Hospl TN37 . . . .**136** D6
Consort Way RH15 . . . .**72** E2
Constable Rd TN40 . . . . . .**174** D1
Constable Way TN40 . . . .**157** C5
Conway Ct 1 Hove BN3 . .**163** B7
9 St Leonards TN38 . . . . .**159** B6
Conway Pl BN3 . . . .**163** A8
Conway St BN3 . . . .**163** B8
Cooden Beach Sta
TN39 . . . .**156** B2
Cooden Cl TN39 . . . .**156** C3
Cooden Dr TN39 . . . .**156** C3
Cooden Ledge TN37 . . . . .**135** E7
Cooden Sea Rd
Bexhill TN39 . . . .**156** B2
Bexhill TN39 . . . .**156** C3
Cook Ave BN23 . . . .**185** E6
Cookham Dene TN40 . . . .**157** C4
Cooksbridge Rd BN2 . . . .**164** E6
Cooksbridge Sta BN8 . . . .**123** A7
Cookson Gdns TN35 . . . .**160** C7
Cookstown Cl TN33 . . . . .**132** F6
Coolham Dr BN2 . . . .**164** E7
Coombe Cl BN27 . . . .**131** B5
Coombe Cotts RH19 . . . . .**21** A6
Coombe Hill Rd RH19 . . . .**10** D6
Coombe La TN5 . . . .**41** C7
Coombe Lea 5 BN3 . . . . .**163** C6
Coombe Lodge BN25 . . . .**180** C3
Coombe Mdw BN2 . . . . . .**177** E2
Coombe Rd
Brighton BN2 . . . .**143** D1
Eastbourne BN20 . . . .**184** C4
Lewes BN7 . . . .**190** B3
Coombe Rise BN2 . . . . . .**177** D7
Coombe Road Prim Sch
BN2 . . . .**143** D1
Coombe Shaw TN33 . . . . .**133** A6
Coombe Terr BN2 . . . .**143** C1
Coombe Vale BN2 . . . . . .**177** D7
Coombers La RH16 . . . . . .**51** B5
Coombs Cl TN31 . . . .**68** C5
Coombs Cotts TN31 . . . . . .**68** C5
Cooper Dr TN39 . . . .**157** B8
Cooper Rd TN31 . . . .**93** A5
Cooper Rise TN37 . . . . . .**136** A5
Coopers Cl RH15 . . . .**73** B5
Coopers Hill BN20 . . . . . .**173** B2
Coopers La
Crowborough TN6 . . . .**25** D4
Poundsbridge TN11,TN3 . . .**6** C7
Coopers Row TN22 . . . . . .**55** D4
Coopers Way BN27 . . . . .**152** A6
Coopers Wood TN6 . . . . . .**25** D4
Copenhagen Ct BN2 . . . . .**165** A3
Copestake Dr RH15 . . . . . .**73** D3
Coplands Plat TN31 . . . . . .**67** B7
Coplands Rise TN31 . . . . . .**67** B7
Coppards Cl RH17 . . . .**74** C4
Coppards La TN31 . . . .**67** C8
Copper Beeches
Brighton BN1 . . . .**142** E1
St Leonards TN37 . . . .**136** C4
Copper Cl RH15 . . . .**72** C4
Copper's Hill TN19 . . . .**61** E4
Coppers Ct TN4 . . . .**8** A8
Coppice Ave BN20 . . . . . .**173** A4
Coppice Cl BN20 . . . .**173** A4
Coppice The Battle TN33 .**113** A3
Hastings TN34 . . . .**136** E1
Pembury TN2 . . . .**9** D7
Scaynes Hill RH17 . . . .**51** F3
Coppice View TN21 . . . . . .**82** B6
Coppice Way RH16 . . . .**50** D3
Copse Cl
East Grinstead RH19 . . . . . .**2** A3
St Leonards TN38 . . . .**135** D3
Copse Hill BN1 . . . .**142** D5
Copse Rd TN39 . . . .**156** E4
Copse The RH16 . . . .**51** B5
Copt Hall TN18 . . . .**48** D3
Copthorne Ct 2 BN3 . . . .**163** C6
Copthorne Ho 19 BN21 . .**184** E4
Copthorne Rd RH19 . . . . . .**1** A4
Copwood Ave TN22 . . . . . .**78** B7
Copwood Rdbt TN22 . . . . .**78** A6
Copyhold La RH17 . . . .**50** A4
Copyhold Rd RH19 . . . .**10** D8
Copythorne Ho 1 RH16 . . .**50** E6
Coral Reef Cl BN23 . . . . .**175** A1
Corbyn Cres BN43 . . . . . .**161** A7
Cordons BN7 . . . .**145** D5
Cormorant Cl BN23 . . . . . .**174** C2
Cornelius Ave BN9 . . . . . .**179** A5
Corner Gn BN2 . . . .**124** D5
Cornfield Cl BN25 . . . .**180** T3
Cornfield Gn BN27 . . . . . .**129** C1
Cornfield La BN21 . . . .**185** A2
Cornfield Rd
Eastbourne BN21 . . . .**185** A2

Cornfield Rd continued
Seaford BN25 . . . . .180 F3
Cornfield Terr
11 Eastbourne BN21 . . . . .185 A2
St Leonards TN37 . . . . . .136 C1
Cornford Cl
Burgess Hill RH15 . . . . . . .72 E5
Crowborough TN6 . . . . . . .26 A1
Pembury TN2 . . . . .9 B6
Portslade-by-S BN41 . . . .141 B2
Cornford La TN2 . . . . .9 B5
Cornford Pk TN2 . . . . .9 C6
Cornish Cl BN23 . . . . . . .174 B4
Cornmill Gdns BN26 . . . .172 E4
Cornwall Ave BN10 . . . . .178 E6
Cornwall Ct
Eastbourne BN20 . . . . . . .184 C5
2 Hove BN3 . . . . .163 C7
Cornwall Gdns
Brighton BN1 . . . . .142 E2
6 East Grinstead RH19 . . .10 F8
Cornwall Ho BN1 . . . . . .142 E2
Cornwall Rd TN39 . . . . . .157 B3
Cornwallis Cl BN23 . . . . .185 F7
Cornwallis Gdns TN34 . . .159 E8
Cornwallis St 5 TN34 . . .159 E8
Cornwallis Terr TN34 . . .159 E8
Coronation Bldgs BN9 . . .179 D7
Coronation Cotts
Burwash TN19 . . . . .62 A6
Northbridge Street TN32 . . .64 C5
Ticehurst TN5 . . . . .31 F2
Coronation Gdns
Battle TN33 . . . . .112 F5
Hurst Green TN19 . . . . . . .44 F3
Coronation Rd RH19 . . . . .10 E7
Coronation St 2 BN2 . . .164 C7
Corseley Rd TN3 . . . . .15 B5
Corsica Cl BN23 . . . . . . .180 F2
Corsica Rd BN25 . . . . . . .180 F1
Costells Edge RH17 . . . . . .51 F3
Costume Mus★ TN40 . . . .157 D4
Cotchford Hill TN7 . . . . . .13 D1
Cotchford La TN7 . . . . . . .13 C1
Cotswold Cl
Eastbourne BN23 . . . . . . .174 C4
Hastings TN34 . . . . .160 B8
Cotswold Pl 7 BN2 . . . . .164 F5
Cotswolds The BN42 . . . .161 E7
Cottage Cl BN9 . . . . .168 D2
Cottage Homes BN6 . . . . .98 E6
Cottage La
Hailsham BN24 . . . . .152 E1
Westfield TN33,TN35 . . . .114 D7
Cottages The BN27 . . . . .129 C3
Cottenden Rd TN5 . . . . . . .43 A6
Cottesmore St Mary's RC
Prim Sch BN3 . . . . .163 D8
Coulstock Rd RH15 . . . . . .72 E4
Council Cotts
Cross-in-H TN21 . . . . .81 C8
Crowborough TN6 . . . . . . .38 A8
Robertsbridge TN32 . . . . . .63 F3
Uckfield TN22 . . . . .78 D1
Council Hos
Ginger's Green BN27 . . . .130 C8
Rushlake Green TN21 . . . . .83 D1
Countess of Thanet's
Almshouses TN8 . . . . .3 F3
County Oak Ave BN1 . . . .143 B6
Courcels BN2 . . . . .164 C3
Course The BN7 . . . . .146 B8
Court Cl Brighton BN1 . . .142 E7
East Grinstead RH19 . . . . . .1 F1
Court Cres RH19 . . . . .1 F1
Court Farm Cl BN9 . . . . .168 A2
Court Farm Rd
Hove BN3 . . . . .142 A2
Newhaven BN9 . . . . .179 C5
Rottingdean BN2 . . . . . . .165 F3
Court House Mus★
BN24 . . . . .175 B6
Court La TN22 . . . . .55 D4
Court Leet 8 BN25 . . . . .180 E2
Court Mdw TN6 . . . . .39 B8
Court Meadow Cl BN2 . . .165 F3
Court Meadow Sch RH17 . .50 A8
Court Ord Cotts BN2 . . . .165 F3
Court Ord Rd BN2 . . . . . .165 F3
Court Rd
Eastbourne BN22 . . . . . . .173 F2
Lewes BN7 . . . . .190 B2
Royal Tunbridge Wells TN4 . .7 F4
Court Royal TN2 . . . . .16 E8
Court The BN2 . . . . .173 B1
Courtenay Gate BN3 . . . .163 B5
Courtenay Terr 7 BN3 . . .163 B5
Courtenwell TN3 . . . . .6 F4
Courthope Ave TN5 . . . . . .29 F4
Courthope Dr TN39 . . . . .156 F5
Courthouse St TN34 . . . . .160 B4
Courtland Rd BN26 . . . . .173 A5
Courtlands
13 Brighton BN3 . . . . . . .189 C3
Dodd's Hill TN22 . . . . .35 D2
Haywards Heath RH16 . . . .50 E3
Newhaven BN9 . . . . .179 C7
5 St Leonards TN38 . . . . .159 B6
Courtlands Pl TN6 . . . . . . .25 E1
Courtlands Rd BN22 . . . . .185 A5
Courtney King Ho 1
BN2 . . . . .164 D4
Courtyard The
East Grinstead RH19 . . . . . .2 B1
12 Eastbourne BN21 . . . .184 F4
Falmer BN1 . . . . .144 C6
Hastings TN34 . . . . .136 A1
Haywards Heath RH16 . . . .50 F4

Courtyard The continued
8 Hove BN3 . . . . .163 D6
Sheffield Green TN22 . . . . .53 C5
Cousley Wood Rd TN5 . . . .30 C7
Coventry Ct BN22 . . . . . .185 D6
Coventry Rd TN38 . . . . . .136 B3
Coventry St BN1 . . . . . . .185 C4
Coverdale Ave TN39 . . . . .156 C3
Coverdale Ct RH19 . . . . . . .1 C4
Covers The BN25 . . . . . . .180 F2
Covert The TN39 . . . . . . .156 C2
Cow La BN26 . . . . .181 F8
Cowden Cl TN18 . . . . .45 E8
Cowden Cross TN8 . . . . . . .4 C7
Cowden Hall La TN21 . . . .107 C5
Cowden La TN18 . . . . .45 E7
Cowden Mews TN8 . . . . . . .4 A5
Cowden Rd BN2 . . . . .177 D4
Cowden Sta TN8 . . . . .4 D8
Cowden Wlk TN38 . . . . . .136 A2
Cowdens Cl BN3 . . . . . . .141 D4
Cowdray Cl TN39 . . . . . . .156 D6
Cowdray Ct 1 BN3 . . . . .163 D7
Cowdray Park Rd TN39 . . .156 C6
Cowfold Rd BN2 . . . . .164 E5
Cowley Dr BN2 . . . . .165 F7
Cownwy Ct BN2 . . . . .165 F1
Cox Gr RH15 . . . . .72 E5
Cox's Cotts BN7 . . . . .99 E7
Coxheath Cl TN38 . . . . . . .135 E7
Crabtree Ave BN1 . . . . . . .143 B5
Crabtree Ho 1 TN38 . . . .159 B6
Crackendale Field BN8 . . .124 E6
Cradle Hill Com Prim Sch
BN25 . . . . .181 A5
Cradle Hill Ind Est BN25 .181 B5
Cradle Hill Rd BN25 . . . . .181 B5
Craig CI TN35 . . . . .135 A6
Craigmore Hall TN6 . . . . . .26 A1
Craignair Ave BN1 . . . . . .142 F7
Cranborne Ave BN20 . . . .188 C8
Cranbourne St BN1 . . . . . .189 A4
Cranbrook 14 BN2 . . . . . .189 C3
Cranbrook Rd TN37 . . . . .136 C1
Cranedown BN7 . . . . .146 B7
Cranfield Rd TN40 . . . . . .157 C4
Crangon Cotts BN20 . . . .187 A4
Cranleigh Ave BN2 . . . . . .177 B5
Cranleigh Cl TN39 . . . . . .157 A4
Cranley Ct 2 BN3 . . . . . .162 D7
Cranmer Ave BN3 . . . . . . .141 F1
Cranmer Cl BN7 . . . . .190 B3
Cranston Ave TN39 . . . . . .157 A4
Cranston Cl TN39 . . . . . . .156 F4
Cranston Rd RH19 . . . . .1 F2
Cranston Rise TN39 . . . . .156 F4
Cranwell Rd TN4 . . . . .7 C4
Crates Yd TN4 . . . . .8 A5
Craven Rd BN2 . . . . .164 D6
Crawford Way RH19 . . . . . .1 F3
Crawley Cres BN22 . . . . . .173 E2
Crawley Rd BN1 . . . . .143 D6
Crayford Rd TN4 . . . . .143 D1
Crazy La TN33 . . . . .113 E7
Crecy Cl TN37 . . . . .135 F7
Creek The 11 TN34 . . . . .160 B4
Crendon Pk TN4 . . . . .8 A8
Crescent Cl
Burgess Hill RH15 . . . . . . .73 B3
Woodingdean BN2 . . . . . .165 B8
Crescent Dr N BN2 . . . . . .165 E7
Crescent Dr S BN2 . . . . . .165 E7
Crescent Mans BN2 . . . . .189 C5
Crescent Pl BN2 . . . . .164 C4
Crescent Rd
Brighton BN2 . . . . .164 B8
Burgess Hill RH15 . . . . . . .73 A3
East Grinstead RH19 . . . . . .1 D1
Royal Tunbridge Wells TN1 . .8 B3
Crescent The
Brighton BN2 . . . . .143 E2
Eastbourne BN20 . . . . . . .173 A3
Eastbourne,Downside
BN20 . . . . .184 B5
Felcourt RH19 . . . . .1 C8
Groombridge TN3 . . . . . . .15 C7
Hastings TN34 . . . . .136 C3
Keymer BN6 . . . . .98 B3
Newhaven BN9 . . . . .168 F1
Southwick BN42 . . . . .161 F7
Crescent Way RH15 . . . . . .73 A3
Crespin Way BN1 . . . . . . .143 C2
Crest Rd BN9 . . . . .168 F1
Crest Way BN41 . . . . .141 B3
Cresta Cl BN26 . . . . .173 A7
Cresta Rd BN10 . . . . .178 C6
Cresta Rd BN9 . . . . .179 A6
Crestway Par BN1 . . . . . . .143 C2
Crestway The BN1 . . . . . . .143 C2
Cricket Ct RH19 . . . . .1 E3
Cricketers Cl TN3 . . . . . . .18 A5
Cricketers Field TN32 . . . .65 E1
Cricketfield BN8 . . . . .76 D8
Cricketfield CT 6 BN25 .180 F2
Cricketfield Rd BN25 . . . . .180 F2
Cricketing La BN27 . . . . . .130 C4
Criers La TN20,TN22 . . . . .57 F7
Crink Hill BN8 . . . . .101 F3
Cripland Cl RH16 . . . . .51 B6
Cripps Ave BN10 . . . . . . .167 D1
Crisp Rd BN7 . . . . .123 A4
Crispin Ct 5 TN40 . . . . . .157 D4
Crittle's Ct TN5 . . . . .29 F4
Crockers Hatch Cnr TN3 . . .6 D2
Crockers La TN31 . . . . . . .67 B8
Crocks Dean BN10 . . . . . .167 D2
Croft Ave BN42 . . . . .161 F7

Croft Cl BN26 . . . . .173 A4
Croft Ct
2 Eastbourne BN21 . . . . .185 B3
7 Seaford BN25 . . . . . . .180 E3
Croft Dr BN41 . . . . .141 A3
Croft La BN25 . . . . .180 E3
Croft Rd Brighton BN1 . . .142 D4
Crowborough TN6 . . . . . . .25 F2
Hastings TN34 . . . . .160 B4
Croft Terr 2 TN34 . . . . . .160 A4
Croft The Bexhill TN40 . . .157 A4
14 Eastbourne BN21 . . . .184 F4
Eastbourne,Willingdon
BN20 . . . . .173 B1
Hassocks BN6 . . . . .97 F5
Hastings TN34 . . . . .160 A4
Lower Dicker BN27 . . . . . .128 B4
Southwick BN42 . . . . .161 E8
Croft Works BN27 . . . . . .152 B7
Crofton Park Ave TN39 . . .156 E3
Croham Rd 11 TN6 . . . . . .25 F3
Cromarty Wlk 17 BN23 . . .185 F8
Cromer Way BN27 . . . . . .129 A1
Cromer Wlk 3 TN34 . . . . .136 A1
Cromleigh Way BN42 . . . .140 E2
Cromwell Ct 3 BN3 . . . . .163 D7
Cromwell Mews RH15 . . . .72 F4
Cromwell Pl 1 RH19 . . . . .10 F7
Cromwell Rd
Burgess Hill RH15 . . . . . . .72 F3
Hove BN3 . . . . .163 C7
Royal Tunbridge Wells TN2 . .8 C3
Cromwell St BN2 . . . . .164 C7
Crooked La BN25 . . . . . . .180 F2
Cross La TN5 . . . . .31 D2
Cross Lane Gdns TN5 . . . . .31 D1
Cross Levels Way BN22,
BN21 . . . . .184 E7
Cross Rd BN42 . . . . .161 D8
Cross St Brighton BN1 . . .189 B4
14 Hove BN1,BN3 . . . . . .163 D5
Polegate BN26 . . . . .173 A6
St Leonards TN37 . . . . . . .159 C7
Cross Way BN7 . . . . .123 A4
Cross-in-Hand CE Prim Sch
TN21 . . . . .81 F7
Crossbush Rd BN2 . . . . . .164 E6
Crossroad Cl BN42 . . . . . .161 D8
Crossway The
Brighton BN1 . . . . .143 B2
Portslade-by-S BN41 . . . .141 A3
Royal Tunbridge Wells TN4 . .7 D2
Crossways BN8 . . . . .148 B4
Crossways Ave
East Grinstead RH19 . . . . . .1 C1
East Grinstead RH19 . . . . . .1 D1
Crossways The
Broad Oak TN31 . . . . .90 B4
Hassocks BN6 . . . . .97 C4
Stone Cross BN24 . . . . . . .174 A6
Crouch Cl BN20 . . . . .173 B1
Crouch La Linkhill TN18 . . .47 D6
Lower Street TN33 . . . . . .133 B3
Seaford BN25 . . . . .180 E2
Crouch The 6 BN25 . . . . .180 F2
Crouchfield Cl 2 BN25 . . .180 F2
Crowborough Ct 4 TN6 . . .25 F3
Crowborough Hill TN6 . . . .26 B1
Crowborough Mews TN6 . .25 E2
Crowborough Rd
Hastings TN35 . . . . .160 E8
Marlpits TN22 . . . . .35 E6
Saltdean BN2 . . . . .177 D4
Crowborough Sta TN6 . . . .38 C8
Crowders La TN33 . . . . . .111 D3
Crowhurst CE Prim Sch
TN33 . . . . .134 F5
Crowhurst Cl BN23 . . . . . .174 A4
Crowhurst La TN39 . . . . . .157 C7
Crowhurst Rd
Brighton BN1 . . . . .143 C7
St Leonards TN38 . . . . . . .135 B3
St Leonards TN38 . . . . . . .135 E2
Crowhurst Sta TN33 . . . . .135 A6
Crowlink Cotts BN20 . . . .186 E7
Crowlink La BN20 . . . . . . .183 A1
Crowmere Ave TN40 . . . . .157 C5
Crowmere Terr TN40 . . . . .157 C5
Crown Cl Hailsham BN27 . .152 A7
1 Hove BN3 . . . . .163 D6
Uckfield TN22 . . . . .78 C8
Crown Ct 23 TN34 . . . . . .160 B4
Crown Gdns BN1 . . . . . . .189 A2
Crown Hill
4 Brighton BN2 . . . . . . .164 C6
Seaford BN25 . . . . .180 E7
Crown Ho TN3 . . . . .20 B5
Crown La TN34 . . . . .160 B4
Crown Point Ho BN6 . . . . .97 F4
Crown Rd
Portslade-by-S BN41 . . . .162 A8
Shoreham-by-S BN43 . . . .161 B8
Crown St Brighton BN1 . . .189 A4
18 Eastbourne BN21 . . . .184 D4
Crowne Ho 8 BN21 . . . . .184 E4
Croxden Way BN22 . . . . . .173 D3
Croxton La BN6 . . . . .51 B6
Croydon Cotts 8 TN6 . . . .25 F5
Crump's Cnr TN22 . . . . . .103 D6
Crunden Rd BN20 . . . . . . .184 C4
Cubitt Way TN38 . . . . . . .135 E4
Cuckfield Cl TN40 . . . . . . .158 C4
Cuckfield Rd
Burgess Hill RH15 . . . . . . .72 E7
Goddards' Green BN6,
RH17 . . . . .72 A4
Cuckmere Ct
Alfriston BN26 . . . . .170 F3

Cuckmere Ct continued
5 Seaford BN25 . . . . . . .180 E3
Cuckmere Dr BN24 . . . . . .174 A5
Cuckmere Ho BN27 . . . . . .175 C7
Cuckmere House Sch
BN25 . . . . .181 C3
Cuckmere Path TN22 . . . . .55 E1
Cuckmere Rd
Newhaven BN9 . . . . .179 A5
Seaford BN25 . . . . .181 B3
Cuckmere Rise BN27 . . . . .82 B8
Cuckmere Way BN1 . . . . . .143 C5
Cuckmere Wlk BN22 . . . . .173 D1
Cuckoo Dr TN21 . . . . .82 A6
Culpepper RH15 . . . . .72 E4
Culpepper Cl BN2 . . . . . . .143 D2
Culross Ave RH16 . . . . . . .50 D5
Culver Cl BN23 . . . . .174 B4
Culverden Ave TN4 . . . . . . .8 A6
Culverden Down TN4 . . . . .7 F5
Culverden Park Rd TN4 . . . .7 F5
Culverden Pk TN4 . . . . .7 F5
Culverden Sq TN4 . . . . .8 A5
Culverden St TN1 . . . . .8 A4
Cumballa Ct BN20 . . . . . .188 F8
Cumberland Ct
3 Bexhill TN40 . . . . .157 D4
Eastbourne BN20 . . . . . . .184 B6
Cumberland Dr BN1 . . . . .142 E2
Cumberland Gdns
10 Royal Tunbridge Wells
TN1 . . . . .8 A2
St Leonards TN38 . . . . . . .159 B8
Cumberland Mews 12 TN1 8 A2
Cumberland Rd
Bexhill TN39 . . . . .157 B7
Brighton BN1 . . . . .142 E2
Cumberland Wlk TN1 . . . . .8 A2
Cumberland Yd 11 TN1 . . .8 A2
Cumnor House Sch RH17 . .34 B5
Cunningham Cl TN4 . . . . . .8 B7
Cunningham Ct 10
BN25 . . . . .180 E2
Cunningham Dr BN23 . . . .185 E7
Cunningham Ho 6
TN39 . . . . .157 B3
Cunningham Rd TN4 . . . . . .8 B7
Curlew Ct
Hailsham BN27 . . . . .152 D7
St Leonards TN38 . . . . . . .135 C1
Curlews The BN43 . . . . . . .161 A8
Currie Rd TN4 . . . . .8 A5
Curwen Pl BN1 . . . . .142 E5
Curzon Ho BN2 . . . . .177 C4
Cuthbert Cl TN39 . . . . . . .157 A7
Cuthbert Rd BN2 . . . . .164 C5
Cutter La 7 TN34 . . . . . . .160 A3
Cypress Cl
Shoreham-by-S BN43 . . . .140 A1
St Leonards TN38 . . . . . . .159 A7
Cypress Gr TN2 . . . . .17 C8
Cypress Mews RH15 . . . . . .73 B4
Cyprus Pl TN31 . . . . .93 B5
Cyprus Rd RH15 . . . . .73 A3
Cyril Richings Bsns Ctr
BN43 . . . . .161 B7

D

D'aubigny Rd BN2 . . . . . . .164 B7
Dacre Pk BN27 . . . . .152 D7
Dacre Rd
Eastbourne BN20,BN21 . . .184 C4
Herstmonceux BN27 . . . . .130 E6
Newhaven BN9 . . . . .179 D7
Dads Hill TN21 . . . . .81 B8
Dagg La TN32 . . . . .65 D3
Dairy Gn TN6 . . . . .38 D8
Dakins The RH19 . . . . .10 E8
Dale Ave Brighton BN1 . . .142 F5
Keymer BN6 . . . . .98 A3
Dale Cres BN1 . . . . .142 F6
Dale Dr BN1 . . . . .143 A6
Dale Hill BN45 . . . . .119 A6
Dale Rd Forest Row RH18 . .11 F1
Lewes BN7 . . . . .146 B4
Dale St TN1 . . . . .8 B4
Dale View BN3 . . . . .141 D2
Dale View Gdns BN3 . . . . .141 D2
Dalehurst TN6 . . . . .38 C7
Dalehurst Rd TN39 . . . . . .157 B7
Dales Cl BN27 . . . . .131 B5
Dallaway Dr BN24 . . . . . . .174 B5
Dallaway Gdns RH19 . . . . . .1 E1
Dallington CE Prim Sch
TN21 . . . . .84 D3
Dallington Rd
Eastbourne BN22 . . . . . . .174 A1
Hove BN3 . . . . .162 F8
Dalmeny Rd TN39 . . . . . . .157 A5
Dalmore Ct 3 TN40 . . . . .157 C3
Dalton Rd BN20 . . . . .188 C3
Damian Way BN6 . . . . .98 B4
Damon Cl BN10 . . . . .178 C7
Dana Lodge BN10 . . . . . . .178 A7
Dane Cl BN25 . . . . .180 D2
Dane Court Cl TN39 . . . . .157 B6
Dane Hts 3 BN25 . . . . . . .180 E2
Dane Rd Seaford BN25 . . . .180 E3
St Leonards TN38 . . . . . . .159 B8
Danehill CE Prim Sch
RH17 . . . . .34 B4

Danehill La RH17 . . . . .33 E5
Danehill Rd BN2 . . . . .164 F5
Daniel Way TN31 . . . . .94 F2
Dannfields Rd BN25 . . . . .180 E3
Danny★ BN6 . . . . .97 A2
Danny Sheldon Ho 14
BN27 . . . . .164 C4
Danum Cl BN27 . . . . .129 C3
Danworth Farm BN6 . . . . .72 A1
Danworth La BN6 . . . . .72 B2
Darby's La TN5 . . . . .30 B2
Darcey Dr BN1 . . . . .143 A6
Darent Cl BN24 . . . . .173 C6
Daresbury Cl TN39 . . . . . .188 C7
Darley Rd BN20 . . . . .188 C3
Darrick Ct 6 BN21 . . . . . .185 A1
Dart Ct RH19 . . . . .2 A3
Dartmouth Cl BN2 . . . . . .143 F1
Dartmouth Cres BN2 . . . . .143 F1
Darvel Down TN33 . . . . . . .86 B2
Darwall Dr BN25 . . . . .181 A3
Darwell Cl
Robertsbridge TN32 . . . . . .64 B3
St Leonards TN38 . . . . . . .135 E1
Darwell Dr BN24 . . . . .174 A5
Davey Dr BN1 . . . . .143 B1
Davey's La TN1 . . . . .8 B4
David Lloyd Club The
BN21 . . . . .184 F8
David Saloman's Ho★
TN3 . . . . .7 D8
Davids Hts TN1 . . . . .8 B4
Davigdor Inf Sch BN3 . . . .163 D6
Davigdor Rd BN3 . . . . . . .163 E7
Davis Cl TN39 . . . . .157 A7
Dawber Bldgs BN27 . . . . .152 B7
Dawes Ho TN19 . . . . .62 A6
Dawlish Cl BN2 . . . . .143 F1
Dawson Terr BN2 . . . . . . .164 C6
Daynes Way RH15 . . . . . . .72 E4
Daytona Quay 18 BN23 . .185 F8
De Cham Ave TN37 . . . . . .159 D8
De Cham Rd TN37 . . . . . . .159 C8
De Chardin Dr TN34 . . . . .137 A5
De Courcel Rd BN2 . . . . . .164 E3
De Grey Cl BN7 . . . . .190 B3
De La Warr Gn BN7 . . . . . .123 B3
De La Warr Par TN40 . . . . .157 F3
De La Warr Pav★ TN40 . . .157 C3
De La Warr Rd
Bexhill TN40 . . . . .157 E5
East Grinstead RH19 . . . . . .1 F1
De Moleyns Cl 1 TN40 . . .157 D4
De Montfort Rd
Brighton BN2 . . . . .164 C7
Lewes BN7 . . . . .123 B1
De Montfort Terr 4
BN7 . . . . .123 B1
De Roos Ct BN21 . . . . . . .184 E5
De Roos Rd BN21 . . . . . . .184 E5
De Walden Mews BN20 . . .188 E8
De Warrenne Rd BN7 . . . . .123 B1
Deacons Dr BN41 . . . . . . .141 C2
Deadman's Cross TN21 . . .83 B5
Deadmans La TN31 . . . . . .93 C6
Deadmantree Hill BN8 . . .101 B3
Deal Ave BN25 . . . . .181 C5
Deals The 7 TN31 . . . . . . .93 B5
Dean Cl
Portslade-by-S BN41 . . . .141 C2
Rottingdean BN2 . . . . . . .177 A6
Dean Court Rd BN2 . . . . . .177 A6
Dean Gdns BN41 . . . . .141 C2
Dean Rd BN25 . . . . .180 F2
Dean St BN1 . . . . .163 E5
Dean Wood Cl BN23 . . . . .174 A4
Deanery Cl BN7 . . . . .190 B4
Deanland Rd BN27 . . . . . .127 B4
Deans Cl Bexhill TN39 . . . .157 B6
Woodingdean BN2 . . . . . .165 E8
Deans Dr TN39 . . . . .157 A6
Deans Mdw BN8 . . . . .101 E5
Deans Rd BN26 . . . . .170 F3
Deanway BN3 . . . . .142 B3
Decimus Burton Way 10
TN37 . . . . .159 C7
Decimus Pl TN1 . . . . .8 B4
Deco Bldg The BN2 . . . . . .143 C1
Decoy Dr BN22 . . . . .173 D1
Deepdene TN5 . . . . .30 A6
Deepdene Gdns TN35 . . . .160 C6
Deepdene Sch BN3 . . . . . .162 D7
Deer Haven BN27 . . . . . . .127 C4
Deer Paddock La 7
BN27 . . . . .152 C7
Deerswood La TN39 . . . . .156 E5
Deeside The BN1 . . . . .143 A7
Deilsfoot Cotts TN6 . . . . . .28 A3
Delamere Ct 3 BN21 . . . .184 F2
Delavall Wlk BN23 . . . . . .185 F6
Delaware Dr TN37 . . . . . . .135 F6
Delaware Rd BN7 . . . . . . .146 A8
Delfryn BN41 . . . . .140 F3
Dell Cl TN38 . . . . .136 A1
Dell Dr TN2 . . . . .8 D4
Dell The
East Grinstead RH19 . . . . . .2 B1
Haywards Heath RH16 . . . .50 C5
Dellney Ave RH16 . . . . .50 F3
Delves Ave TN1 . . . . .8 C4
Delves Cl BN8 . . . . .124 D6
Delves Ho 5 BN8 . . . . . . .124 D6
Delves Way BN8 . . . . .124 D6
Den Hill BN20 . . . . .184 A4

Denbigh Cl TN39 ....156 E4
Denbigh Ct TN39 ....156 E5
Denbigh Rd TN4 ....8 C7
Dencher Rd BN7 ....145 E3
Dene Cl BN20 ....183 B1
Dene Dr BN22 ....173 C1
Dene Path TN22 ....55 D1
Dene Side BN20 ....183 B1
Dene The
  Eastbourne BN20 ....173 A3
  Hastings TN35 ....137 A5
  Hove BN3 ....141 D3
  Uckfield TN22 ....55 D1
Dene Vale BN1 ....142 D5
Dene Way BN1 ....7 A7
Denecroft BN1 ....142 D5
Denehurst Gdns TN35 ....137 A5
Deneside BN1 ....142 D5
Deneway The BN1 ....142 D4
Denham Cl TN38 ....135 F4
Denham Rd RH15 ....72 D3
Denham Rd RH15 ....72 D3
Denham Way TN31 ....94 E2
Denman's Cl RH16 ....51 A8
Denman's La RH16 ....51 A7
Denmark Mews BN3 ......163 B7
Denmark Pl TN34 ....159 F7
Denmark Rd BN41 ....162 E6
Denmark Terr BN1 ......163 E6
Denmark Villas BN3 .....163 B7
Dennis Hobden Cl BN2 ...143 E1
Denton Cl TN31 ....93 A6
Denton Comm Prim Sch
  BN9 ....168 E1
Denton Dr Brighton BN1 ..143 A6
  Newhaven BN9 ....168 E1
Denton Rd
  Eastbourne BN20 ......188 D8
  Newhaven BN9 ....168 E1
Denton Rise BN9 ....168 E2
Dentons The BN20 ......188 D8
Derby Ct 7 BN3 ....163 E7
Derby Pl 6 BN2 ....189 C2
Derek Ave BN3 ....162 D6
Derek Ho BN3 ....162 F6
Dern La TN21 ....106 B7
Dervia Ho BN3 ....163 C7
Derwent Cl BN27 ....129 A1
Derwent Ct BN1 ....189 A3
Derwent Dr TN4 ....7 E5
Derwent Rd BN20 ....188 E8
Desmond Rd BN22 ......185 D5
Desmond Way BN2 ......164 F6
Devil's Dyke Rd BN1 ....141 E7
Devon Villas RH16 ....50 F4
Devonian Ct BN2 ....189 C4
Devonport Ho 4 TN31 ....93 C6
Devonshire Cl 7 TN2 .....16 F8
Devonshire Ct 1 BN3 ...163 C7
Devonshire Lodge 1
  BN22 ....185 C5
Devonshire Pl
  Brighton BN2 ....189 C2
  Eastbourne BN21 .....185 A2
Devonshire Rd
  Bexhill TN40 ....157 C3
  Hastings TN34 ....159 F8
Devonshire Sq TN40 ....157 C3
Dew La TN31 ....92 A8
Dewe Rd BN2 ....143 C1
Dewhurst Cotts TN5 .....29 A7
Dewhurst La TN5 ....29 B8
Dewpond The BN10 .....167 B1
Dexter Dr RH19 ....10 E8
Diamond Cotts RH17 .....74 A5
Diana Cl TN40 ....158 A6
Dickens Cl RH19 ....1 C1
Dickens Way BN23 .....174 E3
Dicklands The BN7 .....167 D8
Diggers The BN1 ....143 B3
Dillingburgh Rd BN20 ...184 C4
Dillon Way TN2 ....8 D7
Dinapore Ho 11 BN2 ....189 C3
Diplock Cl BN2 ....172 F6
Diplocks Bldgs BN27 ....152 A7
Diplocks The BN27 .....152 A8
Diplocks Way BN27 .....152 A7
Diplocks Wlk BN27 .....152 A8
Dirty La RH19 ....11 E7
Ditchling Beacon Nature
  Reserve★ BN6 ....120 D7
Ditchling Bostall BN6 ...120 D7
Ditchling Cl BN23 ......173 F4
Ditchling Common Ctry Pk★
  BN6 ....73 F1
Ditchling Cres BN1 ....143 C5
Ditchling Ct 4 BN1 ....164 B8
Ditchling Dr TN35 .....160 E8
Ditchling Gdns BN1 ....143 B1
Ditchling Mus★ BN6 .....98 C3
Ditchling Pl 1 BN1 ....143 A1
Ditchling Rd
  Brighton BN1,BN2 .....143 B4
  Westmeston BN1,BN6 ...120 D4
Ditchling Rise BN1 ....143 B1
Ditchling St Margaret's CE
  Prim Sch BN6 ....98 D3
Ditchling Way BN27 ....152 B6
Ditton's Cnr BN26 .....173 C6
Ditton's Rd BN26 ......173 D6
Dittons BN26 ....173 C6
Dittons Mews TN38 .....135 E2
Dittons Rd BN21 ....184 E3
Divall's Cotts RH19 ....11 D6

Dixter La TN31 ....67 B8
Dixter Rd TN31 ....67 A6
Dock The BN8 ....148 C3
Dodshill TN6 ....26 A1
Dog Cotts RH19 ....3 B1
Dog Kennel La TN22 .....57 F6
Dogs Hill Rd TN36 ....118 B5
Doleham Cotts TN35 ...115 D5
Doleham Halt TN35 ....115 D5
Doleham Hill TN35 ....115 D5
Doleham La TN35 ......115 B6
Dolphin Ct
  Eastbourne BN20 .....188 E7
  5 Hove BN3 ....163 A6
Dolphin Ind Est BN43 ..161 B2
Dolphin L Ctr The RH16 ..50 D6
Dolphin Mews
  Brighton BN3 ....189 B1
  Shoreham-by-S BN43 ..161 A7
Dolphin Rd
  Haywards Heath RH16 ...50 D4
  Shoreham-by-S BN43 ..161 B2
Dolphin Way BN43 .....161 B7
Dome The★ BN1 ....189 B2
Dominica Ct BN23 .....185 G7
Donald Hall Rd BN2 ...164 D5
Donald Way TN36 ......118 A5
Donkey Mews 4 BN2 ....163 D5
Donnington Rd BN2 ....165 E6
Dorchester TN1 ....8 B6
Dorchester Ct
  2 Brighton BN1 .....163 E5
  3 Eastbourne BN21 ..184 E4
Dordrecht Way TN34 ...136 E1
Dorin Ct TN1 ....8 C3
Dorita Ct BN10 ....178 D5
Dorking Rd TN1 ....8 C6
Dorman's Cl RH7 ....2 A8
Dormans Gdns RH19 .....1 E6
Dormans High St RH7 ....2 A8
Dormans Park Rd
  Dormans Park RH19 ....1 E6
  East Grinstead RH19 ...1 D3
Dormans Sta RH7 ....1 F6
Dormans Station Rd RH7 .1 F7
Dormansland Prim Sch
  RH7 ....2 A8
Dornden Dr TN3 ....7 A4
Dorothy Ave TN3 ....20 A4
Dorothy Ave N BN10 ...178 C7
Dorothy Rd BN3 ....162 D8
Dorothy Stringer High Sch
  BN1 ....142 F3
Dorset Ave RH19 ....1 C3
Dorset Cotts TN7 ....14 B4
Dorset Ct
  6 Eastbourne BN22 ...185 B3
  Hove BN3 ....162 F6
Dorset Gdns
  Brighton BN2 ....189 C2
  East Grinstead RH19 ...1 C3
Dorset Mews BN2 ......189 B3
Dorset Pl Brighton BN2 .189 C2
  Hastings TN34 ....159 E7
Dorset Rd Bexhill TN40 .157 D4
  Bexhill TN40 ....157 C5
  Lewes BN7 ....190 B1
  Royal Tunbridge Wells TN2 .8 D2
Dorset Rd S TN40 .....157 D4
Dorset St BN2 ....189 B2
Doubledays RH15 ....73 B2
Doucegrove TN38 ......136 A1
Douglas Cl BN27 ......129 B2
Douglas Rd TN6 ....27 D1
Douro Stables TN4 ......8 A4
Dove Ct TN22 ....78 C8
Dovedale Gdns BN22 ...173 F2
Dover Cl BN25 ....181 C5
Dover Rd Brighton BN1 .143 A2
  Polegate BN26 ....173 D7
Dowding Way TN2 ....8 D8
Dower Cl BN2 ....165 D3
Down Ave TN3 ....20 A4
Down La TN3 ....28 C8
Down Rd TN39 ....157 A5
Down St TN22 ....54 C5
Down Terr BN2 ....164 C6
Down The BN41 ....141 D4
Down's Rd TN34 ......136 F3
Downash Cl BN2 ......164 E6
Downash Ct TN5 ....32 A3
Downash Ho TN5 ....32 A3
Downes Ct 9 BN43 ....161 C8
Downey Cl TN37 ......136 B6
Downford 15 BN2 .....164 F5
Downhill View BN2 ....165 E7
Downland Ave
  Peacehaven BN10 .....178 E6
  Southwick BN42 .....140 E1
Downland Cl
  Eastbourne BN23 .....174 C4
  Southwick BN42 .....140 D1
  Woodingdean BN2 ....165 B8
Downland Copse TN22 ..78 C8
Downland Cres BN3 ....141 F3
Downland Ct BN41 ....141 A2
Downland Dr BN3 .....141 F3
Downland Rd BN2 .....165 B8
Downlands Ave TN38 ..157 B4
Downlands Cl TN39 ...157 A4
Downlands Com Sch
  BN6 ....97 F3
Downlands Way BN20 ..183 B1
Downline Cl TN21 .....106 F7
Downs Ave BN20 ......184 B6
Downs Cl BN1 ....143 B1
Downs Inf Sch BN1 ....164 B8
Downs Jun Sch BN1 ...143 A1

Downs Park Sch BN41 ..141 B2
Downs Rd
  Burgess Hill RH15 .....72 E4
  Eastbourne BN22 .....173 B2
  Seaford BN25 ....181 A3
Downs The BN25 ....181 A3
Downs Valley Rd BN2 ..165 E8
Downs View
  Ninfield TN33 ....133 B5
  North Chailey BN8 .....75 E7
  Peacehaven BN10 .....167 D2
Downs View Cl
  East Dean BN20 ......183 C1
  North Chailey BN8 .....75 E7
Downs View La BN20 ...183 C1
Downs View Rd BN6 ....97 F3
Downs View Sch BN2 ..165 C8
Downs Villas BN9 .....168 E3
Downs Wlk
  Peacehaven BN10 .....167 B1
  Peacehaven BN10 .....167 C2
Downscroft RH15 ....73 D6
Downside Brighton BN1 .142 D5
  Hove BN3 ....142 B3
  Lewes BN7 ....146 A8
  Shoreham-by-S BN43 ..140 A1
Downside Cl
  Eastbourne BN20 .....184 C3
  Shoreham-by-S BN43 ..140 A1
Downsmeade BN7 ......146 A8
Downsvalley Rd BN20 ..173 A4
Downsview Brighton BN1 .142 A3
  Eastbourne BN20 .....173 A3
  Heathfield TN21 ......82 B8
  Hove BN3 ....141 D3
  Hurstpierpoint BN6 ....97 A5
Downsview Ave BN2 ...165 E8
Downsview Cotts BN8 ..123 A7
Downsview Cres TN22 ..78 D8
Downsview Dr RH17 ....74 C4
Downsview Rd
  Eastbourne BN20 .....173 A3
  Golden Cross BN27 ...127 B3
  Portslade-by-S BN41 ..141 A2
  Seaford BN25 ....181 A3
Downsview Way BN27 ..152 B7
Downsway
  Arlington BN26 ......150 B3
  Southwick BN42 .....140 F1
  Woodingdean BN2 ....144 D1
Downton Cotts TN18 ....46 F4
Draffin La TN31 ....94 D3
Drake Ave BN23 ......185 E7
Drake Ct BN25 ....180 E2
Drake Ho TN39 ....156 E4
Drapers Way TN38 ....136 B2
Draxmont Way BN1 ...142 F3
Drayton Rise TN6 .....156 D4
Drive Lodge 10 BN3 ...163 C7
Drive The
  Burgess Hill RH15 .....73 B4
  Crowborough TN6 .....25 D2
  Hailsham BN27 ......152 B6
  Hellingly BN27 ......129 C5
  Hove BN3 ....163 C7
  Maresfield TN22 ......55 A5
  Maresfield Park TN22 ..55 A7
  Newhaven BN9 ....179 C5
  Royal Tunbridge Wells TN2 .8 B1
  Southwick BN42 .....140 E1
  St Leonards TN38 ....158 F8
  Uckfield TN38 ....78 C8
  Walter's Green TN3 ....5 F5
Drockmill Cl BN26 ....173 C6
Drove Ave BN2 ....144 D2
Drove Cres BN41 .....141 A2
Drove Rd Newhaven BN9 .179 D8
  Portslade-by-S BN41 ..141 A1
  Woodingdean BN2 ....165 B8
Drove The Brighton BN1 .142 D1
  Falmer BN1 ....144 C5
  Newhaven BN9 ....179 E8
  Offham BN7,BN8 .....123 A5
Drovers Cl BN41 ......141 C2
Drovers Way RH15 .....73 C1
Droveway The
  Haywards Heath RH16 ..50 C6
  Hove BN3 ....142 B1
  Hove BN3 ....142 C1
  Lewes BN7 ....146 A5
Drummond Cl RH16 .....50 D4
Drummond Ct RH16 ....50 D4
Drury La TN38 ....136 A2
Drusilla's Park Zoo★
  BN26 ....171 B6
Dryden Wlk BN23 .....174 A1
Duchess Dr BN25 .....180 E6
Dudeney Lodge BN1 ...143 B1
Dudley Inf Sch TN35 ..160 C5
Dudley Lodge TN2 ......8 C4
Dudley Mews 16 BN3 ..163 D5
Dudley Rd Brighton BN1 .143 B1
  Eastbourne BN22 ....185 B4
  Hastings TN35 ......160 C5
  Royal Tunbridge Wells TN1 .8 A4
Dudwell Rd BN2 ......165 E7
Duke Bernard Ct 8
  BN22 ....185 C5
Duke Ho BN8 ....126 B7
Duke Mews 2 TN37 ...136 B2
Duke Rd TN37 ....136 B2
Duke St Bexhill TN39 ..156 F5
  Brighton BN1 ....189 A2
  St Leonards TN37 ....136 B2
Duke Terr TN37 ......136 B2
Duke's Cl TN1 ....189 A2
Duke's Dr BN20 ......188 E7
Duke's Mound BN2 ...164 D4

Dukes Barn Ct RH16 ...51 B7
Dukes Cl BN25 ....180 D5
Dukes Hill TN33 .....112 D6
Dukes La BN1 ....189 A2
Dukes Rd Lindfield RH16 .51 B8
  Royal Tunbridge Wells TN1 .8 C5
Dukesbury Ho BN21 ...184 E3
Dulwich Cl BN25 .....181 B4
Dumb Woman's La TN31 .92 D3
Dumbrell Ct BN7 .....146 B8
Dumbrells Court Rd BN6 .98 D4
Dumbrells Cl BN6 .....98 D4
Dumbrills Cl RH15 .....73 A5
Dumfries Ct 4 TN38 ..136 B1
Dunbar Dr BN7 ......129 A1
Duncan Ho BN10 .....167 D1
Dunclutha Rd TN34 ...136 F4
Duncton Cl RH16 ......50 D4
Duncton Ho BN6 ......97 E4
Dundale Rd TN3 ....9 E1
Dunes Ave TN31 ......94 F2
Dunning's Rd RH19 ...10 E7
Dunorlan Farm Cotts TN2 .8 E4
Dunstall Ave RH15 ....72 E4
Dunstall Farm Rd RH15 .72 F4
Dunstan Gr TN4 ....8 B6
Dunstan Rd TN4 ....8 B6
Dunstans Croft TN20 ..40 C3
Dunster Cl BN1 ......143 B1
Dunvan Cl BN7 ......190 A4
Durham Cl BN2 ......144 A1
Durham Ct
  Eastbourne BN20 ....184 D4
  4 Hove BN3 ....163 B6
Durkins Rd RH19 ......1 D3
Durrell Cl BN23 .....174 F2
Durrington Ct BN1 ...142 D5
Dursley Rd BN22 ....185 A4
Dutchells Way BN22 ..173 E4
Dyall Cl RH15 ....72 E4
Dyke Cl BN3 ....142 B4
Dyke Rd BN1,BN3 ....163 E8
Dyke Road Ave BN1,BN3 142 C3
Dyke Road Dr BN1 ...163 F8
Dyke Road Mews BN1 .189 A4
Dyke Road Pl BN1 ...142 C3
Dymchurch Cl
  Polegate BN26 ......173 C7
  Seaford BN25 ....181 C5
Dymock Cl BN25 .....181 C4
Dymock's The BN6 ....98 D3
Dymond Rd TN38 ....136 A3
Dynevor Rd TN4 ....8 C7

E

Eagle Cl TN22 ....78 C5
Eagle Ct 15 BN2 .....164 C8
Eagle Rd TN31 ....93 C6
Earl St TN34 ....159 F8
Earl's Rd TN4 ....7 F4
Earls Cl BN25 ....180 C5
Earls Gdn BN7 ......190 B4
Earwig Cnr BN7 .....190 C4
East Albany Rd BN25 .180 F3
East Ascent TN38 ....159 C6
East Beach St TN34 ..160 B4
East Beeches Rd TN6 ..26 B2
East Bourne St 22 TN34 160 B4
East Brighton College of
  Media Arts (Sch) BN2 .164 F5
East Cl BN26 ....173 B6
East Cliff TN34 ......93 C6
East Cliff Rd TN4 ......8 A6
East Dean Rd BN20 ..184 D4
East Dean Rise BN25 .181 A4
East Dr BN2 ....164 C6
East End La BN6 ......98 D3
East Gdns BN6 ....98 D3
East Grinstead Sta BN1 .1 D1
East Grinstead Town Mus★
  RH19 ....1 F2
East Hill RH19 ....1 E6
East Hill Cliff Rly★
  TN34 ....160 B4
East Hill Pas 7 TN34 .160 B4
East Hoathly CE Prim Sch
  BN8 ....104 F5
East Lockside BN2 ...165 A3
East Mascalls La RH16 .51 E6
East Meadway BN43 ..161 A6
East Par TN34 ....160 A3
East Point 6 BN43 ...161 A6
East St Brighton BN1 .189 B1
  Coggins Mill TN20 ....40 D3
  Falmer BN1 ....144 C6
  Hastings TN34 ......160 A4
  Lewes BN7 ....190 B2
  Portslade-by-S BN41 ..162 C7
  Rye TN31 ....93 C5
  Seaford BN25 ....180 E3
East Sussex F HQ BN7 .123 B2
East Sussex Music Sch
  BN7 ....190 B2
East Sussex Music Sch
  (Annexe) BN7 ......190 B2
East View TN21 ....82 B6
East View Fields BN7 ..99 E5
East View Terr TN33 ..88 F1
East Way BN7 ....122 F2
East Wick RH16 ....51 C7
Eastbank BN42 ......140 F1
Eastbourne Ave 4 TN35 175 D5
Eastbourne Butterfly Ctr★
  BN22 ....185 D4
Eastbourne Coll BN21 .184 D3

Eastbourne District General
  Hospl BN21 ....184 E7
Eastbourne La BN26 ..183 C7
Eastbourne Miniature Steam
  Rly Pk★ BN23 ....185 A4
Eastbourne Rd
  Brighton BN2 ....143 D1
  East Dean BN20 .....187 D6
  Eastbourne BN20 ....173 B4
  Felbridge RH19 ......1 A5
  Halland BN8 ....104 C6
  Pevensey Bay BN24 ..175 C4
  Seaford BN25 ....181 C3
  Uckfield TN22 ....78 F3
  Westham BN23,BN24 ..174 F4
Eastbourne Sta BN21 .184 F3
Eastbourne Tech Coll
  BN22 ....173 E2
Eastbourne Terr 4
  BN25 ....181 A3
Eastbridge Rd BN9 ...179 E7
Eastbrook Rd BN41 ..162 B5
Eastbrook Way BN42 .162 A7
Eastdale Rd RH15 .....73 D6
Eastergate BN1 ......156 D6
Eastergate Rd BN2 ..143 F4
Eastern Ave
  Polegate BN26 ......173 C7
  Shoreham-by-S BN43 .161 A7
Eastern Cl BN3 ......161 A7
Eastern Concourse BN2 165 D2
Eastern Cotts RH16 ..51 B7
Eastern Pl 7 BN2 ....164 E4
Eastern Rd Brighton BN2 164 D4
  Haywards Heath RH16 ..50 F3
  Lindfield RH16 ......51 C7
  Wivelsfield RH17 ....74 B4
Eastern Ring Rd BN1 .144 C2
Eastern St 21 BN2 ...164 D4
Eastern Terr 10 BN2 .164 D4
Eastern Terrace Mews 9
  BN2 ....164 D4
Eastfield Cres BN1 ...143 A4
Eastgate St BN7 .....190 B2
Eastgate Wharf BN7 .190 B2
Easthill Dr BN41 ....141 B2
Easthill Way BN41 ...141 B1
Eastlands Cl TN4 .....16 E7
Eastlands Rd TN4 .....7 E1
Eastport La BN7 .....190 A4
Eastview Cotts BN8 ..124 C5
Eastway TN39 ......156 D4
Eastwell Pl BN27 ...152 B8
Eastwick Cl BN1 ....143 B4
Eastwood Rd TN39 ..157 A4
Eatenden La TN32,TN33 .87 B3
Eaton Ct 9 BN3 .....163 B7
Eaton Gardens Mans 20
  BN3 ....163 C7
Eaton Gate 17 BN3 ..163 C7
Eaton Gdns BN3 .....163 C7
Eaton Gr BN3 ....163 C7
Eaton Hall 19 BN3 ...163 C7
Eaton Manor 11 BN3 .163 C7
Eaton Pl BN2 ....164 D4
Eaton Rd BN3 ....163 C7
Eaton Villas BN3 ....163 B7
Eaton Wlk TN33 ......88 D1
Ebbisham Ct RH19 .....1 A1
Ebden's Hill TN37 ...136 B8
Ebenezer Rd TN34 ...160 B4
Ecclesden 7 BN2 ....189 C3
Ecmod Rd BN22 .....185 C6
Edburton Ave BN1 ...143 A1
Eden Cl BN24 ....174 A5
Eden Dr TN39 ....156 F4
Eden Rd TN1 ....8 A2
Eden Vale
  Dormans Park RH19 ...1 F5
  East Grinstead RH19 ..1 D4
Eden Wlk 9 TN1 ......8 A2
Edenbridge Rd TN7 ..13 C7
Edensor Rd BN20 ...188 D7
Edgar Rd TN35 .....160 C6
Edgehill BN41 ......140 F2
Edgehill Cl TN21 .....81 F7
Edgeland Terr BN22 .173 F1
Edinburgh Ct
  Eastbourne BN20 ...184 C5
  Seaford BN25 ......180 D3
Edinburgh Rd
  Bexhill TN40 ....157 C5
  8 Brighton BN2 ....164 B8
  Seaford BN25 ......180 D3
  St Leonards TN38 ...158 E7
Edinburgh Way RH19 .10 E7
Edison Rd BN23 ....174 A1
Edith Ave BN10 ....178 B7
Edith Ave N BN10 ..178 C8
Edith Rd TN35 .....160 D7
Edmond Cl BN23 ...185 E8
Edmonton Rd TN39 .157 B7
Edmund Rd TN35 ...160 C6
Edster Ct BN41 ....140 F3
Edward Ave Hove BN3 .142 A3
  Saltdean BN2 ......177 D7
Edward Cl Hove BN3 .142 A3
  Seaford BN25 ......180 A6
Edward Ho BN3 .....162 F6
Edward Rd
  Haywards Heath RH16 .50 E2
  St Leonards TN38 ...158 E7
Edward St Brighton BN2 189 C1
  Lewes BN7 ....190 B2
  Royal Tunbridge Wells TN4 .7 F4
  Rusthall TN4 ....7 C4
Edward Terr TN38 ...136 A4
Edward Way RH15 ...72 D5

Edwin Rd TN35 .160 C6
Effingham Cl BN2 .177 C6
Effingham Dr TN39 .156 D3
Egbert Cl BN23 .185 E8
Egerton Ho BN20 .188 E8
Egerton Rd TN39 .157 B3
Egginton Cl BN1 .144 A5
Egginton Rd BN2 .144 A5
Egles Gr TN22 .78 B8
Egmont Rd BN3 .141 D1
Egremont Pl
Brighton BN2 .189 C2
Hastings TN34 .160 B6
Eight Acre La TN35 .115 D1
Eight Bells Cl TN22 .56 C4
Eileen Ave BN2 .177 B5
Eisenhower Dr TN37 .135 F6
Elder Cl BN41 .141 B2
Elder Pl BN1 .189 B4
Elderwood Cl
Bexhill TN39 .157 C7
Eastbourne BN22 .173 D2
Eldon Rd BN21 .184 C5
Eldred Ave BN1 .142 D5
Eldridge Way TN37 .136 C6
Eleanor Cl Lewes BN7 .123 B2
Seaford BN25 .180 D5
Eleanor Terr TN35 .160 D8
Eley Cres BN2 .165 E3
Eley Dr BN2 .165 E3
Elford St 3 TN34 .159 F8
Elgar Way BN23 .174 E3
Elgin Gdns BN25 .181 C3
Elim Court Gdns TN6 .25 E4
Elim Wlk TN34 .136 F2
Eliot Ho 5 RH16 .50 E3
Elizabeth Ave BN3 .142 A3
Elizabeth Cl Hove BN3 .142 A3
Seaford BN25 .180 A6
Elizabeth Cres RH19 .1 F3
Elizabeth Ct
4 Bexhill TN40 .157 C5
Eastbourne BN20 .184 C5
2 Hailsham BN27 .152 C7
7 Hove BN3 .163 C7
Polegate BN26 .173 A6
Elizabeth Garlick Ct 1
TN1 .8 B4
Elizabeth Rd
Shoreham-by-S BN43 .161 C8
St Leonards TN38 .136 A2
Elizabethan Cl TN33 .132 F2
Ellen Ho 3 BN3 .163 B7
Ellen St Hove BN3 .163 B7
Portslade-by-S BN41 .162 C7
Ellenslea Rd TN37 .159 C7
Ellenwhorne La TN32 .89 A7
Ellerslie La TN39 .156 F6
Elliots Way TN21 .82 A8
Ellis Cl TN34 .159 E7
Ellis Gordon Ct BN9 .179 B7
Ellis Way TN22 .78 A7
Ellison Cl TN6 .25 E4
Elm Ave BN27 .127 C3
Elm Cl Hove BN3 .142 C2
Laughton BN8 .126 C7
Seaford BN25 .181 C3
Elm Cotts Laughton BN8 .126 C7
Upper Dicker BN27 .151 A8
Elm Ct Brighton BN1 .163 E8
4 East Grinstead RH19 .1 D2
Newhaven BN9 .179 B7
Polegate BN26 .173 A6
Portslade-by-S BN41 .162 B8
Elm Dr East Grinstead RH19 .2 A1
Hove BN3 .141 E1
Elm Gn 4 BN27 .129 B1
Elm Gr Brighton BN2 .164 C7
Eastbourne BN22 .173 F1
Lewes BN7 .190 A1
Elm Grove Prim Sch
BN2 .164 C7
Elm Rd BN41 .162 B8
Elm Way TN21 .82 B6
Elmhurst Ave TN2 .9 D8
Elmore Ct BN2 .189 C3
Elmore Rd BN2 .189 C3
Elms Ave BN21 .185 B2
Elms La TN35 .116 F1
Elms Lea Ave BN1 .142 E3
Elms Rd BN21 .185 B2
Elms The BN8 .124 C5
Elmsdown Pl BN27 .152 C7
Elmsmead TN31 .70 B4
Elmstead 4 RH19 .10 E8
Elmstead Rd TN40 .157 E5
Elmwood 12 BN21 .184 F4
Elmwood Cl BN23 .174 C4
Elmwood Gdns BN23 .174 C4
Elphick Pl TN6 .25 F3
Elphick Rd
Broyle Side BN8 .124 F7
Newhaven BN9 .179 C8
Elphick's Pl TN2 .17 B8
Elphinstone Ave TN34 .136 F2
Elphinstone Com Sch
TN34 .160 A6
Elphinstone Gdns TN34 .136 F3
Elphinstone Rd TN34 .136 F2
Elrington Rd BN3 .142 C1
Elsted Cl BN22 .174 A1
Elsted Cres BN1 .143 C6
Elsted Rd TN39 .156 C2
Elven Cl BN20 .183 C1
Elven La BN20 .183 C1
Elvin Cres BN2 .165 E4
Elwood Cl RH15 .72 F1
Elwyn Jones Ct BN1 .142 E4
Ely Ct TN1 .8 B4
Embassy Ct
10 Brighton BN1 .163 D5
4 Haywards Heath RH16 .50 E6
Emerald Quay BN43 .161 A6
Emerson Coll RH18 .12 B3
Emmanuel Rd TN34 .160 A5
Encore Ho TN21 .81 F8
Endcliffe Ct BN20 .188 E8
Endwell Rd TN40 .157 C3
Engalee RH19 .1 C2
English Bsns Pk BN3 .162 E8
English Cl BN3 .162 E8
English's Pas BN7 .190 B2
Enholms La RH17 .34 A4
Ensenada Reef BN23 .175 B1
Enterprise Ctr The
BN21 .184 F3
Enterprise Est BN1 .143 C7
Enys Rd BN21 .184 F4
Epsom Cl TN38 .159 A8
Epsom Ct 6 TN40 .157 E4
Erica Cl BN23 .174 B2
Ericsson Way RH15 .72 D2
Eridge Cl TN39 .157 A4
Eridge Ct TN2 .7 F1
Eridge Dr TN6 .26 A3
Eridge Gdns TN6 .26 A3
Eridge Gn BN7 .123 B2
Eridge La TN3,TN6 .27 B2
Eridge Rd
Crowborough TN6 .26 C6
Eastbourne BN21 .184 D7
Groombridge TN3 .15 D5
Hove BN3 .142 A2
Royal Tunbridge Wells TN2,
TN4 .7 E1
Eridge Sta TN3 .15 E2
Erin Way RH15 .72 E3
Erroll Mans 6 BN3 .162 D7
Erroll Rd BN3 .162 C6
Ersham Rd BN27 .152 B5
Ersham Way BN27 .152 B6
Erskine Park Rd TN4 .7 C4
Esher Cl BN25 .180 F4
Eshton Rd BN22 .185 C5
Eskbank Ave BN1 .143 A7
Eskdale Cl BN23 .174 C4
Esplanade BN25 .180 E2
Esplanade Mews 19
BN25 .180 E2
Esplanade The BN10 .177 F3
Essenden Rd TN38 .159 A7
Essex Cl TN2 .16 F8
Essex Ct BN20 .184 B6
Essex Pl 3 Brighton BN2 .164 C4
Newhaven BN9 .179 C7
Essex Rd TN38 .136 A4
Essex St BN2 .164 C4
Estate Rd BN9 .179 E7
Estcots Dr RH19 .2 A1
Estcots Prim Sch RH19 .2 A1
Etchingham CE Prim Sch
TN19 .44 D2
Etchingham Rd BN23 .174 E1
Etchingham Sta TN19 .44 C1
Ethel St BN3 .163 B7
Ethelred Cl BN23 .185 F8
Etherington Hill TN3 .7 C8
Etherton Way BN25 .181 A4
Ethnam La TN18 .47 E4
Eton Cl BN25 .181 A4
Eton Mews 3 BN21 .185 A3
Eugene Way BN23 .175 B1
Euro Bsns Pk BN9 .168 D1
Eurythmy Sch RH19 .10 E6
Evelyn Ave BN9 .179 C7
Evelyn Ct BN41 .162 A8
Evelyn Glennie Ct 7
BN2 .164 C5
Evelyn Rd BN7 .123 B2
Evelyn Terr BN2 .164 C5
Everest Ho 2 BN3 .162 F7
Eversfield Ct TN37 .159 D7
Eversfield Hospl TN38 .159 A6
Eversfield Mews N 5
TN37 .159 C7
Eversfield Mews S 16
TN37 .159 C7
Eversfield Pl TN37 .159 D7
Eversfield Rd BN21 .184 F4
Evershed Way BN43 .161 B7
Eversley Cl TN37 .136 C2
Eversley Cres TN37 .136 C2
Eversley Ct BN21 .184 F4
Eversley Rd Bexhill TN40 .157 C3
St Leonards TN37 .136 C2
Everton Cotts TN19 .62 B6
Evesham TN38 .136 A3
Ewart St BN2 .189 C3
Ewbank Ho BN3 .163 D7
Ewehurst La TN3 .6 F6
Ewell Ct 5 TN40 .157 E4
Ewhurst Cl TN34 .136 F4
Ewhurst La TN31 .66 F4
Ewhurst Rd BN2 .143 C1
Exceat Cl Brighton BN2 .164 E6
Eastbourne BN23 .174 B4
Excelsior The BN1 .142 D4
Exeter Cl BN22 .173 B2
Exeter St BN1 .163 E8
Exmouth Pl TN34 .160 A4

F

Factory La BN27 .152 A6
Fair Isle Cl BN23 .185 E8
Fair La Robertsbridge TN32 64 B4
Robertsbridge TN32 .64 C4
Fair Mdw TN31 .93 C7
Fair Oak Cl TN21 .82 A7
Fair View Cotts TN5 .30 A6
Fairbanks RH16 .50 E4
Fairbridge Way RH15 .72 F5
Faircrouch La TN5 .29 B5
Fairdene BN42 .140 F1
Fairfax Ave TN37 .135 F7
Fairfield
Herstmonceux BN27 .130 E6
Peacehaven BN10 .178 B7
Fairfield Ave TN2 .8 C5
Fairfield Chase TN39 .156 F4
Fairfield Cl
Burgess Hill RH15 .72 F4
Shoreham-by-S BN43 .140 C1
Fairfield Cotts BN26 .149 D2
Fairfield Cres BN6 .97 A6
Fairfield Gdns
Burgess Hill RH15 .72 F4
Portslade-by-S BN41 .141 B1
Fairfield Lodge BN20 .188 E8
Fairfield Rd
Burgess Hill RH15 .72 F4
East Grinstead RH19 .10 F8
Eastbourne BN20 .184 E1
St Leonards TN37 .136 C6
Fairfield Way RH16 .50 D8
Fairford Cl RH16 .50 E5
Fairglen Cotts TN5 .29 B3
Fairglen Rd TN5 .29 B4
Fairhaven BN7 .99 E1
Fairholme BN7 .190 A1
Fairholme Ct TN6 .25 F1
Fairholme Rd BN9 .168 F1
Fairhurst BN10 .177 F3
Fairisle Cl BN27 .129 A2
Fairlawn 1 RH16 .50 E4
Fairlawn Cres RH19 .1 B2
Fairlawn Dr RH19 .1 B2
Fairlawns 9 Hove BN3 .163 A6
Shoreham-by-S BN43 .161 A8
Fairlawns Dr BN27 .130 E6
Fairlea Cl RH15 .72 F4
Fairlie Gdns BN1 .142 E3
Fairlight TN22 .55 E1
Fairlight Ave
Hastings TN35 .160 D7
Telscombe Cliffs BN10 .177 F3
Fairlight Cl Bexhill TN40 .158 A5
Polegate BN26 .173 A6
Fairlight Ct BN10 .177 F4
Fairlight Field BN8 .124 D5
Fairlight Gdns TN35 .138 F4
Fairlight Pl 8 BN2 .164 C8
Fairlight Prim Sch BN2 .164 C8
Fairlight Rd
Eastbourne BN22 .185 C5
Fairlight TN35 .138 A4
Hastings TN35 .160 E8
Fairlight Wood Cvn Site
TN35 .116 D1
Fairmile Rd TN2 .8 E5
Fairmount Rd TN40 .157 D5
Fairoak BN26 .173 C6
Fairplace RH17 .74 C4
Fairstone Cl TN35 .160 E8
Fairview Cotts TN6 .25 E4
Fairview La TN6 .25 E4
Fairview Rise BN1 .142 D5
Fairway Bsns Ctr BN2 .143 E4
Fairway Cl BN20 .184 C2
Fairway Cres BN41 .141 C2
Fairway The Bexhill TN39 156 F6
Newhaven BN9 .179 A7
St Leonards TN38 .158 F8
Fairway Trad Est BN2 .143 E4
Fairways BN1 .163 E8
Fairways Cl BN25 .181 C2
Fairways Rd BN25 .181 B2
Fairways The TN4 .8 A7
Falaise Rd
Hastings TN34 .159 D7
Newhaven BN9 .168 F1
Falcon Cl BN43 .161 C6
Falcon Way BN27 .129 B3
Falconbury Dr TN39 .156 D3
Falconer Dr TN33 .112 F4
Fallowfield Cl BN3 .141 F2
Fallowfield Cres BN3 .141 F2
Falmer Ave BN2 .177 B6
Falmer Cl BN20 .184 B7
Falmer Gdns BN2 .165 D8
Falmer High Sch BN1 .144 A5
Falmer Hill BN1 .144 B6
Falmer House Rd BN1 .144 B6
Falmer Rd BN2 .165 E5
Falmer Sta BN1 .144 B6
Falmouth Cl BN23 .185 F8
Faraday Ave RH19 .10 F6
Faraday Cl BN22 .173 F1
Faraday Lodge TN2 .8 E5
Farlaine Rd BN21 .184 C6
Farley Bank TN35 .160 B6
Farley Way TN35 .138 E5
Farleys Way TN31 .69 B2
Farlington Ave RH16 .50 F5
Farlington Cl RH16 .50 F5
Farm Cl
East Grinstead RH19 .11 B8
Hassocks BN6 .97 E4
Portslade-by-S BN41 .141 A2
Seaford BN25 .181 B4
Farm Cotts RH16 .50 C3
Farm Gdns TN31 .69 C2
Farm Hill BN2 .165 C8
Farm La Camber TN31 .94 D3
Ditchling BN6 .98 E3
Farm Mews BN3 .163 D6
Farm Rd BN3 .163 D6
Farm Way
Burgess Hill RH15 .73 D1
Southwick BN42 .162 A7
Farm World, Great Knelle
Farm (Childrens Farm)*
TN31 .68 A8
Farman St 15 BN3 .163 D5
Farmcombe Cl TN2 .8 B2
Farmcombe La TN2 .8 B2
Farmcombe Rd TN2 .8 C2
Farmet Ct RH19 .1 C3
Farmland Way BN27 .129 C1
Farmlands Ave BN26 .172 F4
Farmlands Cl
Polegate BN26 .173 A4
St Leonards TN37 .136 C5
Farmlands Ct BN26 .173 A4
Farmlands Way BN26 .172 F5
Farmway Cl BN3 .141 D2
Farncombe Cl RH17 .74 D4
Farncombe Rd BN7 .190 C2
Farne Cl BN27 .129 A2
Farnham Ave BN6 .98 A5
Farnham Beeches TN3 .7 A4
Farnham Cl TN3 .7 A3
Farnham La TN3 .7 A4
Farnham Pl TN3 .7 A3
Farningham Rd TN6 .38 C8
Farnlea RH15 .73 D5
Farnol Ho 6 BN21 .184 D4
Farrance Ct TN1 .8 B4
Farriers Pl BN8 .124 D5
Farriers Way TN22 .78 C6
Farthing Hill TN5 .31 E1
Farthing La BN27,TN33 .109 E4
Farthings The TN6 .26 A3
Fastnet Cl BN23 .185 E8
Faulkners Way RH15 .73 A5
Faversham Rd BN23 .174 D2
Faygate Cl TN39 .157 B8
Faygate Ct BN2 .164 E6
Faygate Rd BN22 .173 E2
Fayre Mdw TN32 .64 C4
Fazan Ct TN5 .29 F4
Fearon Rd TN34 .136 F2
Felbridge Cl RH19 .1 C3
Felbridge Ct RH19 .1 A4
Felbridge Ctr The RH19 .1 A3
Felbridge Pl RH19 .1 A4
Felcourt Cotts RH19 .1 C8
Felcourt La RH19 .1 C8
Felcourt Rd RH19 .1 C7
Feld The RH19 .1 A3
Fellows Rd TN34 .160 B7
Felride RH16 .50 E3
Felwater Ct RH19 .1 A3
Fen Ct TN38 .135 E1
Fennel Wlk BN43 .140 B1
Fennell's Cl BN21 .184 E5
Ferbies TN3 .7 A7
Ferbies Cl TN3 .7 A7
Ferdinand Terr TN3 .15 C7
Ferguson Rd TN29 .96 D2
Fermor Rd TN6 .38 A7
Fermor Row 2 TN6 .37 F8
Fermor Way TN6 .38 A8
Fern Cl BN23 .174 C3
Fern Gn 1 BN27 .129 B1
Fern Rd TN38 .158 F8
Fernbank Sh Ctr TN6 .25 F3
Ferndale TN2 .8 D5
Ferndale Cl TN2 .8 C4
Ferndale Point TN2 .8 C4
Ferndale Rd
Burgess Hill RH15 .73 C2
Hove BN3 .163 D7
Fernhurst Cl BN1 .143 B6
Fernhurst Cres BN1 .143 B5
Fernlea Cl TN35 .114 E4
Ferns The TN1 .8 C4
Fernside 5 RH19 .1 D2
Fernside Ave TN38 .135 F1
Fernwood Rise BN1 .142 D5
Ferrers Rd BN7 .123 B1
Ferring Cl TN31 .93 A6
Ferring Ct BN1 .143 F5
Ferringham TN4 .7 F4
Ferry Hill TN36 .117 E8
Ferry Rd TN31 .93 B5
Festival Gdns TN39 .157 C7
Feversham Cl BN43 .161 B6
Field Cl Burgess Hill RH15 .72 E4
Seaford BN25 .181 B2
Field End TN22 .55 A4
Field View TN32 .64 B3
Field Way TN38 .158 E8
Fielden La TN6 .25 D1
Fielden Rd TN6 .25 D2
Fieldfare Ct BN27 .152 D7
Fields End Cl RH16 .50 F4
Fieldway Broad Oak TN31 .90 C5
Ditchling BN6 .98 D3
Haywards Heath RH16 .50 F8
Fiennes Rd BN27 .130 E6
Figg La TN6 .37 F8
Filching Cl BN26 .172 E3
Filching Ct BN20 .184 B5
Filching Manor Motor Mus*
BN26 .172 D2
Filching Rd BN20 .184 B5
Filder Cl BN22 .185 A6
Filsham Dr TN40 .158 A6
Filsham Rd TN38 .159 A8
Filsham Valley TN38 .158 F7
Filsham Valley Sch
TN38 .158 F7
Finch Ct BN10 .178 A7
Finches Gdns RH16 .51 A8
Finches La RH16 .51 A8
Finches Park Rd RH16 .51 A8
Finches The Bexhill TN40 157 F4
Shoreham-by-S BN43 .161 A8
2 St Leonards TN38 .136 A5
Findon Ave BN2 .177 E6
Findon Cl Bexhill TN39 .156 E3
Hove BN3 .141 F3
Seaford BN25 .181 C3
Findon Rd BN2 .164 F5
Finistere Ave BN23 .185 E8
Finley Ct TN38 .158 F6
Finmere Cl BN22 .185 C6
Finmere Ct BN22 .185 C6
Finmere Rd BN22 .185 C6
Finsbury Lodge 1 BN2 .164 C6
Finsbury Rd BN2 .164 C6
Fir Cl BN2 .165 F7
Fir Grove Rd TN21 .81 B6
Fir Toll Cl TN20 .39 F2
Fir Toll Rd
Woolbridge TN20 .39 C2
Woolbridge TN20 .39 E2
Fir Tree Cl Bexhill TN39 .156 C3
Hailsham BN27 .129 C2
Fir Tree Rd TN4 .7 F3
Fir Tree Way BN6 .98 A4
Fircroft Cl BN1 .142 E3
Firehills Cotts TN35 .138 C3
Firlands RH16 .50 F4
Firle Bostal BN8 .148 A2
Firle CE Prim Sch BN8 .148 B4
Firle Cl Hastings TN35 .160 E8
Seaford BN25 .180 E5
Firle Cres BN7 .122 F2
Firle Dr BN25 .180 E5
Firle Gn TN22 .55 E1
Firle Grange BN25 .180 E5
Firle Pl* BN8 .148 C3
Firle Rd Bexhill TN39 .156 D4
Brighton BN2 .164 D6
Eastbourne BN22 .185 B4
Peacehaven BN10 .178 C8
Ripe BN8 .149 B7
Seaford BN25 .180 E6
Firle Terr BN9 .168 D2
Firs Ct TN4 .7 F6
Firs The TN35 .160 C5
First Ave Bexhill TN40 .157 F5
Camber TN31 .94 F2
Hove BN3 .163 C6
Newhaven BN9 .179 C7
First St TN3 .6 F3
Firstone Ho TN20 .39 F2
Firtoft Cl RH15 .73 B3
Firtree Rd TN34 .160 A6
Firwood Cl
Eastbourne BN22 .173 E1
Heathfield TN21 .82 A8
Firwood Rise TN21 .82 A8
Fisher Cl BN23 .185 F7
Fisher St BN7 .190 B2
Fisher's Gate Cotts TN7 .14 A1
Fishermen's Mus*
TN34 .160 B3
Fishersgate Cl BN41 .162 A7
Fishersgate Fst Sch
BN41 .162 A7
Fishersgate Sta BN41 .162 B7
Fishersgate Terr BN41 .162 A7
Fishmarket Rd TN31 .93 C6
Fishponds La TN35 .114 E3
Fitch Dr BN2 .143 F1
Fitzalan Ct BN10 .178 B7
Fitzalan Ho 10 BN21 .184 F4
Fitzgerald Ave BN25 .180 F2
Fitzgerald Cl BN20 .184 F1
Fitzgerald Ho 8 BN25 .180 E3
Fitzgerald Pk BN25 .180 F2
Fitzgerald Rd BN7 .190 B4
Fitzherbert Ct BN2 .164 D8
Fitzherbert Dr BN2 .164 D8
Fitzjohn Ct BN6 .97 F3
Fitzjohns Rd BN7 .123 B1
Fitzmaurice Ave BN22 .185 B5
Fitzroy Rd BN7 .123 B2
Five Acre Wlk TN34 .136 E1
Five Ashes CE Prim Sch
TN20 .58 B6
Five Ashes Rd TN6 .39 A5
Five Chys La TN22 .57 A6
Five Hos The TN36 .117 E8
Five Villages Ho TN36 .116 F6
Five Ways TN1 .8 B4
Flag Ct BN3 .163 B5
Flamingo Family Fun Pk*
TN34 .160 A3
Flamsteed Rd BN27 .131 A1
Fleetway Ct TN31 .94 F2
Fleming Cl BN23 .174 F2
Fleming Wlk RH19 .10 F6
Fletcher Ave TN37 .135 F7
Fletcher Cl BN27 .152 C7
Fletching CE Prim Sch
TN22 .53 F3
Fletching Cl BN2 .164 F6
Fletching Rd BN22 .174 A2
Fletching St TN20 .40 B3
Flimwell Cl Brighton BN2 164 E5
Eastbourne BN23 .174 A4
Flimwell TN5 .32 D4

Flimwell Cl continued
St Leonards TN38 . . . .**135** D3
Flint Cl
Portslade-by-S BN41 . . . . **141** B2
Seaford BN25 . . . .**180** E6
Flint Halls 5 BN21 . . . . .**184** D3
Flints The BN7 . . . .**145** E5
Flitterbrook La TN21 . . .**83** C4
Florance La TN3 . . . .**15** B6
Florence Ave BN3 . . . . . .**162** D8
Florence Ct BN1 . . . .**142** F2
Florence Pl BN1 . . . .**143** B1
Florence Rd BN1 . . . .**164** A8
Florida Ct TN38 . . . .**158** F6
Floyd Cl TN4 . . . .**8** A7
Fold The BN3 . . . .**162** D7
Folders Cl RH15 . . . .**73** D1
Folders Grange RH15 . . .**73** C1
Folders La RH15 . . . .**73** D1
Foley Cl BN23 . . . .**185** E2
Folkestone Cl BN25 . . . .**181** C5
Folkestone Rd TN31 . . . .**93** F8
Folkington Gdns TN37 . .**136** C5
Folkington Rd BN26 . . . .**172** D5
Follett Holt Ho BN8 . . . .**100** E7
Folly Field BN9 . . . .**179** C6
Fonthill Lodge Sch RH19 .**10** C6
Fonthill Rd BN3 . . . .**163** B8
Fontridge La TN19 . . . . . .**62** E3
Fontwell Ave TN39 . . . . .**156** C5
Foords La BN24 . . . .**174** C7
Foot's La TN19 . . . .**61** B3
Ford Rd TN38 . . . .**135** F2
Fordbrook Hill TN6 . . . . .**37** F2
Fordcombe CE Prim Sch
TN3 . . . .**6** B5
Fordcombe Rd TN3 . . . . . .**6** C4
Foredown Cl
Eastbourne BN20 . . . .**184** C2
Portslade-by-S BN41 . . . .**141** B2
Foredown Dr BN41 . . . . . .**141** C1
Foredown Rd
Portslade Village BN41 . . .**141** B4
Portslade-by-S BN41 . . . .**141** B3
Foredown Tower Countryside
Ctr★ BN41 . . . .**141** B3
Forest Dene
Crowborough TN6 . . . .**26** D1
Royal Tunbridge Wells TN2 . .**8** C1
Forest Fold Cotts TN6 . . .**25** D5
Forest La TN21 . . . .**83** D6
Forest Lodge
Crowborough TN6 . . . .**37** D8
2 East Grinstead RH19 . . .**10** F8
Forest Pk
Crowborough TN6 . . . .**25** D2
Maresfield TN22 . . . .**54** F5
Forest Pl TN1 . . . .**80** F6
Forest Rd Brighton BN1 . .**143** E6
Forest Row RH18 . . . .**12** B2
Royal Tunbridge Wells TN2 . .**8** C1
Forest Ridge RH19 . . . . . .**21** A6
Forest Rise TN6 . . . .**26** D1
Forest Row Bsns Pk
RH18 . . . .**11** F3
Forest Row CE Prim Sch
RH18 . . . .**11** F2
Forest View
Hailsham TN27 . . . .**152** A8
Nutley TN22 . . . .**35** C3
Forest View Rd RH19 . . . .**10** E6
Forest Way
Golden Cross BN27 . . . . .**127** C3
Hastings TN34 . . . .**136** E1
Pembury TN2 . . . .**9** D8
Royal Tunbridge Wells TN2 . .**8** D1
Foresters Ho BN26 . . . . . .**173** A6
Forewood La TN33 . . . . . .**135** A7
Forewood Rise TN33 . . . .**134** F6
Forge Cl
Portslade-by-S BN41 . . . .**141** B2
Staplecross TN32 . . . .**65** E1
Uckfield TN22 . . . .**78** C6
Forge Field TN5 . . . .**42** F6
Forge La TN32 . . . .**65** E1
Forge Lane Cotts TN22 . .**55** A8
Forge Rd TN22 . . . .**15** C2
Forge Rise TN22 . . . .**78** C6
Forge The BN3 . . . .**162** F8
Forge Way
Burgess Hill RH15 . . . .**73** A4
St Leonards TN37 . . . .**136** C5
Forgefield Cotts TN18 . . .**47** A4
Forstal The Cobbarn TN3 . .**15** F3
Pembury TN2 . . . .**9** E8
Forstall TN3 . . . .**7** A4
Fort Gate BN9 . . . .**179** E5
Fort Haven BN43 . . . .**161** C6
Fort La BN22 . . . .**185** D6
Fort Rd Eastbourne BN22 .**185** D6
Newhaven BN9 . . . .**179** D6
Fort Rise BN9 . . . .**179** D5
Forward Cl BN9 . . . .**168** E2
Fosse The BN7 . . . .**190** B2
Foster Cl BN25 . . . .**180** E4
Foster Ct BN3 . . . .**163** E6
Foundry Cl RH15 . . . .**73** B3
Foundry La BN7 . . . .**190** C2
Foundry St BN1 . . . .**189** B3
Fountains Cl
Brighton BN1 . . . .**143** B2
Eastbourne BN22 . . . .**173** E3
Founthill Ave BN2 . . . . . .**177** B5
Founthill Rd BN2 . . . .**177** B5
Fourteen Acre La TN35 . .**115** D4

Fourth Ave BN3 . . . .**163** B6
Fowey Cl BN43 . . . .**161** B6
Fowlers Cl TN39 . . . .**156** E5
Fowly La TN22 . . . .**56** C7
Fox Cl RH15 . . . .**72** F1
Fox Hill RH16 . . . .**50** E1
Fox Hill Cl RH16 . . . .**50** F1
Fox Hill Village RH16 . . . .**50** F1
Fox Hollow BN27 . . . .**152** B6
Fox in the Wood TN5 . . . .**29** C6
Fox Way BN41 . . . .**141** B2
Foxcote TN37 . . . .**136** D5
Foxdown Rd BN2 . . . .**165** F7
Foxglove Cl
Broyle Side BN8 . . . .**125** A7
Burgess Hill RH15 . . . .**72** D4
Foxglove Rd BN23 . . . . . .**174** B3
Foxhall Bexhill BN39 . . . .**156** E5
Peacehaven BN10 . . . .**167** B1
Foxhill Ct 3 RH16 . . . .**50** E3
Foxhole La
Four Throws TN18 . . . .**46** D8
Wadhurst TN5 . . . .**30** B4
Foxhunters Rd BN41 . . . .**140** F3
Foxwarren RH16 . . . .**50** C5
Framble Mount TN22 . . . .**79** B6
Framfield 11 BN2 . . . .**164** F5
Framfield CE Prim Sch
TN22 . . . .**79** B6
Framfield Cl BN1 . . . .**143** E6
Framfield Rd Buxted TN22 .**56** B3
Uckfield TN22 . . . .**78** D6
Framfield Way BN21 . . . .**184** D6
Framroze Ct BN1 . . . .**143** B2
Francis Bird Pl TN37 . . . .**136** C6
Francis Rd RH16 . . . .**51** B8
Francis St BN1 . . . .**189** B4
Francislea RH16 . . . .**50** E2
Frankfield Rise TN2 . . . . . .**8** A1
Franklands Cl RH15 . . . . . .**73** B1
Franklands Gdns RH15 . . .**98** A8
Franklands Way RH15 . . . .**98** A8
Franklin Rd
Brighton BN2 . . . .**164** C7
Portslade-by-S BN41 . . . .**162** C7
Shoreham-by-S BN43 . . . .**140** D1
Franklin St BN2 . . . .**164** C8
Franklynn Ct RH16 . . . . . .**50** F3
Franklynn Rd RH16 . . . . . .**50** F3
Frankton Ave RH16 . . . . . .**51** A3
Frant Ave TN39 . . . .**156** C5
Frant CE Prim Sch TN3 . . .**17** B4
Frant Cl TN39 . . . .**156** C5
Frant Ct TN3 . . . .**17** B3
Frant Green Rd TN3 . . . . .**17** B3
Frant Rd Hove BN3 . . . . . .**142** A2
Royal Tunbridge Wells TN2,
TN3 . . . .**17** A7
Frant Sta TN3 . . . .**17** F5
Frary Wlk TN21 . . . .**82** A3
Fraser Ave BN23 . . . .**185** E7
Freckley Hollow TN33 . . .**111** C1
Fred Emery Ct 16 BN1 . . .**163** E5
Freda Gardham Com Sch
TN31 . . . .**93** D6
Frederic Ho BN2 . . . .**177** B5
Frederick Cotts RH16 . . . .**51** B7
Frederick Gdns BN1 . . . .**189** B3
Frederick Pl BN1 . . . .**189** B3
Frederick Rd TN35 . . . . . .**160** C7
Frederick St BN1 . . . .**189** B3
Frederick Thatcher Pl
TN33 . . . .**112** A5
Free Heath Rd TN3,TN5 . . .**19** C3
Freehold Terr 1 BN2 . . . .**164** C8
Freek's La RH15 . . . .**73** A5
Freeland Cl BN25 . . . .**180** A6
Freeland Ho 5 BN20 . . . .**184** F1
Freeman Ave BN22 . . . . .**173** E1
Freemans Rd BN41 . . . . .**162** A8
Freezeland La TN39 . . . . .**134** A2
Fremlin Cl TN4 . . . .**7** B4
French Gdns RH16 . . . . . .**51** A6
French's Ct 9 BN25 . . . . .**180** E2
Frenches Farm Dr TN21 . .**82** A5
Frenchgate Cl BN22 . . . .**173** F2
Frenchgate Rd BN22 . . . .**173** F2
Freshfield Bank RH18 . . . .**11** E2
Freshfield Cl BN27 . . . . . .**152** B6
Freshfield Crossway
RH17 . . . .**52** C8
Freshfield La RH17 . . . . . .**33** E2
Freshfield Pl BN2 . . . .**164** C5
Freshfield Rd BN2 . . . . . .**164** D6
Freshfield St BN2 . . . .**164** C6
Freshfield Way BN2 . . . . .**164** C5
Freshford Cl BN23 . . . . . .**174** D2
Freshwater Ave TN34 . . .**136** E2
Freshwater Sq BN22 . . . .**173** C3
Freshway BN22 . . . .**173** C3
Frewen Cl TN31 . . . .**67** B7
Frewen Coll TN31 . . . .**67** C5
Frewyn Ct TN38 . . . .**135** F4
Friar Cl BN1 . . . .**143** A4
Friar Cres BN1 . . . .**143** A3
Friar Rd BN1 . . . .**143** A3
Friar Wlk BN1 . . . .**142** F4
Friar's Cres TN35 . . . .**138** B7
Friar's Hill Terr TN35 . . . .**138** A7
Friar's Way TN34 . . . .**136** F4
Friars Bank TN35 . . . .**138** B7
Friars Cl BN6 . . . .**97** E4
Friars Hill TN35 . . . .**137** F7
Friars Mews BN7 . . . .**190** B1
Friars Oak Rd BN6 . . . . . .**97** E5
Friars Rd TN36 . . . .**117** F7
Friars Vale TN6 . . . .**25** C5

Friars Way TN2 . . . .**8** D6
Friars' Ave BN10 . . . .**178** E6
Friars' Wlk BN7 . . . .**190** B2
Friday St BN23 . . . .**174** C3
Fridays The BN20 . . . .**187** B7
Friezland Rd TN4 . . . .**7** D1
Frimley Cl BN2 . . . .**165** F7
Friston Ave BN22 . . . .**173** C1
Friston Cl Brighton BN2 . .**143** F4
Friston BN20 . . . .**183** A1
Seaford BN25 . . . .**180** C4
Friston Downs BN20 . . . .**183** B2
Friston Hill BN20 . . . .**183** A1
Frith Pk RH19 . . . .**1** E3
Frith Rd BN3 . . . .**163** B8
Frobisher Cl BN23 . . . . . .**185** E7
Frobisher Ho BN10 . . . . . .**167** D1
Frog Hole La TN20,TN21 . .**58** C5
Frog La TN1 . . . .**8** A2
Front Cotts TN5 . . . .**31** E1
Fruitfields TN5 . . . .**32** C3
Fry Cres RH15 . . . .**72** E5
Fryatts Way TN39 . . . . . .**156** F6
Fryman's La TN31 . . . .**89** D2
Fulbourne Ho BN20 . . . . .**184** E1
Fulford Cl TN38 . . . .**159** A8
Fuller Cl TN5 . . . .**29** E5
Fuller Rd BN7 . . . .**123** A3
Fuller's Pas BN7 . . . .**190** B2
Fullers La TN31 . . . .**67** B6
Fullwood Ave BN9 . . . . . .**179** B7
Fulmar Cl BN3 . . . .**142** D1
Fulmar Dr RH19 . . . .**2** B3
Fulmer Pl 5 TN40 . . . . . .**157** C4
Furlongs The BN26 . . . . .**170** F3
Furnace Ave TN3 . . . .**20** A3
Furnace La
Beckley Furnace TN31 . . . .**90** D7
Hook Green TN3 . . . .**19** E4
Horam TN21 . . . .**106** D8
Warbleton TN21 . . . .**82** E2
Furnace Way TN22 . . . . . .**78** E7
Furness Rd BN20,BN21 . .**184** F2
Furnival Ct TN2 . . . .**16** F8
Furze Croft Hove BN3 . . .**163** D6
St Leonards TN38 . . . .**159** A8
Furze Hill BN3 . . . .**163** D6
Furze Hill Ct BN3 . . . .**163** E6
Furze Hill Ho BN3 . . . .**163** E6
Furze La RH19 . . . .**1** B4
Furzedene BN3 . . . .**163** D6
Furzefield Ave TN3 . . . .**7** A8
Furzefield Chase RH19 . . .**1** C6
Furzefield Rd RH19 . . . . . .**1** D4
Fyning Pl TN39 . . . .**156** C5
Fyrsway TN35 . . . .**138** E4
Fysie La TN19 . . . .**44** D3**

G

Gables Ct 2 BN21 . . . . . .**185** A3
Gables The TN34 . . . .**136** E3
Gableson Ave BN1 . . . . . .**142** B4
Gage Ridge RH18 . . . .**11** E2
Gages The BN27 . . . .**152** D7
Gainsborough Cres
BN23 . . . .**174** D1
Gainsborough Ho 16
BN3 . . . .**163** C7
Gainsborough La BN26 . .**172** E6
Gainsborough Rd TN40 . .**157** E6
Galley Hill View TN40 . . .**157** E4
Galliers Cl BN1 . . . .**143** B6
Gallipot Hill TN7 . . . .**13** C3
Gallops The BN7 . . . .**123** A4
Gallows Cl BN24 . . . .**174** E6
Gallows La BN24 . . . .**174** E6
Galveston Cl BN23 . . . . . .**185** F7
Gammons Way TN33 . . . .**88** E1
Gander Cl RH15 . . . .**73** A5
Gander Gn RH16 . . . .**50** F7
Gander Ho BN22 . . . .**173** E1
Gander Hill RH16 . . . .**50** F7
Gannet Ho
5 Eastbourne BN21 . . . . .**185** A2
Hove BN3 . . . .**142** B1
Ganton Pl TN38 . . . .**158** F8
Garden Cl
4 Bexhill TN40 . . . .**157** D4
East Grinstead RH19 . . . . .**10** F7
Portslade-by-S BN41 . . . .**162** C8
Shoreham-by-S BN43 . . . .**140** C1
Garden Cotts
Goatham Green TN31 . . . .**89** D8
14 Hastings TN34 . . . . . .**160** B4
Garden Ct Bexhill TN40 . .**157** D5
19 Eastbourne BN21 . . . .**185** A2
Shoreham-by-S BN43 . . . .**140** B1
Garden Ho The BN1 . . . .**189** A3
Garden House La RH19 . . .**10** F7
Garden Mews BN20 . . . . .**188** D8
Garden Rd TN1 . . . .**8** B7
Garden St Lewes BN7 . . .**190** B1
Royal Tunbridge Wells TN1 . .**8** B4
Garden Wood Rd RH19 . . .**10** C8
Gardener St BN41 . . . . . .**162** B8
Gardens The BN42 . . . . . .**161** F7
Gardner Centre Rd BN41 .**144** B6
Gardner Cl BN23 . . . .**185** E7
Gardner Rd BN41 . . . .**162** A7
Gardner St Brighton BN1 .**189** B2
Herstmonceux BN27 . . . . .**130** F6
Gardner Way TN38 . . . . .**159** B6
Gardner's Hill TN11 . . . . . .**70** B6
Garfield Rd BN27 . . . .**152** C7
Garland Rd RH19 . . . .**1** D2
Garnet Dr BN20 . . . .**184** C7
Garnet Ho 13 BN2 . . . . . .**164** C4

Garston Pk TN19 . . . .**62** B6
Garth Cl TN39 . . . .**157** A5
Gatehouse Cl TN39 . . . . .**156** C2
Gatehouse La
Framefield TN22 . . . .**79** C7
Goddards' Green BN6,
RH15 . . . .**72** C4
Gatelands Dr TN39 . . . . .**157** B6
Gatesmead RH16 . . . .**50** F8
Gattons Inf Sch The
RH15 . . . .**72** E3
Gattons The RH15 . . . .**72** E3
Gatwick Farm Cotts RH19 . .**3** A4
Gaudick Cl BN20 . . . .**184** E1
Gaudick Rd BN20 . . . .**184** E1
Gavin Astor Cl TN40 . . . .**158** A6
Geary Pl TN35 . . . .**114** C3
Geering Pk BN27 . . . .**152** D7
Geering Rd BN24 . . . .**174** B5
Geers Wood TN21 . . . .**81** F6
Geerswood Cotts 2
TN21 . . . .**82** A6
Gemini Bsns Ctr BN3 . . . .**163** B8
Gemma BN27 . . . .**152** E7
Geneva Rd BN9 . . . .**179** D6
Genistos The BN6 . . . .**97** E4
Gensing Rd TN38 . . . .**159** C7
George Hill TN32 . . . .**64** B3
George St Brighton BN2 . .**189** B2
Hailsham BN27 . . . .**152** C7
Hastings TN34 . . . .**160** A3
Hove BN3 . . . .**163** B6
Portslade-by-S BN41 . . . .**162** C7
Royal Tunbridge Wells TN2 . .**8** C3
Sparrow's Green TN5 . . . . .**29** F5
Georgia Pl TN2 . . . .**8** C4
Georgian Cl TN40 . . . .**157** E5
Georgian Wlk TN38 . . . . .**158** F8
Gerald Cl RH15 . . . .**73** D3
Gerald Rd BN25 . . . .**180** F1
Gerard St BN1 . . . .**189** B5
German St TN36 . . . .**117** E7
Ghyll Ind Est TN31 . . . . . .**82** A5
Ghyll Rd Crowborough TN6 .**25** E4
Heathfield TN21 . . . .**82** A6
Ghyll Side Rd TN31 . . . . . .**67** B7
Ghyllside BN2 . . . .**143** E1
Ghyllside Ave TN34 . . . . .**136** D4
Ghyllside Dr TN34 . . . . . .**136** D4
Ghyllside Way TN34 . . . .**136** D4
Gibb Cl TN40 . . . .**158** A5
Gibbetts TN40 . . . .**6** F3
Gibbon Rd BN9 . . . .**179** C6
Gibraltar Rise TN21 . . . . . .**82** A7
Gibson Ct BN7 . . . .**190** B3
Giffards Cl RH19 . . . .**1** F1
Gilbert Rd
Eastbourne BN22 . . . .**185** B4
St Leonards TN37,TN38 . . .**159** B8
Gilbert Way BN27 . . . . . .**152** B5
Gilberts Dr BN20 . . . .**187** B8
Gilda Cres BN26 . . . .**173** A6
Gildredge Rd
Eastbourne BN21 . . . .**184** F2
Seaford BN25 . . . .**180** F3
Gilham La RH18 . . . .**11** E2
Gill The TN2 . . . .**9** E8
Gillham Wood Ave
TN39 . . . .**156** D3
Gillham Wood Rd TN39 . .**156** D3
Gilligans The RH15 . . . . . .**72** F5
Gillridge Gn TN6 . . . .**25** F4
Gillman's Dr TN38 . . . . . .**135** F1
Gillman's Hill TN38 . . . . .**136** A1
Gillman's Pk TN38 . . . . . .**135** F1
Gimble Way TN2 . . . .**9** D8
Gingerbread La TN18 . . . .**32** F2
Gipps Cross La TN3 . . . . . .**6** F3
Girton Ho BN3 . . . .**162** F6
Githa Rd TN35 . . . .**160** C6
Glade The
Hailsham BN27 . . . .**151** F6
Mayfield TN20 . . . .**40** F3
Uckfield TN22 . . . .**78** D7
Gladepoint RH16 . . . .**50** E5
Glades The Bexhill TN40 . .**157** E6
East Grinstead RH19 . . . . . .**2** B1
Gladstone Bldgs BN8 . . .**101** E4
Gladstone Cl BN22 . . . . . .**173** F1
Gladstone Pl BN2 . . . .**164** C8
Gladstone Rd
Burgess Hill RH15 . . . .**73** C4
Crowborough TN6 . . . .**25** F1
Portslade-by-S BN41 . . . .**162** B7
Rusthall TN4 . . . .**7** B4
Gladstone Terr
Brighton BN2 . . . .**189** C4
Hastings TN34 . . . .**160** A5
Gladys Ave BN10 . . . .**178** D6
Gladys Rd BN3 . . . .**162** D8
Glanfield Ct TN1 . . . .**8** C5
Glassenbury Dr TN40 . . .**157** F5
Glastonbury Rd BN3 . . . .**162** D6
Gleave Cl RH19 . . . .**2** A2
Glebe Cl Bexhill TN39 . . .**156** D3
Eastbourne BN20 . . . .**184** D3
Lewes BN7 . . . .**146** A8
Southwick BN42 . . . .**161** F7
Glebe Com Mid Sch
BN42 . . . .**161** D8
Glebe Cotts TN33 . . . . . .**134** D4
Glebe Dr BN25 . . . .**180** E3
Glebe The Felbridge RH19 . .**1** A4
Hastings TN34 . . . .**160** B5
Hurstpierpoint BN6 . . . . . .**97** A6
Lindfield RH16 . . . .**51** A8

Glebe The continued
Pembury TN2 . . . .**9** D8
Pett TN35 . . . .**116** F1
Southwick BN42 . . . .**161** F8
Glebe Villas BN3 . . . .**162** D7
Glebelands Cl BN43 . . . . .**161** B8
Glebelands The TN6 . . . . .**25** F2
Glen Cl BN26 . . . .**172** F4
Glen Cotts BN26 . . . .**172** F3
Glen Gordon RH16 . . . . . .**50** E6
Glen Rise BN1 . . . .**142** B5
Glen Rise Cl BN1 . . . .**142** B5
Glen The TN22 . . . .**55** D1
Glen Vue RH19 . . . .**1** E1
Glenburn Cl TN39 . . . . . .**157** C7
Glencoe TN6 . . . .**25** F2
Glendale Ave BN21 . . . . .**184** C5
Glendale Ct TN2 . . . .**8** D6
Glendale Rd
Burgess Hill RH15 . . . .**73** B2
Hove BN3 . . . .**163** D7
Glendor Rd BN3 . . . .**162** E6
Glendyne Cl RH19 . . . .**11** A8
Glendyne Way RH19 . . . . .**11** A8
Gleneagles Cl
Bexhill TN40 . . . .**157** E5
Seaford BN25 . . . .**180** A6
Gleneagles Ct 13 RH16 . . .**50** E4
Gleneagles Dr
Hailsham BN27 . . . .**152** A8
St Leonards TN38 . . . .**158** F7
Glenfalls Ave BN1 . . . . . .**143** A7
Glenfergus 3 RH16 . . . . . .**50** E6
Glengorse TN33 . . . .**112** F3
Glengorse Ct TN33 . . . . . .**112** F3
Glenham Pl RH19 . . . .**21** A5
Glenleigh Ave TN39 . . . . .**156** F6
Glenleigh Park Rd TN39 .**157** A6
Glenleigh Wlk TN32 . . . . .**64** A4
Glenmore Mews 4
BN21 . . . .**185** A3
Glenmore Pk TN2 . . . .**16** F8
Glenmore Rd TN6 . . . .**25** C3
Glenmore Rd E TN6 . . . . .**25** D3
Glenside 1 RH19 . . . .**1** E1
Glenthorn Rd TN39 . . . . .**157** A4
Glenthorne Ho 17 BN21 .**184** F4
Glenview Cl TN35 . . . .**160** D5
Glessing Rd BN24 . . . .**174** B6
Gleton Ave BN3 . . . .**141** D2
Glottenham Farm Cotts
TN32 . . . .**63** F1
Gloucester Ave TN40 . . . .**158** A5
Gloucester Cl
East Grinstead RH19 . . . . .**11** A8
Eastbourne BN20 . . . .**173** C2
Gloucester Cotts 3
TN34 . . . .**160** A4
Gloucester Ct BN23 . . . . .**174** A2
Gloucester Mews 2
BN1 . . . .**189** B3
Gloucester Pas 4 BN1 . . .**189** B3
Gloucester Pl BN1 . . . . . .**189** B3
Gloucester Rd
Brighton BN1 . . . .**189** B3
Burgess Hill RH15 . . . .**72** F3
Turner's Green TN5 . . . . . .**29** F6
Gloucester St BN1 . . . . . .**189** B3
Gloucester Yd 3 BN1 . . . .**189** B3
Glovers La TN39 . . . .**157** C7
Glynde Ave
Eastbourne BN22 . . . .**173** E1
Saltdean BN2 . . . .**177** D6
Glynde Cl BN9 . . . .**168** D2
Glynde Ct Bexhill TN39 . .**156** C3
Polegate BN26 . . . .**173** A6
Glynde Ho BN3 . . . .**163** D6
Glynde Pl★ BN8 . . . .**147** F7
Glynde Rd BN2 . . . .**164** D6
Glynde Sta BN8 . . . .**147** F6
Glyndebourne Ave BN2 .**177** C6
Glyndebourne Gdns
TN37 . . . .**136** C6
Glyndebourne Opera Ho★
BN8 . . . .**124** E2
Glyndebourne Manor Cottage Est
BN24 . . . .**152** F2
Glyne Ascent TN40 . . . . .**157** F5
Glyne Barn Cl TN40 . . . . .**158** A5
Glyne Dr TN40 . . . .**158** A5
Glyne Gap Sch TN40 . . . .**158** A5
Glyne Hall TN40 . . . .**157** D3
Glynleigh 18 BN2 . . . .**189** C3
Glynleigh Dr BN26 . . . . . .**173** C6
Glynleigh Rd BN24 . . . . .**153** A1
Glynn Rd BN10 . . . .**167** C1
Glynn Rd W BN10 . . . .**167** C1
Glynn Rise BN10 . . . .**167** B1
Goatham La TN31 . . . .**89** C5
Gochers Ct BN26 . . . .**164** C2
Godden Cl TN31 . . . .**67** B7
Godden Rd BN8 . . . .**76** C7
Goddens Gill TN31 . . . .**67** B7
Goddens The RH19 . . . . . .**10** E7
Godfrey Cl BN7 . . . .**190** A4
Godwin Rd
Hastings TN35 . . . .**160** C5
Hove BN3 . . . .**141** D1
Goffs The BN21 . . . .**184** E3
Golby Ct BN10 . . . .**178** A7
Gold La BN10 . . . .**167** C2
Goldbridge Rd BN8,TN22 .**76** F7
Goldcrest Dr TN22 . . . .**78** D5
Golden Cross Inn Cvn Pk The
BN8 . . . .**127** C3
Golden Gate Way BN23 .**175** B1
Golden Hill RH15 . . . .**73** D3

Golden Jubilee Way
BN23,BN24 ....173 F4
Golden La 11 BN1 ......163 D5
Golden Miller La BN26 .172 F6
Goldhurst Gn TN36 .....116 E5
Golding Rd BN23 ....174 F2
Goldsmid Mews 10 BN3 163 D6
Goldsmid Rd BN3 ....163 E7
Goldsmith Ct BN3 ......174 E3
Goldsmiths Ave TN6 .....25 D3
Goldstone Cl BN3 ......142 A2
Goldstone Cres BN3 ....142 B2
Goldstone Ct BN3 ......142 A3
Goldstone Ho 4 BN3 ...163 B7
Goldstone La BN3 ......163 B8
Goldstone Prim Sch
  BN3 ....141 E1
Goldstone Rd BN3 ......163 B7
Goldstone Ret Pk BN3 .163 B8
Goldstone St BN3 ......163 B7
Goldstone Villas BN3 ..163 B7
Goldstone Way BN3 ....142 A2
Golf Dr BN1 ....143 B3
Goodensfield TN5 ....29 E5
Goods Station La TN1 ....8 B4
Goodtrees La TN8 ....4 B2
Goodwin Cl BN27 ......129 A2
Goodwins Cl RH19 ....1 D3
Goodwins The TN2 ......7 F1
Goodwood Cl
  Bexhill TN40 ....157 D6
  Eastbourne BN20 ....173 B2
Goodwood Ct 2 BN3 ...163 D7
Goodwood Way BN2 ...143 F3
Gooseberry La TN31 .....67 A3
Gordon Ave BN43 ......161 A7
Gordon Cl RH16 ....50 E6
Gordon Ho RH15 ....73 C4
Gordon Pl TN39 ....157 B6
Gordon Rd Brighton BN1 .142 E4
  Burgess Hill RH15 ......73 C4
  Buxted TN22 ....56 C3
  Crowborough TN6 ....25 F2
  Hailsham BN27 ....152 B7
  Hastings TN34 ....160 A4
  Haywards Heath RH16 ...50 E6
  Portslade-by-S BN41 ..162 C7
  Portslade-by-S,Fishersgate
  BN41 ....162 A7
  Royal Tunbridge Wells TN4 .8 C7
  Shoreham-by-S BN43 ...161 A7
Gore Park Ave BN21 ...184 D4
Gore Park Rd BN21 ....184 D4
Gorham Ave BN2 ......177 A6
Gorham Cl BN2 ....177 A6
Gorham Ct BN10 ......177 E4
Gorham Way BN10 ....177 C4
Goring Ct BN1 ....143 F5
Gorringe Cl
  Eastbourne BN20 ......173 A3
  Shoreham-by-S BN43 ..161 D7
Gorringe Dr BN20 .....173 A3
Gorringe Rd BN22 ....185 A4
Gorringe Valley Rd
  BN20 ....173 A3
Gorse Cl
  Eastbourne BN20 ......184 B5
  Portslade-by-S BN41 ..140 F4
Gorse Dr BN25 ....180 F6
Gorse Hill TN21 ....59 F1
Gorse Rd TN2 ....8 E5
Gorselands TN33 ....88 E1
Gorses TN39 ....156 C2
Gorsethorn Way TN35 .138 E4
Gorseway The TN39 ...156 C5
Gosford Way BN26 ....172 F6
Gote La BN8 ....124 D4
Goudhurst Cl BN23 ....174 D1
Gower Rd RH16 ....50 E3
Gows Croft BN7 ......145 E5
Grace Ct BN6 ....97 E5
Gradwell End BN8 .....100 D7
Graffham Cl BN2 .....164 E6
Grafton St BN2 ....189 C1
Graham Ave
  Brighton BN1 ....142 F5
  Portslade-by-S BN41 ..140 F4
Graham Cl BN41 ......140 F4
Graham Cres BN41 ...140 F4
Grammer Ct BN8 ....75 D7
Grampian Cl
  Eastbourne BN23 .....174 C3
  Royal Tunbridge Wells TN2 .8 D5
Granary Cotts TN33 ..112 E4
Granary Rural Bsns Ctr The
  BN27 ....128 F6
Grand Ave Bexhill TN40 158 A5
  Hassocks BN6 ....97 F4
  Hove BN3 ....163 C6
  Seaford BN25 ....180 D6
Grand Avenue Mans 4
  BN3 ....163 C6
Grand Cres BN2 ......177 A5
Grand Ct
  3 Eastbourne BN21 ..185 A1
  10 St Leonards TN37 .159 C6
Grand Hotel Bldgs 8
  BN21 ....185 A1
Grand Junction Rd BN1 189 B1
Grand Mans 10 BN20 ..185 A1
Grand Par Brighton BN2 189 B2
  Eastbourne BN21 .....185 B2
  Polegate BN26 ....172 F6
  St Leonards TN38 ....159 C6
Grand Parade Mews
  BN2 ....189 B2
Grange Ave TN34 .....136 D4
Grange Cl Brighton BN1 142 E1

Grange Cl continued
  Burgess Hill RH15 ......73 C5
  Crowborough TN6 ......25 C1
  Horam TN21 ....106 F6
Grange Court Dr TN39 .157 B6
Grange Ct
  Eastbourne BN21 .....184 F2
  Hove BN3 ....162 F8
  Lewes BN7 ....190 A1
  9 Southwick BN42 ...161 E7
Grange End BN20 .....184 F1
Grange Gdns
  Eastbourne BN20 .....184 F2
  Rusthall TN4 ....7 A4
Grange Ind Est The
  BN42 ....161 D7
Grange Mus & Art Gallery★
  BN2 ....165 F2
Grange Rd
  Barcombe Cross BN8 ..101 D4
  Eastbourne BN21 .....184 F1
  Hastings TN34 ....136 A5
  Hove BN3 ....162 E8
  Lewes BN7 ....190 A1
  Rusthall TN4 ....7 A4
  Southwick BN42 ......161 E7
  Uckfield TN22 ....78 C7
Grange The
  Barcombe Cross BN8 ..101 D4
  21 Eastbourne BN21 ..185 A2
  Saltdean BN2 ....177 D4
Grangeways BN1 ......142 E5
Grant St BN2 ....189 C1
Grantham Bank BN8 ..101 E4
Grantham Cl BN8 .....100 E7
Grantham Rd BN1 ....143 A1
Grants Hill Ho TN22 ...78 C7
Granville Ct
  2 Eastbourne BN20 ..184 F1
  10 Hove BN3 ....163 B7
  11 Seaford BN25 .....180 E2
Granville Rd
  Eastbourne BN20 .....184 F1
  Hove BN3 ....163 E7
  Royal Tunbridge Wells TN1 .8 C5
Graperies The 3 BN2 ..164 C5
Grasmere BN20 ....184 F1
Grassington Rd BN20 .184 F1
Grasmere Ave BN10 ..177 F4
Grasmere Ct BN10 ...178 A8
Gratton St TN39 .....157 A3
Gravelye Cl RH16 .....51 B5
Gravelye La
  Haywards Heath RH16 .51 B6
  Haywards
  Heath,Franklands Village
  RH16 ....51 A4
Gravett Ct RH15 ....72 F2
Graycoats Dr TN6 .....25 F2
Grays Cotts TN33 ....112 F3
Grays Inf Sch BN9 ...179 D6
Graystone La TN35 ...160 D7
Graywood La BN8 ....105 D6
Graywood Rd BN8 ...105 C6
Grazebrook Cl TN39 ..156 C3
Great Brooms Rd TN4 ..8 C8
Great Cliffe Rd BN23 ..174 E1
Great College St BN2 .164 C4
Great Courtlands TN3 ..7 A3
Great Dixter House & Gdns★
  TN31 ....66 F7
Great Dixter Nurseries★
  TN31 ....66 F7
Great Footway TN3 .....6 F3
Great Hall Arc 3 TN1 ...8 B3
Great Heathmead RH16 .50 D6
Great House Ct 4 RH19 .10 F8
Great Oak TN19 ....45 A3
Great Rough BN8 .....76 A6
Great Sanders Ho TN33 .88 C4
Great Walstead Sch
  RH16 ....51 F1
Great Wilkins BN1 ...144 B5
Great Wood Woodland
  Walks★ TN33 ....113 B5
Greater Paddock BN8 .124 E6
Greatham Ct BN1 .....8 B2
Grecian Rd TN1 ....8 B2
Greeba Ct 8 TN38 ...159 B6
Green Cl Ringmer BN8 .124 E6
  4 Southwick BN42 ...161 E7
Green Ct 3 BN42 ....161 E7
Green Field Cl BN42 ..161 E7
Green Gate BN10 ....167 C1
Green Gr BN27 ....152 B8
Green Hedges TN32 ...63 E4
Green Hedges Ave RH19 .1 D2
Green Hedges Pl RH19 ..1 D2
Green La Bexhill TN39 156 D5
  Broyle Side BN8 ....103 B1
  Crowborough TN6 ......26 B2
  Heathfield TN21 ....82 B6
  Jevington BN26 ......172 C1
  Lewes BN7 ....190 A1
  Seaford BN25 ....180 E2
  South Chailey BN8 ....100 E7
  South Street BN8 ......75 E1
  Wivelsfield RH17 ......74 B3
  Woodingdean BN2 ....165 E6
Green Mdws RH16 ....51 B8
Green Park Cnr RH17 ..74 B4
Green Rd RH17 ....74 B4
Green Ridge BN1 ....142 B5
Green Sq TN5 ....29 F5
Green St BN21 ....184 C4
Green The Blackboys TN22 .80 A6
  Bodiam TN32 ....65 E7
  Catsfield TN33 ......133 E8

Green The continued
  East Dean BN20 ......187 B8
  Ewhurst Green TN32 ...66 B5
  Frant TN3 ....17 B3
  Hailsham BN27 ....129 C2
  Horsted Keynes RH17 ..33 C5
  Hove BN3 ....142 C2
  Langton Green TN3 .....6 E3
  Newick BN8 ....76 D7
  Ninfield TN33 ....133 B5
  Ringmer BN8 ....124 D5
  Rottingdean BN2 ......165 F2
  Sedlescombe TN33 ...113 E8
  Southwick BN42 ......161 E7
  St Leonards TN38 .....159 B8
Green View RH15 ....72 E3
Green Wall BN7 ......190 B2
Green Way TN2 ....8 E8
Green Wlk
  Hailsham BN27 ....129 C1
  Seaford BN25 ....181 B2
Green Wlk The BN22 ..173 B3
Greenacres Brighton BN1 142 F1
  Peacehaven BN10 ....167 C2
  Peacehaven BN10 ....178 A4
  Westfield TN35 ......114 E3
Greenacres Dr
  Hailsham BN27 ....152 C7
  Ringmer BN8 ....124 D4
Greenacres Way BN2 ..152 C8
Greenbank Ave BN2 ..177 D6
Greene TN7 ....146 B4
Greenfield Cl
  Brighton BN1 ....143 A5
  Rusthall TN4 ....7 C5
Greenfield Cres BN1 ..142 F5
Greenfield Dr TN22 ...78 D4
Greenfield Rd
  Burwash TN19 ....62 C7
  Eastbourne BN21 ....184 D4
Greenfields BN27 ....129 A1
Greenfields Cl TN37 ..136 B6
Greenfields Sch RH18 ..11 C1
Greenhill Pk RH17 ....51 A4
Greenhill Way
  Haywards Heath RH17 ..51 A2
  Peacehaven BN10 ....167 C2
Greenlands Cl RH15 ...98 B8
Greenlands Dr RH15 ..98 B8
Greenleaf Gdns BN26 .173 A8
Greenleas Hove BN3 ..141 D2
  Pembury TN2 ....9 C6
Greenstede Ave RH19 ..1 E2
Greenway BN20 ......184 B6
Greenway Ct BN2 ....177 A5
Greenways Bexhill TN39 156 F7
  Haywards Heath RH16 ..50 F6
  Ovingdean BN2 ......165 D3
  Portslade-by-S BN41 ..141 B1
  Southwick BN42 ......140 F1
Greenways Cnr BN2 ..165 D4
Greenways Cres BN43 .140 A1
Greenwell Cl BN25 ...181 B4
Greenwich Rd BN27 ..152 C7
Greenwich Way RH16 ..50 D4
Greenwoods La TN21 ..83 D7
Greggs Wood Rd TN2 ..8 E7
Gregory Ct 2 RH19 .....1 E1
Gregory La BN24 ....174 F5
Gregory Wlk TN33 ...113 E8
Grenada 4 TN39 .....157 A2
Grenada Cl Bexhill TN39 156 D4
  Eastbourne BN23 ....185 G7
Grenham Ct TN35 ....160 C7
Grenville Ho RH16 ....167 D1
Grenville Rd BN24 ...175 C4
Grenville St BN1 .....189 A2
Gresham BN24 ....175 B6
Gresham Cl BN21 ....184 C6
Gresham Way TN38 ..159 A8
Gresley Rd TN38 ....135 F5
Greville Rd TN35 ....160 C7
Grey Alders RH16 .....51 B6
Grey Tower Bglws
  BN24 ....175 C3
Grey Twr Cvn Site BN24 175 C3
Greyfriars BN3 ......163 D8
Greyfriars Pl TN36 ..118 B6
Greyhorses TN39 ....156 B4
Greys Rd BN20 ......184 D3
Greystones Ct TN6 ...25 D4
Grinley Ct 6 TN40 ...157 C4
Grinstead La RH19 ...21 C7
Grinstead Mount 4
  BN2 ....164 F5
Gromenfield TN3 .....15 C7
Groombridge Hill TN3 ..6 D1
Groombridge Pl★ TN3 .15 C8
Groombridge Place Gdns★
  TN3 ....6 A1
Groombridge Rd TN3 ..6 A1
Groombridge St Thomas' CE
  Prim Sch TN3 ....15 C7
Groombridge Sta TN3 .15 C7
Grosvenor Bridge TN1 ..8 B4
Grosvenor Cl BN26 ..172 F5
Grosvenor Cres TN38 .159 A6
Grosvenor Ct
  Brighton BN1 ....142 E3
  Seaford BN25 ....180 D3
Grosvenor Gdns TN38 158 F6
Grosvenor Mans 1 BN3 163 B6
Grosvenor Pk TN1 .....8 A4
Grosvenor Rd
  East Grinstead RH19 ...1 E3
  Royal Tunbridge Wells TN1 .8 A4
  Seaford BN25 ....180 E4

Grosvenor St BN2 ...189 C2
Grosvenor Wlk TN1 ....8 A4
Grove Ave TN1 ....8 A2
Grove Bank 9 BN2 ...189 C3
Grove Ct 12 BN3 .....163 C6
Grove Hill Brighton BN2 189 C3
  Grove Hill BN27 ......129 C2
Grove Hill Gdns TN1 ...8 B2
Grove Hill Rd TN1 .....8 B3
Grove La TN31 ....70 C4
Grove Park Sch TN6 ...25 E1
Grove Rd
  Burgess Hill RH15 .....73 B3
  Eastbourne BN21 ....184 F2
  Hastings TN35 ....160 D8
  Seaford BN25 ....180 F3
Grove Sch The TN38 .135 F1
Grove St BN2 ....189 C3
Grove The Battle TN33 .112 F3
  Bexhill TN39 ....156 F5
  Crowborough TN6 .....25 E1
  Eastbourne BN20 ....184 B7
  Eastbourne,Wannock
  BN20 ....172 A5
  Hailsham BN27 ....152 B6
  Haywards Heath RH16 .51 B3
  Mayfield TN20 ....40 A2
  Newhaven BN9 ......168 E2
  Pembury TN2 ....9 D8
  Rye TN31 ....93 C6
Grove Villa 3 BN1 ...189 A4
Grovebury BN27 .....152 C7
Grovelands Cl RH15 ...72 F1
Grovelands Com Sch
  BN27 ....129 A1
Grovelands Rd BN27 .129 A1
Grovely La TN31 ......84 B1
Grover St 3 TN1 ....8 B4
Growers End BN8 .....76 D7
Guardian Ct BN26 ...172 F7
Guardswell Pl BN25 ..180 F3
Guestling Bradshaw CE Prim
  Sch TN35 ....138 A8
Guestling Rd BN22 ..185 D5
Guildford Rd
  Brighton BN1 ....189 A3
  7 Royal Tunbridge Wells
  TN1 ....8 B3
Guildford St BN1 .....189 A3
Guinness Ct BN9 ....168 E1
Guinness Trust Bglws
  BN9 ....168 E2
Gulderford La TN29,TN31 .71 D3
Guldeford Lane Cnr
  TN31 ....71 D2
Guldeford Rd TN31 ....93 E7
Gun Hill Gun Hill TN21 106 D3
  Lower Dicker BN27,TN21 128 B8
Gun Rd TN22 ....80 A6
Gundreda Rd BN7 ....123 B2
Gunter's La TN39 ...157 A6
Gurth Rd TN35 ......160 C5
Gwent Ct 7 BN2 .....185 C4
Gwydyr Mans 3 BN3 .163 C6
Gwyneth Gr TN40 ...157 F7
Gwynne Gdns RH19 ....1 C2

H

Hackenden Cl RH19 ....1 E3
Hackenden Cotts RH19 ..1 E3
Hackenden La RH19 ....1 E3
Hackhurst La BN27 ..128 B4
Hackhurst Lane Ind Est
  BN27 ....128 B4
Hackwood TN32 ....63 E4
Haddington Cl BN3 ..163 B6
Haddington St 11 BN3 .163 B7
Hadley Ct Polegate BN26 173 A6
  Royal Tunbridge Wells TN4 .7 F6
Hadley Ho 7 BN21 ..184 F3
Hadlow Ave BN23 ...174 B4
Hadlow Cl BN2 ......164 D6
Hadlow Down Rd TN6 ..38 B4
Hadrian Ave BN42 ...162 A4
Hadrian Gdns TN37 .136 A6
Haig Ave BN1 ....143 D6
Hailsham Ave BN2 ..177 D7
Hailsham Com Coll
  BN27 ....152 B8
Hailsham Ct 2 TN40 ..157 C4
Hailsham Rd
  Heathfield TN21 ......82 A6
  Herstmonceux BN27 ..130 E5
  Polegate BN26 ....172 F7
  Stone Cross BN24,BN26 173 F8
Hairpin Croft BN10 ..167 C1
Hale Gn BN8 ....106 A2
Half Mile Dro BN8 ...125 B7
Halfway Sta★ BN2 ...164 C4
Hall La TN27 ....57 C5
Hall's Hole Rd TN2 ....8 E4
Halland Cl BN22 .....173 D1
Halland Rd BN2 .....143 F4
Hallands The RH15 ....73 C4
Hallett Rd BN2 ......164 D7
Halley Pk BN27 ......152 C7
Halley Rd
  Cade Street TN21 .....82 E8
  Wartling BN27 ....131 B1
Halls Cotts TN5 ....29 F5
Hallyburton Rd BN3 ..162 D6
Halsford Cl RH19 ......1 B3
Halsford Gn RH19 .....1 B3
Halsford La RH19 ......1 C3
Halsford Park Prim Sch
  RH19 ....1 C2

Gol – Har 203

Halsford Park Rd RH19 ..1 C2
Halton Cres TN34 ....160 B6
Halton Hts TN34 ....160 B6
Halton Pl TN34 .....160 B6
Halton Rd BN22 ....185 C4
Halton Shaws BN6 ....97 B5
Halton Terr TN34 ....160 B6
Ham Bsns Ctr BN43 .161 A7
Ham La Burwash TN19 ..62 B6
  Lewes BN7 ....190 B1
  Ringmer BN8 ....124 C6
  Scaynes Hill RH17 ....51 E3
Ham Rd BN43 ....161 A7
Hamble Rd BN24 ....173 F5
Hambleton Cl BN23 ..174 D3
Hambrook RH15 ....73 C1
Hamelsham Ct TN33 .152 A8
Hamilton Cl BN41 ...141 A3
Hamilton Ct
  Brighton BN2 ....165 A3
  Royal Tunbridge Wells TN4 ..8 A5
  Seaford BN25 ....180 D7
Hamilton Gdns TN35 .160 D7
Hamilton Ho
  13 Eastbourne BN21 .184 E4
  Royal Tunbridge Wells TN4 ..8 A5
Hamilton Lodge Sch
  BN2 ....164 D5
Hamilton Mans 8 BN3 163 B5
Hamilton Rd BN1 ....189 A4
Hamilton Terr TN39 ..157 A4
Hamlands La BN22 ...173 B3
Hamlin's Cnr BN6 ....72 A6
Hammer La BN27,TN21 107 F5
Hammerwood Pk★ RH19 ..3 C2
Hammerwood Rd RH19 .11 E6
Hammonds Dr BN23 ..185 C7
Hammonds Gdns RH15 72 F1
Hammonds Ridge RH15 72 F1
Hammy Cl BN43 .....161 C8
Hammy La BN43 ....161 B8
Hammy Way BN43 ..161 B8
Hampden Ave BN22 .173 F1
Hampden Cl TN33 ...112 B4
Hampden Gdns BN9 .168 D2
Hampden Park Dr BN22 184 E8
Hampden Park Inf Sch
  BN22 ....173 E2
Hampden Park Sta
  BN22 ....173 F1
Hampden Rd BN2 ...164 C4
Hampden Terr 8 BN22 185 C4
Hampshire Ct
  Brighton BN2 ....189 C1
  6 Eastbourne BN23 .174 E1
Hampstead Rd BN1 ..142 D1
Hampton Pl BN1 ....163 E5
Hampton St 24 BN1 ..163 E6
Hampton Terr 7 BN1 .163 E6
Hampton Way RH19 ..10 F7
Hamsey Cl Brighton BN2 164 C5
  Eastbourne BN20 ....184 B6
Hamsey Com Prim Sch
  BN8 ....123 A8
Hamsey Cres BN7 ...123 A2
Hamsey La
  Cooksbridge BN8 .....123 B7
  Seaford BN25 ....181 C2
Hamsey Rd Saltdean BN2 177 D4
  Saltdean BN2 ....177 D5
  Sharpthorne RH19 ....21 A6
Hamshaw St BN22 ..184 F8
Hamsland RH17 ......33 C4
Hanbury La RH16 .....51 A5
Hangdown Mead Bsns Pk
  RH19 ....21 B5
Hanging Birch La TN21 .81 D1
Hangleton Cl BN3 ...141 D2
Hangleton Gdns BN3 .141 D1
Hangleton Jun & Inf Sch
  BN3 ....141 E2
Hangleton La BN41 ..141 B2
Hangleton Manor Cl
  BN3 ....141 D2
Hangleton Rd BN3 ..141 E2
Hangleton Valley Dr
  BN3 ....141 D4
Hangleton Way BN3 .141 D4
Hankham Hall Rd BN24 174 D7
Hankham Prim Sch
  BN24 ....174 B8
Hankham Rd BN24 ..174 B6
Hankham St BN24 ..174 B8
Hanlye La RH17 ......50 B8
Hannington Pl BN6 ...97 A7
Hanover Cl Bexhill TN40 157 C5
  Seaford BN25 ....180 B6
Hanover Cres BN2 ..189 C4
Hanover Ct Brighton BN2 189 C4
  Eastbourne BN21 ....184 D5
  Haywards Heath RH16 .50 D4
Hanover Lofts BN2 ..189 C3
Hanover Mews BN2 .189 C4
Hanover Rd
  Eastbourne BN22 ....185 C4
  Royal Tunbridge Wells TN1 ..8 A4
Hanover St BN2 .....189 C4
Hanover Terr BN2 ...189 C4
Hanson Rd BN9 ......179 C6
Harbour Barn TN36 ..118 B6
Harbour Ct BN43 ....161 B6
Harbour Ho BN43 ...161 B6
Harbour Quay BN23 .175 A1
Harbour Rd TN31 .....93 D4
Harbour View Cl BN25 180 B6

Harbour View Rd BN9 . . 179 B5
Harbour Way
Shoreham-by-S BN43 . . . . 161 B6
St Leonards TN38 . . . . . . 135 E7
Harbour's Yd TN33 . . . . . 112 E4
Harcourt Cl TN22 . . . . . . 78 C6
Harcourt Rd TN22 . . . . . . 78 D6
Harding Ave BN22 . . . . . 185 B6
Hardrada Rise TN34 . . . . 136 E3
Hardwick Rd
Eastbourne BN21 . . . . . . 185 A2
Hove BN3 . . . . 141 E3
Hardwick Way BN3 . . . . 141 E3
Hardwicke Rd TN34 . . . . 160 B6
Hardy Dr BN23 . . . . 185 F6
Hare Way TN37 . . . . 136 C5
Harebeating Cl BN27 . . . 129 C2
Harebeating Cres BN27 129 C2
Harebeating Dr BN27 . . 129 C2
Harebeating Gdns BN27 129 C2
Harebeating La BN27 . . 129 D1
Harebell Cl BN23 . . . . . . 174 C3
Harebell Dr BN41 . . . . . 141 A3
Harecombe Rd TN6 . . . . . 37 F8
Harecombe Rise TN6 . . . . 37 F8
Haremere Hall Gdns*
TN19 . . . . 44 E2
Haremere Hill TN19 . . . . . 44 D2
Harescroft TN2 . . . . 16 F7
Harewood Cl TN39 . . . . 157 A3
Harewood Ct 8 BN3 . . . 163 C6
Harfield Cl BN9 . . . . 168 F2
Hargate Cl TN2 . . . . 16 F8
Hargreaves Rd BN23 . . . 174 A1
Harison Rd BN25 . . . . . . 181 A4
Harkness Dr TN34 . . . . . 137 B5
Harlands Cl RH16 . . . . . . 50 C6
Harlands Ho RH16 . . . . . . 50 D6
Harlands Mews TN22 . . . . 78 D5
Harlands Prim Sch
Haywards Heath RH16 . . . . 50 D7
Uckfield TN22 . . . . 78 D5
Harlands Rd RH16 . . . . . . 50 D6
Harlequin Gdns TN37 . . . 136 A6
Harlequin La TN6 . . . . 37 E8
Harlequin Pl TN6 . . . . 37 E8
Harley La TN21 . . . . 82 A6
Harley Shute Rd TN38 . . 158 E7
Harley Way TN38 . . . . . . 158 E6
Harmans Dr RH19 . . . . 2 B1
Harmans Mead RH19 . . . . . 2 B1
Harmers Hay Rd BN27 . . 129 B1
Harmers Hill BN8 . . . . 76 C7
Harmony St TN4 . . . . 7 D4
Harmony Wood TN34 . . . 136 F5
Harmsworth Cres BN3 . . 141 E3
Harold Cl BN24 . . . . 175 F7
Harold Dr BN23 . . . . 185 F8
Harold Ho 2 TN2 . . . . 8 C7
Harold Mews 2 TN38 . . . 159 C6
Harold Pl TN34 . . . . 159 F7
Harold Rd TN35 . . . . 160 C5
Harold Terr TN33 . . . . . . 112 F3
Harpers Rd BN9 . . . . 179 C7
Harrier La TN33 . . . . 112 F4
Harriers Ct BN27 . . . . . . 152 D7
Harries Rd TN2 . . . . 8 E7
Harrington Ct BN1 . . . . . 142 E2
Harrington Mans BN1 . . 142 E2
Harrington Pl BN1 . . . . . 143 B2
Harrington Rd BN1 . . . . 142 E2
Harrington Villas BN1 . . 142 F2
Harris Ct BN21 . . . . 185 A3
Harrisons La BN8 . . . . . . 124 E5
Harrow Cl BN25 . . . . 181 A4
Harrow La TN37 . . . . 136 B5
Hart Cl TN22 . . . . 78 A7
Hartfield Ave BN1 . . . . . 143 A5
Hartfield Ho TN22 . . . . . . 78 C6
Hartfield La BN21 . . . . . 184 F4
Hartfield Mdw TN38 . . . 135 D3
Hartfield Rd Bexhill TN39 156 E2
Cowden TN8 . . . . 4 C6
Eastbourne BN21 . . . . 184 F3
Forest Row RH18 . . . . 12 B2
Saltdean BN2 . . . . 177 D5
Seaford BN25 . . . . 181 A3
Harting Combe TN38 . . . 159 B8
Hartington Mans 7
BN21 . . . . 185 A2
Hartington Pl
Brighton BN2 . . . . 164 C8
Eastbourne BN21 . . . . 185 A2
Hartington Rd BN2 . . . . 164 C8
Hartington Terr BN2 . . . 164 C8
Hartington Villas BN3 . . 163 B8
Hartley Ct 10 BN1 . . . . . 189 A4
Hartwood Lodge 6
TN40 . . . . 157 C4
Harvard Cl BN7 . . . . 190 A4
Harvard Rd BN8 . . . . 124 D5
Harvest Cl Lindfield RH16 . 51 B7
Telscombe Cliffs BN10 . . . 167 B2
Harvest Hill RH19 . . . . 10 E8
Harvest Way TN37 . . . . . 136 C5
Harvesters RH16 . . . . 50 D2
Harvey Cl TN38 . . . . 135 F4
Harvey's La BN8,TN22 . . 103 D4
Harveys Way BN7 . . . . . . 190 C2
Harvington Bsns Pk
BN22 . . . . 184 F8
Harwood Cl BN23 . . . . . 185 E7
Harwoods Cl 3 RH19 . . . . 10 F7
Harwoods La RH19 . . . . . 10 F7
Haslam Cres TN40 . . . . . 157 F6
Hasletts Cl TN1 . . . . 8 B6
Hassocks Cl BN23 . . . . . . 173 F4
Hassocks Inf Sch BN6 . . . 97 F4
Hassocks Lodge BN6 . . . . 97 F3
Hassocks Rd BN6 . . . . 97 B5
Hassocks Sta BN6 . . . . 97 E4
Hastings Ave BN25 . . . . . 181 C5
Hastings Castle & 1066
Story* TN34 . . . . 160 A4
Hastings Cl BN26 . . . . . . 173 B7
Hastings Coll of Arts & Tech
TN38 . . . . 159 B6
Hastings Ct TN40 . . . . . . 157 E5
Hastings Ctry Pk*
TN35 . . . . 160 E5
Hastings Ctry Pk Visitor Ctr*
TN35 . . . . 138 C4
Hastings Mus & Art Gall*
TN34 . . . . 159 E7
Hastings Rd Battle TN33 . 113 B2
Bexhill TN40 . . . . 157 E5
Bexhill TN40 . . . . 157 F5
Brighton BN2 . . . . 164 C8
Newenden TN17,TN18 . . . . 48 C6
Pembury TN2 . . . . 9 D6
Pembury TN2 . . . . 9 F5
The Moor TN18 . . . . 45 F6
Hastings Sta TN34 . . . . . 159 E8
Hatch End RH18 . . . . 11 F2
Hatchgate Cl RH17 . . . . . 50 A6
Hatchgate La RH17 . . . . . 50 A6
Hatfield Ct 18 BN3 . . . . 163 C6
Hatherley Rd TN37 . . . . 159 C7
Havana Ct 12 BN23 . . . . 185 F8
Havelock Rd
Bexhill TN40 . . . . 157 C6
Brighton BN1 . . . . 142 F1
Eastbourne BN22 . . . . 185 B4
Hastings TN34 . . . . 159 F7
Haven Brow BN25 . . . . . . 181 A4
Haven CE/Methodist Prim
Sch The BN23 . . . . 185 F7
Haven Cl
Beachlands BN24 . . . . 175 E6
Eastbourne BN22 . . . . 173 B3
Haven Rd TN38 . . . . 158 D6
Haven The BN27 . . . . 152 C6
Haven Way BN9 . . . . 179 B6
Havering Cl TN2 . . . . 8 F6
Hawkenbury Cl TN2 . . . . . 8 D1
Hawkenbury Mead TN2 . . . 8 D1
Hawkenbury Rd TN2,TN3 . . 8 E1
Hawkenbury Way BN7 . . 123 A1
Hawkes Farm Prim Sch
BN27 . . . . 129 B3
Hawkhurst CE Prim Sch
TN18 . . . . 45 F8
Hawkhurst Cl BN23 . . . . 174 D2
Hawkhurst Pl BN1 . . . . . 143 D6
Hawkhurst Rd
Brighton BN1 . . . . 143 D6
Flimwell TN5,TN18 . . . . 32 E2
Hawkhurst Way TN39 . . . 156 E3
Hawkins Cl BN43 . . . . . . 140 D1
Hawkins Cres BN43 . . . . 140 D2
Hawkins Rd BN43 . . . . . 140 D1
Hawkins Way BN27 . . . . 152 B8
Hawks Farm Cl BN27 . . . 129 B2
Hawks Rd BN27 . . . . 129 B2
Hawks Town Cres BN27 . 129 C2
Hawksbridge Cl BN22 . . 173 C3
Hawkstown Cl BN27 . . . 129 B3
Hawkstown Gdns BN27 . 129 B3
Hawkstown View BN27 . 129 B3
Hawkswood Dr BN27 . . . 129 C3
Hawkswood Rd BN27 . . . 129 C3
Hawth Cl BN25 . . . . 180 C4
Hawth Cres BN25 . . . . . . 180 C4
Hawth Gr BN25 . . . . 180 C4
Hawth Hill BN25 . . . . 180 C5
Hawth Park Rd BN25 . . . 180 C4
Hawth Pl BN25 . . . . 180 C4
Hawth Rise BN25 . . . . . . 180 C5
Hawth Valley Ct 1
BN25 . . . . 180 C4
Hawth Way BN25 . . . . . . 180 D4
Hawthorn Ave TN39 . . . . 156 D3
Hawthorn Bank BN2 . . . . 143 F4
Hawthorn Cl
Burgess Hill RH15 . . . . 73 D5
Saltdean BN2 . . . . 177 C6
Hawthorn Ct BN26 . . . . . 173 B6
Hawthorn Pl RH16 . . . . . . 50 C2
Hawthorn Rd
Eastbourne BN23 . . . . 185 C7
Hastings TN35 . . . . 160 D6
Hawthorn Rise BN9 . . . . 179 B7
Hawthorn Way BN41 . . . 141 A3
Hawthorn Wlk TN2 . . . . . . 8 E8
Hawthorne Cl TN21 . . . . . 82 B6
Hawthornes The TN31 . . . 90 B4
Hawthorns The
Burgess Hill RH15 . . . . 73 A5
Hailsham BN27 . . . . 152 A7
The Moor TN18 . . . . 45 F8
Hawthylands Cres BN27 129 B2
Hawthylands Dr BN27 . . 129 B2
Hawthylands Rd BN27 . . 129 B2
Haybourne Cl BN2 . . . . . 164 E7
Haybourne Rd BN2 . . . . . 164 E7
Hayes Cl
Portslade-by-S BN41 . . . . 162 C8
Ringmer BN8 . . . . 124 D5
Hayes La TN31 . . . . 91 C5
Hayes Plat TN31 . . . . 67 C5
Hayland Gn BN27 . . . . . . 129 C1
Hayland Ind Units TN38 135 F5
Haylind Rd RH16 . . . . 51 B5
Hayreed La BN26 . . . . . . 151 A1
Haystoun Cl BN22 . . . . . . 173 C2
Haystoun Ho BN22 . . . . . 173 C2
Haystoun Pk BN22 . . . . . 173 C2
Hayward Rd BN7 . . . . 123 A3
Haywards Heath Coll
RH16 . . . . 50 D6
Haywards Heath Sta
RH16 . . . . 50 E6
Haywards Rd
Brighton BN1 . . . . 143 A6
Haywards Heath RH16 . . . . 50 E3
Haywards Villas RH16 . . . . 50 F3
Haywood Way TN35 . . . . 160 C8
Hazel Bank 3 BN2 . . . . . 189 C4
Hazel Cl Hove BN41 . . . . . 141 C3
Newhaven BN9 . . . . 179 B7
Hazel Court Sec Sch
BN23 . . . . 174 A3
Hazel Ct TN35 . . . . 136 F6
Hazel Gr Burgess Hill RH15 73 B1
Eastbourne BN20 . . . . 173 A3
Hazelbank TN3 . . . . 6 F3
Hazeldene BN25 . . . . 181 B3
Hazeldene Meads BN1 . . 142 D3
Hazeledene La BN8 . . . . . 75 F7
Hazelgrove Gdns 8
RH16 . . . . 50 E4
Hazelgrove Rd RH16 . . . . 50 E4
Hazelholt BN41 . . . . 140 F3
Hazelwood BN1 . . . . 142 D3
Hazelwood Ave BN22 . . . 173 D4
Hazelwood Cl
Bexhill TN39 . . . . 156 C3
Royal Tunbridge Wells TN2 . . 8 D8
Hazelwood Cotts TN5 . . . . 31 D1
Hazelwood Gdns TN37 . . 136 D5
Hazleden Cross RH19 . . . . 10 B6
Headland Ave BN25 . . . . 181 A3
Headland Cl BN10 . . . . . 178 E7
Headway Ct TN4 . . . . 7 B4
Heansill La TN18 . . . . 45 E8
Heasewood RH16 . . . . 50 C3
Heath Cl 9 RH16 . . . . 50 E4
Heath Ct RH16 . . . . 50 E5
Heath Hill Ave BN2 . . . . 144 A2
Heath Rd RH16 . . . . 50 E5
Heath Sq RH16 . . . . 50 D5
Heath Stables BN7 . . . . . 123 A1
Heathcote Dr RH19 . . . . . . 1 C2
Heathdown Cl BN10 . . . . 167 D2
Heather Bank RH16 . . . . . 50 C5
Heather Cl BN23 . . . . 174 B3
Heather Ct 8 BN1 . . . . . 163 E6
Heather Way TN35 . . . . . 138 F4
Heather Wlk TN6 . . . . 26 D1
Heatherdune Rd TN39 . . 157 A5
Heathfield Ave BN2 . . . . 177 D6
Heathfield Cl TN34 . . . . . 136 F5
Heathfield Com Coll
TN21 . . . . 82 E7
Heathfield Cres BN41 . . 140 F3
Heathfield Dr BN41 . . . . 140 F4
Heathfield Gdns TN32 . . . 64 B3
Heathfield L Ctr TN21 . . . 82 D7
Heathfield Rd BN25 . . . . 180 F3
Heathfields TN2 . . . . 8 D4
Heathlands TN35 . . . . . . 114 E3
Heathy Brow BN10 . . . . . 167 B1
Heavegate Rd TN6 . . . . . . 37 C8
Heaven Farm* RH17 . . . . 34 B1
Hebrides Wlk BN23 . . . . 185 E7
Hectors La RH19 . . . . 11 C7
Hedge Barton Trailer Pk
TN3 . . . . 5 F5
Heighton Cl TN39 . . . . . . 156 D3
Heighton Cres BN9 . . . . 168 D2
Heighton Rd BN9 . . . . . . 168 E2
Heights The
Brighton BN1 . . . . 142 B5
Hastings TN35 . . . . 160 E8
6 Haywards Heath RH16 . . 50 E4
Helena Cl BN41 . . . . 141 C2
Helena Ct TN38 . . . . 159 B7
Helena Rd BN2 . . . . 144 C1
Helensdene Wlk TN37 . . 159 D8
Helenswood Sch
Hastings TN34 . . . . 160 B8
St Leonards TN37 . . . . . . 136 D6
Hellingly Cl BN2 . . . . . . 164 F5
Hellingly Com Prim Sch
BN27 . . . . 128 F5
Helvellyn Dr BN23 . . . . . 174 C4
Hempstead Gdns TN22 . . 78 D7
Hempstead La
Hailsham BN27 . . . . 128 F1
Uckfield TN22 . . . . 78 D7
Uckfield TN22 . . . . 78 E8
Uckfield TN22 . . . . 78 E8
Hempstead Rd
Saltdean BN2 . . . . 177 D7
Uckfield TN22 . . . . 78 C7
Hempstead Rise TN22 . . . 78 C7
Hemsley Ho TN21 . . . . 81 F8
Henderson Cl TN34 . . . . 136 F3
Hendon St BN2 . . . . 164 D5
Henfield Cl BN2 . . . . 164 F5
Henfield Rd BN22 . . . . . . 173 E2
Henfield Way BN3 . . . . . 141 F3
Henge Way BN41 . . . . . . 141 B2
Hengist Cl BN23 . . . . 185 F8
Henleaze BN21 . . . . 184 E3
Henley Cl
Royal Tunbridge Wells TN2 . . 8 C4
Rye TN31 . . . . 93 A6
Henley Ct BN2 . . . . 164 F4
Henley Rd BN2 . . . . 164 F4
Henley's Hill BN27 . . . . . 131 F7
Henry Burt Way RH15 . . . 72 E1
Henry Terr 3 TN34 . . . . . 160 B4
Henwood Green Rd TN2 . . 9 E6
Henwoods Cres TN2 . . . . . 9 D6
Henwoods Mount TN2 . . . . 9 E6
Herbert Rd BN1 . . . . 142 F2
Herbrand Wlk TN39 . . . . 156 A1
Hereford Ct
15 Brighton BN2 . . . . 189 C2
1 Eastbourne BN23 . . . . . 174 E1
15 Hove BN3 . . . . 163 C7
Hereford St BN2 . . . . 164 C5
Hereward Rd BN23 . . . . . 185 F8
Hereward Way BN7 . . . . 190 B4
Hermitage La RH19 . . . . . 10 F8
Hermitage Rd RH19 . . . . . . 1 D3
Hermitage The TN34 . . . 159 E8
Herne Down TN6 . . . . 38 A7
Herne Jun Sch TN6 . . . . . 37 F8
Herne Rd TN6 . . . . 37 F8
Heron Cl
Eastbourne BN23 . . . . 174 C2
St Leonards TN38 . . . . . . 158 E8
Uckfield TN22 . . . . 78 D5
Heron Cotts TN18 . . . . . . 48 D3
Heron Ct BN27 . . . . 152 D7
Heron Pl RH19 . . . . 10 F8
Heron Ridge BN26 . . . . . 173 B6
Heron's Tye BN6 . . . . 97 F3
Herons Dale Sch BN43 . . 140 C1
Herons The BN43 . . . . . . 161 A8
Herons Way
Golden Cross BN27 . . . . . 127 C4
Pembury TN2 . . . . 9 E8
Heronsdale Rd BN2 . . . . . 165 F8
Herontye Dr RH19 . . . . 11 A8
Herontye Ho RH19 . . . . . . 10 F7
Herring's Rd TN21,TN33 . 109 F8
Herstmonceux Castle Gdns*
BN27 . . . . 131 A1
Herstmonceux CE Prim Sch
BN27 . . . . 130 E6
Hertford Cl TN38 . . . . . . 136 A4
Hertford Inf Sch BN1 . . . 143 B2
Hertford Jun Sch BN1 . . 143 C2
Hertford Rd BN1 . . . . 143 B2
Heskett Pk TN2 . . . . 9 E6
Hestingas Plat 2 TN34 . 160 B4
Heston Ave BN1 . . . . 142 F7
Hever Cl BN23 . . . . 174 D2
Hever Cres TN39 . . . . . . 156 F5
Heyworth Cl BN2 . . . . . . 165 F8
Heyworth Prim Sch RH16 50 F4
Heyworth Ride RH16 . . . . 50 C3
Hickling Cl BN23 . . . . . . 174 B4
Hickman Way TN34 . . . . . 136 D4
Hickman's Cl RH16 . . . . . 51 B8
Hickman's La RH16 . . . . . 51 A8
Hidden Spring Vineyard &
Orch* TN21 . . . . 107 B8
Hide Hollow BN23 . . . . . 174 D3
Higglers Cl TN22 . . . . 56 C3
High Bank TN35 . . . . 160 C7
High Bank Cl TN35 . . . . 160 C6
High Beach Ho BN25 . . . 180 C3
High Beech Cl TN37 . . . . 135 F6
High Beech Country Club
(Chalet Pk) The TN37 . 135 F6
High Beech La RH16 . . . . . 50 F8
High Beeches TN2 . . . . 8 D6
High Branches TN39 . . . 156 E4
High Broom La TN6 . . . . . 37 E7
High Broom Rd TN6 . . . . . 37 F7
High Brooms Ind Pk TN2 . 8 C8
High Brooms Rd TN4 . . . . . 8 C7
High Brooms Sta TN4 . . . . 8 C7
High Cl East Dean BN20 . 183 C2
Portslade-by-S BN41 . . . . 141 A1
High Cross Fields TN6 . . . 25 F3
High Fords TN36 . . . . . . 116 E5
High Fords Cl TN36 . . . . 116 E5
High Hatch La BN6 . . . . . 72 B4
High Hurst Cl BN8 . . . . . . 76 D7
High Hurstwood CE Prim Sch
TN22 . . . . 37 A1
High Mdw TN31 . . . . 67 B7
High Park Ave BN3 . . . . 141 E3
High Park Cl TN31 . . . . . . 67 A7
High Pk TN31 . . . . 67 A7
High Point RH16 . . . . 51 A3
High Rocks* TN3 . . . . 7 B1
High Rocks La TN3,TN4 . . . 7 C1
High Rocks Sta* TN3 . . . . 7 B1
High St Alfriston BN26 . . . 171 A2
Barcombe Cross BN8 . . . . 101 E4
Battle TN33 . . . . 112 D4
Bexhill TN40 . . . . 157 D5
Blackboys TN22 . . . . 80 A6
Brighton BN2 . . . . 189 C2
Burwash TN19 . . . . 62 A6
Buxted TN22 . . . . 56 C3
Cowden TN8 . . . . 4 B5
Crowborough TN6 . . . . 25 F3
Ditchling BN6 . . . . 98 D3
East Grinstead RH19 . . . . . 10 F8
East Hoathly BN8 . . . . . . 105 A5
Eastbourne BN21 . . . . 184 E3
Etchingham TN19 . . . . 44 C1
Flimwell TN5 . . . . 32 C3
Frant TN3 . . . . 17 C4
Hailsham BN27 . . . . 152 C8
Hartfield TN7 . . . . 13 D4
Hastings TN34 . . . . 160 B4
Heathfield TN21 . . . . 82 A8
Horam TN21 . . . . 106 F8
Hurstpierpoint BN6 . . . . . . 97 A5
Lamberhurst TN3 . . . . 20 B5
Lewes BN7 . . . . 190 A2
High St *continued*
Lindfield RH16 . . . . 51 B8
Maresfield TN22 . . . . 55 B4
Mayfield TN20 . . . . 40 B2
Newhaven BN9 . . . . 179 C7
Newick BN8 . . . . 76 D7
Ninfield TN33 . . . . 133 A6
Nutley TN22 . . . . 35 C3
Pembury TN2 . . . . 9 C6
Pevensey BN24 . . . . 175 B6
Polegate BN26 . . . . 173 A6
Portslade-by-S BN41 . . . . 141 A1
Robertsbridge TN32 . . . . . . 64 B4
Rotherfield TN6 . . . . 39 B8
Rottingdean BN2 . . . . 165 F1
Royal Tunbridge Wells TN1 . . 8 A2
Rye TN31 . . . . 93 C5
Seaford BN25 . . . . 180 E2
Ticehurst TN5 . . . . 31 C1
Uckfield TN22 . . . . 78 C6
Wadhurst TN5 . . . . 29 F4
Westham BN24 . . . . 175 A6
Winchelsea TN36 . . . . 117 F7
High St (School Hill)
TN22 . . . . 55 B4
High Trees
4 Eastbourne BN21 . . . . . 184 F4
Haywards Heath RH16 . . . . 50 F5
Uckfield TN22 . . . . 78 C5
High View
Eastbourne BN21 . . . . 184 E5
Heathfield TN21 . . . . 82 B8
High Wickham TN35 . . . 160 B5
High Woods La TN3 . . . . . . 9 B3
Higham Gdns TN35 . . . . 138 A8
Higham La TN31 . . . . 67 A7
Highbank BN1 . . . . 142 C5
Highbridge La BN7 . . . . . 100 B4
Highbrook Cl BN2 . . . . . . 143 D3
Highcliff Ct BN2 . . . . 177 A5
Highcombe BN20 . . . . . . 188 D7
Highcroft Cres TN21 . . . . 82 A7
Highcroft Lodge BN1 . . . 163 E8
Highcroft Mews BN1 . . . 142 D1
Highcroft Rd RH19 . . . . . . 21 A6
Highcroft Villas BN1 . . . . 163 E8
Highden 2 BN2 . . . . 164 C6
Highdown BN42 . . . . 140 F1
Highdown Cl BN42 . . . . . 140 F1
Highdown Cotts TN17 . . . 20 F3
Highdown Ct BN1 . . . . . . 142 E3
Highdown Rd
Hove BN1,BN3 . . . . 163 E7
Lewes BN7 . . . . 123 A2
Highfield Cl TN2 . . . . 9 D6
Highfield Cres BN1 . . . . 143 A5
Highfield Ct 7 RH16 . . . . 50 E4
Highfield Dr
Hurstpierpoint BN6 . . . . . . 97 C5
St Leonards TN38 . . . . . . 135 D3
Highfield Gdns TN39 . . . 157 C7
Highfield Ind Est N
BN23 . . . . 174 A1
Highfield Ind Est S
BN23 . . . . 174 A1
Highfield Jun Sch BN22 174 A1
Highfield Rd
East Grinstead RH19 . . . . . . 1 D3
Horam TN21 . . . . 106 F7
Royal Tunbridge Wells TN4 . . 8 C7
Highfields Brighton BN1 . 143 E5
Burwash TN19 . . . . 62 A6
Forest Row RH18 . . . . 11 F2
Horsted Keynes RH17 . . . . 33 C4
Rye TN31 . . . . 93 B7
Highgate Flats TN6 . . . . . 27 B1
Highgate Rd RH18 . . . . . . 11 F1
Highgate Works RH18 . . . 11 E1
Highgrove Battle TN33 . . 112 B4
Royal Tunbridge Wells TN2 . 17 A8
Highland Ct RH16 . . . . 50 E4
Highland Grange TN6 . . . . 25 E3
Highland Lodge BN21 . . . 184 F4
Highland Rd RH16 . . . . . . 50 F3
Highlands TN2 . . . . 8 D7
Highlands Ave TN22 . . . . . 78 D4
Highlands Cl
Bexhill TN39 . . . . 156 F7
Crowborough TN6 . . . . 25 E3
Keymer BN6 . . . . 98 A3
Highlands Ct TN6 . . . . 25 E3
Highlands Dr
Burgess Hill RH15 . . . . 73 A4
St Leonards TN38 . . . . . . 159 B7
Highlands Gdns TN38 . . 159 B7
Highlands Mews 2
TN38 . . . . 159 B6
Highlands Rd
Portslade-by-S BN41 . . . . 141 B1
Seaford BN25 . . . . 180 F3
Highlands The
Bexhill TN39 . . . . 156 F7
Cuckfield RH17 . . . . 50 A8
Highlea Cl TN37 . . . . 136 C5
Highleigh 8 BN2 . . . . . . 189 C3
Highsted Pk BN10 . . . . . 167 D2
Highview Ave N BN1 . . . 142 E6
Highview Ave S BN1 . . . 142 E6
Highview Cl
St Leonards TN37 . . . . . . 136 D5
Windmill Hill BN27 . . . . . 131 B5
Highview Ct BN20 . . . . . 184 F1
Highview La TN22 . . . . . . 78 D4
Highview Rd
Brighton BN1 . . . . 142 E6
Broad Oak TN21 . . . . 59 E1
Telscombe Cliffs BN10 . . . 177 F4
Highview Way BN1 . . . . . 142 E6

Highwater View TN37 ...135 F7
Highway Cl BN2 ...143 D2
Highway The
 Brighton BN2 ...143 D3
 Newhaven BN10,BN9 ...179 A6
Highways BN41 ...141 B2
Highwoods Ave TN39 ...156 C6
Highwoods Ct TN39 ...156 E5
Hiham Bglws TN36 ...117 E7
Hiham Gn TN36 ...117 E7
Hilary Cl BN26 ...172 F5
Hilary Lodge 2 BN2 ...164 C5
Hilbert Cl TN2 ...8 C5
Hilbert Rd TN2 ...8 C5
Hilders Farm Cl TN6 ...26 B1
Hilgrove Rd BN2 ...177 D7
Hill Brow BN3 ...142 B3
Hill Cl TN6 ...25 E1
Hill Crest
 Dormans Park RH19 ...1 E6
 Royal Tunbridge Wells TN4 ...8 B8
Hill Crest Ct BN9 ...179 C6
Hill Crest Rd BN9 ...179 D6
Hill Dr BN3 ...142 B3
Hill Farm Way BN42 ...140 E2
Hill Mead TN22 ...35 C4
Hill Rd Eastbourne BN20 ...184 B5
 Fairlight TN35 ...138 C4
 Lewes BN7 ...123 B2
 Newhaven BN9 ...168 F2
 Saltdean BN2 ...177 D5
Hill Rise Newhaven BN9 ...168 F2
 Seaford BN25 ...180 C5
Hill Side BN9 ...179 D7
Hill St Hastings TN34 ...160 A4
 Royal Tunbridge Wells TN1 ...8 B5
Hill Top BN1 ...142 B5
Hill Top Way BN9 ...179 B6
Hill View RH18 ...11 F1
Hill View Rd TN4 ...7 C4
Hillary Cl RH19 ...2 A3
Hillbank BN41 ...140 F3
Hillborough Cl TN39 ...156 D4
Hillbrow (Brighton Univ)
 BN20 ...184 E1
Hillbrow Rd BN1 ...142 D4
Hillbury Gdns TN5 ...31 D1
Hillcrest Brighton BN1 ...142 C5
 Horsted Keynes RH17 ...33 C5
 Rye TN31 ...93 B7
Hillcrest Ave TN39 ...157 A6
Hillcrest Cl RH17 ...51 F3
Hillcrest Ct BN1 ...142 C5
Hillcrest Dr TN2 ...8 D7
Hillcrest La RH17 ...51 F3
Hillcrest Sch TN35 ...137 E6
Hillcroft BN41 ...140 F2
Hillgarth TN4 ...8 A8
Hillman Cl BN7 ...190 C2
Hillrise TN6 ...26 B2
Hillside Brighton BN2 ...143 E2
 6 Crowborough TN6 ...37 F8
 Forest Row RH18 ...11 F4
 Friston BN20 ...183 B1
 Mayfield TN20 ...40 B2
 Portslade-by-S BN41 ...141 C1
 Southwick BN42 ...140 F1
Hillside Ave BN25 ...181 C5
Hillside Cl RH19 ...1 E3
Hillside Cotts TN5 ...30 B8
Hillside Dr TN21 ...106 F7
Hillside Rd Bexhill TN40 ...157 C5
 Hastings TN34 ...136 E5
 Hastings TN34 ...136 E5
Hillside Sch BN41 ...141 B2
Hillside Way
 Brighton BN2 ...143 E2
 Brighton,Westdene BN1 ...142 C4
Hillside Wlk RH16 ...50 C6
Hilltop Dr TN31 ...93 B7
Hillview Ho BN9 ...179 D6
Hillview Rd BN2 ...165 B8
Hillyfield BN7 ...146 B8
Hillyglen Ct TN34 ...159 E8
Hilton Ct 11 RH16 ...50 E4
Hindleap Warren Outdoor
 Education Ctr RH18 ...22 D5
Hindover Cres BN25 ...181 A4
Hindover Rd BN25 ...181 A4
Hinton Cl BN1 ...143 C2
Hippodrome BN1 ...189 A2
Hither Chantlers TN3 ...7 A2
Hoad Rd BN2 ...185 B4
Hoad's Wood Rd TN34 ...160 A7
Hoadleys La TN6 ...25 D5
Hoadswood Cross TN21 ...84 B2
Hoath Hill TN32 ...87 C5
Hoathdown Ave BN9 ...179 A7
Hobart Quay BN23 ...175 A2
Hobbs Cl TN31 ...68 C5
Hobbs La TN31 ...68 D6
Hoblands RH16 ...51 B4
Hobney Rise BN24 ...174 F5
Hockington La BN20 ...173 B1
Hodcombe Cl BN23 ...174 B4
Hoddern Ave BN10 ...178 B8
Hoddern Jun Sch BN10 ...178 B8
Hodshrove La BN2 ...143 E3
Hodshrove Pl BN2 ...143 E3
Hodshrove Rd BN2 ...143 E3
Hoe The TN37 ...136 B6
Hog Hole La TN5 ...30 E8
Hogarth Ho TN38 ...159 A8
Hogarth Rd
 Eastbourne BN23 ...174 D1
 Hove BN3 ...162 F7
Hogs Edge BN2 ...144 A2
Hogtrough La TN36 ...117 E7

Holbrook 16 BN2 ...164 F5
Holbrook Cl BN20 ...188 E8
Holden Park Rd TN4 ...8 A8
Holdings The
 Kingston near Lewes BN7 ...145 F5
 Upper Wellingham BN8 ...124 B7
Hole Farm Cl TN34 ...136 E2
Hollamby Pk BN27 ...152 D7
Holland Ave TN39 ...156 C4
Holland Mews BN3 ...163 D5
Holland Rd BN3 ...163 D6
Holland St BN2 ...189 C3
Hollands Way RH19 ...2 A4
Hollier's Hill TN40 ...157 C6
Hollies The TN20 ...40 A2
Hollin Cl TN4 ...7 F4
Hollingbourne Ct 8
 BN2 ...164 E4
Hollingbury Copse BN1 ...143 A4
Hollingbury Cres BN1 ...143 B2
Hollingbury Ind Est
 BN1 ...143 C7
Hollingbury Park Ave
 BN1 ...143 A2
Hollingbury Pl BN1 ...143 B2
Hollingbury Rd BN1 ...143 B1
Hollingbury Rise BN1 ...143 B2
Hollingbury Rise W
 BN1 ...143 A3
Hollingbury Terr BN1 ...143 A2
Hollingdean La BN1 ...164 B8
Hollingdean Rd BN2 ...164 B8
Hollingdean St BN1 ...143 B1
Hollingdean Terr BN1 ...143 B1
Hollinghurst Cl TN37 ...136 B5
Hollinghurst Rd TN37 ...136 B4
Hollington Cl TN38 ...159 A8
Hollington Old La TN38 ...136 A4
Hollington Park Cl
 TN38 ...136 A1
Hollington Park Rd
 TN38 ...136 A1
Hollington Prim Sch
 TN38 ...136 A4
Hollow La Blackboys TN22 ...80 B4
 Dormansland RH19,RH7 ...2 D6
 East Hoathly BN8 ...105 A4
Hollow The RH16 ...51 B5
Holly Bank 3 BN2 ...189 C5
Holly Bank Ct TN6 ...26 B2
Holly Cl Bexhill TN39 ...156 C6
 Brighton BN1 ...142 E3
 Hailsham BN27 ...152 B6
 Heathfield TN21 ...82 A6
Holly Ct TN6 ...25 E2
Holly Dr TN21 ...82 A6
Holly Pl BN22 ...173 E3
Holly Rd RH16 ...51 A3
Hollybank Gdns TN38 ...136 B1
Hollycroft BN7 ...100 A3
Hollydene Rd TN5 ...29 F6
Hollyshaw TN2 ...8 C2
Hollyshaw Cl TN2 ...8 C2
Hollywood Ct RH16 ...50 E5
Holm Ho RH15 ...72 F3
Holm Oak Cl TN39 ...156 E3
Holmbush Cl
 Haywards Heath RH16 ...50 E2
 Shoreham-by-S BN43 ...140 D2
Holmbush Ct 8 BN43 ...161 C8
Holmbush Ctr BN43 ...140 C1
Holmbush Fst Sch
 BN43 ...140 D1
Holmbush Way BN42 ...140 E1
Holmdale Rd BN9 ...169 A1
Holmebury Ho 11 TN34 ...159 E7
Holmes Ave BN3 ...141 F1
Holmes Cl BN25 ...180 A6
Holmes Farm Cotts
 TN39 ...156 A8
Holmes Hill TN6 ...127 C6
Holmesdale Cl TN5 ...29 C5
Holmesdale Cl TN34 ...159 E6
Holmesdale Gdns TN34 ...159 E7
Holmesdale Rd
 Bexhill TN39 ...157 A4
 Burgess Hill RH15 ...73 A1
Holmewood House Sch
 TN3 ...7 A2
Holmewood Rd TN4 ...8 C7
Holmewood Ridge TN3 ...6 F3
Holmhurst Cl TN4 ...7 F4
Holmhurst La TN37 ...136 B5
Holmhurst St Mary
 TN37 ...136 C6
Holms Cl TN21 ...81 F6
Holmstead BN2 ...189 C4
Holmwood Cl BN6 ...97 F4
Holt Lodge 1 BN2 ...189 C4
Holt The Burgess Hill RH15 ...73 C2
 Hailsham BN27 ...152 A6
 Seaford BN25 ...180 F5
Holters Way BN25 ...180 F5
Holton Hill BN2 ...165 E7
Holtview Rd BN2 ...165 B8
Holtye Ave RH19 ...2 A3
Holtye Pl RH19 ...2 B3
Holtye Rd RH19 ...2 B3
Holy Cross CE Prim Sch
 TN22 ...78 C7
Holyhead Cl BN27 ...129 A1
Holyrood RH19 ...11 A8
Holywell Cl BN20 ...188 E8
Holywell Rd BN20 ...188 E7
Holywell Wlk BN27 ...152 B7
Home Farm Bsns Ctr
 BN1 ...143 D3
Home Farm Ct Frant TN3 ...17 C4

Home Farm Ct continued
 Horsted Keynes RH17 ...33 C5
Home Farm La TN2 ...8 E8
Home Farm Rd BN1,BN2 143 D3
Home Platt RH19 ...21 A6
Home Rd BN1 ...142 E1
Homebush Ave
 Saltdean BN2 ...177 D5
 Saltdean BN2 ...177 F7
Homecoast Ho BN10 ...178 B7
Homedane Ho 7 TN34 ...159 F7
Homedrive Ho BN3 ...163 C8
Homefield Cl BN25 ...180 F4
Homefield Rd BN25 ...180 F4
Homegate Ho 3 BN21 ...184 F3
Homeglade Ho BN20 ...188 E8
Homehill Ho 7 TN40 ...157 C4
Homelands Cl TN39 ...157 A6
Homelatch Ho 1 BN21 ...185 A3
Homelawn Ho 3 TN40 ...157 E4
Homeleigh BN1 ...142 E5
Homeridge Ho BN2 ...177 D5
Homeshore Ho BN25 ...181 A3
Homestall Rd RH19 ...11 E8
Homestead La RH15 ...73 C6
Homestead The TN3 ...15 C7
Hometye Ho BN25 ...180 D3
Homewarr Ho 4 TN40 ...157 E4
Homewood Cl TN3 ...6 F3
Homewood Ho 1 TN22 ...185 B6
Homoepathic Hospl TN1 ...8 A3
Honey Croft BN3 ...141 D4
Honey La BN8 ...149 D5
Honeycrag Cl BN26 ...173 A7
Honeypot La BN7,BN8 ...100 B7
Honeysuckle Cl
 Eastbourne BN23 ...174 B3
 Hailsham BN27 ...152 B5
 St Leonards TN38 ...136 D5
Honeysuckle La BN27 ...127 C3
Honeyway Cl BN26 ...172 F3
Honies Ct TN39 ...157 C6
Hoo Gdns BN20 ...173 B1
Hoo The BN20 ...173 B1
Hood Cl BN23 ...185 E7
Hook Hill TN5 ...31 A6
Hookswood Cl TN6 ...26 A3
Hoopers Cl BN7 ...190 A4
Hoover Cl TN37 ...135 F7
Hop Gdn TN22 ...36 C2
Hope Cotts BN42 ...161 E8
Hopehouse La TN17,TN18 47 C1
Hopfield Gdns TN22 ...78 E8
Hopgarden Cl TN34 ...159 E8
Hoppers Croft La TN19 ...62 B6
Hopwood Gdns TN34 ...159 E8
Horam Manor Caravan Site
 TN21 ...106 F2
Horam Park Cl TN21 ...106 F7
Horebeech La TN21 ...107 A6
Horizon Cl
 Portslade-by-S BN41 ...162 B8
 Royal Tunbridge Wells TN2 ...8 C2
Horleigh Green Rd TN20 .39 C1
Horley Pl BN2 ...164 E6
Hornbeam BN19 ...62 B7
Hornbeam Ave TN39 ...157 A7
Hornbeams The RH15 ...72 D4
Hornblower Cotts TN19 ...44 C1
Hornbuckles Cl BN8 ...100 E7
Hornby Pl BN2 ...144 A1
Hornby Rd BN2 ...144 A1
Horning Cl BN23 ...174 B4
Horns Rd TN18 ...45 D8
Horntye Pk TN37,TN38 ...159 D8
Horntye Rd TN37 ...136 C1
Horsa Cl BN23 ...185 E8
Horsegrove Ave TN5 ...31 F1
Horsegrove La TN6 ...39 B8
Horseshoe Cl TN38 ...136 B2
Horseshoe La TN31 ...68 A1
Horsewalk BN27,TN33 ...154 E7
Horsfield Rd BN7 ...123 B3
Horsgate Ho RH17 ...50 A8
Horsgate La RH17 ...50 A6
Horsham Ave BN10 ...178 C7
Horsham Ave N BN10 ...178 C8
Horsham Cl BN2 ...164 F6
Horsted Ho 1 RH16 ...50 E7
Horsted Keynes Ind Pk
 RH17 ...33 B7
Horsted Keynes Sta
 RH17 ...33 A7
Horsted La Danehill RH17 ...34 A4
 Isfield TN22 ...102 F7
 Sharpthorne RH19 ...21 D1
Horsted Pond La TN22 ...78 A3
Horsted Square Ind Est
 TN22 ...78 A6
Horsye Rd BN2 ...185 B7
Horton Rd BN1 ...143 B1
Hoskins Pl RH19 ...2 A4
Hosmers Field TN6 ...39 D8
Houghton Green La
 TN31 ...70 C2
Houghton La TN31 ...70 C3
Houndean Cl BN7 ...146 A8
Houndean Rise BN7 ...145 F8
Hova Villas BN3 ...163 B6
Hove Bsns Ctr BN3 ...163 B8
Hove Ent Ctr BN41 ...162 C6
Hove General Hospl
 BN3 ...163 A7
Hove Manor 8 BN3 ...163 A6
Hove Mus & Art Gall★
 BN3 ...163 A6
Hove Nuffield Hospl
 BN3 ...162 F7

Hove Park Gdns
 Hove BN3 ...142 B1
 Hove BN3 ...163 B8
Hove Park Rd BN3 ...142 C1
Hove Park Sch & Sixth Form
 Ctr (Upper) BN3 ...142 A1
Hove Park Sch (Lower)
 BN3 ...141 D2
Hove Park Villas BN3 ...163 B8
Hove Park Way BN3 ...142 C1
Hove Pl BN3 ...163 B5
Hove St BN3 ...163 A6
Hove Sta BN3 ...163 B8
Hove Tech Ctr 1 BN3 ...163 A8
Hovedene BN3 ...163 C7
How's Cl TN31 ...90 B5
Howard Ave BN3 ...163 B7
Howard Cl BN27 ...152 D6
Howard Ct Hove BN3 ...142 A4
 Peacehaven BN10 ...178 B7
Howard Gdns TN2 ...8 A1
Howard Ho Bexhill TN39 ...156 E4
 1 Eastbourne BN21 ...185 A1
 Peacehaven BN10 ...167 D1
Howard Pl BN1 ...189 A4
Howard Rd BN2 ...164 C7
Howard Sq BN21 ...185 A2
Howard Terr BN1 ...142 D1
Howards Cres TN39 ...156 C4
Howbourne La TN22 ...56 E5
Howbourne La TN22 ...56 E5
Howe Cl TN31 ...90 B5
Howey Cl RH15 ...168 F1
Howland Cl 4 BN23 ...175 A1
Howlett Cl TN38 ...135 F4
Howlett Dr BN27 ...129 B2
Howletts Cl BN22 ...173 F1
Hoyle Rd BN10 ...178 C7
Hudson Cl BN23 ...185 G7
Hudson Ct BN26 ...185 C6
Huggett's La BN22 ...173 B3
Hughenden Ct 2 TN34 ...136 F2
Hughenden Pl 1 TN34 ...136 F2
Hughenden Rd TN34 ...160 A6
Hughes Rd BN2 ...164 B8
Hughes Way TN22 ...78 C8
Hugletts La TN21 ...83 A7
Humboldt Ct TN2 ...8 D5
Humphrey Lodge RH15 ...73 D3
Humphrey's Gap BN43 ...161 A7
Hundred Acre La BN6,
 RH17 ...74 B2
Hundredhouse La TN31 ...90 F4
Hungershall Park Cl TN4 ...7 E1
Hungershall Pk TN4 ...7 E2
Hunloke Ave BN22 ...185 B6
Hunston Cl BN2 ...165 F7
Hunt's Gate RH17 ...52 E3
Hunters Way
 Royal Tunbridge Wells TN2 ...7 F1
 Uckfield TN22 ...78 B8
Hunting Cl TN40 ...157 C5
Huntingdon Rd TN6 ...25 F1
Huntingdon Way RH15 ...73 D5
Huntington Cl BN7 ...190 C2
Huntley Mill Rd TN5 ...31 E3
Huntleys Pk TN4 ...7 F5
Hurdis Rd BN25 ...180 A6
Hurrell Rd TN34 ...160 B6
Hurst Cres BN41 ...162 B8
Hurst Cl BN1 ...143 C5
Hurst Farm Rd RH19 ...10 D7
Hurst Green CE Sch
 TN19 ...45 A2
Hurst Hill BN1 ...143 C5
Hurst La
 Eastbourne BN21 ...184 D4
 Sedlescombe TN33 ...88 F3
 Windmill Hill BN27 ...131 B5
Hurst Rd
 Eastbourne BN21 ...184 D5
 Hassocks BN6 ...97 D4
Hurst Shaw TN21 ...107 C8
Hurst The TN2 ...8 E7
Hurst Way TN35 ...137 A6
Hurst Wickham Cl BN6 ...97 C5
Hurstfield Cl RH17 ...52 A3
Hurstwood 6 BN2 ...164 F5
Hurstwood Cl TN40 ...158 B5
Hurstpierpoint Coll BN6 ...97 B8
Hurstwood La
 Haywards Heath RH17 ...51 A2
 Royal Tunbridge Wells TN4 ...7 F3
 Sharpthorne RH17,RH19 ...21 D1
Hurstwood Pk TN4 ...7 F3
Hurstwood Rd TN22 ...56 A6
Hurtis Hill TN6 ...37 E7
Hutton Rd BN1 ...143 B3
Hyde Bsns Pk The BN2 ...164 F8
Hyde Cl BN7 ...145 E5
Hyde Gdns BN21 ...185 A2
Hyde Rd BN21 ...184 F2
Hyde Tynings Cl BN20 ...188 D8
Hydehurst Cl TN6 ...25 F1
Hydney St BN22 ...185 C5
Hydneye The BN22 ...173 F1
Hylands Yd 5 TN31 ...93 B5
Hylden Cl BN2 ...165 B8
Hyperion Ave BN26 ...172 E6
Hythe Ave BN38 ...159 B8
Hythe Cl Polegate BN26 ...173 C7
 Seaford BN25 ...181 C5
Hythe Cres BN25 ...181 C4
Hythe Rd BN1 ...143 A2
Hythe View BN25 ...181 C4

I

Ian Cl TN40 ...157 F7
Icklesham CE Prim Sch
 TN36 ...116 E6
Icklesham Dr TN38 ...135 D3
Iden Cl BN2 ...164 E5
Iden Ct TN34 ...136 D3
Iden Hurst BN6 ...97 A7
Iden Rd TN31 ...70 B3
Iden St BN2 ...174 A2
Iden's La TN21 ...82 D8
Ifield Cl BN2 ...177 E6
Ifield Mill Cl BN24 ...174 B5
Iford & Kingston CE Prim Sch
 BN7 ...145 F5
Iford Cl BN9 ...168 D1
Ilex Cl BN42 ...141 A1
Ilex Gn 6 BN27 ...129 B1
Image Cross Flats RH19 ...21 A5
Imberhorne Bsns Ctr
 RH19 ...1 B3
Imberhorne La RH19 ...1 B2
Imberhorne Lower Sch
 RH19 ...1 D3
Imberhorne Sch RH19 ...1 B3
Imberhorne Way RH19 ...1 B3
Impala Gdns TN4 ...8 B6
Imperial Arc BN1 ...189 A2
Independent Bsns Pk The
 RH19 ...1 B3
Ingham Dr BN1 ...143 D6
Ingleside TN38 ...135 E4
Ingleside Dr TN6 ...25 E2
Inglewood Gdns TN38 ...135 E4
Ingram Cres E BN3 ...162 E8
Ingram Cres W BN3 ...162 E8
Ingram Ct BN3 ...162 E7
Ingrams Ave TN39 ...157 C7
Ingrams Ho 4 RH16 ...50 E7
Ingrams Way BN27 ...152 A6
Inholmes RH15 ...73 C3
Inholmes Park Rd RH15 ...73 B3
Inkerman Terr TN31 ...94 A3
Inkpen La RH18 ...11 F1
Innham's Wood TN6 ...25 E4
Innings Dr BN24 ...175 C4
Innovation Dr RH15 ...72 D2
Insley Ct TN39 ...156 F3
Institute Wlk 4 RH19 ...1 E1
Inverness Rd 4 BN2 ...164 C8
Inwood Cres BN1 ...142 E1
Iona Cl BN27 ...129 A3
Iona Way 12 RH16 ...50 E7
Irelands La 7 BN7 ...123 B1
Ironlatch Ave TN38 ...135 F2
Ironlatch Cl TN38 ...135 F2
Ironstone Way TN22 ...78 E7
Ironstones TN3 ...7 B3
Irving Ho TN1 ...8 B5
Isaac's La RH16,RH15 ...50 A2
Isabel Cl BN25 ...180 E5
Isabel Cres BN3 ...162 E8
Isfield Rd Brighton BN1 ...143 C2
 Brighton BN2 ...102 E5
Isfield Sta★ TN22 ...102 E7
Isherwood TN33 ...112 B5
Islingword Pl BN2 ...164 C6
Islingword Rd BN2 ...164 C7
Islingword St BN2 ...189 C3
Ismay Lodge TN39 ...156 F3
Ive Grange TN33 ...132 F5
Iveagh Cres BN9 ...168 D2
Ivor Rd BN2 ...144 C1
Ivors La BN8 ...123 B5
Ivory Pl BN2 ...189 C3
Ivy Cotts BN8 ...104 C6
Ivy Dene La RH19 ...11 D6
Ivy La TN3 ...18 A5
Ivy Mews 13 BN3 ...163 D5
Ivy Pl BN1,BN3 ...163 D5
Ivy Terr BN21 ...184 F3
Ivydene Ind Est RH19 ...11 D7
Ivyhouse Employment Area
 TN35 ...160 B8
Ivyhouse La TN35 ...137 B6

J

Jack O'Dandy Cl BN21 ...184 C7
Jackdaws The TN22 ...78 E4
Jackies La BN8 ...76 B7
Jacks Hill TN7 ...13 D2
Jackson Mews BN9 ...179 C7
Jackson St BN2 ...189 C4
Jacobs Acre TN40 ...157 C5
Jacqueline Du Pre Ct 6
 BN2 ...164 C5
Jamaica Way BN23 ...185 F8
James Ave BN27 ...130 E6
James Bradford Almhouses
 RH16 ...50 C4
Jameson Cres TN38 ...136 A3
Jameson Mews 9
 TN40 ...157 D4
Jameson Rd TN40 ...157 D4
Jane Murray Way BN6,
 RH15 ...72 C5
Janes Cl RH15 ...73 C5
Janes La RH15 ...73 D4
Janeston Ct 4 BN3 ...163 C7
Japonica Cl BN43 ...140 B1

Jardine Ct TN6 .....25 F2
Jarretts Cl 4 TN31 .....93 B5
Jarvis Brook Ctry Pk TN6 38 B8
Jarvis Brook Prim Sch
 TN6 .....38 C7
Jarvisbrook Cl TN39 ...156 D3
Jasmine Cotts TN3 .....15 C7
Jasmine Ct Brighton BN1 142 F6
 Hove BN3 .....163 D7
Jasmine Gn 2 BN27 ....129 B1
Jasmine Way TN39 .....156 F3
Jason Cl BN10 .....178 C7
Jay Cl BN23 .....174 C2
Jay Rd BN10 .....178 E6
Jays The Burgess Hill RH15 72 E4
 Uckfield TN22 .....78 D4
Jefferies RH17 .....33 C4
Jefferies Way TN6 .....25 F4
Jefferson Way TN37 ...135 F6
Jeffreys Way TN22 .....55 D1
Jellicoe Cl BN23 .....185 F7
Jenner's La TN35 .....137 E6
Jephson Cl BN20 .....188 F8
Jerome Cl BN23 .....174 E2
Jersey St BN2 .....189 C3
Jervis Ave BN23 .....185 E6
Jesmond Cl BN3 .....162 E7
Jesmond Rd BN3 .....162 E7
Jesters RH16 .....73 C7
Jevington Cl TN39 .....156 D2
Jevington Ct BN43 .....161 D6
Jevington Dr
 Brighton BN2 .....143 D1
 Seaford BN25 .....180 D4
Jevington Gdns BN21 ...185 A1
Jevington Ho 9 BN21 ..184 D4
Jevington Rd BN26 .....172 D2
Jew St BN1 .....189 B2
Jikack Ind Est BN6 .....72 B4
Jireh Ct RH16 .....50 E5
Joan Hughes Ct BN26 .173 A6
Joan Nightingale Ho
 RH16 .....50 C4
Jobs La BN6 .....72 A6
Joe's La BN27 .....131 B5
John Dann Cl TN22 .....80 A6
John Macadam Way
 TN37 .....136 A6
John Spare Ct TN4 .....8 A6
John St Brighton BN2 ...189 C3
 Royal Tunbridge Wells TN4 ...8 A5
John Whittle Lodge
 BN2 .....143 C1
John's Cross Rd TN32 ..87 C8
Johns Cl BN10 .....167 C2
Johnson Bank 4 BN2 ..164 C7
Johnson Cl TN37 .....135 F6
Johnson Dr RH15 .....73 D3
Johnston Pl 1 BN23 ...175 A1
Jonas Dr TN5 .....29 E5
Jonas La TN5 .....29 E5
Jordan Ct BN3 .....162 E8
Jordans La BN22 .....173 D3
Jordans La E BN22 .....173 D3
Jordans La W BN22 ....173 C3
Jordans The RH19 .....10 E8
Joyce Villas TN21 .....106 E5
Jubilee Cl RH16 .....51 A4
Jubilee Cotts 4 TN6 ...37 F8
Jubilee Ct Brighton BN2 .143 E2
 Peacehaven BN10 .....178 B7
Jubilee Gdns BN25 .....181 A5
Jubilee Ho
 Eastbourne BN22 .....185 B4
 Newhaven BN9 .....179 C7
Jubilee Rd Bexhill TN39 .157 A7
 Burgess Hill RH15 .....72 E2
 Portslade-by-S BN41 ...162 A8
Judge's Terr 1 RH19 ...10 E8
Judges Cl 3 RH19 .....10 E8
Jugg's Rd BN7 .....146 B7
Juggs Cl BN7 .....146 B8
Juggs Rd BN7 .....146 A7
Julian Ct 5 BN43 .....161 C8
Julian Rd BN3 .....163 E7
Junction Cl RH15 .....73 C4
Junction Rd
 Bodiam TN18,TN32 .....46 A3
 Brighton BN1 .....189 A3
 Burgess Hill RH15 .....73 B3
 Cripp's Corner TN32,TN33 ..88 C5
 Eastbourne BN21 .....185 A3
 St Leonards TN37 .....136 B7
 Staplecross TN32 .....65 C5
Junction St BN26 .....173 B6
Juniper Cl
 Portslade-by-S BN41 ...141 B3
 Seaford BN25 .....181 C3
 St Leonards TN38 .....135 E3
Juniper Ct RH16 .....50 C2
Juniper Wlk BN43 .....140 C1
Jury's Gap Coastguard Cotts
 TN31 .....95 E1
Jury's Gap Rd TN29 ...96 F5

K

Kammond Ave BN25 ..181 B5
Kane Hythe Rd TN33 ..111 D6
Karenza Ct TN21 .....164 A8
Katherine Way BN25 ..180 D5
Keaton Ho 2 RH16 .....50 E6
Keats Cl TN38 .....158 F6
Keats Pl RH19 .....1 D1

Keats Wlk BN23 .....174 E3
Kebbell Lodge 12 BN2 .189 C2
Kedale Rd BN25 .....180 E4
Keel Gdns TN4 .....7 E8
Keere St BN7 .....190 A1
Keith Wlk BN23 .....185 F6
Keld Ave TN22 .....78 D6
Keld Cl TN22 .....78 D6
Keld Dr TN22 .....78 D6
Kelly Rd BN3 .....142 D1
Kelsey Cotts BN8 .....124 E6
Kelsey Ct RH15 .....73 D3
Kemble Cl TN2 .....8 E7
Kemp Ct BN2 .....164 E4
Kemp St BN1 .....189 B3
Kemp Town Pl 18 BN2 .164 D4
Kemps Farm Rd TN6 ...26 B1
Kemps Way TN32 .....64 C5
Kemptown Mews 11
 BN2 .....164 E4
Kendal Ct BN9 .....179 E7
Kendal Pk TN4 .....7 E5
Kendal Rd BN3 .....162 F8
Kendall Ct RH16 .....50 F2
Kenilworth Cl BN2 .....144 A2
Kenilworth Rd TN38 ...159 B7
Kenmure Ave BN1 .....143 A7
Kennard Ct RH18 .....11 E3
Kennedy Ave RH19 .....1 D3
Kennedy Cl TN21 .....82 B6
Kennedy Ct TN38 .....136 B3
Kennedy Rd TN40 .....157 E4
Kennedy Way BN9 .....179 B8
Kennel Cnr BN2 .....143 E2
Kennel La TN39 .....156 C4
Kennett Cl BN24 .....173 F5
Kenrith Ct TN4 .....136 E2
Kensington 7 BN23 ....175 A1
Kensington Cl TN38 ...135 D3
Kensington Gdns BN1 .189 B3
Kensington Pl BN1 .....189 B3
Kensington St BN1 .....189 B3
Kent Ave TN38 .....135 D3
Kent Cl Bexhill TN40 ...158 A5
 Shoreham-by-S BN43 ..161 C7
 Winchelsea TN36 .....117 E7
Kent Ct BN20 .....184 B6
Kent Fields BN7 .....145 E5
Kent Ho TN1 .....8 C6
Kent La TN32 .....85 E7
Kent Rd
 Royal Tunbridge Wells TN4 ...8 A6
 St Leonards TN38 .....135 F4
Kent St TN33 .....114 A3
Kent's La BN6 .....99 C7
Kentish Gdns TN2 .....16 E8
Kenton Cl TN39 .....157 A5
Kenton Ct 7 BN21 .....185 A1
Kenton Rd BN3 .....162 D7
Kents Rd RH16 .....50 F3
Kenwards BN1 .....143 D7
Kenwood Ct TN34 .....160 B8
Kenya Ct 2 BN1 .....163 E6
Keppel Rd BN34 .....136 F2
Kepplestone BN20 .....188 E8
Kerrara Terr BN22 .....185 B5
Kerrison Mews 7 BN3 .163 D5
Kestrel Cl Bexhill TN40 .157 E4
 Hove BN3 .....163 D8
Kestrel Ct BN27 .....152 D7
Kestrels The
 Shoreham-by-S BN43 ..161 A8
 St Leonards TN38 .....135 F5
Ketcham Cnr BN24 ....174 E6
Ketche's La RH17,TN22 ..52 E7
Kevin Gdns BN2 .....165 E8
Kew St BN1 .....189 A3
Kewhurst Ave TN39 ...156 D3
Kewhurst Ho TN39 .....156 E4
Key W BN23 .....185 G8
Keymer Ave BN10 .....178 D7
Keymer Cl
 Eastbourne BN23 .....174 E1
 St Leonards TN38 .....158 E6
Keymer Ct RH15 .....73 B2
Keymer End RH16 .....50 D3
Keymer Gdns RH15 ....73 B3
Keymer Ho 18 BN21 ...184 E4
Keymer Par RH15 .....73 B2
Keymer Pk BN6 .....98 B3
Keymer Rd Brighton BN1 .143 B6
 Burgess Hill RH15 .....98 B8
 Hassocks BN6 .....97 F3
Keysford La RH17 .....33 A4
Kibbles La TN4 .....7 E8
Kidbrook RH16 .....51 B6
Kidbrooke Rise RH18 ..11 E2
Kidd's Hill TN7 .....24 A4
Kilburn Terr 6 BN21 ...185 A3
Kilda St 1 BN22 .....185 B4
Kildare Cl TN34 .....160 B8
Kildare Ct BN20 .....184 C3
Kiln Cl TN22 .....78 D4
Kiln Dr TN31 .....93 B8
Kiln La
 Hawkhurst Heath RH16 ...51 B5
 Hooe TN33 .....155 B7
 Isfield TN22 .....102 E3
Kiln Rd BN8 .....125 A8
Kiln The RH15 .....73 C3
Kilnbank TN2 .....8 C7
Kilnbarn Ct RH16 .....50 D3
Kilnbarn Way RH16 ....50 D2
Kilnwood La BN8 .....100 E7
Kilpatrick Cl BN23 .....174 D3

Kimberley Ct TN39 ....157 C6
Kimberley Rd
 Brighton BN2 .....143 D1
 Seaford BN25 .....180 C4
Kindersley Cl RH19 .....2 B3
King Alfred (Swimming Pool
 & Sports Ctr) BN3 ...163 A5
King Charles Pl 10
 BN43 .....161 A6
King Edward Ave TN34 .136 C3
King Edward Cl TN34 ..136 C3
King Edward's Par BN20 188 F8
King George Ave RH19 ..1 C3
King George Rd BN43 ..161 D8
King George V Hill TN1 ..8 C5
King George VI Ave
 BN3 .....142 A3
King George VI Dr BN3 .142 A4
King George VI Mans
 BN3 .....141 F2
King Henry's Rd BN7 ..123 B2
King John Ct 7 BN43 ..161 A6
King Offa Prim Sch
 TN39 .....157 B5
King Offa Way TN40 ...157 C5
King Pl BN1 .....189 A2
King St Brighton BN1 ..189 B2
 East Grinstead RH19 ....1 A6
King Wood Hill TN31 ...90 A3
King's Ave
 Eastbourne BN21 .....184 E5
 Newhaven BN9 .....168 A1
 Rye TN31 .....93 D6
King's Bank La TN31 ...68 A3
King's Cl BN21 .....184 E5
King's Dr BN21 .....184 D7
King's Espl BN3 .....163 A3
King's Gdns BN3 .....163 B5
King's Hill Rd TN19 ....62 B3
King's Manor Com Coll
 BN43 .....161 D8
King's Mead La BN25 ..180 D4
King's Rd
 Brighton BN1,BN3 .....163 C5
 Haywards Heath RH16 ..50 F3
 St Leonards TN37 .....159 C7
Kingfisher Cl TN22 .....78 E5
Kingfisher Ct
 Hailsham BN27 .....152 D7
 Uckfield TN22 .....78 B6
Kingfisher Dr BN23 ....174 C2
Kingfisher Rise RH19 ..10 F8
Kings Chase TN6 .....25 D3
Kings Cl Bexhill TN40 ..157 C4
 Eastbourne BN21 .....184 F5
 Peacehaven BN10 .....167 B1
Kings Copse 9 RH19 ...10 F8
Kings Ct Brighton BN1 .189 B2
 Crowborough TN6 .....25 E2
Kings Ct E 4 BN23 ....185 F8
Kings Ct S 6 BN23 ....185 F8
Kings Ct W 5 BN23 ....185 F8
Kings Dr BN6 .....97 F4
Kings Gate
 Haywards Heath RH16 ..50 E5
 Hove BN3 .....163 C8
Kings Mead Ct BN20 ..188 D7
Kings Mews BN3 .....163 B6
Kings Par BN1 .....143 A2
Kings Pk TN2 .....8 D3
Kings Rd BN42 .....140 E1
Kings Ride
 Alfriston BN26 .....170 F3
 Burgess Hill RH15 .....73 D1
 Seaford BN25 .....180 D4
Kings Toll Rd TN2 .....9 F6
Kings Way RH15 .....73 D2
Kings Well Ct 14 BN25 .180 E2
Kings Wlk 10 TN34 ....159 F8
Kingsbury Rd BN1 .....189 B4
Kingsbury St BN1 .....189 B4
Kingscote Lodge BN1 ..143 F5
Kingscott Cl TN39 .....157 B8
Kingsdale Cl Battle TN33 112 F3
 St Leonards TN37 .....136 C6
Kingsfield Cl BN42 ....161 E8
Kingsfield Cotts BN8 ..149 E8
Kingsfold 2 BN2 .....164 C5
Kingsfold Ct 1 BN25 ..180 F2
Kingsford BN23 .....185 D7
Kingsland 3 BN2 .....184 F1
Kingsland BN43 .....161 C7
Kingsley Cl TN37 .....136 A5
Kingsley Ct
 7 Brighton BN1 .....163 E5
 Wadhurst TN5 .....30 A4
Kingsley Rd
 Brighton BN1 .....142 D1
 Lewes BN7 .....123 B2
Kingsmarsh Cotts TN20 .58 B6
Kingsmead BN25 .....180 E5
Kingsmead Cl BN25 ...180 E4
Kingsmead Way BN25 .180 E4
Kingsmead Wlk BN25 .180 E4
Kingsmere BN1 .....142 E2
Kingsmere Ct 4 BN20 .184 D4
Kingsmere Way BN23 .185 F8
Kingsthorpe Rd BN3 ..162 F8
Kingston Ave BN25 ....181 B3
Kingston Bay Rd BN43 .161 C6
Kingston Broadway
 BN43 .....140 D1
Kingston Buci Fst Sch
 BN43 .....161 B8
Kingston Cl Brighton BN1 143 G6
 Hove BN3 .....141 D2
 Seaford BN25 .....181 B3

Kingston Cl continued
 Shoreham-by-S BN43 ...161 C8
Kingston Cl 17 BN43 ..161 C8
Kingston Gn BN25 .....181 B3
Kingston Ho 15 BN21 .184 F4
Kingston La BN42,BN43 .161 D7
Kingston Quay 18 BN23 185 F8
Kingston Rd
 Eastbourne BN22 .....173 F2
 Lewes BN7 .....146 B7
Kingston Ridge BN7 ...145 D6
Kingston Villas TN21 ..106 E5
Kingston Way
 Seaford BN25 .....181 B3
 Shoreham-by-S BN43 ..140 D1
Kingsway Hove BN3,BN41 163 B5
 Seaford BN25 .....180 D4
Kingsway Ct Hove BN3 .163 C5
 Seaford BN25 .....180 D4
Kingswood Ave TN39 ..156 F6
Kingswood Cl TN2 .....8 D2
Kingswood Flats BN2 ..189 C2
Kingswood Rd TN2 .....8 C3
Kingswood St BN2 .....189 B2
Kinross Ct 5 BN21 ....185 A4
Kinsale Ct 5 BN3 .....163 D7
Kinver La TN40 .....158 A6
Kipling Ave BN3 .....142 A3
Kipling Ct Bexhill TN40 .157 C6
 3 Haywards Heath RH16 ..50 D5
 Rottingdean BN2 .....177 A5
Kipling Way RH19 .....1 C1
Kipling Wlk 1 BN23 ...174 E2
Kirby Dr BN10 .....167 B1
Kirdford Cl RH15 .....73 C1
Kirk Way BN20 .....184 B5
Kirkdale Rd TN1 .....8 A4
Kirkstall Ct BN23 .....173 E3
Kitchenour La TN31 ...68 E5
Kite Cl TN38 .....158 E8
Kites Nest Wlk TN39 ..156 B4
Kitilear Ct TN38 .....163 D6
Knebworth Rd TN39 ...156 F5
Knelle Rd TN32 .....64 A4
Knelle View TN31 .....67 B7
Knepp Cl BN2 .....143 F2
Knight's Ridge TN2 .....9 D7
Knights Cl TN2 .....9 D7
Knights Gate Rd BN1 ..144 C2
Knights Gdn BN27 .....152 B6
Knights Mdw
 Battle TN33 .....112 F4
 Uckfield TN22 .....78 E8
Knights Pk TN2 .....8 F8
Knights Way TN2 .....8 F8
Knightsbridge Cl TN4 ..7 F5
Knightsbridge Ct TN1 ..8 B6
Knockhatch Adventure Pk★
 BN27 .....151 E2
Knole Cl 4 TN40 .....157 D3
Knole Gr RH19 .....1 C3
Knole Rd Bexhill TN40 .157 D3
 Rottingdean BN2 .....177 A5
Knoll Bsns Ctr The BN3 162 D8
Knoll Cl BN3 .....141 D1
Knoll Cres BN22 .....174 A1
Knoll Pl RH16 .....51 B5
Knoll Rd BN22 .....174 A2
Knoll Rise TN38 .....159 A7
Knowle
 Crowborough TN6 .....38 C8
 Langton Green TN3 .....6 F3
Knowle Cotts TN3 .....17 E1
Knowle Ct TN38 .....159 A6
Knowle Hill Bodiam TN32 .65 D8
 Mayfield TN20 .....40 A1
Knowle La BN8 .....104 A6
Knowle Pk
 Crowborough TN6 .....25 D2
 Mayfield TN20 .....40 D1
Knowle Rd TN35 .....138 E5
Knoyle Rd BN1 .....142 E2
Knyveton Ct RH15 .....73 B3
Kylemore BN24 .....175 B6
Kymer Gdns BN6 .....98 A3

L

La Marne Ct TN34 .....136 E2
La Senera Pl BN23 .....175 B1
Laburnum Ave BN3 ....141 E1
Laburnum Ct TN2 .....8 E7
Laburnum Gdns TN40 .157 F6
Laburnum Gn 5 BN27 .129 B1
Laburnum Gr BN1 .....143 B3
Laburnum Way RH16 ..51 B4
Laburnum Wlk BN2 ....173 D3
Labyrinth The 20 BN21 .185 A2
Lacys Hill BN27 .....147 F8
Ladies Mile Brighton BN1 143 B7
 Withyham TN6,TN7 .....14 D4
Ladies Mile Cl BN1 ....142 F6
Ladies' Mile Ct BN1 ...142 E6
Ladies' Mile Rd BN1 ...142 E6
Lady Bee Ind Est BN42 .161 E6
Lady Oak La TN5,TN17 ..32 C7
Lady's Gift Rd TN4 .....7 F8
Ladycross Cl BN25 .....181 C3
Ladyfern Ct TN2 .....8 C4
Ladymead RH15 .....73 C5
Ladysmith Rd BN2 .....164 D8
Lagwood Cl BN6 .....97 F3
Laine Cl BN1 .....142 E3
Laines The BN26 .....170 F3
Lake Dr BN10 .....178 B8
Lake Ho TN39 .....156 D3
Lake House Cl TN39 ...156 D4

Lake Rd TN4 .....7 E4
Lake St TN20,TN6 .....40 D7
Lake View Rd RH19 .....1 F5
Lakehurst La TN33 .....110 B8
Lakelands Cl BN22 .....174 A1
Lakelands Dr TN39 ....156 D4
Lakeman Way TN4 .....8 B7
Lakeside TN2 .....8 E6
Lakeside Ct BN22 .....174 A1
Lakeview 1 BN2 .....164 C5
Laleham Cl
 Eastbourne BN21 .....184 E4
 St Leonards TN37 .....136 C5
Lamberhurst Rd TN3,
 TN12 .....20 C8
Lamberhurst St Mary's CE
 Prim Sch TN3 .....20 B6
Lamberhurst Vineyard★
 TN3 .....20 A4
Lambert Pl BN7 .....190 B4
Lambert Rd BN23 .....174 E3
Lamberts Cotts TN33 ..112 E3
Lamberts Rd TN2 .....8 D8
Lambourn Ave BN24 ..174 A5
Lambourn Cl RH19 .....1 E3
Lambourn Way TN2 .....8 D1
Lambourne Cl BN1 ....143 C2
Lambourne Rd BN1 ...143 C2
Lampington Row TN3 ..6 E3
Lampool Cnr TN22 .....55 A7
Lampool Rdbt TN22 ...55 A7
Lanark Ct BN20 .....184 B6
Lancaster Ct
 16 Eastbourne BN22 ...185 B3
 12 Hove BN3 .....163 A6
Lancaster Dr RH19 .....2 A3
Lancaster House Rd
 BN1 .....144 B7
Lancaster Rd
 Brighton BN1 .....189 A4
 St Leonards TN38 .....135 F5
Lancaster St 7 BN7 ....190 B2
Lancing Cl TN34 .....136 D3
Lancing Ct 5 BN2 .....164 C5
Lancing Way BN26 ....172 F4
Landgate TN31 .....93 C6
Landgate Sq 4 TN31 ...93 C6
Landport Farm Rd BN7 .123 A3
Landport Rd Lewes BN7 .123 B3
 Lewes BN7 .....190 A3
Landsdown Rd BN25 ..181 C5
Landsdowne Way TN40 .157 C5
Landseer Rd BN3 .....163 A8
Lane The Fordcombe TN3 ..6 C5
 Foxhole BN25 .....182 A4
Langdale Cl BN23 .....174 C4
Langdale Gdns BN3 ...162 F6
Langdale Rd BN3 .....162 F6
Langham Cl
 Hastings TN34 .....136 F4
 Ringmer BN8 .....124 D5
Langham Rd
 Hastings TN34 .....136 F4
 Robertsbridge TN32 ....63 F4
Langholm Rd TN3 .....6 F3
Langhurst 9 BN2 .....164 E4
Langley Cl TN39 .....157 B8
Langley Cres BN2 .....144 E1
Langney Gn BN23 .....185 E8
Langney Prim Sch BN23 174 E1
Langney Rd BN21,BN22 .185 B3
Langney Rise BN23 ....174 D2
Langney Sh Ctr BN23 .174 C2
Langridge Cl TN6 .....37 D8
Langridge Dr
 East Grinstead RH19 ...10 E8
 Portslade-by-S BN41 ...141 B3
Langridge La RH16 .....51 A5
Langridge Way RH15 ..72 E5
Langridges Cl BN8 .....76 C7
Langton Cl TN33 .....112 E4
Langton Green Prim Sch
 TN3 .....6 E4
Langton Rd
 Rusthall TN3, TN4 .....7 C3
 Speldhurst TN3 .....7 A7
Langton Ridge TN3 .....7 B3
Langtye La BN26,BN8 ..149 E6
Lansdown Pl BN7 .....190 B1
Lansdown Terr 5 TN21 .82 A6
Lansdowne Cres BN27 .129 B2
Lansdowne Ct
 5 Eastbourne BN21 ....185 A1
 23 Hove BN3 .....163 C6
Lansdowne Dr BN27 ...129 B2
Lansdowne Gdns BN27 129 B2
Lansdowne Mans 11
 BN3 .....163 D6
Lansdowne Mews 7
 BN3 .....163 D6
Lansdowne Pl BN3 ....163 D6
Lansdowne Rd
 Hailsham BN27 .....129 B2
 Hove BN1,BN3 .....163 D6
 Royal Tunbridge Wells TN1 ..8 B4
Lansdowne Sq
 1 Hove BN3 .....163 D5
 8 Royal Tunbridge Wells
 TN1 .....8 B4
Lansdowne St BN3 ....163 D6
Lansdowne Way BN27 .129 B3
Lanthorne Mews
 Royal Tunbridge Wells TN1 ..8 B5
 Royal Tunbridge
 Wells,Calverley Park TN1 ..8 B5
Lapierre Rd BN9 .....179 B7
Lapwing Cl BN23 .....174 C2

Lapwing Ct BN27 ......152 D7
Larch Cl Heathfield TN21 ..82 B5
St Leonards TN38 ......136 A1
Woodingdean BN2 ......165 F7
Larch Gdns BN22 ......173 D3
Larch Way RH16 ......51 B4
Larches Ho RH19 ......2 B4
Larches The RH19 ......2 B4
Lark Hill BN3 ......141 E3
Larke Cl BN43 ......161 C7
Larkfield Cl TN36 ......136 A3
Larkfield Way BN1 ......143 A4
Larkhill TN40 ......157 C4
Larkspur Dr BN23 ......174 B3
Larnach Cl TN22 ......78 D8
Lascelles Terr BN21 ......185 A1
Lashbrooks Rd
 Uckfield TN22 ......78 B7
 Uckfield TN22 ......78 B7
Latimer Rd BN22 ......185 C4
Laton Rd TN34 ......136 F2
Laughton Cl BN23 ......174 A4
Laughton Com Prim Sch
 BN8 ......126 C6
Laughton Lodge BN8 ..126 A8
Laughton Rd
 Ringmer BN8 ......125 D6
 Woodingdean BN2 ......165 F8
Laundry La RH17 ......22 D1
Laurel 2 RH16 ......50 D6
Laurel Bank Bexhill TN40 157 E5
 Royal Tunbridge Wells TN4 ..8 B8
 Wadhurst TN5 ......30 A4
Laurel Cl RH15 ......73 D5
Laurel Dene RH19 ......1 F1
Laurel La TN36 ......116 F5
Laurel Rd TN2 ......8 D7
Laurel Way TN2 ......8 D7
Laurel Wlk TN38 ......135 E3
Laurels The
 4 Brighton BN2 ......189 C5
 1 Crowborough TN6 ......25 F3
 Uckfield TN22 ......78 E8
Lauren Ct TN38 ......158 F7
Lauriston Rd BN1 ......142 E2
Lavant Cl TN39 ......156 C6
Lavant Rd BN24 ......174 B5
Lavender Cl
 Eastbourne BN23 ......174 B3
 Hailsham BN27 ......128 F1
Lavender Gdns TN5 ......31 E1
Lavender Hill BN43 ......140 B1
Lavender Ho BN2 ......189 C1
Lavender St BN2 ......189 C1
Lawes Ave BN9 ......179 C7
Lawns The BN21 ......184 D4
Lawns The
 Eastbourne BN20 ......173 B1
 Eastbourne BN22 ......173 B2
 Eastbourne,Roselands
 BN22 ......185 C5
 Hailsham BN27 ......152 C6
Lawrence Cl BN23 ......174 D1
Lawrence Ho TN22 ......78 C7
Lawrence Rd BN3 ......162 F7
Lawrie La RH16 ......51 B5
Laylands Ct BN41 ......162 A7
Laylands Rd BN41 ......162 A7
Lazanby Ct TN38 ......159 B8
Le Brun Rd BN21 ......184 F5
Lea Ave TN31 ......93 A6
Lea Ct BN9 ......179 C8
Lea Rd BN10 ......178 B8
Leach Ct Brighton BN2 ..164 C5
 Brighton BN2 ......189 C2
Leacroft RH19 ......1 D2
Leaf Hall Rd 10 BN21 ..185 B3
Leaf Hospl (Univ of Brighton)
 BN21 ......184 F4
Leaf Rd BN21 ......185 A3
Leahurst Court Rd BN1 142 E3
Leahurst 1 BN1 ......142 E3
Lealands Cl BN1 ......15 C6
Lealands Dr TN22 ......55 C1
Leamland Wlk BN27 ...152 B7
Leap Cross Small Bsns Ctr
 BN27 ......129 A1
Leas The Burgess Hill RH15 72 F4
 Peacehaven BN10 ......178 F6
 St Leonards TN38 ......159 A6
 Turner's Green TN5 ......30 A4
Leasam La TN31 ......93 B8
Leasingham Gdns TN39 157 A5
Ledsham Ave TN37 ......136 B5
Ledsham Cl TN37 ......136 B5
Ledsham Pk TN37 ......136 B5
Ledsham Way TN37 ......136 B5
Lee Bank BN1 ......189 C3
Lee Rd BN7 ......123 B2
Lee Way BN9 ......179 C8
Leeds Ave BN23 ......185 D7
Leeds Cl TN35 ......160 D8
Leeds La TN20 ......58 D6
Leeford Cotts TN33 ......88 A1
Leeves Cl TN21 ......82 A6
Leeves Way TN21 ......82 A6
Leeward Quay 11 BN23 185 F8
Leggs' La TN3 ......6 E5
Legsheath La RH18,RH19 21 F8
Leicester Ct 5 BN2 ...185 B4
Leicester Dr TN2 ......16 F8
Leicester Rd BN7 ......123 B1
Leicester St BN2 ......189 C2
Leicester Villas BN3 ..162 D7
Leighton Rd TN4 ......8 A7

Leighton Rd
 Horsted Keynes RH17 ......33 C5
 Hove BN3 ......163 A8
Leighton Villas RH17 ...33 C5
Leneda Dr TN2 ......16 E8
Lenham Ave BN2 ......177 B5
Lenham Rd E BN2 ......177 B5
Lenham Rd W BN2 ......177 A5
Lennox Cl BN20 ......184 B5
Lennox Ct TN21 ......82 B8
Lennox Rd BN3 ......162 F8
 Shoreham-by-S BN43 ......161 B8
Lennox St BN2 ......189 C2
Leopald Flats TN39 ...157 B8
Leopold Rd Bexhill TN39 157 B4
 Brighton BN1 ......189 A3
Lepeland BN27 ......129 A1
Lesley Cl RH17 ......157 F7
Leslie Best Ho BN1 ...189 B4
Leslie St BN2 ......185 B4
Letheren Pl BN21 ......184 D3
Leveller End BN8 ......76 D7
Leveller Rd BN8 ......76 D7
Levett Ave BN26 ......173 C6
Levett Cl BN26 ......173 C6
Levett Rd BN26 ......173 C6
Levett Way BN26 ......173 C6
Levetts La TN32 ......46 D1
Lewes Castle ★ BN7 ..190 A2
Lewes Cl Bexhill TN39 ..157 A6
 Saltdean BN2 ......177 E5
Lewes Cres BN2 ......164 E4
Lewes Ct
 5 Eastbourne BN21 ...184 F4
 Falmer BN1 ......144 A4
 Southwick BN42 ......162 A7
Lewes High Sch BN7 ..123 B1
Lewes Ho 7 BN21 ......184 F4
Lewes Mews 12 BN2 ..164 E4
Lewes New Sch The
 BN7 ......190 A2
Lewes Rd
 Brighton BN1,BN2 ......143 C3
 Chelwood Gate RH17 ......22 C1
 Danehill RH17 ......34 B3
 Ditchling BN6 ......98 E2
 Eastbourne BN21 ......184 F5
 Forest Row RH18 ......11 E2
 Horsted Keynes RH17 ......33 C5
 Isfield TN22 ......102 E6
 Laughton BN8 ......126 C7
 Lindfield RH16 ......51 B7
 Newhaven BN9 ......179 C8
 Polegate BN26 ......172 C6
 Ringmer BN8 ......124 D6
 Scaynes Hill RH17 ......51 D4
 Selmeston BN26 ......149 D2
 Uckfield TN22 ......78 D4
Lewes St BN2 ......189 C3
Lewes Sta BN7 ......190 B1
Lewis Ave TN40 ......158 A5
Lewis Cl BN9 ......168 F2
Lewis Ct 6 BN2 ......164 C5
Lewis Rd TN38 ......136 A3
Lewry Cl BN9 ......179 B7
Lexden Cl BN25 ......181 A4
Lexden Dr BN25 ......181 A5
Lexden Lodge Ind Est
 TN6 ......38 D8
Lexden Rd BN25 ......180 F6
Leybourne Cl BN2 ......144 A1
Leybourne Gdns TN37 136 C4
Leybourne Par BN2 ...144 A1
Leybourne Rd BN2 ...144 A1
Leyland Rd BN24 ......175 D4
Leylands Pk RH15 ......73 B4
Leylands Rd RH15 ......73 B4
Library Way TN22 ......78 C7
Lichfield Ct 10 BN2 ...164 F5
Lilac Rd BN2 ......173 D3
Lillesden Cotts TN18 ...45 E7
Lillywhite Cl RH15 ......72 F5
Limden Cl TN5 ......42 F6
Lime Cl Frant TN3 ......17 B3
 St Leonards TN38 ......136 B1
 Uckfield TN22 ......78 D8
Lime Closs BN27 ......130 F5
Lime Hill Rd TN1 ......8 A4
Lime Tree Ave TN22 ...78 D7
Lime Tree Gr RH16 ......51 C7
Lime Tree Terr TN19 ...62 A6
Lime Way TN1 ......82 B6
Limekiln Ct TN6 ......26 C3
Limes La TN22 ......56 D3
Limes The
 14 Eastbourne BN21 ...184 E4
 Felbridge RH19 ......1 A5
Limetree Ave BN22 ...173 D3
Limney Rd BN2 ......164 E7
Limousin Ho BN23 ...185 F8
Linchmere BN2 ......164 F7
Linchmere Ave BN2 ..177 C5
Lincoln Ave BN10 ......178 A7
Lincoln Ave S BN10 ..178 A7
Lincoln Cl
 Eastbourne BN20 ......188 C8
 2 St Leonards TN38 ..136 A4
Lincoln Cotts BN2 ...189 C3
Lincoln Ct
 Eastbourne BN20 ......184 B7
 Hove BN3 ......163 C8
 Peacehaven BN10 ......178 A7
Lincoln Rd BN41 ......162 B7
Lincoln St BN2 ......189 C4
Lincoln Way TN6 ......38 A8
Lincoln Wood RH16 ...50 C5
Linden Ave RH19 ......1 C2

Linden Chase TN22 ...78 D7
Linden Cl
 Eastbourne BN22 ......173 E2
 Royal Tunbridge Wells TN4 ..8 C4
Linden Ct TN22 ......78 C7
Linden Gdns
 Heathfield TN21 ......81 F6
 Royal Tunbridge Wells TN2 ...7 F1
Linden Gr Hailsham BN27 129 C3
 Lindfield RH16 ......51 B7
Linden Park Rd TN2 ...8 A2
Linden Rd TN40 ......157 C5
Lindens The 4 BN2 ...189 C4
Lindfield BN41 ......141 A1
Lindfield Ave BN25 ...181 C2
Lindfield Cl BN2 ......177 B6
Lindfield Ct BN1 ......143 C2
Lindfield Dr BN27 ......152 B7
Lindfield Ent Pk RH16 ...51 C6
Lindfield Prim Sch RH16 51 A7
Lindfield Rd BN22 ...173 C1
Lindfield Sch The BN22 173 D2
Lindon Cl BN20 ......183 B1
Lindsay Cl BN20 ......184 C2
Lindfield Rd RH19 ......1 D3
Link Ho 2 TN6 ......25 F3
Link Rd BN20 ......184 D1
Link The East Dean BN20 183 C2
 Rye TN31 ......93 A5
Link Way TN1 ......8 E8
Linkden Cotts TN18 ...47 E5
Links Ave BN10 ......179 A7
Links Cl Crowborough TN6 ..25 D2
 Portslade-by-S BN41 ......162 C8
 Seaford BN25 ......181 A4
Links Dr TN40 ......157 E4
Links Rd
 Portslade-by-S BN41 ......162 C8
 Seaford BN25 ......181 A4
Links The
 6 Bexhill TN40 ......157 D3
 St Leonards TN38 ......158 F8
Links Way TN31 ......94 C2
Linkswood BN21 ......184 E2
Linkway Eastbourne BN20 184 B7
 Westham BN24 ......174 E6
Linkway The BN1 ......143 B1
Linley Cl Bexhill TN40 ..157 D4
 Hastings TN34 ......160 A4
Linley Dr TN34 ......160 A4
Linnet Cl BN23 ......174 C2
Linnet Gn TN22 ......78 D5
Linosa Ct 17 TN22 ...185 B3
Linthouse BN10 ......167 D2
Linton Cres TN34 ......159 E8
Linton Ct TN34 ......159 E8
Linton Rd Hastings TN34 159 E8
 Hove BN3 ......162 F8
Lion Hill BN23,BN24 ...174 B5
Lion Hill Cotts BN24 ..174 B5
Lion La BN2 ......185 B3
Lion Mews 4 Hove BN3 162 F7
 Uckfield TN22 ......78 D6
Lion St TN31 ......93 C5
Lionel Rd TN40 ......157 E4
Lions Ct BN2 ......164 E5
Lions Dene BN1 ......142 D4
Lions Gdns BN1 ......142 D2
Lions Pl BN25 ......180 F2
Liphook Cl BN1 ......143 C1
Lipscombe Rd TN2 ......8 D6
Liptraps La TN2 ......8 D7
Lismore Rd BN21 ......185 A2
Lister Ave RH19 ......10 F6
Lister Rd BN24 ......174 A1
Litlington Ct 4 BN25 ..180 C4
Little Bayham Cotts TN3 .18 F4
Little Bentswood RH16 ..50 F5
Little Bentswood Cl
 RH16 ......50 F5
Little Black Hill RH16 ...51 B7
Little Common Rd TN39 156 C5
Little Common Sch
 TN39 ......156 D4
Little Copse Rd BN6 ...97 E4
Little Cranfield TN33 ...1 D1
Little Cres BN2 ......177 B5
Little East St
 Brighton BN2 ......189 B1
 Lewes BN7 ......190 B2
Little Footway TN3 ......6 F1
Little George St BN2 ..189 B1
Little Horsted CE Prim Sch
 TN22 ......78 C1
Little Iridge Farm Cotts
 TN19 ......45 C1
Little King St RH19 ......1 E1
Little London Rd TN21 106 F8
Little Mallett TN3 ......6 F3
Little Mount Sion TN1 ...8 A2
Little Paddock
 Crowborough TN6 ......25 E1
 Heathfield TN21 ......82 A7
 Ringmer BN8 ......124 E6
Little Park Cotts TN33 112 C5
Little Pk TN5 ......29 E5
Little Preston St BN1 ..163 B1
Little Ridge Ave TN37 ..136 C5
Little Ridge Com Prim Sch
 TN36 ......136 C5
Little Sherwood Ind Pk
 TN36 ......116 D5
Little Sunnyside TN6 ...25 F1
Little Trogers La TN20 ..40 A4
Little Twitten TN39 ...156 C3
Little Western St 1
 BN1 ......163 B5

Littlemead
 Cooksbridge BN8 ......123 A7
 Nutley TN22 ......35 C3
Littlewood La TN22 ...56 C4
Littleworth Cl BN2 ...165 F7
Living World The ★
 BN25 ......181 F4
Livingstone Ho 5 BN3 163 B7
Livingstone Rd
 Burgess Hill RH15 ......72 F3
 Hove BN3 ......163 B7
Livingstone St BN2 ..164 D5
Lloyd Cl BN3 ......163 C8
Lloyd Rd BN3 ......163 C8
Lockhart Ct RH16 ......50 F2
Lockitt Way BN7 ......145 E5
Locks Cres BN41 ......141 B1
Locks Ct 10 BN42 ......161 E7
Locks Hill BN41 ......141 B1
Lockwood Cl BN2 ......165 E7
Lockwood Cres BN2 ..165 E7
Loder Pl BN1 ......142 F2
Loder Rd BN1 ......142 F2
Lodge Ave BN22 ......173 C1
Lodge Cl
 East Grinstead RH19 ......1 D1
 Lewes BN7 ......146 A8
 Portslade-by-S BN41 ......140 A8
Lodge Hill La BN6 ......98 C4
Lodge La Keymer BN6 ...98 C3
 Royal Tunbridge Wells TN3 ..16 A8
Lodge Rd TN35 ......160 C5
Lodge The Brighton BN2 189 C5
 14 Eastbourne BN21 ...185 A2
Lodsworth BN2 ......164 F7
Lodsworth Cl BN2 ......164 F7
Lomaria Ct TN2 ......8 C4
Lomas La TN18 ......47 F5
Lomond Ave BN1 ......143 B1
London Meed Com Prim Sch
 RH15 ......73 A1
London Rd Bexhill TN39 157 B5
 Brighton BN1 ......189 A4
 Brighton,Withdean BN1 142 D4
 Burgess Hill RH15 ......72 F3
 Crowborough TN6 ......25 E4
 Danehill RH17 ......34 A4
 East Grinstead RH19 ......1 C3
 East Hoathly BN8 ......105 A5
 Flimwell TN5 ......32 D3
 Forest Row RH18 ......11 E4
 Hailsham BN27 ......129 A2
 Hassocks BN6,RH15 ......97 E6
 Hurst Green TN19 ......45 A3
 John's Cross TN32,TN33 ..87 D3
 Maresfield TN22 ......55 B4
 Pyecombe BN1,BN45 ......119 C4
 Royal Tunbridge Wells TN4 ..8 A4
 Royal Tunbridge Wells,Mount Sion
 TN1 ......8 A2
 St Leonards TN37,TN38 ..159 C8
London Road (Brighton) Sta
 BN1 ......164 A8
London Terr BN1 ......189 B4
Loney Ct 1 BN43 ......161 C8
Long Ave TN40 ......158 A6
Long Barn Motor Mus ★
 TN21 ......80 F8
Long Beach Cl BN23 ..175 B1
Long Beach Mews BN23 175 B1
Long Beach View BN23 175 B1
Long Hos TN32 ......85 D5
Long La TN33 ......88 E1
Long Man of Wilmington
 The ★ BN26 ......171 E3
Long Meads TN3 ......7 B4
Long Park Cnr BN6 ......98 D2
Long Slip TN3 ......7 A3
Long Wlk RH16 ......51 B4
Longacre Cl TN37 ......136 C6
Longbury TN22 ......78 C5
Longfield Rd TN2 ......8 D8
Longhill Cl BN2 ......165 E4
Longhill High Sch BN2 165 E4
Longhill Rd BN2 ......165 E4
Longhurst RH15 ......73 D2
Longhurst Cotts BN8 ..75 D7
Longland Rd BN20 ...184 C4
Longley Ind Est BN1 ..189 B4
Longridge Ave BN2 ..177 D5
Longstone Rd BN21 ..185 A3
Longview TN21 ......82 A5
Longview Way TN2 ......8 D7
Lonsdale Gdns TN1 ......8 A3
Looes Barn Cl BN2 ...177 D7
Lookout The BN10 ......167 D3
Loose Farm Barns TN33 113 A2
Loose Farm Cotts TN33 113 A2
Lordine La TN32 ......66 B4
Lords La TN35 ......160 D7
Lords The BN25 ......180 E6
Lordsdale La TN6 ......37 E8
Lordswell La TN6 ......37 D8
Loriners Ct TN3 ......162 D7
Lorna Rd BN3 ......163 D7
Lorne Rd BN1 ......189 B5
Lorraine Ct 2 Hove BN3 163 E7
 11 Hove BN3 ......163 E7
Lorraine Rd BN9 ......179 D7
Lossenham La TN18 ...48 D3
Lottbridge Dro
 Eastbourne BN23 ......185 B7
 Eastbourne BN22 ......173 F1
Lottbridge Rdbt BN23 185 A8
Lovat Mead TN38 ......158 E6

Love La Eastbourne BN20 184 D3
 Mayfield TN20 ......39 F2
 Rye TN31 ......93 B6
Lovegrove Ct BN3 ......162 E8
Lovell Ct 1 BN21 ......184 D4
Lover's Wlk BN1 ......163 F8
Lover's Wlk Cotts BN1 163 F8
Lowdells Cl RH19 ......1 C4
Lowdells Dr RH19 ......1 D4
Lowdells La RH19 ......1 C3
Lower Bevendean Ave
 BN2 ......143 E1
Lower Chalvington Pl
 BN2 ......164 E5
Lower Church Rd RH15 ..72 F3
Lower Cross Cotts TN31 ..91 E2
Lower Dene RH19 ......2 A1
Lower Dr Seaford BN25 ..180 F5
 Southwick BN42 ......140 E1
Lower Glen Rd TN37 ..136 B4
Lower Green Rd
 Pembury TN2 ......9 D7
 Rusthall TN3,TN4 ......7 C6
Lower Hazelhurst TN5 ..31 A4
Lower High St TN5 ......30 A4
Lower Lake TN33 ......112 F1
Lower Market St 6
 BN3 ......163 D5
Lower Mere RH19 ......10 F8
Lower Park Rd TN34 ..136 E1
Lower Pl BN9 ......179 C7
Lower Platts TN5 ......31 A4
Lower Rd
 Eastbourne BN21 ......184 D4
 Forest Row RH18 ......11 F3
 Herstmonceux BN27 ......130 C3
Lower Rock Gdns BN2 189 C1
Lower Roedale Cotts
 BN1 ......143 B3
Lower Saxonbury TN6 ..25 F7
Lower South Rd TN37 136 C1
Lower Sq RH18 ......11 E3
Lower St East Dean BN20 187 B8
Lower Street TN33 ......133 B5
Lower Station Rd BN8 ..76 A6
Lower Village RH16 ......50 C4
Lower Waites La TN35 138 F4
Lowfield Rd RH16 ......50 F3
Lowlands Rd RH15 ......73 B5
Lowlands The BN27 ...129 A1
Lowther Cl BN23 ......174 C3
Lowther Rd BN1 ......143 A2
Loxdale (The Swedish Folk
 High Sch) BN41 ......141 B1
Loxfield Cl TN20 ......40 A2
Loxfield Gdns TN6 ......26 B1
Loxwood Cl Bexhill TN39 156 D5
 Eastbourne BN23 ......173 C1
Loyal Par BN1 ......142 C5
Lucas RH17 ......33 D5
Lucas Cl RH19 ......2 A1
Lucas Grange RH16 ...50 D5
Lucas Shadwell Way
 TN31 ......93 F2
Lucas Way RH16 ......50 D6
Lucastes Ave RH16 ...50 D6
Lucastes La RH16 ......50 C5
Lucastes Rd RH16 ......50 C5
Lucerne Cl BN41 ......141 B1
Lucerne Rd BN1 ......143 A1
Lucinda Way BN25 ...180 F6
Lucraft Rd BN1,BN2 ..144 A5
Lucy Way TN39 ......157 B6
Ludley Hill TN31 ......91 A4
Ludlow Rise BN2 ......144 A1
Ludpit La TN19,TN32 ...63 C9
Luke Lade Ct BN27 ...152 C7
Lulham TN10 ......167 B2
Lullington Ave BN3 ..162 F6
Lullington Cl
 Bexhill TN40 ......158 A6
 Eastbourne BN21 ......184 C7
 Seaford BN25 ......181 B2
Lullington Gdns TN37 136 C5
Lullington Ho 4 BN21 184 E4
Lullington Rd BN26 ..171 A3
Lunce's Hill RH16,RH17 ..73 F8
Lundy Wlk
 7 Eastbourne BN23 ..185 F8
 Hailsham BN27 ......129 A2
Lureland Ct BN10 ......178 C6
Lurgashall RH15 ......73 C1
Lushington La BN21 ..185 A2
Lushington Rd BN21 ..185 A2
Lustrells Cl BN2 ......177 B6
Lustrells Cres BN2 ...177 C6
Lustrells Rd BN2 ......177 B6
Lustrells Vale BN2 ...177 C6
Luther St BN2 ......164 C7
Luton Cl BN21 ......184 C6
Luxford Cl TN22 ......78 C7
Luxford Cotts TN6 ......38 A8
Luxford Dr TN6 ......38 A8
Luxford La TN6 ......38 A8
Luxford Rd
 Crowborough TN6 ......38 A8
 Lindfield RH16 ......51 B7
Luxford's La RH19 ......11 B6
Lychgates Cl TN40 ...157 D5
Lydd Cl BN23 ......174 D2
Lydd Rd TN31 ......94 F2
Lymden La TN5 ......43 A7
Lyminster Ave BN1 ...143 A5
Lynchet Cl BN1 ......143 C3
Lynchet Down BN1 ...143 C2

Lynchet Wlk BN1 ....143 C2
Lynchets Cres BN3 .....141 D3
Lynchets The TN7 .....190 C4
Lynden Ct **1** BN1 ......142 E2
Lyndhurst Ave TN34 ...160 A8
Lyndhurst Ct BN3 ......163 D7
Lyndhurst Rd BN3 ......163 D7
Lynholm Rd BN26 .....173 C6
Lynton Cl
  East Grinstead RH19 .....2 A2
  Hurstpierpoint BN6 ....97 B5
Lynton Park Ave RH4 ....2 A2
Lynton St BN2 ....164 C7
Lynwood TN3 ....15 C6
Lynwood Cl TN37 ......136 D5
Lynwood Rd BN2 ....177 C4
Lyon Cl BN3 ....163 D7
Lyoth La RH16 ....51 C4
Lyoth Villas RH16 .....51 C4
Lytham Ct TN38 ....158 F8

M

Mabb's Hill TN5 ....42 F7
Maberley Rd TN40 .....157 C6
Mackenzie Ho RH19 .....1 A4
Mackerel Hill TN31 .....68 F4
Mackerel's Rocks BN8 ..76 F3
Mackie Ave Brighton BN1 143 A7
  Keymer BN6 ....98 A5
Macmillan Dr BN21 ...184 C5
Macquarie Quay BN23 .185 G8
Madehurst Cl BN2 .....164 D5
Madeira Dr Brighton BN2 164 C4
  Hastings TN34 ....136 C3
Madeira Pk TN2 ....8 B2
Madeira Pl BN2 ....189 C1
Madeira Way BN23 ....185 F8
Mafeking Rd BN2 .....143 D1
Magdalen Cl BN23 ....174 C1
Magdalen Ct **6** TN40 .157 D4
Magdalen Rd
  Bexhill TN40 ....157 D4
  St Leonards TN37 .....159 D7
Magellan Way BN3 ....185 G7
Magna Ct TN40 ....157 B4
Magnolia Cl TN21 ......82 B5
Magnolia Dr BN22 ....173 D2
Magnolia Wlk BN22 ...173 D2
Magpie Cl Bexhill BN39 .156 C6
  St Leonards TN38 .....158 E8
Magpie Rd BN23 ......174 C3
Magreed La TN21 ......59 E2
Maidstone Rd TN2 ......9 E8
Main Rd
  Icklesham TN35,TN36 ..116 D5
  Westfield TN35 ....114 E4
Main St Iden TN31 .....70 B4
  Northiam TN31 ....67 B5
  Peasmarsh TN31 ....69 B2
Mainstone Rd **1** BN3 .162 F7
Maitland Ct TN34 .....136 E6
Major Cl BN1 ....143 B1
Major York's Rd TN4 ....7 F2
Malcolm Ct **6** BN21 ...184 F4
Malcolm Gdns BN26 ...173 A7
Malden Reach **6** BN23 .175 A1
Maldon Rd BN1 ....142 D2
Malines Ave BN10 ....178 B8
Malines Ave S BN10 ..178 A7
Mallard Cl BN22 ......184 F8
Mallard Dr TN22 ....78 E5
Mallard Pl RH19 ....10 F8
Mallett Cl **12** BN25 ...180 E2
Malling Cl BN7 ....190 B4
Malling Down BN7,BN8 .190 C4
Malling Hill BN7 ....190 C3
Malling House (Sussex Pol
  HQ) BN7 ....190 B4
Malling Ind Est BN7 ..190 B4
Malling St Lewes BN7 .190 C2
  Lewes BN7 ....190 C3
Mallory Rd BN3 ....142 C2
Malt House Trad Est
  BN43 ....161 B7
Malthouse Bsns Pk The
  TN31 ....69 C2
Malthouse Ct **14** BN2 .189 C2
Malthouse La
  Brighton BN2 ....189 C3
  Burgess Hill BN6,RH15 ..72 C2
  Burgess Hill RH15 ......72 D4
  Peasmarsh TN31 ....69 B2
  Peasmarsh TN31 ....69 D2
Malthouse Way BN7 ...123 A4
Maltings Barn The BN7 .190 C2
Maltings The
  Burgess Hill RH15 ......72 D4
  Peasmarsh TN31 ....69 B2
Malton Way TN2 ....8 F7
Malvern Cl BN22 .....173 E4
Malvern Ho **1** TN39 ...157 B3
Malvern St **12** BN3 ...163 B7
Malvern Way TN34 ....160 B8
Manaton Ct TN38 .....159 F8
Manchester Rd TN33 ..133 A6
Manchester St BN2 ...189 B1
Mandalay Ct BN1 .....142 D4
Manhattan Ct BN1 ....142 D4
Manhattan Gdns TN35 .160 D8
Manifold Rd BN22 ....185 B4
Mann St TN34 ....159 F8
Manning Cl RH19 ....1 D2
Manor Ave BN6 ....98 A5

Manor Cl Brighton BN2 .164 E5
  Broyle Side BN8 ......124 F7
  Burgess Hill RH15 ......73 D4
  Eastbourne BN20 .....173 B2
  Horam TN21 ....106 F7
  Icklesham TN36 ....116 F5
  Royal Tunbridge Wells TN4 ..7 E3
  Seaford BN25 ....181 B3
  Southwick BN42 ......162 A8
  Uckfield TN22 ....78 C8
Manor Cotts
  Lamberhurst TN3 ......20 B5
  Sedlescombe TN33 .....88 E1
Manor Cres BN2 ......164 E5
Manor Ct
  North Chailey BN8 .....75 D7
  Southwick BN42 ......162 A7
Manor Dr BN10 ....167 B1
Manor End TN22 ....78 C8
Manor Field Prim Sch
  RH15 ....73 C4
Manor Gdns BN2 .....164 E5
Manor Gn BN2 ....164 E5
Manor Hall Fst Sch
  BN42 ....161 F7
Manor Hall Mid Sch
  BN42 ....161 F8
Manor Hall Rd BN42 ..161 F8
Manor Hill BN2 ....164 E6
Manor House Ct TN22 .78 C8
Manor Paddock BN2 ..164 E4
Manor Park Cl BN27 ..129 A3
Manor Park Ct BN26 ..173 A6
Manor Park Rd BN27 ..129 A3
Manor Pk TN4 ....7 E3
Manor Pl BN2 ....164 E4
Manor Prim Sch TN22 .78 D8
Manor Rd Bexhill TN40 .157 D4
  Brighton BN2 ....164 E5
  Burgess Hill RH15 ......73 D3
  East Grinstead RH19 ....1 C2
  Eastbourne BN22 .....174 A2
  Hastings TN34 ....160 A5
  Horam TN21 ....106 F8
  Portslade-by-S BN41 ..141 B1
  Rusthall TN4 ....7 C4
  Seaford BN25 ....181 B3
Manor Rd N BN25 .....181 B3
Manor Terr BN7 ......190 A1
Manor The TN2 ....8 E5
Manor Way Brighton BN2 164 E5
  Crowborough TN6 .....37 E8
  Eastbourne BN20 .....184 B8
  Polegate BN26 ....173 B6
  Uckfield TN22 ....78 C8
Mansell Cl TN39 ......156 C4
Mansell Ct RH15 ....73 B3
Mansell Rd BN43 .....161 B8
Mansers La BN27 .....128 C3
Mansfield Rd BN3 ....162 E7
Mansion Cl RH15 ......73 D3
Manston Way TN34 ...136 C4
Mantell Cl BN1 ....123 C4
Mantell Ho **2** BN2 ...189 C2
Manton Ct BN23 .....185 D8
Manton Rd BN2 ....143 E1
Manvers Rd BN20 ....184 B3
Maple Ave TN39 ......156 C3
Maple Cl Bexhill TN39 .156 C3
  Burgess Hill RH15 ......73 B5
  Haywards Heath RH16 ..51 B3
  Maresfield TN22 ....55 A4
  Royal Tunbridge Wells TN2 ..8 A1
  Woodingdean BN2 ....165 E7
Maple Ct
  Burgess Hill RH15 ......72 D3
  Hailsham BN27 ....152 A8
  Royal Tunbridge Wells TN4 ..7 E4
Maple Dr
  Burgess Hill RH15 ......73 A5
  East Grinstead RH19 ....2 A1
Maple Gdns BN3 .....141 F1
Maple Hts TN37 ......136 B7
Maple Leaf Cl BN9 ...179 B7
Maple Rd
  Eastbourne BN23 .....185 D7
  Peacehaven BN10 ....178 F6
Maple Wlk TN39 ......156 C3
Maplehurst Cl TN37 ..136 B7
Maplehurst Dr TN37 ..136 C8
Maplehurst Rd
  Eastbourne BN22 .....173 D2
  Portslade-by-S BN41 ..141 A1
  St Leonards TN37 .....136 B7
Maplehurst Rise TN37 .136 B7
Mapleleaf Gdns BN26 .173 A8
Maples Cotts TN22 ....80 A6
Maples The BN8 ......124 E6
Maplewood **4** BN1 ..142 E3
Marbles Rd BN8 ....76 D7
Marchants Cl BN6 .....97 A6
Marchants Dr TN31 ....94 E2
Marchants Rd BN6 .....97 A6
Marchants Way RH15 ..72 F5
Marcia Cl BN20 ......184 A8
Marcus Gdns TN37 ...136 A5
Mardan Ct TN38 ......159 F7
Marden Cl BN2 ....144 E1
Marden Ct TN39 .....157 A3
Marden's Hill TN6 .....25 C5
Mare Bay Cl TN38 ....135 E7
Maresfield Dr BN24 ..175 E6
Maresfield Rd BN2 ...164 E5
Margaret Cl BN10 ....178 B7
Margaret St BN2 .....189 C1
Margery Rd BN3 .....162 D8
Marianne Ho TN35 ...160 B5

Marianne Pk TN35 ....160 B5
Marina Bexhill TN40 ..157 C3
  St Leonards TN38 .....159 B6
Marina Arc **7** TN40 ..157 C3
Marina Court Ave **4**
  TN40 ....157 C3
Marina Way BN2 .....164 F3
Marina Wlk BN23 ....185 E8
Marine Ave
  Beachlands BN24 .....175 F6
  Hove BN3 ....162 E6
Marine Cl
  Beachlands BN24 .....175 F6
  Saltdean BN2 ....177 B5
Marine Cotts TN31 .....94 E2
Marine Cres BN25 ....180 F2
Marine Ct
  Newhaven BN9 ....179 D6
  Rottingdean BN2 .....177 A5
  Seaford BN25 ....180 C3
  4 St Leonards TN38 .159 C6
  Telscombe Cliffs BN10 .177 F3
Marine Dr
  Rottingdean BN2 .....165 C2
  Saltdean BN2 ....177 B5
  Seaford BN25 ....180 B5
Marine Gdns BN2 ....189 C1
Marine Hts TN38 .....159 A6
Marine Par Brighton BN2 164 C4
  Eastbourne BN21,BN22 .185 B3
  Hastings TN34 ....160 A3
  Seaford BN25 ....180 C3
Marine Parade Rd **15**
  BN21 ....185 B3
Marine Pk TN38 ......158 F6
Marine Rd
  Eastbourne BN22 .....185 B3
  Pevensey Bay BN24 ...175 D5
Marine Sq BN2 ....164 C4
Marine Terr BN24 ....175 D5
Marine Terrace Mews **7**
  BN2 ....164 C4
Marine View
  3 Brighton BN2 .....189 C2
  Newhaven BN9 ....179 B6
Mariners Quay BN2 ..164 F3
Mariteau Ho TN36 ...117 E7
Marjoram Pl BN43 ...140 B1
Mark Cl BN25 ....181 C2
Mark Cross BN4 .....126 B2
Mark Cross CE Prim Sch
  TN6 ....28 A3
Mark La BN21 ....185 A2
Market La BN7 ....190 B2
Market Pas
  6 Hastings TN34 ....160 A3
  9 St Leonards TN38 .159 C6
Market Pl
  Burgess Hill RH15 ......73 A2
  Haywards Heath RH16 ..50 D6
  16 Royal Tunbridge Wells
  TN2 ....8 A2
Market Rd Battle TN33 .112 C5
  Rye TN31 ....93 C5
Market Sq Battle TN33 .112 D5
  1 Hailsham BN27 ...152 C7
  Hailsham BN27 ....152 C7
  Lewes BN7 ....190 B2
  17 Royal Tunbridge Wells
  TN2 ....8 A2
  Rye TN31 ....93 C5
Market Terr **8** TN38 .159 C6
Markland Way TN22 ...78 A7
Markly La
  Heathfield TN21 ....59 B2
  Rushlake Green TN21 ..83 C3
Markstakes Cnr BN8 ..75 E1
Markstakes La BN8 ....76 C2
Markwick Terr TN38 ..159 B8
Marlborough Cl
  Eastbourne BN23 .....174 D3
  Royal Tunbridge Wells TN4 ..7 E4
  St Leonards TN38 .....136 A1
Marlborough Ct
  Burgess Hill RH15 ......72 E3
  8 Eastbourne BN21 ..184 F3
  1 Hove BN3 ....163 C6
  Newhaven BN9 ....179 C7
Marlborough Dr RH15 .73 C2
Marlborough Ho **12**
  TN37 ....159 C7
Marlborough Mews
  BN1 ....189 A2
Marlborough Pl **6** BN1,
  BN2 ....189 B3
Marlborough St BN1 ..189 A2
Marle Ave RH15 ....73 A4
Marle Green Cotts
  TN21 ....107 B6
Marley Cl TN33 ......112 F4
Marley Gdns TN33 ...112 F4
Marley La TN33 ......113 B6
Marley Rd TN31 ....93 A6
Marley Rise TN33 ....112 F4
Marline Ave TN38 ....136 A4
Marlings The RH16 ....50 C3
Marlinspike The BN43 .161 A6
Marlow Ave BN22 ....185 B6
Marlow Ct Brighton BN2 164 F4
  5 Crowborough TN6 ..37 F8
Marlow Dr
  Haywards Heath RH16 ..51 C4
  St Leonards TN37 .....136 C5
Marlow Rd BN2 ......164 F4

Marlowes The TN40 ..157 E5
Marlpit Cl RH19 ....1 E4
Marlpit Gdns TN5 .....31 E1
Marlpit Rd RH19 ....21 A6
Marlpit The TN5 ....29 E5
Marlpits La TN33 .....133 A7
Marmion Rd BN3 .....162 F7
Marsden Cl BN10 ....178 A7
Marsden Rd BN23 ....174 E1
Marsh Ho **3** BN42 ..161 D7
Marsh Quarter La TN18 ..47 C3
Marshall Ct BN2 .....173 D1
Marshall La BN9 .....179 C7
Marshall Rd BN23 ...185 A8
Marshall Rdbt BN23 ..174 A1
Marshall Way BN3 ...141 F1
Marshalls Row BN1 ..189 B4
Marshfoot La BN27 ..152 D8
Marshlands La TN21 ..82 A7
Marshlands Prim Sch
  BN27 ....152 D8
Marston Ct **10** BN3 ..163 E7
Martello Beach Cvn Pk
  BN24 ....175 C3
Martello Cl TN31 ......93 B4
Martello Ct
  Newhaven BN9 ....168 D2
  Pevensey Bay BN24 ...175 C3
Martello Mews **21** BN25 180 E2
Martello Rd
  Eastbourne BN22 .....185 D6
  Seaford BN25 ....180 E2
Martens Field BN7 ...146 E1
Martha Gunn Rd BN2 .143 E1
Martin Ct BN22 ......173 D1
Martin Rd BN3 ....141 D1
Martineau La TN35 ..137 F5
Martingale Cl TN37 ..136 C5
Martinique Way BN23 .185 G7
Martins The BN10 ....167 B1
Martlet Ho Brighton BN1 .164 A8
  Saltdean BN2 ....177 D4
Martlet The BN3 .....142 D1
Martlets Bexhill TN40 .157 E5
  Eastbourne BN22 .....173 B3
Martlets Ct TN6 ....25 F1
Martlets The
  Broad Oak TN31 ....90 C4
  Burgess Hill RH15 ......73 A3
  Crowborough TN6 .....25 F1
  Hailsham BN27 ....152 A7
  Hastings TN34 ....136 E2
  Lewes BN7 ....190 B4
  South Chailey BN8 ....100 D7
Martletts The
  Burwash Common TN19 ..60 F3
  Ringmer BN8 ....124 E6
Martyn's Cl BN2 .....165 E4
Martyns Pl RH19 ......11 A8
Martyns Way TN38 ...158 A5
Marwick Ct TN38 ....159 B8
Mary Burfield Ct **3** TN21 82 A7
Mary Stanford Cl TN31 .94 A3
Maryan Ct BN27 .....152 B8
Maryland Rd TN2 ......8 D1
Marylands RH16 ......50 F5
Maskelyne Rd BN27 ..131 A1
Mason Cl RH19 ....1 E2
Mason Rd Rye TN31 ...93 A5
  Seaford BN25 ....180 F4
Matlock Rd Brighton BN1 142 D2
  Eastbourne BN20 .....188 E8
Matthew Ho **14** BN3 .163 A6
Maudlin Ct TN37 .....159 C8
Maunsell Ct RH16 ....50 F3
Maunsell Rd TN38 ...135 F5
Maurice Rd BN25 ....180 F1
Maxfield Cl BN20 ....184 B5
Maxfield La TN35 ....115 D2
May Ave BN25 ....181 B3
May Rd BN2 ....164 D7
May Tree Cl BN3 .....162 D8
May Tree Gdns TN40 .157 F6
May Tree Wlk BN3 ...141 E1
Maycroft Pl TN20 .....39 F2
Mayfair Cl BN26 .....172 F4
Mayfair Ct BN20 .....173 B1
Mayfair Mews TN40 ..157 C5
Mayfield Ave BN10 ..178 D6
Mayfield CE Prim Sch
  TN20 ....40 B3
Mayfield Cl BN1 .....142 F5
Mayfield Ct Bexhill TN39 .156 C4
  Broad Oak TN21 ....59 E1
  Burgess Hill RH15 ......73 B3
  Saltdean BN2 ....177 C6
Mayfield Flat TN21,TN22 .81 A8
Mayfield La Durgates TN5 .29 D4
  St Leonards TN38 .....135 D2
Mayfield Pk TN5 ....29 E5
Mayfield Pl BN22 ....185 A4
Mayfield Rd
  Mark Cross TN6 ....28 A2
  Rotherfield TN6 ....39 A7
  Royal Tunbridge Wells TN4 ..7 F4
Mayfield Way TN40 ...157 E5
Mayflower Ct
  Haywards Heath RH16 ..50 F4
  11 Shoreham-by-S BN43 .161 A6
Mayflower Rd RH16 ...50 F4
Mayflower Sq BN1 ...189 B4
Mayhew Way BN3 ....190 B3
Mayhouse Rd RH15 ..72 F1
Maynard's Green Com Prim
  Sch TN21 ....82 A2
Mayne Waye TN34 ...160 B8

Mayo Ct **5** BN2 .....164 B8
Mayo La TN39 ....157 A8
Mayo Rd BN2 ....164 B8
Mayo Rise TN39 .....157 A8
Maypole Cotts TN22 ..56 B8
Maypole Rd
  Ashurst Wood RH19 ....11 E6
  East Grinstead RH19 ....1 D2
Maytham Rd TN17 ....49 C7
Maytree Cotts BN8 ...100 C7
Mayvern Ct **5** TN6 ...25 F3
Mayview Cl TN21 .....59 E1
Maywood Ave BN22 ..173 E2
Maze Hill TN38 ......159 B7
Maze Hill Terr TN38 ..159 B7
Mcbechie Ho RH19 .....1 D3
McIndoe Rd RH19 ......1 D3
McMichaels Way TN19 .45 A3
McNair Ct BN3 ....162 E7
McWilliam Rd BN20 ..144 C1
Meachants Ct BN20 ..173 B2
Meachants La BN20 ..173 B2
Mead Sch The TN2 .....8 A1
Mead The TN39 ......156 D4
Meadow Bank TN33 ..112 F4
Meadow Cl
  Hailsham BN27 ....129 B1
  Hove BN3 ....142 B3
  Portslade-by-S BN41 ..141 B2
  Rottingdean BN2 .....165 F3
  Southwick BN42 .....162 A8
  St Leonards TN38 .....136 A4
Meadow Cres TN39 ..157 C7
Meadow Dr RH16 .....51 B6
Meadow Hill Rd **6** TN1 ..8 B3
Meadow Ho BN8 .....100 E7
Meadow La
  Burgess Hill RH15 ......72 F1
  Lindfield RH16 ....51 B6
  Sedlescombe TN33 .....88 D1
Meadow Par BN2 ....165 F3
Meadow Pl TN22 ......78 C8
Meadow Rd
  Groombridge TN3 .....15 C7
  Hailsham BN27 ....152 A6
  Royal Tunbridge Wells TN1 ..8 A4
  Rusthall TN4 ....7 C4
Meadow Rise TN21 ..106 F7
Meadow The TN2 ......9 E4
Meadow Vale BN2 ...165 E5
Meadow View
  Rotherfield TN6 ....39 B7
  Union Street TN5 ......32 A3
  Westfield TN35 ....114 E4
Meadow View Cotts
  TN19 ....45 A3
Meadow Way
  Fairlight Cove TN35 ..138 C4
  Heathfield TN21 ....82 A5
  Seaford BN25 ....181 B3
Meadowcroft Cl RH19 ..1 C2
Meadowlands Ave
  BN22 ....173 D1
Meadows BN6 ....97 F5
Meadows Rd BN22 ...173 B2
Meadows The
  Crowborough TN6 .....25 F2
  Hove BN3 ....141 C3
  Lewes BN7 ....190 C4
  St Leonards TN37 .....136 C5
Meadowside TN33 .....88 E1
Meadowside Cotts TN5 .31 F1
Meadowsweet Cl TN38 .135 C2
Meadowview
  Brighton BN2 ....143 A1
  Lower Street TN33 ....133 B5
Meads Ave Bexhill TN39 .156 C4
  Hove BN3 ....141 C3
Meads Brow BN20 ....188 D8
Meads Cl BN3 ....141 C3
Meads Ct BN20 ......184 E1
Meads Gate BN20 ....188 E8
Meads Prim Sch The
  RH19 ....10 E7
Meads Rd Bexhill TN39 .156 C4
  Eastbourne BN20 .....184 E1
  Seaford BN25 ....180 F3
Meads St BN20 ......188 E8
Meads The Brighton BN1 .143 D5
  Burgess Hill RH15 ......72 F3
  East Grinstead RH19 ..10 E7
  Royal Tunbridge Wells TN2 ..8 C2
Meadsway BN20 ......188 E8
Meadway Cres BN3 ..141 F2
Meadway Ct BN42 ...161 D8
Meadway The
  Brighton BN2 ....164 F5
  Shoreham-by-S BN43 .161 A6
Mealla Cl BN7 ....190 A4
Medina Dr BN24 .....174 D5
Medina Pl BN3 ....163 B6
Medina Terr Hove BN3 .163 B5
  St Leonards TN38 .....159 A6
Medina Villas BN3 ...163 B6
Medmerry Hill BN2 ..143 C5
Medway Crowborough TN6 .26 C1
  Hailsham BN27 ....129 A2
Medway Dr
  East Grinstead RH19 ..10 D3
  Forest Row RH18 .....12 A2
Medway La BN24 ....174 A5
Medway Rd TN1 ....8 B5
Medway View RH18 ...12 A2
Meeching Ct BN9 ....179 D7
Meeching Pl BN9 ....179 C7
Meeching Rd BN9 ...179 D7
Meeching Rise BN9 ..179 C7

Meeching Valley Prim Sch BN9 ...179 B7
Meeds Rd RH15 ...73 A2
Meeting House La BN1 ...189 B2
Megrims Hill TN18 ...47 A6
Melbourne Rd BN22 ...185 B4
Melbourne St BN2 ...164 C8
Melfort Rd TN6 ...25 D1
Melrose Ave BN41 ...141 A4
Melrose Cl Brighton BN1 ...143 C2
  Hailsham BN27 ...152 A8
Melrose Ho TN6 ...25 E1
Melvill La BN20 ...173 B1
Melville Rd BN3 ...163 E7
Mendip Ave BN23 ...174 D3
Mendip Gdns TN34 ...160 B7
Mendip Wlk TN2 ...8 D5
Menzies St BN38 ...136 B2
Meon Cl BN24 ...174 A5
Mercatoria TN38 ...159 C6
Mercer St TN1 ...8 B5
Mercers TN3 ...7 A3
Mercia Cl [1] TN40 ...157 C4
Mercread Rd BN25 ...180 F3
Meres La TN20 ...58 D7
Merevale BN1 ...143 B2
Merewood Ct BN21 ...184 E4
Mereworth Rd TN4 ...8 A6
Meridian Com Prim Sch BN10 ...167 C1
Meridian Ctr BN10 ...178 C8
Meridian Ind Est The BN10 ...178 C7
Meridian Rd BN7 ...123 E1
Meridian Way
  East Grinstead RH19 ...1 F3
  Peacehaven BN10 ...178 C7
Merivale TN35 ...137 A6
Merlin Cl BN3 ...163 D8
Merlin Ct BN27 ...152 E7
Merlin Way RH19 ...2 A3
Merlynn [12] BN21 ...185 A2
Mermaid Pas [3] TN31 ...93 B3
Mermaid St TN31 ...93 B5
Merrimac Ho [1] TN40 ...157 C4
Merrimede Ct TN38 ...159 A7
Merriments Gdns★ TN19 45 B5
Merriments La TN18, TN19 ...45 D5
Merrion Cl TN4 ...8 B7
Merrion Way TN4 ...8 B7
Merston Cl BN2 ...165 E6
Merton Ct
  [7] Bexhill TN40 ...157 E4
  Brighton BN2 ...165 A3
Meryon Ct TN31 ...93 C5
Metcalfe Ave BN9 ...179 B8
Metropole Ct
  [12] Brighton BN1 ...163 E5
  [11] Eastbourne BN22 ...185 B3
Mewetts Ct BN20 ...173 B3
Mews Rd TN38 ...159 C6
Mews The Brighton BN1 ...142 E2
  East Hoathly BN8 ...105 A5
  Pembury TN2 ...9 C6
  [5] Royal Tunbridge Wells TN1 ...8 B3
  Seaford BN25 ...181 B4
Meyners Cl BN3 ...141 C3
Michael Fields RH18 ...11 E2
Michael Hall Sch RH18 ...11 D1
Michel Cl BN20 ...183 C1
Michel Dene Cl BN20 ...183 C1
Michel Dene Rd BN20 ...183 C1
Michel Gr BN21 ...184 E4
Michelbourne Ct RH15 ...72 E1
Michele Cl [5] TN38 ...136 B1
Michelham Dr BN23 ...174 A4
Michelham Priory★ BN27 ...151 B7
Michelham Rd TN22 ...55 C1
Michelson Cl TN38 ...135 F4
Micklefield Way BN25 ...181 B3
Middle Cl TN33 ...86 B2
Middle Dr TN22 ...55 A6
Middle Farm Countryside Ctr★ BN8 ...148 F4
Middle Field TN2 ...9 E8
Middle Furlong BN25 ...180 F3
Middle La TN21 ...83 E3
Middle Rd
  Bells Yew Green TN3 ...18 A5
  Brighton BN1 ...142 E1
  Hastings TN34 ...160 D8
  Shoreham-by-S BN43 ...161 B7
Middle Row [1] RH19 ...10 E7
Middle St Brighton BN1 ...189 A2
  Falmer BN1 ...144 C6
  [9] Hastings TN34 ...159 F8
  Portslade-by-S BN41 ...162 B6
Middle Street Prim Sch BN1 ...189 A2
Middle Village RH16 ...50 C2
Middle Way
  Burgess Hill RH15 ...73 B3
  Lewes BN7 ...123 A4
Middle Wlk TN2 ...8 E8
Middleham Cl BN24 ...124 C4
Middleham Way BN23 ...174 C4
Middlesex Ct [4] BN22 ...185 A4
Middlesex Rd TN40 ...157 D3
Middleton Ave BN3 ...162 D6
Middleton Dr BN2 ...185 E7
Middleton Rise BN1 ...143 E5
Middleway TN31 ...131 B5
Midfields Cl RH15 ...73 B3
Midfields Dr RH15 ...73 B3

Midfields Wlk RH15 ...73 B4
Midhurst Rd BN22 ...173 F2
Midhurst Rise BN3 ...143 B6
Midhurst Wlk BN3 ...141 F4
Midway Rd BN2 ...165 C8
Midway The TN4 ...7 D2
Mighell St BN2 ...189 C2
Milchester Ho BN20 ...188 E8
Milcote Ave BN3 ...162 F8
Mildenhall Dr TN37 ...136 B3
Mildmay Cl BN8 ...124 D6
Mildmay Rd BN7 ...123 A1
Mile End Cotts BN1 ...142 E6
Mile Oak Cres BN42 ...140 F1
Mile Oak Gdns BN41 ...141 A1
Mile Oak Prim Sch BN41 ...140 F3
Mile Oak Rd
  Portslade-by-S BN41 ...140 F3
  Southwick BN42 ...140 F1
Miles Wlk BN3 ...163 B6
Milestones TN21 ...82 B8
Milfoil Dr BN30 ...174 B3
Military Rd TN30, TN31 ...70 F3
Mill Brooks BN8 ...100 D7
Mill Cl East Grinstead RH19 ...10 E7
  Friston BN20 ...183 A1
  Hastings TN35 ...160 E8
  Heathfield TN21 ...81 F7
  Polegate BN26 ...172 F4
  Portslade-by-S BN41 ...141 C1
  Ringmer BN8 ...124 E5
  South Chailey BN8 ...100 D7
  Staplecross TN32 ...65 E2
  Westfield TN35 ...114 E5
Mill Cnr TN31 ...67 A3
Mill Cotts RH19 ...10 E7
Mill Cres TN31 ...25 F3
Mill Dr Crowborough TN6 ...25 F3
  Hove BN3 ...142 A3
  Seaford BN25 ...181 A3
Mill Dro Seaford BN25 ...180 A5
  Uckfield TN22 ...78 C6
Mill Gap Rd BN21 ...184 F4
Mill Gdns Heathfield TN21 ...82 A5
  Ringmer BN8 ...124 D5
Mill Green Ind Est RH16 ...50 E6
Mill Green Rd RH16 ...50 E6
Mill Hill Cl RH16 ...50 E7
Mill Ho BN2 ...173 A7
Mill La Barcombe BN8 ...101 D2
  Clayton BN6, BN45 ...119 E2
  Crowborough TN6 ...25 E2
  Dormans Park RH7 ...1 F8
  East Hoathly BN8 ...105 A5
  Flackley Ash TN31 ...68 F3
  Goddards' Green BN6 ...72 A3
  Hastings TN35 ...137 E5
  Hellingly BN27 ...129 A6
  Hooe Common TN33 ...132 F2
  Mark Cross TN6 ...28 A3
  Portslade-by-S BN41 ...141 B1
  Punnett's Town TN21 ...83 D6
  Rodmell BN7 ...167 D8
  South Chailey BN8 ...100 D7
  Uckfield TN22 ...78 C6
  Westfield TN35 ...114 E5
Mill Mead BN8 ...124 E5
Mill Path BN8 ...124 E5
Mill Pk RH15 ...73 B3
Mill Race BN6 ...97 E8
Mill Rd Brighton BN1 ...142 C6
  Burgess Hill RH15 ...73 B3
  Eastbourne BN21 ...184 E6
  Hailsham BN27 ...152 D6
  Heathfield TN21 ...81 F7
  Lewes BN7 ...190 C4
  Portslade-by-S BN41 ...162 B7
  Ringmer BN8 ...124 D5
  Rye TN31 ...93 C7
  Winchelsea TN36 ...117 E8
Mill Rd Ind Est BN41 ...162 B7
Mill Rise Brighton BN1 ...142 C5
  Heathfield TN21 ...82 A8
  Robertsbridge TN32 ...64 A3
Mill Row BN1 ...189 A3
Mill St BN1 ...144 C7
Mill Stream Mdw RH16 ...50 D7
Mill View BN8 ...124 C4
Mill View Cl BN24 ...174 D6
Mill View Hospl BN3 ...141 E1
Mill View Rd TN39 ...157 B7
Mill Way
  East Grinstead RH19 ...10 E7
  Polegate BN26 ...172 E4
Mill Wood RH15 ...73 B3
Milland Rd TN40 ...157 E6
Milland Rd BN27 ...129 B1
Millbank RH15 ...73 B4
Millberg Rd BN25 ...181 C4
Millbrook Bsns Pk TN6 ...38 D8
Millbrook Cl TN21 ...107 A7
Millbrook Gdns BN20 ...184 B6
Millbrook Ind Est TN6 ...38 D8
Millbrook Rd TN6 ...26 A3
Millcroft BN1 ...142 C5
Millcroft Ave BN42 ...140 E1
Millcroft Gdns BN42 ...140 E1
Millcross Rd BN41 ...141 B1
Milldown Rd BN25 ...180 F3
Miller's Hill TN35 ...114 E6
Miller's Rd BN1 ...142 E1
Millers Rise BN27 ...152 A6
Millfield [2] Bexhill TN40 ...157 C4
  Ninfield TN33 ...133 A6
Millfield Cl Newick BN8 ...76 C7
  Seaford BN25 ...181 B4

Millfield Cotts [8] BN2 ...164 D4
Millfield Ct [3] TN40 ...157 C4
Millfield Rise TN40 ...157 C4
Millfields BN26 ...173 A7
Millfields Ct BN26 ...173 A7
Millham Cl TN39 ...156 F5
Millington Ct TN22 ...78 C6
Millrace The BN26 ...172 F4
Millstream Cl TN3 ...5 D2
Millstream Gdns BN26 ...172 F4
Millward Rd BN24 ...175 C3
Millwood Cl TN22 ...55 C4
Millwood La TN22 ...55 C4
Millwood Rd TN39 ...157 A8
Millyard Cres BN2 ...165 D7
Milner Flats BN2 ...189 C2
Milner Rd BN2 ...143 D1
Milnthorpe Gdns BN20 ...188 E8
Milnthorpe Rd
  Eastbourne BN20 ...188 E8
  Hove BN3 ...162 F8
Milton Cres
  East Grinstead RH19 ...10 C8
  Eastbourne BN21 ...184 C4
Milton Ct [6] RH16 ...50 D5
Milton Dr
  Royal Tunbridge Wells TN2 ...8 D7
  Southwick BN42 ...161 F8
Milton Rd Brighton BN2 ...189 C4
  Eastbourne BN21 ...184 C4
  Haywards Heath RH16 ...50 D6
Milton St BN24 ...174 B7
Milward Cres TN34 ...160 A4
Milward Ct [3] BN43 ...161 C8
Milward Rd TN34 ...160 A5
Mimosa BN2 ...173 A4
Mimosa Ct BN1 ...143 B3
Mimram Rd BN24 ...174 A5
Mindelheim Ave RH19 ...2 B2
Minnels The BN6 ...98 A3
Minsted Sq TN39 ...156 C2
Minster TN26 ...173 A7
Mint The TN31 ...93 B5
Mistley Cl TN40 ...158 A4
Mitchelldean BN10 ...167 C1
Mitre Ho [23] BN1 ...163 E5
Mitre Way TN33 ...112 E4
Mitten Rd TN40 ...157 C4
Moat Croft Ct BN21 ...184 E3
Moat Croft Rd BN21 ...184 E4
Moat Farm TN2 ...17 A7
Moat Ho BN21 ...184 E3
Moat La Cowden TN8 ...4 E7
  Waldron TN21 ...80 D2
  Westfield TN33 ...114 E3
Moat Lake Cotts TN21 ...80 F4
Moat Rd RH19 ...1 E2
Mocatta Way RH15 ...72 D5
Modena Rd BN3 ...162 F7
Moira House Sch BN20 ...188 D8
Mole Cl BN24 ...174 A5
Molesey Ct TN22 ...78 C7
Molesworth St BN3 ...162 F8
Molyneux Almshouses TN4 ...7 B4
Molyneux Ct TN4 ...7 B4
Molyneux Park Gdns TN4 ...7 F4
Molyneux Park Rd TN4 ...7 F4
Mona Rd BN22 ...185 B5
Monarch Gdns
  Eastbourne BN23 ...174 F1
  Seaford BN25 ...181 A5
  St Leonards TN37 ...136 A5
Monarch Ho BN2 ...185 E5
Monastery Gdns TN6 ...39 B8
Monceux Rd
  Eastbourne BN21 ...184 C4
  Herstmonceux BN27 ...130 E6
Monckton Way BN7 ...145 E5
Monger's Mead BN8 ...101 E4
Monk Cl BN1 ...143 E6
Monk's Ho★ BN7 ...146 E1
Monks La Lewes BN7 ...190 A1
  Newbury's TN5 ...30 B8
Monks Way Lewes BN7 ...190 A4
  Northiam TN31 ...67 B8
Monks' Wlk TN36 ...117 E7
Monson Rd TN1 ...8 B4
Monson Way [5] TN1 ...8 B4
Montacute Gdns TN7 ...2 F2
Montacute Rd
  Lewes BN7 ...146 A8
  Royal Tunbridge Wells TN2 ...8 A1
Montacute Way TN22 ...78 D8
Montague Cl BN43 ...161 D7
Montague Ct
  [6] Brighton BN2 ...164 C4
  [2] Shoreham-by-S BN43 ...161 D7
Montague Pl BN2 ...164 C4
Montague St [4] BN2 ...164 C4
Montague Way BN24 ...174 F5
Montana Cl TN38 ...135 E6
Montargis Way TN6 ...26 A1
Montefiore Rd BN3 ...163 E7
Monteith Cl TN3 ...7 A3
Monterey Cl TN39 ...156 E3
Monterey Ct BN1 ...142 E3
Monterey Gdns TN39 ...156 E3
Monterey Wharf [5] BN23 ...175 A1
Montes Hill RH16 ...51 F8
Monteswood La RH16, RH17 ...52 B8
Montford Cl BN43 ...161 D7
Montfort Cl BN24 ...174 F6
Montfort Rd BN24 ...174 F6
Montgomery Rd
  Hastings TN35 ...137 D5

Montgomery Rd continued
  Royal Tunbridge Wells TN4 ...8 B7
Montgomery St BN3 ...163 A7
Montgomery Terr [2] BN3 ...163 A7
Montpelier Cres BN1 ...163 E6
Montpelier Lodge [9] BN1 ...163 E6
Montpelier Pl BN1 ...163 E6
Montpelier Rd BN1 ...163 E6
Montpelier St BN1 ...163 E6
Montpelier Terr BN1 ...163 E6
Montpelier Villas BN1 ...163 E6
Montpellier Apartments [25] BN1 ...163 E6
Montreal Rd BN2 ...189 C3
Montserrat [2] TN39 ...157 A2
Monument View BN2 ...164 D6
Moon's La RH7, TN8 ...2 E1
Moonrise Way BN27 ...127 C3
Moons Hill TN33 ...133 B6
Moons Yd TN6 ...39 B8
Moor Hall Dr TN33 ...132 F6
Moor Hill TN18 ...45 F8
Moor La Ringmer BN8 ...125 B3
  Westfield TN35 ...114 E3
Moor Pl TN19 ...1 D1
Moor The TN18 ...45 F8
Moore Pk BN27 ...152 D7
Moore's La TN31 ...90 E8
Moorhen Cl TN38 ...158 E8
Moorhurst Rd TN35 ...135 F5
Moorings The
  Eastbourne BN20 ...188 E8
  Felbridge RH19 ...1 A3
  Lewes BN7 ...190 C2
  Shoreham-by-S BN43 ...161 C6
Moray Wlk BN27 ...129 A2
Morecambe Rd BN1 ...143 A6
Morehouse Farm Bsns Ctr RH17 ...74 A6
Morestead BN10 ...167 D1
Moreton Ct BN41 ...162 B8
Morgan Cl TN39 ...157 B8
Morgay Wood La TN35 ...115 E2
Morlais Pl TN36 ...118 B6
Morlais Ridge TN36 ...118 B6
Morland Dr TN3 ...20 B5
Morlands TN33 ...133 B5
Morley Cl BN7 ...146 B8
Morley Lodge BN2 ...189 C4
Morley St BN2 ...189 C3
Morningside Cl BN25 ...180 F4
Mornington Cres BN3 ...162 D7
Mornington Mans [4] BN3 ...162 D7
Morris Rd BN7 ...190 C2
Mortain Pk BN27 ...152 D7
Mortain Rd BN24 ...174 F6
Mortimer Gdns BN3 ...172 F4
Mortimer Mews BN3 ...163 A8
Mortimer Rd
  Eastbourne BN25 ...185 A6
  Hove BN3 ...162 F8
Morton Rd RH19 ...10 E7
Moscow Rd TN35 ...160 C7
Moss Ho BN21 ...184 F2
Motcombe Ct [9] TN40 ...157 D3
Motcombe Inf Sch BN21 ...184 C5
Motcombe La BN21 ...184 D4
Motcombe Rd BN21 ...184 D4
Motte Field TN7 ...13 E4
Mottins Hill TN6 ...38 D8
Moulsecoomb Prim Sch BN2 ...143 E3
Moulsecoomb Sta BN2 ...143 D2
Moulsecoomb Way BN2 ...143 F4
Mount Caburn Cres BN10 ...167 C2
Mount Cl BN9 ...179 F6
Mount Dr BN2 ...177 C6
Mount Edgcumbe Rd TN4 ...8 A3
Mount Ephraim TN4 ...8 A4
Mount Ephraim Ct TN4 ...8 A4
Mount Ephraim Rd TN1 ...7 F4
Mount Harry Rd BN1 ...123 A2
Mount Idol View TN39 ...157 A8
Mount Joy TN33 ...112 D5
Mount Pl BN7 ...190 A2
Mount Pleasant
  Blackboys TN22 ...80 A6
  Brighton BN2 ...189 C2
  Crowborough TN6 ...38 B7
  Durgates TN5 ...29 C5
  Lamberhurst TN3 ...19 E6
  Lewes BN7 ...190 A2
  Spithurst BN8 ...101 C5
  The Moor TN18 ...45 F8
  Uckfield TN22 ...78 C6
Mount Pleasant Ave [2] TN1 ...8 B3
Mount Pleasant Cres [2] TN34 ...136 F1
Mount Pleasant Ct TN34 ...160 A6
Mount Pleasant La BN20 ...20 F4
Mount Pleasant Rd
  Hastings TN34 ...160 A6
  Royal Tunbridge Wells TN1 ...8 A3
Mount Rd
  Eastbourne BN20 ...188 E8
  Hastings TN35 ...160 C6
  Newhaven BN9 ...179 F8
Mount Sion TN1 ...8 A1
Mount St Battle TN33 ...112 D5
  Lewes BN7 ...190 A1

Mount The
  Hailsham BN27 ...152 C6
  St Leonards TN38 ...159 B7
  Uckfield TN22 ...78 C8
Mount View Terr TN27 ...152 C6
Mount Zion Pl BN1 ...189 A3
Mountain Ash Cl BN27 ...152 A8
Mountbatten Cl TN37 ...137 D5
Mountbatten Ct BN3 ...162 E8
Mountbatten Dr BN23 ...185 F2
Mountfield & Whatlington CE Prim Sch TN32 ...87 D7
Mountfield Ct [4] TN1 ...8 B3
Mountfield Gdns TN1 ...8 B3
Mountfield La TN32 ...86 C8
Mountfield Rd
  Eastbourne BN22 ...173 E1
  Lewes BN7 ...190 B1
  Royal Tunbridge Wells TN1 ...8 B3
Mountfield Villas TN32 ...87 C5
Mountfields BN1 ...143 C2
Mountney Bridge Bsns Pk BN24 ...174 F4
Mountney Dr BN24 ...175 F2
Mountney Rd BN24 ...184 C4
Mountreed TN20 ...58 B7
Mowden Sch BN3 ...142 D1
Moy Ave BN22 ...185 B5
Moyne Cl BN3 ...141 E1
Muddles Gn BN8 ...127 E7
Muirfield Cl [16] RH16 ...50 E4
Muirfield Rise TN38 ...158 F8
Mulberry Cl Bexhill TN39 ...156 C4
  Brighton BN1 ...142 E3
  Eastbourne BN22 ...173 E3
  Shoreham-by-S BN43 ...140 D1
Mulberry Ct BN26 ...173 A6
Mulberry La BN6 ...98 D3
Mulberry Pk TN22 ...55 B5
Mulberry Way TN37 ...82 B5
Mulberry Wlk TN37 ...136 D5
Mullany Bsns Pk BN27 ...127 B4
Munns Dr RH15 ...73 B4
Munster Cotts BN8 ...101 E4
Munster Gn BN8 ...101 E4
Murray Ave BN9 ...179 B8
Museum of Local History★ TN33 ...112 D4
Museum of Rural Life★ TN32 ...64 D2
Museum of Shops★ BN21 ...185 A2
Musgrave Ave RH19 ...10 E8
Mushroom Field BN7 ...145 E5
Muskerry Ct TN4 ...7 B4
Muster Ct RH16 ...50 D4
Muster Gn N RH16 ...50 D4
Muster Gn S RH16 ...50 D4
Mutton Hall Hill TN21 ...82 B8
Mutton Hall La TN21 ...82 B8
Mutton Hill RH7 ...2 B7
Myrtle Cotts [3] TN6 ...25 F3
Myrtle Rd
  Crowborough TN6 ...25 F3
  Eastbourne BN22 ...185 D6

N

Namrik Mews BN3 ...163 A6
Nan Kemp's Grave BN7 ...145 E6
Nan Tucks La TN22 ...56 C2
Nanson Rd BN1 ...143 D6
Naomi Cl BN20 ...184 C1
Napier Ho [3] BN2 ...164 C7
Napier Rd
  Royal Tunbridge Wells TN2 ...8 D2
  St Leonards TN38 ...135 E4
Nash Cl RH17 ...52 B4
Natal Rd BN2 ...143 D1
Neale Cl RH19 ...1 B3
Neath Rd TN31 ...96 A2
Neaves La BN8 ...125 A5
Neill's Cl BN9 ...179 C7
Neills Rd TN3 ...19 C2
Nelson Dr BN23 ...185 E6
Nelson Ho TN39 ...156 E4
Nelson Pl [17] BN2 ...189 C3
Nelson Rd Hastings TN34 ...160 A5
  Royal Tunbridge Wells TN2 ...8 D2
Nelson Row BN2 ...189 C2
Neptune Ct BN2 ...164 F3
Nesbitt Rd BN2 ...143 D1
Nestor Ct BN1 ...163 E8
Nether La TN22 ...35 C3
Netherfield CE Prim Sch TN33 ...86 C2
Netherfield Gn BN2 ...165 F8
Netherfield Hill TN33 ...112 C7
Netherfield Hill Cotts TN33 ...112 B7
Netherfield Rd TN33 ...111 F8
Netherfield Way TN33 ...86 D2
Netherwood Cl TN34 ...136 F5
Nettleton Ct BN1 ...143 B1
Nevill Ave
  Eastbourne BN22 ...173 E1
  Hove BN3 ...141 F1
Nevill Cl Crowborough TN6 ...37 C8
  Hove BN3 ...142 A2
Nevill Cotts BN6 ...98 D2

Nevill Cres BN7 ....123 A1
Nevill Ct Crowborough TN6 .37 C8
Hove BN3 ....142 A1
Nevill Gate TN2 ....8 B1
Nevill Gdns BN3 ....142 A2
Nevill Gn TN22 ....55 D1
Nevill Lodge TN2 ....8 C4
Nevill Pk TN4 ....7 E3
Nevill Pl BN3 ....142 A1
Nevill Rd Crowborough TN6 .25 F3
Hove BN3 ....142 A2
Lewes BN7 ....123 A2
Rottingdean BN2 ....165 F1
Uckfield TN22 ....55 D1
Nevill Ridge TN4 ....7 D3
Nevill St TN2 ....8 A2
Nevill Terr
7 Crowborough TN6 .....25 F3
1 Lewes BN7 ....123 A1
Royal Tunbridge Wells TN2 ..7 F2
Nevill Way BN3 ....142 A2
Neville Rd
3 Eastbourne BN22 .....185 B4
Peacehaven BN10 ......178 D6
New Barn Cl
Hailsham BN27 ....152 C6
Portslade-by-S BN41 ...141 B2
Shoreham-by-S BN43 ...140 B1
New Barn La TN22 ....78 C5
New Barn Rd
Rottingdean BN2 ....165 F3
Shoreham-by-S BN43 ...140 B1
New Church Rd BN3 .....162 E7
New Coastguards Cotts 6
BN25 ....180 C4
New College Cl BN23 ...174 C4
New Cotts
Crowborough TN6 ......38 C8
Eastbourne BN20 ......188 D8
Poundford TN20 ....58 B6
Scaynes Hill RH17 ......51 F1
The Moor TN18 ....45 B7
New Cut Mountfield TN32 .87 C5
Westfield TN35 ....114 E4
New Dorset St BN1 .....189 A3
New England Ho BN1 ...189 B4
New England La
Rye TN31 ....93 C8
Sedlescombe TN33 .....113 F6
New England Rd
Brighton BN1 ....189 A4
Haywards Heath RH16 ...50 F4
Royal Tunbridge Wells TN4 ..8 A7
New England Rise BN41 141 A4
New England St BN1 ....189 B4
New Farthingdale RH7 ....2 A8
New Horizons Sch
TN38 ....136 A4
New Langney Ct BN23 ..174 E1
New Lydd Rd TN31 ......94 E2
New Moorsite TN35 .....114 F3
New Park Ave TN40 ....157 C4
New Pl Eastbourne BN21 .184 D3
Uckfield TN22 ....78 C5
New Pond Hill TN21 .....81 D6
New Rd Brighton BN2 ...189 B2
Crowborough TN6 ......25 F3
Eastbourne BN22 .....185 B4
Fairlight TN35 ....138 D4
Hailsham BN27 ....129 C4
Hastings TN35 ....160 D6
Keymer BN6 ....98 B2
Lewes BN7 ....190 A2
Mill Corner TN31 ....67 B3
Newhaven BN9 ....168 D1
Polegate BN26 ....173 B6
Ringmer BN8 ....124 D3
Rotherfield TN6 ....39 C8
Rye TN31 ....93 D6
Saint's Hill TN11 ....6 A8
Uckfield TN22 ....78 D3
New Steine BN2 ....189 C1
New Steine Mews BN2 .189 C2
New Upperton Rd 7
BN21 ....184 E4
New Way La BN6 ....97 B2
New Winchelsea Rd
TN31,TN36 ....93 B3
Newark Pl BN2 ....189 C3
Newbury Cotts TN5 .....30 B8
Newbury La TN5 ....30 C8
Newcomen Rd TN4 ......8 A5
Newdigate Ho 2 TN40 .157 E4
Newells Cl BN2 ....144 E1
Newfield La BN9 ....179 C7
Newfield Rd BN9 ......179 C7
Newgate Rd TN37 .....136 C1
Newhaven Fort* BN9 .179 D5
Newhaven Harbour Sta
BN9 ....179 D6
Newhaven Hts BN9 ....179 C7
Newhaven Local & Maritime
Mus* BN9 ....168 D1
Newhaven Rd BN25 ....180 B5
Newhaven Sq BN9 .....179 D7
Newhaven St BN2 .....189 C3
Newhaven Town Sta
BN9 ....179 D8
Newhaven Wlk TN38 ..136 A3
Newick CE Prim Sch
BN8 ....76 C6
Newick Cl BN25 ....181 C2
Newick Dr BN8 ....76 C7
Newick Hill BN8 ....76 C8
Newick House Sch RH15 .73 C1

Newick La TN20,TN21 ....59 C5
Newick Rd Brighton BN1 .143 E4
Eastbourne BN20 .....184 C6
Newington Ct TN5 ......31 E1
Newlands TN3 ....7 A3
Newlands Ave TN39 ...157 B5
Newlands Cl
Hastings TN34 ....136 E5
Keymer BN6 ....98 B3
Newlands Cres RH19 .....1 D2
Newlands Manor Sch
BN25 ....181 A4
Newlands Park Way BN8 76 C7
Newlands Pl RH18 ......11 F3
Newlands Rd
Rottingdean BN2 ......177 A5
Royal Tunbridge Wells TN4 ..8 B7
Newlands Rise TN4 ......8 A6
Newlands Sch BN25 ...181 B4
Newlands Way TN4 ......8 B7
Newlyn Ct 14 TN40 ....157 D3
Newmans Way TN35 ...160 D8
Newmarket Rd BN2 ....164 C8
Newmarket Terr 12
BN2 ....164 C8
Newnham Rd TN21 .....82 A6
Newnham Way TN21 ...82 A7
Newport Rd RH15 ......72 F5
Newport St BN2 ....189 C4
Newstead 5 BN1 ......189 A4
Newtimber Dr BN41 ...141 A1
Newton Ave RH19 .....10 F6
Newton Cl RH16 ....51 B7
Newton Ct RH16 ....50 E5
Newton Pk BN27 ......152 D7
Newton Rd Lewes BN7 .123 B2
Lindfield RH16 ....51 C7
Peacehaven BN10 .....178 C7
Royal Tunbridge Wells TN1 ..8 B4
Newton Willows TN3 ....15 C7
Newton's Hill TN7 ......13 D3
Newtown Rd BN3 ......163 B8
Newts Way TN38 ......135 E1
Nicholson Ct BN23 ....174 E1
Nicolson Dr BN43 .....161 A8
Nightingale Cl
East Grinstead RH19 ...10 D7
Eastbourne BN23 .....174 C2
Haywards Heath RH16 ..50 F4
Nightingale Cotts TN35 114 D4
Nightingale La RH15 ...72 F1
Nightingale Rise TN22 .78 D4
Nightingales The
Royal Tunbridge Wells TN4 ..8 A5
Uckfield TN22 ....78 E5
Nile St BN1 ....189 B2
Ninfield CE Prim Sch
TN33 ....133 B5
Ninfield Pl BN2 ....164 E7
Ninfield Rd TN39 .....157 B7
Nizells Ave BN3 ....163 E4
Noahs Ark La RH16 ....51 C7
Noble Ct BN3 ....162 E7
Nodes La BN27 ....129 F4
Noel Gn RH15 ....73 B4
Noel Rise RH15 ....73 B4
Nolan Rd BN2 ....165 E7
Nook Cl TN35 ....160 D7
Nook The TN22 ....78 D4
Norbury Cl TN6 ....25 C4
Nore Rd BN9 ....179 B6
Norfolk Bldgs 5 BN1 .163 E5
Norfolk Cl TN39 ......157 B7
Norfolk Ct
4 Brighton BN1 ....163 E5
4 Eastbourne BN22 ...185 C4
Norfolk Dr TN38 ......135 F4
Norfolk Ho 2 TN37 ...159 C7
Norfolk Mews 6 BN1 .163 E5
Norfolk Pl 3 BN1 .....163 E5
Norfolk Rd Brighton BN1 163 E6
Royal Tunbridge Wells TN1 ..8 B2
Norfolk Sq BN1 ....163 E5
Norfolk St BN1 ....163 E5
Norfolk Terr BN1 .....163 E6
Norfolk Way TN22 .....78 C8
Norlington Ct BN8 ....124 D6
Norlington Fields BN8 .124 D6
Norlington La BN8 ....124 D7
Norman Cl Battle TN33 .112 F4
Seaford BN25 ....180 B6
Norman Ct 6 TN34 ...159 E7
Norman Rd
Burgess Hill RH15 .....73 A3
Hove BN3 ....162 E6
Newhaven BN9 ....179 C7
Pevensey Bay BN24 ...175 D4
Royal Tunbridge Wells TN1 ..8 B5
St Leonards TN37 ....159 C6
Normandale TN39 ....156 F3
Normandale Ho TN39 .156 F3
Normandy Cl 7 RH19 ..10 F8
Normandy Ct 2 TN39 .157 B3
Normandy Ho 3 TN39 163 C6
Normandy Rd TN34 ...136 C3
Normanhurst 10 BN2 .189 C3
Normans TN39 ....156 F3
Normans Gdns 6 RH19 1 E1
Normans' Bay Sta BN24 176 C8
Normansal Cl BN25 ...181 A6
Normansal Park Ave
BN25 ....181 A6
Normandland TN3 ......36 B2
Normanton St 8 BN2 .164 C7
Norstead Gdns TN4 ....8 A5
North Ave BN20 .....184 B5
North Bank BN6 ....97 E4
North Barnes La BN7 .100 A5

North Beeches Rd TN6 ..26 A2
North Camp La BN25 ..180 F5
North Cl Polegate BN26 .173 B7
Portslade-by-S BN41 ..141 A4
North Common Rd BN8,
RH17 ....74 E5
North Crescent Ind Est
BN27 ....152 A7
North Ct Hassocks BN6 .97 E4
Lewes BN7 ....190 C2
North Dr Brighton BN2 .164 C6
Dormans Park RH19 .....2 B6
North End BN6 ....98 D4
North Farm Cotts BN41 141 A2
North Farm Rd TN2 ......8 C8
North Gdns BN1 ....189 A3
North Heath Cl BN27 ...129 C2
North La
Portslade-by-S BN41 ...141 A3
Three Oaks TN35 .....115 E5
North Pl BN1 ....189 B2
North Point 1 BN43 ...161 A6
North Quay Rd BN9 ...179 D8
North Rd Alfriston BN26 .170 F3
Bexhill TN39 ....157 C7
Bodle Street Green BN27 .109 C2
Brighton BN1 ....189 B3
Brighton,Preston BN1 ..142 E1
Haywards Heath RH16 ..51 A4
Pevensey Bay BN24 ...175 D5
Portslade-by-S BN41 ...141 A3
Ringmer BN8 ....124 D6
St Leonards TN37 ....136 C1
North Road Cotts BN8 .124 D6
North Row TN2 ....78 C8
North Salts TN31 ......93 C6
North St Alfriston BN26 .171 A3
Brighton BN1 ....189 B2
Cowden TN8 ....4 A6
Eastbourne BN21 .....185 B3
Hailsham BN27 ....152 B8
Hellingly BN27 ....129 A7
Lewes BN7 ....190 B3
Lower Horsebridge BN27 .107 A2
Lower Horsebridge BN27 .128 F4
Mayfield TN20 ....40 B3
Portslade-by-S BN41 ..162 C7
Punnett's Town TN21 ..83 D6
Roser's Cross TN21 ....80 F5
Rotherfield TN6 ....39 B8
Royal Tunbridge Wells TN2 .8 C3
St Leonards TN38 ....159 C7
Winchelsea TN36 .....117 E8
North St Quadrant BN1 189 A2
North Terr TN6 ....160 C6
North Trade Rd TN33 .112 B4
North Way Lewes BN7 .123 A2
Newhaven BN9 ....179 C8
Seaford BN25 ....180 F5
North-South Rd BN1 ..144 B7
Northampton Way 1
TN38 ....136 A4
Northbourne Rd BN22 .185 C6
Northbridge St TN32 ...64 B5
Northcliffe Cl BN25 ...180 F4
Northcote La BN10 ...167 A1
Northdown Cl BN9 ...179 C6
Northdown Rd BN9 ...179 B6
Northdown Terr RH19 ...1 D3
Northease Cl BN2 .....141 D2
Northease Dr BN3 ....141 E3
Northease Gdns BN3 .141 E3
Northease Wall BN7 ..146 D3
Northerlea BN41 ......141 A1
Northern Ave BN26 ..173 B7
Northfield BN26 ......172 F5
Northfield Cl BN25 ...180 F5
Northfield Cotts TN22 .102 D3
Northfield Rise
Hove BN3 ....141 D4
Rottingdean BN2 .....177 A4
Northfield Way BN1 ..143 A4
Northfields TN3 ....7 A8
Northfields Bsns Pk
BN27 ....128 A4
Northgate Cl BN1 ....165 F2
Northiam CE Prim Sch
TN31 ....67 B5
Northiam Rd
Broad Oak TN31 ......90 A6
Eastbourne BN20,BN21 .184 C4
Northiam Rise TN38 ..135 D2
Northiam Sta* TN31 ..48 C2
Northlands Ave RH16 ..51 B4
Northlands Cotts TN32 .46 C1
Northlands Wood Com Prim
Sch RH16 ....51 B4
Northridge TN31 ......67 A7
Northumberland Ct
BN22 ....174 A2
Northway RH15 ....73 C4
Northwood Ave BN2 .177 E5
Norton Cl BN3 ....163 B6
Norton Dr BN2 ....144 C3
Norton Rd Hove BN3 ..163 B6
Newhaven BN9 ....179 E7
Norton Terr BN2 .....179 E7
Norton Wall BN7 .....146 C4
Norway Rd BN22 .....185 D6
Norway St BN41 .....162 C7
Norwich Cl BN2 ......144 A2
Norwich Cres BN2 ...143 F2
Norwich Dr BN2 .....144 A2
Norwich House Rd BN1 144 B7
Norwood Rd TN4 ......7 D1
Nottidge Rd TN4 ......7 D1
Novington La BN7 ...100 A3

Nuffield Hospl TN2 .....8 C3
Nunnery La TN11 ......5 F8
Nunnery Stables 5
BN7 ....123 B1
Nursery Cl
Hailsham BN27 ....152 C6
Haywards Heath RH16 ..50 D5
Polegate BN26 ....173 B6
Portslade-by-S BN41 ..140 E4
Shoreham-by-S BN43 ..161 B8
Union Street TN5 .....32 B3
Nursery Field TN22 ....56 C4
Nursery La
Maresfield Park TN22 ..55 B7
Nutley TN22 ....35 C4
Uckfield TN22 ....78 D4
Waldron Down TN21,TN22 .80 E8
Windmill Hill BN27 ...131 B5
Nursery Path BN27 ...152 B6
Nursery Rd TN4 ....8 B8
Nursery The RH15 ....73 C4
Nursery Way TN21 ....81 E7
Nutbourne Cl BN23 ...174 E2
Nuthatch Rd BN23 ...174 C2
Nuthurst Cl BN2 .....164 F6
Nuthurst Pl BN2 .....164 F5
Nutley Ave BN2 ......177 D4
Nutley CE Prim Sch
TN22 ....35 C5
Nutley Cl Hove BN3 ..141 F3
Rye TN31 ....93 A6
Nutley Mill Rd BN24 ..174 B5
Nutley Windmill* TN22 .35 F1
Nye Cl Ditchling BN6 ..98 D1
Westmeston BN6 .....120 D8
Nye Rd RH15 ....73 C3
Nyetimber Hill BN2 ..143 E2
Nym Cl BN2 ....100 E7

O

Oak Ave BN27 ....127 C3
Oak Bank RH16 ......50 F7
Oak Cl BN1 ....142 E3
Oak Croft RH19 ......11 A8
Oak Field The TN35 ..116 F1
Oak Hall Pk RH15 ....73 B1
Oak Ho 3 TN2 ....8 C7
Oak Lodge TN2 ....8 D2
Oak Pas 8 TN34 .....160 A4
Oak Rd 3 Bexhill TN40 .157 C5
Royal Tunbridge Wells TN2 ..8 A1
Oak Terr TN31 ....67 B6
Oak Tree Cl
East Grinstead RH19 ...1 C3
Eastbourne BN23 ....174 C4
Royal Tunbridge Wells TN2 ..8 A1
Oak Tree Cotts
Burgess Hill RH15 .....73 B3
Danehill RH17 ....34 A4
Oak Tree Ct TN22 ....78 D8
Oak Tree La BN23 ...174 C4
Oak Tree Way BN27 .129 C2
Oakapple Rd BN42 ..140 E1
Oakdale Rd
Haywards Heath RH16 ..50 F3
Royal Tunbridge Wells TN4 ..7 F4
Oakdene Ave BN41 ...140 E3
Oakdene Cl BN41 ....140 E3
Oakdene Cres BN41 .140 E3
Oakdene Gdns BN41 .140 E3
Oakdene Rise BN41 ..140 E4
Oakdene Way BN41 ..140 E4
Oakdown Ct TN19 ....61 A4
Oakendene BN2 ......143 F4
Oakenfield RH15 .....73 A5
Oakfield Cl RH16 .....51 A7
Oakfield Court Rd TN2 .8 C3
Oakfield Rd TN35 ....160 C7
Oakfield The TN31 ....93 B8
Oakfield Way
Bexhill TN39 ....156 C6
East Grinstead RH19 ...1 F3
Oakhill Cotts TN31 ....68 C4
Oakhill Dr TN31 ......90 B5
Oakhurst RH16 ....50 D8
Oakhurst Cl TN34 ....136 E5
Oakhurst Dr TN6 .....26 A3
Oakhurst Gdns RH19 ...1 C2
Oakhurst La RH16 ....50 D8
Oakhurst Rd TN33 ...112 D7
Oakland Dr TN32 .....63 D4
Oakland Villas TN3 ...15 B7
Oaklands
Crowborough TN6 .....26 B1
6 Eastbourne BN23 ..185 A4
South Chailey BN8 ...100 C7
Westham BN24 ......174 D6
Oaklands Ave BN2 ...177 D5
Oaklands Cl BN26 ...173 B6
Oaklands Rd
Groombridge TN3 .....15 B6
Haywards Heath RH16 ..50 D5
Oaklands Way BN27 .152 A6
Oaklea Cl TN37 ......136 C5
Oaklea Cl TN7 ....13 D4
Oaklea Way TN22 ....78 C8
Oakleaf Ct BN26 .....173 A7
Oakleaf Dr BN26 .....173 A7
Oakleigh Dr TN31 ....82 B6
Oakleigh Rd TN39 ...156 C4
Oakley Cl RH15 ......11 B7
Oakley Cotts RH19 ...11 C5
Oakley Ct TN22 ......78 D6
Oakley Ho BN1 ......189 C2

Oakley Sch TN2 ....9 A5
Oakmead Rd RH15 ...72 F1
Oakmede Way BN8 ..124 D5
Oakmeeds Com Coll
RH15 ....73 A2
Oakroyd Cl RH15 ....73 D5
Oaks Cl TN19 ....63 B8
Oaks Forstal TN18 ...47 C5
Oaks The
Burgess Hill RH15 ....72 F4
East Grinstead RH19 ...11 B8
Haywards Heath RH16 ..51 A4
Haywards Heath RH16 ..51 C4
Heathfield TN21 ......82 B6
St Leonards TN37 ...136 D5
Oaktree BN8 ....101 E4
Oakwood Hill RH16 ...50 D4
Oakwood Ave TN39 ..157 B7
Oakwood Cl
Burgess Hill RH15 ....73 B2
Hastings TN34 ....136 F3
Oakwood Dr TN22 ....78 E8
Oakwood Pk
Forest Row RH18 .....11 F3
Nutley TN22 ....35 C4
Oakwood Rd
Burgess Hill RH15 ....73 B2
Haywards Heath RH16 ..50 D4
Oakwood Rise TN2 ....8 E7
Oakwood Sch BN22 .173 D3
Oast Cl TN2 ....8 D7
Oast House Dr TN31 ..92 F4
Oast House Field TN36 .116 F6
Oast House Rd TN36 .116 F5
Oasthouse Cl TN37 ..136 D5
Oathall Ave RH16 .....50 D6
Oathall Com Coll RH16 .50 D6
Oathall Rd RH16 .....50 E6
Oban Rd TN37 ....136 B3
Observatory Science Ctr
The* BN27 ....131 C1
Observatory View BN27 .152 D7
Ocean Bldg The BN1 .189 A3
Ocean Ct BN23 ......185 F7
Oceania 4 TN39 .....157 B3
Ochiltree Cl TN34 ...160 A8
Ochiltree Rd TN34 ...160 A8
Ocho Rios Mews 9
BN23 ....185 F8
Ockenden Way BN6 ..97 C3
Ockley Hill BN6,RH15 .98 B6
Ockley La
Burgess Hill RH15 .....98 B3
Keymer BN6 ....98 B4
Ockley Way BN6 .....98 B3
Ockling Piece BN21 ..184 D5
Ocklynge Ave 3 BN21 .184 D5
Ocklynge Cl BN39 ...156 C5
Ocklynge Ct 2 BN21 .184 D4
Ocklynge Jun Sch BN20 184 D4
Ocklynge Rd BN21 ...184 D4
Ockman La 1 TN31 ...93 C5
Octagon The BN2 ....164 F3
Offa Ct TN40 ....157 C4
Offa Rd TN35 ....160 D7
Offham Cl
Eastbourne BN23 .....173 F2
Seaford BN25 ....180 F5
Offham Ct 3 BN25 ..180 C4
Offham Rd BN7 ......123 B2
Offham Terr BN7 ....190 A2
Okehurst Rd BN21 ...184 C3
Old Barn Cl BN20 ...173 B1
Old Barn Ct RH16 ....50 C7
Old Barn Way BN42 .162 A7
Old Ben Homes BN25 .180 C4
Old Boat Cnr BN1 ...143 D8
Old Boat Wlk BN1 ...143 B7
Old Brickyard TN31 ..93 A5
Old Camp Rd BN20 ..184 C2
Old Church Rd TN38 .136 A4
Old Coastguard Cotts
BN9 ....179 D6
Old Coastguards TN35 .139 C7
Old Convent The RH19 ..1 E2
Old Court Cl BN1 ....142 F4
Old Dr BN26 ....172 F6
Old Dro BN23 ....174 C3
Old Farm Cl RH17 ....51 A2
Old Farm Rd
Bexhill TN39 ....157 B6
Brighton BN1 ....142 F5
Old Fire Station The 5
BN22 ....185 A3
Old Foord Cl BN8 ...100 D7
Old Forest La TN6 ....38 E8
Old Forewood La TN33 .134 F7
Old Forge La TN22 ....36 A1
Old Fort Rd BN43 ...161 B6
Old Gardens Cl TN2 ..17 B8
Old Ghyll Rd TN21 ....82 A5
Old Harbour Farm La
TN36 ....118 B5
Old Harrow Rd TN37 .136 B4
Old Heath Cl BN24 ..104 C6
Old Hop Garden The
TN31 ....69 C2
Old House Gdns TN34 .136 F4
Old House La
Langton Green TN3 .....6 D4
Uckfield TN22 ....78 E4
Old Humphrey Ave 1
TN34 ....160 B4
Old La
Crowborough,Poundfield
TN6 ....26 B1
Crowborough,St John's
TN6 ....25 D3

Old La *continued*
Mayfield TN20 . . . . .40 A2
Old London Rd
Brighton BN1 . . . . .142 E6
Hastings TN35 . . . . .160 C6
Old Lydd Rd TN35 . . . . . . .94 E2
Old Malling Way BN7 . .190 A4
Old Manor Cl TN40 . . . .157 D4
Old Mansion Cl BN20 . .184 A8
Old Market Cotts
 17 Hove BN3 . . . . .163 D5
 3 Seaford BN25 . . . . . . .180 E3
Old Mill Cl Brighton BN1 .142 E5
Hailsham BN27 . . . . .129 A3
Portslade-by-S BN41 . . . .162 A7
Old Mill Ct TN6 . . . . .25 E1
Old Mill La BN26 . . . . . . .172 F4
Old Mill Pk TN39 . . . . . . .157 A6
Old Mill Wlk TN33 . . . . .112 D5
Old Mint Ho★ BN24 . . . .175 B6
Old Motcombe Mews **11**
 BN21 . . . . .184 D4
Old Nursery Cl TN18 . . . .47 B5
Old Orch BN25 . . . . .181 B5
Old Orchard Pl BN27 . . .152 B7
Old Orchard Rd BN21 . .184 F2
Old Parish La BN2 . . . . .165 C8
Old Park RH17 . . . . .50 A6
Old Patcham Mews
 BN1 . . . . .142 E6
Old Place BN1 . . . . .165 F1
Old Rd East Grinstead RH19 . .1 F1
Magham Down BN27 . . . .130 A4
Old Rectory Gdns BN42 161 D8
Old Riding School The
 TN3 . . . . .15 B2
Old River Way TN36 . . . .118 B7
Old Roar Rd TN37 . . . . .136 C5
Old School Cl
 Polegate BN26 . . . . .173 A7
 Ringmer BN8 . . . . .124 C4
Old School Cotts BN7 . . .99 E5
Old School Ct RH16 . . . . .51 B5
Old School Fields TN22 .78 C5
Old School Ho BN27 . . . .131 B5
Old School Pl RH15 . . . . .72 F2
Old Shoreham Rd
 Portslade-by-S BN3,BN41 .162 C8
 Southwick BN42 . . . . . . .140 E1
Old Station Rd TN5 . . . . .29 E6
Old Steine BN1 . . . . .189 B2
Old Stone Link **2** RH19 . .10 E8
Old Swan Ct TN22 . . . . .152 D6
Old Timbers La TN22 . . . .78 C6
Old Top Rd TN35 . . . . . .160 D8
Old Town Hall Mus★
 TN34 . . . . .160 A4
Old Viaduct Ct **10** BN2 .164 C8
Old Wardsdown TN5 . . . .32 B3
Old Wickham La RH16 . . .50 E7
Old Willingdon Rd
 BN20 . . . . .183 B2
Old Wish Rd BN21 . . . . .184 F1
Old World Cotts TN31 . . .94 C3
Oldaker Rd BN8 . . . . .76 D7
Olde Place Mews BN2 . .165 F1
Oldfield Ave BN20 . . . . .173 A4
Oldfield Cres
 Hailsham BN27 . . . . .129 B1
 Southwick BN42 . . . . . . .161 E8
Oldfield Rd BN6 . . . . .98 A4
Oldlands Ave BN6 . . . . . . .98 A4
Oldlands Hall TN22 . . . . .36 D4
Oldlands Hill TN22 . . . . .36 C2
Olive Rd BN3 . . . . .162 D8
Oliver Cl Crowborough TN6 .26 A1
Hastings TN34 . . . . .159 E7
Oliver Ho **10** BN3 . . . . . .163 B5
Olivers Mews TN33 . . . . .112 E4
Olives Mdw TN22 . . . . . . .78 D7
Olivier Cl BN2 . . . . .164 C5
Onslow Rd BN1 . . . . .142 C2
Open Mkt The BN1 . . . . .189 B4
Orange Row BN1 . . . . . . .189 B2
Orchard Ave BN3 . . . . . .142 A1
Orchard Bsns Ctr TN2 . . .8 D8
Orchard Cl Fairwarp TN22 .36 B2
Hastings TN34 . . . . .136 F2
Haywards Heath RH16 . . . .50 D8
Royal Tunbridge Wells TN2 . .8 D6
Scaynes Hill RH17 . . . . . .51 F3
Southwick BN42 . . . . . . .161 F8
Orchard Cnr RH16 . . . . . .51 B5
Orchard Cotts TN6 . . . . . .39 B8
Orchard Gdns BN3 . . . . .142 B1
Orchard Gr TN2 . . . . .9 C7
Orchard Grange BN27 . .128 C3
Orchard La Ditchling BN6 . .97 F4
Hassocks BN6 . . . . .97 F3
Orchard Mews BN9 . . . . .168 E2
Orchard Par BN2 . . . . . . .173 A3
Orchard Rd Bexhill TN40 .157 C6
Burgess Hill RH15 . . . . . .72 E3
Hove BN3 . . . . .142 B1
Lewes BN7 . . . . .190 C3
Orchard Rise TN3 . . . . . .15 B7
Orchard The
 Broad Oak TN31 . . . . . . .90 B4
 Etchingham TN19 . . . . . . .44 C1
 Hassocks BN6 . . . . .97 F3
 Nutley TN22 . . . . .35 C4
 Shoreham-by-S BN43 . . . .140 C1
Orchard View Pk BN27 . .131 B6
Orchard Way
 Burgess Hill RH15 . . . . . .72 F3
 East Grinstead RH19 . . . . .1 E1
 Haywards Heath RH16 . . .50 D8
 Peasmarsh TN31 . . . . .69 C1

Orchard Way *continued*
 Sedlescombe TN33 . . . . . .88 E1
Orchards Sh Ctr RH16 . . .50 E4
Orchards The BN2 . . . . .143 E3
Orchid Cl BN23 . . . . .174 B3
Orchid Pk RH16 . . . . .51 C6
Orchid View BN1 . . . . . . .143 C6
Orchidhurst TN2 . . . . .8 D7
Ore Bsns Pk TN35 . . . . . .160 B6
Ore Pl TN34 . . . . .137 A5
Ore Sta TN34 . . . . .160 A6
Oriental Pl BN1 . . . . .163 E5
Orion Cl BN27 . . . . .152 D7
Orion Par BN6 . . . . .97 F3
Orkney Ct BN20 . . . . . . .184 B6
Orlando Ho BN1 . . . . . . .164 A8
Ormerod Ave TN38 . . . . .136 A4
Ormerod Ct RH16 . . . . . .50 E5
Orpen Rd BN3 . . . . .142 D1
Orwell BN24 . . . . .174 B5
Osbern Cl TN39 . . . . .156 C3
Osborne Ct TN34 . . . . . .136 E2
Osborne Ct
 Polegate BN26 . . . . .173 A7
 7 Shoreham-by-S BN43 .161 C8
Osborne Hill TN6 . . . . . . .38 C8
Osborne Rd
 Brighton BN1 . . . . .143 A2
 Crowborough TN6 . . . . . .38 C8
 Eastbourne BN20 . . . . . .184 B4
Osborne Villas BN3 . . . . .163 B6
Osmers Hill TN5 . . . . . . .29 F7
Osmond Gdns BN3 . . . . .163 E7
Osmond Rd BN3 . . . . . . .163 E7
Osmunda Bank RH19 . . . .1 E6
Osmunda Ct TN2 . . . . .8 C4
Osprey Dr TN22 . . . . .78 C5
Osprey Ho **18** BN1 . . . . .163 E5
Ospringe Pl TN2 . . . . .8 F6
Oswald Ct TN40 . . . . . . .157 D4
Otham Court La BN26 . . .173 B8
Otham Pk BN27 . . . . . . .152 D7
Otham Rd BN22 . . . . .174 A2
Ottafield Ct RH16 . . . . . .50 F6
Otteham Cl BN26 . . . . . .173 B6
Otterbourne Pl RH19 . . . .1 B1
Oulton Cl BN2 . . . . .165 D5
Our Lady of Lourdes RC Prim
 Sch BN2 . . . . .165 F1
Ousedale Cl BN7 . . . . . .123 B1
Outlook Ave BN10 . . . . . .178 F6
Outlook The BN20 . . . . . .183 A1
Oval Cl BN10 . . . . .167 C2
Over St BN1 . . . . .189 B3
Overdown Rise BN41 . . . .140 F4
Overhill BN42 . . . . .140 E1
Overhill Dr BN1 . . . . . . .142 E5
Overhill Gdns BN1 . . . . .142 E5
Overhill Way BN1 . . . . . .142 E6
Overton Shaw RH19 . . . . .1 E4
Ovingdean Cl BN2 . . . . . .165 D5
Ovingdean Hall Sch
 BN2 . . . . .165 D4
Ovingdean Rd BN2 . . . . .165 D5
Owen Cl RH15 . . . . .72 F1
Owl House Gdns★ TN3 . .19 E7
Owls Gdns TN5 . . . . .42 F5
Owlsbury Cross TN21 . . . .83 B5
Ox Lea TN3 . . . . .7 A3
Oxbottom Cl BN8 . . . . . . .76 B6
Oxenbridge La TN19 . . . . .63 C8
Oxenbridge Row TN19 . . .63 B8
Oxendean Gdns BN22 . . .173 B4
Oxford Ct BN1 . . . . .189 B4
Oxford Mews BN3 . . . . . .163 C7
Oxford Pl BN1 . . . . .189 B4
Oxford Rd
 8 Eastbourne BN22 . . . .185 B4
 St Leonards TN38 . . . . . .136 A3
Oxford St BN1 . . . . .189 B4
Oxford Terr **9** TN34 . . . .160 B4
Oxshott Ct **3** TN40 . . . .157 F4
Oyster Creek TN31 . . . . . .94 A3

P

Pacific Dr BN23 . . . . .175 B2
Pacific Heights N **11**
 BN23 . . . . .175 A1
Pacific Heights S **10**
 BN23 . . . . .175 A1
Packer Cl RH19 . . . . .2 A3
Packham Way RH15 . . . . .72 F4
Paddock Bexhill TN40 . . .157 D6
 Fordcombe TN3 . . . . .6 B5
Paddock Cotts BN24 . . . .175 A6
Paddock La BN41 . . . . . .140 F3
Paddock Field BN1 . . . . .144 B5
Paddock Gdns
 East Grinstead RH19 . . . . .10 E7
 Polegate BN26 . . . . .172 F4
Paddock La BN7 . . . . . . .190 A2
Paddock Rd Lewes BN7 . .190 A2
 St Leonards TN37 . . . . . .136 C5
Paddock Terr BN7 . . . . . .190 A2
Paddock The
 Eastbourne BN22 . . . . . .173 F2
 Hove BN3 . . . . .142 F1
 Maresfield TN22 . . . . .55 A4
 Northiam TN31 . . . . .67 B7
 Pembury TN2 . . . . .9 C6
 Walter's Green TN3 . . . . . .5 F5
Paddockhall Rd RH16 . . . .50 D5
Paddocks The Cowden TN8 . .4 B7
 Hailsham BN27 . . . . .129 A2
 Haywards Heath RH16 . . .50 C3
 Plumpton Green BN7 . . . . .99 E6

Paddocks The *continued*
 Rodmell BN7 . . . . .167 D8
Padgham Cnr TN21 . . . . .109 E8
Padgham La TN21 . . . . . .109 D8
Padua Ho BN2 . . . . .165 F8
Padua House Flats BN2 .165 F8
Pages Ave TN39 . . . . . . .156 F2
Pages Cl TN21 . . . . .81 E7
Pages Hill TN21 . . . . .81 E7
Pages La TN39 . . . . .156 E3
Pagets The BN8 . . . . .76 D7
Pagham Cl BN23 . . . . . . .174 B4
Pain's Flat RH15,RH17 . .72 D8
Paine's Cnr TN21 . . . . . . .60 C4
Paines Cotts TN31 . . . . . .94 A3
Palace Ct **11** TN34 . . . . . .159 E7
Palace Pier BN1 . . . . .189 B1
Palace Pl BN1 . . . . .189 B1
Palesgate La TN6 . . . . . . .26 C2
Palesgate Way BN20 . . . .184 B5
Palliser Rd BN23 . . . . . . .185 E6
Palm Ct **2** BN3 . . . . .163 D6
Palma Cl BN26 . . . . .173 A7
Palmeira Ave BN3 . . . . . .163 D6
Palmeira Avenue Mans **24**
 BN3 . . . . .163 C6
Palmeira Ct BN3 . . . . . . .163 C6
Palmeira Grande **9**
 BN3 . . . . .163 D6
Palmeira Ho **6** BN3 . . . . .163 D7
Palmeira Mans **21** BN3 .163 C6
Palmeira Pl BN3 . . . . . . .163 D7
Palmeira Sq BN3 . . . . . . .163 C6
Palmer Ho BN8 . . . . .100 C7
Palmers Row BN27 . . . . .152 B7
Palmerston Rd BN9 . . . . .168 F1
Palmyra Pl BN23 . . . . . . .185 G8
Panama Reach BN23 . . . .185 G8
Pangdean La BN6,RH15 . .72 C3
Pangdene Cl RH15 . . . . . .72 F1
Pankhurst Ave BN2 . . . . .164 D6
Pankhurst Cl TN39 . . . . . .157 A8
Pankhurst Rise TN39 . . . .157 A8
Pannel La TN35,TN36 . . .116 E2
Pannell Cl RH19 . . . . .1 D1
Pannett RH15 . . . . .72 E4
Pantiles The
 20 Royal Tunbridge Wells
 TN2 . . . . .8 A2
 ★ Royal Tunbridge Wells TN2 . .8 A2
Parade The
 Beachlands BN24 . . . . . .175 F6
 Brighton BN1 . . . . .142 B4
 Crowborough TN6 . . . . . .25 F3
 East Grinstead RH19 . . . . .1 B3
 Hove BN3 . . . . .141 E2
 Pevensey Bay BN24 . . . . .175 E5
Paradise Cl BN20 . . . . . .184 D2
Paradise Dr BN20 . . . . . .184 D2
Paradise Family L Pk★
 BN9 . . . . .168 D1
Paragon Cl BN20 . . . . . . .172 F3
Parham Cl BN2 . . . . .164 D5
Parham Ho **13** BN3 . . . . .163 D7
Park Apartments The
 BN1 . . . . .142 D4
Park Ave Bexhill TN39 . . .157 B8
 Eastbourne BN21,BN22 . .184 D7
 Hastings TN34 . . . . .136 D3
 Hove BN3 . . . . .162 E4
 Keymer BN6 . . . . .98 A2
 Shoreham-by-S BN43 . . . .161 A8
 Telscombe Cliffs BN10 . . .178 A8
Park Cl Brighton BN1 . . . .143 E5
 Burgess Hill RH15 . . . . . .72 F4
 Eastbourne BN20 . . . . . .184 D3
 Hailsham BN27 . . . . .152 D3
 Hastings TN34 . . . . .136 D3
 Hove BN3 . . . . .141 E3
 Hurstpierpoint BN6 . . . . . .97 A6
 Portslade-by-S BN41 . . . .141 B1
Park Cnr BN8 . . . . .104 F2
Park Cres Brighton BN2 . .189 C4
 Crowborough TN6 . . . . . .25 F3
 Forest Row RH18 . . . . . . .12 A2
 Hastings TN34 . . . . .136 D2
 Portslade-by-S BN41 . . . .162 A8
 Rottingdean BN2 . . . . . . .165 F1
Park Crescent Pl BN2 . . .189 C4
Park Crescent Rd BN2 . . .189 C4
Park Crescent Terr BN2 .189 C4
Park Croft BN26 . . . . .173 A5
Park Ct **11** Brighton BN2 .164 C6
 Brighton,Patcham BN1 . . .142 E6
 Brighton,Preston BN1 . . .142 F1
 Burgess Hill RH15 . . . . . .73 A3
 4 Haywards Heath RH16 . .50 E4
 Hove BN3 . . . . .163 D7
 Peacehaven BN10 . . . . . .178 B7
Park Dr TN34 . . . . .136 D2
Park Drive Cl BN9 . . . . . .168 F2
Park E RH16 . . . . .50 F2
Park Farm Bsns Pk RH17 74 B2
Park Farm Cl TN19 . . . . . .63 B6
Park Gate Brighton BN1 . .163 F8
 Hailsham BN27 . . . . .129 D3
 Hove BN3 . . . . .163 D6
Park Gates **16** BN21 . . . .185 A2
Park Hill BN2 . . . . .189 C2
Park La
 Ashurst Wood RH19 . . . . .11 D6
 Battle TN33 . . . . .112 D4
 Bexhill TN39 . . . . .157 A6
 6 Crowborough TN6 . . . .25 F3
 Eastbourne BN21 . . . . . .184 C8
 Laughton BN8 . . . . .126 C7
 Southwick BN42 . . . . . . .161 D7
 Whatlington TN32 . . . . . . .88 A5

Park Lodge
 10 Eastbourne BN21 . . .185 A2
 Hove BN3 . . . . .163 D8
Park Lodge Ct TN38 . . . .159 B7
Park Manor BN1 . . . . . . .142 D3
Park Mead Prim Sch
 BN27 . . . . .151 A7
Park Par TN6 . . . . .50 E4
Park Rd Bexhill TN39 . . . .157 B3
 Brighton BN1 . . . . .143 C6
 Burgess Hill RH15 . . . . . .73 A3
 Crowborough TN6 . . . . . .25 F3
 Dormans Park RH19 . . . . . .1 F6
 East Grinstead RH19 . . . . .1 C1
 Forest Row RH18 . . . . . . .12 A2
 Hailsham BN27 . . . . .129 B4
 Haywards Heath RH16 . . . .50 E4
 Heathfield TN21 . . . . .82 B7
 Heathfield TN21 . . . . .82 C5
 Lewes BN7 . . . . .190 A2
 Peacehaven BN10 . . . . . .178 F6
 Rottingdean BN2 . . . . . . .165 F1
 Royal Tunbridge Wells TN4 . .8 B5
 Seaford BN25 . . . . .180 D3
 Shoreham-by-S BN43 . . . .161 A8
Park Rise BN3 . . . . .141 E3
Park Road Terr **4** BN2 . .189 C2
Park Royal BN3 . . . . .163 C6
Park Shaw TN33 . . . . .88 E1
Park Sq BN2 . . . . .164 F3
Park St Brighton BN2 . . . .189 C2
 Falmer BN1 . . . . .144 C6
 Royal Tunbridge Wells TN2 . .8 C3
Park Terr BN21 . . . . .165 F1
Park The Crowborough TN6 .25 F4
 Rottingdean BN2 . . . . . . .177 A5
Park View Brighton BN2 . .164 C6
 Brighton,Preston BN1 . . .163 E8
 Buxted TN22 . . . . .56 C4
 Hastings TN34 . . . . .136 D2
 Haywards Heath RH16 . . . .50 E6
 Herstmonceux BN27 . . . .130 E5
 Northiam TN31 . . . . .67 A6
 Peasmarsh TN31 . . . . . . .69 B2
Park View Cl BN10 . . . . . .167 A1
Park View Rd Hove BN3 . .142 F1
 Westfield TN35 . . . . .114 E4
Park View Rise BN10 . . . .178 A8
Park View Terr BN1 . . . . .163 E8
Park Village BN1 . . . . . . .144 B8
Park Village The BN1 . . .144 A8
Park Villas TN21 . . . . .82 B6
Park W RH15 . . . . .50 F2
Park Way Hastings TN34 . .136 D3
 Southwick BN42 . . . . . . .161 F8
Park Way Cl BN42 . . . . . .161 F8
Park Wood Rd TN34 . . . . .136 F6
Parker Cl BN21 . . . . .184 E5
Parker Ct BN41 . . . . .141 B2
Parker Rd TN34 . . . . .160 A7
Parkfield Ave BN22 . . . . .173 E1
Parkfield Way RH15 . . . . .50 C3
Parkhurst Rd TN40 . . . . .157 C3
Parkland Inf Sch BN22 . .173 D1
Parkland Jun Sch BN22 .173 D1
Parklands Maresfield TN22 55 A5
 Royal Tunbridge Wells TN4 . .8 C8
 Shoreham-by-S BN43 . . . .161 C8
Parklands Rd BN6 . . . . . . .97 F3
Parkmead BN2 . . . . .189 C4
Parkmore Terr BN1 . . . . .189 A5
Parks The BN41 . . . . .141 B3
Parks Yd TN33 . . . . .112 D4
Parkside Burgess Hill RH15 72 F3
 East Grinstead RH19 . . . . .1 C1
 Heathfield TN21 . . . . .82 B6
 Keymer BN6 . . . . .98 A4
 Shoreham-by-S BN43 . . . .140 A4
Parkside Com Prim Sch
 TN21 . . . . .82 C5
Parkside Rd BN5 . . . . . . .180 F4
Parkstone Par TN34 . . . . .136 D4
Parkstone Rd TN34 . . . . .136 D4
Parkstone Terr TN34 . . . .136 D4
Parkview
 Hurstpierpoint BN6 . . . . . .97 A5
 Royal Tunbridge Wells TN2 . .8 D4
Parkview Rd TN22 . . . . . . .55 D1
Parkway BN20 . . . . .184 B8
Parkwood BN1 . . . . .70 B4
Parkwood Cl TN2 . . . . .8 C6
Parnell Ct **3** BN3 . . . . . . .163 B6
Parochial Terr BN2 . . . . .189 B2
Parrock La TN7 . . . . .12 C4
Parry Cl BN23 . . . . .174 E3
Parsonage Cl TN4 . . . . . . .7 B5
Parsonage La
 Icklesham TN36 . . . . .116 F6
 Lamberhurst TN3 . . . . . . .20 B6
 Westfield TN35 . . . . .114 C4
Parsonage Rd
 Eastbourne BN24 . . . . . .184 D4
 Rusthall TN4 . . . . .7 B5
Parsons Cl TN38 . . . . . . .135 F4
Partridges La TN5 . . . . . . .28 C5
Parve Ct TN40 . . . . .157 C4
Pashley Down Cty Inf Sch
 BN20 . . . . .184 B4
Pashley Manor Gdns★
 TN5 . . . . .44 B7
Pashley Rd BN20 . . . . . . .184 C2
Paston Ho BN1 . . . . .163 D6
Paston Pl BN2 . . . . .164 D4
Pasture Hill Rd RH16 . . . .50 D5
Patagonia Ho TN2 . . . . . . .8 C3
Patcham By-Pass BN1 . .142 E6
Patcham Grange BN1 . . .142 D6
Patcham High Sch BN1 .142 F6

Patcham House Special Sch
 BN1 . . . . .142 E6
Patcham Inf Sch BN1 . . .142 E6
Patcham Jun Sch BN1 . . .142 F6
Patcham Mill Rd BN24 . . .174 B5
Patchdean BN1 . . . . .142 E5
Patching Lodge **5** BN2 . .164 C5
Paton Rd TN39 . . . . .157 A8
Paul Cl BN27 . . . . .129 A3
Pavilion Bldgs BN1 . . . . .189 B2
Pavilion Cl BN6 . . . . .97 E5
Pavilion Ct **15** BN1 . . . . .163 E7
Pavilion Par BN2 . . . . . . .189 B2
Pavilion Rd BN1 . . . . . . .144 C7
Pavilion Ret Pk BN2 . . . .143 C1
Pavilion St BN2 . . . . .189 B2
Pavilion Way RH19 . . . . . .10 E8
Paxhill Pl TN38 . . . . .135 E4
Paygate Rd TN33 . . . . . . .113 E7
Payne Ave BN3 . . . . .162 F8
Payne Terr BN1 . . . . .143 B1
Paynsbridge Way TN21 .107 A7
Paynters Way BN8 . . . . . .76 C7
Paynton Rd TN37 . . . . . .136 B3
Paythorne Cl BN42 . . . . .140 D1
Payton Dr RH15 . . . . .72 F2
Payton Ho RH15 . . . . .73 D3
Peace Cl BN1 . . . . .143 C1
Peacehaven Com Sch
 BN10 . . . . .178 C8
Peacehaven Inf Sch
 BN10 . . . . .178 B7
Peacock Ind Est BN3 . . . .163 D7
Peacock La BN1 . . . . .142 E4
Peakdean Cl BN20 . . . . . .183 B2
Peakdean La BN20 . . . . . .183 B2
Pearl Ct **3** BN21 . . . . . . .185 A2
Pearse Pl TN3 . . . . .20 B5
Peartree Cl RH15 . . . . . . .72 E3
Peartree Field TN36 . . . .116 F6
Peartree Hill TN5 . . . . . . .42 E4
Peartree Rd TN39 . . . . . .156 D6
Peasmarsh CE Prim Sch
 TN31 . . . . .69 B1
Pebble Rd BN24 . . . . .175 C5
Pebsham Comm Prim Sch
 TN40 . . . . .158 A5
Pebsham Dr TN40 . . . . . .158 A6
Pebsham La TN38,TN40 . .158 A6
Peckham Cl BN7 . . . . .190 A4
Peel Rd BN2 . . . . .164 C4
Peelings La BN24 . . . . . .174 C6
Peelings Manor Barns
 BN24 . . . . .174 B6
Peeps La TN6 . . . . .39 A6
Pegasus Way RH19 . . . . . .2 B3
Pegwell Cl TN34 . . . . . . .136 E2
Pelham Arc **1** TN34 . . . . .160 A3
Pelham Cl
 Peacehaven BN10 . . . . . .167 D1
 Westham BN24 . . . . .174 F5
Pelham Cres
 Hailsham BN27 . . . . .152 C6
 Hastings TN34 . . . . .160 A3
Pelham Ct **4** BN25 . . . . . .180 E2
Pelham Pl TN34 . . . . .160 A3
Pelham Place Cotts
 RH16 . . . . .51 A7
 Seaford BN25 . . . . .180 E2
Pelham Rd Lindfield RH16 .51 A6
 Seaford BN25 . . . . .180 E2
Pelham Rise BN10 . . . . . .167 D1
Pelham Sq BN1 . . . . .189 B3
Pelham St Brighton BN1 . .189 B3
 Hastings TN34 . . . . .159 E3
Pelham Terr
 Brighton BN1 . . . . .143 C3
 Lewes BN7 . . . . .190 A3
Pelham Yd **7** BN25 . . . . .180 E2
Pell Cl TN5 . . . . .30 A6
Pellbrook Rd BN7 . . . . . .123 B3
Pellings Farm Cl TN6 . . . .26 B2
Pellings Rise TN6 . . . . . . .26 B3
Pells CE Prim Sch BN7 . .190 A3
Pelwood Rd TN31 . . . . . . .95 C3
Pembroke Ave BN3 . . . . .163 A7
Pembroke Cl BN27 . . . . . .129 C5
Pembroke Cres BN3 . . . . .163 A7
Pembroke Ct
 2 Hove BN3 . . . . .163 A6
 St Leonards TN37 . . . . . .159 C8
Pembroke Gdns BN3 . . . .163 A6
Pembroke Ho **6** BN21 . . .184 F3
Pembury Cl
 Haywards Heath RH16 . . . .51 B3
 Pembury TN2 . . . . .9 D7
Pembury Gr TN39 . . . . . .157 A7
Pembury Grange TN2 . . . .9 A6
Pembury Hospl TN2 . . . . . .9 B7
Pembury Rd
 Eastbourne BN23 . . . . . .174 D1
 Royal Tunbridge Wells TN2 . .8 E4
Pembury Sch TN2 . . . . . . .9 D8
Pendean RH15 . . . . .73 C1
Pendragon Ct BN3 . . . . . .163 A8
Pendrill Pl TN5 . . . . .29 F5
Penhale Rd BN22 . . . . . . .185 D5
Penhurst Cl
 Eastbourne BN24 . . . . . .174 A1
 St Leonards TN37 . . . . . .136 D5
Penhurst Dr TN40 . . . . . .158 A6
Penhurst La TN33 . . . . . .110 E6
Penhurst Pl BN2 . . . . . . .164 F6
Penland Ct TN34 . . . . . . .159 D6
Penland Ct **9** TN40 . . . . .157 E4
Penland Rd Bexhill TN40 .157 E5

Penland Rd continued
Haywards Heath RH16 ....50 D7
Penn Cres
Haywards Heath RH16 .....51 A5
Ringmer BN8 ....124 D5
Penn Yd TN2 ....9 C6
Pennett Ho RH16 ....50 D7
Pennine Rise TN34 ....160 B8
Pennine Way BN23 ....174 D3
Pennine Wlk TN2 ....8 D5
Pennington Ho RH16 .....51 A3
Penny La TN20 ......40 D5
Pennybridge La TN20 ....40 D5
Penrith Way BN23 .....174 C4
Penrose Ct 12 TN40 .....157 D3
Pensford Dr BN23 .....174 D3
Penshurst Rd TN11,TN3 ...6 E8
Penstock Terr TN1 ....93 F3
Penstone Ct 4 BN43 ...161 C8
Pentland Cl
Eastbourne BN23 ....174 E3
St Leonards TN37 ....136 C5
Pentlands BN26 ....183 C7
Pepper Dr RH15 ....72 F1
Pepper Hall Cotts RH17 .74 B5
Peppercombe Rd BN20 .184 B4
Pepys Wlk BN23 ....174 E3
Percival Cres BN22 .....173 F3
Percival Mans 20 BN2 ..164 C4
Percival Rd BN22 ....173 F3
Percival Terr 14 BN2 ...164 D4
Percy & Wagner Almshouses
5 BN2 ....189 C4
Percy Rd TN35 ....160 C7
Percy Terr TN4 ....8 A6
Peredur Ctr for the Arts
RH19 ....10 E6
Perrone Ct TN22 ....78 C7
Perry Ave RH19 ....1 E3
Perry Hill BN2 ....177 C7
Perryfields RH15 ....72 E4
Perryhill Cotts TN7 ......13 E8
Perryhill La TN7 ....13 E8
Perryman's La TN22 .....34 D3
Perrymans La TN22 .....36 F1
Perrymans's Cross TN31 ..92 B7
Perrymount Rd RH16 .....50 E5
Perth Cl BN25 ....181 C3
Perth Ct 4 BN21 ....185 A4
Perth Rd TN37 ....136 B3
Peter Gladwin Prim Sch
BN41 ....141 B2
Peter James Cl TN31 .....94 E2
Peter James La TN35 ...138 C6
Peterhouse TN40 ....157 D5
Petersfield TN2 ....9 E7
Petland Gdns RH16 ......50 F3
Petlands Rd RH16 ....50 E3
Pett Cl BN2 ....164 F6
Pett La TN36 ....117 A4
Pett Level Rd TN35 .....139 B7
Pett Rd TN35 ....138 C8
Petworth Dr RH15 ....73 A4
Petworth Ho 14 BN2 ....163 D7
Petworth Pl BN22 ....173 E2
Petworth Rd BN1 ....143 B6
Pevensey & Westham CE
Prim Sch BN24 ....175 A6
Pevensey & Westham Sta
BN24 ....174 F3
Pevensey Bay Rd BN23 .175 A2
Pevensey Bay Sta BN24 175 C6
Pevensey Castle ★
BN24 ....175 A6
Pevensey Cl
3 Bexhill TN39 ....157 B3
Pevensey Bay BN24 .....175 D4
Pevensey Park Rd BN24 174 F6
Pevensey Rd
7 Bexhill BN2 ....164 C8
Eastbourne BN21,BN22 ..185 B3
Newhaven BN9 ....179 B5
Polegate BN26 ....173 C6
St Leonards TN38 ....159 B7
Peverells The BN25 .....181 A5
Peyton Cl BN23 ....185 F7
Philip Cole Cl 16 TN34 ..160 B4
Philip Ct 8 BN1 ....163 C7
Phoenix Brewery Halls
BN2 ....189 C4
Phoenix Cl
Eastbourne BN23 ....185 G8
Hailsham BN27 ....152 E7
Phoenix Cres BN42 .....161 D8
Phoenix Cswy BN7 ......190 B2
Phoenix Ct 9 BN22 ....185 B3
Phoenix Dr BN23 ....175 A1
Phoenix Ho 10 TN6 ......25 F3
Phoenix Ind Est BN7 ...190 B2
Phoenix La RH19 ....11 E6
Phoenix Pl Brighton BN2 189 C3
Lewes BN7 ....190 B2
Phoenix Rise BN2 ......189 C3
Phoenix Way BN42 .....161 D8
Phyllis Ave BN10 ....178 B8
Piazza The BN23 ....185 F8
Picardy Cl TN33 ....112 E4
Picardy Rd BN23 ....185 E8
Piccadilly La TN20 ......40 C1
Pick Hill TN21 ....106 D4
Pickers Gn RH16 ....51 A8
Picketts La TN22 ....54 D8
Pickforde La TN5 ....31 D1
Picton St BN2 ....164 C7

Piddinghoe Ave BN10 ..178 D6
Piddinghoe Cl BN10 ....178 D7
Piddinghoe Mead BN9 ..168 B6
Pierpoint Mews 9
BN23 ....175 A1
Pilgrim Ct RH16 ....51 A5
Pilgrims Way TN34 .....136 F4
Pilmer Rd TN6 ....25 F4
Pilot Ho 1 BN2 ....189 C2
Pilot Rd TN34 ....160 B8
Piltdown Cl Bexhill TN39 .157 B4
Hastings TN34 ....136 E1
Piltdown Rd BN2 ......164 F6
Piltdown Rise TN22 ......78 D8
Piltdown Way BN22 ....174 A4
Pinders St TN35 ....160 D6
Pine Ave TN34 ....160 B8
Pine Ct BN25 ....180 F5
Pine Gr Crowborough TN6 .25 E2
East Grinstead RH19 ......1 B3
Pine Tree Cl
Hurstpierpoint BN6 ......97 B5
Newhaven BN9 ....179 C7
Pine Tree Rd TN21 ......82 A6
Pine Trees BN6 ....97 D4
Pine Trees Ct BN6 ......97 D4
Pine Way BN27 ....152 A7
Pine Way Cl RH19 ......10 E7
Pine Wlk TN22 ....78 D8
Pineham Copse RH16 ...50 F4
Pinehurst RH15 ....73 A1
Pinehurst Wlk TN34 ...160 B7
Pines The
2 Brighton BN2 ....189 C4
Hastings TN34 ....160 B7
Haywards Heath RH16 ...51 B4
Hove BN3 ....163 E6
Pinewood 5 BN1 ....142 E3
Pinewood Chase TN6 ...25 D3
Pinewood Cl
Brighton BN1 ....142 D2
Eastbourne BN22 ......173 D2
Seaford BN25 ....180 F4
Pinewood Ct RH16 ......50 D2
Pinewood Rd TN2 ....8 D5
Pinewood Way
Haywards Heath RH16 ...50 D2
St Leonards TN38 ......135 E3
Pinewoods TN39 ....156 E4
Pinewoods Ct TN39 ....156 E4
Pinfold 4 RH16 ....50 D6
Pinfold Cl BN2 ....165 E6
Pinton Hill TN5 ....31 B3
Pinwell Rd BN7 ....190 B1
Pipe Pas BN7 ....190 A2
Piper's Green TN2 ....78 D4
Pipers Cl Bexhill TN40 ..157 C5
Hove BN3 ....141 C3
Wadhurst TN5 ....30 A4
Pipers Field TN22 ....78 D4
Pipers Yd TN20 ....40 C3
Pipit Mdw TN22 ....78 D5
Pippin Cl BN27 ....131 B5
Pit La BN6 ....97 A5
Pitcairn Ave BN23 .....175 B2
Pitreavie Dr BN27 .....152 A8
Pitt Dr BN25 ....181 A5
Pitt Gdns BN2 ....165 D7
Place La BN25 ....180 E3
Plainfields Ave BN1 ....143 A7
Plaistow Cl BN2 ....164 F6
Plashett Park Gates
TN22 ....102 F5
Plat The TN31 ....67 B6
Platt The Dormansland RH7 ..2 A8
Frant TN3 ....17 B1
Haywards Heath RH16 ...51 B4
Plaw Hatch La RH18,RH19 21 E5
Playden Cl 1 BN2 ......164 E4
Playden Gdns TN34 ....160 B8
Playden La TN31 ....70 C3
Pleasant Row 25 TN34 ..160 B4
Pleasant View Cotts TN6 .25 E4
Pleasant View Rd TN6 ...25 F4
Plemont Gdns TN39 ....157 A6
Pleyden Rise TN39 .....155 F4
Plough La TN37 ....136 B5
Plover Cl BN23 ....174 C2
Plover Ct Hailsham BN27 152 D7
St Leonards TN38 ....135 E3
Plum Tree Cotts TN18 ...45 E8
Plumey Feather Cotts
TN3 ....14 E3
Plumpton Bostall BN6,
BN7 ....121 E6
Plumpton Cl
Bexhill TN40 ....157 C6
Eastbourne BN23 ......174 A4
Plumpton Coll BN6 ....121 D8
Plumpton Cross BN7 ....99 E3
Plumpton Crossways
BN7,BN8 ....74 F1
Plumpton La BN7 ....99 E3
Plumpton Prim Sch BN7 .99 F5
Plumpton Race Course
BN7 ....99 E4
Plumpton Rd BN2 ......164 D6
Plumpton Sta BN7 ......99 E5
Plymouth Ave BN2 .....143 F1
Plymouth Cl BN23 .....185 F8
Plynlimmon Rd TN34 ...160 A4
Pocock's Rd BN21 .....184 D5
Poels Ct RH19 ....1 E2
Polegate By-Pass BN26 172 F7
Polegate Prim Sch
BN26 ....173 A7
Polegate Sta BN26 .....173 A6

Polegate Windmill ★
BN26 ....173 A5
Polesden Rd TN2 ....8 D2
Polley Cl TN2 ....9 D7
Pollington Pl TN6 ....25 F2
Pomper La BN6 ....72 A2
Pond Cl TN31 ....90 B5
Pond Way RH19 ....2 B1
Pondcroft Rd RH16 .....51 B7
Pondside RH16 ....50 C3
Pondsyde Ct BN25 .....180 F4
Ponswood Rd TN38 ....136 B2
Pont Cl TN21 ....83 C6
Pook Reed Cl TN21 .....81 F6
Pook Reed La TN21 .....81 F6
Pool Pas BN1 ....189 B1
Pool Valley BN2 ....189 B1
Poona Rd TN1 ....8 B2
Popes Ct BN2 ....143 B1
Popes Row Cotts TN17 ..20 F2
Poplar Ave BN3 ....141 E3
Poplar Cl Bexhill TN39 ..157 A7
Brighton BN1 ....142 F2
Hove BN3 ....141 E3
Poplar Mews RH16 .....50 C2
Poplar Wlk BN22 ......173 D3
Poplars The BN6 ....98 A3
Poppinghole La TN32 ...87 E8
Popps La TN39 ....156 C3
Poppyfield TN31 ....70 C1
Port Hall Ave BN1 .....163 E8
Port Hall Mews BN1 ...163 E8
Port Hall Pl BN1 ....163 E8
Port Hall Rd BN1 ......163 E8
Port Hall St BN1 ....163 E8
Port Rd BN22 ....174 A1
Port View BN9 ....168 E2
Porters Way BN26 .....173 B6
Portfield Ave BN1 .....143 A6
Portfield Cl TN40 ......157 D5
Portland Ave BN3 ......162 E7
Portland Bsns Pk BN3 ..162 E8
Portland Cl TN21 ......129 A1
Portland Cotts 11 TN34 .159 F8
Portland Ho 5 RH19 ....10 F8
Portland La BN3 ....162 D7
Portland Mews 19 BN2 .164 C4
Portland Pl
18 Brighton BN2 ....164 C4
13 Hastings TN34 ......159 F8
Portland Rd
Burgess Hill RH15 ....72 F3
East Grinstead RH19 ....10 F8
Hove BN3 ....162 E7
Portland Road Trad Est
BN3 ....162 D8
Portland Sq TN21 ....82 D7
Portland St BN1 ....189 A2
Portland Terr
15 Hastings TN34 ......159 F8
Newhaven BN9 ....168 D2
Portland Villas
16 Hastings TN34 ......159 F8
Hove BN3 ....162 D7
Portlands The BN23 ....185 G7
Portsdown Way BN20 ..173 B3
Portside BN2 ....164 F3
Portslade Com Coll
Portslade-by-S BN41 ...140 F2
Portslade-by-S BN41 ...141 A1
Portslade Com Coll (Lower)
BN41 ....141 A3
Portslade Inf Sch BN41 .162 B8
Portslade Sta BN3 .....162 C8
Portsmouth La RH16 .....50 F8
Portsmouth Wood RH16 .50 F8
Portsmouth Wood Cl
RH16 ....50 F8
Portsmouth Wood Dr
RH16 ....50 F8
Posey Cotts TN31 ......131 B5
Possingworth Cl TN21 ...80 F7
Post Horn Cl RH18 ......12 B1
Post Horn La RH18 ......12 B2
Post Office Pas 10 TN34 160 A4
Post Office Sq TN1 ....8 A3
Potato La BN8 ....124 F5
Potman's La TN33,TN39 133 F4
Pottens Mill La TN21 ....59 F4
Potter's La BN7 ....190 A1
Potteries Cotts BN27 ...128 D3
Potteries The TN22 ......78 D4
Potters Field BN8 ......124 D6
Potters La RH15 ....72 F1
Pottery Cl TN31 ....90 A2
Pottery Cotts BN6 ......74 A1
Pottery La TN31 ....90 A2
Pottingfold Rd TN31 ....93 A6
Potts Marsh Ind Est
BN24 ....174 F4
Pouchlands Dr BN8 ....100 C7
Pound Cl BN23 ....185 F6
Pound Cnr BN8 ....101 D4
Pound Gate BN6 ....97 D3
Pound La Alfriston BN26 .171 A7
Framefield TN22 ....79 E7
Laughton BN8 ....126 C7
Pound The RH15 ....72 F4
Poundfield Farm TN6 ...26 B2
Poundfield Rd
Crowborough TN6 ....26 B2
Sandhurst TN18 ....47 B5
Poundsbridge Hill TN11,
TN3 ....6 D7
Poveys Cl RH15 ....72 D3
Powder Mill La TN4 ......8 B8
Powdermill Cl TN4 ....8 C8

Powdermill La
Battle TN33 ....112 C1
Goatham Green TN31,TN33 .89 D3
Powell Gdns BN9 ......168 D1
Powell Rd BN8 ....76 D7
Powis Gr BN1 ....189 A3
Powis Rd BN1 ....163 E6
Powis Sq BN1 ....163 E6
Powis Villas BN1 ......189 A3
Poynings Cl BN25 ......181 C2
Poynings Dr BN3 ......141 F3
Poynter Rd BN3 ....163 A8
Pratt's Folly La TN6 .....25 E1
Prescott Gdns RH15 ....73 A3
Preston Cir BN1 ....189 B4
Preston Dro BN1 ....142 F2
Preston Gr TN22 ....79 B6
Preston Grange BN1 ...142 E1
Preston Manor Mus ★
BN1 ....142 E1
Preston Park Ave BN1 .142 F1
Preston Park Sta BN1 ..142 D2
Preston Rd Bexhill TN39 157 B7
Brighton BN1 ....163 F8
Preston St BN1 ....163 E5
Preston Village Mews
BN1 ....142 E1
Prestonville Ct
2 Brighton BN1 ....163 E7
1 Brighton BN1 ....189 A4
Prestonville Rd BN1 ....189 A4
Pride View BN24 ......174 B5
Prideaux Ct BN21 .....184 E5
Prideaux Rd BN21 .....184 E5
Primrose Acre BN27 ...127 B3
Primrose Cl
Burgess Hill RH15 ......72 D4
Eastbourne BN23 ......174 B3
Primrose Hill
Bexhill TN39 ....156 F6
Fairlight Cove TN35 ....138 F5
Primrose La RH18 ....12 A1
Primrose Way BN27 ....127 B3
Prince Albert St BN1 ...189 B2
Prince Charles Cl BN42 141 A1
Prince Charles Rd BN7 .190 C4
Prince Edward's Rd
BN7 ....123 B1
Prince Of Wales Ct BN3 162 F6
Prince Regent's Cl BN2 164 E4
Prince Regent's Ct 2
BN2 ....164 E4
Prince William Par
BN7 ....185 F6
Prince's Cres BN2 .....189 C5
Prince's Ho BN1 ....189 B2
Prince's Pl BN1 ....189 B2
Prince's Rd Brighton BN2 164 B8
St Leonards TN37 ......159 D7
Prince's St Brighton BN2 189 B2
Royal Tunbridge Wells TN2 ..8 C3
Prince's Terr BN2 ......164 E4
Princes Ave BN3 ....163 A6
Princes Cl Seaford BN25 .180 E5
Uckfield TN22 ....78 A7
Princes Cres BN3 ......163 A6
Princes Ct 6 BN3 ......163 A6
Princes Field BN26 ....150 B3
Princes Rd BN23 ......185 E5
Princes Sq BN3 ....163 A6
Princess Dr BN25 ......180 D5
Princess Royal Hospl The
RH16,RH17 ....51 A2
Principal Cl TN39 ......155 F5
Prinkle La BN27 ....109 C1
Prinsep Rd BN3 ....163 A8
Prior's Way TN8 ....4 A6
Priory Ave TN34 ....136 E1
Priory Cl Hastings TN34 .136 E1
Pevensey Bay BN24 ....175 D5
Priory Cres BN7 ....190 A1
Priory Ct Bexhill TN40 ..157 C5
Brighton BN1 ....163 F8
1 Eastbourne BN20 ....184 F1
Lewes BN7 ....190 B1
Priory Flats BN7 ......190 A1
Priory Ho BN7 ....190 B1
Priory Hts BN20 ....184 A5
Priory La BN23 ....174 E3
Priory Meadow Sh Ctr
TN34 ....159 F8
Priory Orch 8 BN23 ....174 E1
Priory Rd
Burgess Hill RH15 ....73 A1
Eastbourne BN23 ......174 E2
Forest Row RH18 ....11 D2
Hassocks BN6 ....97 E5
Hastings TN34 ....160 B5
Priory Sch BN7 ....190 C1
Priory St Hastings TN34 .159 F7
Lewes BN7 ....190 A1
Priory The Brighton BN1 142 D5
5 Hove BN3 ....163 B5
Priory View TN34 ......160 A5
Priory Way RH16 ....50 F4
Promenade BN10 ......178 C6
Promenade The BN24 ..175 D4
Prospect Cotts
Burwash TN19 ....62 B6
Crowborough TN6 ......25 E3
Lamberhurst TN3 ....20 A3
Prospect Gdns 12 BN21 .184 D4
Prospect Pl TN34 ......159 E7
Prospect Rd
Heathfield TN21 ....82 B6
Royal Tunbridge Wells TN4 ..7 F7
Royal Tunbridge
Wells,Camden Park TN2 ..8 C3

Prospect Terr TN21 .....82 A7
Provence Ho BN23 .....174 F1
Providence Cotts
Crowborough TN6 ....25 D4
Groombridge TN3 ....15 C7
Providence Pl BN1 .....189 B4
Prowting Mead TN3 ....156 C4
Pudding Cake La TN22 ..78 C7
Pulborough Ave BN22 .173 E2
Pulborough Cl BN2 .....164 F7
Pump Ho The BN3 .....162 D8
Pump La TN22 ....79 D4
Pump Terr TN1 ....8 A2
Punnetts Town Com Prim
Sch TN21 ....83 B6
Purbeck Cl BN23 ......174 C4
Purbeck Ho BN1 ....189 C2
Putlands Cres TN39 ....157 A8
Pyecombe BN45 ....119 A6

Q

Quadrangle The BN8 ...105 C5
Quadrant BN1 ....189 A2
Quadrant The
Eastbourne BN21 ......184 E4
Keymer BN6 ....98 A4
Quail St BN27 ....152 D7
Quakers La RH16 ....51 A5
Quantock Cl
Eastbourne BN23 ......174 D3
Royal Tunbridge Wells TN2 ..8 D7
Quantock Gdns TN34 ..160 B7
Quarry Bank Rd BN1 ...143 B2
Quarry Cl RH15 ....73 D3
Quarry Cotts TN5 ....29 D7
Quarry Cres TN34 .....160 A5
Quarry Hill
Haywards Heath RH16 ...50 C6
St Leonards TN38 ......159 B7
Quarry Ho TN38 ....159 B6
Quarry La BN25 ....181 A5
Quarry Rd Hastings TN34 160 A5
Newhaven BN9 ....179 D5
Royal Tunbridge Wells TN1 ..8 B5
Quarry Rise RH19 ....2 A3
Quarry Terr TN34 ......136 F1
Quarry View 1 TN6 .....37 F8
Quay Ct BN43 ....161 B6
Quay The 5 BN43 .....161 A6
Quay Units BN10 ......178 D7
Quebec Cl Bexhill TN39 .157 A5
Eastbourne BN23 ......185 F7
Quebec Mans TN38 ....159 A8
Quebec Rd TN38 ......136 A4
Quebec St BN2 ....189 C3
Queen Alexandra Ave
BN3 ....142 A3
Queen Anne's Cl BN7 ..190 A2
Queen Caroline Cl BN3 142 A3
Queen Elizabeth Ave
RH15 ....73 A2
Queen Mary Ave BN3 ..142 A3
Queen Sq BN1 ....189 A2
Queen St TN18 ....47 B5
Queen Victoria Ave
BN3 ....142 A3
Queen Victoria Hospl The
RH19 ....1 F3
Queen's Ave 3 TN34 ..159 F7
Queen's Cres BN23 ....185 E7
Queen's Ct RH16 ....50 F6
Queen's Gdns
Brighton BN1 ....189 B3
Eastbourne BN21 ......185 B3
Hove BN3 ....163 C5
Royal Tunbridge Wells TN4 ..8 B6
Queen's Par
Eastbourne BN22 ......173 F1
Hove BN3 ....141 E2
Queen's Park Prim Sch
BN2 ....164 C5
Queen's Park Rd BN2 ..164 C6
Queen's Park Rise BN2 164 C6
Queen's Park Terr BN2 164 C6
Queen's Pl Brighton BN1 189 B4
Hove BN3 ....163 B5
Queen's Rd Brighton BN1 189 A3
East Grinstead RH19 .....1 E1
Eastbourne BN23 ......185 D7
Hastings TN34 ....159 F8
Lewes BN7 ....190 B4
Royal Tunbridge Wells TN4 ..8 B6
Queen's Wlk RH19 ....1 E1
Queens App TN22 ....55 D1
Queens Cotts TN5 ....29 E6
Queens Cres RH15 ......73 A2
Queens Ct 8 TN39 .....157 B3
Queens Dr Hassocks BN6 .97 F4
Maresfield TN22 ....54 F4
Queens Par 8 TN34 ....159 F8
Queens Park Gdns
BN25 ....180 C4
Queens Park Mews
BN2 ....164 C6
Queens Rd
Crowborough TN6 ....25 F1
Haywards Heath RH16 ...50 E6
Herstmonceux BN27 ...130 E5
Southwick BN42 ....140 E1
Queens Sq TN34 ....159 F8
Queensbury Mews BN1 .163 E5
Queensdown Sch BN1 ..143 C3
Queensdown School Rd
BN1,BN2 ....143 D2
Queensmount TN20 .....58 B7
Queensway Brighton BN2 164 D6

Queensway continued
East Grinstead RH19 . . . . . .1 E1
Seaford BN25 . . . . . .181 A6
St Leonards TN37,TN38 . . . .135 E5
Querneby Cl BN43 . . . . .161 D7
Quickbourne La TN31 . . . . .67 C7
Quinnell Dr BN27 . . . . .129 B2
Quintin Cl BN27 . . . . .152 A5
Quintins The BN27 . . . . .152 C8

R

Radcliffe Cl TN37 . . . . .136 C3
Radinden Dr BN3 . . . . .142 D1
Radinden Manor Rd
BN3 . . . . .163 D8
Radnor Ho RH16 . . . . .50 D6
Radnor Mews TN38 . . . . .135 E2
Ragged Dog La TN21 . . . . .81 B3
Raglan Ct Brighton BN1 . . . .189 A4
Pevensey Bay BN24 . . . .175 C3
Railway App
East Grinstead RH19 . . . . . .1 E1
Newhaven BN9 . . . . .179 D7
Railway Cotts Cowden TN8 . . .4 D8
Horsted Keynes RH17 . . . . .33 A8
Ripe BN8 . . . . .149 A6
St Leonards TN38 . . . . .158 F6
Railway La BN7 . . . . .190 B2
Railway Rd BN9 . . . . .179 D7
Railway St BN1 . . . . .189 A3
Railway View TN6 . . . . .38 C8
Rainey Ct 20 BN21 . . . . .185 B3
Raleigh Cl BN23 . . . . .185 E7
Ramsay Way BN23 . . . . .185 F7
Ramslye Rd TN4 . . . . .16 E8
Ranalah Est BN9 . . . . .179 D8
Randiddles Cl BN6 . . . . .97 B4
Randolph Ho TN39 . . . . .156 E5
Randolph La TN39 . . . . .70 B3
Ranelagh Ct BN23 . . . . .185 E6
Ranelagh Villas BN3 . . . .163 B8
Rangemore Dr BN21 . . . .184 D6
Rankine Rd TN2 . . . . .8 D7
Rannoch Rd TN6 . . . . .25 D2
Rannoch Rd W TN6 . . . . .25 D2
Ranscombe Hill BN8 . . . . .147 A6
Ranscombe La BN8 . . . . .147 A6
Ranworth Cl BN23 . . . . .174 B4
Raphael Rd BN3 . . . . .162 F7
Rapson's Rd BN20 . . . . .173 A3
Rastrick Cl RH15 . . . . .72 F1
Rattle Rd BN24 . . . . .174 D6
Ratton Dr BN20 . . . . .184 B7
Ratton Gdn BN20 . . . . .184 B7
Ratton Rd BN21 . . . . .184 E4
Ratton Sch BN20 . . . . .184 C7
Raven Ct Battle TN33 . . . .112 F4
St Leonards TN38 . . . . .135 E3
Ravens TN39 . . . . .156 C3
Ravens Croft BN20 . . . .188 F8
Ravens BN20 . . . . .188 F8
Ravenside Ret & L Pk
TN40 . . . . .158 A4
Ravenswood BN6 . . . . .97 E4
Ravenswood Ave TN6 . . . . .8 D6
Ravenswood Dr BN2 . . . .165 F6
Ravenswood Rd RH15 . . . .73 B3
Ravine Cl TN34 . . . . .160 A7
Rayford Cl BN10 . . . . .178 C7
Rayford Ct
2 Bexhill TN40 . . . . .157 D4
15 Seaford BN25 . . . . .180 E2
Raymond Cl BN25 . . . . .181 A5
Rayner Cl TN6 . . . . .25 F3
Raystede Ctr for Animal
Welfare ★ BN8 . . . . .103 D1
Readers TN11 . . . . .69 F5
Reading Rd BN2 . . . . .164 D5
Reba Ct BN2 . . . . .177 D4
Rectory Cl Burwash TN19 . . .62 B6
East Hoathly BN8 . . . . .105 A5
Eastbourne BN20 . . . . .184 D3
Hove BN3 . . . . .162 D7
Newhaven BN9 . . . . .179 C6
Shoreham-by-S BN43 . . . .161 D4
St Leonards TN38 . . . . .136 B2
Rectory Ct 15 BN43 . . . .161 C8
Rectory Field TN7 . . . . .13 E4
Rectory La Beckley TN31 . . . .67 F4
Rye TN31 . . . . .93 C8
Winchelsea TN36 . . . . .117 E7
Rectory Pk TN35 . . . . .116 E7
Rectory Rd
Newhaven BN9 . . . . .168 E2
Shoreham-by-S BN43 . . . .161 D7
Rectory Way TN40 . . . . .157 D5
Red Barn Mews TN33 . . . .112 D4
Red Dyke Cotts BN24 . . . .173 F6
Red Lake Com Prim Sch
TN35 . . . . .160 D8
Red Lake Terr TN35 . . . .160 D8
Red Lion Mobile Home Pk
TN33 . . . . .132 G2
Red Oak TN18 . . . . .45 E8
Red Oast Cotts TN5 . . . . .32 C3
Redbridge La TN6 . . . . .37 D5
Redbrook La TN22 . . . . .56 D4
Redford Cl BN23 . . . . .174 E1
Redford Ct TN39 . . . . .156 F4
Redgate Rd RH19 . . . . .1 B3
Redgeland Rise TN38 . . . .135 F2
Redgill La BN8 . . . . .53 B1
Redhill Cl BN1 . . . . .142 C5
Redhill Dr BN1 . . . . .142 C5

Redleaf Cl TN2 . . . . .8 D6
Redman King Ho BN20 . . . .184 F2
Redmayne Dr TN34 . . . .159 E7
Redoubt Rd BN22 . . . . .185 C4
Redoubt The ★ BN22 . . . .185 C4
Redshank Ct BN27 . . . .152 D7
Redvers Rd BN2 . . . . .143 D1
Redward Bsns Pk BN3 . . . .185 B7
Redwood Dr TN16 . . . . .50 D3
Reed Ct BN2 . . . . .190 A4
Reed Ho BN8 . . . . .100 E7
Reed Pond Wlk RH16 . . . .51 A4
Reedham Rd BN23 . . . .174 B4
Reedswood Dr
Broad Oak TN31 . . . . .90 A4
St Leonards TN38 . . . . .158 E8
Reeves Ct TN3 . . . . .6 B5
Reeves Hill BN1 . . . . .143 D5
Reeves Terr TN5 . . . . .31 E1
Refectory Rd BN1 . . . .144 B7
Regal Dr 10 RH19 . . . . .10 F8
Regency Cl TN22 . . . . .78 E4
Regency Ct Brighton BN1 142 D3
12 Eastbourne BN20 . . . .185 A1
Regency Gdns TN38 . . . .159 A8
Regency Hall 21 TN2 . . . . .8 A2
Regency Ho TN2 . . . . .8 B2
Regency Mews
15 Brighton BN1 . . . . .163 E5
11 Eastbourne BN20 . . . .185 A1
Regency Rd BN1 . . . . .189 A4
Regency Sq BN1 . . . . .163 E5
Regent Arc BN1 . . . . .189 B2
Regent Bsns Pk RH15 . . . .72 E2
Regent Hill BN1 . . . . .189 A2
Regent Pl Heathfield TN21 . .82 A4
Royal Tunbridge Wells TN2 . .8 D3
St Leonards TN37 . . . . .135 F7
Regent Row BN1 . . . . .189 A2
Regent Sq TN31 . . . . .93 C6
Regent St BN1 . . . . .189 B2
Regents Cl BN25 . . . . .180 E5
Regina Ct TN4 . . . . .7 F4
Reginald Rd TN39 . . . .157 B4
Regnum Rd BN22 . . . . .173 E4
Reigate Rd BN1 . . . . .142 D1
Renascent Ho 18 BN21 . . .185 B3
Renfields RH16 . . . . .50 C3
Renown Ct TN40 . . . . .157 D6
Resting Oak Hill BN8 . . . .100 F3
Reynolds Dr TN40 . . . .157 E5
Reynolds La TN4 . . . . .7 F7
Reynolds Rd
Eastbourne BN23 . . . . .174 E1
Hove BN3 . . . . .162 F7
Reynoldstown La BN26 . . .172 F6
Ribbetts Cotts BN6 . . . . .97 A5
Ribbetts Ho BN6 . . . . .97 A5
Riccards La TN33 . . . . .88 A2
Rices Hill RH19 . . . . .1 E1
Rich Ind Est BN9 . . . . .168 E1
Richard Allen Ct BN2 . . . .143 C1
Richard Beau Nash
Apartments TN1 . . . . .8 B4
Richardson Ct 5 BN3 . . . .162 F7
Richardson Rd Hove BN3 162 F7
Royal Tunbridge Wells TN4 . .8 A5
Richborough TN34 . . . .136 D4
Richington Way BN25 . . . .181 B5
Richland Cl TN35 . . . . .160 F6
Richmead Gdns TN20 . . . .40 B2
Richmond Ave TN39 . . . .156 F3
Richmond Cl TN39 . . . .157 A3
Richmond Ct
9 Hove BN3 . . . . .163 E7
Seaford BN25 . . . . .180 E3
Richmond Gdns 2 BN2 189 C3
Richmond Gr TN39 . . . .157 A2
Richmond Hts 12 BN2 . . . .189 C4
Richmond Mews BN25 . . . .180 E3
Richmond Par BN2 . . . .189 C3
Richmond Pl
Brighton BN2 . . . . .189 B3
Eastbourne BN21 . . . . .184 F4
Royal Tunbridge Wells TN2 . .8 B1
Richmond Rd
Bexhill TN39 . . . . .157 A3
Brighton BN2 . . . . .164 B8
Pevensey Bay BN24 . . . .175 D5
Seaford BN25 . . . . .180 E3
Richmond Sq RH19 . . . . .1 D2
Richmond St
Brighton BN2 . . . . .189 C3
Hastings TN35 . . . . .160 C6
Richmond Terr
Brighton BN2 . . . . .189 C4
2 Seaford BN25 . . . . .180 E3
Richmond Way RH19 . . . .10 F8
Riddens Cl BN7 . . . . .99 E5
Riddens La BN7 . . . . .99 E6
Riddens The BN7 . . . . .99 E5
Riddlesdale Ave TN4 . . . .8 A6
Ride The BN1 . . . . .142 F1
Riders Bolt TN39 . . . . .156 E5
Ridge Cl Nutley TN22 . . . .35 C5
Portslade-by-S BN41 . . . .141 A4
Ridge Rd BN1 . . . . .144 D2
Ridge The
Groombridge TN3 . . . . .15 A6
St Leonards TN34,TN37 . . .136 D6
Winchelsea Beach TN36 . . .118 C6
Ridge View BN1 . . . . .143 E5
Ridge W The TN37 . . . .136 A7
Ridge Way RH17 . . . . .51 B2
Ridgelands Cl BN20 . . . .184 C3
Ridgeside Ave BN1 . . . .142 E5

Ridgeway
East Grinstead RH19 . . . . .10 E7
Hurst Green TN19 . . . . .45 A3
Pembury TN2 . . . . .9 D7
Southwick BN41,BN42 . . . .140 F1
The Moor TN18 . . . . .45 E8
Ridgeway Cl
Heathfield TN21 . . . . .82 A8
Southwick BN42 . . . . .140 F1
Ridgeway Gdns BN2 . . . .165 E7
Ridgeway The
Burgess Hill RH15 . . . . .73 B4
Friston BN20 . . . . .183 B1
Herstmonceux BN27 . . . .130 E6
Seaford BN25 . . . . .180 F4
Ridgewaye The TN4 . . . . .8 A8
Ridgewood Ave BN2 . . . .177 C7
Ridgewood Cl TN22 . . . . .78 D4
Ridgewood Gdns
Bexhill TN40 . . . . .157 F4
Hastings TN34 . . . . .136 E5
Ridgewood Ind Pk TN22 . . . .78 E4
Ridgway Cl BN2 . . . . .165 D8
Ridgway Paddock BN7 . . .145 E6
Ridgway The BN2 . . . .165 D8
Ridings The Bexhill TN39 . .156 F8
Burgess Hill RH15 . . . . .73 C2
Newick BN8 . . . . .76 C7
Ovingdean BN2 . . . . .165 C4
Royal Tunbridge Wells TN2 . .8 F6
Seaford BN25 . . . . .180 F5
St Leonards TN37 . . . . .136 F5
Telscombe Cliffs BN10 . . . .167 B2
Rigden Rd BN3 . . . . .142 C1
Riley Rd BN2 . . . . .143 C1
Rill Wlk RH19 . . . . .2 B1
Ringle Gn TN18 . . . . .47 C5
Ringles Cross TN22 . . . . .55 D2
Ringmer Bsns Pk BN8 . . . .124 F6
Ringmer Cl BN1 . . . . .143 E4
Ringmer Com Coll BN8 . . .124 E6
Ringmer Dr BN1 . . . . .143 E4
Ringmer Pk Cotts BN8 . . .124 E5
Ringmer Prim Sch BN8 . . .124 E6
Ringmer Rd
Brighton BN1 . . . . .143 E4
Newhaven BN9 . . . . .179 B6
Seaford BN25 . . . . .180 E2
Ringmer Way BN23 . . . .174 A4
Ringwood Cl BN23 . . . . .185 B5
Ringwood Ct 6 BN22 . . . .185 C5
Ringwood Rd
Bexhill TN39 . . . . .157 C7
Eastbourne BN22 . . . . .185 B5
Ripe La BN8 . . . . .126 E2
Ripley Chase BN21 . . . .184 E3
Ripley Cl BN23 . . . . .174 E2
Risden La TN18 . . . . .46 D7
Rise Park Gdns BN23 . . . .174 B4
Rise The
East Grinstead RH19 . . . . .10 F8
Haywards Heath RH16 . . . .51 B5
Horam TN21 . . . . .106 F7
Portslade-by-S BN41 . . . .140 F2
Riseden Rd TN5 . . . . .29 C1
Rising The BN23 . . . . .174 E2
Risings The BN25 . . . . .180 F4
Rissom Ct BN1 . . . . .142 E2
Ritz Blgs TN1 . . . . .8 A3
River La BN26 . . . . .171 A3
River Way TN2 . . . . .78 C6
Riverbourne Ho 10
BN22 . . . . .185 B4
Riverbridge Cotts TN33 . .113 E8
Riverdale BN7 . . . . .190 A3
Riverhall Hill TN5 . . . . .31 E3
Riverside Forest Row RH18 . 11 E3
Hadlow Down TN22 . . . . .57 D1
Southwick BN42 . . . . .161 E7
Riverside Bsns Ctr
BN43 . . . . .161 A7
Riverside Gdns TN6 . . . . .38 C8
Riverside Ho BN9 . . . .179 D6
Riverside Ind Est BN7 . . .190 B3
Riverside N BN9 . . . . .179 D7
Riverside Rd BN43 . . . .161 A6
Riverside S BN9 . . . . .179 D6
Rixons Cl RH17 . . . . .33 C5
Rixons Orch RH17 . . . . .33 C5
RNLI Lifeboat Mus ★
BN21 . . . . .185 A1
Robert Lodge BN2 . . . .164 F4
Robert St BN1 . . . . .189 B3
Robert Tressell Cl TN34 . .136 E1
Robert Tressell Workshops
7 TN34 . . . . . . .159 F8
Robert's Hill TN36 . . . .117 E8
Roberts Row TN31 . . . . .68 C5
Robertsbridge Com Coll
TN32 . . . . .63 F4
Robertsbridge Sta TN32 . .64 A4
Robertson Pas TN34 . . . .159 F7
Robertson Rd BN1 . . . .142 D1
Robertson St TN34 . . . .159 F7
Robertson Terr 1 TN34 . .159 F7
Robertsons Hill TN34 . . . .160 B6
Robian Cl TN22 . . . . .55 A4
Robin Cl
East Grinstead RH19 . . . . .1 F2
Eastbourne BN23 . . . . .174 C2
Robin Ct TN39 . . . . .157 A3
Robin Davis Cl BN2 . . . .143 E1
Robin Dene BN2 . . . . .165 F4
Robin Hill TN39 . . . . .156 D4
Robin Post La BN26 . . . .151 B1
Robin Rd RH15 . . . . .72 D2
Robin Rise RH16 . . . . .50 F3
Robinia Lodge BN1 . . . .142 E2

Robins Reach BN27 . . . .127 B3
Robins Row BN41 . . . .141 A1
Robinson Rd BN9 . . . .179 C8
Robinsons Ct BN22 . . . .185 C6
Robsack Ave TN35 . . . .135 E2
Robsack Wood Com Prim Sch
TN38 . . . . .135 E2
Rochdale Ho TN1 . . . . .8 C5
Rochdale Rd TN1 . . . . .8 C6
Rochester Cl
Eastbourne BN20 . . . . .188 C8
5 Hove BN3 . . . . .163 D6
Rochester Ct 4 BN3 . . . .163 D6
Rochester Gdns BN3 . . . .163 D6
Rochester Ho TN6 . . . . .26 C1
Rochester Rd 4 TN37 . . . .136 B2
Rochester St BN2 . . . .164 D5
Rochester Way TN6 . . . . .26 C1
Rochford Way BN25 . . . .180 B6
Rochmans Way TN6 . . . . .38 A8
Rock Channel TN31 . . . . .93 C5
Rock Channel Quay TN31 93 C5
Rock Cl Hastings TN35 . . . .160 D8
12 Southwick BN42 . . . .161 E7
Rock Cotts TN3 . . . . .17 B1
Rock Gr BN2 . . . . .164 E4
Rock Hall Cotts TN22 . . . .78 D8
Rock La TN35 . . . . .137 D7
Rock Pl BN2 . . . . .189 C1
Rock St BN2 . . . . .164 E4
Rock Villa Rd TN1 . . . . .8 A4
Rock's Hill TN35 . . . .114 E7
Rock-a-Nore Par TN34 . .160 B4
Rock-a-Nore Rd TN34 . . .160 B3
Rockall Ave BN23 . . . .185 F8
Rockall Dr BN27 . . . . .129 A2
Rockhurst Dr BN20 . . . .184 B6
Rockington Way TN6 . . . .38 B8
Rocklands Cotts BN27 . . .131 B5
Rocklands Holiday Pk
TN35 . . . . .160 D5
Rocklands La TN35 . . . .160 C5
Rockmead Rd TN35 . . . .138 F4
Rocks La TN22 . . . . .55 F7
Rocks Park Prim Sch
TN22 . . . . .78 B8
Rocks Park Rd TN22 . . . . .78 B7
Rocks The RH19 . . . . .11 D6
Rocky La RH16 . . . . .50 D1
Roderick Ave
Peacehaven BN10 . . . . .178 B7
Peacehaven BN10 . . . . .178 C8
Roderick Ave N BN10 . . . .167 C2
Roderick Ct BN10 . . . . .178 C8
Rodmell Ave BN2 . . . . .177 D5
Rodmell CE Prim Sch
BN7 . . . . .146 E1
Rodmell Ct 5 BN25 . . . .180 C4
Rodmell Pl BN1 . . . . .143 A6
Rodmell Rd
Royal Tunbridge Wells TN2 . .8 A2
Seaford BN25 . . . . .181 B2
Rodmill Dr BN21 . . . . .184 D6
Rodmill Rd BN21 . . . . .184 D5
Rodney Cl BN23 . . . . .185 F7
Rodwell TN6 . . . . .26 C1
Roebuck St 18 TN34 . . . .160 B4
Roedale Ct 1 BN1 . . . .143 B1
Roedale Rd BN1 . . . . .143 B1
Roedean Cl Bexhill TN39 . .157 A5
Seaford BN25 . . . . .181 A4
Roedean Cres BN2 . . . .165 A4
Roedean Ct BN2 . . . . .164 F4
Roedean Hts BN2 . . . .165 A4
Roedean Path BN2 . . . .165 A3
Roedean Rd
Brighton BN2 . . . . .164 F4
Royal Tunbridge Wells TN2 . .8 A1
Roedean Sch BN2 . . . .165 C3
Roedean Terr BN2 . . . .165 B3
Roedean Vale BN2 . . . .165 B3
Roedean Way BN2 . . . .165 B3
Roeheath BN8 . . . . .75 F4
Roffrey Ave BN22 . . . .173 C1
Rolfe Dr RH15 . . . . .73 D3
Romaine Cl RH15 . . . . .73 D5
Roman Cl BN25 . . . . .180 B6
Roman Cres BN42 . . . .161 E8
Roman Croft BN21 . . . .184 E4
Roman Rd Hove BN3 . . . .162 D6
Southwick BN42 . . . . .161 E8
Roman Way
Southwick BN42 . . . . .161 E8
Uckfield TN22 . . . . .78 E7
Romans Way BN24 . . . .174 E6
Romany Cl BN41 . . . . .162 B8
Romford Rd TN2 . . . . .9 F7
Romney Cl BN25 . . . .181 C4
Romney Ct 8 TN40 . . . .157 C4
Romney Rd
Polegate BN26 . . . . .173 B7
Rottingdean BN2 . . . . .177 A5
Romney St BN22 . . . . .185 C5
Romsey Cl BN1 . . . . .143 C2
Rookery Cl Brighton BN1 . .168 E2
Newhaven BN9 . . . . .168 E2
Rookery La
Rushlake Green TN21 . . . .83 E2
Winchelsea TN36 . . . . .117 F7
Rookery The BN23 . . . .174 C4
Rookery Way
Haywards Heath RH16 . . . .51 B4
Newhaven BN9 . . . . .168 F2
Rookhurst Rd TN40 . . . .157 F5
Rookley Cl TN2 . . . . .8 D2
Rookwood Cl TN22 . . . . .78 E8

Que – Row **213**

Roopers TN3 . . . . .7 A7
Roosevelt Ct TN38 . . . .136 B3
Rope Wlk Hailsham BN27 152 B8
Rye TN31 . . . . .93 C6
Rope Wlk The TN18 . . . .47 B5
Roper's Gate TN2 . . . . .7 E1
Rosary RH15 . . . . .73 B2
Rose Cotts Danehill RH17 . .34 A4
Forest Row RH18 . . . . .11 F3
Rose Ct BN6 . . . . .97 E4
Rose Gr BN27 . . . . .127 B3
Rose Hill BN2 . . . . .189 C4
Rose Hill Cl BN1 . . . .189 B4
Rose Hill Ct BN1 . . . .189 B4
Rose Hill Sch TN4 . . . . .7 E5
Rose Hill Terr BN1 . . . .189 B4
Rose Walk Cl BN25 . . . .179 C7
Rose Wlk BN25 . . . . .180 F4
Rose Wlk The BN9 . . . .179 C7
Rosebarn Cl RH15 . . . . .73 C1
Rosebery Ave
Eastbourne BN22 . . . . .173 E1
Woodingdean BN2 . . . . .165 C8
Rosedale Pl BN2 . . . .173 D3
Rosedene Cl BN2 . . . .165 E6
Rosefield Cotts TN32 . . . .65 E1
Rosehill Gdns TN6 . . . . .26 C1
Rosehill Wlk TN1 . . . . .8 A3
Roseland Ct 2 BN22 . . . .185 C5
Roselands Bexhill TN39 . . .156 F6
Sedlescombe TN33 . . . . .88 E1
Roselands Ave
Eastbourne BN22 . . . . .185 C5
Wellbrook TN22 . . . . .39 F1
Roselands Cl BN22 . . . .185 C5
Roselands Inf Sch BN22 . .185 B5
Roseleigh Gdns RH17 . . . .51 F3
Rosemary Cl
Haywards Heath RH16 . . . .50 B3
Peacehaven BN10 . . . . .167 C1
Rosemary Dr BN43 . . . .140 C1
Rosemary Gdns TN19 . . . .62 B2
Rosemary La
Guestling Green TN35 . . . .138 D6
Stonecrouch TN5 . . . . .32 A5
Rosemount
Lower Dicker BN8,BN27 . . .128 A7
Muddles Green BN8 . . . .127 F7
Rosemount Cl BN25 . . . .180 A6
Rosetti Rd BN24 . . . . .175 D4
Roseveare Rd BN22 . . . .185 C6
Rossdale TN4 . . . . .8 D5
Rossington Cl BN21 . . . .184 D5
Rosslyn Ave BN43 . . . .161 A7
Rosslyn Rd BN43 . . . .161 A7
Rotary Lodge BN1 . . . .143 E6
Rotary Point BN41 . . . .141 B1
Rothbury Rd BN1 . . . .162 D7
Rother Ave BN24 . . . .173 F5
Rother Cl Burwash TN19 . . .62 B6
Crowborough TN6 . . . . .38 A7
Rother Ct TN39 . . . . .157 B6
Rother Ho TN21 . . . . .82 A8
Rother Ironworks The 5
TN31 . . . . .93 C5
Rother Rd BN25 . . . . .181 A1
Rother Valley Rly ★ TN32 . .64 A4
Rother View
Burwash TN19 . . . . .62 B7
Etchingham TN19 . . . . .44 C1
Rotherfield Ave
Bexhill TN40 . . . . .157 D4
Eastbourne BN23 . . . . .174 A4
Hastings TN34 . . . . .160 B5
Rotherfield Cl BN1 . . . .143 B6
Rotherfield Cres BN1 . . . .143 B5
Rotherfield La TN20 . . . . .39 F4
Rotherfield Prim Sch
TN6 . . . . .39 B8
Rotherfield Rd TN6 . . . . .38 E8
Rotherhill Rd TN6 . . . . .38 A7
Rotherhurst La TN6 . . . . .39 B6
Rothermead TN20 . . . . .39 F1
Rotherview TN32 . . . . .64 C5
Rothley Chase RH16 . . . .50 F4
Rothsay Ct TN38 . . . . .159 B7
Rothsay Rd TN38 . . . . .159 B7
Rothwell Ct BN9 . . . .179 A7
Rotten Row Lewes BN7 . . .146 B8
Lewes BN7 . . . . .190 A1
Rottingdean Pl BN2 . . . .165 F4
Rotunda Rd BN23 . . . .185 D8
Rotyngs The BN2 . . . . .165 F2
Rough Brow BN25 . . . .181 A4
Rough Field RH19 . . . . .1 D4
Rough The BN8 . . . . .76 C7
Round Hill Cres BN2 . . . .164 B8
Round Hill Rd 2 BN2 . . . .164 B8
Round Hill St BN2 . . . .164 B8
Roundacres Way TN40 . . . .157 E6
Roundel The TN37 . . . .136 D5
Roundhay Ave BN10 . . . .178 E6
Roundhill Rd TN2 . . . . .8 D1
Roundhouse Cotts TN21 . .82 D7
Roundway BN1 . . . . .143 E5
Roundwood La RH16 . . . .50 F8
Roundwood Rd TN37 . . . .136 B5
Rowan Ave
Eastbourne BN22 . . . . .173 D3
Hove BN3 . . . . .141 E1
Rowan Cl
Haywards Heath RH16 . . . .51 B4
Heathfield TN21 . . . . .82 A3
Portslade-by-S BN41 . . . .141 A1
Seaford BN25 . . . . .181 C3

Rowan Cl *continued*
St Leonards TN37 ......**136** D6
Rowan Ct Brighton BN1 ..**142** E1
Polegate BN26 ....**173** A6
Rowan Gdns TN40 ....**157** F6
Rowan Ho
⬛6 Brighton BN2 ......**189** C4
Royal Tunbridge Wells TN4 ...**7** E4
Rowan Tree Rd TN2 ....**7** E1
Rowan Way BN2 ....**165** E4
Rowan's Ct BN7 ....**190** A4
Rowanden Ct BN2 ....**177** C4
Rowans The
Burgess Hill RH15 ......**72** A3
Hurstpierpoint BN6 ....**97** A7
Rowbarns TN33 ......**112** C6
Rowe Ave BN10 ....**178** B7
Rowe Ave N BN10 ....**178** B8
Rowsley Rd BN20 ....**188** D7
Royal Alexandra Hospl for
Sick Children The BN1 **189** A3
Royal Chase TN4 ......**7** F4
Royal Cres BN2 ....**164** C4
Royal Crescent Mans ⬛10
BN2 ....**164** C4
Royal Crescent Mews ⬛8
BN2 ....**164** C4
Royal Ct TN34 ......**136** E5
Royal Dr BN25 ....**180** E6
Royal George Ct RH15 ..**72** F3
Royal George Par BN43 **140** C1
Royal George Rd RH15 ..**72** E3
Royal Mews TN38 ....**159** A6
Royal Military Rd TN36 ..**118** A8
Royal Oak La TN22 ....**56** B8
Royal Par
Eastbourne BN22 ......**185** C4
Eastbourne BN22 ......**185** D5
Royal Pavilion ★ BN1 ..**189** B2
Royal Sovereign View
BN23 ....**185** F6
Royal Sussex Cres BN20 **184** B5
Royal Sussex St BN7 ..**190** B1
Royal Sussex Cty Hospl
BN2 ....**164** D4
Royal Terr ⬛4 TN37 ..**159** C7
Royal Victoria Place Sh Ctr
TN1 ....**8** B4
Royles Cl BN2 ......**177** A6
Royston Cl BN20 ....**183** A1
Royston Gdns TN40 ..**157** F6
Rubislaw ⬛3 BN21 ....**184** F4
Rudyard Cl BN2 ....**165** E8
Rudyard Kipling Prim Sch
BN2 ....**165** E7
Rudyard Rd BN2 ....**165** E8
Rue De Bayeux TN33 ..**112** D5
Ruffet Ct TN2 ....**7** E1
Rufus Cl BN7 ......**190** A2
Rugby Cl BN25 ....**181** B4
Rugby Ct ⬛5 BN2 ....**164** E4
Rugby Pl BN2 ......**164** E4
Rugby Rd BN1 ......**143** A1
Rumbolds La RH16 ....**50** D2
Rumsey Ct TN6 ......**25** F1
Rusbridge La BN7 ..**190** C2
Rush Ct ⬛4 BN2 ....**185** B3
Rushers Cross TN20 ..**40** E5
Rushes The RH16 ....**51** C4
Rushetts TN3 ....**6** F4
Rushey Cl BN8 ......**124** E5
Rushlake Cl BN1 ....**143** E5
Rushlake Cres BN21 ..**184** D6
Rushlake Rd BN1 ....**143** E5
Rushlye Cl TN3 ......**17** F5
Rushmere Rise TN38 ..**135** E1
Rushwood RH16 ....**51** B4
Ruskin Pl BN3 ......**162** F7
Ruskin Rd
Eastbourne BN20 ......**173** B1
Hove BN3 ....**162** F8
Rusper Ho ⬛16 BN21 ..**184** E4
Rusper Rd Brighton BN1 **143** D6
Eastbourne BN20 ......**184** B6
Ruspers BN21 ....**73** D2
Russell Cotts ⬛5 BN21 **184** E4
Russell Cres ⬛2 BN1 ..**189** A4
Russell Ct ⬛5 TN34 ..**160** A3
Russell Mews ⬛14 BN1 **163** E5
Russell Pl BN1 ......**189** A2
Russell Rd BN1 ......**189** A2
Russell Row BN7 ....**190** A4
Russell Sq BN1 ......**189** A2
Russell St TN34 ....**159** F8
Russet Cl BN26 ....**173** C6
Russett Way BN27 ..**131** B5
Rusthall Grange TN4 ..**7** D4
Rusthall High St TN4 ..**7** C4
Rusthall Pk TN4 ......**7** D4
Rusthall Rd TN4 ......**7** D4
Rustic Cl BN10 ....**167** B1
Rustic Pk BN10 ....**167** B2
Rustic Rd BN10 ....**167** B2
Rustington BN20 ....**188** F8
Rustington Rd BN1 ..**143** A5
Rustlings Cl RH16 ....**51** B5
Rustwick TN4 ....**7** D4
Rutherfords Bsns Pk
TN33 ....**113** B7
Rutland Cl BN21 ....**184** D6
Rutland Ct
⬛3 Eastbourne BN23 ..**174** E1
Hove BN3 ....**162** F6
Rutland Gdns BN3 ..**162** F7
Rutland Rd BN3 ....**163** A7

Rutley Cl TN32 ......**64** C5
Ruxley Cl BN23 ....**174** D2
Rydal Cl TN4 ....**7** E5
Rydal Dr TN4 ....**7** E5
Rydal Way BN23 ....**174** C4
Ryde Ct BN3 ......**141** D1
Ryde Rd BN2 ......**164** D7
Ryders TN3 ....**7** A3
Rye Cl Polegate BN26 ..**173** C7
Saltdean BN2 ....**177** F6
Seaford BN25 ....**181** C4
Rye Harbour Local Nature
Reserve ★ TN31 ....**94** B1
Rye Harbour Nature
Reserve
★ Rye TN36 ....**93** C2
★ Winchelsea Beach TN36 **118** F8
Rye Rd Four Throws TN18 ..**46** D8
Hastings TN35 ......**137** D5
Iden TN30 ....**70** A8
Peasmarsh TN31 ......**69** E2
Rye Sta TN31 ......**93** B6
Ryecroft ⬛12 Brighton BN2 **164** F5
Haywards Heath RH16 ..**50** E3
Ryefield Cl BN21 ....**184** C7
Ryelands Dr BN2 ....**143** D3
Rylstone Rd BN22 ..**185** C4
Rymers CI TN2 ....**8** D7
Rymill Rd TN38 ....**136** A3
Ryst Wood Rd RH18 ..**12** B1

S

Sackville Cl
East Grinstead RH19 ....**1** C3
Lewes BN7 ....**190** A2
Sackville Coll ★ RH19 ..**1** F1
Sackville Com Coll RH19 **11** A8
Sackville Ct Bexhill TN40 **157** D5
⬛3 East Grinstead RH19 ..**10** F8
Sackville Gdns
East Grinstead RH19 ....**1** C3
Hove BN3 ....**162** F6
Sackville La RH19 ....**1** C3
Sackville Rd Bexhill TN39 **157** B3
Eastbourne BN22 ......**173** F2
Hailsham BN27 ......**152** C6
Hove BN3 ....**163** A7
Sackville Trad Est BN3 ..**163** B8
Sacred Heart RC Prim Sch
TN35 ....**160** B5
Sacred Heart Sch TN5 ..**29** D5
Saddler's Ct ⬛6 TN38 ..**159** B6
Saddlers Cl RH15 ....**73** D1
Sadler Way BN8 ....**124** D4
Saffreys Ct TN38 ....**159** B7
Saffron Cl BN43 ....**140** C1
Saffron Gate BN3 ....**163** C7
Saffron Gdns BN26 ..**170** F3
Saffrons Ct BN21 ....**184** E2
Saffrons Mead ⬛9 BN20 **184** F2
Saffrons Pk BN20 ....**184** E1
Saffrons Rd BN21 ....**184** F2
Saffrons The RH15 ....**72** F5
Saint Hill Gn RH19 ....**10** D4
Saint Hill Manor ★ RH19 **10** C4
Saint Hill Rd RH19 ....**10** C5
Saints Hill TN11 ......**6** A3
St Agnes Rd RH19 ....**1** E2
St Aidan's Ct ⬛3 BN25 **185** C5
St Andrew's CE Inf Sch
BN22 ....**185** D6
St Andrew's CE Prim Sch
BN3 ....**163** B7
St Andrew's Ct BN9 ..**179** B7
St Andrew's Dr BN25 ..**180** B6
St Andrew's La BN7 ..**190** B2
St Andrew's Rd
Bexhill TN40 ....**157** C5
Brighton BN1 ....**143** A1
Portslade-by-S BN41 ..**162** C7
St Andrew's Sch BN20 ..**188** D7
St Andrew's Sq ⬛6 TN34 **159** F8
St Andrew's Villas
TN34 ....**160** A4
St Andrews Cl BN27 ..**129** A1
St Andrews Rd RH15 ..**73** C4
St Ann's Ct BN3 ....**163** D7
St Ann's Ct BN24 ..**175** D4
St Anne's Cl TN40 ..**157** D5
St Anne's Cres ⬛3 BN7 **123** C4
St Anne's Ct
⬛6 Brighton BN1 ....**189** A4
⬛9 Brighton BN2 ....**164** C4
St Anne's Gdns BN6 ..**98** A3
St Anne's Ho ⬛7 BN1 **189** A4
St Anne's Rd BN21 ..**184** F4
St Anne's Sch BN7 ....**146** B8
St Anne's Terr ⬛6 BN7 **123** B1
St Annes Gn TN19 ....**62** A6
St Annes Rd BN20 ..**173** B3
St Annes Well Ho ⬛6
BN3 ....**163** D6
St Anns Mans ⬛5 BN1 **163** E7
St Anthony's Ave BN23 **185** E8
St Anthonys BN8 ....**124** E6
St Aubyn's Cres BN1 ..**162** F7
St Aubyn's Gdns ⬛13 BN3 **163** A6
St Aubyn's Mead BN2 **177** A5
St Aubyn's Rd
Eastbourne BN22 ......**185** B3
Portslade-by-S BN41 ..**162** C7
Portslade-by-S,Fishersgate
BN41 ....**162** A7

St Aubyns BN3 ......**163** B6
St Aubyns Mans BN3 ..**163** A5
St Aubyns S BN3 ....**163** A5
St Aubyns St BN2 ..**165** F1
St Augustine's CE Prim Sch
RH17 ....**25** C4
St Augustine's Cl TN39 **156** F3
St Augustine's RC Prim Sch
TN4 ....**8** A7
St Augustines Cl RH17 ..**51** F3
St Barnabas CE Prim Sch
TN1 ....**8** B5
St Barnabas' Cl TN1 ..**8** B5
St Bartholomew's CE Prim
Sch BN1 ....**189** B4
St Bede's Prep Sch
BN20 ....**188** E7
St Bede's Sch BN27 ..**151** A8
St Bernadette's RC Prim Sch
BN1 ....**142** E2
St Boswells Cl BN27 ..**152** A8
St Brelades BN21 ....**185** B2
St Catherine's CE TN37 **159** D8
St Catherine's Ct ⬛8
RH19 ....**1** D2
St Catherine's Terr ⬛6
BN3 ....**163** B5
St Christopher's Rd BN6 **97** A6
St Christopher's Sch
BN3 ....**163** A6
St Clement's Caves ★
TN34 ....**160** A4
St Clement's Ct BN21 ..**184** D6
St Clements Pl ⬛5 TN38 **159** C6
St Crispians BN25 ....**180** A5
St Crispians St BN25 ..**180** D3
St Cuthmans Cl BN2 ..**164** F6
St David's Ave TN40 ..**157** C5
St David's St BN10 ..**178** B8
St David's Rd TN4 ....**8** B6
St Davids Cl BN22 ..**173** D4
St Denys BN21 ......**184** E4
St Dominic TN38 ....**136** A4
St Edmund's Rd RH16 ..**50** F3
St Edward's Cl RH19 ..**1** C1
St Elizabeth's BN25 ..**180** F4
St Francis Chase TN39 **157** A5
St Francis Cl RH16 ..**50** F2
St George's Ho BN6 ..**97** B5
St George's La BN6 ....**97** B5
St George's Mews BN1 **189** B3
St George's Pk TN2 ..**16** B7
St George's Pl
Brighton BN1 ....**189** B3
Hurstpierpoint BN6 ....**97** B5
St George's Rd
Bexhill TN40 ....**157** C5
Brighton BN2 ....**164** D4
Eastbourne BN22 ......**185** B4
Hastings TN34 ......**160** A5
St George's Terr ⬛5
BN2 ....**164** C4
St Georges Ct
⬛11 Bexhill TN40 ....**157** D3
East Grinstead RH19 ....**1** C3
Royal Tunbridge Wells TN4 ...**8** A5
St Georges Mount ⬛14
TN37 ....**159** C7
St Giles CE Prim Sch
RH17 ....**33** C6
St Giles Cl
Shoreham-by-S BN43 ..**161** B8
Winchelsea TN36 ....**117** E7
St Gregory's Catholic Comp
Sch TN4 ....**8** A7
St Helen's Ave TN34 ..**136** E3
St Helen's Cres
Hastings TN34 ......**136** E2
Hove BN3 ....**141** D3
St Helen's St TN34 ....**136** E2
St Helen's Down TN34 **160** A7
St Helen's Dr BN3 ....**141** D3
St Helen's Park Rd
TN34 ....**136** E3
St Helen's Rd
Brighton BN2 ....**164** D7
Hastings TN34 ......**136** D2
St Helena La BN7 ....**74** E1
St Helena's St ⬛1 BN21 **184** E4
St Helens's Wood Rd
TN34 ....**136** E5
St Heliers Ave BN3 ..**162** E7
St James BN24 ......**176** D8
St James Ct RH19 ....**1** D1
St James La TN22 ....**35** C4
St James Rd BN22 ..**185** C4
St James St BN7 ....**190** A1
St James Wlk BN8 ....**75** E1
St James' Ave TN40 ..**157** D6
St James' CE Inf Sch TN2 **8** C4
St James' CE Jun Sch TN2 **8** C4
St James' Cl TN40 ..**157** C7
St James' Cres TN40 ..**157** D7
St James' Ho ⬛13 BN2 **189** C2
St James' Pk TN1 ......**8** C5
St James' Rd
Bexhill TN40 ....**157** C6
Royal Tunbridge Wells TN1 ...**8** C5
St James' Ave BN2 ..**189** C2
St James's Ct TN1 ..**8** B4
St James's Pl BN2 ..**189** B2
St James's Rd
East Grinstead RH19 ....**1** D1
Hastings TN34 ......**136** F1
St James's St BN2 ..**189** C2
St James's Street Mews
BN2 ....**189** C2

St John Bank BN8 ..**100** D8
St John the Baptist RC Sch
BN2 ....**164** D5
St John's Ave RH15 ..**72** F4
St John's CE Prim Sch
TN6 ....**25** C4
St John's CE Prim Sch
BN7 ....**8** B7
St John's Cl
Crowborough TN6 ......**25** C3
East Grinstead RH19 ....**1** E2
South Chailey BN8 ....**100** D7
St John's Dr BN24 ..**174** E6
St John's Hill BN7 ..**190** A1
St John's Ho BN21 ..**188** F8
St John's Meads CE Prim Sch
BN20 ....**188** D7
St John's Mount ⬛8 BN2 **189** C2
St John's Pk TN4 ......**8** A8
St John's Pl
Brighton **189** C2
⬛22 Hove BN3 ......**163** C6
St John's Rd
Bexhill TN40 ....**157** D6
Crowborough TN6 ......**25** D4
East Grinstead RH19 ....**1** E2
Eastbourne BN20 ......**188** F8
Haywards Heath RH16 ..**50** E2
Hove BN3 ....**163** C5
Polegate BN26 ......**173** C5
Royal Tunbridge Wells TN4 ...**8** A6
Seaford BN25 ......**180** E2
St John's Res Sch BN2 ..**164** D5
St John's St BN7 ....**190** B2
St John's Terr BN7 ..**190** A2
St Johns
Burgess Hill RH15 ......**73** A3
Polegate BN26 ......**173** A6
St Johns Rd RH15 ....**73** A3
St Joseph's Cl BN3 ..**163** A8
St Joseph's RC Prim Sch
Brighton BN2 ....**143** C1
Haywards Heath RH16 ..**50** E4
St Joseph's Trad Est ⬛3
BN3 ....**163** A8
St Josephs Bsns Pk ⬛2
BN3 ....**163** A8
St Josephs Way RH16 ..**50** E4
St Julian's La BN43 ..**161** D7
St Julians Cl BN43 ..**161** C7
St Keyna Ave BN3 ..**162** D6
St Kilda Mans ⬛5 BN21 **184** F3
St Kitts BN3 ....**157** A2
St Kitts Dr BN23 ....**185** G7
St Laurence Cl BN10 ..**167** A1
St Lawrence CE Prim Sch
BN6 ....**97** C6
St Lawrence Mews
BN23 ....**175** A1
St Lawrence Pl BN23 ..**175** A1
St Lawrence Rd TN39 ..**157** B7
St Lawrence Way
Eastbourne BN23 ......**175** A1
Hurstpierpoint BN6 ....**97** A7
St Leonard's Ave BN3 ..**162** C7
St Leonard's Gdns BN3 **162** D7
St Leonard's Pl BN20 ..**184** C3
St Leonard's Rd
⬛9 Brighton BN2 ....**164** C8
Eastbourne BN21 ......**185** A3
Hove BN3 ....**162** C7
St Leonards CE Prim Sch
TN38 ....**159** A7
St Leonards Cl BN9 ..**168** E7
St Leonards Ct TN38 ..**159** A6
St Leonards Pk RH19 ..**1** E1
St Leonards Rd
Bexhill TN40 ....**157** C3
Newhaven BN9 ......**168** F2
St Leonards Terr BN26 **172** F7
St Leonards Warrior Square
Sta TN38 ....**159** C7
St Leonards-Mayfield Sch
TN20 ....**40** A3
St Louie BN42 ......**162** A8
St Lucia ⬛1 TN39 ....**157** A2
St Lucia Wlk ⬛3 BN23 **185** F8
St Luke's CE Inf Sch BN2 **164** C6
St Luke's Inf Sch BN2 ..**164** C6
St Luke's Jun Sch BN2 ..**164** C6
St Luke's La BN9 ....**179** C7
St Luke's Rd
Brighton BN2 ....**164** C6
Royal Tunbridge Wells TN4 ...**8** B6
St Luke's Terr BN2 ..**164** C6
St Lukes Cl RH15 ....**73** A3
St Margaret's Ave RH19 **1** F6
St Margaret's CE Prim Sch
BN2 ....**177** A6
St Margaret's Pl BN1 ..**189** A2
St Margaret's Rd
East Grinstead RH19 ....**1** F3
St Leonards TN37 ....**159** D7
St Margaret's Rise
BN25 ....**180** A6
St Margaret's Terr
TN37 ....**159** D7
St Margarets BN2 ....**177** A6
St Margarets Cres TN39 **156** B8
St Margarets Terr ⬛8
BN3 ....**163** B5

St Mark's Mews ⬛13
BN2 ....**164** E4
St Mark's Rd TN2 ....**16** F7
St Mark's St BN2 ....**164** E4
St Marks Cl TN39 ....**156** D5
St Marks Field TN22 ..**57** B5
St Martin's Ct ⬛6 BN2 **189** C5
St Martin's Flats ⬛6 BN2 **164** C7
St Martin's La BN7 ..**190** A1
St Martin's Pl BN2 ..**164** C7
St Martin's St BN2 ..**189** C5
St Martins TN33 ....**112** D5
St Martins CE Prim Sch
BN2 ....**164** C8
St Martins Cres BN9 ..**168** D1
St Martins Ho BN8 ..**124** E6
St Martins Rd BN22 ..**173** D5
St Mary Magdalen RC Prim
Sch BN1 ....**163** C5
St Mary Magdalene RC
Sch TN40 ....**157** F6
St Mary Magdalene St
BN2 ....**189** C5
St Mary Star of the Sea RC
Prim Sch TN37 ....**159** D8
St Mary the Virgin CE Prim
Sch TN7 ....**13** D4
St Mary's CE Sch RH19 ..**1** D2
St Mary's Cl
Cackle Street TN31 ....**90** A2
Eastbourne BN22 ......**173** B2
Ticehurst TN5 ....**31** D1
St Mary's Cnr ⬛3 BN21 **184** D3
St Mary's Cotts
Battle TN33 ....**112** E3
Bexhill TN39 ......**156** F8
⬛4 Eastbourne BN20 ..**184** D3
St Mary's Ct
⬛2 Eastbourne BN21 ..**184** D3
⬛8 St Leonards TN37 ..**159** C7
St Mary's Farmhouse
TN33 ....**112** E3
St Mary's Gdns TN33 ..**112** E3
St Mary's La Bexhill TN39 **156** F8
Speldhurst TN3 ....**7** A8
Ticehurst TN5 ....**31** D1
St Mary's Pl BN2 ....**189** C2
St Mary's RC Prim Sch
Crowborough TN6 ......**26** A2
Portslade-by-S BN41 ..**162** B7
St Mary's Rd
Burgess Hill RH15 ......**72** F4
Eastbourne BN21 ......**184** D4
Hastings TN34 ......**160** A5
St Mary's Rd W RH15 ..**72** E4
St Mary's Sch
Bexhill TN40 ....**157** E6
Maynard's Green TN21 ..**82** A1
St Mary's Sq ⬛17 BN2 **164** D4
St Mary's Terr
Battle TN33 ....**112** F3
Hastings TN34 ......**160** A5
St Mary's Villas TN33 ..**112** E3
St Mary's Wlk BN27 ..**152** C7
St Mary-in-the-Fields
TN20 ....**40** B2
St Marys TN21 ......**80** B2
St Marys Ave BN27 ..**152** C7
St Marys Cotts ⬛18 TN38 **159** C7
St Marys Garth TN22 ..**56** C4
St Marys Mead TN22 ..**56** B3
St Marys Pl ⬛3 BN43 ..**161** A6
St Matthew's Dr TN38 ..**136** C1
St Matthew's Gdns
TN38 ....**136** B1
St Matthew's High Brooms CE
Prim Sch TN4 ....**8** B8
St Matthew's Rd TN38 ..**136** B1
St Matthews Ct BN2 ..**164** C5
St Mellion Cl BN21 ..**151** F8
St Michael's CE Prim Sch
TN31 ....**70** C2
St Michael's Pl
Brighton BN1 ....**163** E6
⬛8 Hastings TN34 ..**159** E7
St Michael's Prim Sch
TN7 ....**14** B5
St Michael's Rd
Portslade-by-S BN41 ..**162** B7
Royal Tunbridge Wells TN4 ...**8** B7
St Michael's Terr BN7 **190** B4
St Michaels Cl
Crowborough TN6 ......**38** B7
Stone Cross BN24 ....**174** A6
St Michaels Rd RH19 ..**1** E2
St Nicholas Cl RH16 ..**51** A6
St Nicholas La BN7 ..**190** B2
St Nicholas Lodge BN1 **189** A2
St Nicholas Pl ⬛2 BN43 **161** A6
St Nicholas Rd
Brighton BN1 ....**189** A3
Portslade-by-S BN41 ..**162** B7
St Nicholas' CE Jun Sch
BN41 ....**162** B9
St Nicolas & St Mary CE Fst &
Mid Sch BN43 ....**161** A8
St Nicolas Cl BN24 ..**175** B6
St Olive's Cl TN21 ..**81** C7
St Pancras Gdns BN7 **146** B8
St Pancras Gn BN7 ..**145** C2
St Pancras RC Prim Sch
BN7 ....**123** D1
St Pancras Rd BN7 ..**146** B8
St Patrick's Cres TN40 **157** C5
St Patrick's Rd BN3 ..**163** A7
St Paul's CE Prim Sch
BN1 ....**189** A3

St Paul's CE Prim Sch
  TN37 . . . . .136 D1
St Paul's Cl RH16 . . . . . . .50 F5
St Paul's Ct Rusthall TN4 . . .7 C4
  St Leonards TN37 . . . . . . .159 D8
St Paul's Pl TN37 . . . . . .159 D8
St Paul's RC Coll 50 F5
St Paul's Rd TN37 . . . . . .136 C1
St Paul's St Brighton BN2 189 C5
  Rusthall TN4 . . . . .7 C4
St Pauls CE Inf Sch TN4 . .7 B4
St Pauls CE Jun Sch TN4 . .7 B4
St Pauls Cl TN37 . . . . . . .173 D3
St Peter & St Paul CE Prim
  Sch TN40 . . . . .157 C4
St Peter's Ave BN10 . . . .178 A8
St Peter's CE Prim Sch
  TN2 . . . . .8 C3
St Peter's Cl Hove BN3 . .141 F2
  Seaford BN25 . . . . .180 E5
St Peter's Com Inf Sch
  BN41 . . . . .162 B7
St Peter's Cres TN40 . . . .157 D5
St Peter's Mews TN40 . . .157 D5
St Peter's Pl BN1,BN2 . . .189 B3
St Peter's RC Prim Sch
  East Grinstead RH19 . . . . . .1 C1
  Shoreham-by-S BN43 . . . .161 A8
St Peter's Rd
  Portslade-by-S BN41 . . . .162 B7
  Seaford BN25 . . . . .180 E5
  St Leonards TN37 . . . . . .159 C8
St Peter's St
  Brighton BN1 . . . . .189 B3
  Royal Tunbridge Wells TN2 . .8 C3
St Peters Mead TN6 . . . . .39 A7
St Peters Pl TN7 . . . . . .190 A2
St Peters Rd RH15 . . . . . .73 A4
St Peters Row TN3 . . . . . . .6 A5
St Philip's Ave BN22 . . . .185 B5
St Philip's RC Prim Sch
  TN22 . . . . .78 C5
St Philips Ct TN2 . . . . .8 D6
St Philips Mews 3 BN3 162 F7
St Richard's Ct BN3 . . . .141 D1
St Richard's Flats BN41 162 B7
St Richard's RC Coll
  TN40 . . . . .157 E4
St Richards Ho 3 TN38 159 C7
St Richards Rd BN41 . . . .162 B7
St Saviour's Rd TN38 . . . .158 F6
St Saviours TN22 . . . . . . .78 D6
St Saviours Ct 1 BN1 . .164 B8
St Stephens Ct TN1 . . . . . .8 B5
St Swithun's Cl RH19 . . . . .1 F1
St Swithun's La BN7 . . . .190 A1
St Swithun's Terr BN7 . .190 A1
St Thomas 5 TN39 . . . . .157 A2
St Thomas a Becket RC Inf
  Sch BN21 . . . . .184 F5
St Thomas a Becket RC Jun
  Sch BN21 . . . . .184 F5
St Thomas CE Prim Sch
  TN36 . . . . .117 F7
St Thomas Ct BN7 . . . . .190 C2
St Thomas of Canterbury Ct
  TN20 . . . . .40 A2
St Thomas's Rd TN34 . . .160 A5
St Thomas's St TN36 . . . .117 F7
St Vincent's Ct BN2 . . . .165 A3
St Vincents Flats TN37 . .136 B4
St Vincents Pl BN20 . . . .184 E1
St Vincents Rd TN38 . . . .158 F6
St Wilfred's Ct 5 RH16 . .50 E4
St Wilfred's Pl BN25 . . . .181 B3
St Wilfrid's CE Prim Sch
  RH16 . . . . .50 F3
St Wilfrid's Ct BN27 . . . .152 B8
St Wilfrid's Gn BN27 . . . .152 C8
St Wilfrids RC Prim Sch
  RH15 . . . . .72 F2
St Wilfrid's Way RH16 . . .50 E4
St Wilfrids Rd RH15 . . . . .73 B4
Salcey Cl TN38 . . . . .135 E2
Salehurst CE Prim Sch
  TN32 . . . . .64 B4
Salehurst Gdns TN38 . . . .135 D2
Salehurst Rd BN21 . . . . .184 C4
Salisbury Cl BN27 . . . . . .173 C2
Salisbury Ct BN25 . . . . . .180 E4
Salisbury Rd
  Bexhill TN40 . . . . .157 B5
  Eastbourne BN20 . . . . . .188 C8
  Hove BN3 . . . . .163 C6
  Langton Green TN3 . . . . . . .6 F3
  Royal Tunbridge Wells TN4 . .8 C8
  Seaford BN25 . . . . .180 E3
  St Leonards TN37 . . . . . .136 C1
Salisbury Rd TN21 . . . . . .81 B8
Salisbury Yd TN37 . . . . . .136 C1
Sally Ct 3 BN2 . . . . . . .185 B3
Salomons Rd TN4 . . . . . . .7 C4
Saltcote La TN31 . . . . . . .93 C7
Saltcote Mews TN31 . . . . .93 C7
Saltdean Cl TN39 . . . . . .156 E3
Saltdean Dr BN2 . . . . . . .177 C5
Saltdean Park Rd BN2 . . .177 C6
Saltdean Prim Sch BN2 . .177 D6
Saltdean Vale BN2 . . . . . .177 D6
Saltdean Way TN39 . . . . .156 D3
Salters La TN34 . . . . . . .160 B4
Saltwood Rd BN25 . . . . .181 C4
Salvador Cl BN24 . . . . . .175 A2
Salvadori Ct TN2 . . . . .9 D6
Salvington Cres TN39 . . . .156 F4
Samoa Way BN23 . . . . . .175 B2
San Feliu Ct RH19 . . . . . . .2 B2

San Jose Cl TN35 . . . . . .160 C6
San Juan Ct BN23 . . . . . .185 G7
Sancroft Rd BN20 . . . . . .184 B3
Sanctuary The BN20 . . . . .184 B4
Sand Hill La BN8,TN22 . . .104 B8
Sand Rd TN3 . . . . .20 A4
Sandbanks Cl BN27 . . . . .152 A5
Sandbanks Gdns BN27 . .152 B5
Sandbanks Gr BN27 . . . .152 B6
Sandbanks Way
  Hailsham BN27 . . . . .152 A6
  Hailsham BN27 . . . . .152 B6
Sandbrook BN6 . . . . .97 F3
Sanders Ho BN3 . . . . . . .162 E8
Sanderstead 1 BN2 . . . .164 F5
Sandfield Rd TN11 . . . . . . .6 A7
Sandford Mews BN23 . . . .174 D3
Sandgate Cl BN25 . . . . . .181 C5
Sandgate Rd BN1 . . . . . .143 C4
Sandhawes Hill RH19 . . . . .2 A4
Sandhill La
  Churches Green BN27 . . . .109 B6
  Crowborough TN6 . . . . . . .26 E7
Sandhurst Ave
  Pembury TN2 . . . . .9 E6
  Woodingdean BN2 . . . . . .144 D1
Sandhurst Cl
  Royal Tunbridge Wells TN2 . . .8 C6
  Sandhurst Cross TN18 . . . .47 A4
Sandhurst Gdns TN34 . . .136 F6
Sandhurst Ho TN2 . . . . . . .8 D5
Sandhurst La TN39 . . . . .156 B6
Sandhurst Mews TN34 . . .174 E1
Sandhurst Pk 8 BN2 . . . .8 C6
Sandhurst Prim Sch
  TN18 . . . . .47 C5
Sandhurst Rd 1 TN18 . . . .47 C5
Sandhurst Vineyards★
  TN18 . . . . .47 C5
Sandore Cl BN25 . . . . . .181 A4
Sandore Rd BN25 . . . . . .181 A4
Sandown Cl
  Eastbourne BN23 . . . . . .174 B4
  Royal Tunbridge Wells TN2 . . .8 F6
Sandown Ct BN3 . . . . . . .141 D1
Sandown Gr TN2 . . . . .8 F6
Sandown Ho TN6 . . . . . . .25 F3
Sandown Pk TN2 . . . . .8 F6
Sandown Prim Sch
  TN34 . . . . .160 C8
Sandown Rd
  Brighton BN2 . . . . .164 D7
  Hastings TN35 . . . . .160 C7
  Southwick BN42 . . . . . . .161 E8
Sandown Way TN40 . . . . .157 C6
Sandpiper Wlk BN23 . . . .174 C2
Sandpit Cotts BN6 . . . . . .99 C2
Sandridge TN6 . . . . .25 F1
Sandridge Cl
  East Grinstead RH19 . . . . .11 A3
  Hove BN3 . . . . .142 A3
  Seaford BN25 . . . . .181 A6
Sandringham Dr BN3 . . . .142 A3
Sandringham Hts TN38 . .135 D3
Sandringham Lodge 17
  BN3 . . . . .163 C6
Sandringham Mews TN4 . .8 A5
Sandrock Hall TN34 . . . . .136 F5
Sandrock Hill TN33,
  TN38 . . . . .135 A4
Sandrock Ho TN2 . . . . . . .8 D4
Sandrock Pk TN34 . . . . . .136 F5
Sandrock Rd TN2 . . . . .8 C4
Sandrocks Way RH16 . . . . .50 E2
Sandwich Dr BN23 . . . . . .158 F8
Sandwich St BN22 . . . . . .185 C6
Sandy Cl TN37 . . . . .136 B5
Sandy Cross Cotts TN21 . .82 A5
Sandy Cross La 1 TN21 . .82 B5
Sandy La
  Chelwood Gate RH17 . . . . .34 C8
  Coleman's Hatch TN7 . . . . .23 D6
  East Grinstead RH19 . . . . . .1 F1
  Framefield TN22 . . . . .79 A7
  Horam TN21 . . . . .81 E2
Sandy Vale RH16 . . . . . . .50 E2
Sanshaw Ct BN21 . . . . . .184 E3
Santa Cruz Dr BN23 . . . .185 F7
Santer Ho TN18 . . . . .45 E4
Santos Wharf 19 BN23 . . .185 F8
Sanyhils Ave BN1 . . . . . .142 F7
Saunders Cl
  Hastings TN34 . . . . .160 A5
  Uckfield TN22 . . . . .78 A8
Saunders Hill BN1 . . . . . .143 D7
Saunders Park Ho 2
  BN2 . . . . .164 C8
Saunders Park Rise
  BN2 . . . . .143 C1
Saunders Park View
  BN2 . . . . .143 C1
Saunders Rd TN4 . . . . .7 E1
Saunders Way TN31 . . . . .95 A2
Savill Rd RH16 . . . . .51 A8
Sawyard Cotts TN22 . . . . .53 C5
Sawyers Cl RH15 . . . . . . .73 C3
Saxby Cl BN23 . . . . .174 E1
Saxby Rd Bexhill TN39 . . .157 A5
  Burgess Hill RH15 . . . . . . .72 D4
Saxon Cl BN2 . . . . .177 C6
Saxon Ct Hove BN3 . . . . .162 D6
  Pevensey Bay BN24 . . . . .175 D5
Saxon Ground BN21 . . . . .184 E4
Saxon La BN25 . . . . .180 E2
Saxon Mount Sch TN38 . .158 E4
Saxon Pl BN21 . . . . .184 C6
Saxon Rd Hastings TN35 .160 D7

Saxon Rd continued
  Hove BN3 . . . . .162 D6
  Newhaven BN9 . . . . .179 C7
Saxon Rise TN40 . . . . . . .157 E4
Saxon St TN37 . . . . .159 C6
Saxonbury 16 BN2 . . . . .189 C3
Saxonbury Cl TN6 . . . . . . .25 C2
Saxonhurst Ct TN37 . . . . .136 B4
Saxons TN37 . . . . .156 F3
Saxonwood Rd TN33 . . . .112 C5
Sayerland La BN26 . . . . . .173 A8
Sayerland Rd BN26 . . . . .173 A8
Sayers The 5 RH19 . . . . . .1 C1
Scamps Hill RH16 . . . . . . .51 C6
Scanlon Cl BN20 . . . . . . .173 A3
Scarborough Rd BN1 . . . .142 D1
Scarletts Cl TN22 . . . . . . .78 B7
Scaynes Hill Rd RH16 . . . .51 D6
Sceptre BN1 . . . . .142 E2
Schofield Way BN23 . . . . .185 F7
School Cl
  Burgess Hill RH15 . . . . . .72 F2
  1 Southwick BN42 . . . . .161 E7
School Cotts
  East Chiltington BN7 . . . .100 A3
  Maresfield TN22 . . . . .55 B4
School Field BN8 . . . . . .101 E5
School Hill
  Barcombe Cross BN8 . . . .101 E4
  Lamberhurst TN3 . . . . .20 B6
  Old Heathfield TN21 . . . . .82 D5
  Winchelsea TN36 . . . . . .117 E8
School La
  Ashurst Wood RH19 . . . . .11 A6
  Blackboys TN22 . . . . .80 A6
  Crowborough TN6 . . . . . . .25 F1
  Crowborough,St John's
    TN6 . . . . .25 D4
  Danehill RH17 . . . . .34 B5
  Forest Row RH18 . . . . . . .11 F2
  Hadlow Down TN22 . . . . . .57 B5
  Nutley TN22 . . . . .35 C5
  Peasmarsh TN31 . . . . .69 B2
  Polegate BN26 . . . . .173 A7
  Pyecombe BN45 . . . . . . .119 C6
  Saltdean BN2 . . . . .177 C6
School Path BN8 . . . . . . .101 D4
School Pl TN40 . . . . .158 A5
School Rd Hastings TN35 .160 C7
  Hove BN3 . . . . .162 F8
School Rise
  Brighton BN2 . . . . .164 E6
  Royal Tunbridge Wells TN2 . . .7 F1
School Terr TN32 . . . . . . .64 C5
Schwerte Way 5 TN37 . . .159 E7
Science Park Rd BN1 . . . .144 B7
Science Park Sq BN1 . . . .144 B6
Scotland St BN2 . . . . . . .189 C3
Scotney Castle★ TN3 . . . .20 D3
Scotney Castle Gdns★
  TN3 . . . . .20 D3
Scotsford Cl TN21 . . . . . . .59 F1
Scotsford Hill TN20 . . . . . .40 E1
Scotsford Rd TN21 . . . . . .59 F2
Scott Rd BN3 . . . . .162 F7
Scotts Acre TN31 . . . . . . .94 E2
Scotts Way TN2 . . . . .16 E8
Scrace Hill Terr RH16 . . . .73 F8
Scraper's Hill BN8 . . . . . .128 A8
Scrase Lodge RH15 . . . . . .73 D3
Scutes Cl TN34 . . . . .160 A7
Sea Cotts 5 BN25 . . . . . .180 F2
Sea Ct BN24 . . . . .175 D4
Sea Ho 14 BN42 . . . . . . .161 E7
Sea Rd Bexhill TN40 . . . . .157 D3
  Camber TN31 . . . . .94 F2
  Fairlight Cove TN35 . . . . .139 A5
  Pevensey Bay BN24 . . . . .175 D5
  St Leonards TN38 . . . . . .158 F6
  Winchelsea Beach TN36 . . .118 B7
Sea-Saw Way BN2 . . . . . .164 F7
Seabeach La BN22 . . . . . .185 C5
Seabourne Rd TN40 . . . . .158 A6
Seacliffe BN10 . . . . .177 F3
Seafield Cl BN25 . . . . . . .181 B5
Seafield Rd BN3 . . . . . . .163 B6
Seaford Ct BN12 . . . . . . .180 E2
Seaford Head Com Coll
  Seaford BN25 . . . . .180 F2
  Seaford BN25 . . . . .181 A2
Seaford Mus of Local
  History★ BN25 . . . . .180 E1
Seaford Prim Sch BN25 180 E4
Seaford Rd
  Eastbourne BN22 . . . . . .185 C5
  Hove BN3 . . . . .162 C6
  Newhaven BN9 . . . . .179 F8
Seaford Sta BN25 . . . . . .180 E3
Seagrave Cl BN25 . . . . . .180 A6
Seagrove Way BN25 . . . . .180 F5
Searle Ave BN10 . . . . . . .178 E6
Seaside BN22,BN23 . . . . .185 C5
Seaside Pas TN38 . . . . . .158 F6
Seaside Rd
  Eastbourne BN21 . . . . . .185 B3
  St Leonards TN38 . . . . . .158 F6
Seaside Rdbt BN23 . . . . .185 D7
Seaside Way TN38 . . . . . .158 F6
Seattle Dr BN23 . . . . . . .175 A1
Seaview Ave BN10 . . . . . .178 D6
Seaview Cotts TN36 . . . . .116 C5
Seaview Est BN42 . . . . . .161 F7
Seaview Ho BN9 . . . . . . .179 D6
Seaview Terr
  Newhaven BN9 . . . . .168 F1
  Peacehaven BN10 . . . . . .178 E6
  Woodingdean BN2 . . . . . .165 B8

Seaview Terr
  Icklesham TN31 . . . . . . .116 E5
  2 Rye TN31 . . . . .93 C5
Seaville Dr
  Eastbourne BN23 . . . . . .185 D8
  Pevensey Bay BN24 . . . . .175 D8
Second Ave Bexhill TN40 .157 C5
  Camber TN31 . . . . .94 F2
  Hove BN3 . . . . .163 C6
  Newhaven BN9 . . . . .179 C6
Second Rd BN10 . . . . . . .178 A7
Sedgebrook Gdns TN34 136 E2
Sedges The BN38 . . . . . . .135 E1
Sedgewick Rd TN40 . . . . .157 C6
Sedlescombe CE Prim Sch
  TN33 . . . . .88 E1
Sedlescombe Gdns
  TN38 . . . . .136 B2
Sedlescombe Organic
  Vineyard★ TN32 . . . . . . .88 D5
Sedlescombe Rd N
  TN37 . . . . .136 B4
Sedlescombe Rd S
  TN38 . . . . .136 B1
Sefton Chase TN6 . . . . . . .26 A3
Sefton Rd BN41 . . . . .140 F3
Sefton Way TN6 . . . . .26 A3
Segrave Cl BN7 . . . . .123 B2
Selba Dr BN2 . . . . .143 C3
Selborne Pl BN3 . . . . . . .163 C7
Selborne Rd BN3 . . . . . . .163 C6
Selby Cl TN22 . . . . .78 D5
Selby Ct RH16 . . . . .50 E3
Selby Gdns TN22 . . . . . . .78 D5
Selby Rd
  Eastbourne BN21 . . . . . .184 D5
  Uckfield TN22 . . . . .78 D6
Selby Rise TN22 . . . . .78 D5
Selham Cl BN1 . . . . .143 D6
Selham Dr BN1 . . . . .143 D6
Selham Pl BN1 . . . . .143 D6
Selhurst Rd BN2 . . . . . . .165 E6
Sellbourne Pk TN3 . . . . . .17 C4
Selmeston Cl TN34 . . . . .136 D1
Selmeston Ct 2 BN25 . .180 C4
Selmeston Ho 8 BN21 . .184 D4
Selmeston Pl BN2 . . . . . .164 F6
Selmeston Rd BN2 . . . . . .164 F5
Selsey Cl BN1 . . . . .143 E6
Selsfield Cl BN21 . . . . . . .184 D6
Selsfield Dr BN2 . . . . . . .143 D3
Selwyn Dr BN21 . . . . . . .184 E4
Selwyn Ho 10 BN21 . . . .184 D4
Selwyn Park Ct 9 BN21 .184 D4
Selwyn Rd BN21 . . . . . . .184 E4
Semley Lodge BN6 . . . . . .97 E4
Semley Rd Brighton BN1 .143 A1
  Hassocks BN6 . . . . .97 E4
Sempstead La TN31,TN32 66 C4
Senlac Gdns TN33 . . . . . .112 C5
Senlac Ct TN33 . . . . .112 C5
Senlac Gn TN22 . . . . .78 E8
Senlac Pl TN3 . . . . .15 C7
Senlac Rd BN9 . . . . .179 D7
Senlac Way TN37 . . . . . .136 C5
Sergison Cl RH15 . . . . . . .50 C5
Sergison Rd RH16 . . . . . . .50 D5
Setfords Field BN8 . . . . . .75 E1
Sett The BN41 . . . . .141 B4
Sevelands Cl BN2 . . . . . .164 F7
Seven Acre Ct TN37 . . . .136 A5
Seven Dials BN1 . . . . . . .189 A4
Seven Sisters Ctry Pk★
  BN25 . . . . .182 A2
Seven Sisters Rd BN23 . . .173 C3
Seven Sisters Sheep Ctr★
  BN20 . . . . .187 B7
Seven Sisters Visitor Ctr★
  BN25 . . . . .181 F4
Sevenfields RH15 . . . . . . .72 D4
Sevenoaks Rd BN23 . . . . .174 D2
Seville St BN2 . . . . .164 C7
Sewell Ave TN40 . . . . . . .157 D5
Seymour Cotts TN6 . . . . . .27 D1
Seymour Ho 5 BN2 . . . .164 D4
Seymour Sq 3 BN2 . . . .164 D4
Seymour St 4 BN2 . . . .164 D4
Seymour Villas TN34 . . . .160 A7
Shaftesbury Ct TN22 . . . . .78 C8
Shaftesbury Pl BN1 . . . . .164 A8
Shaftesbury Rd
  Brighton BN1 . . . . .189 B5
  Royal Tunbridge Wells TN4 . .8 A5
Shakespeare St BN3 . . . .163 A8
Shakespeare Wlk BN23 . .174 D2
Shalesbrook La RH18 . . . . .12 A1
Shalfleet Cl BN23 . . . . . .174 B3
Shandon Cl TN2 . . . . .8 C4
Shands BN6 . . . . .97 F3
Shanklin Cl BN23 . . . . . .174 B4
Shanklin Ct
  11 Brighton BN2 . . . . . .164 C8
  Hove BN3 . . . . .141 D1
Shanklin Rd BN2 . . . . . . .164 C8
Shannon Cl BN10 . . . . . .167 B1
Shannon Way BN10 . . . . .185 F8
Sharp's Cnr TN21 . . . . . .106 E8
Sharpthorne Cres BN41 . .141 C1
Sharrow Ct RH16 . . . . . . .50 C5
Shaw The TN12 . . . . .67 B7
Shawcross Ho 5 BN1 . . .142 E2
Shawfield TN6 . . . . .26 B2
Shaws Cnr TN11 . . . . .67 B7
Shearbarn Holiday Pk
  TN35 . . . . .160 E2
Shedden Ct TN21 . . . . . . .82 A8

Sheddingdean Bsns Ctr
  RH15 . . . . .72 F5
Sheddingdean Cl RH15 . . .73 A4
Sheddingdean Com Prim Sch
  RH15 . . . . .73 A5
Sheddingdean Ct RH15 . .72 F4
Sheddingdean
  Neighbourhood Ctr
  RH15 . . . . .73 A5
Sheen Rd BN2 . . . . .185 B4
Sheep Pen La 3 BN25 . .181 A3
Sheep Plain TN6 . . . . .37 D8
Sheep Wlk BN2 . . . . .165 F1
Sheepbell Cl BN41 . . . . . .141 B3
Sheepcote La
  Chalvington BN27 . . . . . .150 C8
  Golden Cross BN27 . . . . .127 C3
Sheepfair BN7 . . . . .123 A2
Sheepfold The BN10 . . . .167 C1
Sheepsetting La TN21 . . . .81 E7
Sheepstreet La TN19,TN5 .43 E5
Sheepwash La TN22 . . . . .80 C8
Sheerwater Cres TN34 . . .136 D4
Sheerwater Terr TN34 . . .136 D4
Sheffield Mill La TN22 . . . .53 C8
Sheffield Park Gdn★
  TN22 . . . . .53 D5
Sheffield Park Sta★
  TN22 . . . . .53 A4
Sheffield Park Way
  BN23 . . . . .174 A4
Sheiling Rd TN6 . . . . .25 E3
Shell La 9 TN34 . . . . . . .160 A3
Shelldale Ave BN41 . . . . .162 B7
Shelldale Cres BN41 . . . .162 B8
Shelldale Rd BN41 . . . . . .162 B8
Shelley Cl BN7 . . . . .123 B3
Shelley Ct 4 RH16 . . . . . .50 D5
Shelley Pk 4 TN21 . . . . . .82 A7
Shelley Rd
  East Grinstead RH19 . . . . . .1 D1
  Hove BN3 . . . . .162 F7
  Ringmer BN8 . . . . .124 C5
Shelley Wlk 3 BN23 . . . .174 D2
Shelley Wood RH15 . . . . .72 D4
Shenfield Way BN1 . . . . .143 D3
Shenstone RH16 . . . . .51 B8
Shepham Ave BN2 . . . . . .177 D6
Shepham La BN26 . . . . . .173 A1
Shepherd St 3 TN38 . . . .159 C6
Shepherd's Cl TN39 . . . . .156 D4
Shepherd's Hill TN7 . . . . .23 D8
Shepherd's Way TN35 . . .138 E4
Shepherds Cl
  Eastbourne BN22 . . . . . .173 F3
  Piddinghoe BN9 . . . . . . .168 B2
  Ringmer BN8 . . . . .124 E5
Shepherds Cot BN10 . . . .167 D2
Shepherds Croft BN1 . . . .142 C4
Shepherds Ct TN35 . . . . .138 E4
Shepherds Mead RH15 . .72 F2
Shepherds Way
  Ringmer BN8 . . . . .124 E5
  South Chailey BN8 . . . . . .100 C3
  Uckfield TN22 . . . . .78 C5
Shepherds Wlk
  Crowborough TN6 . . . . . . .26 C1
  Hassocks BN6 . . . . .97 F3
  Royal Tunbridge Wells TN2 . . .8 D4
Shepherdsgrove La RH19 . .3 A4
Sheppard Way TN41 . . . .141 A3
Sheppey Wlk BN27 . . . . .129 C5
Sheppeys RH16 . . . . .50 D2
Shepway Par BN25 . . . . .180 E3
Shepway The BN25 . . . . .181 B4
Sheraton Cl BN21 . . . . . .184 F2
Sherborne Ct 5 BN21 . . .184 D4
Sherborne Cl
  Hove BN3 . . . . .141 D3
  Royal Tunbridge Wells TN2 . . .8 D2
Sherborne Rd BN3 . . . . . .141 D3
Sherbourne Way BN3 . . . .141 D3
Sheridan Mans BN3 . . . . .163 A8
Sheridan Pl RH19 . . . . .1 C1
Sheridan Terr BN3 . . . . . .163 A8
Sheriff's La TN6 . . . . .39 D7
Sheringham Cl TN32 . . . . .65 E2
Sherrington Rd BN2 . . . . .165 F8
Sherwood Dr TN34 . . . . .136 F1
Sherwood Dr RH16 . . . . . .50 C5
Sherwood Gn BN27 . . . . .152 B6
Sherwood Park Com Prim
  Sch TN2 . . . . .8 D6
Sherwood Pl TN3 . . . . .6 E3
Sherwood Rd
  Royal Tunbridge Wells TN2 . .8 E5
  Seaford BN25 . . . . .180 F4
Sherwood Rise BN25 . . . .180 F4
Sherwood Way TN2 . . . . . .8 D6
Shinewater Ct BN23 . . . . .174 B3
Shinewater La BN23 . . . . .174 B4
Shinewater Prim Sch
  BN23 . . . . .174 B4
Shinewater Rdbt BN23 . . .174 B3
Shingle Ct TN38 . . . . . . .135 E2
Shingle Rd BN43 . . . . . . .161 A6
Shining Cliff TN34 . . . . . .136 F4
Ship St Brighton BN1 . . . .189 A2
  East Grinstead RH19 . . . . .10 E7
  Newhaven BN9 . . . . .179 C6
Ship Street Gdns BN1 . . .189 A2
Shipley Cl TN39 . . . . .156 D3
Shipley Mill Cl BN24 . . . .174 B5
Shipley Rd BN2 . . . . .165 E7

Shipwreck Heritage Ctr★
TN34 . . . .**160** B3
Shipyard La TN31 . . . . . .**93** C5
Shirlea View TN33 . . . . .**112** E4
Shirley Ave BN3 . . . .**142** B2
Shirley Cl BN43 . . . .**161** D8
Shirley Dr Hove BN3 . . . .**142** C2
St Leonards TN37 . . . . . .**136** B4
Shirley Gdns TN4 . . . .**7** C5
Shirley Gr TN4 . . . .**7** C5
Shirley Mews BN3 . . . . . .**163** B7
Shirley Rd BN3 . . . .**163** C8
Shirley St BN3 . . . .**163** B7
Shirleys BN6 . . . .**98** E2
Shoreham Beach Com Fst
Sch BN43 . . . .**161** A6
Shoreham By-Pass
BN41,BN43 . . . .**140** D2
Shoreham Coll BN43 . . . .**161** D7
Short Brow BN25 . . . . . .**181** A4
Short Brow Cl BN22 . . . .**173** B3
Shortdean Pl BN21 . . . . .**184** D4
Shortgate La
Laughton BN8 . . . .**126** B8
Shortgate BN8 . . . .**104** B2
Shortgate Rd BN2 . . . . . .**143** F4
Shortlands BN22 . . . .**173** C1
Shorts Cl RH16 . . . .**50** E3
Shotters RH15 . . . .**72** E1
Shovelstrode La RH19 . . .**11** D8
Showfields Rd TN2 . . . . . .**7** F1
Shropshire Ct BN20 . . . . .**184** B7
Shrub La TN19 . . . .**62** C7
Shrublands Ct TN2 . . . . . .**8** C4
Shrublands The TN39 . . .**156** E3
Sicklehatch La TN21 . . . .**82** B2
Sidcup Dr TN23 . . . .**174** D2
Sidehill Dr BN41 . . . .**140** F2
Sidehills BN8 . . . .**101** D4
Sidley Com Prim Sch
TN39 . . . .**157** C7
Sidley Gn TN39 . . . .**157** C7
Sidley Rd BN22 . . . .**185** C5
Sidley St TN39 . . . .**157** C7
Sidney Cl TN2 . . . .**16** F8
Sidney Tidy Ho **5** BN2 .**164** C6
Silchester Rd TN38 . . . . .**159** C7
Sillwood Ct **8** BN1 . . . . .**163** E5
Sillwood Hall **2** BN1 . .**163** E5
Sillwood Pl **17** BN1 . . . .**163** E5
Sillwood Rd BN1 . . . .**163** E5
Sillwood St BN1 . . . .**163** E5
Sillwood Terr **22** BN1 . .**163** E5
Silva Cl TN40 . . . .**158** A6
Silvan Rd TN38 . . . .**135** E4
Silver Bank Cotts TN19 . .**64** B8
Silver Birches
Brighton BN1 . . . .**142** E1
Haywards Heath RH16 . . . .**51** A4
Silver Ct RH19 . . . .**1** C2
Silver Hill TN19 . . . .**45** B1
Silver Strand E **8** BN23 **175** A1
Silver Strand W BN23 . . .**175** A1
Silverdale BN6 . . . .**98** B3
Silverdale Ave BN3 . . . . .**163** D7
Silverdale Ct BN27 . . . . .**152** B8
Silverdale La
Royal Tunbridge Wells TN4 . . .**8** B6
Sandhurst Cross TN18 . . . .**46** F5
Silverdale Prim Sch
TN38 . . . .**136** B3
Silverdale Rd
Burgess Hill RH15 . . . .**73** B2
Eastbourne BN20 . . . .**184** F1
Hove BN3 . . . .**163** D7
Royal Tunbridge Wells TN4 . . .**8** B6
Silverden Cotts TN18 . . . .**46** F4
Silverhill Ave TN37 . . . . .**136** C4
Silverlands Rd **1** TN37 .**136** B2
Silvester Rd TN40 . . . . . .**157** C5
Silwood Cl TN2 . . . .**8** E7
Simmonds Ct TN4 . . . .**7** B4
Simons Cl TN6 . . . .**26** A1
Singleton Mill Rd BN24 . .**174** C5
Singleton Rd BN1 . . . . . .**143** A6
Singleton Way RH15 . . . . .**73** C1
Singleton Wlk TN40 . . . .**158** B6
Sinnock Sq **17** TN34 . . .**160** B4
Sion Wlk **8** TN1 . . . .**8** A2
Sir David's Pk TN4 . . . . . .**7** C7
Sir Henry Fermor CE Prim
Sch TN6 . . . .**26** A2
Six Bells Mews TN31 . . . .**67** C5
Skinner's La TN33 . . . . . .**133** D8
Skinners' Sch The TN4 . . . .**8** A6
Skippers Hill Manor Sch
TN20 . . . .**58** B7
Skyline View BN10 . . . . .**167** D1
Slade The TN3 . . . .**20** A3
Sleeches Cross TN3 . . . . .**17** B2
Sleepers Stile Rd TN5 . . . .**19** B1
Slider's La Fletching TN22 .**53** A7
Furner's Green TN22 . . . . .**34** B1
Slides The TN38 . . . .**135** F3
Slimbridge Rd RH15 . . . . .**72** F3
Slindon Ave BN10 . . . . . .**178** D6
Slindon Cres BN23 . . . . .**174** E1
Slinfold Cl BN2 . . . .**164** D5
Sliverick's La TN33 . . . . .**109** F7
Sloane Ct **4** BN2 . . . . . .**164** C5
Sloe La BN26 . . . .**171** A3
Slonk Hill Rd BN43 . . . . .**140** A1
Sloop La RH17 . . . .**52** D5
Slugwash La RH17 . . . . . .**74** F7
Small Acre BN27 . . . .**127** B3

Smeatons La TN36 . . . . .**118** B5
Smith Cl TN33 . . . .**133** B5
Smithlands La BN8 . . . . .**106** A3
Smithy The
Best Beech Hill TN5 . . . . . .**29** A3
Uckfield TN22 . . . .**78** B6
Smithy's Cl TN37 . . . . . .**136** C5
Smolletts RH19 . . . .**10** C8
Smugglers Cl BN26 . . . . .**170** F3
Smugglers La TN6 . . . . . .**25** D5
Smugglers Way TN35 . . .**138** F4
Snape La TN35 . . . .**29** D1
Snape View TN5 . . . .**29** F4
Snatt's Rd TN22 . . . .**55** C1
Snednore BN7 . . . .**145** F5
Snipe Cl TN2 . . . .**9** E8
Snowdon Cl BN23 . . . . . .**174** D3
Snowdrop La RH16 . . . . . .**51** C4
Snowflakes La RH16 . . . . .**51** D6
Soames Ct RH15 . . . .**72** F4
Solomon's La TN22 . . . . . .**87** C4
Solomons Cl BN23 . . . . .**175** B2
Solway BN27 . . . .**129** A2
Solway Ave BN1 . . . .**142** F7
Somerhill Ave BN3 . . . . .**163** D7
Somerhill Ct **10** BN3 . . . .**163** D7
Somerhill Jun Sch BN3 . .**163** D6
Somerhill Lodge BN3 . . . .**163** D6
Somerhill Rd BN3 . . . . . .**163** D7
Somerset Ct
Eastbourne BN23 . . . .**174** E1
3 Hove BN3 . . . .**163** C7
Somerset Point **1** BN2 .**164** C4
Somerset Rd **8** A6
Somerset St BN2 . . . .**164** C5
Somerset Villas TN3 . . . . .**15** C7
Somerville Cl BN3 . . . . . .**185** E7
Somerville Gdns TN4 . . . . .**7** F4
Sompting Cl BN2 . . . .**164** F7
Sompting Ct **3** BN43 . . .**161** B8
Sorrel Cl BN23 . . . .**174** C3
Sorrel Dr BN23 . . . .**174** C3
South Ave Brighton BN2 .**164** C5
Eastbourne BN20 . . . .**184** B5
Hurstpierpoint BN6 . . . . . .**97** A5
South Bank BN6 . . . .**97** E4
South Brooks Rd BN29 . . .**96** F2
South Cl
Beachlands BN24 . . . .**175** F6
Burgess Hill RH15 . . . .**72** E1
Hailsham BN27 . . . .**152** B6
South Cliff Bexhill TN39 .**156** F2
13 Eastbourne BN20 . . . .**185** A1
Eastbourne BN20 . . . .**188** F8
South Cliff Ave
Bexhill TN39 . . . .**156** C2
Eastbourne BN20 . . . .**184** F1
South Cliff Twr BN20 . . . .**188** F8
South Coast Rd
Peacehaven BN10 . . . .**178** D6
Telscombe Cliffs BN2,
BN10 . . . .**177** E4
South Ct Lewes BN7 . . . .**190** C2
Royal Tunbridge Wells TN4 . . .**8** A6
South Downs TN7 . . . .**99** E5
South Downs Bsns Pk
BN7 . . . .**190** C3
South Downs Sch Com Specl
The BN20 . . . .**184** B4
South Dr RH15 . . . .**72** B3
South Gr TN1 . . . .**8** A2
South La Newhaven BN9 .**179** D7
Wood's Corner TN21 . . . . . .**84** E2
South Lodge **9** BN2 . . .**164** F5
South Lodge Cl RH15 . . . .**72** F4
South Lynn Dr BN21 . . . .**184** F1
South Malling CE Prim Sch
BN7 . . . .**190** C4
South Pl BN7 . . . .**190** B2
South Point **9** BN43 . . .**161** A6
South Rd Brighton BN1 . .**142** E1
Hailsham BN27 . . . .**152** B6
Haywards Heath RH16 . . . .**50** E4
Newhaven BN9 . . . .**179** D7
Wivelsfield Green RH17 . . . .**74** D4
South Rd Mews BN1 . . . .**142** E1
South Rough BN8 . . . .**76** C7
South Side TN21 . . . .**59** E1
South St Brighton BN1 . .**189** A2
Crowborough TN6 . . . .**25** E1
Ditchling BN6 . . . .**98** D3
East Hoathly BN8 . . . .**104** F4
Eastbourne BN21 . . . .**185** A2
Falmer BN1 . . . .**144** C6
Lewes BN7 . . . .**190** C2
Mayfield TN20 . . . .**40** B2
Portslade-by-S BN41 . . . . .**141** A1
Rotherfield TN6 . . . .**39** B8
Seaford BN25 . . . .**180** E2
St Leonards TN37 . . . .**159** C7
South Terr
Broad Oak TN21 . . . .**59** E1
Hastings TN34 . . . .**159** F8
Westfield TN35 . . . .**114** E3
South Undercliff TN31 . . .**93** C5
South View Ditchling BN6 .**98** E5
11 Eastbourne BN21 . . .**184** E4
Hastings TN34 . . . .**160** B4
Newhaven BN9 . . . .**168** E2
South View Cl TN19 . . . . .**44** F3
South View Rd
Crowborough TN6 . . . .**25** D4
Royal Tunbridge Wells TN4 . . .**8** B7
Turner's Green TN5 . . . . . .**29** F6
South Way Lewes BN7 . . .**123** A1
Newhaven BN9 . . . .**179** D7
Seaford BN25 . . . .**181** C1

South Woodlands BN1 . .**142** E5
Southall Ave BN7 . . . . . .**143** D2
Southampton Cl **16**
BN23 . . . .**185** F8
Southampton St BN2 . . .**189** C3
Southborough CE Prim Sch &
Tunbridge Wells Language
Unit TN4 . . . .**7** E8
Southbourne Rd BN22 . .**185** C6
Southcliffe BN7 . . . .**190** C4
Southcourt Ave TN39 . . .**156** F2
Southdown Ave
Brighton BN1 . . . .**143** A1
Eastbourne BN20 . . . .**173** A3
Hastings TN34 . . . .**160** B2
Lewes BN7 . . . .**146** A8
Peacehaven BN10 . . . .**178** B6
Portslade-by-S BN41 . . . . .**162** C8
Southdown Cl
Haywards Heath RH16 . . . .**50** D2
Newhaven BN9 . . . .**179** B6
Southdown Com Sch
BN23 . . . .**174** B3
Southdown Cotts BN20 . .**173** B3
Southdown Ct
3 Hailsham BN27 . . . . .**152** C7
Polegate BN26 . . . .**172** F6
Southdown Ho
7 Eastbourne BN20 . . . .**184** F1
9 Eastbourne BN20 . . . .**185** A1
Southdown Jun Sch
BN9 . . . .**179** C7
Southdown Mews BN2 . .**164** C5
Southdown Pl
Brighton BN1 . . . .**143** A1
Lewes BN7 . . . .**190** A1
Southdown Rd
Brighton BN1 . . . .**143** A1
Eastbourne BN20 . . . .**184** C7
Newhaven BN9 . . . .**179** B6
Portslade-by-S BN41 . . . . .**141** A2
Seaford BN25 . . . .**181** A2
Southwick BN42 . . . .**161** E7
Southease Sta BN8 . . . . .**168** A7
Southerden Cl TN37 . . . .**152** C7
Southern Ave BN26 . . . . .**173** B6
Southern Cross BN41 . . .**162** B8
Southern Rd BN22 . . . . .**173** F2
Southern Ring Rd BN1 . .**144** B6
Southfield BN26 . . . .**172** F5
Southfield Rd TN4 . . . .**8** A6
Southfields Speldhurst TN3 .**7** A7
Turner's Green TN5 . . . . . .**29** F6
Southfields Ct **9** BN21 .**184** F3
Southfields Rd BN21 . . . .**184** F3
Southfields Way TN4 . . . .**8** B8
Southgate TN4 . . . .**7** F3
Southlands RH19 . . . .**10** E7
Southlands Ave TN39 . . .**157** A7
Southlands Ct **1** BN43 .**161** B8
Southlands Gen Hospl
BN43 . . . .**140** B1
Southlands Rd TN39 . . . .**157** A7
Southmead Cl TN20 . . . . .**40** D3
Southmount BN1 . . . . . .**143** B1
Southon Cl BN41 . . . .**140** F3
Southover CE Prim Sch
BN7 . . . .**190** A1
Southover High St BN7 . .**190** A1
Southover Manor Ho
BN7 . . . .**190** A1
Southover Pl BN2 . . . . . .**189** C4
Southover Rd BN7 . . . . . .**190** A1
Southover St BN2 . . . . . .**189** C3
Southport Cl TN38 . . . . .**158** F7
Southridge Rd TN6 . . . . . .**37** E8
Southridge Rise TN6 . . . . .**37** E8
Southview RH15 . . . .**72** D3
Southview Cl
Crowborough TN6 . . . .**25** E1
Shoreham-by-S BN43 . . . . .**161** C7
Southwick BN42 . . . .**161** E7
Southview Dr TN22 . . . . . .**78** D8
Southview Rd
Peacehaven BN10 . . . .**178** C8
Southwick BN42 . . . .**161** E8
Southwater Cl BN2 . . . . .**164** D6
Southwater Rd TN37 . . . .**159** C8
Southway RH15 . . . .**72** D3
Southway Jun Sch RH15 . .**72** D3
Southwick Cl RH19 . . . . . .**1** D2
Southwick Ho **6** RH19 . .**1** D2
Southwick Sq BN42 . . . . .**161** E7
Southwick St BN42 . . . . .**161** E8
Southwick Sta BN42 . . . .**161** E7
Southwood Ave TN4 . . . . .**8** A6
Southwood Cl TN38 . . . .**136** A1
Southwood Rd TN4 . . . . . .**7** B5
Sovereign Bsns Pk RH15 .**72** E2
Sovereign Cl
Hastings TN34 . . . .**160** A8
Seaford BN25 . . . .**181** A5
Sovereign Ct
Bexhill TN40 . . . .**157** E5
Brighton BN2 . . . .**165** A3
Eastbourne BN22 . . . .**185** C5
Sovereign Dr
Burgess Hill RH15 . . . .**72** E2
Eastbourne BN22 . . . .**185** E6
Sovereign Ho TN38 . . . . .**159** A6
Sovereign Mews TN38 . .**159** A6
Spa Ct **4** BN3 . . . .**163** B5
Spa Ind Pk TN2 . . . .**8** E8
Spa Valley Rly★ TN3 . . . .**15** D7
Spaldings The TN38 . . . .**135** E4
Spanish Ct RH15 . . . .**73** B4
Sparke Gdns TN33 . . . . .**133** A6
Sparrow Way RH15 . . . . .**72** D3

Sparrows Green Rd TN5 . .**29** F5
Sparrows The BN10 . . . . .**167** C1
Spatham La BN6 . . . .**98** F4
Speckled Wood TN35 . . .**160** C7
Speldhurst CE Prim Sch
TN3 . . . .**7** A7
Speldhurst Rd TN3 . . . .**7** B8
Speldhurst Rd
Langton Green TN3 . . . .**6** F4
Royal Tunbridge Wells TN3,
TN4 . . . .**7** E8
Spencer Ave BN3 . . . . . .**141** D3
Spencer Mews **6** TN1 . . .**8** A2
Spencer Rd BN21 . . . . . .**185** A2
Spences Field BN7 . . . . .**190** C3
Spences La BN7 . . . .**190** C3
Spicers Cl RH15 . . . .**72** F5
Spindlewood Country Holiday
Pk TN35 . . . .**160** C8
Spindlewood Dr TN39 . . .**156** C4
Spinnals Gr BN42 . . . . . .**161** D7
Spinney Cl BN6 . . . .**97** C5
Spinney The Battle TN33 .**112** F2
Bexhill TN39 . . . .**156** D3
Burgess Hill RH15 . . . .**73** B5
Golden Cross BN27 . . . . . .**127** B3
Hassocks BN6 . . . .**97** F5
Haywards Heath TN34 . . . .**136** E1
Haywards Heath RH16 . . . .**50** D8
Hove BN3 . . . .**142** C3
Robertsbridge TN32 . . . . . .**63** F3
Spinneys The
Heathfield TN21 . . . .**82** B6
Lewes BN7 . . . .**190** B2
Spital Rd BN7 . . . .**123** B1
Spithurst Rd BN8 . . . . . .**101** E6
Spode La TN8 . . . .**4** A7
Sponden La TN18 . . . .**47** A7
Sportcentre Rd BN1 . . . .**144** A6
Spotted Cow La TN22 . . . .**56** E5
Spout Hill TN6 . . . .**27** D1
Spray Hill TN3 . . . .**20** B4
Spray's La TN33,TN35 . . .**114** B4
Spring Cl BN20 . . . .**173** B1
Spring Copse RH19 . . . . . .**1** F4
Spring Gdns
Brighton BN1 . . . .**189** B2
Glynde BN8 . . . .**147** F5
Lewes BN7 . . . .**190** B2
Rusthall TN4 . . . .**7** B4
6 Southwick BN42 . . . .**161** E7
Spring Hill Northiam TN31 .**67** B7
Saint's Hill TN11,TN3 . . . . . .**6** A7
Spring La Bexhill TN39 . .**156** C5
Burwash TN19 . . . .**61** F6
Clayton BN6 . . . .**119** E8
Poundford TN20 . . . .**58** A5
Spring Lodge Cl BN23 . . .**174** E2
Spring Mdw RH18 . . . . . .**11** F1
Spring Pk TN21 . . . .**82** A8
Spring St Brighton BN1 . .**163** E5
St Leonards TN37 . . . .**136** C1
Spring Stps TN36 . . . . . .**117** F8
Spring Way RH19 . . . .**2** A4
Springate Rd BN42 . . . . .**161** F8
Springett Almshouses
TN18 . . . .**45** E8
Springett Ave BN8 . . . . .**124** D5
Springett Cotts BN8 . . . .**124** D5
Springfield RH19 . . . .**1** D4
Springfield Ave BN10 . . .**177** F4
Springfield Cl
Crowborough TN6 . . . .**26** B2
Westham BN24 . . . .**174** F6
Springfield Cotts
Cackle Street TN31 . . . .**90** A2
Rotherfield TN6 . . . .**39** B8
Springfield Rd
Bexhill TN40 . . . .**157** C6
Brighton BN1 . . . .**164** A8
Eastbourne BN22 . . . .**185** B4
Groombridge TN3 . . . .**15** C7
St Leonards TN38 . . . .**136** B1
Springfield Valley TN38 .**135** F1
Springfields TN5 . . . .**31** E1
Springfields Farm Ind Est
RH17 . . . .**73** F5
Springhead TN2 . . . .**8** D5
Springhead Way TN6 . . . .**37** E8
Springside Wlk TN38 . . .**135** F1
Springview Apartments
TN2 . . . .**8** D6
Springwood Rd TN21 . . . .**82** A8
Spruce Cl BN22 . . . .**173** D2
Spruce Ho TN4 . . . .**7** E4
Spur Rd BN26 . . . .**173** B5
Spurway Pk BN26 . . . . . .**173** B5
Squab La BN27 . . . .**130** A5
Square The
Beachlands BN24 . . . .**175** F6
Brighton BN1 . . . .**142** E6
Cowden TN8 . . . .**4** B6
Hailsham BN27 . . . .**152** A7
Wadhurst TN5 . . . .**30** A4
Squires Farm Ind Est
TN22 . . . .**79** D1
Squirrel Cl Bexhill TN39 .**156** E5
St Leonards TN38 . . . .**135** F3
Squirrel Way TN2 . . . .**8** E5
Squirrel Wlk BN27 . . . . .**127** B3
Squirrels Drey BN27 . . . .**127** B3
Stable Ctyd TN22 . . . .**23** A1
Stable Mews TN37 . . . . .**136** C5
Stabledene Way TN2 . . . . .**9** D6
Stablefield TN35 . . . .**114** E4
Stables La **9** BN21 . . . .**185** A3

Stables The
Ponts Green TN33 . . . . . .**110** D2
The Moor TN18 . . . .**45** E8
Stacey's Cnr TN21 . . . . . .**85** A5
Stafford Ct Brighton BN2 .**189** C2
2 Eastbourne BN23 . . . .**174** E1
Stafford Ho
10 Eastbourne BN21 . . .**184** F1
Keymer BN6 . . . .**98** A3
Stafford Jun Sch BN22 . .**185** A6
Stafford Rd Brighton BN1 **163** E8
Royal Tunbridge Wells TN2 . . .**8** B4
Seaford BN25 . . . .**180** F3
Stafford Way BN6 . . . .**98** A3
Stag Rd TN3 . . . .**8** D8
Stainsby St **1** TN37 . . .**159** C7
Stalkers La BN8 . . . .**105** E5
Stalkhurst Camping & Cvn Pk
TN35 . . . .**137** B5
Stamford **6** RH16 . . . . .**50** D6
Stamford Bldgs BN8 . . . .**148** E5
Stamford Ct TN35 . . . . . .**160** B6
Stamford Lodge **2** BN1 **142** E2
Stanam Rd TN2 . . . .**9** E6
Standard Hill TN33 . . . . .**132** F5
Standard Hill Cl TN33 . . .**132** F6
Standean Cl BN1 . . . .**143** D6
Standen★ RH19 . . . .**10** C4
Standen Cl RH19 . . . .**1** A4
Standen St
Royal Tunbridge Wells TN4 . . .**8** A5
Standen Street TN17 . . . . .**47** B3
Stanford Ave
Brighton BN1 . . . .**143** A1
Hassocks BN6 . . . .**97** E4
Stanford Cl Hassocks BN6 .**97** E4
Hove BN3 . . . .**142** C1
Stanford Ct BN1 . . . .**163** E8
Stanford Inf Sch BN1 . . .**163** F8
Stanford Jun Sch BN1 . . .**163** F8
Stanford Rd BN1 . . . .**163** E8
Stanford Terr BN6 . . . .**97** E4
Stanhope Pl **1** TN38 . . .**159** C6
Stanhope Rd TN1 . . . .**8** C5
Stanier Rd TN38 . . . .**135** F2
Stanley Ave BN41 . . . . . .**140** F3
Stanley Ave S BN41 . . . . .**140** F3
Stanley Ct **3** BN2 . . . . .**164** C4
Stanley Deason L Ctr
BN2 . . . .**164** F5
Stanley Rd Brighton BN1 .**189** B4
2 Eastbourne BN22 . . . .**185** B4
Hastings TN34 . . . .**159** E8
Peacehaven BN10 . . . .**167** B1
Portslade-by-S BN41 . . . . .**162** A8
Royal Tunbridge Wells TN1 . . .**8** B5
Stanley St BN2 . . . .**189** C4
Stanmer BN1 . . . .**143** F8
Stanmer Ave BN2 . . . . . .**177** D7
Stanmer Ct BN1 . . . .**143** A2
Stanmer Dr BN22 . . . . . .**173** D1
Stanmer Ho BN1 . . . .**143** B2
Stanmer Park Rd BN1 . . .**143** B2
Stanmer St BN1 . . . .**143** B2
Stanmer Villas BN1 . . . . .**143** B2
Stansfield Rd BN7 . . . . . .**123** B2
Stanstead Cres BN2 . . . .**165** E4
Stansted Rd BN23 . . . . . .**185** A4
Staplecross Methodist Prim
Sch TN32 . . . .**65** E2
Staplefield Dr BN2 . . . . .**143** F3
Stapley Ct BN3 . . . .**162** D8
Stapley Rd BN3 . . . .**141** F8
Star Ho TN3 . . . .**20** B8
Star La Alfriston BN26 . . .**171** A3
Blackboys TN22 . . . .**80** B3
Mayfield TN20 . . . .**40** B2
Star Mews TN20 . . . .**40** B2
Star Rd **6** BN21 . . . . . .**184** E4
Starboard Ct BN2 . . . . . .**164** C5
Starborough Cotts RH7 . . .**1** F5
Starfield TN6 . . . .**25** E1
Starling Cl RH15 . . . .**72** C3
Starr's Cotts **10** TN34 . .**160** B4
Starr's Green La TN33 . . .**113** A3
Starrs Mead TN33 . . . . . .**113** A3
Starvecrow La TN31 . . . . .**91** D6
Starwell Cl TN34 . . . .**136** D3
Station App Battle TN33 .**112** E3
Eastbourne BN22 . . . .**173** F1
Etchingham TN19 . . . .**44** C1
Falmer BN1 . . . .**144** B6
Hassocks BN6 . . . .**97** F4
Hastings TN34 . . . .**159** E8
Heathfield TN21 . . . .**82** A7
Horsted Keynes RH17 . . . .**33** A7
Hove BN3 . . . .**163** B8
Mayfield TN20 . . . .**39** F2
Rye TN31 . . . .**93** B6
Seaford BN25 . . . .**180** E3
St Leonards TN37 . . . .**159** C7
Station App E BN6 . . . . . .**97** E4
Station App W BN6 . . . . . .**97** E4
Station Cl
Plumpton Green BN7 . . . . .**99** E5
Town Row TN6 . . . .**27** C1
Station Cotts
Crowhurst TN33 . . . .**135** A6
Hassocks BN6 . . . .**97** E4
Winchelsea TN36 . . . .**92** D1
Station Mews TN32 . . . . .**64** A3
Station Par **11** BN21 . . .**184** F3
Station Rd
Arlington BN26 . . . .**150** B2
Bexhill TN40 . . . .**157** C6
Brighton BN1 . . . .**142** D3
Burgess Hill RH15 . . . .**73** B2
Crowhurst TN33 . . . .**134** F5

Station Rd *continued*
East Grinstead RH19 1 D1
Forest Row RH18 11 F3
Groombridge TN3 15 C7
Hailsham BN27 152 C6
18 Hastings TN34 159 F8
Heathfield TN21 82 A7
Hellingly BN27 129 A5
Horsted Keynes RH17 33 C5
Hurst Green TN19 45 A3
Isfield TN22 102 D8
Lewes BN7 190 B1
Mayfield TN20 40 A2
Newhaven BN9 168 F1
North Chailey BN8 75 F7
Northiam TN31 67 B8
Plumpton Green BN7 99 E6
Polegate BN26 173 A6
Portslade-by-S BN3,BN41 162 C7
Robertsbridge TN32 64 B4
Rockrobin TN5 29 C6
Seaford BN25 180 B5
Sharpthorne RH19 21 A6
7 Southwick BN42 161 E7
Stonegate TN5 42 E5
Town Row TN6 27 C1
Winchelsea TN36 92 E1
Withyham TN7 14 B5
Station Road Ind Est BN27 152 C6
Station St Brighton BN1 189 B3
8 Eastbourne BN21 185 A3
Lewes BN7 190 B2
Staveley Rd BN20 188 E8
Steellands Rise TN5 31 F1
Steep Hill TN31 89 E2
Steep Rd TN6 38 D3
Steine Gdns BN2 189 B2
Steine La BN1 189 B2
Steine St BN2 189 B1
Stennings The RH19 1 C2
Stephen's Rd TN4 8 B6
Stephens Cl BN8 124 D5
Stephens Rd BN1 143 B2
Stephenson Dr RH19 10 F7
Stevens Cl TN39 157 C7
Stevens Ct BN3 162 E7
Stevenson Cl BN23 174 E3
Stevenson Rd
Brighton BN2 164 C5
1 St Leonards TN37 136 B3
Stewards Inn La BN7 190 A1
Stewart Rd TN4 8 C7
Steyne Cl 4 BN25 180 F2
Steyne Ct 18 BN25 180 E2
Steyne Rd BN25 180 F2
Steyne The BN25 180 E2
Steyning Ave Hove BN3 141 F3
Peacehaven BN10 178 C7
Steyning Cl BN25 181 C2
Steyning Ct 7 BN3 163 B7
Steyning Rd
Rottingdean BN2 177 A5
Seaford BN25 181 C2
Stiles The BN27 152 C7
Stirling Ave BN25 181 C4
Stirling Cl
Burgess Hill RH15 73 C4
Seaford BN25 181 C3
Stirling Court Rd RH15 73 C4
Stirling Ct 5 BN3 163 C7
Stirling Pl BN3 163 A6
Stirling Rd TN38 135 F5
Stirling Way RH19 2 B3
Stock Dale TN35 138 F4
Stockland Green Rd TN3 7 B8
Stockland La TN22 57 B6
Stockleigh Ct 15 TN38 159 C7
Stockleigh Rd TN38 159 C7
Stocks Mdw TN33 133 B5
Stockwell Ct
Burgess Hill RH15 72 F3
1 Haywards Heath RH16 50 E3
Stockwell Rd RH19 10 E6
Stoddards La TN31 67 F6
Stoke Brunswick Sch RH19 11 E7
Stoke Cl BN25 181 B3
Stoke Manor Cl BN25 181 B4
Stokes Ho 6 TN39 157 A4
Stone Cotts TN3 19 F4
Stone Court La TN2 9 E8
Stone Cross Mayfield TN20 39 F7
Stone Cross BN24 174 B5
Stone Cross Prim Sch BN24 174 A5
Stone Cross Rd
Crowborough TN6 38 A7
Wadhurst TN5 30 A4
Stone Cross Windmill* BN24 174 B5
Stone Pit La TN18 47 E5
Stone Quarry Rd RH17 34 D7
Stone Row TN3 6 B5
Stone Row Cotts TN3 6 D1
Stone St Brighton BN1 163 E5
12 Hastings TN34 159 F8
Royal Tunbridge Wells TN1 8 B4
Stone Works Cotts TN31 93 F3
Stonebeach Rise TN38 135 F7
Stonebridge La TN22 79 F5
Stonecott Cl TN6 37 F8
Stonecroft Cl BN3 141 E4
Stonecross Rd BN2 143 F4
Stonedene Cl RH18 12 B2
Stonefield Pl 2 TN34 159 F8
Stonefield Rd TN34 159 F8
Stonefield Way RH15 72 F5
Stonegate CE Prim Sch TN5 42 F5
Stonegate Cl BN23 174 A4
Stonegate Ct TN5 42 F5
Stonegate Rd TN5 30 C1
Stonegate Sta TN5 42 D3
Stonegate Way TN21 82 B8
Stoneham Cl BN7 190 A4
Stoneham Rd BN3 162 F7
Stonehaven Ct 5 TN40 157 D3
Stonehill BN8,TN21 106 C3
Stonehouse Dr
Hastings,Beauport Park TN33,TN38 113 F1
St Leonards TN38 136 A2
Stonehurst Ct 10 BN2 164 C6
Stonehurst La TN20,TN22 57 D7
Stoneleigh Ave BN1 142 F6
Stoneleigh Cl
Brighton BN1 142 F6
East Grinstead RH19 1 F1
Stonelink Cl TN37 135 F7
Stonepark Dr RH18 12 A2
Stonepound Crossroads BN6 97 D4
Stonepound Rd BN6 97 E4
Stonery Cl BN41 141 A2
Stonery Rd BN41 141 A2
Stonestile La TN35 136 F8
Stonewall Park Rd TN3 6 F3
Stonewood Cl
Royal Tunbridge Wells TN4 8 A8
Seaford BN25 181 C4
Stoney La Hailsham BN27 152 C7
Shoreham-by-S BN43 161 C8
Stoneywish Nature Reserve* BN6 98 E3
Storrington Cl BN3 141 E2
Stour Cl BN24 173 F5
Straight Half Mile TN22 55 B5
Strand TN31 93 B5
Strand Ct 1 TN31 93 B5
Strand Hill TN36 117 F7
Strand Mdw TN19 62 B7
Strand The BN2 165 A3
Stratford St TN1 8 C5
Strathenden Ct 16 BN25 180 E2
Strathfield Cl RH16 50 F4
Strawberry Cl TN2 16 E7
Strawberry Fields TN31 67 A7
Strawlands BN7 99 E6
Stream La
Fairlight Cove TN35 139 A5
Sedlescombe TN33 88 C2
The Moor TN18 46 A7
Stream Lane Cotts TN18 46 A7
Stream Pit La TN18 47 B5
Stream Pk RH19 1 A3
Streamside Cl TN34 136 E3
Streat Bostall BN6 121 C6
Streat La BN6 99 C4
Streatfield Gdns TN21 81 F8
Streatfield Ho TN22 78 C8
Streatfield Rd
Heathfield TN21 81 F8
Uckfield TN22 78 B7
Streele La TN22 56 D1
Streele View TN22 78 E8
Street End La
Broad Oak TN21 59 E1
Broad Oak TN21 59 E5
Street The
Framefield TN22 79 B6
Kingston near Lewes BN7 145 E5
Litlington BN26 182 A8
Muddles Green BN8 127 E8
Sedlescombe TN33 88 E1
Selmeston BN26 149 E3
West Firle BN8 148 B3
Westmeston BN6 120 F8
Wilmington BN26 171 F6
Streetlands TN33 88 E1
Stretton Ct 6 BN3 162 F7
Stringer Way BN1 142 F3
Stringwalk The BN27 152 C7
Stroma Gdns BN27 128 F2
Strome Ho TN39 157 C7
Strongs Pas 5 TN34 160 B4
Strood Gate RH17 74 C5
Strood Rd TN37 136 C2
Stuart Ave BN21 184 C6
Stuart Cl TN2 16 F8
Stuart Way RH19 10 F7
Stubb La TN31 90 D2
Stud Cotts BN27 151 A8
Studdens La BN27 108 D1
Sturdee Cl BN23 185 F7
Sturdee Pl TN34 160 A3
Sturton Pl BN27 152 B7
Sudeley Pl BN2 164 D4
Sudeley St BN2 164 D4
Sudeley Terr 6 BN2 164 D4
Suffolk Ct 5 BN22 185 C4
Suffolk Ho 16 TN40 157 D3
Suffolk Rd TN39 157 C7
Suffolk St BN3 162 F8
Sugar La RH17 33 C4
Sugworth Cl RH16 50 D7
Sullington Cl BN2 143 F4
Sullington Way BN43 161 A8
Sumach Cl BN22 173 E2
Summer Cl BN41 162 A7
Summer Ct BN20 188 D7
Summer Hayes BN9 179 C7
Summer Hill TN38 159 A8
Summer Hill Rd TN39 156 F6
Summercourt BN27 152 B8
Summerdale Rd BN3 141 D2
Summerdown Cl BN20 184 D3
Summerdown La BN20 183 C1
Summerdown Rd BN20 184 D3
Summerfields Ave BN27 152 A8
Summerheath Rd BN27 152 B8
Summerhill Cl RH16 50 F7
Summerhill Dr RH16 51 A7
Summerhill Grange RH16 50 F7
Summerhill La RH16 50 F7
Summerlands Rd BN22 173 C2
Summersdeane BN42 140 F1
Summervale Rd TN4 7 E1
Sun La 8 TN34 160 A3
Sun St BN7 190 A2
Sunhill Ct TN2 9 C6
Sunningdale Cl
10 Bexhill TN40 157 E4
Hailsham BN27 129 A1
Seaford BN25 181 A2
Sunningdale Dr TN38 158 F7
Sunninghill Ave BN3 141 F2
Sunninghill Cl BN3 141 E2
Sunnybank TN5 32 E3
Sunnybank Cl TN20 40 B2
Sunnybrooke Cl TN22 78 D7
Sunnycroft Cl RH17 51 E2
Sunnydale Ave BN1 143 A6
Sunnydale Cl BN1 143 A6
Sunnyside Cvn Pk BN25 180 B4
Sunnyside Rd TN4 7 C4
Sunnywood Ct RH16 50 D3
Sunnywood Dr RH16 50 D3
Sunset Ave BN27 127 C3
Sunset Cl
Beachlands BN24 175 F6
Peacehaven BN10 167 B1
Sunstar La BN26 172 E6
Sunte Ave RH16 50 F7
Sunte Cl RH16 50 E7
Sunview Ave BN10 178 D6
Surrenden Cl BN1 142 F4
Surrenden Cres BN1 142 E4
Surrenden Holt BN1 142 F3
Surrenden Lodge BN1 142 F2
Surrenden Pk BN1 143 A4
Surrenden Rd BN1 142 F3
Surrey Cl
Royal Tunbridge Wells TN2 16 F8
Seaford BN25 180 D4
Surrey Ho 12 BN2 164 D4
Surrey Rd BN25 180 C4
Surrey St BN1 189 A3
Susan's Rd BN21 185 A3
Susans Cl BN8 105 A5
Sussex Amb HQ BN7 190 B2
Sussex Ave BN27 152 B8
Sussex Cl Bexhill TN39 156 F5
Hailsham BN27 152 B8
Royal Tunbridge Wells TN2 8 C1
Sussex Cotts RH19 21 A6
Sussex Ct
Eastbourne BN22 185 B5
2 Haywards Heath RH16 50 E3
15 Hove BN3 163 C6
4 Shoreham-by-S BN43 161 A6
Sussex Cty Cricket Gd BN3 163 C7
Sussex Downs Coll BN21 184 E7
Sussex Downs Coll (Cliffe Bldg) BN7 190 B1
Sussex Downs Coll (Southover Bldg) BN7 190 B1
Sussex Eye Hospl BN2 164 D4
Sussex Farm Mus & Nature Trails* TN21 106 E7
Sussex Gdns
East Dean BN20 183 C1
Haywards Heath RH17 51 B3
Sussex Ho
6 Eastbourne BN21 185 A2
Telscombe Cliffs BN10 177 F3
Sussex House Bsns Pk BN3 162 F8
Sussex Hts 13 BN1 163 E5
Sussex Mews
4 Brighton BN2 164 E4
19 Royal Tunbridge Wells TN2 8 A2
Sussex Nuffield Hospl BN2 165 C8
Sussex Pl BN2 189 C3
Sussex Rd
Haywards Heath RH16 50 E3
Hove BN3 163 B5
St Leonards TN38 159 A6
Sussex Sq Brighton BN2 164 E4
17 Haywards Heath RH16 50 E4
Sussex St BN2 189 C2
Sussex Terr BN2 189 C3
Sussex View BN3 163 D7
Sussex Way
Burgess Hill RH15 72 E5
Telscombe Cliffs BN10 177 F3
Sutherland Ave TN39 157 A4
Sutherland Cl 1 TN39 157 A4
Sutherland Rd
Brighton BN2 164 C5
Royal Tunbridge Wells TN1 8 B3
Sutton Ave
Peacehaven BN10 178 B7
Seaford BN25 181 A3
Sutton Ave N BN10 178 B8
Sutton Cl BN2 144 E1
Sutton Cotts BN7 146 B3
Sutton Croft La 6 BN25 180 E3
Sutton Dro BN25 180 F4
Sutton Mews BN25 181 A4
Sutton Par BN25 181 A4
Sutton Park Rd BN25 180 E3
Sutton Pl TN40 157 E4
Sutton Rd
Eastbourne BN21 185 A3
Seaford BN25 181 A3
Sutton Wall BN7 146 D4
Suttons Ind Pk TN36 118 A7
Suttons The Camber TN31 95 A1
St Leonards TN38 135 F2
Swaine's Pas 6 TN34 160 B4
Swaines Way TN21 82 A6
Swainham La TN38 135 B4
Swainsthorpe Cl RH16 50 F3
Swale Cl BN24 174 A5
Swallow Bank TN38 135 F2
Swallow Cl BN23 174 C2
Swallow Ct TN22 78 D5
Swallow Dr Battle TN33 112 F4
Royal Tunbridge Wells TN2 8 F6
Swallow Rest RH15 72 C3
Swallows The BN10 167 B1
Swan Ave 9 TN34 160 A4
Swan Barn Cvn Site BN27 152 D5
Swan Bsns Ctr BN27 152 D6
Swan Cl BN8 100 E7
Swan Ct BN8 100 E7
Swan Rd BN27 152 D6
Swan Terr TN34 160 A4
Swanborough Cotts BN7 146 A4
Swanborough Dr BN2 164 F7
Swanborough Dro BN7 145 F4
Swanborough Hollow BN7 146 A4
Swanborough Pl BN2 164 F7
Swanley Cl BN23 174 D2
Swann Cl RH15 73 D3
Swannee Cl BN10 167 D1
Swans Ghyll RH18 11 E3
Swansbrook La TN21 106 E2
Swaylands Ave TN6 37 F7
Sweda Ct 13 BN2 164 D4
Sweeps Hill Cl TN2 9 D7
Sweethaws La TN6 37 C6
Sweetings La TN3,TN5 19 D1
Sweetlands BN6 98 B5
Swife La TN21 60 D5
Swift Cl Burgess Hill RH15 72 D3
Crowborough TN6 25 D1
Uckfield TN22 78 D5
Swiftsden Cotts TN19 44 F6
Swinburne Ave BN22 173 C3
Swingate Cross BN27 129 C5
Swissland Hill RH19,RH7 1 E7
Swynford Dr 1 TN38 136 A5
Sybron Way TN6 38 D8
Sycamore Cl
Bexhill TN39 156 C4
Eastbourne BN22 173 D3
Heathfield TN21 82 B6
Hove BN41 141 C3
Seaford BN25 181 C3
St Leonards TN38 136 A1
Woodingdean BN2 165 E8
Sycamore Cotts TN2 9 C6
Sycamore Ct TN22 78 D8
Sycamore Dr
East Grinstead RH19 2 A1
Hailsham BN27 152 B5
Sycamores The
Peacehaven BN10 167 D1
St Leonards TN37 159 C8
Sydenham Ct TN40 157 D3
Sydney Cl TN38 136 B3
Sydney Little Rd TN38 135 D4
Sydney Rd
Eastbourne BN22 185 B4
Haywards Heath RH16 50 E6
Sydney St BN1 189 B3
Sylvan Cl RH16 51 B4
Sylvester Way BN3 141 C3
Symbister Rd BN41 162 C7
Syresham Gdns RH16 50 F4

T

Tackleway TN34 160 B4
Taddington Ho 2 BN22 185 C4
Taddington Rd 1 BN22 185 C4
Tainter's Brook TN22 78 E8
Talbot Cres BN1 143 D6
Talbot Pk TN2 8 D5
Talbot Rd TN18 45 F8
Talbot Terr BN7 190 A2
Tall Ash Dr TN37 136 C4
Tall Timbers BN27 127 B4
Talland Par 5 BN25 180 E2
Tamar Cl BN24 174 A5
Tamarack Cl BN22 173 D2
Tamerisk Stps 24 TN34 160 B4
Tamplin Terr BN2 189 C3
Tamworth Rd BN3 162 F7
Tan Yard Cotts TN36 117 F8
Tanbridge Rd BN23 174 F2
Tandridge Rd BN3 162 E6
Tangier La TN3 17 B6
Tanglewood Coppice TN39 156 E3
Tangmere Cl TN39 156 E3
Tangmere Rd BN1 143 A6
Tanhouse La TN31 68 F2
Tanneries The BN27 129 F4
Tanners Cross RH16 50 C2
Tanners Field RH17 74 A5
Tanners Way TN6 26 A1
Tanners' Brook BN7 190 B1
Tanyard TN18 47 B5
Tanyard Ave RH19 11 A8
Tanyard Cotts
Battle TN33 112 E3
Buxted TN22 56 C1
Tanyard La
Chelwood Common RH17, TN22 34 C4
Winchelsea TN36 117 F8
Tapsell's La TN5 29 D5
Tarland Ho TN2 8 D3
Tarner Rd BN2 189 C3
Tarragon Way BN43 140 C1
Tarring Cl BN9 168 D2
Tas Combe Way BN20 173 B2
Tasmania Way BN23 175 A2
Tate Cres RH15 72 F5
Taunton Gr BN2 144 A1
Taunton Pl BN2 144 A1
Taunton Rd BN2 143 F1
Taunton Way BN2 144 A1
Tavistock 8 BN21 185 A2
Tavistock & Summerhill Sch RH16 50 F7
Tavistock Down BN1 143 C2
Taylor Cl TN38 135 F4
Taylor Ct 1 TN2 8 C7
Taylor St TN4 8 A8
Tea Garden La TN3 7 C2
Teal Ct Hailsham BN27 152 D7
St Leonards TN38 135 E3
Teasley Mead TN3 5 C4
Tedder Rd TN4 8 B7
Tedder Terr TN35 137 D5
Teg Cl BN41 141 C2
Teise Cl TN2 8 D2
Teknol Ho RH15 72 E2
Telegraph St 12 BN2 164 C4
Telford Rd TN38 136 A5
Telham Cl TN34 137 A5
Telham La TN33 112 E1
Telscombe Cliffs Prim Sch BN10 178 A8
Telscombe Cliffs Way BN10 178 A8
Telscombe Pk BN10 167 C2
Telscombe Rd
Eastbourne BN23 174 F2
Peacehaven BN10 167 D2
Temple Gdns BN1 163 E6
Temple Gr RH15 72 D4
Temple Grove Sch TN22 36 E3
Temple Hts 14 BN1 163 E6
Temple St BN1 163 E6
Tenantry Down Rd BN2 164 E8
Tenantry Rd BN2 164 D8
Tennis Cl BN27 152 B7
Tennis Rd BN3 162 E6
Tennyson Ct 5 RH16 50 D5
Tennyson Rise RH19 10 C8
Tennyson Wlk BN23 174 E3
Tenterden Cl BN23 174 D2
Tenterden Rise TN34 136 E2
Terminus Ave TN39 157 A3
Terminus Pl
9 Brighton BN1 189 A4
6 Hailsham BN27 152 C7
Terminus Rd
Bexhill TN39 157 B3
Blackboys TN22 80 A6
Brighton BN1 189 A4
Eastbourne BN21 185 A3
Framefield TN22 79 F6
Terminus St BN1 189 A3
Terrace Rd TN37 159 C7
Terraces The BN2 189 C1
Tescombe Grange BN10 177 F3
Teynham Ho BN2 177 C4
Thackeray Cl BN23 174 E3
Thakeham Cl TN40 158 A6
Thalia Ho TN40 157 B4
Thames Cl BN2 189 C2
Thanet Way TN34 136 E2
Thatchers Cl RH15 73 D1
Thatchings The BN26 173 A5
Theaklen Dr TN38 136 B2
Theobald Ho 1 BN1 189 B3
Theobalds Gn TN21 82 A5
Theobalds Rd RH15 73 D6
Theodore Cl TN2 8 E7
Third Ave Bexhill TN40 157 F6
Hove BN3 163 B6
Newhaven BN9 179 C6
Third Rd BN10 178 A7
Third St TN3 6 F3
Thirlmere Rd TN4 7 E5
Thomas Brassey Cl TN37 136 B5
Thomas Peacocke Com Coll TN31 93 B6
Thomas St Lewes BN7 190 C3
Royal Tunbridge Wells TN4 8 A5
Thomas Turner Dr BN8 105 A5
Thompson Rd
Brighton BN1 143 C1
Newhaven BN9 168 F2
Thorn Cotts TN35 116 A4
Thornbank Cres TN39 156 F3
Thornbush Cres BN41 141 B3
Thorndean Rd BN2 143 D3
Thornden Ct TN17 49 A8
Thornden La TN17 49 A8
Thorne Cres TN39 133 E1

Thornfield Gdns TN2 .....8 F5
Thornhill Ave BN1 ....143 A7
Thornhill Cl BN3 ......141 E2
Thornhill Rise BN41 ...141 A4
Thornhill Way BN41 ...141 A3
Thornhurst RH15 ....73 C1
Thorns The BN35 ....138 A8
Thornsdale 5 BN2 .....189 C3
Thornton Ct 5 BN2 ...185 B3
Thornwell Rd BN26 ....171 F4
Thornwood Cl BN22 ....173 E2
Thorny Cl BN21 ....82 A7
Three Gables TN2 ......35 C4
Three Leg Cross Rd TN5 .31 D3
Three Oaks La TN5 .....29 D7
Three Oaks Sta TN35 ..115 D2
Thunders Hill BN27 ....128 A4
Thurrock Cl BN20 ......173 B4
Thyme Cl BN43 ....140 C4
Thyssel La TN31 ....67 B6
Tibbs Mill La TN22,TN6 ...37 E2
Ticehurst Ave TN39 ...155 F5
Ticehurst CE Prim Sch
TN5 ....43 D8
Ticehurst Cl Bexhill TN39 155 F4
Hastings TN35 ....160 C7
Ticehurst Ct TN38 ....159 B7
Ticehurst Rd BN2 .....164 C5
Tichborne Cotts RH16 ..51 C6
Tichborne St BN1 ......189 B2
Tickerage La TN22 .....79 F6
Tidebrook TN5,TN20 ....40 F7
Tidebrook Gdns BN23 ..174 F2
Tideswell Rd BN21 ....185 A3
Tideway Com Sch BN9 .179 B6
Tidy St BN1 ....189 B3
Tilbury Ct BN2 ....189 C2
Tilbury Way BN2 ......189 C3
Tile Barn Cl TN22 .....102 D8
Tile Barn Rd TN38 ....135 E4
Tile Kiln BN8 ....124 D6
Tilebarn Ct RH16 ......50 E2
Tilekiln La TN35 ......160 E8
Tilers Cl RH15 ....73 D3
Tilford Ct 1 BN40 ....157 F4
Tilgate Cl Brighton BN2 164 D6
Eastbourne BN21 ....184 D7
Tilgate Dr TN39 ......156 D3
Tilley La BN27 ....131 E6
Tilling Green Inf Sch
TN31 ....93 A5
Tillingham Ave TN31 ..93 B6
Tillingham Cl BN24 ..174 A5
Tillingham Ct TN31 ..93 A5
Tillingham La TN31 ..92 A6
Tillingham View TN31 .90 B5
Tillingham Way BN24 .174 A5
Tillington BN2 ....164 F7
Tillington Terr TN35 ..160 C6
Tillstone Cl BN2 ......143 D2
Tillstone St BN2 ......189 C2
Tilsmore 17 BN2 ......164 F5
Tilsmore Cnr TN21 ....81 F7
Tilsmore Rd TN21 .....81 F7
Timber Yard Cotts BN7 .190 C2
Timberlaine Rd BN24 .175 C4
Timberley Gdns TN22 .78 C4
Timberley Rd BN22 ...173 D1
Timbers BN27 ....152 C8
Tindal Cl BN1 ....73 D3
Tinker's La TN21 ......57 E3
Tinkers La TN5 ....31 E3
Tintagel Ct BN3 ......163 A8
Tintern Cl Brighton BN1 .143 B1
Eastbourne BN22 ....173 E3
Tisbury Rd BN3 ......163 C6
Titchfield Cl RH15 ....73 D1
Tithe Barn Field TN36 .116 F5
Titian Rd BN3 ....162 F4
Tiverton Dr TN40 .....157 E5
Tivoli BN1 ....142 E2
Tivoli Cres BN1 ......142 D1
Tivoli Cres N BN1 ....142 D2
Tivoli Pl BN1 ....142 D2
Tivoli Rd BN1 ....142 D2
Tobago 6 TN39 ......157 A2
Tobias Sch of Art RH19 ..10 E6
Tolkien Rd BN13 ......174 F2
Toll La Dodd's Hill TN22 ..35 F1
Fairway TN22 ....36 A1
Toll Wood Rd TN21 ...106 F7
Tollgate Lindfield RH16 ...51 B8
Peacehaven BN10 ....167 B1
Tollgate Com Jun Sch
BN23 ....185 D7
Tollgate Gdns BN23 ..185 D7
Tollgate Lock TN31 ...93 B4
Tollgate The TN32 ....65 E1
Tollgates TN33 ....112 B4
Tollwood Pk TN6 ......26 B1
Tollwood Rd TN6 .....38 B8
Tompset's Bank RH18 ..11 E1
Tomtits La RH18 ......11 E1
Tonbridge Rd TN2 ....9 A7
Tonbridge Way TN31 .94 E2
Tongdean Ave BN3 ...142 C2
Tongdean La BN1 .....142 C4
Tongdean Pl BN3 .....142 C3
Tongdean Rd BN3 ....142 C3
Tongdean Rise BN1 ..142 C4
Top Cross Rd TN40 ...158 A7
Top Dr TN22 ....55 A6
Top Hill Cl BN41 .....140 F2
Top Rd RH19 ....21 B5

Tor Rd BN10 ....167 C1
Tor Rd W BN10 ....167 C2
Torcross BN2 ....143 E1
Torfield Cl TN34 .....160 B4
Torfield Ct BN21 .....184 E4
Torfield Ho TN34 .....160 B4
Torfield Rd BN21 .....184 E4
Torfield Sch TN34 ....160 B5
Toronto Terr
Brighton BN2 ....164 C6
Lewes BN7 ....190 A2
Torrance Cl BN3 .....141 F1
Totland Rd BN2 ......164 D7
Tott Hill BN6 ....97 B5
Tott Yew Rd BN20 ...173 A4
Tottington Way BN43 .140 B1
Tovey Cl BN21 ....184 D6
Tower Cl
Beachlands BN24 ...175 F7
East Grinstead RH19 ...1 E2
Tower Ct
East Grinstead RH19 .....1 E2
Uckfield TN22 ....55 D1
Tower Ho Brighton BN1 .142 E2
Burgess Hill RH15 ...73 B2
Tower Mill Pl BN26 ..173 A5
Tower Rd Brighton BN2 .164 C6
St Leonards TN37 ....135 F7
Tower Rd W TN37,TN38 .159 B8
Tower Ride Uckfield TN22 .55 D1
Uckfield TN22 ....55 C1
Tower St Heathfield TN21 .82 B8
Rye TN31 ....93 C6
Tower View TN22 .....78 D8
Towergate BN1 ......142 E2
Towerscroft Ave TN37 .136 C5
Town Hill TN3 ....20 A4
Town Place Farm Cotts
RH17 ....52 C7
Town Wall 2 TN31 ....93 B5
Towner Art Gall & Mus★
BN21 ....184 D3
Townlands Rd TN5 ....29 F4
Tozer Ct BN41 ....162 B7
Traders Pas 6 TN31 ..93 B5
Trafalgar Cl
Peacehaven BN10 ...167 C1
St Leonards TN37 ...135 F7
Trafalgar Cotts 8 TN34 .160 B4
Trafalgar Ct BN1 ....189 B3
Trafalgar Gate BN2 ..164 F3
Trafalgar Ho 8 TN40 .157 D3
Trafalgar La BN1 ....189 B3
Trafalgar Mews 9
BN22 ....185 C4
Trafalgar Pl BN1 ....189 B3
Trafalgar Rd BN41 ..162 B8
Trafalgar St BN1 ....189 B3
Trafalgar Terr BN1 ..189 B3
Tram Rd TN31 ....94 A2
Transit Rd BN9 ......179 D7
Travellers La TN35 ..160 C8
Trebilco Cl TN2 ......8 D7
Treblers Rd TN6 .....38 E6
Tredcroft Rd BN3 ....142 C2
Treemaines Rd BN23 .174 F2
Treemans Rd (Lewes Rd)
RH17 ....33 B2
Treetops Cl BN2 ....165 E8
Tremola Ave BN2 ....177 C6
Trenches Rd TN6 ....25 F1
Trevelyan Pl RH16 ...50 E5
Trevor Gdns BN8 ....147 F6
Treyford Cl BN2 .....144 E1
Triangle Ho 4 RH16 .50 F3
Triangle Rd RH16 ....50 E3
Triangle The BN20 ...173 B3
Triangle Way RH15 ..72 D5
Trickland Cotts TN22 .53 C5
Trinity Cl TN2 ....8 D4
Trinity Cotts TN31 ...71 F2
Trinity Ct BN6 ......97 B5
Trinity Field BN8 ...124 E6
Trinity Mews 3 TN34 .159 E7
Trinity Pl BN21 .....185 B2
Trinity Rd BN6 .....97 A6
Trinity St Brighton BN2 .189 C4
10 Hastings TN34 ...159 E7
Trinity Trees BN21 ..185 A2
Trinity Villas 2 TN34 .159 E7
Tristan Gdns TN4 ....7 D4
Trojans Plat TN36 ...117 E7
Troon Cl BN25 ......180 A6
Troon Ct RH16 ....50 E4
Trossachs Cl BN23 ..174 D3
Troy Cl TN6 ....26 A1
Trujillo Ct BN23 ....185 G8
Truleigh Cl BN2 .....165 F7
Truleigh Dr BN41 ...141 A4
Truleigh Way BN43 .140 A1
Truman Dr TN35 ....135 F6
Trumpet La BN27 ...109 C2
Tubwell La
Crowborough TN6 ...38 D7
Horam TN21 ....81 F2
Tudor Ave TN38 ....159 A7
Tudor Cl
East Grinstead RH19 ..10 F8
Hove BN3 ....141 F2
Rottingdean BN2 ...177 A6
Seaford BN25 ......180 D4
Tudor Ct Bexhill TN39 .156 F4
Royal Tunbridge Wells TN2 ..7 E1
Tudor Gdns RH15 ....72 F2
Tudor Rose Pk BN10 .178 F6
Tudor Wlk TN22 ....79 B5
Tugwell Rd BN22 ...173 F2
Tumulus Rd BN2 ....177 C7

Tunbridge Wells Gram Sch
for Boys TN4 ....8 A7
Tunbridge Wells Gram Sch
for Girls TN4 ....8 A6
Tunbridge Wells High Sch
TN2 ....8 F5
Tunbridge Wells Ind Hospl
The TN3 ....6 B3
Tunbridge Wells Mus★
TN1 ....8 B4
Tunbridge Wells Rd
Argos TN20,TN6 .....39 E5
Mark Cross TN3,TN6 ...28 A5
Tunbridge Wells Sta TN1 ..8 A3
Tunbridge Wells Trade Pk
TN2 ....8 D8
Tunbridge Wells West Sta★
TN2 ....7 F1
Tunnel Rd TN1 ......8 B4
Tuppen Ho BN7 .....145 E5
Tuppenney Cl TN35 ..160 C7
Turkey Cock La 2 TN31 .93 C6
Turkey La RH15 .....73 B3
Turkey Rd TN39 ....156 E7
Turley Cotts TN3 ....7 A8
Turnberry TN38 .....158 F7
Turnberry Ct 14 RH16 .50 E4
Turnberry Dr BN27 .152 A8
Turner Cl Bexhill TN40 .157 E5
Eastbourne BN23 ...174 D1
Turner Ct RH19 .....2 A3
Turner's Hill Rd RH19 .10 B6
Turners Cotts TN31 .68 C5
Turners Green La TN5 .29 F6
Turners Green Rd TN5 .29 F6
Turners Mill Cl RH16 .50 D7
Turners Mill Rd RH16 .50 D6
Turners Way RH15 ..72 F4
Turnpike Cl
Broyle Side BN8 ....125 A8
Peacehaven BN10 ..167 C1
Turnpike Piece BN1 .144 B6
Turret Ct TN3 ....1 C3
Turton Cl BN2 ......164 D5
Tuscan Ct BN10 ....177 F3
Tutts Barn Ct BN21 .184 F5
Tutts Barn La BN22 .185 A5
Tuxford Rd TN4 .....7 B5
Tweedsmuir Cl BN23 .174 C3
Twineham Cl BN2 ...164 F7
Twineham Rd BN21 .184 D7
Twitten Cl 2 BN42 ..161 E7
Twitten The Bexhill TN39 .156 D4
Burgess Hill RH15 ..73 B4
Crowborough TN6 ..25 E1
Ditchling BN6 ......98 D3
Southwick BN42 ...161 E7
Twyford Cres TN37 .136 C4
Twyford Rd BN1 ...143 E6
Twyfords TN6 ......25 E1
Twyhurst Ct RH19 ..1 D3
Twysden Cotts TN18 ..47 A4
Tye Cl BN2 ....177 D4
Tye Hill Rd BN26 ...151 A4
Tye View BN10 ....167 A1
Tyedean Rd BN10 ..177 F4
Tyhurst Pl TN22 ....78 C6
Tyler's Gn RH16,RH17 .50 B4
Tylers La TN35 ......35 C1
Tyndale Ave TN39 ..156 C3
Tyson Pl 9 BN2 ....189 C2

U

Uckfield Cl BN2 .....164 F6
Uckfield Com Coll TN22 .78 D8
Uckfield Com Hospl
TN22 ....78 D6
Uckfield Rd
Poundgate TN6 .....37 B7
Upper Wellingham BN8 .124 B7
Uckfield Sta TN22 ...78 C6
Uckham La TN33 ....112 E6
Udiam Cotts TN32 ...65 C5
Udimore Rd TN31 ...91 C3
Under Rd BN27 .....130 B3
Undercliff
St Leonards TN38 ...159 B6
St Leonards TN38 ...159 C6
Undercliff Terr 7 TN38 .159 C6
Underdown Rd BN42 .161 E8
Underhill TN22 .....55 B5
Underhill La Clayton BN6 119 E8
Westmeston BN6 ...120 C8
Underwater World★
TN34 ....160 B3
Unicorn Ho 1 TN34 .160 A4
Union Cnr BN27 ....129 B3
Union Rd BN2 ......189 C4
Union Sq 22 TN2 ...8 A2
Union St Brighton BN1 .189 B2
11 St Leonards TN38 .159 C7
Union Street TN5 ...32 B3
Univ of Brighton
Brighton BN1 ....189 B2
Eastbourne BN20 ...188 D8
Falmer BN1 ....144 B6
Univ of Brighton
(Cockcroft/Watts Annexes)
BN2 ....143 D2
Univ of Brighton (St Peter's
Ho) BN2 ....189 B3
Univ of Sussex BN1 ..144 A7
Updown Hill RH16 ..50 C7
Upland Rd BN20 ...184 C3
Uplands Cl Bexhill TN39 .156 F6
Uckfield TN22 ......55 C1

Uplands Com Tech Coll
TN5 ....30 A4
Uplands Dr TN22 ...55 D1
Uplands Pk TN21 ..59 E1
Uplands Rd BN1 ...143 C2
Uplands Sch BN1 ..143 C2
Uplands The TN38 .159 B7
Upper Abbey Rd BN2 .164 D4
Upper Ave BN21 ...185 A4
Upper Bedford St BN2 .164 C4
Upper Belgrave Rd
BN25 ....180 F5
Upper Bevendean Ave
BN2 ....143 E1
Upper Broomgrove Rd
TN34 ....160 B7
Upper Carlisle Rd BN20 188 D8
Upper Chalvington Pl
BN2 ....164 C5
Upper Church Rd TN37 .136 C2
Upper Chyngton Gdns
BN25 ....181 B4
Upper Cl RH18 .....11 F2
Upper Clarence Rd
TN37 ....136 C2
Upper Cumberland Wlk
TN1 ....8 B1
Upper Dr The BN3 ..163 D8
Upper Duke's Dr BN20 .188 C7
Upper Dunstan Rd TN4 ..8 B6
Upper Gardner St BN1 .189 B3
Upper Glen Rd TN37 .136 A5
Upper Gloucester Rd
BN1 ....189 A3
Upper Greenwoods La
TN21 ....83 C6
Upper Grosvenor Rd TN1,
TN4 ....8 B6
Upper Hamilton Rd
BN1 ....189 A5
Upper Hollingdean Rd
BN1 ....143 B1
Upper Horsebridge Rd
BN27 ....129 A3
Upper King's Dr BN20 .173 B1
Upper Kingston La
BN42,BN43 ....140 D1
Upper Lake TN33 ...112 E4
Upper Lewes Rd BN2 .189 C4
Upper Lodges BN1 ..143 B2
Upper Market St 5
BN3 ....163 D5
Upper Maze Hill TN38 .159 B7
Upper Nellington TN3 ...7 B4
Upper North St BN1 .189 A2
Upper Park Pl 7 BN2 .189 C2
Upper Park Rd TN37 .136 C1
Upper Platts TN5 ...31 F1
Upper Profit TN3 ....7 A3
Upper Ratton Dr BN20 .184 B8
Upper Rock Gdns BN2 .189 C2
Upper Roedale Cotts
BN1 ....143 B4
Upper Sea Rd TN40 .157 D4
Upper Sherwood Rd
BN25 ....181 A4
Upper Shoreham Rd
Shoreham-by-S BN43 .140 B1
Shoreham-by-S BN43 .140 D1
Shoreham-by-S BN43 .141 A8
Upper South Rd TN37 .136 C1
Upper Sq RH18 .....11 E3
Upper St East Dean BN20 187 B8
Rusthall TN4 ....7 D4
Upper St James's St
BN2 ....189 C1
Upper St Johns RH15 73 A4
Upper Stables RH16 .50 C3
Upper Station Rd TN21 .82 A7
Upper Stephens TN3 ...7 A3
Upper Sudeley St 7
BN2 ....164 D4
Upper Valley Rd BN9 .179 B6
Upper Wellington Rd 5
BN2 ....164 C7
Upper Winfield Ave
BN1 ....142 F6
Upper Wish Hill BN20 .184 B8
Upperton Gdns BN21 .184 F3
Upperton La BN21 ..184 F3
Upperton Rd BN21 ..184 F4
Upton Ave BN42 ...140 E1
Upton Quarry TN3 ..6 F3
Upwick Rd BN20 ...184 C3

V

Val Mascal TN38 ...136 A1
Val Prinseps Rd BN24 .175 C4
Vale Ave Brighton BN1 .142 E7
Royal Tunbridge Wells TN1 ..8 A3
Vale Cl BN25 ....181 B4
Vale Ct BN41 ....162 B7
Vale Gdns BN41 ...162 B7
Vale Rd Battle TN33 .112 B5
Haywards Heath RH16 ...50 E2
Mayfield TN20 .....40 B2
Portslade-by-S BN41 .162 C7
Royal Tunbridge Wells TN1 ..8 A4
Saltdean BN2 ......177 D7
Seaford BN25 .....181 A4
St Leonards TN37 ..136 A4
Vale The BN2 ......165 E5
Vale View Rd TN21 .82 B6
Valebridge Cl RH15 .73 C6
Valebridge Dr RH15 .73 C5
Valebridge Rd RH15 .73 C6

Valence Rd BN7 ...123 B1
Valentine Ct
2 Eastbourne BN21 .185 A2
14 Hove BN3 ....163 C7
Valentine Dr RH15 ..72 E4
Valerie Cl BN41 ....141 C2
Vallance Cl RH15 ...72 E4
Vallance Ct 7 BN3 .163 A6
Vallance Gdns BN3 .163 A6
Vallance Rd BN3 ..163 A6
Vallensdean Cotts BN41 141 C2
Valley Cl Brighton BN1 .142 C4
Newhaven BN9 .....179 B8
Valley Dene BN9 ...179 B7
Valley Dr Brighton BN1 .142 C4
Seaford BN25 ......181 A5
Valley Rd
Crowborough TN6 ..25 F1
Lewes BN7 ....146 A8
Newhaven BN9 .....179 A7
Newhaven BN9 .....179 B7
Peacehaven BN10 ..167 C2
Portslade-by-S BN41 .141 A2
Rusthall TN4 ....7 D4
Valley Rise BN25 ...180 F4
Valley Side Rd TN35 .160 C7
Valley View TN22 ..53 A8
Valley View Cl TN6 .25 F1
Valley View Cvn Site
TN32 ....64 C4
Valverde Ho 13 BN3 .163 C7
Van Allen Bldg The
BN2 ....189 C1
Van Allen Mews BN2 .189 C1
Vanbrugh Ct 21 BN3 .163 C7
Vancouver Rd BN23 .175 B2
Vantage Wlk 1 TN38 .136 B1
Varndean Cl BN1 ...142 E3
Varndean Coll BN1 .142 F3
Varndean Dr BN1 ...142 E3
Varndean Gdns BN1 .142 E3
Varndean Holt BN1 .142 F3
Varndean Rd BN1 ..142 E3
Varndean Sch BN1 .143 A3
Vega Cl BN27 ......152 D7
Ventnor Cl BN23 ...174 B4
Ventnor Villas BN3 .163 B6
Venture Cl TN40 ...157 F4
Verbania Way RH19 ..2 B1
Verdant Cl TN34 ...159 D8
Vere Rd BN1 ....189 B5
Veric 12 BN3 ......163 C7
Vermont Rd TN4 ....7 C4
Vermont Way TN37 .135 F6
Vernon Ave
Peacehaven BN10 ..178 C6
Woodingdean BN2 .165 C8
Vernon Cl BN23 ...185 E7
Vernon Ct 3 BN1 ..163 E6
Vernon Gdns 4 BN1 .163 E6
Vernon Lodge 9 BN21 .185 A2
Vernon Rd
Royal Tunbridge Wells TN1 ..8 C6
Uckfield TN22 ......78 D6
Vernon Terr BN1 ...163 E7
Vernons Rd BN8 ...76 C7
Veronica Way BN2 .189 C1
Verrall's Wlk BN7 ..190 A1
Verulam Pl TN37 ...159 E7
Viaduct Rd BN1 ...189 B4
Vian Ave BN23 ....185 F7
Vicarage Cl
Newhaven BN9 ....168 E2
Ringmer BN8 ......124 D5
Seaford BN25 .....180 F3
Vicarage Dr BN20 .184 D3
Vicarage Field BN27 .152 C8
Vicarage La
Burwash Common TN19 ...61 A3
Eastbourne BN20 ..184 D3
Hailsham BN27 ....152 C8
Hellingly BN27 ....129 A6
Rottingdean BN2 ..165 F1
Scaynes Hill RH17 .51 F3
Westfield TN35 ....114 D3
Vicarage Rd
Burwash Common TN19 ...61 A3
Eastbourne BN20 ..184 D3
Hailsham BN27 ....152 C7
Hastings TN34 .....160 A5
Vicarage Terr BN2 .165 F1
Vicarage Way
Hurst Green TN19 ..45 A3
Ringmer BN8 ......124 D5
Viceroy Lodge 10 BN3 .163 A6
Victor Cl BN25 ....180 E5
Victoria Ave
Burgess Hill RH15 ..72 E3
Hastings TN35 .....160 C8
Peacehaven BN10 ..167 C2
Victoria Bsns Ctr RH15 ..72 E2
Victoria Cl
Burgess Hill RH15 ..72 F2
Polegate BN26 ....172 F7
Victoria Cotts
High Cross TN6 ....39 C6
2 Hove BN3 ....163 B5
St Leonards TN37 .136 A5
Stone Cross BN24 .174 B7
Victoria Ct 6 Hove BN3 .163 C6
Portslade-by-S BN41 .162 C8
St Leonards TN38 .159 B6
Victoria Dr BN20,BN21 .184 C5
Victoria Gdns
Burgess Hill RH15 ..72 F2
Eastbourne BN20 ..184 C4
Victoria General Hospl
BN7 ....123 A1

Victoria Gr **7** BN3 ....163 C6
Victoria Ind Est RH15 ...72 E2
Victoria Mans BN21 ......185 B2
Victoria Mews BN2 ....165 F1
Victoria Pl **6** BN1 ....163 E6
Victoria Rd Bexhill TN39 .157 B4
  Brighton BN1 ....163 E6
  Burgess Hill RH15 ......72 E2
  Crowborough TN6 ....38 C8
  Eastbourne BN20 ......184 C5
  Hailsham BN27 ....152 C7
  Haywards Heath RH16 ...51 A3
  Mayfield TN20 ....40 A3
  Polegate BN26 ....172 F7
  Portslade-by-S BN41 ...162 C8
  Royal Tunbridge Wells TN1 ....8 A4
  Southwick BN42 ....161 D7
  St Leonards TN37 ......159 D7
  Windmill Hill BN27 .....131 B5
Victoria Road Trad Est
  BN41 ....162 C8
Victoria St BN1 ....163 E6
Victoria Terr
  Burwash TN19 ....62 A6
  1 Hove BN3 ....163 B5
Victoria Way
  Burgess Hill RH15 ......72 E2
  East Grinstead RH19 ...10 F7
  Winchelsea Beach TN36 .118 A5
Victory Mews BN2 ....165 A3
View Bank TN35 ....160 D6
View Rd BN10 ....178 C8
View Terr RH7 ....2 A8
Views Path TN6 ....51 B4
Views Wood Path TN22 ..55 D1
Viking Cl BN25 ....180 B6
Viking Way BN23 ....185 F8
Villa Rd TN37 ....159 D7
Village Barn The BN2 ...142 E7
Village Cl Bexhill TN39 ..156 C4
  Portslade-by-S BN41 ...141 B2
Village Mews BN39 .....156 C4
Village The
  Alfriston BN26 ....170 F7
  Alfriston,Alciston BN26 ..170 D8
  Eastbourne BN20 ......188 D8
Village Way BN1 ....144 C6
Village Wks BN8 ....105 A5
Villiers Cl BN2 ....165 E8
Villiers Ct BN1 ....189 B3
Vincent Cl BN23 ....185 F7
Vine Cotts TN6 ....38 C7
Vine Farm Cotts BN8 ...104 A5
Vine Pl BN1 ....189 A3
Vine Sq BN22 ....185 D6
Vine St BN1 ....189 B3
Vinehall Cl TN34 ....137 A5
Vinehall Rd TN32 ....87 E5
Vinehall Sch TN32 ....87 E5
Vineries The
  Burgess Hill RH15 ......73 D3
  Eastbourne BN23 ......174 D2
  Hove BN3 ....163 E6
Vines Cross Rd
  Brighton BN2 ....164 F7
  Horam TN21 ....107 B7
Vineyard La TN5 ....31 C2
Vintry The
  Eastbourne BN21 ......184 C7
  Nutley TN22 ....35 C4
Virgin's Croft TN33 .....112 D6
Virgin's La TN33 ....112 D6
Volks Electric Rly ★
  BN1,BN2 ....164 C4
Vue Gris Nez TN36 ......118 B5

W

Wade Cl BN23 ....185 F7
Wadhurst Bsns Pk TN5 ..29 B7
Wadhurst CE Prim Sch
  TN5 ....29 F5
Wadhurst Cl
  Eastbourne BN22 ......173 F2
  St Leonards TN37 ......136 B5
Wadhurst La TN33 ....111 E6
Wadhurst Rd Frant TN3 ..17 D1
  Mark Cross TN6 ....28 C3
Wadhurst Rise BN2 .....164 F5
Wadhurst Sta TN5 ....29 C6
Wadlands Brook Rd RH19 .1 D5
Wagg Cl RH19 ....2 A1
Waghorns La TN22 ......57 C6
Wainwright Rd TN39 ....135 D3
Wainwright Rd TN39 ....157 B4
Waite Cl BN7 ....190 B3
Waites La TN35 ....138 E5
Wakefield Rd BN2 ....189 C5
Wakehams Cl TN39 .....157 C7
Waldegrave Ct BN2 .....177 D7
Waldegrave Rd BN1 .....143 A1
Waldegrave St **4** TN34 .159 F8
Walden Terr TN34 ....112 E4
Waldene Cl TN34 ....136 F2
Waldron Ave BN1 ....143 D6
Waldron Ct BN22 ....184 D8
Waldron Ct TN21 ....82 B8
Waldron Pl BN1 ....143 D6
Waldron Rd BN8 ....105 A5
Waldron Thorns TN21 ...82 A7
Waldshut Rd BN7 ....123 A3
Wales Farm Cotts BN7 ..124 E1
Walesbeech Rd BN2 ....177 D4
Walhatch Cl RH18 ......11 F2
Walker Cl BN23 ....185 F7
Walks The TN3 ....15 C8
Wall Hill Rd RH18,RH19 ..11 E5

Wallace Cl TN2 ....17 A8
Wallands Com Prim Sch
  BN7 ....123 A2
Wallands Cres BN7 .....190 A2
Walled Gdn The TN22 ...55 D4
Wallers TN3 ....7 A8
Wallington Twrs **4**
  TN40 ....157 F4
Wallis Ave BN23 ....185 E7
Wallis Cl TN6 ....26 A1
Wallis Field TN3 ....15 B6
Wallis Ho RH19 ....1 E1
Wallis Pl BN23 ....185 E8
Wallis Way RH15 ....72 E4
Wallsend Rd BN24 ......175 C6
Walmer Cres BN2 ....144 B1
Walmer Rd BN25 ....181 C4
Walnut Cl Brighton BN1 .142 E3
  Heathfield TN21 ....82 B6
Walnut Cl BN26 ....173 A6
Walnut Pk RH16 ....51 B4
Walnut Tree Wlk BN20 ..184 B8
Walnut Way TN4 ....8 C8
Walnut Wlk BN26 ....173 A6
Walpole Rd BN2 ....164 D5
Walpole Terr BN2 ....164 D5
Walpole Wlk BN23 ......174 E3
Walshes Rd TN6 ....38 B7
Walsingham Cl BN22 ...173 D3
Walsingham Rd BN3 ....162 F6
Walter May Ho **14** BN2 .164 F5
Walters Green Rd TN11 ..5 F6
Walton Bank TN11 ......143 E5
Walton Cl
  Eastbourne BN23 ......174 E3
  St Leonards TN37 .....136 C5
Walton Pk TN39 ....156 F4
Walwers La BN7 ....190 B2
Wanderdown Cl BN2 ....165 E4
Wanderdown Dr BN2 ...165 E4
Wanderdown Rd BN2 ...165 D4
Wanderdown Way BN2 ..165 E4
Wannock Ave BN20 .....172 F3
Wannock Cl TN40 ....158 A6
Wannock Dr BN26 ......172 F5
Wannock Gdns BN26 ...172 F3
Wannock La BN20,BN26 .172 F3
Wannock Rd
  Eastbourne BN22 ......185 D5
  Polegate BN26 ....172 F5
War Meml Hos BN20 ....184 C6
War Meml Hospl TN6 ...25 M4
Warberry Park Gdns TN4 .2 E7
Warbleton Cl BN2 ....164 E5
Warburton Cl
  East Grinstead RH19 ...11 A8
  Eastbourne BN21 ......184 C8
  Uckfield TN22 ....78 D8
Ward Cl TN5 ....29 C5
Ward Way TN39 ....157 A6
Warden Ct RH17 ....50 A6
Wardsbrook Rd TN5 .....43 D7
Ware Ct TN5 ....73 D3
Warelands RH15 ....72 F1
Warenne Rd BN3 ....141 C4
Wares Field TN22 ....78 D4
Wares Rd TN22 ....78 D4
Warleigh Rd BN1 ....189 B5
Warmdene Ave BN1 .....142 F6
Warmdene Cl BN1 ......142 F5
Warmdene Rd BN1 .....142 F6
Warmdene Way BN1 ....142 F6
Warminster Rd BN24 ...175 D5
Warner Ct RH15 ....73 A3
Warnham Cl TN3 ....163 C5
Warnham Gdns TN39 ...156 E2
Warnham Rise BN1 .....143 A5
Warren Ave BN2 ....165 C8
Warren Cl
  Crowborough TN6 .....25 C1
  Eastbourne BN20 ......188 C8
  Friston BN20 ....183 B1
  Lewes BN7 ....146 B8
  Roser's Cross TN21 ....81 A6
  St Leonards TN38 .....158 E8
  Woodingdean BN2 .....165 B8
Warren Cnr TN21 ....81 A8
Warren Cotts
  Mayfield TN20 ....40 C3
  North Chailey BN8 ....75 F7
Warren Ct
  9 Crowborough TN6 ..25 C1
  Southwick BN42 ....140 E1
Warren Dr BN7 ....146 A8
Warren Farm La TN3 ...16 B4
Warren Gdn TN6 ....25 E2
Warren Hill BN20 ......184 A1
Warren La Friston BN20 .183 B1
  North Chailey BN8 ....75 E8
  Roser's Cross TN21 ...81 A7
Warren Lodge BN10 ...167 A1
Warren Rd
  Crowborough TN6 .....25 C1
  Fairlight TN35 ....138 C4
  Woodingdean BN2 ....165 B8
Warren Ridge
  Crowborough TN6 .....25 D2
  Frant TN3 ....17 C3
Warren Rise RH16 .....165 B8
Warren The
  Burgess Hill RH15 ....73 C1
  Mayfield TN20 ....40 C2
  Ticehurst TN5 ....31 C1
Warren Way
  North Chailey BN8 ....75 F8
  Telscombe Cliffs BN10 .167 A1

Warren Way continued
  Woodingdean BN2 .....165 D8
Warren Wood TN6 ......25 D1
Warrenwood BN8 ....53 A1
Warrior Cl BN41 ....141 B2
Warrior Ct TN37 ....159 D7
Warrior Gdns TN37 .....159 C7
Warrior Ho BN20 ....188 E8
Warrior Sq
  6 Eastbourne BN22 ..185 C4
  St Leonards TN37 .....159 D7
Warrs Hill La BN8 ......75 B8
Wartling Cl TN38 ......135 F3
Wartling Dr TN39 ......155 F5
Wartling Rd
  Eastbourne BN22 ......185 D6
  Wartling BN27 ....131 C2
Warwick Ct
  8 Eastbourne BN23 ..174 E1
  8 Hove BN3 ....163 E7
Warwick Mount **2** BN2 .164 C4
Warwick Pk TN2 ....8 B1
Warwick Rd Bexhill TN39 .156 F5
  4 Royal Tunbridge Wells
  TN1 ....8 A2
  Seaford BN25 ....180 E3
Washington Ave TN37 ...135 F6
Washington Rd RH16 ...51 A5
Washington St BN2 .....189 C4
Washwell La TN5 ....29 F3
Wassall La TN17 ....48 E7
Watchbell La **3** TN31 ..93 C5
Watchbell St TN31 ......93 C5
Water Mint Cl TN38 .....135 E1
Waterbury Hill RH17 ....33 B5
Waterdown Rd TN4 .....7 E1
Waterdyke Ave BN42 ...161 E7
Waterfield TN2 ....17 A7
Waterford Cl BN10 .....167 C2
Waterfrets Cotts TN3 ...6 F5
Waterfront BN2 ....164 F3
Waterfront The BN23 ...185 G8
Watergate BN3 ....157 B8
Watergate La BN7 ......190 A1
Waterhall Rd BN1 ......142 C6
Waterloo Cl TN37 ......135 F7
Waterloo Ho **9** BN3 ...162 D5
Waterloo Pas **15** TN34 .160 B4
Waterloo Pl
  1 Brighton BN1 .....189 C3
  13 Hastings TN34 ....160 B4
  Lewes BN7 ....190 B2
Waterloo Sq BN26 .....171 A3
Waterloo St BN3 ....163 D5
Watermen's Cl TN34 ...136 F3
Watermill Cl
  Bexhill TN39 ....157 B7
  Polegate BN26 ....173 A5
Watermill Dr TN38 .....135 D3
Watermill La
  Bexhill TN39 ....134 B2
  Clayhill TN31 ....67 D2
  Icklesham TN35,TN36 ..116 C3
Watermill Lane Cotts
  TN35 ....138 C8
Waters Cotts TN39 .....30 A4
Waters Edge **13** BN43 ..161 A6
Waterside
  Crowborough TN6 ....25 F2
  East Grinstead RH19 ..2 B1
Waterside Cl TN35 .....160 C7
Waterside Ctr BN7 .....190 A3
Waterworks RH18 .....11 F3
Waterworks Cotts
  Friston BN20 ....183 A1
  1 Hastings TN34 ....159 F8
  Hove BN3 ....142 A2
Waterworks Rd
  Eastbourne BN22 .....185 A4
  1 Hastings TN34 ....136 F1
Watling Cl **5** BN42 ...161 E7
Watling Ct **8** BN42 ...161 E7
Watling Rd BN42 ......161 E7
Wattle's Wish TN33 ....112 C6
Watts Cl TN5 ....29 F4
Watts La BN21 ....184 E4
Watts Lodge RH15 ....73 D3
Watts' Palace La TN31 ..89 D7
Waverley Cres BN1 ....143 C1
Waverley Ct
  4 Hastings TN34 ....159 E7
  3 Seaford BN25 .....180 F2
Waverley Dr TN2 ....8 F6
Waverley Gdns BN24 ...175 D5
Wayfaring Down BN26 ..172 D3
Wayfield Ave BN3 ......141 F1
Wayfield Cl BN3 ....141 F1
Wayford Cl BN23 ......174 D2
Wayland Ave BN1 ......142 C3
Wayland Hts BN1 ......142 C4
Wayside Brighton BN1 ..142 D6
  Friston BN20 ....183 B1
Wayside Wlk TN21 .....81 F6
Weald Ave BN3 ....162 F8
Weald Cl
  Barcombe Cross BN8 ..101 E4
  Lewes BN7 ....190 A3
Weald Rd RH15 ....72 E3
Weald Rise RH16 ......50 E1
Weald The RH19 ......1 F4
Weald View
  Barcombe Cross BN8 ..101 E4
  Staplecross TN32 .....29 F8
  Turner's Green TN5 ...29 F6
Wealden Cl TN6 ....25 D3
Wealden Cotts TN19 ...61 C3
Wealden Ho TN21 .....82 A8

Wealden Ind Est TN6 ...38 C8
Wealden Pk BN22 .....173 C1
Wealden View BN19 ...62 E7
Wealden Way
  Bexhill TN39 ....156 C6
  Haywards Heath RH16 .50 D4
Wealdview Rd TN21 ....81 F7
Weare Rd TN4 ....8 C8
Weatherby Cl BN21 ....184 C8
Weavers Cl RH15 .....73 D1
Weavers La BN26 ......170 F3
Weavers Rock La TN37 .82 C5
Wedderburn Rd BN20 ..173 B1
Week La BN8 ....124 D2
Weir Wood Cotts RH18 .11 C3
Weir Wood Resr (Nature
  Reserve) ★ RH19 ......10 D1
Welbeck Ave Hove BN3 .162 E6
  Royal Tunbridge Wells TN4 ..8 C8
  St Leonards TN38 .....159 A7
Welbeck Cl
  Burgess Hill RH15 ....73 D4
  Eastbourne BN20 .....173 D3
Welbeck Ct Hove BN3 ..162 E6
  9 Seaford BN25 .....180 E3
Welbeck Dr RH15 .....73 D5
Welbeck Mans BN3 ...162 E6
Welesmere Rd BN2 ...177 A7
Welkin (Brighton Univ)
  BN20 ....184 E1
Welkin The RH16 .....51 B8
Welland Cl TN6 ....38 A8
Wellcombe Cres BN20 ..188 D7
Weller Rd TN4 ....7 C4
Wellesley Cl
  Bexhill TN39 ....156 D3
  Crowborough TN6 ....25 D1
Wellesley Ct **19** TN34 ..160 B4
Wellesley Rd **7** BN21 ..185 A3
Wellfield RH19 ....11 C7
Wellgreen La BN7 .....145 F5
Wellhouse La RH15 ...98 C7
Wellhouse Pl BN7 .....190 A2
Wellingham La BN24 ...124 A7
Wellington Cl **3** BN23 .175 A1
Wellington Ct
  4 Eastbourne BN22 ..185 C5
Wellington Gdns TN33 ..112 C5
Wellington Ho **17** TN34 .159 F8
Wellington Lodge BN7 ..152 B8
Wellington Mews TN34 .159 F8
Wellington Pk **1** BN25 .181 A3
Wellington Pl
  6 Hastings TN34 ....159 F7
  Sparrow's Green TN5 ..29 F5
Wellington Quay BN23 ..175 A1
Wellington Rd
  Brighton BN2 ....189 C4
  Hastings TN34 ....160 A4
  Newhaven BN9 ......168 C5
  Peacehaven BN10 ....178 E6
  Portslade-by-S BN41 ..162 B6
Wellington Sq TN34 ...159 F8
Wellington St
  Brighton BN2 ....164 C7
  Lewes BN7 ....190 B2
Wellington Terr **14**
  TN34 ....159 F8
Wellington Town Rd RH19 .1 D2
Wellingtonia Ct **8** BN1 .142 E3
Wellis Ct TN38 ....159 A8
Wellis Gdns TN38 .....159 A8
Wellplace Cotts TN36 ..116 F5
Wells Chase BN7 ......99 E6
Wells Cl
  Eastbourne BN20 .....188 C8
  Plumpton Green BN7 ..99 E6
  Royal Tunbridge Wells TN1 ..8 A4
Wells Ho TN4 ....7 F4
Wells Lea RH19 ......1 D4
Wells Mdw RH19 .....1 D4
Wellsbourne **8** BN2 ...164 F5
Wellsbourne Rd BN24 ..174 A5
Wellsmead Pk BN20 ...188 D8
Welsley Mews TN6 ....25 F2
Wendale Dr BN10 .....167 D2
Wendover Grange **8**
  BN3 ....163 A6
Wenham Gdns BN8 ...104 C5
Went Hill Gdns BN22 ..173 B3
Went Hill Pk BN25 ....181 A3
Went La BN20 ....183 C1
Went Way BN20 ......187 B8
Wenthill Cl BN25 .....187 B8
Wentworth Cl
  Bexhill TN40 ....157 F5
  Hailsham BN27 ....129 A1
Wentworth Ct BN23 ...185 E6
Wentworth St BN2 ....189 C1
Wentworth Way TN38 ..158 E8
Wessex Rd BN2 ......189 C5
West Ascent TN38 ....159 B6
West Beach BN25 .....180 B4
West Beeches Rd TN6 ..26 B2
West Blatchington Inf Sch
  BN3 ....141 E4
West Blatchington Jun Sch
  BN3 ....141 E4
West Blatchington Windmill
  (dis) ★ BN3 ....141 F2
West Cl Alfriston BN26 ..170 F3
  Polegate BN26 ....173 B7
West Comm RH16 .....50 F8
West Common Dr RH16 .51 A7
West Dean Rise BN25 ..181 A4
West Down Rd TN39 ...157 A5
West Dr BN2 ....164 C6

Vic – Wes **219**

West End BN27 ....130 E6
West Furlong Ct BN6 ..97 A5
West Furlong La BN6 ..97 A5
West Gate BN7 ....99 E6
West Hill
  Dormans Park RH19 ...1 E6
  East Grinstead RH19 ..10 D8
West Hill Arc **3** TN34 ..160 A3
West Hill Cliff Rly ★
  TN34 ....160 A4
West Hill Ct
  Eastbourne BN21 .....184 E4
  4 St Leonards TN38 .159 B6
West Hill Mews TN38 ..158 F6
West Hill Pl BN1 ......189 A3
West Hill Rd
  Brighton BN1 ....189 A3
  St Leonards TN38 ....159 A6
West Hill St BN1 ......189 A4
West Ho **15** BN21 ....185 A2
West Hoathly Rd RH19 .10 A3
West Hove Inf & Jun Schs
  BN3 ....162 F7
West La RH19 ....10 D8
West Leigh RH19 .....10 E7
West Mallion RH16 ....50 F3
West Par TN39 ....157 B2
West Park Cres RH15 ..72 D4
West Point **8** BN43 ..161 A6
West Quay BN25 .....179 D6
West Rd Kilndown NT17 .20 F3
  Portslade-by-S BN41 ..162 A7
  Pyecombe BN45 .....119 A6
West Rise Com Inf Sch
  BN23 ....174 C2
West Rise Jun Sch
  BN23 ....174 C2
West St Alfriston BN26 ..170 F3
  Brighton BN1 ....189 A2
  Burgess Hill RH15 ...72 E4
  Ditchling BN6 ....98 D3
  Dormansland RH7 ....2 A8
  East Grinstead RH19 ..10 E8
  Eastbourne BN21 .....184 E4
  Hastings TN34 ....160 A3
  Lewes BN7 ....190 B2
  Mayfield TN20 ....40 A2
  Portslade-by-S BN41 ..162 C7
  Rottingdean BN2 .....165 F1
  Rye TN31 ....93 C5
  Seaford BN25 ....180 C3
West St Leonards Prim Sch
  TN38 ....158 F8
West St Leonards Sta
  TN38 ....158 F7
West Street La TN21 ...81 F7
West Terr
  Eastbourne BN21 .....184 F2
  Herstmonceux BN27 ..130 E6
West Undercliff TN31 ..93 A5
West View Hastings TN34 160 B6
  Hove BN3 ....163 C8
  Lindfield RH16 ....51 B6
  Seaford BN25 ....180 E2
  Uckfield TN22 ....55 D1
West View Cotts RH16 ..51 B6
West View Ct **17** BN25 ..180 E2
West View Gdns RH19 ...10 E8
West View Terr BN9 ...168 D2
West Way BN3 ....141 D2
Westaway Dr TN39 ....157 A4
Westbourne Ct TN39 ...156 C2
Westbourne Gdns BN3 .163 A7
Westbourne Gr BN3 ...163 A7
Westbourne Pl BN3 ...163 A6
Westbourne St BN3 ...163 A6
Westbourne Villas BN3 .162 F6
Westbrook
  Forest Row RH18 ....11 E3
  Saltdean BN2 ....177 C6
Westbrook La TN35 ...114 E5
Westbrook Terr TN2 ...8 D1
Westbrook Way BN42 ..161 F7
Westcliff Man BN20 ...188 B4
Westcombe **11** BN1 ...163 E7
Westcourt BN27 ......152 B7
Westcourt Dr TN39 ...156 F3
Westdean Ave BN9 ...179 A5
Westdean Cl TN37 ....136 C6
Westdene Dr BN1 .....142 C5
Westdene Prim Sch
  BN1 ....142 C5
Westdown Ho **4** BN21 .185 A2
Westdown La TN19 ...61 A3
Westdown PK TN19 ...61 A3
Westdown Rd BN25 ...180 D4
Westergate Rd BN2 ...143 A6
Westerham Rd BN23 ..174 D1
Westerings The **4** TN21 .82 A6
Westerleigh Cl BN3 ...159 A8
Western Ave Battle TN33 112 C5
  Polegate BN26 ....173 B7
Western Concourse
  BN2 ....164 F3
Western Ct BN9 ......179 C6
Western Espl BN41 ...162 D6
Western Gdns TN6 ....38 D8
Western Rd Bexhill TN40 .157 C3
  Burgess Hill RH15 ...72 E3
  Crowborough TN6 ....38 C7
  Eastbourne BN22 .....185 B4
  Hailsham BN27 ......152 A8
  Haywards Heath RH16 .50 F4
  Hove BN1,BN3 ....163 E5
  Hurstpierpoint BN6 ...97 A7

Western Rd continued
Lewes BN7 . . . . .123 B1
Newhaven BN9 . . . . .179 C6
Newick BN8 . . . . .76 C7
Pevensey Bay BN24 . . . .175 D4
Royal Tunbridge Wells TN1 . .8 C5
St Leonards TN37 . . . . . .159 C7
Turner's Green TN5 . . . . . .29 F6
Western Road Prim Sch
BN7 . . . . .190 A1
Western St BN1 . . . . .163 E5
Western Terr 21 BN1 . . . .163 E5
Westfield Ave BN2 . . . . .177 D7
Westfield Ave N BN2 . . .177 D7
Westfield Ave S BN2 . . .177 D7
Westfield Cl
Brighton BN1 . . . . .143 A4
Five Ashes TN20 . . . . .58 B6
Polegate BN26 . . . . .173 A7
Westfield Cres BN1 . . . . .143 A5
Westfield Ct BN26 . . . . . .173 A4
Westfield La TN35,TN37 . .136 C8
Westfield Prim Sch
TN35 . . . . .114 E4
Westfield Rd BN21 . . . . .184 D6
Westfield Rise BN2 . . . . .177 E7
Westgate St BN7 . . . . . . .190 A2
Westham 18 BN2 . . . . . . .164 F5
Westham TN39 . . . . .156 E3
Westham Dr BN24 . . . . . .175 F6
Westhill Dr RH15 . . . . .72 C3
Westland Ct BN41 . . . . . .162 A7
Westlands Rd RH16 . . . . . .51 B5
Westlords BN21 . . . . .184 C8
Westmeston Ave BN2 . . .177 B6
Westminster Cl BN2 . . . .173 D4
Westminster Cres TN34 . .160 A8
Westmoreland Cl TN38 . .135 F3
Westmoreland Ct TN22 . . .78 C5
Westmorland Ct
16 Brighton BN1 . . . . . .163 E5
Eastbourne BN20 . . . . . .184 B7
Westmount 3 BN2 . . . . .164 C6
Westmount BN42 . . . . . . .161 D8
Westpoint BN8 . . . . .76 C7
Westville Rd TN39 . . . . . .157 A4
Westway TN2 . . . . .9 D7
Westway Cl BN41 . . . . . . .140 E4
Westway Gdns BN41 . . . .140 E4
Westwood Rd TN4 . . . . .7 C5
Wharf Rd
Eastbourne BN21 . . . . . .184 F3
Hove BN3 . . . . .162 D6
Whatlington Rd TN33 . . .112 E7
Whatlington Way TN38 . .135 D2
Wheatfield Ct TN37 . . . . .136 C4
Wheatfield Way BN2 . . . .143 F3
Wheatland Cl BN10 . . . . .167 B2
Wheatsheaf Ct RH15 . . . . .72 F5
Wheatsheaf Gdns BN2 . .190 C3
Wheatsheaf La RH17 . . . . .50 A6
Wheel Farm Bsns Pk
TN35 . . . . .114 D4
Wheel La TN35 . . . . .114 D3
Wheeler Ct RH16 . . . . .50 F2
Wheelers La TN22 . . . . . . .57 D6
Wheelers Lane Cotts
TN22 . . . . .57 D5
Wheelwright Cl BN22 . . .173 D4
Wheelwright La RH15 . . . .73 D1
Whichelo Pl BN2 . . . . . . .164 C6
Whiffens Ct BN27 . . . . . . .152 A6
Whincroft Pk TN6 . . . . . . .37 D8
Whipping Post La BN2 . . .165 F1
Whippingham Rd BN2 . . .164 C7
Whippingham St BN2 . . .164 C8
Whistler Ct BN1 . . . . .142 F1
Whitbread Cl BN23 . . . . .174 B4
White Bear Pas 3 TN1 . . . .8 A2
White Chys TN6 . . . . .26 A1
White Ct BN26 . . . . .170 F2
White Hill BN7 . . . . .190 A2
White Hill Ave TN39 . . . .156 E4
White Hill Dr TN39 . . . . . .156 E4
White House Prim Sch
BN27 . . . . .152 B8
White Lodge Hove BN3 . .163 C8
Royal Tunbridge Wells TN1 . .8 C4
White Rock TN34,TN37 . .159 E7
White Rock Gdns 7
TN34 . . . . .159 E7
White Rock Pleasure
Grounds★ TN34 . . . . . .159 E7
White Rock Rd TN34,
TN37 . . . . .159 E7
White St BN2 . . . . .189 C2
White Way
Alfriston BN26 . . . . .170 F1
Lewes BN7 . . . . .146 B1
White's Cl BN6 . . . . .97 A7
Whitebread La TN31 . . . . .67 E8
Whitecross St BN1 . . . . .189 B3
Whitefield Rd TN4 . . . . .8 A6
Whitefriars Rd TN34 . . . .160 A5
Whitegate Cl TN4 . . . . .8 A8
Whitegates Cl BN8 . . . . .100 E7
Whitegates La TN5 . . . . . .29 D8
Whitegates Pk TN35 . . . .114 D2
Whitehall Par 3 RH19 . . . . .1 E1
Whitehawk Cl BN2 . . . . . .164 E5
Whitehawk Cres BN2 . . .164 E5
Whitehawk Hill Rd BN2 .164 D5
Whitehawk Prim Sch
BN2 . . . . .164 E6

Whitehawk Rd
Brighton BN2 . . . . .164 E6
Brighton BN2 . . . . .164 F5
Whitehawk Way BN2 . . .164 F6
Whitehill Cl
Crowborough TN6 . . . . . . .25 F1
Eastbourne BN20 . . . . . .184 B5
Whitehill Ct TN39 . . . . . .156 E5
Whitehill Inf Sch TN6 . . . . .25 F2
Whitehill Rd TN6 . . . . .37 F8
Whitehouse Ave TN39 . . .157 B7
Whitehouse La TN21 . . . . .81 B4
Whitelot Cl BN42 . . . . . . .140 E2
Whitelot Way BN42 . . . . .140 E2
Whiterock Pl BN42 . . . . . .161 E7
Whitesmith BN8 . . . . .105 B1
Whitesmith La BN8 . . . . .105 B1
Whitethorn Dr BN1 . . . . .142 B4
Whiteway BN25 . . . . .180 E6
Whiteway La BN2 . . . . . . .177 A6
Whiteways Cotts BN7 . . .146 C2
Whitfeld La BN8 . . . . .123 C6
Whitley Rd BN21 . . . . . . .185 B5
Whittinghame Gdns
BN1 . . . . .142 F3
Whittington Coll RH19 . . . . .1 A4
Whittington's Way TN34 .160 B8
Whittle Dr BN23 . . . . .174 A1
Whittlewood Cl TN38 . . .135 E2
Whitworth Rd TN37 . . . . .136 B3
Whybourne Crest TN2 . . . .8 D1
Whydown Hill TN33 . . . . .113 E6
Whydown Rd TN39 . . . . .156 B7
Wick Hall BN3 . . . . .163 D6
Wick Hurst Rd BN41 . . . .141 A3
Wickets The RH15 . . . . . . .72 F5
Wickham Ave TN39 . . . . .157 B3
Wickham Cl RH16 . . . . . . .50 E7
Wickham Dr BN6 . . . . .97 C5
Wickham Gdns TN4 . . . . . . .7 D5
Wickham Hill BN6 . . . . . . .97 C4
Wickham La BN7,BN8 . . .100 E3
Wickham Rock La TN36 .117 C5
Wickham Way RH16 . . . . . .50 E7
Wickhurst Cl BN41 . . . . . .140 F2
Wickhurst Rise BN41 . . . .140 F3
Wicklands Ave BN2 . . . . .177 D5
Widbury TN3 . . . . .6 F3
Widdicombe Way BN2 . .143 E2
Wigmore Cl BN1 . . . . .143 B1
Wilbury Ave BN3 . . . . . . .163 C8
Wilbury Cres BN3 . . . . . . .163 C8
Wilbury Gdns BN3 . . . . . .163 C8
Wilbury Gr BN3 . . . . .163 C6
Wilbury Grange BN3 . . . .163 C6
Wilbury Lodge 13 BN3 . .163 C6
Wilbury Rd BN3 . . . . .163 C6
Wilbury Villas BN3 . . . . . .163 C7
Wilby Ave BN42 . . . . .140 E1
Wild Park Ctr BN2 . . . . . .143 E3
Wild Park Nature Trail★
BN2 . . . . .143 D5
Wilderness Gdns TN31 . . .67 B7
Wilderness La TN22 . . . . . .57 C3
Wilderness Pk TN6 . . . . . . .25 E2
Wilderness Rd BN6 . . . . . .97 A6
Wilderness Rise RH19 . . . . .2 A6
Wilderness The RH16 . . . . .51 B8
Wilderness Wood Visitor
Ctr★ TN22 . . . . .57 D4
Wilderwick Rd RH19,RH7 . .2 A7
Wildwood BN23 . . . . .174 C4
Wilfrid Rd BN3 . . . . .141 D1
Wiliamson Cott Homes
BN3 . . . . .163 A7
Wilkins Way TN40 . . . . . .157 F6
Wilkinson Cl BN2 . . . . . . .165 F3
Wilkinson Way BN25 . . . .180 E4
Willard Cl BN22 . . . . .185 A6
Wille Cotts BN7 . . . . .190 C1
Willetts Cotts TN3 . . . . . . .5 C4
Willetts Field BN8 . . . . . .127 E8
Willetts La TN3 . . . . .5 C4
William Allen La RH16 . . .51 B6
William Parker Sch
TN34 . . . . .136 D4
William Rd TN38 . . . . . . .158 E7
William St Brighton BN2 .189 B2
Portslade-by-S BN41 . . . .162 B7
Royal Tunbridge Wells TN4 . .8 A5
William Street Trad Est
BN41 . . . . .162 B7
William Sutton Ho BN1 .189 B2
Williams Ct 7 BN23 . . . .174 E1
Williams Rd BN43 . . . . . .161 C8
Willicombe Ho TN2 . . . . . . .8 D4
Willicombe Pk TN2 . . . . . . .8 D4
Willingdon Ave
Bexhill TN39 . . . . .157 A4
St Leonards TN38 . . . . . .136 A5
Willingdon Cl
Eastbourne BN20 . . . . . .173 B1
St Leonards TN38 . . . . . .136 A5
Willingdon Com Sch
BN20 . . . . .172 F4
Willingdon Ct BN20 . . . . .173 B3
Willingdon Dro BN23 . . . .174 B2
Willingdon La BN26 . . . . .183 C7
Willingdon Park Dr
BN22 . . . . .173 B2
Willingdon Prim Sch
BN20 . . . . .173 A3
Willingdon Rd
Brighton BN2 . . . . .143 E1
Eastbourne BN20,BN21 . .184 C6
Willingdon Way
Eastbourne BN22 . . . . . .173 B2
St Leonards TN38 . . . . . .136 A5

Willingford La TN19 . . . . .61 C2
Willoughby Cres BN22 . .185 C6
Willow Ave BN27 . . . . . . .129 B1
Willow Bank TN32 . . . . . . .64 B3
Willow Cl
East Grinstead RH19 . . . . . .1 D1
Etchingham TN19 . . . . .63 B8
Heathfield TN21 . . . . .82 B8
Hurstpierpoint BN6 . . . . . . .97 A7
Woodingdean BN2 . . . . . .165 E8
Willow Ct 4 Hove BN3 . .163 D7
Polegate BN26 . . . . .173 A6
Willow Dr Bexhill TN39 . .156 C5
Polegate BN26 . . . . .173 A5
Seaford BN25 . . . . .181 C3
Willow End TN34 . . . . . . .136 F4
Willow Est The BN9 . . . . .179 E8
Willow Gdns BN6 . . . . .97 A7
Willow Ho BN6 . . . . .97 E5
Willow La TN36 . . . . .118 B6
Willow Lodge 8 RH19 . . . .10 F8
Willow Mead 8 RH19 . . . .10 F8
Willow Mews
19 Eastbourne BN22 . . .185 B3
Robertsbridge TN32 . . . . . .64 B3
Willow Pk RH16 . . . . .51 B4
Willow Stream Ct TN35 . .115 C3
Willow Tree Rd TN2 . . . . . . .7 F1
Willow Way BN6 . . . . .97 A8
Willow Wlk
Eastbourne BN22 . . . . . .173 D2
Newhaven BN9 . . . . .179 C8
Royal Tunbridge Wells TN2 . .8 E8
Willowbed Wlk TN34 . . . .136 E5
Willowbrook Way BN6 . . .98 A3
Willowdowne Cl BN3 . . . .163 A5
Willowfield Rd BN22 . . . .185 B4
Willowfield Sq 7 BN22 . .185 B3
Willowmead TN6 . . . . .37 E8
Willows Cl TN22 . . . . .78 D8
Willows Mobile Home Pk The
BN27 . . . . .129 A3
Willows Rise TN22 . . . . . . .79 B3
Willows The
Barcombe Cross BN8 . . . .101 E5
2 Eastbourne BN22 . . . .189 C5
Burgess Hill RH15 . . . . . . .73 B5
Hassocks BN6 . . . . .97 E4
St Leonards TN37 . . . . . .136 A6
Wilman Rd TN4 . . . . .8 B7
Wilmington Cl
Brighton BN1 . . . . .143 A5
Hassocks BN6 . . . . .97 F4
Wilmington Gdns BN21 . .185 A1
Wilmington Par BN1 . . . .142 F5
Wilmington Rd
Hastings TN34 . . . . .160 A7
Newhaven BN9 . . . . .179 B6
Seaford BN25 . . . . .180 D4
Wilmington Sq BN21 . . . .185 A1
Wilmington Way
Brighton BN1 . . . . .143 A5
Haywards Heath RH16 . . . .51 A5
Wilmot Ct 6 BN43 . . . . . .161 C8
Wilmot Rd BN43 . . . . .161 C8
Wilson Ave BN2 . . . . .164 F6
Wilson Gr TN22 . . . . .78 A7
Wilson's Cross BN27 . . . .131 F7
Wilton 1 RH16 . . . . .50 D6
Wilton Ave BN22 . . . . . . .173 D2
Wilton Ho TN38 . . . . .158 F6
Wilton Rd TN40 . . . . .157 C3
Wiltshire Ct BN23 . . . . . . .174 E1
Wiltshire Ho 16 BN2 . . . .189 C2
Wiltshire Way TN2 . . . . . . .8 D7
Winceby Cl TN39 . . . . . . .156 E2
Winchcombe Rd BN22 . . .185 A4
Winchelsea La
Cock Marling TN31,TN36 . .92 C1
Hastings TN35 . . . . .137 E5
Winchelsea Mus★ TN36 .117 E7
Winchelsea Rd
Eastbourne BN22 . . . . . .185 D6
Guestling Green TN35 . . . .137 F7
Hastings TN35 . . . . .160 D8
Rye TN31 . . . . .93 B5
Winchelsea Sta TN36 . . . .92 D1
Winchester Cl BN25 . . . . .181 C5
Winchester Ho BN22 . . . .173 E3
Winchester St BN1 . . . . . .189 B5
Winchester Way BN22 . . .173 C2
Wincombe Rd BN1 . . . . . .142 D1
Windermere Cres BN22 . .185 C5
Windermere Ct 9 BN22 . .164 C6
Windermere Rd RH16 . . . .50 F4
Windgrove Cotts TN33 . . .112 C6
Windgrove Ho TN33 . . . . .112 D6
Winding St 21 TN34 . . . . .160 B4
Windlesham Ave BN1 . . . .163 E6
Windlesham Cl
Crowborough TN6 . . . . . . .25 F1
Portslade-by-S BN41 . . . .141 A1
Windlesham Ct 14 BN1 . .163 E7
Windlesham Gdns BN1,
BN3 . . . . .163 E7
Windlesham Ho 15 BN1 . .163 E6
Windlesham Mans 17
BN3 . . . . .163 E7
Windlesham Rd BN1 . . . . .163 E6
Windlesham Sch BN1 . . . .163 E8
Windmill Ave BN6 . . . . . . .97 F3
Windmill Cl
Eastbourne BN21 . . . . . .184 D6
Heathfield TN21 . . . . .82 B8
Hove BN3 . . . . .141 F2

Windmill Ct
Royal Tunbridge Wells TN2 . .8 C3
Winchelsea Beach BN36 . .118 B6
Windmill Dr Bexhill TN39 .157 B6
Brighton BN1 . . . . .142 C6
Burgess Hill RH15 . . . . . . .73 A4
Windmill Gn BN24 . . . . . .174 C5
Windmill La
Ashurst Wood RH19 . . . . .11 C7
Cousley Wood TN5 . . . . . . .30 C8
Durgates TN5 . . . . .29 E4
East Grinstead RH19 . . . . . .1 D3
Friston BN20 . . . . .183 A1
Windmill Par BN42 . . . . . .140 E1
Windmill Park Cvn Pk
TN36 . . . . .118 B6
Windmill Pl BN26 . . . . . . .173 A5
Windmill Rd
Polegate BN26 . . . . .173 A6
Southwick BN42 . . . . .140 E1
St Leonards TN38 . . . . . .136 E1
Windmill St
Brighton BN2 . . . . .189 C3
Royal Tunbridge Wells TN2 . .8 C3
Windmill Terr 20 BN2 . . .189 C3
Windmill View BN1 . . . . .143 B7
Windmill Way TN36 . . . . .118 B7
Windmills Jun Sch The
BN6 . . . . .98 A3
Windover Cres BN7 . . . . .123 A2
Windover Way BN22 . . . .173 B3
Windsor Bsns Units TN6 . .38 C8
Windsor Cl
Eastbourne BN23 . . . . . .174 C5
Haywards Heath RH16 . . . .50 E2
Hove BN3 . . . . .142 A3
Seaford BN25 . . . . .180 B6
Windsor Ct Brighton BN1 .189 A2
Brighton,Withdean BN1 . .142 D4
Crowborough TN6 . . . . . . .38 C8
8 Eastbourne BN22 . . . .185 B3
Polegate BN26 . . . . .173 A7
Windsor Lodge 5 BN3 . . .163 B6
Windsor Pl
Crowborough TN6 . . . . . . .38 C8
East Grinstead RH19 . . . . .11 A8
Hastings TN34 . . . . .136 F2
Windsor Rd Bexhill TN39 .157 B4
Crowborough TN6 . . . . . . .38 C8
Hailsham BN27 . . . . .152 B6
St Leonards TN37 . . . . . .136 B3
Windsor St BN1 . . . . .189 A2
Windsor Way
Polegate BN26 . . . . .173 A7
Winchelsea Beach BN36 . .118 A6
Windward Quay 10
BN23 . . . . .185 F8
Wineham Way TN40 . . . . .157 F4
Winfield Ave BN1 . . . . . . .142 F6
Winfield Cl Brighton BN1 .142 F5
Portslade-by-S BN41 . . . .141 A3
Wingate Cl TN38 . . . . . . .136 A1
Wingle Tye Rd RH15 . . . . .98 A8
Wingrove Ho BN2 . . . . . . .171 A3
Winkfield Ct RH16 . . . . . . .50 D5
Winkhurst Way RH15 . . . . .73 D1
Winkney Rd BN22 . . . . . . .173 F3
Winnals Pk RH16 . . . . .50 D5
Winscote Cl TN6 . . . . .25 D1
Winston 3 BN27 . . . . .152 B7
Winston Cres BN23 . . . . .185 D7
Winston Dr TN39 . . . . . . .156 F4
Winstone Scott Ave TN3 . .6 C4
Winterbourne Cl
Hastings TN34 . . . . .159 D8
Lewes BN7 . . . . .146 A2
Winterbourne Hollow
BN7 . . . . .146 B8
Winterbourne La BN7 . . .146 A8
Winterbourne Mews
BN7 . . . . .146 B8
Winterton Way BN43 . . . .161 B6
Winton Ave BN22 . . . . . . .177 A5
Winton St BN26 . . . . .171 A4
Wisden Ave RH15 . . . . . . .72 E5
Wiseacre TN3 . . . . .20 A3
Wish Ct BN3 . . . . .162 E8
Wish Hill BN20 . . . . .173 B1
Wish Rd
Eastbourne BN21 . . . . . .185 A2
Hove BN3 . . . . .162 E6
Wish St TN31 . . . . .93 B5
Wish Tower Puppet Mus★
BN21 . . . . .185 A1
Wish Ward TN31 . . . . .93 B5
Wishing Tree Cl TN38 . . .135 F2
Wishing Tree La TN38 . . .135 F1
Wishing Tree Rd TN38 . . .135 F2
Wishing Tree Rd N
TN38 . . . . .136 A4
Wiston Ct 12 BN43 . . . . . .161 C8
Wiston Rd BN2 . . . . .164 F6
Wiston Way BN2 . . . . .164 F6
Withdean Ave BN1 . . . . . .142 D2
Withdean Cl BN1 . . . . .142 D3
Withdean Court Ave
BN1 . . . . .142 D3
Withdean Cres BN1 . . . . .142 E3
Withdean Ct 7 BN1 . . . . .142 E3
Withdean Hall 9 BN1 . . . .142 D3
Withdean Rd BN1 . . . . . . .142 D3
Withdean Rise BN1 . . . . . .142 D3
Withdean Stad (Brighton &
Hove Albion FC) BN1 . .142 D4
Witherenden Rd TN20 . . . .41 A7
Withy Bush RH15 . . . . .72 E5
Withyham Ave BN2 . . . . .177 C5
Withyham Cl BN22 . . . . . .173 F1

Withyham Rd
Bexhill TN39 . . . . .156 C2
Groombridge TN3 . . . . . . .15 B7
Wittersham La TN31 . . . . . .70 B5
Wittersham Rd Iden TN31 . .70 B7
Potman's Heath TN17,
TN30 . . . . .49 D4
Wittersham Road Sta★
TN17 . . . . .49 D6
Wivelsfield Prim Sch
RH17 . . . . .73 F6
Wivelsfield Rd
Haywards Heath RH16 . . . .50 E2
Saltdean BN2 . . . . .177 C7
Wivelsfield Sta RH15 . . . . .73 C4
Woburn Cl BN22 . . . . .129 A1
Woburn Pl BN1 . . . . .143 F5
Woburn Way BN22 . . . . . .173 D3
Wode Rd TN33 . . . . .133 A3
Wolfe Cl TN6 . . . . .38 A8
Wolseley Rd
Brighton BN1 . . . . .143 D6
Portslade-by-S BN41 . . . .162 A8
Royal Tunbridge Wells TN4 . .8 C7
Wolstead Lodge 3 RH16 . .50 F3
Wolstonbury Cl BN6 . . . . .97 B4
Wolstonbury Ct RH15 . . . .73 B2
Wolstonbury Rd BN3 . . . .163 E7
Wolstonbury Way RH15 . .73 B2
Wolverstone Dr BN1 . . . . .143 C2
Wood Park BN2 . . . . .131 D2
Wood Ride RH16 . . . . .50 D3
Wood St
East Grinstead RH19 . . . . . .1 D1
Royal Tunbridge Wells TN1 . .8 B4
Wood's Pas 4 TN34 . . . . .160 B4
Woodbourne Ave BN1 . . .143 A4
Woodbrook Rd TN34 . . . . .136 F2
Woodbury Ave RH19 . . . . . .2 B1
Woodbury Cl
East Grinstead RH19 . . . . .11 B8
Royal Tunbridge Wells TN4 . .8 A5
Woodbury Park Gdns TN4 . .8 B5
Woodbury Park Rd TN4 . . . .8 B5
Woodcombe TN34 . . . . . . .136 F4
Woodcote Rd RH18 . . . . . .11 F2
Woodcrest Rd BN2 . . . . . . .72 F1
Woodcroft RH15 . . . . .72 F5
Woodcroft Dr BN21 . . . . .184 C7
Woodcutters RH17 . . . . . . .51 F3
Woodgate Mdw BN7 . . . . .99 E2
Woodgate Rd BN22 . . . . . .185 C5
Woodhams Cl TN33 . . . . .112 D5
Woodhill Pk TN2 . . . . .9 C6
Woodhouse Cl BN3 . . . . . .162 E7
Woodhouse Rd BN3 . . . . .162 E7
Woodingdean Prim Sch
BN2 . . . . .165 C8
Woodland Ave
Burgess Hill RH15 . . . . . . .73 C4
Eastbourne BN22 . . . . . .173 C1
Hove BN3 . . . . .142 B3
Woodland Cl
Burgess Hill RH15 . . . . . . .73 C4
Hove BN3 . . . . .142 B2
Royal Tunbridge Wells TN4 . .8 C7
Woodland Cres RH15 . . . . .73 C4
Woodland Ct BN3 . . . . . . .142 B4
Woodland Dr BN3 . . . . . . .142 B4
Woodland Mews TN21 . . . .82 B6
Woodland Par BN3 . . . . . .142 B3
Woodland Rd TN4 . . . . .8 C7
Woodland Rise TN40 . . . . .157 E4
Woodland Vale Rd
TN37,TN38 . . . . .159 C8
Woodland Way
Brighton BN1 . . . . .142 F4
Crowborough TN6 . . . . . . .37 F8
Crowhurst TN33 . . . . .134 F4
Fairlight Cove TN35 . . . . .138 E4
Heathfield TN21 . . . . .82 B6
Woodland Wlk BN2 . . . . .165 D4
Woodlands Hove BN3 . . . .142 C2
Pembury TN2 . . . . .9 F4
Woodlands Cl
Hailsham BN27 . . . . .129 C2
Heathfield TN21 . . . . .82 B5
Peacehaven BN10 . . . . . .167 B1
Peasmarsh TN31 . . . . .69 C2
Uckfield TN22 . . . . .78 D8
Woodlands Rd
East Grinstead RH19 . . . . . .2 A4
Haywards Heath RH16 . . . .50 F4
Woodlands The
Brighton BN1 . . . . .142 E4
Hastings TN34 . . . . .136 E5
Woodlands Way TN34 . . . .136 E6
Woodleigh Rd RH15 . . . . . .73 C4
Woodmans Oak TN33 . . . . .88 A3
Woodpecker Cres RH15 . . .72 F4
Woodpecker Dr BN27 . . . .152 A8
Woodpecker La BN27 . . . .127 B3
Woodpecker Rd BN23 . . . .174 B2
Woodpecker Way
Golden Cross BN27 . . . . . .127 B3
Uckfield TN22 . . . . .78 D5
Woodridge Cl RH16 . . . . . .51 A3
Woodruff Ave BN3 . . . . . .142 B3
Woods Green Cotts TN5 . . .29 F6
Woods Ground RH17 . . . . .74 B4
Woods Hill Cl RH19 . . . . . .11 D1
Woods Hill La RH19 . . . . . .11 D1
Woods Ho BN3 . . . . .163 A8
Woodsgate Ave TN40 . . . .157 C6
Woodsgate Pk TN39 . . . . .157 B6
Woodsgate Way TN2 . . . . . .9 B6
Woodside Broad Oak TN31 . .90 B5
Crowborough TN6 . . . . . . .25 E2

Woodside *continued*
Kilndown TN17 . . . .**20** F2
Woodside Ave BN1 . . . .**142** D2
Woodside Cl TN2 . . . .**9** E6
Woodside Lodge BN1 . .**142** D2
Woodside Rd Pembury TN2 .**9** E6
Rusthall TN4 . . . .**7** D4
Woodside Terr BN27 . . . .**151** F4
Woodside Way BN27 . . .**152** A4
Woodsland Cl BN6 . . . . .**97** F4
Woodslands Rd BN6 . . . . .**97** F4
Woodspring Cl TN37 . . .**136** B5
Woodstock RH19 . . . .**1** C2
Woodstock Rd TN39 . . .**156** C6
Woodview Cl BN1 . . . . .**143** D6
Woodville Ct 9 TN39 . . .**157** B3
Woodville Rd TN39 . . . .**157** B3
Woodward Cl BN23 . . . .**185** E7
Woodwards Cl RH15 . . . .**73** B1
Woolven Cl RH15 . . . .**72** E1
Worcester Ct
5 Eastbourne BN23 . . . . .**174** E1
1 Hove BN3 . . . .**163** E6
Worcester Villas BN3 . .**162** C7
Worcester Way BN27 . . .**131** B5

Wordsworth Dr BN23 . . .**174** E2
Wordsworth Rise 6 RH19 . .**1** C1
Wordsworth St BN3 . . . .**163** A7
Workhouse La
Icklesham TN36 . . . .**116** F5
Westfield TN35 . . . .**114** E3
Worsham Ct TN39 . . . .**156** C4
Worsham La TN40 . . . .**157** F7
Worsted La RH19 . . . .**11** B8
Wray Cl RH19 . . . .**11** D6
Wren Cl Burgess Hill RH15 **72** D3
Heathfield TN21 . . . .**82** A7
Wren Ct Battle TN33 . . . .**112** F4
St Leonards TN38 . . . .**135** E3
Wrentham Ho RH15 . . . . .**73** B3
Wrestwood Ave BN22 . .**173** C1
Wrestwood Cl TN40 . . . .**157** D6
Wrestwood Rd TN40 . . .**157** D6
Wrotham Cl
Eastbourne BN23 . . . .**174** D1
Hastings TN34 . . . .**136** E5
Wroxham Rd BN23 . . . . .**174** B4
Wyatts La RH17 . . . .**33** D5
Wyberlye Rd RH15 . . . . . .**73** A4
Wybourne Rise TN2 . . . . .**17** B8

Wychperry Rd RH16 . . . . .**50** D5
Wychurst Gdns TN40 . . .**157** D6
Wyck Ct BN41 . . . .**162** A7
Wykeham Ct TN34 . . . . .**159** E8
Wykeham Rd TN34 . . . . .**159** E8
Wykeham Terr BN1 . . . . .**189** A2
Wykeham Way RH15 . . .**73** C2
Wynberg Cotts TN6 . . . .**39** C6
Wyndham St BN2 . . . . . .**189** C1
Wynnes Mews BN3 . . . .**163** A7
Wynnstay RH15 . . . .**73** B2
Wyshe The BN45 . . . .**119** C6
Wythwood RH16 . . . .**50** E1

Y

Yardley St BN1 . . . .**189** B5
Yarrow Rd BN7 . . . .**123** B2
Yates Cl TN31 . . . .**95** A2
Yeomans BN8 . . . .**125** A7
Yesterdays World Mus★
TN33 . . . .**112** D4
Yew Ct 1 RH19 . . . .**1** D2
Yew La RH19 . . . .**1** B3

Yew Tree Cl
Broyle Side BN8 . . . .**124** F7
Hastings TN34 . . . .**136** E6
Heathfield TN21 . . . .**82** A6
Yew Tree Cotts
Burgess Hill RH15 . . . .**73** B3
Groombridge TN3 . . . .**15** F8
Yew Tree Rd TN4 . . . .**8** B8
Yewtree La TN6 . . . .**39** E8
Yielding's Cl BN21 . . . . .**184** D5
York Ave
East Grinstead RH19 . . . . . .**11** A8
Hove BN3 . . . .**163** E6
York Bldgs 5 TN34 . . . . .**159** F7
York Ct 13 BN3 . . . .**163** E7
York Gdns 4 TN34 . . . .**159** F7
York Gr BN1 . . . .**189** A4
York Ho BN41 . . . .**162** B8
York Mansions E 13
BN3 . . . .**163** E6
York Mansions W 12
BN3 . . . .**163** E6
York Pl Brighton BN1 . . . .**189** B3
Hove BN3 . . . .**163** E6

York Rd Bexhill TN40 . . . .**158** A5
Burgess Hill RH15 . . . .**72** D2
Eastbourne BN21 . . . .**184** F2
Hove BN1,BN3 . . . .**163** E6
Peacehaven BN10 . . . .**178** E6
Royal Tunbridge Wells TN1 . . .**8** A4
St Leonards TN37 . . . .**136** C2
York Villas BN1 . . . .**189** A4
Yorklands BN3 . . . .**142** B4
Yorkshire Ct BN20 . . . . .**184** B7
Youl Grange BN20 . . . . .**184** D1
Youngsmere Cl BN1 . . . .**143** B6
Ypres Tower Mus★ TN31 **93** C5
Yvonne Robertson Ho
TN40 . . . .**157** D5
Zion Gdns BN1 . . . .**189** A2

Addresses

Name and Address	Telephone	Page	Grid reference

NG	NH	NJ	NK
NM	NN	NO	NP
NR	NS	NT	NU
NX	NY	NZ	
SC	SD	SE	TA
SH	SJ	SK	TF	TG
SM	SN	SO	SP	TL	TM
SR	SS	ST	SU	TQ	TR
SW	SX	SY	SZ	TV

Any feature in this atlas can be given a unique reference to help you find the same feature on other Ordnance Survey maps of the area, or to help someone else locate you if they do not have a Street Atlas.

The grid squares in this atlas match the Ordnance Survey National Grid and are at 500 metre intervals. The small figures at the bottom and sides of every other grid line are the National Grid kilometre values (**00** to **99** km) and are repeated across the country every 100 km (see left).

To give a unique National Grid reference you need to locate where in the country you are. The country is divided into 100 km squares with each square given a unique two-letter reference. Use the administrative map to determine in which 100 km square a particular page of this atlas falls.

The bold letters and numbers between each grid line (**A** to **F**, **1** to **8**) are for use within a specific Street Atlas only, and when used with the page number, are a convenient way of referencing these grid squares.

Example   *The railway bridge over DARLEY GREEN RD in grid square B1*

Step 1: Identify the two-letter reference, in this example the page is in **SP**

Step 2: Identify the 1 km square in which the railway bridge falls. Use the figures in the southwest corner of this square: Eastings **17**, Northings **74**. This gives a unique reference: **SP 17 74**, accurate to 1 km.

Step 3: To give a more precise reference accurate to 100 m you need to estimate how many tenths along and how many tenths up this 1 km square the feature is (to help with this the 1 km square is divided into four 500 m squares). This makes the bridge about **8** tenths along and about **1** tenth up from the southwest corner.

This gives a unique reference: **SP 178 741**, accurate to 100 m.

Eastings (read from left to right along the bottom) come before Northings (read from bottom to top). If you have trouble remembering say to yourself "Along the hall, THEN up the stairs"!

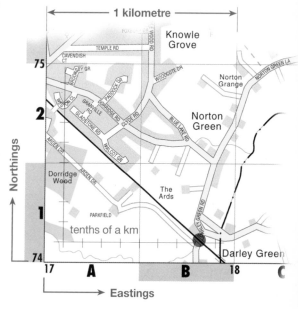

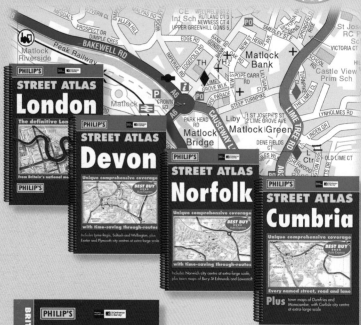